ADVANCED PROGRAMMING IN CLIPPER™ WITH C

ADVANCED PROGRAMMING IN CLIPPER™ WITH C

Stephen J. Straley
with David Karasek

Addison-Wesley Publishing Company, Inc.

Reading, Massachusetts Menlo Park, California New York
Don Mills, Ontario Wokingham, England Amsterdam Bonn Sydney
Singapore Tokyo Madrid Bogota Santiago San Juan

Many of the designations used by manufacturers and sellers to distinguish their products are claimed as trademarks. Where those designations appear in this book and Addison-Wesley was aware of a trademark claim, the designations have been printed in initial capital letters.

Code Base is a registered trademark of Sequiter Software.
Microsoft C is a registered trademark of Microsoft Corporation.
FUNCky is a trademark of dLESKO Associates.
Clipper and *Nantucket* are registered trademarks of Nantucket Corporation.
CP/M is a registered trademark of Digital Research, Inc.
Get-It is a trademark of Communications Horizon.
SJS_LIB, *Steve Straley's Accounting Package*, and *Steve Straley's CLIRMA Library* are trademarks of Four Seasons Publishing.
Steve Straley's ToolKit is a registered trademark of Four Seasons Publishing.

Cover design by Doliber Skeffington

Set in 10-point Times Roman by Context, Inc.

ISBN 0-201-51735-3

ABCDEFGHIJ-HA-89
First printing, December 1989

DEDICATION

To Joe King for being not only a business partner
but a true friend as well;
to Dale Porter who renewed my hope, spirit, and faith
in many things; it came at no better time.
And to my family: Mom, Aunt Pat, Sharon, Robert, Nicole,
and now to Kristina Lynn, the newest member of the clan;
no matter what others may say or do, be true and honest to yourself,
for reality will eventually fall into place. — S.S.

This book is dedicated to Wilann, my wife,
and Elizabeth and Marc, my children. — D.K.

ABOUT THE AUTHORS

Stephen J. Straley, formerly the senior support engineer at Nantucket, was directly involved in the early stages of Clipper development. Mr. Straley is the author of the first comprehensive book on Clipper: *Programming in Clipper*. He worked for the First Boston Corporation, specializing in Clipper connectivity to mainframe data, and now has his own software and educational publishing firm, which developed such packages as Steve Straley's ToolkiT, Clirma, and Accounting Package and produces a biweekly newsletter, "FROM the Desk of Steve Straley (D.O.S.S.)". As an authorized trainer for Nantucket, Mr. Straley conducts the Clipper Seminar Series across the country and has been one of the highest-rated instructors at both Clipper Developer Conferences. Mr. Straley is currently President of SJS & Associates, which has offices in New York and in Los Angeles.

David Karasek is a C and Clipper software developer and, as a member of Stephen J. Straley & Associates, coauthored, with Mr. Straley, the CLIRMA library for mainframe communication with Clipper. His specialties are PC-mainframe communications and customized user interfaces. Since being employed at National Broadcasting Company in New York and at the First Boston Corporation, Mr. Karasek has spent the past 10 years in systems development.

TABLE OF CONTENTS

PREFACE

After writing the first book on Clipper and seeing the flood of such publications since that time, many people may wonder why I would write another book on this topic. The answer lies in listening to the users, reading the mail responding to the newsletter, and talking to the leaders in the industry. The need for more advanced topics, more tricks and tips, has become clear. While many people want to begin to learn the C language (the parent language of Clipper), most are either intimidated, hesitant, or reluctant to try. Finally, there is a need to continue the educational path my first book created. Since that time, more software products have been developed, additional applications have been marketed, and enhanced seminars have been conducted through my office, and as a result, the needs of the Clipper programming community have grown. This book will guide you further along that path.

The first half of this book focuses on Clipper-based tricks, theories, and problem-solving techniques. As with most of my examples, this is all accomplished in 100 percent Clipper code. One of the goals in writing this book is to give you a new, fresh, innovative look at Clipper; it is no longer just a dBASE-like compiler. Taking the time to understand the underlying principles involved will yield benefits for you in the present as well as the future. If your "dBlinders" were still present with the first book, remove them now. There is no place for them. Your programming, testing, and developing environment should be Clipper, not the interpreter (any interpreter). The intent of this book is to help you make better applications, develop more user-friendly software, and to ease your programming demands.

However, sometimes Clipper's internal working, its design or intent, or its implementation may fall short for providing everything to everyone. For those rare occasions, Clipper's ability to open its architecture up to outside languages can solve this problem. The "Extend System" is as simple as it sounds: It extends the Clipper system to outside routines and/or functions. However, only a small percentage of the Clipper user base is equipped to handle this challenge, and there are many people who want to learn C, and be completely in control of the situation and of the language. Yet learning a new language is only as easy as the demand is big or the point of reference is clear. We seem to be able to learn a new language if the demand to make something work is so great that we tear into the task, or we can learn the new languages by importing some theories from other language to the new language. The latter will be our base. Therefore, the second half of this book teaches you how to program in C from a Clipper point of view. By cross-referencing C topics with their Clipper-based counterparts, by demonstrating C code equivalent for Clipper commands and/or functions, by sticking to the theories of good, structured programming, you will eventually be able to handle complex C-related issues. Add that to an extensive look at the core Clipper language and your applications will take on new dimensions; your programming style will take on new meaning.

And a word is now offered to those skeptics worried about the future. This should reassure some doubting souls present in our midst by showing and demonstrating the power and life of Clipper. Indeed, the soul of Clipper is alive and well; the tricks within this book are not bound by time or by version numbers. It has been my intent to get the Clipper programmers out of the verb-oriented world of the past and into the structured and procedural methods of today. And while we continue to bat about the ideas of object-oriented programming, we know that the ideas outlined in this book can set you on the path to the future. As well as looking to the future and what it may hold for us, the main theme of this book is simple: get the job done fast, professionally, on time, and under budget (getting paid for the work is a topic left for other publications). This is, or should be, the essence of any programmer's goal: to accomplish the task, to provide a service that did not exist (or was done as well as) before, and to become more astute about the techniques of problem solving. This book should help you attain that level.

Read each chapter and try to apply it to your current programming needs. Try some of the example programs to see how problems get solved in Clipper. Take the time to read and understand the "why" behind every "how." I can't force you to learn and to think; you must do that. I assure you that in doing this you will begin to see new directions and applications for the language and for your programming. Remember the three rules that must be applied to your coding style and your programming techniques: think, mix and match, and ask yourself "what if?"

The power of Clipper is not in the individual commands and functions; it is in its ability to create something new and exciting from mixing and matching the various commands and functions together. I have often said that the main difference between a president like Teddy Roosevelt and one like Calvin Coolidge was in their approaches to the laws and the job. Both men worked within the same constitutional frame, yet one seemed to be effective while the other silently went through the motions. Historians have noted that Mr. Coolidge looked at the Constitution and acted in those areas that the laws "said" he could. Mr. Roosevelt, on the other hand, looked at the laws and did everything he could except what he was told he "could not" do. The ability to look at the Clipper manual, or my previous book, to read the commands and functions, and to try everything that is not explicitly forbidden is the key to being a successful Clipper programmer. Remove the dBlinders: they are preventing you from thinking, from mixing and matching, and from asking yourself "what if." If you can accomplish this, you will embark on a new journey filled with "why not's" instead of "cannot's," on a course laced with "how to's" and not "if only I could's." So sit back, have your computer ready with a pad of paper and pencil by your side, and begin the first steps into a new world, a new voyage...one you will employ and enjoy. Happy Clipping!

Stephen J. Straley

ACKNOWLEDGMENTS

There are so many individuals who deserve my heart-felt thanks. First, to my coauthor, David Karasek. With our CLIRMA library, he believed in the theories and direction of our company and was willing to help us reach our goals. I admire and respect this man for all that he has done. To my friendly force of supporters, associates, and close friends who have come to push me as hard as I push myself: David Dodson, Essor Maso, Joe King, Les Squires, Joe Booth, Dave Schwartz, and Jim Tamburrino. And finally, to my colleagues in the industry who have welcomed me and my views and have worked with me in striking an accord of progress for the end user: Dirk Lesko, Neil Weicher, John Halovanic, Corey Schwartz, Ray Love, Gary Beam, Tom Rettig, Fritz Koenig, David Kalman, and David Irwin.

—S.J.S.

Many thanks to James H. Carr, Technical Trainer in C and C++, Bell Labs, Craig Lau at National Broadcasting Company for his support, and to Ken Soyer at Sequiter Software.

—D.K.

INTRODUCTION

Regardless of the perception of the many, many magazines, Clipper is a language as well as a DBMS package. While it may not be in the same format as other languages, it makes up for that with power and performance. In the three years since I left Nantucket, I have been pushing the language to do more for more people. During that time, and in my move to the East Coast, I became involved with banking institutions and major corporations. In those organizations, the idea of structured programming is not unfamiliar. Additionally, I found that many of these places had a mixture of programmers: C programmers and dBASE-like programmers. Eventually, I took a job with one such company, and I found that the two camps, C and dBASE (Clipper), did not get along. C programmers almost felt contempt for all others; in their minds, there would never be a replacement for the C language. They felt that Clipper was unstructured and that they, the programmers, did not have as much control over the environment and the machine with Clipper as they did with the C language. On the other side, many of the Clipper programmers I met looked at the C language with a mixture of fear and disdain; it was too complicated for them to learn. To them, the idea of having several additional libraries handling the database, screen, networking, and communication information, not to mention the concept of an INCLUDE file, made them back away from the language quietly and quickly.

The bridge between the two must be forged. When deadlines are critical and getting the job finished (and under budget) is important, these minute differences must be left outside of the board room. Clipper gets the job done; so does C. One is neither better than the other, nor worse. Clipper should, however, get more people into the programming cycle, which in turn would increase department productivity and performance potential. End users within the company will see a fresher evolution of their tools, and company profits will eventually increase. C programmers must not keep their prejudices about the Clipper language, referring to it as "the dBASE compiler." This mind set prohibits team work and unit growth. On the other side, Clipper programmers need not accept their language as "the dBASE compiler" and refer to it as just another language that gets the job completed. If the C language were enveloped with a database manager, a screen manager, an indexing routine, and a verb intensive command set, C would probably be called something like, oh, I don't know. . . maybe, Clipper?

You see, it is just a question of how we look at the issue. But instead of looking at the language, we should look at the problems within the MIS departments of the major corporations. There are just too many applications that need to be written in order to effectively move the industry to the next plateau. Indeed, there are many new and exciting hardware issues being developed, but we, as programmers, should look at the existing world and consider the real potential of solving today's problems. Tomorrow's potential will only be important if people are getting the answers to today's dilemmas. Of all the languages I have seen, only Clipper give me all of the potential in one package. It is the intent of this book to show you, the Clipper programmer, some of this power and to educate you to the other side of the world, the C world. And to those C programmers who may be reading this book: It is our intent to squash your prejudices and preconceived notions about Nantucket's Clipper compiler. It, too, has a place on your programming shelf.

HOW TO USE THIS BOOK

Before reading any further, take a few moments to read this section. This book is neither guide nor cookbook. In it the philosophy of Clipper is looked at in all areas, from all angles. In *Programming in Clipper, 2nd Edition* (Addison-Wesley), the Clipper command and function library is laid out, as are as the basic enhanced features of the compiler. That knowledge should be firmly within your grasp if you are to get the fullest benefit from this book. Remember, it is not what you remember that counts; it is what you know. Individual command or function syntax is easy to remember, especially with the assistance of our previous book at your side or even *The Guide to Clipper: An On-Line Help System for Clipper*. In either case, you will memorize those functions and commands you use most frequently; the rest may be looked up. As long as you know where to get the information, you will be safe. However, the command and function base is only one part of the Clipper language. In this book, we will stretch what you think you know to new heights. Because of this difference, we suggest that you take plenty of notes as you read each chapter. In addition, read each chapter again and again, in its entirety, if you can, in order to gain the most from each topic. This way, your thinking processes will alter and grow. When this happens, ultimately your applications will reflect that change. We intend to enlarge your perceptions of the Clipper language. A better title for the book might be *Advanced Techniques and the Philosophy of Clipper*.

Each chapter will take you into new ideas and areas; as you read, envision the implementation of each idea in your current and future projects. Do not simply copy the ideas from these pages to your applications; embellish, enhance, and manipulate them. Let the code work through your mind, and play with the nuances of the language; get your hands and mind dirty! Each section of each chapter will emphasize an issue and show how Clipper solves problems that relate to it. While we may not offer a particular point relevant to your needs, the philosophy of the language and the specific coding examples should give you new avenues to consider as future problems appear. Again, look at the coding examples and relate the issues and code extracts to your needs.

Once we have done that, we will begin to teach you the fundamentals of the C language. As we did with Clipper in taking off the "dBlinders," we want to remove your potential fear of and confusion with the C language. With this in mind, your trip in the Clipper world, with C-like overtones, will give your applications new luster and professionalism. "Anything that can be done will be done" should be your motto and Clipper and C will be your tools. With this is mind, these are a few rules to maintain while reading this book.

1. THINK. This book will not teach you the fundamentals. We will stretch your past knowledge; it's time to take the training wheels off. To get the most from this book you will have to read it and then think, ponder the thoughts, the code, the topic, and the impact it will have in the future.

2. MIX & MATCH. Too many times we look at a problem and assume there is a one-to-one solution for it. Many times we find ourselves at an impasse because we have the preconceived notion that for every problem, there is only one solution. The beauty of the Clipper language is the ability to mix and match individual unique features and functions to yield some interesting results. The power of the language unfolds more potential when we mix and match the commands and functions of the language.

3. GENERALIZE TO MODULARIZE TO UTILIZE. Stretch a specific function to work in many different areas. Take older validation functions and make them work across several fields instead of just one. When we start to look at the concepts behind individual functions and begin to generalize them through the use of parameter passing and type checking, we will begin to get more utility from our modularized functions. When this happens, our potential to explore new programming avenues will elevate.

4. REMAIN CLOSE TO THE NATIVE LANGUAGE. Just because you know C, or think you do, does not mean you should assume that Clipper is incapable of meeting your needs. Too many times, programmers would rather piece together C code than think the problem through in the Clipper language. Try to use the native language as long as you can. Indeed, there are case where it is impossible to achieve a net result using the Clipper language. Normally, these situations call for the use of a mouse, graphics, extensive networking functions, or even communications. There is no other solution other than programming these extended features in C and linking them into the Clipper environment. However, there are some cases where it is more efficient to program a problem in Clipper than in C. In those cases, think the problem through in Clipper before resorting to C language.

5. ASK "WHAT IF" AND TRY IT. Look at the functions and the syntax of the language and take a few moments to ask yourself "what if. . . What if I used this function in conjunction with that function, what would I get?" Do not be a lazy, glorified dot-prompter. You are a professional: think like one. Regardless of time constraints and contractual obligations, as long as you can think, push yourself to push the language. No one else can do more for you than you can.

There is a special appendix in the back of the book. It contains one Clipper program that will generate all of the databases, indexes, text files, and ancillary information that is used by all of the routines and programs found in this book.

Finally, use this book in conjunction with *Programming in Clipper, 2nd Edition.* Together, your journey into the Clipper world will be more enjoyable, fascinating, and above all else, profitable.

CHAPTER ONE

Parsing Strings, Macros, and Array Technology

In every seminar conducted, one advanced topic rises above all others and shines through as being the most important function within the Clipper dialect. The function that always comes to mind as the most important is the one function that can be used to generate menus, database structures, windows, subdirectory names and paths, complex relational operations, and much more. Each of these topics pertain to different areas of an application, yet all perform at higher levels when based on the same function: the parser. So why is this function so important and how can it be used throughout an application? This chapter answers that question and more.

It is not an exaggeration to say that the Parsing() function is involved in every application developed. As we began to push the limits of the ToolkiT — Release 2 and the Accounting Package, we found that by letting the parser pull out the necessary information in a long string, we not only save on memory, but on coding effort as well. Ironically, it is the concept of the parser that makes Clipper work on the inside; therefore, it is no surprise that the same concept should apply to Clipper-based applications as well.

A parsing routine is a function that removes information from a string of data, alters the original string to contain the original value of the string less the removed value, and returns the extract. The key element of a parser is the concept of a delimiter. This is the character that tells the function when the extract ends and the remaining string value begins. Our mind thinks like a parser. For example, when we read, we parse out the information in blocks known as words, and those words are delimited by the space character. Working with computers is similar but much more powerful in many ways. It would be very difficult to train our minds to ignore a space character as a delimiter and to view another character as that special character. For a function, and for the computer, this switch is simple. For example, let's consider the following string:

```
"Lions/Tigers/Bears/Cubs (thought I was going to say something else)"
```

Now, assign it to a variable:

```
variable = "Lions/Tigers/Bears/Cubs " + ;
           "(thought I was going to say something else)"
```

Now, let's parse out information from this string, based on the number of occurrences of the "/ " character. If we were to display the results to the screen, we would see the following:

```
Lions
Tigers
Bears
Cubs (thought I was going to say something else)
```

Notice that the parsing character, or delimiter, is removed from both the extract and the remaining value in the string. Also, note that the number of displayed items is based on the number of delimiters plus one.

The only trouble with this concept is its operation. For example, we know that the parser should return a value: that portion of the string that has been extracted. However, it also implies that the string has been modified for the next operation. This means that the parser needs to return the value of the remaining string. The problem is that a function can only return a single value. One way to get around this problem is by initializing a PUBLIC variable that can be accessed at any level, at any time, and can be altered within the Parsing() routine. This yields the value for the extract, while altering the value of the PUBLIC variable, thus, generating two values. While this is close to parsing in concept, the practice and implementation of a PUBLIC variable for a parsing string becomes unwieldy and unstructured. However, if we turn our attention to one of the unique features within the Clipper language, our answer is at hand. Remember, in *Programming in Clipper, 2nd Edition* (Addison-Wesley) we talked about the idea of parameters by reference and by value. The following briefly reviews this.

When parameters are passed by value, the subroutines that acquire the parameters can look at the parameters' values but cannot alter their contents. This means that any parameter that was passed by value and modified in the subroutine will reattain its original value on leaving the subroutine. Technically, only the value of the parameter is passed to the subroutine and not the address point. On the other hand, if we were to pass the address point of the parameter to the subroutine, the subroutine could alter the value of the variable, which would remain changed when control returned to the calling routine.

Passing a parameter by reference means that the subroutine can have its own value while modifying the value of the passed parameter. This would therefore seem to imply that the subroutine yields more than one value. This is precisely what we need. In Clipper, we know that we can pass a parameter to a function by reference by simply adding the "@" character in front of the name of the variable. Therefore, using the above example, the call to the parsing function would look something like this:

```
? Parsing(@variable, "/")
```

Looking at this sample, we can see that the value of the Parsing() function is that portion of the string to the left of the "/ " character. Additionally, we can see that the Parsing() function has altered the value of the string variable by giving it everything to the right of the "/ " character. In a programming environment, this is probably how the function may be called:

```
DO WHILE !EMPTY(variable)
    ? Parsing(@variable, "/")
ENDDO
```

As you can see, as the Parsing() function alters the value of the string named **variable,** it is then tested in the DO WHILE command. The Parsing() function should perform until no element is found. At this point the passed string (by reference) is set to a null byte and the value of the function is the original string. On the last iteration of the function, we can see that the potential value for the string **variable** will be a null byte, which in turn will terminate the DO WHILE loop. Before going any further, let's take a look at a simple Parsing() function.

```
********************
* ***********************************************
* * The following procedure(s)/function(s) are  *
* * part of Steve Straley's ToolkiT(tm) -       *
* * Release 2, published by Four Seasons        *
* * Publishing Co., Inc.  All Rights Reserved   *
* * Information: 212-599-2141 / 800-662-2278    *
* * All Rights Reserved                         *
* ***********************************************

FUNCTION Parsing

   PARAMETERS _getstr

   * This function is the string parser.  Basically, return the
   * beginning fragment of a string, adjust the string, and if
   * passed by reference, alter the contents of the original
   * string.

   PRIVATE _location, _tempback
   _location = IF(EMPTY(AT("+", _getstr)),  ;
                  AT("/", _getstr), AT("+", _getstr))
   _tempback = IF(!EMPTY(_location), SUBSTR(_getstr, 1, ;
                 _location - 1), _getstr)
   _getstr = IF(!EMPTY(_location), SUBSTR(_getstr, ;
                 _location + 1), "")
   RETURN(_tempback)

* End of File
```

This function was used in both editions of *Programming in Clipper* (Addison-Wesley) where it was called Getnum() and used by the Mpop() function. Since then, the function has been altered to encompass a tighter control on the parameter checking and to allow additional terminating characters. Now, we have a newer version that first appeared in the ToolkiT — Release 2, which was renamed the Parsing() function:

```
********************
* ***********************************************
* * The following procedure(s)/function(s) are  *
* * part of Steve Straley's ToolkiT(tm) -       *
* * Release 2, published by Four Seasons        *
* * Publishing Co., Inc.  All Rights Reserved   *
* * Information: 212-599-2141 / 800-662-2278    *
* * All Rights Reserved                         *
* ***********************************************

FUNCTION Parsing

   PARAMETERS _getstr, _forcode
```

```
   * _getstr is the string to be parsed
   * _forcode is the code that parses.

   * This function is the string parser.  Basically, return the
   * beginning fragment of a string, adjust the string, and if
   * passed by reference, alter the contents of the original
   * string.

   PRIVATE _forcode, _location, _tempback

   IF PCOUNT() = 2
      IF TYPE("_forcode") = "L"
         _thechar = "|"
      ELSE
         _thechar = _forcode
      ENDIF
      _forcode = .T.
   ELSE
      _forcode = .F.
   ENDIF

   IF _forcode
      _location   = AT(_thechar, _getstr)
   ELSE
      _location   = IF(EMPTY(AT("+", _getstr)),  ;
                    AT("/", _getstr), AT("+", _getstr))
   ENDIF

   _tempback = IF(!EMPTY(_location), SUBSTR(_getstr, ;
                  1, _location - 1), _getstr)
   _getstr = IF(!EMPTY(_location), SUBSTR(_getstr, ;
                  _location + 1), "")
   RETURN(_tempback)

* End of File
```

IMPLICATIONS OF A PARSER

A parser can take on many forms and can be used for many purposes. If properly used, it can save time and effort. The compiler itself needs to have some type of parse within Clipper.exe in order to understand the words and phrases of each command line of your PRG files. There, the terminating character for each element of a command line is commonly a blank space. Sometimes, with special words or clauses in a command line, the format of the number of spaces can be as little as 0 characters. In those cases, key words and/or phrases would have been previously recognized by the compiler to prepare it for the next key word or phrase. These key words could in essence butt up against one another. For example, the IF() function can rest against the "="; however, the IF command needs a blank space to delimit it from the next portion of the command line. Other than those exceptions, the programmer can dictate the format number of blank characters he or she wants in a command line. In other words, Clipper.exe did not want to use the “/ ” character as a delimiting character for its parse because it would no make sense. To prove this, consider the following command line:

```
DO WHILE .T.
```

What are the key elements of this line? First, there is the basic command DO WHILE (which consists of a DO and a WHILE statement), and there is the conditional statement, the logical true (.T.). Now, if the delimiter for Clipper was the “/ ” character, Clipper would take this command line as one entire string and not as three separate entities. Therefore, we can see that the space character is the delimiter. This is determined not by Nantucket, but by the format of the language. The data, in this case, is the syntax of the language set, and Clipper’s parser must adhere to the rules. Otherwise, we would all be coding differently. So you see, the format of the data that is to be viewed and parsed is critical.

In this chapter, we will be looking at several examples of how a parser can be employed in an application to save time and effort.

PARSING OUT THE COLORS

One of the most natural strings in the Clipper language that can be easily parsed is the individual colors yielded by the SETCOLOR() function. Even in the default mode of “W/N, I/W,,,I/W”, which can be seen by a simple SETCOLOR(“”) call, each element in the string can be seen individually. For example, we can pick up the standard foreground color or, perhaps, the unselected background color. This sample code shows just that:

```
********************
* Name      Color1.prg
* Author    Stephen J. Straley
* Date      July 1, 1989
* Notice    Copyright (c) 1989 Stephen J. Straley & Associates
*           All Rights Reserved
* Compile   Clipper Color1 -m
* Release   Summer 87
* Link      PLINK86 FI Color1 LIB Clipper LIB Extend;
* Note      This shows how the color string can be parsed
*           into many different elements.
*
********************

CLEAR SCREEN
SET COLOR TO W+/N, N/W
maincolor = STRTRAN(STRTRAN(SETCOLOR(), ",", "/"), "+", ";")
? SETCOLOR()
DO WHILE !EMPTY(maincolor)
   ? STRTRAN(Parsing(@maincolor), ";", "+")
ENDDO
```

```

* ***********************************************
* * The following procedure(s)/function(s) are  *
* * part of Steve Straley's ToolkiT(tm) -       *
* * Release 2, published by Four Seasons        *
* * Publishing Co., Inc.  All Rights Reserved   *
* * Information: 212-599-2141 / 800-662-2278    *
* * All Rights Reserved                         *
* ***********************************************

FUNCTION Parsing

   PARAMETERS _getstr

   * This function is the string parser.  Basically, return the
   * beginning fragment of a string, adjust the string, and if
   * passed by reference, alter the contents of the original
   * string.

   PRIVATE _location, _tempback

   _location    = IF(EMPTY(AT("+", _getstr)), ;
                     AT("/", _getstr), AT("+", _getstr))

   _tempback = IF(!EMPTY(_location), ;
                  SUBSTR(_getstr, 1, _location - 1), _getstr)
   _getstr = IF(!EMPTY(_location), ;
                SUBSTR(_getstr, _location + 1), "")
   RETURN(_tempback)

* End of File
```

The trick here is to use the STRTRAN() function to replace every occurrence of the "," character with the "/ " character (our delimiter) and to strip every blank space from the string. Additionally, we need to replace every occurrence of the "+" character with another character. In the above example, this is the ";" character. The reason for this is the versatility of the Parsing() function. The Parsing() function has been coded to accept either the "/ " character or the "+" character; and since the "+" character means something specific to the colors, it is important to replace it with another character and to swap it back to its original value once the parsing operation is complete.

The implementation of this technology is just as important. It is generally accepted that the individual elements of the screen's colors can be concatenated to make one large string, which in turn can be used by the SETCOLOR() function to reset the colors of the system. In the past, each individual element of the screen's color had to be kept in a separate variable if the programmer wanted to give the end user the ability to toggle through each color band on each color fragment. Running the following program will show the four different bands of color and how to toggle through them.

```
001 : ********************
002 : * Name      Makecolr.prg
003 : * Author    Stephen J. Straley
004 : * Date      July 1, 1989
005 : * Notice    Copyright (c) 1989 Stephen J. Straley & Associates
006 : *           All Rights Reserved
007 : * Compile   Clipper Makecolr -m
008 : * Release   Summer 87
009 : * Link      PLINK86 FI Makecolr LIB Clipper LIB Extend;
010 : * Note      This allows the colors to be changed on the fly
011 : *           and is available in the ToolkiT and Scrinit()
012 : *           functions.  The unselected option does not
013 : *           work with characters and needs to be corrected
014 : *           in Clipper.
015 : *
016 : ********************
017 :
018 : CLEAR SCREEN
019 : @ 0,0 SAY "Press the HOT keys to change the colors!"
020 : value = Altercolor(5)
021 : CLEAR SCREEN
022 : ? value
023 :
024 : * **********************************************
025 : * * The following procedure(s)/function(s) are  *
026 : * * part of Steve Straley's ToolkiT(tm) -       *
027 : * * Release 2, published by Four Seasons        *
028 : * * Publishing Co., Inc.  All Rights Reserved   *
029 : * * Information: 212-599-2141 / 800-662-2278    *
030 : * * All Rights Reserved                         *
031 : * **********************************************
032 :
033 : FUNCTION Altercolor
034 :
035 :     PARAMETERS _p, _l, _v
036 :
037 :     _rsomething = (PCOUNT() = 1)
038 :
039 :     PRIVATE _trow, _tcol, _topt, _tcolor
040 :
041 :     _atrow = IF((TYPE("_p") = "N"), _p, ROW())
042 :
043 :     _trow   = IF((_atrow > 20), 2, _atrow)
044 :     _tcol   = COL()
045 :     _topt   = 1
046 :     _tcolor = SETCOLOR()
047 :     _hcolor = SETCOLOR()
048 :     scrframe= IF((TYPE("scrframe") != "C"), CHR(201) + ;
049 :               CHR(205) + CHR(187) + CHR(186) + CHR(188) + ;
050 :               CHR(205) + CHR(200) + CHR(186) + CHR(32), ;
051 :               scrframe)
052 :     SET KEY ASC("+") TO Upfor
053 :     SET KEY ASC("-") TO Downfor
054 :     SET KEY ASC("1") TO Normal
```

```
   SET KEY ASC("2") TO Bright
   SET KEY ASC("3") TO Blinking
   SET KEY ASC("4") TO Putback
   SET KEY 5 TO  Upback
   SET KEY 24 TO Downback
   Pushscreen(_trow+1,0,_trow+3,78)
   DO WHILE .T.
      SETCOLOR(_tcolor)
      STORE 0 TO _upfor, _downfor, _upback, _downback, ;
                 _normal, _bright, _blink
      @ _trow+1,0, _trow+3,78 BOX scrframe
      @ _trow+1,1 SAY " ESC to Quit, +/- Foreground, " +;
                  CHR(24) + CHR(25) + " Background "
      @ _trow+3,1 SAY " (1) Normal, (2) Bright, (3) " +;
                      "Blinking, (4) Original "
      @ _trow+2,2  PROMPT " Standard "
      @ _trow+2,12 PROMPT " Enhanced "
      @ _trow+2,22 PROMPT " Border "
      @ _trow+2,30 PROMPT " Background "
      @ _trow+2,42 PROMPT " Unselected "

      @ _trow+2,55 SAY Fill_out(SETCOLOR(), 23)

      MENU TO _topt
      IF _topt = 0
         EXIT
      ELSE
         _tcolor = Manipcol(_topt, _tcolor)
      ENDIF
   ENDDO
   Popscreen(_trow+1,0,_trow+3,78)
   SET KEY ASC("+") TO
   SET KEY ASC("-") TO
   SET KEY ASC("1") TO
   SET KEY ASC("2") TO
   SET KEY ASC("3") TO
   SET KEY ASC("4") TO
   SET KEY 5 TO
   SET KEY 24 TO
   @ _trow, _tcol SAY ""
   SETCOLOR(_hcolor)
   RETURN(_tcolor)

********************

FUNCTION Manipcol

   PARAMETERS pickcolor, _colors

   _colors = STRTRAN(STRTRAN(_colors, "/", "|"), "," , "/")

   _a = STRTRAN(PARSING(@_colors, ","), "|", "/")
   _b = STRTRAN(PARSING(@_colors, ","), "|", "/")
   _c = PARSING(@_colors)
```

```
109 :     _d = PARSING(@_colors)
110 :     _e = STRTRAN(PARSING(@_colors, ","), "|", "/")
111 :
112 :     IF     pickcolor = 1
113 :        DO CASE
114 :        CASE _bright = 1
115 :           _a = SUBSTR(_a, 1, 1) + "+" + SUBSTR(_a, 2)
116 :        CASE _blink  = 1
117 :           _a = SUBSTR(_a, 1, 1) + "*" + SUBSTR(_a, 2)
118 :        CASE _normal = 1
119 :           _a = STRIPFROM(_a, "+*")
120 :        CASE _upfor = 1 .OR. _downfor = 1
121 :           _a = FRONT(_a, _upfor = 1)
122 :        CASE _upback = 1 .OR. _downback = 1
123 :           _a = BACK(_a, _upback = 1)
124 :        ENDCASE
125 :        _a = STRTRAN(STRTRAN(_a, "**", "*"), "++", "+")
126 :
127 :     ELSEIF pickcolor = 2
128 :        DO CASE
129 :        CASE _bright = 1
130 :           _b = SUBSTR(_b, 1, 1) + "+" + SUBSTR(_b, 2)
131 :        CASE _blink  = 1
132 :           _b = SUBSTR(_b, 1, 1) + "*" + SUBSTR(_b, 2)
133 :        CASE _normal = 1
134 :           _b = STRIPFROM(_b, "+*")
135 :        CASE _upfor = 1 .OR. _downfor = 1
136 :           _b = FRONT(_b, _upfor = 1)
137 :        CASE _upback = 1 .OR. _downback = 1
138 :           _b = BACK(_b, _upback = 1)
139 :        ENDCASE
140 :        _b = LTRIM(STRTRAN(STRTRAN(_b, "**", "*"), "++", "+"))
141 :
142 :     ELSEIF pickcolor = 3
143 :        DO CASE
144 :        CASE _upfor = 1 .OR. _downfor = 1
145 :           _c = STRTRAN(FRONT(_c, _upfor = 1), "/", "")
146 :        ENDCASE
147 :
148 :     ELSEIF pickcolor = 4
149 :        DO CASE
150 :        CASE _upfor = 1 .OR. _downfor = 1
151 :           _d = STRTRAN(FRONT(_d, _upfor = 1), "/", "")
152 :        ENDCASE
153 :
154 :     ELSEIF pickcolor = 5
155 :        DO CASE
156 :        CASE _bright = 1
157 :           _e = SUBSTR(_e, 1, 1) + "+" + SUBSTR(_e, 2)
158 :        CASE _blink  = 1
159 :           _e = SUBSTR(_e, 1, 1) + "*" + SUBSTR(_e, 2)
160 :        CASE _normal = 1
161 :           _e = STRIPFROM(_e, "*+")
162 :        CASE _upfor = 1 .OR. _downfor = 1
```

```
163 :           _e = FRONT(_e, _upfor = 1)
164 :        CASE _upback = 1 .OR. _downback = 1
165 :           _e = BACK(_e, _upback = 1)
166 :      ENDCASE
167 :      _e = LTRIM(STRTRAN(STRTRAN(_e, "**", "*"), "++", "+"))
168 :    ENDIF
169 :
170 :    RETURN(_a + "," + _b + "," + _c + "," + _d + "," + _e)
171 :
172 : *******************
173 :
174 : FUNCTION Front
175 :
176 :    PARAMETERS _tchar, upit
177 :
178 :    * if upit, then go forward with the incement
179 :    * if not, go backwards
180 :    * determine if _tchar is of character or numeric type
181 :
182 :    _hold = PARSING(@_tchar)
183 :
184 :    IF SUBSTR(_hold, 1, 1)$"0123456789"    && number type
185 :       _g = VAL(SUBSTR(_hold, 1, 1))
186 :       _g = _g + IF(upit, 1, -1)
187 :       IF _g > 9
188 :          _g = 0
189 :       ELSEIF _g < 0
190 :          _g = 9
191 :       ENDIF
192 :       _hold = TRANSFORM(_g, "9") + SUBSTR(_hold, 2)
193 :    ELSE                             && character type
194 :       format = "N B G BGR RBW I X "
195 :       _g = STRIPFROM(SUBSTR(_hold, 1, 2), "*+")
196 :       _posit = AT(_g, format) + IF(upit, 2, -2)
197 :       IF _posit > 17
198 :          _posit = 1
199 :       ELSEIF _posit < 1
200 :          _posit = 17
201 :       ENDIF
202 :       IF SUBSTR(_hold, 2, 1)$"*+"    && Only one character
203 :          _hold = TRIM(SUBSTR(format, _posit, 2)) + ;
204 :                  SUBSTR(_hold, 2)
205 :       ELSE
206 :          _hold = TRIM(SUBSTR(format, _posit, 2)) + ;
207 :                  SUBSTR(_hold, 3)
208 :       ENDIF
209 :    ENDIF
210 :    RETURN(_hold + "/" + _tchar)
211 :
212 :
213 : *******************
214 :
215 : FUNCTION Back
216 :
```

```
217 :     PARAMETERS _tchar, upit
218 :
219 :     _hold = _tchar
220 :     _tchar = PARSING(@_hold)
221 :
222 :     IF SUBSTR(_hold, 1, 1)$"0123456789"    && number type
223 :         _g = VAL(SUBSTR(_hold, 1, 1))
224 :         _g = _g + IF(upit, 1, -1)
225 :         IF _g > 9
226 :             _g = 0
227 :         ELSEIF _g < 0
228 :             _g = 9
229 :         ENDIF
230 :         _hold = TRANSFORM(_g, "9") + SUBSTR(_hold, 2)
231 :     ELSE                            && character type
232 :         format = "N B G BGR RBW I X "
233 :         _g = STRIPFROM(SUBSTR(_hold, 1, 2), "*+")
234 :         _posit = AT(_g, format) + IF(upit, 2, -2)
235 :         IF _posit > 17
236 :             _posit = 1
237 :         ELSEIF _posit < 1
238 :             _posit = 17
239 :         ENDIF
240 :         IF SUBSTR(_hold, 2, 1)$"*+"    && Only one character
241 :             _hold = TRIM(SUBSTR(format, _posit, 2)) + ;
242 :                     SUBSTR(_hold, 2)
243 :         ELSE
244 :             _hold = TRIM(SUBSTR(format, _posit, 2)) + ;
245 :                     SUBSTR(_hold, 3)
246 :         ENDIF
247 :     ENDIF
248 :     RETURN(_tchar + "/" + _hold)
249 :
250 : ******************
251 :
252 : PROCEDURE Upfor
253 :
254 :     STORE 1 TO _upfor
255 :     KEYBOARD CHR(13)
256 :
257 : ******************
258 :
259 : PROCEDURE Downfor
260 :
261 :     STORE 1 TO _downfor
262 :     KEYBOARD CHR(13)
263 :
264 : ******************
265 :
266 : PROCEDURE Normal
267 :
268 :     STORE 1 TO _normal
269 :     KEYBOARD CHR(13)
270 :
```

```
271 : *******************
272 :
273 : PROCEDURE Bright
274 :
275 :     STORE 1 TO _bright
276 :     KEYBOARD CHR(13)
277 :
278 : *******************
279 :
280 : PROCEDURE Blinking
281 :
282 :     STORE 1 TO _blink
283 :     KEYBOARD CHR(13)
284 :
285 : *******************
286 :
287 : PROCEDURE Putback
288 :
289 :     _tcolor = _hcolor
290 :     KEYBOARD CHR(13)
291 :
292 : *******************
293 :
294 : PROCEDURE Upback
295 :
296 :     STORE 1 TO _upback
297 :     KEYBOARD CHR(13)
298 :
299 : *******************
300 :
301 : PROCEDURE Downback
302 :
303 :     STORE 1 TO _downback
304 :     KEYBOARD CHR(13)
305 :
306 : *******************
307 :
308 : FUNCTION Parsing
309 :
310 :     PARAMETERS _getstr
311 :
312 :     * This function is the string parser.  Basically, return the
313 :     * beginning fragment of a string, adjust the string, and if
314 :     * passed by reference, alter the contents of the original
315 :     * string.
316 :
317 :     PRIVATE _location, _tempback
318 :
319 :     _location   = AT("/", _getstr)
320 :
321 :     _tempback = IF(!EMPTY(_location), ;
322 :                 SUBSTR(_getstr, 1, _location - 1), _getstr)
323 :     _getstr = IF(!EMPTY(_location), ;
324 :                 SUBSTR(_getstr, _location + 1), "")
```

```
325 :     RETURN(_tempback)
326 :
327 : ********************
328 :
329 : PROCEDURE Pushscreen
330 :
331 :     PARAMETERS push1, push2, push3, push4, pushsave, ;
332 :               pushscr, pushbord, pushshad
333 :
334 :     IF TYPE("sc_level")="U" .OR. TYPE("allscreens")="U"
335 :        PUBLIC allscreens[20], sc_level
336 :        AFILL(allscreens, "")
337 :        sc_level = 2
338 :     ENDIF
339 :     scrframe = CHR(218) + CHR(196) + CHR(191) + CHR(179) + ;
340 :                CHR(217) + CHR(196) + CHR(192) + CHR(179) + ;
341 :                CHR(32)
342 :
343 :     DO CASE
344 :     CASE PCOUNT() = 4   && 4 parameters means No border,
345 :        pushsave = .T.   && No Frame, Just save the area
346 :        pushscr = .T.
347 :        pushbord = .F.
348 :        pushshad = .F.
349 :     CASE PCOUNT() = 5   && 5 parameters mean Save area
350 :        pushscr = .T.    && without border logic
351 :        pushbord = .F.
352 :        pushshad = .F.
353 :     CASE PCOUNT() = 6
354 :        pushbord = .T.
355 :        pushshad = .F.
356 :     CASE PCOUNT() = 7
357 :        pushshad = .F.
358 :     ENDCASE
359 :
360 :     IF pushsave
361 :        push_temp = ""
362 :        IF pushshad
363 :           allscreens[sc_level] = ;
364 :              SAVESCREEN(push1,push2,push3 + 1, push4 + 1)
365 :        ELSE
366 :           allscreens[sc_level] = ;
367 :              SAVESCREEN(push1,push2,push3,push4)
368 :        ENDIF
369 :        sc_level = IF(sc_level=20, sc_level, sc_level+1)
370 :     ENDIF
371 :
372 :     IF pushbord
373 :        IF !pushscr
374 :           IF TYPE("scrframe") = "U"
375 :              @ push1, push2 TO push3, push4 DOUBLE
376 :           ELSE
377 :              @ push1,push2,push3,push4 BOX ;
378 :                 SUBSTR(scrframe, 1, 8)
```

```
379 :              ENDIF
380 :          ELSE
381 :              IF TYPE("scrframe") = "U"
382 :                  @ push1, push2 CLEAR TO push3, push4
383 :                  @ push1, push2 TO push3, push4 DOUBLE
384 :              ELSE
385 :                  @ push1, push2, push3, push4 BOX scrframe
386 :              ENDIF
387 :          ENDIF
388 :          IF pushshad
389 :              SHADOW(push1, push2, push3, push4)
390 :          ENDIF
391 :      ENDIF
392 :
393 : ********************
394 :
395 : PROCEDURE Popscreen
396 :
397 :      PARAMETERS pop1, pop2, pop3, pop4, popshad
398 :
399 :      IF PCOUNT() = 4
400 :          popshad = .F.
401 :      ENDIF
402 :      sc_level = IF(sc_level = 1, sc_level, sc_level - 1)
403 :      pop_temp = allscreens[sc_level]
404 :      IF popshad
405 :          RESTSCREEN(pop1, pop2, pop3+1, pop4+1, pop_temp)
406 :      ELSE
407 :          RESTSCREEN(pop1, pop2, pop3, pop4, pop_temp)
408 :      ENDIF
409 :      allscreens[sc_level+1] = ""
410 :
411 : ********************
412 :
413 : FUNCTION Shadow
414 :
415 :      PARAMETERS shada, shadb, shadc, shadd, shadde
416 :
417 :      IF PCOUNT() = 4
418 :          shadde = CHR(177)
419 :      ENDIF
420 :
421 :      shad_color = SETCOLOR()
422 :      SETCOLOR( STRTRAN( shad_color, "+", "" ) )
423 :
424 :      FOR shadx = shada+1 TO shadc+1
425 :          @ shadx, shadd+1 SAY shadde
426 :      NEXT
427 :      @ shadx-1,shadb+1 SAY REPLICATE(shadde, shadd-shadb)
428 :
429 :      SETCOLOR( shad_color )
430 :      RETURN(.F.)
```

```
431 :
432 : ********************
433 :
434 : FUNCTION Fill_out
435 :
436 :     PARAMETERS fill_a, fill_b
437 :
438 :     * fill_a = the string to be filled out
439 :     * fill_b = the Length to fill out the string to
440 :
441 :     IF PCOUNT() = 1
442 :         fill_b = 80
443 :     ELSE
444 :         IF TYPE("fill_b") = "C"
445 :             fill_b = VAL(b)
446 :         ENDIF
447 :         fill_b = IIF(fill_b <= 1, 80, fill_b)
448 :     ENDIF
449 :
450 :     IF fill_b <= LEN(fill_a)
451 :         RETURN(fill_a)
452 :     ENDIF
453 :     RETURN(fill_a + SPACE(fill_b - LEN(fill_a)))
454 :
455 : ********************
456 :
457 : FUNCTION Stripfrom
458 :
459 :     PARAMETERS _stripstr, _what_strp
460 :
461 :     PRIVATE _qaz, _retstr
462 :
463 :     IF PCOUNT() != 2
464 :         RETURN ("")
465 :     ENDIF
466 :
467 :     * _what_strp may be longer than one element
468 :     * for one element, STRTRAN() is as effective
469 :
470 :     _retstr = ""
471 :
472 :     FOR _qaz = 1 TO LEN(_stripstr)
473 :         IF (SUBSTR(_stripstr, _qaz, 1)) $ _what_strp
474 :         ELSE
475 :             _retstr = _retstr + SUBSTR(_stripstr, _qaz, 1)
476 :         ENDIF
477 :     NEXT
478 :     RETURN(_retstr)
479 :
480 : * End of File
```

PARSING A LIST-BOX

One of the first functions every developer thinks about is a list-box type of function. In the Summer '87 release of Clipper, we have the DBEDIT() and ACHOICE() functions that approach this concept. However, prior to this release, we were left to our own devices. Moreover, many developers like making their own DBEDIT()-like list-box function. Again, turning back to *Programming in Clipper, 2nd Edition* (Addison-Wesley), the Mpop() function [or Pop() function] was designed to do just that. The Mpop() function is still used over the DBEDIT() function for several reasons. First, the Mpop() function is changeable; the programmer has complete control over the function. With the use of the DBEDIT() function, the developer is left to the designs of Nantucket. While in some cases this may be acceptable, in this case it may not be. In testing examples, a simpler version of the Mpop() function can take up as much as 7K less room in memory than the DBEDIT() function. In either event, the Parsing() function is used to choose which fields to display.

In a practical environment, consider the following code extract:

```
mcode = Chart->code
@ 10,10 GET mcode VALID Goodones(@mcode)
READ

  ******************

  FUNCTION Goodones

     PARAMETERS value

     SEEK value
     IF !FOUND()
        *
        * perform a list-box
        *
        RETURN(.F.)
     ELSE
        RETURN(.T.)
     ENDIF
```

In this brief example, we can see that if an invalid code is entered, the function Goodones() will not be able to find the value. Therefore, a list-box may be displayed, allowing the user to point to the desired item in a windowed area and shoot that item into the GET directly. This method is commonly referred to as a point-and-shoot list-box. The problem most commonly encountered by the developer is to decide which fields to display in the windowed area. Many times, the programmer will simply put the field that is involved with the GET. However, in this example, it can be predicted that the end user will have trouble with the GET because it is a code field. In addition, we can predict with a high degree of certainty that the description for the code is somewhere in the database or in a related database. If it is not, not only will this example not pertain to your programming style, but it is likely that your end-user base has a few choice words to say. In any event, if a description field or additional related fields are available, it may be more than adequate to display those fields in the windowed area as well. Now, with this logic, we have a case where the list-box will show multiple fields and the function must be able to separate the fields to show from those that should be hidden. Consider the following coding extract:

```
Mpop(10,40,8,20,"A", ..., "2+3+10")
```

Here, within the windowed area beginning at 10,40 and continuing on for 8 rows and 20 columns, fields 2, 3, and 10 will be displayed. In this string, we can see that some type of parse is performed on the string of fields and that the delimiter used is the "+" character. While this function was used in *Programming in Clipper, 2nd Edition* (Addison-Wesley), we have used the same parsing technology to work with the DBEDIT() function. Consider the following:

```
001 : ********************
002 : * Name      Listbox.prg
003 : * Author    Stephen J. Straley
004 : * Date      July 1, 1989
005 : * Notice    Copyright (c) 1989 Stephen J. Straley & Associates
006 : *           All Rights Reserved
007 : * Compile   Clipper Listbox -m
008 : * Release   Summer 87
009 : * Link      PLINK86 FI Listbox LIB Clipper LIB Extend;
010 : * Note      This shows how the Parsing() function can assist
011 : *           in the information listed in a list-box.
012 : *
013 : ********************
014 :
015 : SELECT B
016 : USE Filenos
017 : INDEX ON File_name TO Tempname
018 : SELECT A
019 : USE Disknos INDEX Disknos
020 : CLEAR SCREEN
021 : mfile = SPACE(10)
022 : mmore = SPACE(20)
023 : SET KEY 9 TO Inquire
024 : @  8,10 SAY "Press ESC to quit, TAB for Listing"
025 : @ 10,10 SAY "What file do you want? " GET mfile ;
026 :        VALID Lookfor()
027 : @ 12,10 SAY "Just an extra GET for display" GET mmore
028 : READ
029 : CLEAR SCREEN
030 :
031 : ********************
032 :
033 : PROCEDURE Inquire
034 :
035 :    KEYBOARD "?" + CHR(13)
036 :
037 : ********************
```

```
038 :
039 : FUNCTION Lookfor
040 :
041 :    SELECT Filenos
042 :    passback = Lookup(@mfile, "5", "6/7/8/9/20", .T.)
043 :    SELECT Disknos
044 :    RETURN(passback)
045 :
046 : * ********************************************
047 : * * The following procedure(s)/function(s) are  *
048 : * * part of Steve Straley's ToolkiT(tm) -       *
049 : * * Release 2, published by Four Seasons        *
050 : * * Publishing Co., Inc.  All Rights Reserved   *
051 : * * Information: 212-599-2141 / 800-662-2278    *
052 : * * All Rights Reserved                         *
053 : * * ********************************************
054 :
055 : FUNCTION Lookup
056 :
057 :    * make sure that the type of the variable and the
058 :    *      type of the data field are the same
059 :    * make sure that the fields in the field list are available
060 :    * make sure that the field in the get list is available
061 :    * verify window coordinates
062 :    * make sure that the database is available
063 :    * verify all parameters
064 :
065 :    PARAMETER _var, _gets, _says, _stuff
066 :
067 :    IF PCOUNT() < 3
068 :       RETURN(.F.)
069 :    ELSEIF EMPTY(ALIAS())
070 :       RETURN(.F.)
071 :    ELSEIF TYPE("_gets") + TYPE("_says") != "CC"
072 :       RETURN(.F.)
073 :    ENDIF
074 :
075 :    PRIVATE _gname, _old, _qaz
076 :
077 :    _gname = FIELD(VAL(_gets))
078 :
079 :    && Get field is not there
080 :
081 :    IF EMPTY(_gname)
082 :       RETURN(.F.)
083 :    ENDIF
084 :
085 :    && The data types do not match
086 :
087 :    IF TYPE("_var") != TYPE(_gname)
088 :       RETURN(.F.)
089 :    ENDIF
090 :
091 :    && Seek to see if it is there...
```

```
092 :
093 :    SEEK _var
094 :    IF FOUND()
095 :       RETURN(.T.)
096 :    ELSE
097 :       GO TOP
098 :    ENDIF
099 :
100 :    _stuff = IF(TYPE("_stuff") != "L", .F., _stuff)
101 :
102 :    _old = _says
103 :    _cnt = 0
104 :    _tot = 0
105 :    DO WHILE !EMPTY(_old)
106 :       _tot = _tot + 1
107 :       _sname = FIELD(VAL(Parsing(@_old)))
108 :
109 :       && the SAY is not there
110 :
111 :       _cnt = _cnt + IF((EMPTY(_sname)), 1, 0)
112 :
113 :    ENDDO
114 :
115 :    DECLARE _show[_tot - _cnt]
116 :    _old = _says
117 :    _cnt = 1
118 :    DO WHILE !EMPTY(_old)
119 :       _sname = FIELD(VAL(Parsing(@_old)))
120 :       IF !EMPTY(_sname)
121 :          _show[_cnt] = Upperlower(_sname)
122 :          _cnt = _cnt + 1
123 :       ENDIF
124 :    ENDDO
125 :
126 :    _lookrow = ROW()
127 :    IF _lookrow > 16
128 :       _lookrow = 4
129 :    ENDIF
130 :
131 :    _lookcol = COL()
132 :    IF _lookcol > 60
133 :       _lookcol = 60
134 :       _lookrow = _lookrow + 1
135 :    ENDIF
136 :
137 :    _lookscr = SAVESCREEN(_lookrow-1,_lookcol-1,_lookrow + 7, ;
138 :             _lookcol + (79 - _lookcol))
139 :    @ _lookrow - 1, _lookcol - 1 CLEAR TO _lookrow + 7, ;
140 :             _lookcol + (79 - _lookcol)
141 :    @ _lookrow - 1, _lookcol - 1 TO _lookrow + 7, ;
142 :             _lookcol + (79 - _lookcol) DOUBLE
143 :
144 :    DBEDIT(_lookrow, _lookcol, _lookrow + 6, _lookcol + ;
145 :          (78 - _lookcol), _show)
```

```
146 :    IF LASTKEY() = 13
147 :       _var = &_gname.
148 :       IF _stuff
149 :          KEYBOARD CHR(13)
150 :       ENDIF
151 :    ENDIF
152 :    RESTSCREEN(_lookrow - 1, _lookcol - 1, _lookrow + 7, ;
153 :               _lookcol + (79 - _lookcol), _lookscr)
154 :    RETURN(.F.)
155 :
156 : ********************
157 :
158 : FUNCTION Upperlower
159 :
160 :    PARAMETERS _upla
161 :
162 :    * Take the parameter string and uppercase the first
163 :    * letter, lowercasing all other letters
164 :
165 :    IF PCOUNT() != 1
166 :       RETURN("")
167 :    ENDIF
168 :    RETURN(UPPER(SUBSTR(_upla, 1, 1)) + LOWER(SUBSTR(_upla,2)))
169 :
170 : ********************
171 :
172 : FUNCTION Parsing
173 :
174 :    PARAMETERS _getstr
175 :
176 :    PRIVATE _location, _tempback
177 :
178 :    _location   = IF(EMPTY(AT("+", _getstr)), ;
179 :                  AT("/", _getstr), AT("+", _getstr))
180 :    _tempback = IF(!EMPTY(_location), ;
181 :                  SUBSTR(_getstr, 1, _location - 1), _getstr)
182 :    _getstr = IF(!EMPTY(_location), ;
183 :                  SUBSTR(_getstr, _location + 1), "")
184 :    RETURN(_tempback)
185 :
186 : * End of File
```

In this program, the Parsing() function is used to separate the fields to be listed in the DBEDIT() that are called by the Lookup() function on line 42. Many times, as you can see, even though the fifth field in the Filenos work area is the information we want, the end user will see fields 6 through 9 and field 20. Within the actual Lookup() function, we initialize an array named **_show[]** that will contain the names of the fields that will be passed to the DBEDIT() function on lines 144 and 145. After the array has been properly initialized to accommodate the number of elements in the string passed by the Lookup() function, the names of the fields are placed in their proper place. In lines 118 through 124, we continue to parse the string **_old** until there are no more values to be looked at. Since we are passing

_old by reference, its value will change as we pluck off individual items in the string. Remember, we must process the inner functions first, expanding to the outer functions eventually. Looking at line 119 closely, we see that the Parsing() function will be called first, with its value being passed to the Clipper's VAL() function (taking the VAL() of the field numbers that are in string format) and then passing it directly to the FIELD() function that will return the name of the field in that position. If the result from this complex expression is NOT EMPTY(), the name of the field is placed in the array named **_show[]** and the **_cnt** position. At that point (line 122), the counter for the array is then incremented. The rest is simple.

PARSING A MENU

The next obvious and ideal area for a parser is literal information. Most common in this category is menu information, both prompt text and message text for each corresponding text. For example, the old way to code for a menu screen would be the following:

```
********************
* Name      Aprompt.prg
* Author    Stephen J. Straley
* Date      July 1, 1989
* Notice    Copyright (c) 1989 Stephen J. Straley & Associates
*           All Rights Reserved
* Compile   Clipper Aprompt -m
* Release   Summer 87
* Link      PLINK86 FI Aprompt  LIB Clipper LIB Extend;
* Note      This shows what a standard PROMPT menu would
*           look like.
*
********************

CLEAR SCREEN
option = 1
@ 1,20 TO 15,60
SET WRAP ON
SET MESSAGE TO 24 CENTER
DO WHILE .T.
   @  2,30 PROMPT " Chart of Accounts " MESSAGE ;
           "Modify Chart of Account Information"
   @  4,30 PROMPT " Transactions       " MESSAGE ;
           "Modify Transactions not yet Posted"
   @  6,30 PROMPT " Post and Balance   " MESSAGE ;
           "Post Transactions and Balance Accounts"
   @  8,30 PROMPT " General Listings   " MESSAGE ;
           "Create General Listings for General Ledger"
   @ 10,30 PROMPT " Reports            " MESSAGE ;
           "Trial Balance, Statement of Income, Balance Sheets"
   @ 12,30 PROMPT " End of Period      " MESSAGE ;
           "Perform End of Period Transactions"
   @ 14,30 PROMPT " Quit Program       " MESSAGE ;
```

```
                "Exit Program to DOS"
   MENU TO option
   IF option = 7 .OR. EMPTY(option)
      EXIT
   ENDIF
ENDDO
CLEAR SCREEN

* End of Program
```

Take a look at this example. There are several PROMPT commands with literal text on each command line. Additionally, the only variance in the actual PROMPT section is the relative row coordinate for each PROMPT line. This means that there is, in essence, a great deal of duplication and wasted space. It would seem to be more practical to have a long prompt string, with each prompt item delimited by a special character, a beginning row and column position, and a function that would parse the information for each prompt line, increment the relative row position, and display the prompt. While this may sound difficult, it is, in essence, simpler than it sounds. Before getting into the actual function, let us take a look at how the preceding coding example would look in this new unparsed format.

```
********************
* Name      Bprompt.prg
* Author    Stephen J. Straley
* Date      July 1, 1989
* Notice    Copyright (c) 1989 Stephen J. Straley & Associates
*           All Rights Reserved
* Compile   Clipper Bprompt -m
* Release   Summer 87
* Link      PLINK86 FI Bprompt LIB Clipper LIB Extend;
* Note      This shows what the MENUS would look like with
*           a single function call, the use of the Parsing()
*           function, and some muscle from the ToolkiT
*
********************

CLEAR SCREEN
option = 1
@ 1,20 TO 15,60
SET WRAP ON
SET MESSAGE TO 24 CENTER
DECLARE menus[7], messages[7]
menus = "Chart of Accounts/Transactions/" +;
        "Post and Balance/General Listings/" +;
        "Reports/End of Period/Quit Program"
mess  = "Modify Chart of Account Information/" + ;
        "Modify Transactions not yet Posted/" + ;
        "Post Transactions and Balance Accounts/" +;
        "Create General Listings for General Ledger/" +;
        "Trial Balance, Statement of Income, Balance Sheets/" +;
        "Perform End of Period Transactions/" +;
        "Exit Program to DOS"
```

```

DO WHILE !EMPTY(option) .AND. ;
         (option != Occurence("/", menus)+1)
   option = MAKEMENU(menus, 2, 30, option, 3, .T., 2, ;
                     15, "", mess)
   @ 23,00 SAY option
ENDDO
CLEAR SCREEN

* ************************************************
* * The following procedure(s)/function(s) are  *
* * part of Steve Straley's ToolkiT(tm) -        *
* * Release 2, published by Four Seasons         *
* * Publishing Co., Inc.  All Rights Reserved    *
* * Information: 212-599-2141 / 800-662-2278     *
* * All Rights Reserved                          *
* ************************************************

FUNCTION Parsing

   PARAMETERS _getstr

   * This function is the string parser.  Basically, return the
   * beginning fragment of a string, adjust the string, and if
   * passed by reference, alter the contents of the original
   * string.

   PRIVATE _location, _tempback

   _location   = IF(EMPTY(AT("+", _getstr)), ;
                   AT("/", _getstr), AT("+", _getstr))

   _tempback = IF(!EMPTY(_location), ;
                 SUBSTR(_getstr, 1, _location - 1), _getstr)
   _getstr = IF(!EMPTY(_location), ;
               SUBSTR(_getstr, _location + 1), "")
   RETURN(_tempback)

********************

FUNCTION Fill_out

   PARAMETERS _filla, _fillb

   * _filla = the string to be filled out
   * _fillb = the length to fill out the string to

   IF PCOUNT() = 1
      _fillb = 80
   ELSE
      IF TYPE("_fillb") = "C"
         _fillb = VAL(b)
      ENDIF
```

```
085 :        _fillb = IIF(_fillb <= 1, 80, _fillb)
086 :     ENDIF
087 :
088 :     IF _fillb <= LEN(_filla)
089 :        RETURN(_filla)
090 :     ENDIF
091 :     RETURN(LEFT(_filla + SPACE(_fillb - LEN(_filla)),_fillb))
092 :
093 : ********************
094 :
095 : FUNCTION Occurence
096 :
097 :     PARAMETERS _astring, _bstring
098 :
099 :     PRIVATE _clipper_bug
100 :
101 :     _clipper_bug = LEN(_bstring) - ;
102 :              LEN(STRTRAN(_bstring, _astring,"") )
103 :     RETURN( INT(_clipper_bug / LEN(_astring)) )
104 :
105 : ********************
106 :
107 : FUNCTION Makemenu
108 :
109 :     PARAMETERS _choices, _menrow, _mencol, _menstart, ;
110 :               _mentype, _topdown, _spacing, _botrow, ;
111 :               _tqfill, _messages, _helpprog
112 :
113 :     PRIVATE _thismen, _lowerlvl, _uptohere, _themen, _qaz, ;
114 :             _brow, _bcol, _showit, _messit
115 :
116 :     IF TYPE("_menstart") = "C"
117 :        && Using Pop-Help, the name of the menu
118 :        _thismen = &_menstart.
119 :        && variable should be passed and not the value:
120 :        _lowerlvl = .T.
121 :     ELSE             && here is where it should check it out.
122 :        _thismen = _menstart
123 :        _lowerlvl = .F.
124 :     ENDIF
125 :
126 :     DO CASE
127 :     CASE PCOUNT() < 4
128 :        RETURN(0)
129 :     CASE PCOUNT() = 4
130 :        _mentype = 1
131 :        _topdown = .T.
132 :        _spacing = 1
133 :        _botrow = 24
134 :        _tqfill = 0
135 :        _messages = ""
136 :     CASE PCOUNT() = 5
137 :        _topdown = .T.
138 :        _spacing = 1
```

```
139 :        _botrow = 24
140 :        _tqfill = 0
141 :        _messages = ""
142 :     CASE PCOUNT() = 6
143 :        _spacing = 1
144 :        _botrow = 24
145 :        _tqfill = 0
146 :        _messages = ""
147 :     CASE PCOUNT() = 7
148 :        _botrow = 24
149 :        _tqfill = 0
150 :        _messages = ""
151 :     CASE PCOUNT() = 8
152 :        _tqfill = 0
153 :        _messages = ""
154 :     CASE PCOUNT() = 9
155 :        _messages = ""
156 :     ENDCASE
157 :
158 :
159 :     _helpprog = IF( TYPE("_helpprog") = "U", ;
160 :                 PROCNAME(), _helpprog )
161 :
162 :     DECLARE _themen[OCCURENCE("/",_choices)+1]
163 :     _uptohere = OCCURENCE("/",_choices) + 1
164 :     FOR _qaz = 1 TO LEN(_themen)
165 :        _themen[_qaz] = PARSING(@_choices)
166 :     NEXT
167 :
168 :     IF EMPTY(_tqfill)
169 :        _tqfill = LENGTH_EL(_themen)
170 :     ENDIF
171 :
172 :     STORE _menrow TO _brow
173 :     STORE _mencol TO _bcol
174 :
175 :     FOR _qaz = 1 TO LEN(_themen)
176 :
177 :        IF _qaz > 32    && This tests to see if there are more
178 :           EXIT         && than 32 elements for a MENU TO command.
179 :        ENDIF
180 :
181 :        _showit = _themen[_qaz]
182 :
183 :        IF !EMPTY(_messages)
184 :           _messit = PARSING(@_messages)
185 :        ELSE
186 :           _messit = ""
187 :        ENDIF
188 :
189 :        DO CASE
190 :        CASE _mentype = 1       && Numbers In Front
191 :           _showit = FILL_OUT(" " + CHR(IF(_qaz > 9, 55, ;
192 :                     48) + _qaz) + "> " + _showit, _tqfill + 4)
```

```
193 :        CASE _mentype = 2          && <> separators
194 :           _showit = SUBSTR(_showit, 1, 1)
195 :        CASE _mentype = 3          && 1 space in front and in back
196 :           _showit = FILL_OUT(" " + _showit, _tqfill + 2)
197 :        ENDCASE
198 :        IF _mentype = 2
199 :           @ _brow, _bcol SAY "< >" + ;
200 :              SUBSTR( _themen[_qaz], 2)
201 :        ENDIF
202 :        @ _brow, _bcol + IF(_mentype=2, 1, 0) PROMPT ;
203 :                         _showit MESSAGE _messit
204 :
205 :        IF _qaz + 1 <= LEN(_themen)
206 :           IF _topdown        && top down type of menu
207 :              _brow = _brow + _spacing
208 :              IF _brow > _botrow
209 :                 _brow = _menrow
210 :                 _bcol = _bcol + _tqfill + 5
211 :              ENDIF
212 :           ELSE               && right to left type of menu
213 :              DO CASE
214 :              CASE _mentype = 1
215 :                 t_col = _bcol + LEN(_showit) + ;
216 :                         LEN(_themen[_qaz]) + 4
217 :
218 :              CASE _mentype = 2
219 :                 t_col = _bcol + LEN(_showit) + ;
220 :                         LEN(_themen[_qaz]) + 3 + ;
221 :                         LEN(_themen[_qaz])
222 :
223 :              CASE _mentype = 3
224 :                 t_col = _bcol + LEN(_showit) + ;
225 :                         LEN(_themen[_qaz]) + 2
226 :
227 :              OTHERWISE
228 :                 t_col = _bcol + LEN(_showit) + ;
229 :                         LEN(_themen[_qaz]) + 1
230 :
231 :              ENDCASE
232 :              IF t_col > 80
233 :                 _brow = _brow + 1
234 :                 _bcol = _mencol
235 :              ELSE
236 :                 _bcol = _bcol + IF(_mentype = 2, ;
237 :                         LEN(_themen[_qaz])+ 3, 0) + ;
238 :                         LEN(_showit) + 1
239 :              ENDIF
240 :           ENDIF
241 :        ENDIF
242 :        _showit = ""
243 :     NEXT
244 :     scrcursor = .F.
245 :     SET CURSOR OFF
246 :     IF _lowerlvl
```

```
247 :        MENU TO &_menstart
248 :           _thismen = &_menstart.
249 :     ELSE
250 :        MENU TO _thismen
251 :     ENDIF
252 :     SET CURSOR ON
253 :     RETURN(_thismen)
254 :
255 : ********************
256 :
257 : FUNCTION Long_elem
258 :
259 :     PARAMETERS _array, _delimit
260 :
261 :     _delimit = IF((TYPE("_delimit") = "U"), "/", _delimit)
262 :
263 :     IF PCOUNT() = 0
264 :        RETURN(-1)
265 :     ELSEIF TYPE("_array") != "A"
266 :        IF TYPE("_array") != "C"
267 :           RETURN(-1)
268 :        ELSE
269 :           * turn the string into an array
270 :           _choices = _array
271 :           DECLARE _array[Occurence(_delimit, _choices) + 1]
272 :           _uptohere = Occurence(_delimit, _choices) + 1
273 :           FOR _qaz = 1 TO LEN(_array)
274 :              _array[_qaz] = Parsing(@_choices)
275 :           NEXT
276 :        ENDIF
277 :     ENDIF
278 :
279 :     * This function returns the longest character element
280 :     * in an array.
281 :
282 :     PRIVATE _the_ret_val, _the_element, _downtoit, _dtype
283 :
284 :     _the_ret_val = 0
285 :     _the_element = ""
286 :     FOR _downtoit = 1 TO LEN(_array)
287 :        IF TYPE("_array[_downtoit]") != "U"
288 :           _dtype = _array[_downtoit]
289 :           IF TYPE("_dtype") = "C"
290 :              IF LEN(_dtype) > LEN(_the_element)
291 :                 _the_element = _dtype
292 :                 _the_ret_val = _downtoit
293 :              ENDIF
294 :           ENDIF
295 :        ENDIF
296 :     NEXT
297 :     RETURN(_the_ret_val)
298 :
299 : ********************
300 :
```

```
301 : FUNCTION Length_el
302 :
303 :    PARAMETERS _aarray, _delimit
304 :
305 :    _delimit = IF((TYPE("_delimit") = "U"), "/", _delimit)
306 :
307 :    IF PCOUNT() = 0
308 :       RETURN(-1)
309 :    ELSEIF TYPE("_aarray") != "A"
310 :       IF TYPE("_aarray") != "C"
311 :          RETURN(-1)
312 :       ELSE
313 :          * turn the string into an array
314 :          _choices = _aarray
315 :          DECLARE _aarray[Occurence(_delimit, _choices) + 1]
316 :          _uptohere = Occurence(_delimit, _choices) + 1
317 :          FOR _qaz = 1 TO LEN(_aarray)
318 :             _aarray[_qaz] = Parsing(@_choices)
319 :          NEXT
320 :       ENDIF
321 :    ENDIF
322 :
323 :    * This function returns the length of the longest
324 :    * element in the array. Good for formatting purposes
325 :
326 :    RETURN(IF( (Long_elem(_aarray) < 1) , 0, ;
327 :           LEN(_aarray[Long_elem(_aarray)])))
328 :
329 : * End of File
```

In the above example, we modified the Makemenu() function so that it is simpler than the Makemenu() function found in the ToolkiT. This will, however, make no difference in our discussion.

At first glance, this program may appear to be more extensive than the Aprompt program. However, you can see that we have eliminated the necessity to "hard-code" every menu command in place; we have reduced the number of PROMPT commands to just one internal PROMPT called by a function; and we now not only have the ability to customize the menu style by a single parameter, but, by reducing the menu prompts and messages to strings, we can further reduce our code size by placing these strings in text files. This technology, further touched upon in the chapter pertaining to Data-Driven Technology, allows us to modify a menu or a message without recompiling or relinking the application together.

In this example, the Makemenu() function on line 35 returns either the numeric value for the operation picked or a 0 to signify that the Esc key has been pressed. Normally, we would have an extensive DO CASE or IF structure immediately following line 36. Here, the Parsing() function is used to lay out not only the PROMPTs but the messages for those prompts as well. Even more staggering is the concept in lines 33 and 34. Here, the DO

WHILE loop will continue if the value of the variable **option** is not equal to 0 and the value of **option** does not equal the number of occurrences plus one, and the "/ " character appears in the string containing the menu items. Look at the last portion of the string **menus**; the last PROMPT will be "Quit Program." Further, there are six "/ " characters in the **menus** string with the quit option being the seventh menu choice. This means that the DO WHILE command is programmed in such a way that if additional menu items should be required, or if some need to be removed or consolidated, the same piece of code would work. Here is one of the fundamental principles that brought on the movement of object-oriented programming: Program to minimize change. If the menu items, which are strings, should happen to be altered, the basic construction of the DO WHILE loop need not be reprogrammed.

In the Makemenu() function, several parameters tell it how to parse the **menus** string and to build the menu. For example, the sixth parameter on line 35 tells the menu that it is a top-down menu, unlike a Lotus-like menu, which goes across the top from left to right. The style of the menu is picked via the fifth parameter's value (3) and the number of spaces between each PROMPT line (2), the value in the seventh parameter. We can see that once the Makemenu() function has been coded, choosing the style of the menu and laying it out becomes an easy task. We have parameterized to utilize; we have taken the commands PROMPT and MENU TO and elevated them to new heights using the concepts that underlie a string parser.

PARSING FOR AN ARRAY

The Summer '87 release of Clipper includes a useful function named ASORT(). It is designed to sort the contents of an array in ascending order. The information within the array must all be of the same data type in order for the sorting operation to work properly. However, this function seems to have one shortcoming: It works only on one array at a time. While this may not sound like a big problem, consider the following possibility. As the programmer, you choose to give your client the ability to view the current directory. This can be achieved easily with the ADIR() function. Along with the names of the files on the directory, you opt to provide the DOS date and time stamp as well as the size of the file. In essence, you are trying to give your customer a screen quite similar to many of the DOS utilities, such as Norton's Commander and XTREE. Each piece of information fits in each array. That is, the information for the first file seen by the ADIR() function is placed in the first element position in each of the four arrays: names[], sizes[], dates[], and times[]. At the very beginning, the four arrays are in sync; the specified size located in the first position corresponds with the name of the file in the same element location.

Now let's consider the possibility of letting the user sort the information in any of the four arrays. For example, the client wants to see the names of the files in alphabetical order or, maybe, in date order since the last update (good for backup purposes). Obviously we could ASORT() any one of these four arrays, based on the desire (and whim) of the client. This is where the trouble will appear. While the ASORT() function will work perfectly with any one of the four arrays, it will have a difficult time keeping track of all four. Therefore, if the names[] array is sorted, the information in the other arrays may not sort in the same order. That is, the names, dates, times, and sizes may not line up correctly across the screen. The trouble with the ASORT() function is that it does not understand any potential link between multiple arrays. However, the Parsing() function can solve this problem. First, take a look at the code example and test program.

```
001 : ********************
002 : * Name      Masort.prg
003 : * Author    Stephen J. Straley
004 : * Date      July 14, 1989
005 : * Notice    Copyright (c) 1989 Stephen J. Straley & Associates
006 : *           All Rights Reserved
007 : * Compile   Clipper Masort -m
008 : * Release   Summer 87
009 : * Link      PLINK86 FI Masort LIB Clipper Lib Extend;
010 : * Note      This shows how to sort many arrays
011 : *           without C or ASM
012 : *
013 : ********************
014 :
015 :
016 : CLEAR SCREEN
017 : DECLARE new[ADIR("*.*")], old[ADIR("*.*")], ;
018 :         used[ADIR("*.*")], blue[ADIR("*.*")]
019 : ADIR("*.*", new, old, used, blue)
020 :
021 : IF LEN(new) < 5
022 :    WAIT "You need more files in this directory!"
023 :    QUIT
024 : ENDIF
025 :
026 : item = new[LEN(new)-4]
027 : @ 0,0 SAY "The " + DAYWORD(LEN(new)-4) + ;
028 :          " item is " + new[LEN(new)-4]
029 : @ 1,0 SAY " with a size of " + STR(old[LEN(old)-4])
030 : SHOWIT()
031 : @ 24,00 SAY "Working...."
032 : MARRYSORT(new, old, used, blue)
033 : @ 24,00
034 : value = ASCAN(new, item)
035 : @ 0,0 SAY "It is now the " + DAYWORD(value) + ;
036 :          " item in the array: " + new[value]
037 : @ 1,0 SAY " ... and the size of this went " + ;
038 :          "with it! --> " + STR(old[value])
039 : SHOWIT()
040 :
041 : ********************
042 :
043 : PROCEDURE Showit
044 :
045 :    @ 2,0 CLEAR
```

```
046 :     FOR x = 1 TO LEN(new)
047 :        ? new[x], old[x],used[x],blue[x]
048 :        INKEY(.1)
049 :        IF ROW() > 20
050 :           @ 2,0 CLEAR
051 :        ENDIF
052 :     NEXT
053 :     ?
054 :     WAIT
055 :
056 : * *******************************************
057 : * * The following procedure(s)/function(s) are  *
058 : * * part of Steve Straley's ToolkiT(tm) -       *
059 : * * Release 2, published by Four Seasons        *
060 : * * Publishing Co., Inc.  All Rights Reserved   *
061 : * * Information: 212-599-2141 / 800-662-2278    *
062 : * * All Rights Reserved                         *
063 : * *******************************************
064 :
065 : *******************
066 :
067 : FUNCTION Marrysort
068 :
069 :     PARAMETERS _a, _b, _c, _d, _e, _f
070 :
071 :     * _a is the main array to be sorted
072 :     * _b - _f are the anciliary array's
073 :
074 :     PRIVATE _many, _cstr, _end, _qaz, _value, ;
075 :             _backto, _oldstr
076 :
077 :     _many = PCOUNT()
078 :
079 :     _cstr = ""
080 :     _end  = LEN(_a)
081 :     DECLARE _temp[LEN(_a)]
082 :     ACOPY(_a, _temp)
083 :     ASORT(_a)
084 :     FOR _x = 1 TO _end
085 :        _value = _a[_x]
086 :        _cstr = _cstr + LTRIM(TRANSFORM(ASCAN(_temp, ;
087 :                _value), "9999")) + "/"
088 :     NEXT
089 :     _cstr = SUBSTR(_cstr, 1, LEN(_cstr)-1)
090 :     FOR _qaz = 2 TO _many
091 :        _oldstr = _cstr
092 :        _backto = "_" + CHR(64+_qaz)
093 :        FOR x = 1 TO _end
094 :           IF _qaz = 2
095 :              _temp[x] = _b[VAL(PARSING(@_oldstr))]
096 :           ELSEIF _qaz = 3
097 :              _temp[x] = _c[VAL(PARSING(@_oldstr))]
098 :           ELSEIF _qaz = 4
099 :              _temp[x] = _d[VAL(PARSING(@_oldstr))]
```

```
         ELSEIF _qaz = 5
            _temp[x] = _e[VAL(PARSING(@_oldstr))]
         ELSEIF _qaz = 6
            _temp[x] = _f[VAL(PARSING(@_oldstr))]
         ENDIF
      NEXT
      ACOPY(_temp, &_backto.)
   NEXT
   RETURN(.T.)

********************

FUNCTION Parsing

   PARAMETERS _getstr, _forcode

   * _getstr is the string to be parsed
   * _forcode is the code that parses.

   * This function is the string parser.  Basically,
   * return the beginning fragment of a string, adjust
   * the string, and if passed by reference, alter the
   * contents of the original string.

   PRIVATE _forcode, _location, _tempback

   IF PCOUNT() = 2
      IF TYPE("_forcode") = "L"
         _thechar = "|"
      ELSE
         _thechar = _forcode
      ENDIF
      _forcode = .T.
   ELSE
      _forcode = .F.
   ENDIF

   IF _forcode
      _location   = AT(_thechar, _getstr)
   ELSE
      _location   = IF(EMPTY(AT("+", _getstr)), ;
              AT("/", _getstr), AT("+", _getstr))
   ENDIF

   _tempback = IF(!EMPTY(_location), SUBSTR(_getstr, ;
               1, _location - 1), _getstr)
   _getstr = IF(!EMPTY(_location), SUBSTR(_getstr, ;
               _location + 1), "")
   RETURN(_tempback)

********************

FUNCTION Dayword

```

```
154 :     PARAMETER _indate
155 :
156 :     PRIVATE _inday, _inval
157 :
158 :     IF TYPE("_indate") = "D"
159 :        _inday = STR(DAY(_indate), 2)
160 :        _inval = VAL(_inday)
161 :     ELSEIF TYPE("_indate") = "N"
162 :        _inval = _indate
163 :        _inday = STR(_indate)
164 :     ELSE
165 :        RETURN("")
166 :     ENDIF
167 :
168 :     _inval = IF((_inval > 100), PLACES(_inval, 2), _inval)
169 :
170 :     IF _inval > 3 .AND. _inval < 21
171 :        _inday = _inday + "th"
172 :     ELSE
173 :        _inval = VAL(RIGHT(_inday,1))
174 :        _inday = _inday + SUBSTR("thstndrdthththththth", ;
175 :                 (_inval * 2)+1,2)
176 :     ENDIF
177 :     RETURN(LTRIM(TRIM(_inday)))
178 :
179 : ******************
180 :
181 : FUNCTION Places
182 :
183 :     PARAMETERS _thenumber, _places
184 :
185 :     IF PCOUNT() != 2
186 :        RETURN(0)
187 :     ELSEIF _places < 1
188 :        RETURN(0)
189 :     ENDIF
190 :
191 :     _places = INT(_places)
192 :
193 :     PRIVATE _base
194 :
195 :     _base = INT(_thenumber) / (10 * _places)
196 :
197 :     _base = _base - INT(_base)
198 :
199 :     RETURN( INT(_base * (10 * _places)))
200 :
201 : * End of File
```

We must be careful with the concept of sorting arrays. First, we copy the original array, which will be the master array for the sort, to a temporary array. Next we take each element in each of the ancillary arrays and adjust it, based on the new order found in the first array.

Finally, we copy the temporary array back to the original array. While this may sound simple, let us take a step-by-step approach and study the flow of the program.

On lines 17 through 19, we have DECLAREd four arrays that will be used to contain the directory information: file names, sizes, dates, and time stamps. Since arrays are passed by reference in Clipper, we know that if we pass the name of the array to a function or to a procedure, the contents of the arrays can be altered in either the function or the procedure and be reflected once program control is returned to the main module. Looking at this example, the call to the Marrysort() function will use this technology. But first, a call to the Showit() procedure allows us to simply display the contents of the four arrays to the screen.

Now, let's explore the operation of the Marrysort() function. Let's start with lines 81 through 83. Here, a new array called **_temp[]** is DECLAREd and the contents from the main array, **_a[]**, is copied into it. This copy will be the base from which all things will come. After this, we sort the contents of the original array via Clipper's ASORT() function on line 83. Then in lines 84 through 88, the individual items within the sorted array are stored to a temporary variable named **_value**. From here, we will look for the position of the item in the old array **_temp[]**, convert the number to a string, and store it to another variable named **_cstr**. The "/ " character has been added to this string. In other words, if the file named "TEMP.BAT" was found in the fourth position, followed by the file "SSAP.BAT" found in the third position, the portion of the string **_cstr** would look like this: " 4/ 3/ ". Finally, after each element's original position has been logged into the string, we remove the final "/ " character on line 89. This means that we have built a string that, when parsed, will point to the old values in all of the other arrays.

From lines 90 to 107, we are going through each array that is passed to the function. The condition for the FOR...NEXT loop is based on 2 (the second array) to **_many**, which was initialized to the value of PCOUNT(), the number of arrays passed to the function. For every pass through the main FOR...NEXT loop, we have to make a copy of the string that has the element order because eventually, after it has been completely parsed, it will be a null byte. Line 92 is critical; on this command line, the string "_" plus the character from CHR(62 + **_qaz**) is stored to the string **_backto**. Digging deeper we see that on the first pass through the FOR...NEXT loop, the value returned from the CHR() function will be the letter "B," which, when stored with the character "_", is the name of the second parameter on line 69. If we were to macro expand this string, we would be working with the second array passed to the Marrysort() function, since arrays are passed by reference. After this we go through an internal FOR...NEXT loop, using the dummy array named **_temp[]** to contain the items from each of the passed arrays. The items pulled from these arrays will be the positional values from the parsed string that was built on lines 84 through 88. After each item has been adjusted, the ACOPY() function copies the temporary array to the macro expanded string **_backto**, which is one of the five ancillary arrays. Upon completion of both loops, the function will eventually return a logical true (.T.).

For clarity, a massive IF...ELSEIF...ELSE...END structure was used on lines 94 through 104. However, these lines could have been reduced to the single command line:

```
_temp[x] = &_backto.[VAL(PARSING(@_oldstr))]
```

Keep in mind that the function would fractionally slow down because of the constant need to macro expand the variable **_backto**.

USING THE PARSING() FUNCTION FOR DIRECTORIES AND PATHS

Many C and ASM enthusiasts have always wanted the ability to obtain the names of all of the subdirectories on the current logged drive. In the past, this could not be done in the Clipper environment without also using C or Assembler. The other option was to use the DOS TREE.COM program to build a text file with all of the names of the subdirectories and from this, extract the unwanted information in order to build a table for future reference. The need for such a utility has wide implications. For example, in an accounting program, it is common to use multiple subdirectories to house multiple-company information. Others may desire the ability to use one master program and toggle between subdirectories containing separate pieces of information for different departments or categories. In either event, the ability to have the program "know" which directories are present, their names, and their order structure (that is, which subdirectory is a parent and which is a child) is fundamental. And to carry this concept one step further, it may be very nice indeed to build a pop-up window containing the names of the subdirectories from which the user can select the proper one using the keyboard cursor keys.

Once we know if a subdirectory exists, would it not be more "user friendly" to obtain all of the names of the subdirectories on any given drive? Indeed it would and with the low-level file functions, it is a very simple task.

```
********************
* Name     Subs.prg
* Author   Stephen J. Straley
* Notice   Copyright (c) 1989 Stephen J. Straley & Associates
*          All Rights Reserved
* Date     June 1, 1989
* Compile  Clipper Subs -m
* Release  Summer '87
* Link     Plink86 Fi Subs LIB Clipper, Extend
* Note     This program will show how the names of the
*          subdirectories can be obtained using the
*          low-level file functions.
*
* ************************************************
* * The following procedure(s)/function(s) are   *
* * part of Steve Straley's ToolkiT(tm) -         *
* * Release 2, published by Four Seasons          *
* * Publishing Co., Inc.  All Rights Reserved     *
* * Information: 212-599-2141 / 800-662-2278      *
* * All Rights Reserved                           *
* ************************************************
```

```
022 : *
023 : ********************
024 :
025 : CLEAR SCREEN
026 :
027 :     PRIVATE _root, _dstring, peus, seats
028 :
029 :     _root = "\*."
030 :     _dstring = "+\"
031 :
032 :     peus = 1    && I didn't want to use a ROW,;
033 :                 && so a peu will do
034 :     seats = 2  && Same thing for the COL...
035 :     DO WHILE .T.
036 :        _search = Parsing(@_dstring)
037 :        IF EMPTY(_dstring)
038 :           EXIT
039 :        ENDIF
040 :        _path = "C:" + _search + _root
041 :        DECLARE _temp[1]
042 :        _temp[1] = ""
043 :        _howmany = ADIR(_path, .F., .F., .F., .F., _temp)
044 :        IF !EMPTY(_howmany)
045 :           DECLARE _temp[_howmany], _names[_howmany]
046 :           ADIR(_path, _names, .F., .F., .F., _temp)
047 :           FOR x = 1 TO LEN(_temp)
048 :              IF _temp[x] = "D"
049 :                 IF _names[x] = "." .OR. _names[x] = ".."
050 :                    *
051 :                    * this is for the current directory, which
052 :                    * we already know the name of, and the
053 :                    * parent directory.
054 :                    *
055 :                 ELSE
056 :                    _dstring = _dstring + _search + "\" + ;
057 :                               _names[x] + "+"
058 :
059 :                    * This is the display area
060 :
061 :                    @ peus, seats SAY SUBSTR(_names[x], 1, 12)
062 :
063 :                    peus = peus + 1
064 :
065 :                    IF peus > 20
066 :                       seats = seats + 14
067 :                       peus = 1
068 :                    ENDIF
069 :                    IF seats > 65
070 :                       @ 24, 0 SAY " More.. "
071 :                       INKEY(0)
072 :                       CLEAR SCREEN
073 :                       peus = 1
074 :                       seats = 2
075 :                    ENDIF
```

```
076 :                 ENDIF
077 :              ENDIF
078 :           NEXT
079 :        ENDIF
080 :        IF "\\"$_dstring
081 :           _dstring = STRTRAN(_dstring, "\\", "\")
082 :        ENDIF
083 :     ENDDO
084 :     @ 24, 0 SAY " Press any key .... "
085 :     INKEY(0)
086 :
087 : ********************
088 :
089 : FUNCTION Parsing
090 :
091 :     PARAMETERS getstring
092 :
093 :     whereat    = IF(EMPTY(AT("+", getstring)), ;
094 :                  AT("/", getstring), AT("+", getstring))
095 :     newstring = IF(!EMPTY(whereat), ;
096 :                  SUBSTR(getstring, 1, whereat - 1), getstring)
097 :     getstring = IF(!EMPTY(whereat), ;
098 :                  SUBSTR(getstring, whereat + 1), "")
099 :     RETURN(newstring)
100 :
101 : * End of File
```

The entire concept is centered around the Parsing() function and the fact that the path variable name **_dstring** (lines 56 and 57) is built with some assistance from the ADIR() function, then parsed with the Parsing() function. In essence, we push and pop the names of the subdirectories on the same variable.

PARSING A STRUCTURE

We will be going into more detail with this next topic in the Data-Driven Technology chapter of this book. However, let's consider the following code fragment now:

```
********************
* Name      Data1.prg
* Author    Stephen J. Straley
* Date      July 1, 1989
* Notice    Copyright (c) 1989 Stephen J. Straley & Associates
*           All Rights Reserved
* Compile   Clipper Data1 -m
* Release   Summer 87
* Link      PLINK86 FI Data1 LIB Clipper LIB Extend;
* Note      This shows how the structure of a database
*           can sit in an array and be easily modified
*           and/or saved to disk to save space.
*
```

```
********************

CLEAR SCREEN

@ 24,00 SAY "Initializing Chart of Account File." +;
              "   One Moment"

PRIVATE tfile,tfile1,tfile2,tfile3,extmess,

tfile  = "CHART"
tfile1 = "CHT_ACCT"
tfile2 = "CHT_DESC"
tfile3 = "CHT_KEY"

DECLARE _temp[13]
_temp[ 1] = "INTERNAL/N/8"
_temp[ 2] = "ACCOUNT/C/16"
_temp[ 3] = "DESC/C/28"
_temp[ 4] = "NORMAL/C/1"
_temp[ 5] = "BALANCE/N/12/2"
_temp[ 6] = "CONS_ACCT/N/8"
_temp[ 7] = "RPT_LEVEL/N/2"
_temp[ 8] = "POSTING/C/1"
_temp[ 9] = "MAST_CONS/C/16"
_temp[10] = "ACCT_TYPE/C/1"
_temp[11] = "CATEGORY/C/2"
_temp[12] = "CASH/L/1"
_temp[13] = "HISTORY/L/1"
Dbfmake(tfile, _temp)
USE (tfile)
APPEND BLANK
CLEAR SCREEN
@ 0,0 SAY "Please view all of the fields!"
DBEDIT(1,0,3,79)
CLEAR SCREEN

* *********************************************
* * The following procedure(s)/function(s) are  *
* * part of Steve Straley's ToolkiT(tm) -       *
* * Release 2, published by Four Seasons        *
* * Publishing Co., Inc.  All Rights Reserved   *
* * Information: 212-599-2141 / 800-662-2278    *
* * All Rights Reserved                         *
* *********************************************

FUNCTION Dbfmake

   PARAMETERS _thefile, _thearray

   IF PCOUNT() != 2
      RETURN(.F.)
   ENDIF

   PRIVATE _qaz, _atemp, _warray
```

```
068 :
069 :       IF TYPE("_thefile")+TYPE("_thearray") != "C"
070 :          RETURN(.F.)
071 :       ELSE
072 :          && One field, don't ask me why!
073 :          IF TYPE("_thearray") = "C"
074 :             _warray = .F.
075 :          ELSEIF TYPE("_thearray") = "A"
076 :             _warray = .T.
077 :          ELSE
078 :             RETURN(.F.)
079 :          ENDIF
080 :       ENDIF
081 :
082 :       CREATE Template
083 :       USE Template
084 :       IF _warray
085 :          FOR _qaz = 1 TO LEN(_thearray)
086 :             IF TYPE("_thearray[_qaz]") = "U"
087 :                USE
088 :                ERASE Template.dbf
089 :                RETURN(.F.)
090 :             ENDIF
091 :             _atemp = ""
092 :             _atemp = _thearray[_qaz]
093 :             AP_IT(PARSING(@_atemp), PARSING(@_atemp), ;
094 :                   VAL(PARSING(@_atemp)), IF(  (EMPTY(_atemp)), ;
095 :                   0, VAL(PARSING(@_atemp)) ) )
096 :          NEXT
097 :       ELSE
098 :          _atemp = _thearray
099 :          AP_IT(PARSING(@_atemp), ;
100 :                PARSING(@_atemp), VAL(PARSING(@_atemp)), ;
101 :                IF(  (EMPTY(_atemp)), 0, VAL(PARSING(@_atemp))))
102 :       ENDIF
103 :       USE
104 :       CREATE (_thefile) FROM Template
105 :       ERASE Template.dbf
106 :       USE
107 :       RETURN( DOSERROR() = 0 )
108 :
109 : *******************
110 :
111 : FUNCTION Ap_it
112 :
113 :       PARAMETERS _apa, _apb, _apc, _apd
114 :
115 :       * _apa = the field name
116 :       * _apb = the field data type
117 :       * _apc = the field length
118 :       * _apd = the field decimal
119 :
120 :       * This function call is to replace the
121 :       * REPLACE field_name WITH ...
```

```
122 :    * Now: AP_IT("Lastname","C",1)
123 :
124 :    * This function replaces the parameters into
125 :    * a STRUCTURE EXTENDED database which is
126 :    * previously created and open.
127 :
128 :    IF PCOUNT() = 3
129 :       _apd = 0
130 :    ENDIF
131 :
132 :    LOCATE ALL FOR UPPER(field_name) == UPPER(_apa)
133 :    IF FOUND()
134 :       RETURN(0)
135 :    ELSE
136 :       APPEND BLANK
137 :       IF _apc > 255  && For CHAR fields GREATER than 255 bytes
138 :          REPLACE field_name WITH _apa, field_type WITH _apb, ;
139 :                  field_len WITH INT(_apc % 256), ;
140 :                  field_dec WITH INT(_apc / 256)
141 :       ELSE
142 :          REPLACE field_name WITH _apa, field_type WITH _apb, ;
143 :                  field_len WITH _apc, field_dec WITH _apd
144 :       ENDIF
145 :    ENDIF
146 :    RETURN(RECNO())
147 :
148 : ******************
149 :
150 : FUNCTION Parsing
151 :
152 :    PARAMETERS _getstr
153 :
154 :    * This function is the string parser.  Basically, return the
155 :    * beginning fragment of a string, adjust the string, and if
156 :    * passed by reference, alter the contents of the original
157 :    * string.
158 :
159 :    PRIVATE _location, _tempback
160 :
161 :    _location  = IF(EMPTY(AT("+", _getstr)), ;
162 :                   AT("/", _getstr), AT("+", _getstr))
163 :
164 :    _tempback = IF(!EMPTY(_location), ;
165 :                SUBSTR(_getstr, 1, _location - 1), _getstr)
166 :    _getstr = IF(!EMPTY(_location), ;
167 :                SUBSTR(_getstr, _location + 1), "")
168 :    RETURN(_tempback)
169 :
170 : * End of File
```

The first thing that should become apparent is the content of this fragment. It is a database structure. We should be able to note the number of potential fields and their individual qualities. We can see how the Parsing() function could potentially help take this array of information and create a database from it. In most generic applications, it is ideal to have the executable program generate the various database files, ancillary .DBT files (if applicable), and associated index files. This will save on distribution disks for such a program and simplify the startup procedure every application requires. However, such a procedure will have many redundant parts. For example, here is a code fragment from an older version of Steve Straley's Accounting Package:

```
********************
* Name      Data2.prg
* Author    Stephen J. Straley
* Date      July 1, 1989
* Notice    Copyright (c) 1989 Stephen J. Straley & Associates
*           All Rights Reserved
* Compile   Clipper Data2 -m
* Release   Summer 87
* Link      PLINK86 FI Data2 LIB Clipper LIB Extend;
* Note      This shows how, with hard-coding techniques,
*           the data file structure from DATA1.PRG is
*           duplicated!
*
********************

CLEAR SCREEN

@ 24,00 SAY "Initializing Chart of Account File." +;
            "   One Moment"

PRIVATE tfile,tfile1,tfile2,tfile3,extmess

tfile  = "CHART"
tfile1 = "CHT_ACCT"
tfile2 = "CHT_DESC"
tfile3 = "CHT_KEY"
CREATE Template
USE Template
DO Ap_it WITH "INTERNAL",     "N",  8
DO Ap_it WITH "ACCOUNT",      "C", 16
DO Ap_it WITH "DESC",         "C", 28
DO Ap_it WITH "NORMAL",       "C",  1
DO Ap_it WITH "BALANCE",      "N", 12,  2
DO Ap_it WITH "CONS_ACCT",    "N",  8
DO Ap_it WITH "RPT_LEVEL",    "N",  2
DO Ap_it WITH "POSTING",      "C",  1
DO Ap_it WITH "MAST_CONS",    "C", 16
DO Ap_it WITH "ACCT_TYPE",    "C",  1
DO Ap_it WITH "CATEGORY",     "C",  2
DO Ap_it WITH "CASH",         "L",  1
DO Ap_it WITH "HISTORY",      "L",  1
CREATE (tfile) FROM Template
ERASE Template.dbf
USE (tfile)
APPEND BLANK
```

```
46 : CLEAR SCREEN
47 : @ 0,0 SAY "Please view all of the fields!"
48 : DBEDIT(1,0,3,79)
49 : CLEAR SCREEN
50 :
51 : * ************************************************
52 : * * The following procedure(s)/function(s) are   *
53 : * * part of Steve Straley's ToolkiT(tm) -         *
54 : * * Release 2, published by Four Seasons          *
55 : * * Publishing Co., Inc.  All Rights Reserved     *
56 : * * Information: 212-599-2141 / 800-662-2278      *
57 : * * All Rights Reserved                           *
58 : * * ************************************************
59 :
60 : FUNCTION Ap_it
61 :
62 :     PARAMETERS _apa, _apb, _apc, _apd
63 :
64 :     * _apa = the field name
65 :     * _apb = the field data type
66 :     * _apc = the field length
67 :     * _apd = the field decimal
68 :
69 :     * This function call is to replace the
70 :     * REPLACE field_name WITH ...
71 :     * Now: AP_IT("Lastname","C",1)
72 :
73 :     * This function replaces the parameters into
74 :     * a STRUCTURE EXTENDED database which is
75 :     * previously created and open.
76 :
77 :     IF PCOUNT() = 3
78 :         _apd = 0
79 :     ENDIF
80 :
81 :     LOCATE ALL FOR UPPER(field_name) == UPPER(_apa)
82 :     IF FOUND()
83 :         RETURN(0)
84 :     ELSE
85 :         APPEND BLANK
86 :         IF _apc > 255  && For CHAR fields GREATER than 255 bytes
87 :             REPLACE field_name WITH _apa, field_type WITH _apb, ;
88 :                     field_len WITH INT(_apc % 256), ;
89 :                     field_dec WITH INT(_apc / 256)
90 :         ELSE
91 :             REPLACE field_name WITH _apa, field_type WITH _apb, ;
92 :                     field_len WITH _apc, field_dec WITH _apd
93 :         ENDIF
94 :     ENDIF
95 :     RETURN(RECNO())
96 :
97 : * End of File
```

By making a function that will not only create the structure-extended database, but the indexes as well, we can save on code space within the application, Additionally, we can store the structure of the to-be-created database into an array, pass the array to the generic function, and create the designated database. And from this, we could carry this concept even further. We could incorporate the index keys in a large string, only to be parsed and analyzed. As discussed further in this book, we can place each of these arrays in the text file, read in said text files, and then call the function that generates the databases. This means that the structures of the databases can be modified and adjusted outside of the application, which will save not only on the development time, but on the size of the application as well.

VARIABLE LENGTH FIELDS

Up to this point, the Parsing() function has been used in a variety of ways. A unique variance on the ability to store a database structure to an array and parse out each field element and its characteristics, is the possibility of using the Parsing() function to create variable length fields. This concept may come in handy when manipulating downloaded mainframe data.

Now, if we are really adventurous, this technique should immediately imply that you, the developer, are not tied to the .DBF file format. You code your own database file structure, use whatever technique you selected, and build a sophisticated application. Of course, along with the Parsing() function you would need the assistance of the low-level file functions, which are discussed at length later in this book. However, the fact remains that Clipper, with the concept of parsing desired information from large sets of data, gives you the chance to create not only fantastic applications but new structures that could influence the database-management community as well.

We could embellish the parsing concept to go even further; consider this:

```
memvar = "7/0, 0/7"
```

This is nothing more than a parse of the command line, assigning the value on the right to the name of the variable on the left. The "=" symbol is the delimiter, and with this we can now look at the possibility of initializing our memory variables outside of the Clipper application. This not only is theory; it is reality, as you will see in the chapter on Data-Driven Technology.

SUMMARY

The conclusion is simple: A parsing function is vital to the future of application development in Clipper. It frees the developer from the mediocrity and limitations of the interpreters and gives one pure power limited only by one's imagination. And the limits for the

Parsing() function are not limited to these examples. Consider that Clipper was written in C, and C was written in C. Both languages contain parsers of one type or another. Clipper developers could, with very little effort, create a parsing situation in which they could build their own preprocessors for Clipper or, better yet, the next generation of Clipper interpreters and compilers. As you can see, by adding a programming concept to the Clipper concept and architecture, the potential is incredible.

CHAPTER TWO

Mastering DBEDIT()

Before getting into the main issue of this chapter, a couple of key points need to be established. Understanding the concepts and philosophy of this chapter is the key to mastering the subtleties of the Clipper language. This is a chapter not just on one function, but on one mind-set: unlimited possibilities. This may sound like an exaggeration, but be assured it is not. It is our intent that you will walk away from this chapter asking yourself "what if." Nothing short of that will suffice. The first cornerstone that must be laid is simple. Although we will be exploring many angles of the DBEDIT() function, the same principles can be applied to ACHOICE() and MEMOEDIT(). It will be your task to take the necessary time to transfer the concepts from this function to the other two. The second cornerstone, as mentioned earlier, is your thinking process. The approach to the DBEDIT() function, as documented in this chapter, opens up new possibilities to database-management technology, the Clipper language, and your programming style — which will eventually affect your personal functions and libraries. Take time to study the examples and the direction the DBEDIT() function takes with each example. Think about how this could affect your current projects and future applications. We are not suggesting a complete retrofit of previous programming assignments; let them go. But do spend adequate time to allow this new direction to settle in your mind. Indeed, there will be roadblocks as you try to learn this and apply it to other areas of database-management programming. Do not despair. Keep trying. Good Clipper programmers do not want the world handed to them on golden platters; good programmers constantly practice their trade. The idea of practice means to try new things and new approaches, to shuck the haphazard, mundane, and stale code of the past. Without this commitment, you will look at these examples and say, "that's nice." We want you to say, "what if?"

THE BASICS

Before we go any further, let us define the DBEDIT() function in its complete form:

FUNCTION: **DBEDIT()**

Syntax:

DBEDIT([<expN1> [, <expN2> [, <expN3> [, <expN4>]]]]
[, <expC1> [, <expC2> [, <expC3> [, <expC4> [, <expC5>
[, <expC6> [, <expC7>]]]]]]])

Detailed:

<expN1> = <top row coordinate>
<expN2> = <top column coordinate>
<expN3> = <bottom row coordinate>
<expN4> = <bottom column coordinate>
<expC1> = <array of column expressions>
<expC2> = <keystroke function name>
<expC3> = <array of picture expressions>
<expC4> = <array of headings for columns>
<expC5> = <array of characters for heading separator>

<expC6> = <array of characters for column separator>
<expC7> = <array of footings for columns>

Returns: <logical expression>

If used, the function specified in the keystroke-function-name parameter will receive the following two values from the DBEDIT() function:

Value 1 = mode
Value 2 = column pointer

These two values can be accepted by the keystroke function, provided there is a PARAMETER statement within the code definition of the function.

The values for **mode** can be the following:

mode = 0 = Idle; any cursor movement keys have been handled
and there are no further keys pending
mode = 1 = Attempt to cursor past BOF()
mode = 2 = Attempt to cursor past EOF()
mode = 3 = Database file is empty
mode = 4 = Any keystroke exception

The value for the **column pointer** is determined by the number of elements in the array <expC1>. If <expC1> is not passed to the DBEDIT() function, the number of fields in the active database will be used. This is the most critical point that could be made; we must look at each expression, each field, each value in terms of the display columns. This will be apparent as we delve further into this topic.

Once the keystroke function has completed its operation, it will return one of the following values to the DBEDIT() function:

Keystroke() = 0 = Quit DBEDIT()
Keystroke() = 1 = Continue DBEDIT()
Keystroke() = 2 = Continue DBEDIT(); however, force the data to
be reread and refresh the screen/windowed area
Keystroke() = 3 = Append Mode

The append mode is very tricky to control and program properly. It is not a recommended value for the Keystroke() function.

Throughout this chapter, we will be referring to these tables and this listing.

SIMPLE HEADER AND FOOTER INFORMATION

Some of the simpler items to mention with the DBEDIT() function are the header array <expC4>, the footer array <expC7>, and the area of information between the two. However, one basic point must be understood before we tackle these three simple issues. While the manual and other reference texts may explain that the items in the array passed to the DBEDIT() function are normally fields or "expressions," there is a far easier definition that we will use. Think of each item in each array as being a string of information that will get expanded whenever the DBEDIT() function needs to move the cursor or the record pointer in the file or refresh the screen. In addition, think of each array subscript as a column; the number of items in the array will generate the number of columns that may be viewed by the DBEDIT() function. Usually we think of this as being the number of fields. In most examples, the array of field names equates to the number of columns that can be viewed by the DBEDIT() function. But as we go further into this chapter, you will see that this is not always the case.

When dealing with a statement in which the information passed in the arrays are strings that will be "expanded" when DBEDIT() processes the information, think of it as a macro. Consider the following code extract:

```
steve = "Hello There"
dave = "steve"
? &dave.
```

Normally, if the variable dave was displayed via the "?," the word "steve" would appear on the screen. By expanding the value, or macroing, the variable dave, the value of the variable steve ("Hello There") is displayed. This is the concept of macro expansion: going one level deeper in the variable symbol table for an answer. Now, let's consider a typical DBEDIT() field array (assuming there are four fields in the database that is active for the DBEDIT() function):

```
USE Test
DECLARE fields[FCOUNT()] && Number of fields in active database
fields[1] = "NAME"
fields[2] = "AGE"
fields[3] = "PAID"
fields[4] = "B_DAY"
```

Calling the DBEDIT() function, the code in the program would look something like this:

```
DBEDIT(10,10,20,70, fields)
```

The name of the array containing the columns for the display area is passed by reference (note that all arrays in Clipper are passed by reference). Additionally, the names of the fields in the database Test are individually placed in each subscript position in the array named fields[]. Notice that these subscript elements are strings, yet, when the DBEDIT()

function is in action, the contents of the fields are displayed in the column area. Using the previous explanation of macro expansion, we can see that by expanding the name of the fields for each column and for each record, we would get the contents of that field and not the name of the field. We are, in essence, going one level deeper to get the desired information.

Throughout this chapter, no other point about the use of the DBEDIT() function is so vital. The information passed to the function is individually expanded for the number of specified columns and for the number of records in the active database.

When working with the array for the heading and/or footing information, here is another important tip. The window coordinates, as specified by the first four parameters passed to the DBEDIT() function, apply to the entire function. In other words, if the windowed area is 10,10,20,70, as in the example above, the number of the available row for any display information is 11. Removing one row for the line drawn to separate the header area from the display area leaves 10 available rows for display information. If there is some heading and footing information, the number of available rows to be used for the actual information in the active database is lessened by those amounts. Again, if we were to set up a heading banner using four lines of the windowed area as well as assigning two lines to the footing area, we would have no right to complain when DBEDIT() uses only four rows to display the information within the database.

So, how do we get multiple lines in the heading area, the footing area, and the basic information within those two areas. For this, let's consider the following example:

```
********************
* Name     Dbedit1.prg
* Author   Stephen J. Straley
* Date     July 4, 1989
* Notice   Copyright (c) 1989 Stephen J. Straley & Associates
* Compile  Clipper Dbedit1 -m
* Release  Summer 87
* Link     PLINK86 FI Dbedit1 LIB Extend LIB Clipper;
* Note     This is the first demonstration of the DBEDIT()
*          function.
*
********************

CLEAR SCREEN
SET WRAP ON
SET SCOREBOARD OFF
@  0,0 SAY "Steve Straley & Associates"
IF !FILE("ONTAP.*")
   CLEAR SCREEN
   @ 0,0 SAY "Please create the data files first!"
   QUIT
ENDIF
```

```
23 : USE Ontap
24 : DECLARE dispit[FCOUNT()], title[FCOUNT()]
25 : FOR x = 1 TO FCOUNT()
26 :    dispit[x] = FIELDNAME(x)
27 : NEXT
28 : title[1] = "Name of; file"
29 : title[2] = FIELDNAME(2)
30 : title[3] = "Date Stamp"
31 : title[4] = "Time Stamp"
32 : @ 4,0 TO 21,79 DOUBLE
33 : DBEDIT(5,1,20,78,dispit, .F., .F., title)
34 : CLOSE ALL
35 : CLEAR SCREEN
36 :
37 : * End of File
```

Looking at line 28, we can see that the contents of the first subscript in the array **title[]** will be the string "Name of; file." This means that over the first column the header will consist of two lines, the first being "Name of " and the second being "file." With this, we must point out a few obstacles that may come into play. While it is obvious that the semicolon is the character that forces DBEDIT() to display a new line either in the header area or in the footer area (this will not work for the data area), it has a subtle impact on the total region available for data display. In other words, if the windowed area allotted for the DBEDIT() function to work in (using the four screen coordinates) is only twelve rows, and if four rows are taken by header information using semicolons and another five rows are reserved for the footer area, it should be no surprise that you see only three rows of data. So be careful; the header and footer rows detract from the potential area for the DBEDIT() function. Also, a dual centering effect is in operation with the DBEDIT() function. First, Clipper will automatically try to center the entire screen within the windowed area. Second, Clipper will try to make each column area be the width of the data expression, the width of the header for that column, or the width of the footer for that column, whichever is greater. This means that multiple header/footer lines may be beneficial if you are trying to fit more information onto a screen.

The next thing to note is the default information passed to the header array (the eighth parameter in line 33). If no header line is passed to a column, the name of the field for that column position will be displayed. While this may be beneficial in some cases, note that most databases are designed with fields that are either symbolic for some greater meaning, with some encrypted code, or with the "_" character separating two words (e.g., "LAST_NAME"). In all three cases, the names of these fields, in uppercase lettering, will appear in the header area, provided that no header array or expression is passed to the DBEDIT() function to begin with.

From these beginning steps, let us move onto the next phase: working with DBEDIT() and list-box technology.

LIST-BOX TECHNOLOGY

The biggest trouble when you use DBEDIT() for a list-box on a VALID clause is with its return value. Here is a sample of this in use:

```
@ 10,10 GET mstate VALID DBEDIT(9,25,15,50)
```

The DBEDIT() function will either return a logical true (.T.) or a logical false (.F.), which is fine for the VALID clause but is useless for the variable in the GET statement. A list-box should allow the user to point to a piece of data and have the program analyze that piece and its value. This means that a proper list-box should either (a) return the record number the user pointed to or (b) return the contents of the fields at the record selected by the user. The desired field is not important because the programmer generally knows what field is required. For example, in the above fragment, the programmer would not be interested in the field with the zip code or in the contents of that field. Based on the correlation of the data element in the GET, the programmer has only two things to worry about; however, DBEDIT() is not concerned with either value in its generic form. The trick is to build a user-defined function surrounding the DBEDIT() function, which in turn would evaluate the results from such a list-box call, manipulate the value of the involved variable, and return a value to the VALID clause. Below is an example of this.

```
********************
* Name      Lookitup.prg
* Author    Stephen J. Straley
* Date      July 1, 1989
* Notice    Copyright (c) 1989 Stephen J. Straley & Associates
* Compile   Clipper Lookitup -m
* Release   Summer 87
* Link      PLINK86 FI Lookitup LIB Clipper LIB Extend;
* Note      This shows how a DBEDIT() call must be inside of a
*           user-defined function when working in conjunction
*           with a VALID clause.
*
********************

SELECT B
USE Filenos
INDEX ON File_name TO Tempname
SELECT A
USE Disknos INDEX Disknos
CLEAR SCREEN
mfile = SPACE(10)
mmore = SPACE(20)
SET KEY 9 TO Inquire
@  8,10 SAY "Press ESC to quit, TAB for Listing"
@ 10,10 SAY "What file do you want? " GET mfile ;
        VALID Lookfor(@mfile, "5", "5/6/7/8/9/20", .T.)
@ 12,10 SAY "Just an extra GET for display" GET mmore
READ
WAIT ALIAS()
```

```
030 : CLEAR SCREEN
031 :
032 : ********************
033 :
034 : PROCEDURE Inquire
035 :
036 :    KEYBOARD "?" + CHR(13)
037 :
038 : * ***********************************************
039 : * * The following procedure(s)/function(s) are  *
040 : * * part of Steve Straley's ToolkiT(tm) -        *
041 : * * Release 2, published by Four Seasons         *
042 : * * Publishing Co., Inc.  All Rights Reserved    *
043 : * * Information: 212-599-2141 / 800-662-2278     *
044 : * * All Rights Reserved                          *
045 : * * ***********************************************
046 :
047 : FUNCTION Lookfor
048 :
049 :    * make sure that the type of the variable and the
050 :    *      type of the data field are the same
051 :    * make sure that the fields in the field list are available
052 :    * make sure that the field in the get list is available
053 :    * verify window coordinates
054 :    * make sure that the database is available
055 :    * verify all parameters
056 :
057 :    PARAMETER _var, _gets, _says, _stuff
058 :
059 :    rettu = SELECT()
060 :    SELECT Filenos
061 :
062 :    IF PCOUNT() < 3
063 :       SELECT(rettu)
064 :       RETURN(.F.)
065 :    ELSEIF EMPTY(ALIAS())
066 :       SELECT(rettu)
067 :       RETURN(.F.)
068 :    ELSEIF TYPE("_gets") + TYPE("_says") != "CC"
069 :       SELECT(rettu)
070 :       RETURN(.F.)
071 :    ENDIF
072 :
073 :    PRIVATE _gname, _old, _qaz
074 :
075 :    _gname = FIELD(VAL(_gets))
076 :
077 :    && Get field is not there
078 :
079 :    IF EMPTY(_gname)
080 :       SELECT(rettu)
081 :       RETURN(.F.)
082 :    ENDIF
083 :
```

```
084 :     && The data types do not match
085 :
086 :     IF TYPE("_var") != TYPE(_gname)
087 :        SELECT(rettu)
088 :        RETURN(.F.)
089 :     ENDIF
090 :
091 :     && Seek to see if it is there...
092 :
093 :     SEEK _var
094 :     IF FOUND()
095 :        SELECT(rettu)
096 :        RETURN(.T.)
097 :     ELSE
098 :        GO TOP
099 :     ENDIF
100 :
101 :     _stuff = IF(TYPE("_stuff") != "L", .F., _stuff)
102 :
103 :     _old = _says
104 :     _cnt = 0
105 :     _tot = 0
106 :     DO WHILE !EMPTY(_old)
107 :        _tot = _tot + 1
108 :        _sname = FIELD(VAL(Parsing(@_old)))
109 :
110 :        && the SAY is not there
111 :
112 :        _cnt = _cnt + IF((EMPTY(_sname)), 1, 0)
113 :
114 :     ENDDO
115 :
116 :     DECLARE _show[_tot - _cnt]
117 :     _old = _says
118 :     _cnt = 1
119 :     DO WHILE !EMPTY(_old)
120 :        _sname = FIELD(VAL(Parsing(@_old)))
121 :        IF !EMPTY(_sname)
122 :           _show[_cnt] = Upperlower(_sname)
123 :           _cnt = _cnt + 1
124 :        ENDIF
125 :     ENDDO
126 :
127 :     _lookrow = ROW()
128 :     IF _lookrow > 16
129 :        _lookrow = 4
130 :     ENDIF
131 :
132 :     _lookcol = COL()
133 :     IF _lookcol > 60
134 :        _lookcol = 60
135 :        _lookrow = _lookrow + 1
136 :     ENDIF
```

```
137 :
138 :       _lookscr = SAVESCREEN(_lookrow-1,_lookcol-1,_lookrow + 7, ;
139 :                  _lookcol + (79 - _lookcol))
140 :       @ _lookrow - 1, _lookcol - 1 CLEAR TO _lookrow + 7, ;
141 :                  _lookcol + (79 - _lookcol)
142 :       @ _lookrow - 1, _lookcol - 1 TO _lookrow + 7, ;
143 :                  _lookcol + (79 - _lookcol) DOUBLE
144 :
145 :       DBEDIT(_lookrow, _lookcol, _lookrow + 6, _lookcol + ;
146 :          (78 - _lookcol), _show)
147 :       IF LASTKEY() = 13
148 :          _var = &_gname.
149 :          IF _stuff
150 :             KEYBOARD CHR(13)
151 :          ENDIF
152 :       ENDIF
153 :       RESTSCREEN(_lookrow - 1, _lookcol - 1, _lookrow + 7, ;
154 :                  _lookcol + (79 - _lookcol), _lookscr)
155 :       SELECT(rettu)
156 :       RETURN(.F.)
157 :
158 : ********************
159 :
160 : FUNCTION Upperlower
161 :
162 :       PARAMETERS _upla
163 :
164 :       * Take the parameter string and uppercase the first
165 :       * letter, lowercasing all other letters
166 :
167 :       IF PCOUNT() != 1
168 :          RETURN("")
169 :       ENDIF
170 :       RETURN(UPPER(SUBSTR(_upla, 1, 1)) + LOWER(SUBSTR(_upla,2)))
171 :
172 : ********************
173 :
174 : FUNCTION Parsing
175 :
176 :       PARAMETERS _getstr
177 :
178 :       PRIVATE _location, _tempback
179 :
180 :       _location  = IF(EMPTY(AT("+", _getstr)), ;
181 :                   AT("/", _getstr), AT("+", _getstr))
182 :       _tempback = IF(!EMPTY(_location), ;
183 :                   SUBSTR(_getstr, 1, _location - 1), _getstr)
184 :       _getstr = IF(!EMPTY(_location), ;
185 :                   SUBSTR(_getstr, _location + 1), "")
186 :       RETURN(_tempback)
187 :
188 : * End of File
```

As you can see, the VALID clause on line 26 makes reference to a user-defined function named Lookfor() that is further defined beginning on line 47. Since the DBEDIT() function returns only a logical expression, it becomes a useless tool as is when applied as a look-up function. In most cases, the programmer would want either the record number of the item in the database chosen by the end user from the pick list or the actual item and subsequent value. Therefore, the user-defined function Lookfor() is considered to "surround" the DBEDIT() function in order to obtain the proper information. In this function, the variable mfile is passed by reference, which means that if the function Lookfor() changes the value of the parameter _var, it will directly affect the value of mfile. Further, the second parameter to the function is a "get" field while the third parameter is a list of "say" fields. The concept is simple: Every list-box will have one-to-multiple display items in a windowed area. This list may or may not include the desired field. In the case of a code database for attorney fees, it is not impossible to imagine a list-box with the descriptive names, yet the actual returned, or "get," value will be the actual code. It is, therefore, important to perceive the display list as being a separate entity.

Scanning down through the rest of the code, a call to the DBEDIT() function is finally made on lines 145 and 146. Again, since the function returns only a logical expression, we must work around this and code our function accordingly. Now, imagine the user using the cursor keys to scan through this database, looking for the appropriate item. As soon as the proper choice appears in the highlighted bar, the end user will probably press the Enter key. At that point, the DBEDIT() function will cease, leaving the record pointer still sitting on the record of the field the end user was last on. At that point, testing to see if the value of LASTKEY() is 13, we simply find the value of the GET field and replace the value of **_var** with that value. Of course, another possibility would be to have the end user abort the list-box operation. The Esc key would probably be pressed, DBEDIT() would terminate, and the value of LASTKEY() would be 27, not 13. In either case, the function Lookfor() would return a value of a logical false (.F.), keeping the VALID from being completed and the cursor would remain on the GET field. This is important. By forcing a logical false value, the GET would remain, and if the value of the variable **mfile** was changed via **_var**, the value would appear in the GET area. In essence, we are using Clipper's GET logic to potentially display the information chosen within the GET area. To avoid having the end user press the Enter key again, that keystroke is automatically stuffed to the KEYBOARD (line 150) if the value of the passed parameter **_stuff** is set to a logical true (.T.).

By taking these first steps, you have just taken your first major leap into the new world of Clipper programming. Rest assured, the best is yet to come.

RESIZING THE DBEDIT() WINDOW

We have seen how we can get one column of information to display but have several pieces of data within that single area. To circumvent DBEDIT()'s shortcomings, in a practical setting, we must turn to our first usage of a user-defined function to handle all keystrokes. Now, let us take a deeper look at this technique.

One of the first things that must be said about this function is in conjunction with any active SET KEY TO command. (This pertains to the ACHOICE() and the MEMOEDIT() functions as well.) Try to turn off any conflicting or colliding SET KEY TO command prior to the call to the function. In other words, say we had a help system in our application. The default command line would look something like this:

```
SET KEY 28 TO Help
```

However, within the keystroke-exception function, we choose to design a help screen within the DBEDIT() function, and in order to be consistent, we program the function to test for the LASTKEY() being 28. Now, whenever the F1 key is pressed within the DBEDIT() function, Clipper will attempt to evaluate the keystroke and will collide within itself as the SET KEY TO logic tries to grab at it. Sometimes, the help screen within the DBEDIT() will work, and sometimes the Help system will work. Try to avoid this at all cost. Either choose to turn off all SET KEY logic prior to the call and program in those calls within the keystroke exception function or avoid calls to those keys within that same keystroke function.

Moving along, let's take a look at how we can use the keystroke function to change the window area of the DBEDIT() function and how we can test for special keystrokes, both cursor and noncursor keys.

```
********************
* Name      Dbedit3.prg
* Author    Stephen J. Straley
* Date      July 4, 1989
* Notice    Copyright (c) 1989 Stephen J. Straley & Associates
* Compile   Clipper Dbedit3 -m
* Release   Summer 87
* Link      PLINK86 FI Dbedit3 LIB Extend LIB Clipper;
* Note      This program shows how a bottom row value could
*           be used to resize a DBEDIT() window area.
*
********************

   CLEAR SCREEN
   SET WRAP ON
   SET SCOREBOARD OFF
   @ 0,0 SAY "Press ESC to QUIT of R for RESIZE WINDOW"
   @ 0,RIGHTJUST("SJS & Associates", 80) SAY "SJS & Associates"
   IF !FILE("ONTAP.*")
      @ 10,10 CLEAR TO 20,70
      @ 10,10 TO 20,70 DOUBLE
      @ 12,15 SAY "The files you need to run this program are not"
      @ 14,15 SAY "available.  Please compile, link, and execute"
      @ 16,15 SAY "DATA.PRG in order to produce the proper data"
      @ 18,15 SAY "set.  Any Key to Quit..."
      INKEY(0)
      CLEAR SCREEN
```

```
028 :        QUIT
029 :    ENDIF
030 :    USE Ontap
031 :    DECLARE dispit[FCOUNT()]
032 :    FOR x = 1 TO FCOUNT()
033 :        dispit[x] = FIELDNAME(x)
034 :    NEXT
035 :
036 :    bot_row = IF(FILE("Bottom.row"),VAL(MEMOREAD("Bottom.row")), 20)
037 :
038 :    SAVE SCREEN
039 :    DO WHILE .T.
040 :       @ 4,00 CLEAR
041 :       @ 4,0 CLEAR TO bot_row,79
042 :       @ 4,0 TO bot_row,79 DOUBLE
043 :       DBEDIT(5,1,bot_row-1,78,dispit, "INPUTIT")
044 :       IF LASTKEY() = 27
045 :          EXIT
046 :       ENDIF
047 :    ENDDO
048 :    MEMOWRIT("Bottom.row", STR(bot_row))
049 :    RESTORE SCREEN
050 :    CLOSE ALL
051 :
052 : *******************
053 :
054 : FUNCTION Inputit
055 :
056 :    PARAMETERS instat, fld_pnt
057 :
058 :    whatkey = LASTKEY()
059 :
060 :    IF instat = 0
061 :       RETURN(1)
062 :    ELSEIF instat = 1 .OR. instat = 2
063 :       KEYBOARD IF( (instat = 2), CHR(31), CHR(30))
064 :       RETURN(1)
065 :    ELSEIF instat = 3
066 :       WAIT "Nothing in the Database"
067 :       RETURN(0)
068 :    ELSE
069 :       IF CHR(whatkey)$"Rr"
070 :          SET CURSOR ON
071 :          @ 24,00 SAY "New Bottom Row Value => " ;
072 :                  GET bot_row PICT "##" ;
073 :                  VALID bot_row >= 8 .AND. bot_row <= 22
074 :          READ
075 :          GO TOP
076 :       ENDIF
077 :       RETURN(0)
078 :    ENDIF
```

```
079 :    RETURN(1)
080 :
081 : * ***********************************************
082 : * * The following procedure(s)/function(s) are  *
083 : * * part of Steve Straley's ToolkiT(tm) -       *
084 : * * Release 2, published by Four Seasons        *
085 : * * Publishing Co., Inc.  All Rights Reserved   *
086 : * * Information: 212-599-2141 / 800-662-2278    *
087 : * * All Rights Reserved                         *
088 : * ***********************************************
089 :
090 : FUNCTION Rightjust
091 :
092 :    PARAMETERS right_st, right_col
093 :
094 :    IF PCOUNT() = 1
095 :       right_col = 79
096 :    ENDIF
097 :    RETURN(IF(LEN(right_st) > right_col, right_st, ;
098 :           right_col - LEN(right_st)))
099 :
100 : * End of File
```

As with most of the examples in this book, there are several items of interest in this little program. First, note the initialization of the variable **bot_row** on line 36. In essence, that line says that if the file "Bottom.row" is on the disk, take the VAL() of the value from the MEMOREAD() of the file and assign it to the variable; otherwise, start off with a value of 20. Once inside of the main loop on lines 39 through 47, the DBEDIT() display window is controlled via the value from the variable **bot_row**. Looking at the screen region set up by the DOUBLE, we can see that the windowed area for the DBEDIT() is inside that screen region.

Once this is established, let us move onto the string "INPUTIT" located at the end of line 43. This is the name of the user-defined function that will be called after the call to the DBEDIT() is in operation. The phrasing is critical and will be embellished upon in a moment. However, it is important to note that at every clock tick in the computer, a call will be made to the Inputit() function from the DBEDIT() function. Remember, two values will be passed to the user-defined function automatically. This concept is similar to the SET KEY TO command where the associated procedure will receive up to three parameters. Here, the two parameters are received as seen on line 56: There are two variables that will contain the status of the DBEDIT() and the field pointer that the end user is currently resting on. From here, we assign the value of LASTKEY() to a variable named whatkey. Through testing the value of the instat and whatkey variables, we can achieve many new features within the DBEDIT() function.

For example, if the status of DBEDIT() is either a 1 or a 2, indicating an attempt to cursor beyond the beginning or end of the file, line 62 would hold true. At that point, the

KEYBOARD command in conjunction with the IF() function is used to stuff the keyboard with the appropriate key to send the DBEDIT() function the opposite way. In other words, if the BOF() is experienced, the keyboard is stuffed with the character that would send DBEDIT() to the EOF(), and the opposite would hold true coming the other way. Again, the philosophy of mixing and matching Clipper commands and functions in order to achieve a new effect hold true. If the key pressed by the end user within the DBEDIT() function is an exception key, the condition on line 68 would hold true. We then test the results from the LASTKEY() call and, if the key pressed is a member of the string "Rr", the IF command on line 69 would be true as well. Looking at this, we can see that an @...SAY...GET command on the bot_row variable is present. Basically the program flow would be simple; if the end user presses either "R" or "r" within the DBEDIT() function, the @...SAY...GET would be called and the end user would be asked to enter a new value for the bot_row variable. Providing the value for this variable falls within the range specified in the VALID clause on line 74; the READ would then be completed, forcing the record pointer to the top of the file on line 75. Once this is completed, the function Inputit() has to return a value back to the DBEDIT() function. In this case (line 77), the value is 0. This value tells DBEDIT() to terminate, which means the program flow would then jump to line 44 and following. Another test is made to evaluate the value of LASTKEY(). If it is not the ASCII value of the Esc key, the loop would continue with a new call to the DBEDIT() function, this time with a new value stored in the **bot_row** variable. Since that variable was initialized prior to the call to the Inputit() function, it is said to be "higher in memory," and as such, the Inputit() function can manipulate the value of the variable bot_row directly.

If the Esc key is pressed within the Inputit() function, the value returned from that function to the DBEDIT() function is still 0, forcing program flow to return again to line 44. This time, the IF on line 44 would evaluate to a logical true (.T.) and EXIT out of the loop on line 47. Immediately after the termination of the loop, the MEMOWRIT() function writes the new value of bot_row to the file in case the program is restarted by the end user, thus keeping the value of the resized area. This type of configurable software allows for greater participation on the part of the end user and eliminates fear. Additionally, as the end user requires less and less information to run the application, it provides the ability to reduce the amount of visual space required for either list-boxes and/or online help.

It is not our intent to show how compatible, faster, or more powerful Clipper is over any interpreter. Providing a better service to the end user, better applications, and better software is key. The Clipper dialect allows us the opportunity to accomplish this goal as well as giving us enough free time to enjoy our potential profits.

DISPLAYING RECNO() — RELATED AND SPECIFIC TEXT INFORMATION

In this step, we begin to tie the DBEDIT() function to more than a single database. We can display information within the windowed area that is not part of the active database, or we can display information in other work areas in other databases. Consider the following sample program:

```
01 : ********************
02 : * Name      Dbedit4.prg
03 : * Author    Stephen J. Straley
04 : * Date      November 1, 1988
05 : * Notice    Copyright (c) 1988-9 Stephen J. Straley & Associates
06 : * Compile   Clipper Dbedit4 -m
07 : * Release   Summer 87
08 : * Link      PLINK86 FI Dbedit4 LIB Extend LIB Clipper;
09 : * Note      This shows the use of a user defined function as
10 : *           part of the expressions listing.
11 : *
12 : ********************
13 :
14 :     CLEAR SCREEN
15 :     SET WRAP ON
16 :     SET SCOREBOARD OFF
17 :     @ 0,0 SAY "Steve Straley & Associates"
18 :     IF !FILE("ONTAP.*")
19 :         @ 10,10 CLEAR TO 20,70
20 :         @ 10,10 TO 20,70 DOUBLE
21 :         @ 12,15 SAY "The files you need to run this program are not"
22 :         @ 14,15 SAY "available.  Please compile, link, and execute"
23 :         @ 16,15 SAY "DATA.PRG in order to produce the proper data"
24 :         @ 18,15 SAY "set.  Any Key to Quit..."
25 :         INKEY(0)
26 :         CLEAR SCREEN
27 :         QUIT
28 :     ENDIF
29 :     USE Ontap
30 :     DECLARE dispit[FCOUNT()+1], title[FCOUNT()+1]
31 :     FOR x = 1 TO FCOUNT()
32 :         dispit[x+1] = FIELDNAME(x)
33 :         title[x+1]  = UPPERLOWER(FIELDNAME(x))
34 :     NEXT
35 :     dispit[1] = "RECNO()"
36 :     title[1]  = "Record;Number"
37 :     @ 4,0 TO 21,79 DOUBLE
38 :     DBEDIT(5,1,20,78,dispit, .F., .F., title)
39 :     CLOSE ALL
40 :     CLEAR SCREEN
41 :
42 : * ********************************************
43 : * * The following procedure(s)/function(s) are  *
44 : * * part of Steve Straley's ToolkiT(tm) -        *
45 : * * Release 2, published by Four Seasons         *
46 : * * Publishing Co., Inc.  All Rights Reserved   *
47 : * * Information: 212-599-2141 / 800-662-2278    *
48 : * * All Rights Reserved                          *
49 : * ********************************************
50 :
51 : ********************
52 :
53 : FUNCTION Upperlower
54 :
```

```
55 :     PARAMETERS upla
56 :
57 :     RETURN(UPPER(SUBSTR(upla, 1, 1)) + ;
58 :            LOWER(SUBSTR(upla,2)))
59 :
60 : * End of File
```

Again, keeping the concept of the column in mind, we can see that the number of columns that will be displayed will be the number of fields in the Ontap database (line 29) plus 1. This is established by the DECLARE command on line 30. In the FOR loop on lines 31 through 34, the two arrays dispit[] and title[] are filled with the names of the fields and the Upperlower() of their names beginning with the second column, not the first. Notice on lines 35 and 36 that the first column (or subscript position) for both arrays is the string of "RECNO()" and the title for the header area (taking up two lines) of "Record;Number". Remember that earlier we mentioned that DBEDIT() will take the names of the fields and macro expand them to get their number? The same concept will hold true here. Taking the string of the name of a Clipper function, if it is macro expanded, would net the actual record number for each record in the first column of the DBEDIT() windowed area. As long as the function is available in the Clipper application, the names of functions can be passed to each array subscript to be expressed in their respective column positions for each record. In this case, the RECNO() function is part of the internal Clipper.lib and part of the database engine within it. Therefore, we know that this function will be part of the application.

It should be noted at this point that if there was no title[] array, the name of the function would appear as the header for the first column. In other words, the string "RECNO()" would appear at the top of the column where the record numbers appear.

Of course, this is not all that can be accomplished. Stretching the technology mentioned above, let's now get the DELETE key involved both in the display region and in the keystroke-exception function.

```
********************
* Name      Dbedit5.prg
* Author    Stephen J. Straley
* Date      November 1, 1988
* Notice    Copyright (c) 1988-9 Stephen J. Straley & Associates
* Compile   Clipper Dbedit5 -m
* Release   Summer 87
* Link      PLINK86 FI Dbedit5 LIB Extend LIB Clipper;
* Note      This demonstration shows more versatility with
*           the DBEDIT() function.
*
********************

   CLEAR SCREEN
   SET WRAP ON
   SET SCOREBOARD OFF
```

```
17 :     @  0,0 SAY "Steve Straley & Associates"
18 :     @ 24,0 SAY "Press ESC to Quit / DEL to RECALL or DELETE file"
19 :     IF !FILE("ONTAP.*")
20 :        @ 10,10 CLEAR TO 20,70
21 :        @ 10,10 TO 20,70 DOUBLE
22 :        @ 12,15 SAY "The files you need to run this program are not"
23 :        @ 14,15 SAY "available.  Please compile, link, and execute"
24 :        @ 16,15 SAY "DATA.PRG in order to produce the proper data"
25 :        @ 18,15 SAY "set.  Any Key to Quit..."
26 :        INKEY(0)
27 :        CLEAR SCREEN
28 :        QUIT
29 :     ENDIF
30 :     USE Ontap
31 :     DECLARE dispit[1]
32 :     dispit[1] = "SHOWITEMS()"
33 :     header = "Files on Disk..."
34 :     SAVE SCREEN
35 :     @ 5,0 CLEAR TO 20,79
36 :     @ 5,0 TO 20,79 DOUBLE
37 :     DBEDIT(6,1,19,78,dispit, "INPUTIT", .F., header)
38 :     RESTORE SCREEN
39 :     CLOSE ALL
40 :
41 : *******************
42 :
43 : FUNCTION Inputit
44 :
45 :     PARAMETERS instat
46 :
47 :     whatkey = LASTKEY()
48 :     IF whatkey = 27
49 :        RETURN(0)
50 :     ELSEIF whatkey = 7
51 :        IF DELETED()
52 :           RECALL
53 :        ELSE
54 :           DELETE
55 :        ENDIF
56 :     ENDIF
57 :
58 :     IF instat = 2
59 :        KEYBOARD CHR(31)
60 :     ELSEIF instat = 1
61 :        KEYBOARD CHR(30)
62 :     ENDIF
63 :     RETURN(1)
64 :
65 : *******************
66 :
67 : FUNCTION Showitems
68 :
69 :     RETURN(IF(DELETED(), " *** ", "      ") + UPPER(files)  + ;
```

```
70 :        " using " + TRANSFORM(sizes, "@B 999,999,999 bytes. ") +;
71 :        "  Added => " + DTOC(datestamp) + " / " + times )
72 :
73 : * End of File
```

First, let's take a look at lines 31 and 32. We have DECLARED an array called dispit[] to contain only one element. That element is the name of a user-defined function called Showitems(). Using our past discussions as a base, we read this to mean that within the windowed area of DBEDIT(), only one column will appear (since dispit[] has only one element in it). In that one column will be the value of the function Showitems() that will have a value for each record that DBEDIT() was able to display within the windowed area. Since only one column will be displayed, we do not necessarily need to create another array for the header information. As stated in your favorite reference guide, the DBEDIT() function can take either a string or an array. If a string is passed (in this case, line 33 is for the header information) that string will be used for each columned area. Since we have only one column defined, the value of the variable header will be displayed only once.

Once the column and header information have been defined, the actual call to the DBEDIT() function is finally made (line 37). For every clock tick passed by within the DBEDIT() function, a call will be made to the user-defined function passed to the DBEDIT() function: INPUTIT(). Before we pick apart that function, scan down to line 67 and following. Here is the definition of the Showitems() function. As you can see, the function has taken several pieces of information and made one large string, beginning with a call to Clipper's IF() function. For every record that will be displayed by the DBEDIT() function, this function will be called to yield a display value, and that value is the RETURN value from this large string on lines 69 through 71. Note that the expression starts off by testing to see if the record is DELETED() or not. If it is, a series of asterisks appears; otherwise, a few blank spaces will be the value of the IF() function. After this, a few of the fields in the Ontap database are concatenated together, along with literal text. Remember, this function's value will be expressed for every record that is displayed by the DBEDIT() function; this is no different from passing a name of a field to the DBEDIT() function and having it macro expand the field name for every record.

You will notice that the highlighted bar representing the record pointer extends the entire width of the DBEDIT() window. This is because we have defined only one column; remember, line 32 is the DECLARE command. Even though we have created a situation in which multiple pieces of information are defined within that one column, DBEDIT() and Clipper still look to the database with one column in mind. Let's now look at the function Inputit(), which will process all of the keystrokes.

Beginning on line 43, the parameter instat is the mode of the DBEDIT() function. For example, on lines 58 through 62, if the mode of DBEDIT() is either past the top or bottom of the file, the value of the variable instat will be either 2 or 3. In either case, the KEYBOARD will be stuffed with the appropriate character to force DBEDIT() to page through the database in the opposite direction. This means that the wraparound effect, discussed in the previous example, is accomplished. However, please note the ELSEIF condition on line 50: There the value of the LASTKEY() being pressed must be a CHR(7) in order to make line 50 a true expression. The key on the keyboard that represents CHR(7) is the Del key. Therefore, if the Delete key is pressed and if the record is deleted, DELETED() on line 51 would be a true expression. Then the record would be RECALLed; otherwise, the record would be marked for deletion. After this has taken place, the user-defined function Inputit() will return a 1 to the DBEDIT() function, forcing DBEDIT() to continue processing. However, when control is given back to DBEDIT(), it will try to express the value passed to it for that particular column. In this case, once the Inputit() function has RETURNed a 1 to DBEDIT(), DBEDIT() in turn will make a call to the Showitems() function. If the end user presses the Delete key, the record will then be marked (if not previously marked) for deletion, the Inputit() function tells DBEDIT() to continue processing, only to then recall the Showitems() function, which notes the record being marked and displays the three asterisks returned from the IF() function on line 69. This means that you do not need to go through any fancy coding exercise to get the tagged information properly marked on the screen. The DBEDIT() function takes care of it for you.

We have now started to look deeper than the manual may indicate. Building on the simple, a complex user information system can be built with a single call to the DBEDIT() function. Information across several databases may be displayed and keystrokes analyzed for program flow and direction. Even with all of this, we have just scratched the surface of the DBEDIT() function.

LOCKING FIELDS IN DBEDIT()

Many non-Clipper people would claim that the DBEDIT() function is not like the BROWSE command in many interpreters. They are correct, but for this, we are grateful. The DBEDIT() function is much more than a simple BROWSE. It is also far more powerful. One of the main features of a BROWSE is the ability to lock on a field within the windowed area, allowing the user to scan across several windows, keeping the "key" field displayed as well. In addition, the abilities to pick the field and add information while "browsing" may be equally desirable. While some may say these are tasks for the interpreters, consider the following before making any assessment:

```
********************
* Name      Nextedit.prg
* Author    Stephen J. Straley
* Date      July 10, 1989
* Notice    Copyright (c) 1989 Stephen J. Straley & Associates
* Compile   Clipper Nextedit -m
* Release   Summer 87
* Link      PLINK86 FI Nextedit LIB Extend LIB Clipper;
* Note      This shows how the user can lock one field on
*           the screen  and also edit a memo field
*           by using a MEMOEDIT() function inside of this
*           function.
```

```
013 : *
014 : ********************
015 :
016 :     IF !FILE("NOTAP.*")
017 :         @ 10,10 CLEAR TO 20,70
018 :         @ 10,10 TO 20,70 DOUBLE
019 :         @ 12,15 SAY "The files you need to run this program are not"
020 :         @ 14,15 SAY "available.  Please compile, link, and execute"
021 :         @ 16,15 SAY "DATA.PRG in order to produce the proper data"
022 :         @ 18,15 SAY "set.  Any Key to Quit..."
023 :         INKEY(0)
024 :         CLEAR SCREEN
025 :         QUIT
026 :     ENDIF
027 :     USE Notap
028 :     DO Mainmenu
029 :
030 : ******************
031 :
032 : PROCEDURE Mainmenu
033 :
034 :     CLEAR SCREEN
035 :     SET WRAP ON
036 :     SET SCOREBOARD OFF
037 :     @ 0,0 SAY "Steve Straley & Associates"
038 :     @ 23,0 SAY "'P' to Pick a Field / Arrow Key to Pan Across / " + ;
039 :                "'E' to Edit a Field"
040 :     @ 24,0 SAY "Press ESC to Quit / DEL to RECALL or DELETE file"
041 :
042 :     IF ISCOLOR()
043 :         highlite = "R/W, G/N"
044 :         normal   = "W/B, B/W"
045 :     ELSE
046 :         highlite = "W+*/N, N/W"
047 :         normal   = "W/N, N/W"
048 :     ENDIF
049 :
050 :     original = SETCOLOR()
051 :
052 :     DECLARE dispit[3]
053 :     fieldlist = FIELDNAME(1)
054 :     dispit[1] = "SHOWIT1(fieldlist)"
055 :     dispit[2] = "SHOWIT2(fieldlist)"
056 :     dispit[3] = "SHOWIT3(fieldlist)"
057 :     @ 5,0 CLEAR TO 20,75
058 :     @ 5,0 TO 20,75 DOUBLE
059 :     DO WHILE .T.
060 :         header = "Locked field is &fieldlist."
061 :         DBEDIT(6,1,19,74,dispit, "INPUTIT", .F., header)
062 :         IF LASTKEY() = 27
063 :             EXIT
064 :         ENDIF
```

```
065 :     ENDDO
066 :     CLOSE ALL
067 :     CLEAR SCREEN
068 :
069 : ********************
070 :
071 : FUNCTION Inputit
072 :
073 :     PARAMETERS instat
074 :
075 :     SETCOLOR(original)
076 :
077 :     IF instat = 0    && Idle mode
078 :        Sidebar()
079 :     ENDIF
080 :
081 :     whatkey = LASTKEY()
082 :
083 :     IF whatkey = 27 .AND. instat = 4    && ESC and keyboard
084 :        RETURN(0)                        && exception
085 :
086 :     ELSEIF CHR(whatkey)$"Pp"
087 :        fieldlist = FIELDNAME(PICKAFIELD())
088 :        RETURN(0)
089 :
090 :     ELSEIF CHR(whatkey)$"Ee"    && Perform Editstatus
091 :        Editit()
092 :
093 :     ELSEIF whatkey = 7          && Deleted status
094 :        IF DELETED()
095 :           RECALL
096 :        ELSE
097 :           DELETE
098 :        ENDIF
099 :     ENDIF
100 :
101 :     IF instat = 2              && Performs Wrap-around
102 :        KEYBOARD CHR(31)
103 :     ELSEIF instat = 1
104 :        KEYBOARD CHR(30)
105 :     ENDIF
106 :     RETURN(1)
107 :
108 : ********************
109 :
110 : FUNCTION Showit1
111 :
112 :     PARAMETERS whichfield
113 :
114 :     IF DELETED()
115 :        SETCOLOR(highlite)
116 :     ELSE
```

```
      SETCOLOR(normal)
   ENDIF

   RETURN(  FILL_OUT( ISDELETED() + STRVALUE(&whichfield.)  + ;
          " | " + TRANSFORM(sizes, "@B 999,999,999 bytes. ") + ;
          "  | " + DTOC(datestamp) + " / " + times + " | " + ;
          TRANSFORM(per_used, "999 % used"), 73) )

*******************

FUNCTION Showit2

   PARAMETERS whichfield

   IF DELETED()
      SETCOLOR(highlite)
   ELSE
      SETCOLOR(normal)
   ENDIF

   RETURN( FILL_OUT( ISDELETED() + STRVALUE(&whichfield.) + ;
           " | " + SUBSTR(comment, 1, 30) + " | " + ;
           SUBSTR(file_use, 1, 30), 73))

*******************

FUNCTION Showit3

   PARAMETERS whichfield

   IF DELETED()
      SETCOLOR(highlite)
   ELSE
      SETCOLOR(normal)
   ENDIF

   RETURN( FILL_OUT( ISDELETED() + STRVALUE(&whichfield.) + ;
           " | " + subdrive, 73) )

*******************

FUNCTION Isdeleted

   RETURN( IF(DELETED(), " *** ", "     ") )

*******************

PROCEDURE Sidebar

   @ 5,76 CLEAR TO 20,78
   @ 5,76 TO 20,78

   IF !(LASTREC() = RECNO())
```

```
170 :        @ 7 + (RECNO() - INT(LASTREC() / 12)) / ;
171 :              INT(LASTREC() / 12) ,77 SAY CHR(177)
172 :     ELSE
173 :        @ 19,77 SAY CHR(177)
174 :     ENDIF
175 :
176 : *******************
177 :
178 : FUNCTION Pickafield
179 :
180 :     SAVE SCREEN
181 :     newopt = 1
182 :     SET TYPEAHEAD TO 0      && Trick #1
183 :     @ 2,0 CLEAR TO 22,79
184 :     @ 2,0 TO 22,79 DOUBLE
185 :     @ 4,5 SAY "Pick the field you want"
186 :     FOR x = 1 to FCOUNT()
187 :        @ 4+x,6 PROMPT FIELDNAME(x)
188 :     NEXT
189 :     MENU TO newopt
190 :     SET TYPEAHEAD TO 64    && Trick #2
191 :     KEYBOARD CHR(0)        && Trick #3
192 :     SET CURSOR OFF
193 :     RESTORE SCREEN
194 :     RETURN( IF(EMPTY(newopt), 1, newopt) )
195 :
196 : *******************
197 :
198 : PROCEDURE Editit
199 :
200 :     SAVE SCREEN
201 :     @ 2,0 CLEAR TO 22,79
202 :     @ 2,0 TO 22,79 DOUBLE
203 :     @ 4,5 SAY "Edit Appropriate Fields..."
204 :     @  7,10 SAY "File Name => " GET Notap->files
205 :     @  8,10 SAY "     Size => " GET Notap->sizes
206 :     @  9,10 SAY "     Time => " GET Notap->times
207 :     @ 10,10 SAY "     Date => " GET Notap->datestamp
208 :     @ 11,10 SAY " Subdrive => " GET Notap->subdrive
209 :     @ 12,10 SAY "        % => " GET Notap->per_used
210 :     @ 13,10 SAY " Comments => "
211 :     @ 14,10 SAY " File Use => "
212 :     CLEAR GETS
213 :     SET CURSOR ON
214 :     @ 13,24 TO 20,77
215 :     REPLACE Notap->comment WITH ;
216 :             MEMOTRAN(MEMOEDIT(Notap->comment, 14,25,19,76,;
217 :             .T.,"FINISHIT"), "", "")
218 :     @ 13,24 CLEAR TO 20,78
219 :     @ 13,24 SAY SUBSTR(comment, 1, 20)
220 :     @ 14,24 TO 20,77
221 :     REPLACE Notap->file_use WITH ;
222 :             MEMOTRAN(MEMOEDIT(Notap->file_use, 15,25,19,76,;
223 :             .T.,"FINISHIT"), "", "")
```

```
224 :     @ 14,24 CLEAR TO 20,78
225 :     @ 14,24 SAY SUBSTR(file_use, 1, 20)
226 :     @ 17,5 SAY "Any Key to Return..."
227 :     SET CURSOR OFF
228 :     INKEY(0)
229 :     RESTORE SCREEN
230 :
231 : ******************
232 :
233 : FUNCTION Finishit
234 :
235 :     PARAMETERS _a, _b
236 :
237 :     IF LASTKEY() = 27 .OR. LASTKEY() = 23
238 :        RETURN(0)
239 :     ELSEIF LASTKEY() = 13
240 :        KEYBOARD CHR(23)
241 :     ENDIF
242 :     RETURN(1)
243 :
244 : * *********************************************
245 : * * The following procedure(s)/function(s) are  *
246 : * * part of Steve Straley's ToolkiT(tm) -        *
247 : * * Release 2, published by Four Seasons        *
248 : * * Publishing Co., Inc.  All Rights Reserved   *
249 : * * Information: 212-599-2141 / 800-662-2278    *
250 : * * All Rights Reserved                         *
251 : * *********************************************
252 :
253 : *******************
254 :
255 : FUNCTION Fill_out
256 :
257 :     PARAMETERS fill_a, fill_b
258 :
259 :     * fill_a = the string to be filled out
260 :     * fill_b = the Length to fill out the string to
261 :
262 :     IF PCOUNT() = 1
263 :        fill_b = 80
264 :     ELSE
265 :        IF TYPE("fill_b") = "C"
266 :           fill_b = VAL(b)
267 :        ENDIF
268 :        fill_b = IIF(fill_b <= 1, 80, fill_b)
269 :     ENDIF
270 :
271 :     IF fill_b <= LEN(fill_a)
272 :        RETURN(fill_a)
273 :     ENDIF
274 :     RETURN(fill_a + SPACE(fill_b - LEN(fill_a)))
275 :
276 : *******************
277 :
```

```
278 : FUNCTION Upperlower
279 :
280 :    PARAMETERS upla
281 :
282 :    RETURN(UPPER(SUBSTR(upla, 1, 1)) + LOWER(SUBSTR(upla,2)))
283 :
284 : ********************
285 :
286 : FUNCTION Strvalue
287 :
288 :    PARAMETERS showstring
289 :
290 :    DO CASE
291 :    CASE TYPE("showstring") = "C"
292 :       RETURN(showstring)
293 :    CASE TYPE("showstring") = "N"
294 :       RETURN(STR(showstring))
295 :    CASE TYPE("showstring") = "M"
296 :       RETURN(" ")
297 :    CASE TYPE("showstring") = "D"
298 :       RETURN(DTOC(showstring))
299 :    OTHERWISE
300 :       RETURN(IF(showstring, "True", "False"))
301 :    ENDCASE
302 :
303 : * End of File
```

In this example, we are making the DBEDIT() function do much more than previously thought possible. This is because we are mixing and matching many of the Clipper commands and functions together in order to achieve a different effect. In the above example, we have the capability of showing a record's position in a database, which is similar to a Macintosh function; the color of the highlighted bar is different if the record is tagged for deletion; the ability to pick a "locked" field is available; and the ability to edit a record while in a DBEDIT() mode is completely diagrammed.

Starting from the beginning, note that three columns will be displayed. We get that by looking at lines 54 through 56: on line 52 the DECLARE command creates the array **dispit**[] to 3. Also, it is vital to perceive that the global variable named **fieldlist** is global in nature because it is initialized at the topmost level of the program. This variable is initialized to a beginning value of the name of the first field in the Notap database, and that name is also a parameter passed to the Showit1(), Showit2(), and Showit3() functions, as seen in their string representations on lines 54 through 56. Using the first of these functions as the next step in this discussion, jump down to line 110 for the beginning of the definition of the Showit1() function. Focus on lines 120 and following and on the name of the variable on the PARAMETER command line: whichfield. Remember, the element in the first position of the array dispit[] will be macro expanded for every record in the database. This means that the string in the variable fieldlist will be passed to this function for every record, and that name is now in a variable named whichfield. If we internally macro expanded that variable, we would get the actual contents of that field for that record. So, on line 120, the

STRVALUE() function is taking the macro expansion of the name of the field we are locking in the first position and returning its string value.

Looking at the other two functions, you will note that the first three calls made in each RETURN command (lines 137 and 153) are identical. Also, it should be noted that the width of the DBEDIT() window (line 61) is 73 characters (taking the specified last column position minus the first column position), and that the ToolkiT's Fill_out() function takes the concatenated string built in each of the three Showit() functions and fills out the string to be 73 characters in length (lines 123, 139, and 154). Therefore, each column takes up one complete DBEDIT() screen. Even though the end user presses the right arrow key and moves from Showit1() to Showit2(), it appears to be a new screen. To us, it is just another column. Again, to the end user, it will appear that the first field is "locked," appearing in the same position from one column to the next. This is because the first three calls in all three Showit() functions are identical.

At this point, it should be briefly pointed out that in all three Showit() functions, the color of the system is changed whether or not the record is marked for deletion. These two variables, **highlite** and **normal**, are initialized on lines 42 through 48. In that logic, it must also be understood that the main color of the system is initialized to a variable named **original** on line 50.

Moving onto line 60, the single header string is initialized to a variable appropriately named variable and will say "Locked field is" plus the name of the field stored to the variable **fieldlist**. Initially, this will be the name of the field in the first position in the Notap database. Also, this means that the same header line will be used for all three columns, since only a string is passed to the DBEDIT() function. And with that, we finally have the call to the DBEDIT() function on line 61.

Obviously, the rest of the guts of this program is within the Inputit() function that is called by the DBEDIT() function. This function begins on line 71. The **instat** variable is the variable for the status of the DBEDIT() function whenever this function is called. Notice that the first action taken within the function is to reset the color of the system back to the value of **original**. Consider this: Whether or not a record is marked, the color of the displayed area, the highlighted bar, those records marked for deletion, and of those marked for deletion with the highlighted bar will all yield different colors. Since DBEDIT() generates a highlighted bar showing which element the record pointer of the database is currently at, that bar uses a color that is different from the color of the records before and after the current value for RECNO(). Since we have modified what the potential colors of the system could be within each of the three Showit() functions, we need to reset the color back to the **original** value before pressing onward. Therefore, any other action taken within the Inputit() function will be done in the **original** color of the system.

Next, if the function notes that DBEDIT() is idle, or **instat** has a value of 0, a call to the Sidebar() procedure is made. The definition of that function is made on lines 164 through 174. It must be pointed out that this function or technology, as it stands, will only work on databases without active indexes. Other factors must be considered if an index file is in use. In any event, a little box is drawn to the right of the DBEDIT() windowed area. Next, a ratio is calculated: Since there are 12 active rows within the windowed area set aside by line 167, a ratio for the number of records per display row must be obtained. That ratio is then matched up with the current RECNO() value, which, in turn, is added to the numeric value of 7. Basically, as the value of RECNO() increases, the row on which the CHR(177) is will also increase. However, the increase is proportional to the number of available rows the windowed area has. This means as the end user moves down in the database, a Macintosh-like sidebar gauge will be seen to the right of the function. Remember, this will only be called if DBEDIT() is seen as idle.

Moving back to the Inputit() function, the check for the Delete key is made on lines 93 through 99 and will perform as mentioned in the previous example. Additionally, the wraparound effect is still in force since that, too, is programmed into the function on lines 101 through 105. Therefore the two remaining topics appear on lines 86 through 88 and 90 through 91.

Lines 86 through 88 are the condition to allow the end user to pick the field that will be in the first position of each of the displayed columns. Looking at the expression on line 86, it should be obvious that if the end user picks either the "P" or the "p," a call to the Pickafield() function will eventually be made. The value from the Pickafield() function must be numeric and is then passed to Clipper's FIELDNAME() function. That function's value is then passed to the variable **fieldlist**, which is the name of the global variable containing the name of the "locked" field. At that point, the Inputit() function RETURNs a 0, forcing DBEDIT() to quit. Paraphrasing the next few operations, which can be studied by looking closely at the main loop on lines 59 through 65, the DBEDIT() function will be recalled, this time with a different value for **fieldlist**, and thus, a new "locked" field will be in place.

Moving onto the Pickafield() function on lines 178 through 194, several new operations are made. First, on line 182 we are taking advantage of a nuance in Clipper that allows us not to have extra memory variables cluttering up our system. Consider this possibility: In this function, several PROMPTs are made, thus creating a menu of choices (lines 186 through 189). If the end user presses the Esc key, that should equate out to "keep the first field as the locked field" as seen by the return value on line 194. This should set the value of the **fieldlist** variable and then exit out of the DBEDIT() function. But looking to the main loop, lines 62 through 64, we see that if the value of LASTKEY() is the Esc key, the loop is terminated and no further call to the DBEDIT() function is made. Since the Esc key was pressed at the Pickafield() level and not at the Inputit() level, the program must be told not to quit in this case. This leads to the trick on line 182. It was discovered that if the TYPEAHEAD buffer is SET to 0, the code calling the LASTKEY() function will be turned off. Therefore, if the Esc key is pressed within the MENU, the value of LASTKEY() is not trapped. What is trapped is either the letter "P" or "p," which were the only two possible key values to get to this level. After a choice is picked from the menu of field names (lines 186 through 188), the TYPEAHEAD buffer is turned back on and the keyboard is stuffed with a CHR(0), or a null byte, thus clearing it of all values. This will prevent another call to this Procedure, since the value of LASTKEY() is still the ASCII value of either the letter "P" or "p."

Finally, the editing capabilities within the Inputit() function must be discussed. As with the ability to let the end user pick a field with either the letters "P" or "p," the letters "E" or "e" make a call to the Editit() procedure (lines 90 and 91). Looking at line 198, which begins the Editit() definition, it can be quickly seen that not every field is being updated. Since there is no index on, only those fields that are not involved with any potential key information are updated. However, for display purposes, the information is in a GET only to be quickly CLEARed on line 212. The real trick starts on line 215 and following. The **comment** and **file_use** fields are long character strings in the Notap database. Both on lines 215 and 216 and on lines 221 and 223, the information is replaced with value from the MEMOEDIT()/MEMOTRAN() functions. Within these functions, the Finishit() function will be called for every keystroke seen by the MEMOEDIT() function. Before going further, the power of Clipper should now be noted. Remember our location: a function within MEMOEDIT(), which is in a user-defined function, called by another function, which in turn is called by the DBEDIT(), which in turn was called by the MAINMENU procedure. The power to mix and match to create new possibilities and effects is the difference between a good and a mediocre Clipper programmer.

Finally, looking at the Finishit() function (lines 233 through 242), if the Enter key is pressed while inside of the MEMODIT() function, the KEYBOARD will be stuffed with CHR(23), which writes the memo or string and completes the function. This effect keeps the MEMOEDIT() working like a GET: We can move from one GET to the next by pressing the Enter key. Here, we can do the same.

So, in a quick overview, we have the ability to change the colors of the tagged, untagged, highlighted, and unhighlighted areas of the DBEDIT() window; graphically point to the relative RECNO() position in the database; issue a PROMPT and MENU TO command within DBEDIT(); turn off the LASTKEY() function; change the value of a locked field; call a MEMOEDIT() function; and simulate a GET with the function called by the MEMOEDIT(). Not bad for a simple "browse" function.

Testing for FILTER conditions and allowing for a special gateway to DOS is also quite practical.

```
********************
* Name      Dbfilt.prg
* Author    Stephen J. Straley
* Date      July 1, 1989
* Notice    Copyright (c) 1989 Stephen J. Straley & Associates
* Compile   Clipper Dbfilt -m
* Release   Summer 87
* Link      PLINK86 FI Dbfilt LIB Extend LIB Clipper;
* Note      This shows how to lock one field on the screen
```

```
010 : *           Multiple Calls to the function.
011 : *           Working without a SET FILTER TO command
012 : *           Seeking a condition within a subset
013 : *           Change the controlling index on the fly
014 : *
015 : ********************
016 :
017 : CLEAR SCREEN
018 : SELECT B
019 : USE Filenos INDEX Filenos, Filesub, Filetype
020 : SELECT A
021 : USE Disknos INDEX Disknos
022 : SET RELATION TO sub_no INTO Filenos
023 : Scanbyme()
024 :
025 : *******************
026 :
027 : PROCEDURE Scanbyme
028 :
029 : DECLARE db1[4], db2[4]
030 : DECLARE hd1[4], hd2[4]
031 : db1[1] = "ASHOW1()"
032 : db1[2] = "ASHOW2()"
033 : db1[3] = "ASHOW3()"
034 : db1[4] = "ASHOW4()"
035 : db2[1] = "BSHOW1()"
036 : db2[2] = "BSHOW2()"
037 : db2[3] = "BSHOW3()"
038 : db2[4] = "BSHOW4()"
039 : hd1[1] = "      Disk Number               Name"
040 : hd1[2] = "      Disk    Number of;    Number    " + ;
041 :          " Sub Drives           Comments"
042 : hd1[3] = "      Disk Number    Date Added    " + ;
043 :          "Available Bytes"
044 : hd1[4] = SPACE(35) + "Available    Original;    " + ;
045 :          "Disk Number  Date Updated      " + ;
046 :          "Bytes          Drive"
047 : hd2[1] = " File Name         Sub Directory "
048 : hd2[2] = " File Name         File Comments "
049 : hd2[3] = " File Name             Size           " + ;
050 :          "Date          Time"
051 : hd2[4] = " File Name             Type           " + ;
052 :          "Description"
053 : Pushscreen(4,3,13,77,.T.,.T.,.T.,.T.)
054 : var = " Scan Catalogued Information "
055 : @ 4,5 GET var
056 : CLEAR GETS
057 : DO WHILE .T.
058 :    BEGIN SEQUENCE
059 :       SELECT 1
060 :       DBEDIT(5,4,12,76,db1,"PROCESS1", "", hd1)
061 :       EXIT
062 :    END
063 : ENDDO
```

```
@ 24,00
Popscreen(4,3,13,77,.T.)

*******************

FUNCTION Ashow1

   RETURN(FILL_OUT( ISDELETED() + A->disk_no + ;
          SPACE(1) + CHR(186) + SPACE(1) + ;
          A->sub_no + SPACE(1) + CHR(186) + ;
          SPACE(1) + B->sub_name, 71) )

*******************

FUNCTION Ashow2

   RETURN(FILL_OUT( ISDELETED() + A->disk_no + ;
          SPACE(1) + CHR(186) + SPACE(1) + A->disk_name, 71))

*******************

FUNCTION Ashow3

   RETURN( FILL_OUT( ISDELETED() + A->disk_no + ;
          SPACE(1) + CHR(186) + SPACE(1) + ;
          PRINTDATE(A->date_add, 1) +  ;
          SPACE(1) + CHR(186) + SPACE(1) + ;
          TRANSFORM(A->bytes_left, ;
          "@B 999,999,999 bytes"), 71) )


*******************

FUNCTION Ashow4

   RETURN( FILL_OUT( ISDELETED() + A->disk_no + ;
           SPACE(1) + CHR(186) + SPACE(1) + ;
           PRINTDATE(A->date_up, 1) + ;
           SPACE(1) + CHR(186) + SPACE(1) + ;
           IF(A->hardflop, "Floppy   ", "Hard Disk") + ;
           SPACE(1) + CHR(186) + SPACE(1) + ;
           A->drivelet, 71) )

*******************

FUNCTION Process1

   PARAMETERS  _mode


   IF _mode != 0
      IF LASTKEY() = 9
         whichone = INDEXWIN()

```

```
118 :        ELSEIF LASTKEY() = 27
119 :            RETURN(0)
120 :
121 :        ELSEIF LASTKEY() = 300    && Alt Z
122 :            SAVE SCREEN
123 :            CLEAR SCREEN
124 :            SET CURSOR ON
125 :            ? "Type EXIT to Return to DBFILT.EXE"
126 :            RUN Command
127 :            SET CURSOR OFF
128 :            RESTORE SCREEN
129 :
130 :        ELSEIF LASTKEY() = 13
131 :            express = "B->sub_no = '" + sub_no + "'"
132 :            lookup = A->sub_no
133 :            SELECT B
134 :            SEEK lookup
135 :            IF !FOUND()
136 :               SELECT A
137 :               RETURN(1)
138 :            ENDIF
139 :            top1 = ROW() + 1
140 :            range1 = 19 - (top1 + 1)
141 :            Pushscreen(top1,5,20,75,.T.,.T.,.T.,.T.)
142 :            DO WHILE .T.
143 :               DBEDIT(top1+1,6,19,74,db2,"PROCESS2",.F.,hd2)
144 :               IF LASTKEY() = 27
145 :                  EXIT
146 :               ENDIF
147 :            ENDDO
148 :            Popscreen(top1,5,20,75,.T.)
149 :            SELECT A
150 :            RETURN(2)
151 :        ENDIF
152 :     ELSE
153 :        @ 24,00 SAY SPACE(80)
154 :     ENDIF
155 :     RETURN(1)
156 :
157 : ******************
158 :
159 : FUNCTION Bshow1
160 :
161 :     IF !(&express.)
162 :        RETURN(FILL_OUT(" ", 69))
163 :     ELSE
164 :        RETURN(FILL_OUT(ISDELETED() + file_name + ;
165 :               SPACE(1) + CHR(186) + SPACE(1) + sub_name,69))
166 :     ENDIF
167 :
168 : ******************
169 :
170 : FUNCTION Bshow2
171 :
```

```
172 :    IF !(&express.)
173 :       RETURN(FILL_OUT(" ", 69))
174 :    ELSE
175 :       RETURN(FILL_OUT(ISDELETED() + file_name + ;
176 :             SPACE(1) + CHR(186) + SPACE(1) + file_comm,69))
177 :    ENDIF
178 :
179 : *******************
180 :
181 : FUNCTION Bshow3
182 :
183 :    IF !(&express.)
184 :       RETURN(FILL_OUT(" ", 69))
185 :    ELSE
186 :       RETURN(FILL_OUT(ISDELETED() + file_name + ;
187 :             SPACE(1) + CHR(186) + SPACE(1) + ;
188 :             TRANSFORM(file_size, "@B 999,999,999 bytes") + ;
189 :             SPACE(1) + CHR(186) + SPACE(1) + ;
190 :             DTOC(file_date) + SPACE(1) + CHR(186) + ;
191 :             SPACE(1) + file_time, 69) )
192 :    ENDIF
193 :
194 : *******************
195 :
196 : FUNCTION Bshow4
197 :
198 :    IF !(&express.)
199 :       RETURN(FILL_OUT(" ", 69))
200 :    ELSE
201 :       RETURN(FILL_OUT(ISDELETED() + file_name + ;
202 :             SPACE(1) + CHR(186) + SPACE(1) + IF(is_arc, ;
203 :             " Archive File ", " Normal File  ") + ;
204 :             SPACE(1) + CHR(186) + SPACE(1) + file_comm, 69))
205 :    ENDIF
206 :
207 : *******************
208 :
209 : FUNCTION Process2
210 :
211 :    PARAMETERS _mode2
212 :
213 :    whatkey = LASTKEY()
214 :
215 :    IF _mode2 != 4
216 :       @ 24,00
217 :       @ 24,00 SAY INDEXKEY(INDEXORD())
218 :       DO CASE
219 :       CASE whatkey = 13
220 :          RETURN(1)
221 :       CASE whatkey = 31 .OR. whatkey = 1
222 :          SEEK lookup
223 :       CASE whatkey = 3
224 :          IF !(&express.)
225 :             KEYBOARD CHR(18) && + CHR(19)
```

```
226 :          ENDIF
227 :       CASE whatkey = 24
228 :          IF !(&express.)
229 :             KEYBOARD CHR(5) && + CHR(19)
230 :          ENDIF
231 :       CASE whatkey = 5
232 :          IF !(&express.)
233 :             KEYBOARD CHR(24) && + CHR(19)
234 :          ENDIF
235 :       CASE whatkey = 18
236 :          IF !(&express.)
237 :             KEYBOARD CHR(3) && + CHR(19)
238 :          ENDIF
239 :       ENDCASE
240 :    ELSE
241 :       DO CASE
242 :       CASE CHR(whatkey)$"Ff"
243 :          SET CURSOR ON
244 :          afile = SPACE(12)
245 :          @ 24,00 SAY "Enter Name of File to " + ;
246 :                   "Find => " GET afile PICT "@!"
247 :          READ
248 :          SET CURSOR OFF
249 :          IF !EMPTY(afile)
250 :             _noworder = INDEXORD()
251 :             SET ORDER TO 1
252 :             SEEK A->sub_no + (TRIM(afile))
253 :             SET ORDER TO (_noworder)
254 :             IF !FOUND()
255 :                SET ORDER TO 1
256 :                SEEK lookup
257 :                SET ORDER TO (_noworder)
258 :             ENDIF
259 :          ENDIF
260 :          @ 24,00 CLEAR
261 :          RETURN(2)
262 :
263 :       CASE whatkey = 9
264 :          whichone = INDEXWIN()
265 :          SET ORDER TO (whichone)
266 :          RETURN(2)
267 :
268 :       CASE whatkey = 27
269 :          RETURN(0)
270 :
271 :       CASE whatkey = 300    && Alt Z
272 :          SAVE SCREEN
273 :          CLEAR SCREEN
274 :          SET CURSOR ON
275 :          ? "Type EXIT to Return to DBFILT.EXE"
276 :          RUN Command
277 :          SET CURSOR OFF
278 :          RESTORE SCREEN
279 :
```

```
280 :       ENDCASE
281 :    ENDIF
282 :
283 :    RETURN(1)
284 :
285 : *******************
286 :
287 : FUNCTION Isdeleted
288 :
289 :    RETURN (IF(DELETED(), "*** ", "     "))
290 :
291 : *******************
292 :
293 : FUNCTION Indexwin
294 :
295 :    _indexit = 1
296 :    _number = 1
297 :    DECLARE elements[15]
298 :    AFILL(elements, "")
299 :    FOR z = 1 TO 15
300 :       SET ORDER TO (z)
301 :       elements[z] = INDEXKEY(INDEXORD())
302 :       IF z != 1          && This is equal to <>
303 :          IF elements[z-1] = elements[z]
304 :             _number = z - 1
305 :             EXIT
306 :          ENDIF
307 :       ENDIF
308 :    NEXT
309 :    tcolor = SETCOLOR()
310 :    SETCOLOR(Reverse())
311 :
312 :    Pushscreen(0,50,_number+1,78,.T.,.T.,.T.,.T.)
313 :    FOR z = 1 TO _number
314 :       saying = TRANSFORM(z, " 99>> ") + elements[z]
315 :       @ z,51 PROMPT SUBSTR(FILL_OUT(saying, 27), 1, 27)
316 :    NEXT
317 :    MENU TO _indexit
318 :    IF _indexit = 0
319 :       _indexit = 1
320 :    ENDIF
321 :    SETCOLOR(tcolor)
322 :    Popscreen(0,50,_number+1,78,.T.)
323 :    RETURN(_indexit)
324 :
325 : * **********************************************
326 : * * The following procedure(s)/function(s) are  *
327 : * * part of Steve Straley's ToolkiT(tm) -        *
328 : * * Release 2, published by Four Seasons         *
329 : * * Publishing Co., Inc.  All Rights Reserved    *
330 : * * Information: 212-599-2141 / 800-662-2278     *
331 : * * All Rights Reserved                          *
332 : * **********************************************
333 :
```

```
334 : FUNCTION Fill_out
335 :
336 :     PARAMETERS fill_a, fill_b
337 :
338 :     * fill_a = the string to be filled out
339 :     * fill_b = the Length to fill out the string to
340 :
341 :     IF PCOUNT() = 1
342 :         fill_b = 80
343 :     ELSE
344 :         IF TYPE("fill_b") = "C"
345 :             fill_b = VAL(b)
346 :         ENDIF
347 :         fill_b = IIF(fill_b <= 1, 80, fill_b)
348 :     ENDIF
349 :
350 :     IF fill_b <= LEN(fill_a)
351 :         RETURN(fill_a)
352 :     ENDIF
353 :     RETURN(fill_a + SPACE(fill_b - LEN(fill_a)))
354 :
355 : ********************
356 :
357 : PROCEDURE Pushscreen
358 :
359 :     PARAMETERS push1, push2, push3, push4, pushsave, ;
360 :                pushscr, pushbord, pushshad
361 :
362 :     IF TYPE("sc_level")="U" .OR. TYPE("allscreens")="U"
363 :         PUBLIC allscreens[20], sc_level
364 :         AFILL(allscreens, "")
365 :         sc_level = 2
366 :     ENDIF
367 :     scrframe = CHR(218) + CHR(196) + CHR(191) + CHR(179) + ;
368 :                CHR(217) + CHR(196) + CHR(192) + CHR(179) + ;
369 :                CHR(32)
370 :
371 :     DO CASE
372 :     CASE PCOUNT() = 4   && 4 parameters means No border,
373 :         pushsave = .T.  && No Frame, Just save the area
374 :         pushscr = .T.
375 :         pushbord = .F.
376 :         pushshad = .F.
377 :     CASE PCOUNT() = 5   && 5 parameters mean Save area
378 :         pushscr = .T.   && without border logic
379 :         pushbord = .F.
380 :         pushshad = .F.
381 :     CASE PCOUNT() = 6
382 :         pushbord = .T.
383 :         pushshad = .F.
384 :     CASE PCOUNT() = 7
385 :         pushshad = .F.
386 :     ENDCASE
387 :
```

```
388 :    IF pushsave
389 :       push_temp = ""
390 :       IF pushshad
391 :          allscreens[sc_level] = ;
392 :             SAVESCREEN(push1,push2,push3 + 1, push4 + 1)
393 :       ELSE
394 :          allscreens[sc_level] = ;
395 :             SAVESCREEN(push1,push2,push3,push4)
396 :       ENDIF
397 :       sc_level = IF(sc_level=20, sc_level, sc_level+1)
398 :    ENDIF
399 :
400 :    IF pushbord
401 :       IF !pushscr
402 :          IF TYPE("scrframe") = "U"
403 :             @ push1, push2 TO push3, push4 DOUBLE
404 :          ELSE
405 :             @ push1,push2,push3,push4 BOX ;
406 :                SUBSTR(scrframe, 1, 8)
407 :          ENDIF
408 :       ELSE
409 :          IF TYPE("scrframe") = "U"
410 :             @ push1, push2 CLEAR TO push3, push4
411 :             @ push1, push2 TO push3, push4 DOUBLE
412 :          ELSE
413 :             @ push1, push2, push3, push4 BOX scrframe
414 :          ENDIF
415 :       ENDIF
416 :       IF pushshad
417 :          SHADOW(push1, push2, push3, push4)
418 :       ENDIF
419 :    ENDIF
420 :
421 : ********************
422 :
423 : PROCEDURE Popscreen
424 :
425 :    PARAMETERS pop1, pop2, pop3, pop4, popshad
426 :
427 :    IF PCOUNT() = 4
428 :       popshad = .F.
429 :    ENDIF
430 :    sc_level = IF(sc_level = 1, sc_level, sc_level - 1)
431 :    pop_temp = allscreens[sc_level]
432 :    IF popshad
433 :       RESTSCREEN(pop1, pop2, pop3+1, pop4+1, pop_temp)
434 :    ELSE
435 :       RESTSCREEN(pop1, pop2, pop3, pop4, pop_temp)
436 :    ENDIF
437 :    allscreens[sc_level+1] = ""
438 :
439 : ********************
440 :
441 : FUNCTION Shadow
```

```
442 :
443 :    PARAMETERS shada, shadb, shadc, shadd, shadde
444 :
445 :    IF PCOUNT() = 4
446 :        shadde = CHR(177)
447 :    ENDIF
448 :
449 :    shad_color = SETCOLOR()
450 :    SETCOLOR( STRTRAN( shad_color, "+", "" ) )
451 :
452 :    FOR shadx = shada+1 TO shadc+1
453 :        @ shadx, shadd+1 SAY shadde
454 :    NEXT
455 :    @ shadx-1,shadb+1 SAY REPLICATE(shadde, shadd-shadb)
456 :
457 :    SETCOLOR( shad_color )
458 :    RETURN(.F.)
459 :
460 : ********************
461 :
462 : FUNCTION Printdate
463 :
464 :    PARAMETERS in_date, p_option
465 :
466 :    IF PCOUNT() = 1
467 :        p_option = 1
468 :    ENDIF
469 :
470 :    DO CASE
471 :    CASE p_option = 1
472 :        RETURN(CMONTH(in_date) + " " + DAYWORD(in_date) + ;
473 :               ", " + LTRIM(TRIM(STR(YEAR(in_date)))))
474 :    CASE p_option = 2
475 :        RETURN(CDOW(in_date) + ", the " + DAYWORD(in_date) + ;
476 :               " of " + CMONTH(in_date) + ", " + ;
477 :               LTRIM(TRIM(STR(YEAR(in_date)))))
478 :    CASE p_option = 3
479 :        RETURN(CDOW(in_date) + ", the " + DAYWORD(in_date) + ;
480 :               " of " + CMONTH(in_date))
481 :    CASE p_option = 4
482 :        RETURN("The " + DAYWORD(in_date) + " of " + ;
483 :               CMONTH(in_date) + ", " + ;
484 :               LTRIM(TRIM(STR(YEAR(in_date)))))
485 :    CASE p_option = 5
486 :        RETURN(CDOW(in_date) + ", " + CMON(in_date) + " " + ;
487 :               LTRIM(TRIM(STR(DAY(in_date),2))) + ;
488 :               ", " + STR(YEAR(in_date),4))
489 :    CASE p_option = 6
490 :        RETURN(CMONTH(in_date) + " " + ;
491 :               LTRIM(TRIM(STR(DAY(in_date)))) + ", " + ;
492 :               LTRIM(TRIM(STR(YEAR(in_date)))))
493 :    CASE p_option = 7
494 :        RETURN(SUBSTR(DTOS(in_date),1, 4) + ;
495 :               "-" + SUBSTR(DTOS(in_date), 5,2) + "-" + ;
```

```
496 :               SUBSTR(DTOS(in_date),7))
497 :     OTHERWISE
498 :        RETURN(DTOC(in_date))
499 :     ENDCASE
500 :
501 : ********************
502 :
503 : FUNCTION Dayword
504 :
505 :     PARAMETER in_date
506 :
507 :     IF TYPE("in_date") = "D"
508 :        in_day = STR(DAY(in_date),2)
509 :        in_val = VAL(in_day)
510 :     ELSEIF TYPE("in_date") = "N"
511 :        in_val = in_date
512 :        in_day = STR(in_date)
513 :     ELSE
514 :        RETURN("")
515 :     ENDIF
516 :
517 :     IF in_val > 3 .AND. in_val < 21
518 :        in_day = in_day + "th"
519 :     ELSE
520 :        in_val = VAL(SUBSTR(in_day,2,1))
521 :        in_day = in_day + ;
522 :           SUBSTR("thstndrdthththththth", (in_val * 2)+1,2)
523 :     ENDIF
524 :     RETURN(LTRIM(TRIM(in_day)))
525 :
526 : ********************
527 :
528 : FUNCTION Reverse
529 :
530 :     PARAMETERS _a
531 :
532 :     * _a is the color string to reverse
533 :
534 :     IF PCOUNT() = 0
535 :        _a = SETCOLOR()
536 :     ENDIF
537 :
538 :     PRIVATE _b      && _b is the SAY color string
539 :
540 :     _b = STRTRAN(SUBSTR(_a, 1, AT(",", _a)-1), "+", "")
541 :
542 :     RETURN(SUBSTR(_b, AT("/", _b)+1) + "/" + ;
543 :           SUBSTR(_b, 1, AT("/", _b)-1))
544 :
545 : * End of File
```

In this example, we have only two files to consider: Filenos and Disknos. Both are selected in separate work areas and one is RELATED into the other: the Disknos database will move the pointer in the Filenos database based on the value of the **sub_no** field. One of the assumptions this technology makes is that no filter expression will be outside of the basic construction of the active index. If the filter is to work outside of the scoping parameters within the active index, this technique will not work and the alternate COPY FILE TO should be used. Of course, selective indexing and other related topics may circumvent this problem in the future; however, to avoid this situation, try to involve only those indexes with desired subsections. The naming convention for the arrays and the user-defined functions called by the DBEDIT()s for both work areas is simplistic. First, the two main arrays that will hold the column information are suffixed with the letters **db**. The prefix to the array pertains to the numeric work area. In other words, the array for the first work area is called **db1[]** while the second array is called **db2[]**. Since the header information will be different for all of the columns in all work areas, the arrays for the header information follow the same standard; **hd1[]** pertains to the header information for the columns in the first database while **hd2[]** pertains to the header information for the columns in the second database. Within each of the column arrays, reference to the functions with root names such as "SHOW" are listed. The prefix is either the letter "A" or the letter "B," while the suffix to the name of the function is a numeric representation for the column. In other words, the name of the function showing information from the first work area in the second column will be named "ASHOW2()" while the name of the function for the second work area for the fourth column will be named "BSHOW4." These values are assigned to the two arrays, **db1[]** and **db2[]** on lines 31 through 38.

Once the main call to the first DBEDIT() function on line 60 is made, the keystroke function named Process1() will be in control and at the heart of this technology. The definition for that function is on lines 109 through 154. Now let us picture the flow of this program. The end user has two databases to work with, one moving the pointer of the other. As the record number in the "mother" database moves, it relates to the "child" database. The record pointer is moved via the cursor keys in the DBEDIT() function. Once an item is reached, the end user may wish more detailed information present in the "child" database. Instincts would lead the end user to press the Enter key; therefore, we have a test for this key in the Process1() function on lines 130 through 150. This is the beginning of the filtering possibility. Starting with line 131, we have the variable **express** being initialized and set to a value; this variable will be somewhat PUBLIC in nature for it will be accessible for all called routines from this point in the program. Looking at the expression we can see that the variable is first set to the string "B->sub_no = '" plus the value from the A->sub_no field, followed by a single quotation mark character ('). Considering that we are on a record when we get to this spot in the program, and let's say, that the value of the A->sub_no field is 10000, the value of the variable **express** will be the string "B->sub_no = '10000'." If we were to macro expand this string, we would get the evaluation of it, which would be a logical value. A logical true (.T.) would be the value if the value of B->sub_no did equal the string '10000'; otherwise, a logical false would be returned.

After this string is built, the second work area is SELECTed and a SEEK is performed on the value of A->sub-no. This should position us at the top of the filter condition. If the FOUND() (line 135) is (.F.), the function will simply tell the first DBEDIT() to continue processing. Otherwise, a few screen variables are initialized and another call to DBEDIT() is made, this time involving the functions named in the **db2[]** array and calling the Process2() function for the keystrokes.

Let us, here, take a quick look at the four Bshow() functions, on lines 157 through 204. From the first function for the first column, you can see the variable **express** is being expanded. Remember, this will take place for every record that DBEDIT() will try to display within the specified windowed area. If the value of the macro expansion returns a logical false, the Bshow1() function will RETURN 69 blank spaces; however, if the value of the **expression** is a logical true (.T.), the string in the first column of this DBEDIT() will involve the Isdeleted() function, the **file_name** field, and the **sub_name** field. Looking at the other three similar functions, we see that this pattern holds true. This means that if a record does not meet the filter condition, a blank string will be displayed. This will achieve our visual effect for reaching the pseudo end-of-file marker. Now, we must test for the actual physical movement within the database. To do this, we should now look at the code for the Process2() function.

This function begins on line 206 and follows down through line 282. Of specific interest are lines 217 through 238. Here, the value of the variable **_mode2** will not be 4 if any of the normal cursor keys are pressed, if DBEDIT() is idle, or if the cursor is actually going beyond the physical beginning or end of file markers. In this case, all we need to test for is that the key entered is not a keystroke exception. We then need to evaluate the actual value for the LASTKEY() in the system. On these lines, each of the possible keystrokes is tested. If the Enter key is pressed (line 219), the function continues normally. If the Home or Ctrl PgUp keys are pressed, the original SEEK is performed, which will simulate the repositioning of the top of the file. The value of 3 for the **whatkey** variable represents the PgDn action; 24 is for down one record, 5 is for up one record, and 18 is for PgUp. In DBEDIT(), the designated action always takes place before the call to the Process2() function; therefore, we can test to see if the new value for the record pointer still meets the expanded value of the variable **express.** If it does, everything continues as expected; however, if it does not, lines 224, 227, 231, and 235 will stuff the KEYBOARD with the appropriate key to send DBEDIT() in the opposite direction. In other words, if the end user presses the PgDn key, the display will be adjusted accordingly, the value tested against the current record; if the expression is not satisfied, the PgUp key will be stuffed to the keyboard. This effect is far faster than the standard SET FILTER TO &**express.**

In the case of both DBEDIT()s, the Tab key is ASCII value 9 and will make a call to the Indexwin() function. This happens on line 116 and again on line 263. If the Tab key is pressed, a pop-up window will be displayed, allowing the end user to choose the controlling index. This decision is made on the expression of the key in the various files.

Finally, the ability to jump out to DOS quickly is provided in both functions. If the end user presses the Alt-Z combination, the CASE test for line 270 will be true as well as the ELSEIF condition on line 121. Typing "EXIT" at the command line returns control to the program.

DBEDIT() AS A DEBUGGER

Using DBEDIT() for debugging purposes is not at all an uncommon wish, and it is one that can be put together quickly with very little effort. First, let's look at a program example and then discuss each command item.

```
001 : ********************
002 : * Name      Dbstats()
003 : * Author    Stephen J. Straley
004 : * Date      July 14, 1989
005 : * Notice    Copyright (c) 1989 Stephen J. Straley & Associates
006 : * Compile   Clipper Dbstats -m
007 : * Release   Summer 87
008 : * Link      PLINK86 FI Dbstats  LIB Clipper LIB Extend;
009 : * Note      This routine is a modification of the Stats()
010 : *           in Steve Straley's ToolkiT - Release 2
011 : *
012 : *           It shows how the DBEDIT() function can be used
013 : *           to modify records of a database.  Appropriate
014 : *           networking locks need to be added if this routine
015 : *           will be executed on a network.
016 : *
017 : ********************
018 :
019 : SELECT E
020 : USE Ontap INDEX Ontap
021 : SELECT D
022 : USE Disknos INDEX Disknos
023 : SELECT C
024 : USE Filenos INDEX Filenos, Filesub, Filetype
025 : SELECT B
026 : USE Notap INDEX Notap
027 : SELECT A
028 : USE Trans
029 : Stats()
030 : CLOSE ALL
031 :
032 : ******************
033 :
034 : PROCEDURE Stats
035 :
036 :     PARAMETERS _p2, _l2, _v2
037 :
038 :     PRIVATE _poprow, _popcol, _ocolor, _retto, _dummy, _sel
039 :
040 :     _retto = SELECT()
041 :     _temp = ""
042 :     _poprow = ROW()
043 :     _popcol = COL()
044 :     _ocolor = SETCOLOR()
045 :     SETCOLOR(IF((ISCOLOR() .AND. ;
046 :        !(IF(TYPE("scrmono")="U", .T., ;
```

```
047 :        scrmono))), "W/B", ""))
048 :
049 :    IF TYPE("scrcursor") = "U"
050 :       scrcursor = .T.
051 :    ENDIF
052 :    SET CURSOR OFF
053 :    SET SCOREBOARD OFF
054 :
055 :    PUSHSCREEN()
056 :    @ 0,0 CLEAR
057 :    TEXT
058 :
059 :                    System Statistics
060 :
061 :                    Disk / File Status....
062 :
063 :    Available Diskspace
064 :            Selected Area
065 :         Working Database
066 :                    ***
067 :         Number of Fields
068 :        Number of Records
069 :    Key of Primary Index
070 :    Date of Last Updated
071 :          Size of Header
072 :       Byte Size / Record
073 :           Filter Set At
074 :         File Relation Is
075 :    Value for Selected
076 :           Record Number
077 :
078 :
079 :    Press ESC key to Return / ENTER for detail
080 :       + or - Keys to scan through work areas!
081 :            Up or Down Arrow to SKIP
082 : ENDTEXT
083 :
084 :    DO WHILE .T.
085 :       SET CURSOR OFF
086 :       SETCOLOR(REVERSE())
087 :       @  6,23 SAY DISKSPACE(0) ;
088 :              PICT "999,999,999,999 bytes"
089 :       @  7,23 SAY SELECT()   ;
090 :              PICT "@B"
091 :       @  8,23 SAY FILL_OUT(IF(EMPTY(THE_DBF()), ;
092 :              "None in Use", THE_DBF()), 15)
093 :       @ 10,23 SAY FCOUNT()  PICT "@B"
094 :       @ 11,23 SAY LASTREC() PICT "@B"
095 :       @ 12,23 SAY FILL_OUT(IF(EMPTY(INDEXKEY(0)), ;
096 :              "None Available", ;
097 :              SUBSTR(UPPER(INDEXKEY(0)), 1, 20)), 20)
098 :       @ 13,23 SAY FILL_OUT(IF(EMPTY(LUPDATE()), ;
099 :              "Not in Use", DTOC(LUPDATE())), 12)
100 :       @ 14,23 SAY HEADER()  PICT "@B"
```

```
101 :        @ 15,23 SAY RECSIZE() PICT "@B"
102 :        @ 16,23 SAY FILL_OUT(IF(EMPTY(DBFILTER()), ;
103 :              "None Set", SUBSTR(UPPER(DBFILTER()), ;
104 :              1, 19)), 20)
105 :        @ 17,23 SAY FILL_OUT(IF(EMPTY(DBRELATION()), ;
106 :              "None Set", SUBSTR(UPPER(DBRELATION()), ;
107 :              1,19)), 20)
108 :        @ 18,23 SAY FILL_OUT(IF(EMPTY(DBRSELECT()), ;
109 :              "None Set", SUBSTR(UPPER(DBRSELECT()), ;
110 :              1, 19)), 20)
111 :        @ 19,23 SAY TRANSFORM(RECNO(), "@B999999999999999999")
112 :        @ 3,0 SAY ""
113 :        SETCOLOR(_ocolor)
114 :        _dummy = INKEY(0)
115 :        IF _dummy = 27
116 :           EXIT
117 :        ELSEIF CHR(_dummy) = "+"
118 :           _sel = SELECT()
119 :           _sel = IF(_sel = 250, 1, _sel+1)
120 :           SELECT (_sel)
121 :
122 :        ELSEIF CHR(_dummy) = "-"
123 :           _sel = SELECT()
124 :           _sel = IF(_sel = 1, 250, _sel-1)
125 :           SELECT (_sel)
126 :
127 :        ELSEIF _dummy = 24   && Down arrow
128 :           SKIP
129 :           IF EOF()
130 :              GO TOP
131 :           ENDIF
132 :
133 :        ELSEIF _dummy = 5   && Up arrow
134 :           SKIP - 1
135 :           IF BOF()
136 :              GO BOTTOM
137 :           ENDIF
138 :
139 :        ELSEIF _dummy = 13  && Show Structure of the database
140 :           DISPSTRU()
141 :
142 :           ENDIF
143 :     ENDDO
144 :
145 :     SELECT (_retto)
146 :     SETCOLOR(_ocolor)
147 :     SET CURSOR (scrcursor)
148 :     POPSCREEN()
149 :     @ _poprow, _popcol SAY ""
150 :
151 : * ***********************************************
152 : * * The following procedure(s)/function(s) are  *
153 : * * part of Steve Straley's ToolkiT(tm) -        *
154 : * * Release 2, published by Four Seasons         *
```

```
155 : * * Publishing Co., Inc.  All Rights Reserved    *
156 : * * Information: 212-599-2141 / 800-662-2278     *
157 : * * All Rights Reserved                          *
158 : * **********************************************
159 :
160 : *******************
161 :
162 : FUNCTION Popscreen
163 :
164 :     PARAMETERS _pop1, _pop2, _pop3, _pop4, _popshad, _popstype
165 :
166 :     PRIVATE _poptemp
167 :
168 :     scr_level = IF(scr_level = 1, scr_level, scr_level - 1)
169 :
170 :     IF PCOUNT() = 4
171 :        _popshad = .F.
172 :     ELSEIF PCOUNT() = 0
173 :        _pop1 =IF( EMPTY(SUBSTR(allwindows[scr_level],1,2)),;
174 :                0, SUBSTR(allwindows[scr_level], 1, 2))
175 :        _pop2 =IF(EMPTY(SUBSTR(allwindows[scr_level],4,2)),0,;
176 :                SUBSTR(allwindows[scr_level], 4, 2))
177 :        _pop3 =IF(EMPTY(SUBSTR(allwindows[scr_level],7,2)),24,;
178 :                SUBSTR(allwindows[scr_level], 7, 2))
179 :        _pop4 =IF(EMPTY(SUBSTR(allwindows[scr_level],10,2)),79,;
180 :                SUBSTR(allwindows[scr_level],10, 2))
181 :        _popshad = SUBSTR(allwindows[scr_level],13)
182 :        IF _popshad $ ".T..F."
183 :           _popshad = &_popshad.
184 :        ELSEIF EMPTY(_popshad) .OR. TYPE("_popshad") != "L"
185 :           _popshad = .F.
186 :        ENDIF
187 :        _popstype = 1
188 :     ELSEIF PCOUNT() = 5
189 :        _popstype = 1
190 :     ENDIF
191 :
192 :     _poptemp = ""
193 :
194 :     _poptemp = allscreens[scr_level]
195 :     SETCOLOR(allcolor[scr_level])
196 :
197 :     IF _popshad
198 :        DO CASE
199 :        CASE _popstype = 1
200 :           RESTSCREEN(_pop1, _pop2, _pop3+1, _pop4+2, _poptemp)
201 :        CASE _popstype = 2
202 :           RESTSCREEN(_pop1, _pop2-1, _pop3+1, _pop4, _poptemp)
203 :        CASE _popstype = 3
204 :           RESTSCREEN(_pop1-1, _pop2-1, _pop3, _pop4, _poptemp)
205 :        CASE _popstype = 4
206 :           RESTSCREEN(_pop1-1, _pop2, _pop3, _pop4+2, _poptemp)
207 :        ENDCASE
208 :     ELSE
```

```
209 :        RESTSCREEN(_pop1, _pop2, _pop3, _pop4, _poptemp)
210 :     ENDIF
211 :
212 :     allwindows[scr_level+1] = ""
213 :     allscreens[scr_level+1] = ""
214 :     allcolor[scr_level+1]   = ""
215 :     RELEASE _poptemp
216 :     RETURN(scr_level)
217 :
218 : ********************
219 :
220 : FUNCTION Pushscreen
221 :
222 :     PARAMETERS _push1, _push2, _push3, _push4, _pushsave, ;
223 :                _pushscr, _pushbord, _pushshad
224 :
225 :     * This is the first function/procedure that is used
226 :     * to draw a screen and push the screen stack.  The screen
227 :     * stack is stored in the array "allscrens," the color stack
228 :     * is stored in the array "allcolor," and the window
229 :     * logic is housed in the "allwindows" array.  The stack
230 :     * counter is housed in the "scr_level" variable.
231 :     *
232 :     * The return value is the
233 :
234 :     IF TYPE("allscreens") != "A"
235 :        PUBLIC allscreens[20], scr_level, allcolor[20], ;
236 :               allwindows[20]
237 :        scr_level = 2
238 :        AFILL(allscreens, "")
239 :        AFILL(allcolor, "")
240 :        AFILL(allwindows, "")
241 :     ENDIF
242 :
243 :     IF EMPTY(PCOUNT())     && No Parameters!
244 :        _push1    = 0
245 :        _push2    = 0
246 :        _push3    = 24
247 :        _push4    = 79
248 :        _pushsave = .T.
249 :        _pushscr  = .F.
250 :        _pushbord = .F.
251 :        _pushshad = .F.
252 :
253 :     ELSEIF PCOUNT() = 4  && No border, No Frame, Just save
254 :        _pushsave = .T.
255 :        _pushscr = .T.
256 :        _pushbord = .F.
257 :        _pushshad = .F.
258 :
259 :     ELSEIF PCOUNT() = 5  && Save area without border logic
260 :        _pushscr = .T.
261 :        _pushbord = .F.
262 :        _pushshad = .F.
```

```
263 :
264 :     ELSEIF PCOUNT() = 6
265 :        _pushbord = .T.
266 :        _pushshad = .F.
267 :
268 :     ELSEIF PCOUNT() = 7
269 :        _pushshad = .F.
270 :
271 :     ENDIF
272 :
273 :     IF _pushsave
274 :        allscreens[scr_level] = ""
275 :        IF _pushshad
276 :           allscreens[scr_level] = SAVESCREEN(_push1, ;
277 :              _push2, _push3 + 1, _push4 + 2)
278 :        ELSE
279 :           allscreens[scr_level] = SAVESCREEN(_push1, ;
280 :              _push2, _push3, _push4)
281 :        ENDIF
282 :        allcolor[scr_level] = SETCOLOR()
283 :        IF _pushshad
284 :           allwindows[scr_level] = TRANSFORM(_push1, "99") + ;
285 :              "/" + TRANSFORM(_push2, "99") + "/" + ;
286 :              TRANSFORM(_push3+1, "99") + "/" + ;
287 :              TRANSFORM(_push4+2, "99") + "/.T."
288 :        ELSE
289 :           allwindows[scr_level] = TRANSFORM(_push1, "99") + ;
290 :              "/" + TRANSFORM(_push2, "99") + "/" + ;
291 :              TRANSFORM(_push3, "99") + "/" + ;
292 :              TRANSFORM(_push4, "99") + "/.F."
293 :        ENDIF
294 :        scr_level = IF(scr_level = 20, scr_level, scr_level + 1)
295 :     ENDIF
296 :
297 :     IF _pushbord      && Yes, I want a border!
298 :        IF !_pushscr   && No, I Just want a frame, hold the filling
299 :           IF TYPE("scrframe") = "U"
300 :              @ _push1, _push2 TO _push3, _push4 DOUBLE
301 :           ELSE
302 :              @ _push1, _push2, _push3, _push4 BOX ;
303 :                 SUBSTR(scrframe, 1, 8)
304 :           ENDIF
305 :        ELSE
306 :           IF TYPE("scrframe") = "U"
307 :              @ _push1, _push2 CLEAR TO _push3, _push4
308 :              @ _push1, _push2 TO _push3, _push4 DOUBLE
309 :           ELSE
310 :              @ _push1, _push2, _push3, _push4 BOX scrframe
311 :           ENDIF
312 :        ENDIF
313 :     ENDIF
314 :
315 :     RETURN(scr_level-1)
```

```
316 :
317 : ********************
318 :
319 : FUNCTION Reverse
320 :
321 :     PARAMETERS _a
322 :
323 :     * _a is the color string to reverse
324 :
325 :     IF PCOUNT() = 0
326 :        _a = SETCOLOR()
327 :     ENDIF
328 :
329 :     PRIVATE _b
330 :
331 :     * _b is the SAY color string
332 :
333 :     _b = STRTRAN(SUBSTR(_a, 1, AT(",", _a)-1), "+", "")
334 :
335 :     RETURN(SUBSTR(_b, AT("/", _b)+1) + "/" + ;
336 :            SUBSTR(_b, 1, AT("/", _b)-1))
337 :
338 : ********************
339 :
340 : FUNCTION Fill_out
341 :
342 :     PARAMETERS _filla, _fillb
343 :
344 :     * _filla = the string to be filled out
345 :     * _fillb = the Length to fill out the string to
346 :
347 :     IF PCOUNT() = 1
348 :        _fillb = 80
349 :     ELSE
350 :        IF TYPE("_fillb") = "C"
351 :           _fillb = VAL(b)
352 :        ENDIF
353 :        _fillb = IIF(_fillb <= 1, 80, _fillb)
354 :     ENDIF
355 :
356 :     IF _fillb <= LEN(_filla)
357 :        RETURN(_filla)
358 :     ENDIF
359 :     RETURN(LEFT(_filla + SPACE(_fillb - LEN(_filla)),_fillb))
360 :
361 : ********************
362 :
363 : FUNCTION The_dbf
364 :
365 :     * This function returns the alias/dbf
366 :     * name of the given select area/number
367 :
368 :     PARAMETERS _whicha
369 :
```

```
370 :    IF PCOUNT() = 0
371 :        RETURN(ALIAS(SELECT()))
372 :    ELSE
373 :        _whicha = IF(TYPE("_whicha")="C", ;
374 :            ASC(UPPER(_whicha))-64, _whicha)
375 :    ENDIF
376 :    RETURN(ALIAS(_whicha))
377 :
378 : ********************
379 :
380 : PROCEDURE Clear_area
381 :
382 :    PARAMETERS _clr1, _clr2, _clr3, _clr4
383 :
384 :    scr_level = IF(TYPE("scr_level") = "U", 0, scr_level)
385 :
386 :    IF EMPTY(PCOUNT())
387 :        IF TYPE("allwindows") != "A"
388 :            _clr1 = -1
389 :            _clr2 = -1
390 :            _clr3 = 25
391 :            _clr4 = 80
392 :        ELSE
393 :            IF scr_level <= 1
394 :                _clr1 = -1
395 :                _clr2 = -1
396 :                _clr3 = 25
397 :                _clr4 = 80
398 :            ELSE
399 :                _clr1 = VAL(SUBSTR(allwindows[scr_level - 1], ;
400 :                        1, 2))
401 :                _clr2 = VAL(SUBSTR(allwindows[scr_level - 1], ;
402 :                        4, 2))
403 :                _clr3 = VAL(SUBSTR(allwindows[scr_level - 1], ;
404 :                        7, 2))
405 :                _clr4 = VAL(SUBSTR(allwindows[scr_level - 1], ;
406 :                        10, 2))
407 :                IF _clr1 = -1
408 :                    _clr1 = -1
409 :                    _clr2 = -1
410 :                    _clr3 = 25
411 :                    _clr4 = 80
412 :                ENDIF
413 :            ENDIF
414 :        ENDIF
415 :    ENDIF
416 :
417 :    PRIVATE _qaz
418 :
419 :    DO CASE
420 :    CASE (_clr3 - _clr1 > 1) .AND. (_clr4 - _clr2 > 1)
421 :        SCROLL(_clr1 + 1, _clr2 + 1, _clr3 - 1, _clr4 - 1,0)
422 :
423 :    && 1 column
```

```
424 :      CASE (_clr3 - _clr1 > 1) .AND. !(_clr4 - _clr2 > 1)
425 :         FOR _qaz = _clr1+1 TO _clr3-1
426 :            @ _qaz,_clr2+1 SAY " "
427 :         NEXT
428 :
429 :      && 1 Row
430 :      CASE !(_clr3 - _clr1 > 1) .AND. (_clr4 - _clr2 > 1)
431 :         @ _clr1+1,_clr2 SAY SPACE((_clr4-_clr2)-2)
432 :      ENDCASE
433 :
434 : *******************
435 :
436 : FUNCTION Dispstru
437 :
438 :      PARAMETERS _area
439 :
440 :      IF PCOUNT() = 0
441 :         _area = SELECT()
442 :      ELSE
443 :         _area = IF(TYPE("_area") != "N", SELECT(), _area)
444 :      ENDIF
445 :      _area = LTRIM(STR(_area))
446 :
447 :      PRIVATE _t1[FCOUNT()], _t2[FCOUNT()], _t3[FCOUNT()], ;
448 :              _t4[FCOUNT()]
449 :      PRIVATE _ret, _qaz, _count, _oldcol
450 :
451 :      _ret    = SELECT()
452 :      _oldcol = SETCOLOR()
453 :
454 :      SELECT &_area.
455 :
456 :      AFIELDS(_t1, _t2, _t3, _t4)
457 :      _count = 2
458 :
459 :      IF TYPE("scrcursor") = "U"
460 :         scrcursor = .T.
461 :      ENDIF
462 :      SET CURSOR OFF
463 :      SETCOLOR(IF((TYPE("scrmono") = "U"), "", ;
464 :         IF( (ISCOLOR() .AND. !scrmono), ;
465 :         "7/1,0/7,N,N,0/7", "7/0,0/7,N,N,0/7" )))
466 :
467 :      PUSHSCREEN(0,0,20,75,.T.,.T.)
468 :      @ 1,3  SAY " Structure For " + ALIAS() + " "
469 :      @ 2,5  SAY "Names        Types    Len. Dec."
470 :      @ 4,37 SAY "  Date Last Update: " + DTOC(LUPDATE())
471 :      @ 5,37 SAY "  Number of Records: " + LTRIM(STR(LASTREC()))
472 :      @ 6,37 SAY "  Number of Fields: " + LTRIM(STR(FCOUNT()))
473 :      @ 7,37 SAY " Length of a Record: " + LTRIM(STR(RECSIZE()))
474 :      @ 8,37 SAY "    % of Disk Used: "
475 :      @ 9,37 SAY "     Active Filter: " + ;
476 :             IF(EMPTY(DBFILTER()), "None Set", ;
477 :             SUBSTR(UPPER(DBFILTER()), 1, 19))
```

```
@ 10,37 SAY "       Current Area: " + LTRIM(STR(SELECT()))
@ 11,37 SAY "   Current Rec. No.: " + LTRIM(STR(RECNO()))
@ 12,37 SAY "    Active Relation: " + ;
        IF(EMPTY(DBRELATION()), "None Set", ;
        SUBSTR(UPPER(DBRELATION()), 1,19))
@ 13,37 SAY "   Active Index Key: " + ;
        IF(EMPTY(INDEXKEY(0)), "None Available", ;
        SUBSTR(UPPER(INDEXKEY(0)), 1, 15))
@ 14,37 SAY "Related Information: " + ;
        IF(EMPTY(DBRSELECT()), "None Set", ;
        SUBSTR(UPPER(DBRSELECT()), 1, 19))
FOR _qaz = 1 TO FCOUNT()
   IF _count != 14
      @ _count+2, 4 SAY TRANSFORM(_qaz, "999") + ". "
      @ ROW(), 10  SAY _t1[_qaz]
      @ ROW(), 22 SAY _t2[_qaz]
      @ ROW(), 27 SAY _t3[_qaz] PICT "@B"
      @ ROW(), 33 SAY TRANSFORM(_t4[_qaz], "99")
      @ ROW(), 36 SAY CHR(179)
   ELSE
      @ _count+4,4 SAY "Any Key for next screen or " + ;
                       "Q to Quit, D for Data Display"
      _qaz = _qaz - 1
      INKEY(0)
      IF CHR(LASTKEY()) $ "qQ"
         EXIT
      ELSEIF CHR(LASTKEY()) $ "Dd"
         PUSHSCREEN(2,4,18,73,.T.,.T.)
         @ 18,6 SAY " ESC to Return "
         DBEDIT(3,5,17,72,"","Editfunc")
         POPSCREEN(2,4,18,73)
         _qaz = 0
      ELSE
         Clear_area(2,4,20,36)
      ENDIF
      _count = 1
   ENDIF
   _count = _count + 1
NEXT
Clear_area(17,3,20,75)
@ 19,4 SAY "Any Key to Exit, D for Data Display"
_qaz = _qaz - 1
INKEY(0)
IF CHR(LASTKEY()) $ "Dd"
   PUSHSCREEN(2,4,22,73,.T.,.T.)
   @ 21,6 SAY " ESC to Return / E to Edit "
   DBEDIT(3,5,17,72,"", "Editfunc")
   POPSCREEN(2,4,22,73)
   _qaz = 0
ELSE
   Clear_area(2,4,20,36)
ENDIF
POPSCREEN(0,0,20,75)
SELECT (_ret)
```

```
532 :     SET CURSOR(scrcursor)
533 :     SETCOLOR(_oldcol)
534 :     RETURN("")
535 :
536 : *******************
537 :
538 : FUNCTION Editfunc
539 :
540 :     PARAMETERS _edit1, _edit2
541 :
542 :     IF CHR(LASTKEY()) $ "Ee"
543 :        *
544 :        * _edit2 is the column pointer.  Since the
545 :        * columns are synonymous with the pointing
546 :        * field, this will work.  It will NOT work
547 :        * for those examples where a UDF is passed
548 :        * as a column expression.
549 :        *
550 :        _editname = FIELD(_edit2)
551 :        SET CURSOR ON
552 :        @ 21,06 SAY SPACE(60)
553 :        _memvar = &_editname.
554 :        @ 21,06 SAY "Edit &_editname. :" GET _memvar
555 :        READ
556 :        SET CURSOR OFF
557 :        IF UPDATED()
558 :           REPLACE &_editname. WITH _memvar
559 :        ENDIF
560 :        @ 21,06 SAY SPACE(60)
561 :        @ 21,6 SAY " ESC to Return / E to Edit "
562 :     ENDIF
563 :
564 :     IF LASTKEY() = 27
565 :        RETURN(0)
566 :     ENDIF
567 :     RETURN(1)
568 :
569 : * End of File
```

This routine shows how the DBEDIT() function can be used in conjunction with a few other functions to provide a good debugging or system statistic utility. This example relies on the concept of multiple databases being opened at one time: Lines 19 through 28 do this. As you can see, several databases, memo files (automatically USEd), and ancillary index files are open in work areas E through A. Once they are open, a call to the Stats() procedure is made.

Here, a simple screen is drawn (lines 60 through 81) with the main processing loop beginning on line 85 and concluding on line 143. Once the screen is displayed, the end user can press several activation keys to get the procedure to do something. For example, if the plus or minus keys are pressed, the SELECT work area is adjusted accordingly: either up or down one work area. Note on lines 119 and 124, if the movement from one work area to another goes beyond the first or 250th work area, the work area pointer is positioned at either the first or last work area. In other words, the work areas are "wrapped around" by continually pressing either the "+" or the "-" keys. Also, movement within the database is allowed; line 127 allows the down arrow key to SKIP one record and the up arrow key (line 133) to SKIP back up one record. In either case, if the EOF() or BOF() functions yield a logical true (.T.), the record pointer for that database is also wrapped around. Finally, the last key to be tested is the Enter key, which will then make a call to the Dispstru() function.

The definition for this is on lines 434 and following. The Dispstru() function will show additional information on the chosen work area, as well as the structure of the database, which is contained in four arrays that are initialized on lines 447 and 448. These arrays are set to the value of FCOUNT() (the number of fields in that database) and are subsequently filled with their appropriate values via the AFIELDS() functions provided by Clipper. Once the structure is shown, the end user can press the "D" (or "d") key to make a call to DBEDIT() function, either on line 507 or on line 524. Notice that if the fifth parameter is not passed or is a null byte, the default values for DBEDIT() for that parameter will be used. In this case, this is the column parameter and will default to the actual fields in that database. Once inside DBEDIT(), if the letter "E" is pressed, the Editfunc() function will take over. Here, beginning on line 536 and following, the function allows the end user to edit the field that the highlighted bar was last on. Remember, DBEDIT() will automatically pass two pieces of information to the keystroke function: the status of DBEDIT() and the column pointer. In this case, since there is a one-to-one relationship between the column pointer and the field number, we can take this value when the letter "E" is pressed, find out the name and the contents of that field, and allow the end user to modify the contents. The Editfunc() will terminate the appropriate DBEDIT() if the Esc key is pressed.

This routine allows the end user to quickly scan through all of the work areas; view the filters, relations, and disk status; move through the database; scan individual field information; and, finally, modify the contents of individual fields.

Now we have reached the point that requires all of our efforts in piecing this next step together.

DBEDIT(): ALL THINGS TO ALL PROGRAMMERS

Now we have the ability to put this together, including the ability to modify information on the fly, have relative windowing with colors, multiple calls to the DBEDIT() function, and much more. To better see this, let's look at the code that is involved:

```
********************
* Name       Alldb.prg
* Author     Stephen J. Straley
* Notice     Copyright (c) 1989 Stephen J. Straley & Associates
*            All Rights Reserved.
* Date       July 10, 1989
```

```
0007 : * Compile  Clipper Alldb -m
0008 : * Release  Summer '87
0009 : * Link     Plink86 Fi Alldb LIB Clipper, Extend
0010 : * Note     This program intends to show the REAL Tricks and
0011 : *          Tips of Clipper.  In this program, the hidden
0012 : *          subtleties of Clipper and many of its nuances
0013 : *          come through.  For this example, DBEDIT() is pushed
0014 : *          to new heights.
0015 : *
0016 : *          This program is an EXPANDED program from the
0017 : *          original program part of the
0018 : *          "Programming in Clipper, 2nd Edition" Published by
0019 : *          Addison-Wesley; All rights reserved.
0020 : *
0021 : *********************
0022 :
0023 : CLEAR SCREEN
0024 :
0025 : SELECT 3
0026 : USE Statcode
0027 : INDEX ON status TO Statcode
0028 : GO TOP
0029 : DECLARE a3[FCOUNT()+1]
0030 : FOR x = 1 TO FCOUNT()
0031 :    a3[x+1] = FIELD(x)
0032 : NEXT
0033 : a3[1] = "DELETED()"
0034 :
0035 : SELECT 2
0036 : USE Trans
0037 : INDEX ON account TO Trans
0038 : GO TOP
0039 :
0040 : DECLARE a2[2]
0041 : a2[1] = "TOTALS1()"
0042 : a2[2] = "TOTALS2()"
0043 :
0044 : SELECT 1
0045 : USE Clients
0046 : INDEX ON account TO Clients
0047 : SET RELATION TO account INTO trans, ;
0048 :                 TO status INTO statcode
0049 : GO TOP
0050 :
0051 : DECLARE a1[FCOUNT()+ 2], names[FCOUNT()+2], ;
0052 :         picture[FCOUNT()+2], footer[FCOUNT()+2]
0053 :
0054 : AFILL(footer, "")
0055 : footer[1] = "These Fields;modified or "
0056 : footer[2] = "Can NOT be;looked at!"
0057 : a1[1] = "RECNO()"
0058 : names[1] = "Record #"
0059 : a1[2] = [IF( DELETED() , "Marked", "       ")]
```

```
names[2] = "Deleted"

FOR x = 3 TO LEN(a1)
  a1[x] = FIELD(x-2)
  names[x] = Upperlower(FIELD(x-2))
  names[x] = names[x] + SPACE(20-LEN(names[x]))
NEXT
a1[3] = "C->descript"
a1[17]= [IF(A->paired, "Yes", "No ")]
AFILL(picture, SPACE(30))
picture[11] = "$ 999,999,999,999.99          "
FOR y = 3 TO LEN(names)
   names[y] = Mess_cent(LTRIM(TRIM(Upperlower(names[y]))), 20)
   picture[y] = LTRIM(TRIM(picture[y]))
NEXT
picture[1] = "@B"
picture[2] = "@Y"

SET WRAP ON
CLEAR SCREEN
KEYBOARD CHR(19) + CHR(19)

newtemp    = ""
bottom     = 12
expression = ""
maincolor  = SETCOLOR()

@ 0,0 SAY "Browse Client Account."
@ 0,63 SAY "F1 for Keystrokes"
@ 1,0 SAY REPLICATE(CHR(205), 80)
DO WHILE LASTKEY() != 27
   @ 2,0 CLEAR
   Op(A->(DBEDIT(2,1,bottom,79,a1, "Func1", picture, names, ;
      CHR(205), SPACE(1) + CHR(186) + SPACE(1), CHR(205), ;
      footer)))
ENDDO
CLEAR SCREEN

***************

FUNCTION Func1

   PARAMETERS p1, p2

   value = LASTKEY()

   IF p2 = 1
      KEYBOARD CHR(4) + CHR(4)
   ELSEIF p2 = 2
      KEYBOARD CHR(4)
   ENDIF

   DO CASE
   CASE value = 32 .AND. p1 = 4
```

```
0114 :        * Edit a field
0115 :        IF    p2 = 3  && edit the STATUS field
0116 :           newtemp = "A->" + FIELD(1)
0117 :           @ 23,00 SAY "What is the new code (? to list) : " ;
0118 :                     GET &newtemp. VALID Goodcode(&newtemp.)
0119 :           Sjsread()
0120 :           @ 23,00
0121 :
0122 :        ELSEIF p2 = 4  && edit the TRANS field with all TRANS
0123 :           old = A->account
0124 :           @ 23,00 SAY "Enter Account Number " GET account ;
0125 :                   PICT REPLICATE("X", LEN(account))
0126 :           IF Sjsread()
0127 :              @ 24,00 SAY "Adjusting"
0128 :              Op(B->(Changeit("B->account", "A->account", ;
0129 :                   "B->account = old", "Show_rec(24,11)")))
0130 :              @ 23,00 CLEAR
0131 :           ENDIF
0132 :           @ 23,00 CLEAR
0133 :
0134 :        ELSEIF p2 = 12 && Calc. from TRANS base
0135 :           SET KEY 99 TO Additup()
0136 :           SET KEY 67 TO Additup()
0137 :           @ 23,00 SAY "Enter new DUE amount, 'C'= calculate):";
0138 :                   GET due PICT "999999999999999.99"
0139 :           Sjsread()
0140 :           SET KEY 99 TO
0141 :           SET KEY 67 TO
0142 :           @ 23,00
0143 :
0144 :        ELSEIF p2 = 17  && Can't edit this direct because of ()!
0145 :           @ 23,00 SAY "Is a PAIRED account? "
0146 :           Op(A->(Changeit("A->paired", "Verify()")))
0147 :           @ 23,00
0148 :
0149 :        ELSE
0150 :           temp = FIELD(p2-2)
0151 :           @ 23,00 SAY "O.k. Edit "+ Upperlower(FIELD(p2-2))+;
0152 :                   " =>" GET &temp.
0153 :           IF !Sjsread()
0154 :              @ 24,00 SAY "Value left unchanged!  Any Key...."
0155 :              INKEY(0)
0156 :           ENDIF
0157 :           @ 23,00 CLEAR
0158 :        ENDIF
0159 :        RETURN(2)
0160 :
0161 :     CASE value = -9
0162 :        Pushscreen(7,10,14,60,.T.,.T.,.T.,.T.)
0163 :        IF p2 != 3
0164 :           ret_rec = B->(RECNO())
0165 :           expression = "B->account = [" + A->account + "]"
0166 :           tally = 0.00
0167 :           @ 10, 18 SAY " Working on Record # "
```

```
0168 :
0169 :               Op(B->(Sum_it("B->now_due", @tally, ;
0170 :                  "B->account = A->account", 10, 37)))
0171 :
0172 :               Op(B->(Tallyback()))
0173 :               Op(B->(Seekit(A->account)))
0174 :               Op(B->(DBEDIT(8,11,13,59, a2, "FUNC2", "", ;
0175 :                     "Accounting Totals")))
0176 :               Op(B->(Gotoit(ret_rec)))
0177 :            ELSE
0178 :               expression = ""
0179 :               ret_rec = C->(RECNO())
0180 :               Op(C->(DBEDIT(8, 11, 13, 59, a3, "func2")))
0181 :               Op(C->(Gotoit(ret_rec)))
0182 :            ENDIF
0183 :            Popscreen(7,10,14,60,.T.)
0184 :
0185 :         CASE CHR(value)$"Rr"
0186 :            @ 24,00 SAY "Enter New Bottom Parameter => " ;
0187 :               GET bottom PICT "##" VALID ;
0188 :                  bottom >= 12 .AND. bottom <= 23
0189 :            Sjsread()
0190 :            IF LASTKEY() != 27
0191 :               KEYBOARD CHR(4)
0192 :               RETURN(0)
0193 :            ELSE
0194 :               @ 24,00
0195 :            ENDIF
0196 :
0197 :         CASE CHR(value)$"Pp"
0198 :            @ 24,00 SAY "PACK all of the data files? "
0199 :            IF Verify()
0200 :               @ 24,00
0201 :               @ 24,00 SAY "Working on the 3rd Datafile"
0202 :               Op(C->(Packit()))
0203 :               @ 24,00 SAY "Working on the 2nd Datafile"
0204 :               Op(B->(Packit()))
0205 :            ENDIF
0206 :            @ 24,00
0207 :            @ 24,00 SAY "Working on the 1st Datafile"
0208 :            Op(A->(Packit()))
0209 :            @ 24,00 SAY "All Finished.  Any key to return....."
0210 :            INKEY(0)
0211 :            @ 24,00
0212 :            GO TOP
0213 :            RETURN(2)
0214 :
0215 :         CASE value = 27 .AND. p1 != 0
0216 :            RETURN(0)
0217 :
0218 :         CASE value = 28
0219 :            dbshowit = 1
0220 :            Pushscreen(5,12,20,67,.T.,.T.,.T.,.T.)
0221 :            DO WHILE .T.
```

```
0222 :            @  6,13 PROMPT Fill_out(" ESC to Quit DBEDIT()", 54)
0223 :            @  7,13 PROMPT Fill_out(" F1  - This screen", 54)
0224 :            @  8,13 PROMPT Fill_out(" F10 - Another DBEDIT() / "+;
0225 :                    "Detailed Information", 54)
0226 :            @  9,13 PROMPT Fill_out(" ALT A - Add Record to " + ;
0227 :                    "database", 54 )
0228 :            @ 10,13 PROMPT Fill_out(" ALT E - Edit Record " +;
0229 :                    "currently selected by DBEDIT()", 54 )
0230 :            @ 11,13 PROMPT Fill_out(" ALT V - View Record " +;
0231 :                    "currently selected by DBEDIT()", 54 )
0232 :            @ 12,13 PROMPT Fill_out(" ALT S - Search for a" +;
0233 :                    " value", 54 )
0234 :            @ 13,13 PROMPT Fill_out(" All Arrow & Directional "+;
0235 :                    "Keys default as expected", 54 )
0236 :            @ 14,13 PROMPT Fill_out(" R or r - Resize Window"+;
0237 :                    " Area", 54 )
0238 :            @ 15,13 PROMPT Fill_out(" P - PACK data files... ", ;
0239 :                    54 )
0240 :            @ 16,13 PROMPT Fill_out(" DEL to Delete/Recall ",;
0241 :                    54 )
0242 :            @ 19,13 SAY "Any Key to Continue..."
0243 :            MENU TO dbshowit
0244 :            IF dbshowit = 0
0245 :               EXIT
0246 :            ELSEIF dbshowit > 3
0247 :            ELSE
0248 :               Pushscreen(6 + dbshowit, 15, 12 + dbshowit, 53, ;
0249 :                          .T.,.T.,.T.,.T.)
0250 :               DO WHILE .T.
0251 :                  file = "HELPTXT" + ;
0252 :                       TRANSFORM(dbshowit, "9") + ".TXT"
0253 :                  contents = MEMOREAD(file)
0254 :                  @ 12 + dbshowit, 18 SAY " Press ESC to Exit "
0255 :                  nomore = .F.
0256 :                  MEMOEDIT(contents, 7 + dbshowit, 16, ;
0257 :                     11 + dbshowit, 52, .F.,"Editthis", 36 )
0258 :                  IF nomore
0259 :                     EXIT
0260 :                  ENDIF
0261 :               ENDDO
0262 :               Popscreen(6+dbshowit, 15, 12+dbshowit, 53, .T.)
0263 :            ENDIF
0264 :         ENDDO
0265 :         Popscreen(5,12,20,67,.T.)
0266 :
0267 :      CASE value = 287   && Alt G
0268 :         search = SPACE(LEN(A->account))
0269 :         @ 24,00 SAY "Account Number to go to => " GET search
0270 :         Sjsread()
0271 :         SEEK LTRIM(TRIM(search))
0272 :         @ 24,00 CLEAR
0273 :
0274 :      CASE value = 286   && Alt A
```

```
0275 :        @ 23,00 SAY "Would you like to Add a record? "
0276 :        IF Verify()
0277 :           Op(B->(Append())) &&  SELECT 2
0278 :                              &&   APPEND BLANK
0279 :             Op(A->(Append())) &&  SELECT 1
0280 :                              &&   APPEND BLANK
0281 :           Pushscreen(1,0,22,76,.T.,.T.,.T.,.T.)
0282 :           The_record(3)
0283 :           Op(B->(Changeit("B->account", "A->account")))
0284 :           Popscreen(1,0,22,76,.T.)
0285 :           CALL __cclr
0286 :           KEYBOARD CHR(1)
0287 :        ENDIF
0288 :        @ 23,00 SAY SPACE(37)
0289 :        RETURN(2)
0290 :
0291 :     CASE value = 274  && Alt E / Edit
0292 :        Pushscreen(1,0,22,76,.T.,.T.,.T.,.T.)
0293 :        The_record(2)
0294 :        Popscreen(1,0,22,76,.T.)
0295 :        KEYBOARD CHR(1)
0296 :        RETURN(2)
0297 :
0298 :     CASE value = 7 .AND. p1 != 0
0299 :        IF DELETED()
0300 :           * This was the OLD way of doin' things.
0301 :           * RECALL
0302 :           * SELECT B
0303 :           * RECALL ALL FOR B->account = A->account
0304 :
0305 :           Op(A->(D_or_r(.F.)))
0306 :           Op(B->(D_or_r(.F., "B->account = A->account")))
0307 :
0308 :        ELSE
0309 :           * DELETE
0310 :           * SELECT B
0311 :           * DELETE ALL FOR B->account = A->account
0312 :
0313 :           Op(A->(D_or_r(.T.)))
0314 :           Op(B->(D_or_r(.T., "B->account = A->account")))
0315 :
0316 :        ENDIF
0317 :        RETURN(2)
0318 :
0319 :     CASE value = 303  && Alt V
0320 :        Pushscreen(1,0,22,76,.T.,.T.,.T.,.T.)
0321 :        KEYBOARD "A"  && Just to get things started!
0322 :        @ 22,2 SAY "  ESC to Return / UP and DOWN arrows work "
0323 :        DO WHILE INKEY(0) != 27
0324 :           IF LASTKEY() = 24
0325 :              SKIP
0326 :              IF EOF()
0327 :                 GO TOP
0328 :              ENDIF
```

```
0329 :            ELSEIF LASTKEY() = 5
0330 :               SKIP - 1
0331 :               IF BOF()
0332 :                  GO BOTTOM
0333 :               ENDIF
0334 :            ELSEIF LASTKEY() = 1
0335 :               GO TOP
0336 :            ELSEIF LASTKEY() = 6
0337 :               GO BOTTOM
0338 :            ENDIF
0339 :            The_record()
0340 :            CLEAR GETS
0341 :         ENDDO
0342 :         Popscreen(1,0,22,76,.T.)
0343 :         KEYBOARD CHR(1)
0344 :
0345 :      CASE KEYS(value)
0346 :         DO CASE
0347 :         CASE value = 19
0348 :            IF p2 = 1  && The first two fields are OFF limits!
0349 :               KEYBOARD CHR(4)
0350 :            ENDIF
0351 :
0352 :         CASE (value = 5 .OR. value = 24)
0353 :            IF p1 = 1
0354 :               @ 24,00 SAY " [ Top of File ]"
0355 :            ELSEIF p1 = 2
0356 :               @ 24,00 SAY " [ Bottom of File ] "
0357 :            ELSE
0358 :               @ 24,00 SAY "                       "
0359 :            ENDIF
0360 :         ENDCASE
0361 :
0362 :      OTHERWISE
0363 :         IF p1 != 0
0364 :            @ 23,00 SAY ;
0365 :               "Invalid Keystroke.  Any Key to Try Again..."
0366 :            @ 24,00 SAY value
0367 :            INKEY(0)
0368 :            @ 23,0 CLEAR
0369 :         ENDIF
0370 :
0371 :      ENDCASE
0372 :
0373 :      RETURN(1)   && When all else fails....
0374 :
0375 : ********************
0376 :
0377 : FUNCTION Keys
0378 :
0379 :      PARAMETERS the_val
0380 :
0381 :      IF the_val = 5   && Up arrow
0382 :         RETURN(.T.)
```

```
0383 :      ELSEIF the_val = 13  && ENTER Key
0384 :          RETURN(.T.)
0385 :      ELSEIF the_val = 4  && Right Arrow
0386 :          RETURN(.T.)
0387 :      ELSEIF the_val = 24  && Down Arrow
0388 :          RETURN(.T.)
0389 :      ELSEIF the_val = 19  && Left Arrow
0390 :          RETURN(.T.)
0391 :      ELSEIF the_val = 3  && Page Down
0392 :          RETURN(.T.)
0393 :      ELSEIF the_val = 18  && Page Up
0394 :          RETURN(.T.)
0395 :      ELSEIF the_val = 6  && End Key
0396 :          RETURN(.T.)
0397 :      ELSEIF the_val = 1  && Home Key
0398 :          RETURN(.T.)
0399 :      ELSEIF the_val = 29
0400 :          KEYBOARD CHR(4)
0401 :          RETURN(.T.)
0402 :      ELSEIF the_val = 23  && Control W
0403 :          RETURN(.T.)
0404 :      ELSE
0405 :          RETURN(.F.)
0406 :      ENDIF
0407 :
0408 : ********************
0409 :
0410 : FUNCTION Editthis
0411 :
0412 :      PARAMETERS e1, e2, e3  && This is for the help system
0413 :
0414 :      IF LASTKEY() = 28
0415 :          *
0416 :          * do another edit, this time in edit mode!
0417 :          *
0418 :          Pushscreen(2,4,12,44,.T.,.T.,.T.,.T.)
0419 :          SET FUNCTION 10 TO CHR(23)
0420 :          @ 12, 6 SAY " Press F10 to save! "
0421 :          SET CURSOR ON
0422 :          contents = MEMOEDIT(contents, 3, 5, 11, 43, .T.)
0423 :          SET CURSOR OFF
0424 :          IF LASTKEY() = 23
0425 :              MEMOWRIT(file, contents)
0426 :          ENDIF
0427 :          KEYBOARD CHR(23)
0428 :          SET FUNCTION 10 TO
0429 :          Popscreen(2,4,12,44,.T.)
0430 :          RETURN(23)
0431 :
0432 :      ELSEIF LASTKEY() = 27
0433 :          nomore = .T.
0434 :          RETURN(27)
0435 :      ENDIF
0436 :      RETURN(0)
```

```
0437 :
0438 : ********************
0439 :
0440 : PROCEDURE The_record
0441 :
0442 :    PARAMETERS rec_way
0443 :
0444 :    IF PCOUNT() = 0
0445 :       rec_way = 1
0446 :    ENDIF
0447 :
0448 :    a 2, 3 SAY CHR(32) + CHR(17) + CHR(32) + IF(rec_way = 1, ;
0449 :       "View", IF(rec_way = 2, "Edit", "Add")) + ;
0450 :       " - Only Mode " + CHR(16) + CHR(32)
0451 :    a 2, 50 SAY " Record: " + TRANSFORM(RECNO(), "aB9999")
0452 :    FOR qaz = 1 TO FCOUNT()
0453 :       * If the variable 'temp' is not initialized at the
0454 :       * topmost section of the program, then it will bomb
0455 :       * whenever a READ is issued because temp is a local,
0456 :       * private variable and will not appear on the stack
0457 :       * once the call to the procedure 'THE_RECORD()' is
0458 :       * made.
0459 :       temp = FIELD(qaz)
0460 :       IF temp = "STATUS"
0461 :          newtemp = "A->" + temp
0462 :          a qaz+ IF((rec_way = 3), 2, 3), ;
0463 :             Right_just(Upperlower(FIELD(qaz)), 20) SAY ;
0464 :             Upperlower(FIELD(qaz)) + " > "  GET &newtemp. ;
0465 :             VALID Goodcode(&newtemp.)
0466 :       ELSE
0467 :          a qaz+ IF((rec_way = 3), 2, 3), ;
0468 :             Right_just(Upperlower(temp), 20) SAY ;
0469 :             Upperlower(temp) + " > "  GET &temp.
0470 :       ENDIF
0471 :    NEXT
0472 :    start_here = ROW()
0473 :    IF rec_way = 3    && Add mode, add to account file as well
0474 :       SELECT 2
0475 :       FOR y = 2 TO FCOUNT()
0476 :          temp = "B->" + FIELD(y)
0477 :          a start_here + y, Right_just(Upperlower(FIELD(y)), ;
0478 :             20) SAY Upperlower(FIELD(y)) + " > "  GET &temp.
0479 :       NEXT
0480 :    ENDIF
0481 :    SELECT 1
0482 :    IF rec_way = 1
0483 :       CLEAR GETS
0484 :    ELSE
0485 :       * Within this function, the cursor is turned off and
0486 :       * on again AFTER the read, a few other items are
0487 :       * checked as well, and the public variable called
0488 :       * SCRCURSOR is toggled.  This is used for the pop-up
0489 :       * routines in the ToolkiT.  Additionally, the function
0490 :       * will return a logical false if the ESC key is pressed
```

```
0491 :        * or if the READ is NOT Updated().
0492 :
0493 :        Sjsread()
0494 :
0495 :    ENDIF
0496 :
0497 : ******************
0498 :
0499 : FUNCTION Totals1
0500 :
0501 :    IF !(&expression.)
0502 :        RETURN(Fill_out(" ", 58 ))
0503 :    ELSE
0504 :        RETURN(ISTHERE() + B->account + " " + CHR(186) + ;
0505 :                 " " + DTOC(adate) + " " + CHR(186) + ;
0506 :                 TRANSFORM(now_due, "999,999,999,999.99") + ;
0507 :                 " " + CHR(186) + IF(B->paid, " Yes ", " No  "))
0508 :    ENDIF
0509 :
0510 : ******************
0511 :
0512 : FUNCTION Totals2
0513 :
0514 :    IF !(&expression.)
0515 :        RETURN(Fill_out(" ", 58 ))
0516 :    ELSE
0517 :        RETURN(Fill_out(ISTHERE() + B->account + " " + ;
0518 :                 CHR(186) + " " + A->name + " " + CHR(186) + ;
0519 :                 " " + A->Contact, 58 ) )
0520 :    ENDIF
0521 :
0522 : ******************
0523 :
0524 : FUNCTION Isthere
0525 :
0526 :    RETURN(IF(DELETE(), " " + CHR(16) + SPACE(3), SPACE(5)) )
0527 :
0528 : ******************
0529 :
0530 : FUNCTION Func2
0531 :
0532 :    PARAMETERS q1, q2
0533 :
0534 :    newvalue = LASTKEY()
0535 :
0536 :    IF q1 = 4
0537 :       DO CASE
0538 :       CASE newvalue = 27
0539 :           CALL __cclr
0540 :           RETURN(0)
0541 :
0542 :       CASE newvalue = 28
0543 :           Pushscreen(7,12,19,67,.T.,.T.,.T.,.T.)
0544 :           @  8,15 SAY "ESC to Quit DBEDIT()"
```

```
0545 :          @  9,15 SAY "F1  -  This screen"
0546 :          @ 10,15 SAY "F10 -  Another DBEDIT() / " + ;
0547 :                        "Detailed Information"
0548 :          @ 11,15 SAY "ALT A - Add Record to database"
0549 :          @ 12,15 SAY "ALT E - Edit Record currently " + ;
0550 :                        "selected by DBEDIT()"
0551 :          @ 13,15 SAY "ALT V - View Record currently " +;
0552 :                        "selected by DBEDIT()"
0553 :          @ 14,15 SAY "All Arrow and Directional Keys " +;
0554 :                        "default as expected"
0555 :          @ 15,15 SAY "DEL Key to Delete or Recall a " +;
0556 :                        "record."
0557 :          @ 18,15 SAY "Any Key to Continue..."
0558 :          INKEY(0)
0559 :          Popscreen(7,12,19,67,.T.)
0560 :          CALL __cclr
0561 :          RETURN(1)
0562 :
0563 :       CASE newvalue = -8
0564 :          IF SELECT() = 3
0565 :             Op(C->(Changeit("A->status", "C->status")))
0566 :             KEYBOARD CHR(27)
0567 :          ENDIF
0568 :
0569 :       CASE newvalue = 274
0570 :          @ 24,00 SAY "Would you like to Edit a Record? "
0571 :          IF Verify()
0572 :             @ 24,00
0573 :             SET CURSOR ON
0574 :             IF SELECT() = 3
0575 :                Pushscreen(12,20,16,70,.T.,.T.,.T.,.T.)
0576 :                Codescr("Edit")
0577 :                Sjsread()
0578 :                Popscreen(12,20,16,70,.T.)
0579 :             ELSE
0580 :                Pushscreen(14,25,21,65,.T.,.T.,.T.,.T.)
0581 :                Op(B->(Changeit("B->account", "A->account")))
0582 :                Op(B->(Changeit("B->adate", "DATE()")))
0583 :                Transscr("Edit")
0584 :                Sjsread()
0585 :                Popscreen(14,25,21,65,.T.)
0586 :             ENDIF
0587 :             SET CURSOR OFF
0588 :          ELSE
0589 :             @ 24,00
0590 :          ENDIF
0591 :          KEYBOARD ""
0592 :          Tallyback()
0593 :          RETURN(2)
0594 :
0595 :       CASE newvalue = 286
0596 :          @ 24,00 SAY "Would you like to Add a Record? "
0597 :          IF Verify()
0598 :             @ 24,00
```

```
0599 :                APPEND BLANK
0600 :                SET CURSOR ON
0601 :                IF SELECT() = 3
0602 :                    Pushscreen(12,20,16,70,.T.,.T.,.T.,.T.)
0603 :                    Codescr("Add")
0604 :                    Sjsread()
0605 :                    Popscreen(12,20,16,70,.T.)
0606 :                ELSE
0607 :                    Pushscreen(14,25,21,65,.T.,.T.,.T.,.T.)
0608 :                    Op(B->(Changeit("B->account", "A->account")))
0609 :                    Op(B->(Changeit("B->adate", "DATE()")))
0610 :                    Transscr("Add")
0611 :                    Sjsread()
0612 :                    Popscreen(14,25,21,65,.T.)
0613 :                ENDIF
0614 :                SET CURSOR OFF
0615 :              ELSE
0616 :                @ 24,00
0617 :              ENDIF
0618 :              KEYBOARD ""
0619 :              Tallyback()
0620 :              RETURN(2)
0621 :
0622 :          CASE newvalue = 7
0623 :              Op(IF( DELETED(), D_or_r(.F.), D_or_r(.T.) ) )
0624 :
0625 :          OTHERWISE
0626 :              CALL __cclr
0627 :
0628 :          ENDCASE
0629 :      ELSEIF q1 = 1       && At the TOP of the file
0630 :          IF SELECT() = 3  && Codescreen Only!!
0631 :              KEYBOARD CHR(30)
0632 :          ENDIF
0633 :
0634 :      ELSEIF q1 = 2       && At the BOTTOM of the file
0635 :          IF SELECT() = 3  && Codescreen Only!!
0636 :              KEYBOARD CHR(31)
0637 :          ENDIF
0638 :
0639 :      ELSE
0640 :          IF !EMPTY(expression)
0641 :              DO CASE
0642 :              CASE newvalue = 3
0643 :                  IF !(&expression.)
0644 :                      KEYBOARD CHR(18)
0645 :                  ENDIF
0646 :              CASE newvalue = 24
0647 :                  IF !(&expression.)
0648 :                      KEYBOARD CHR(5)
0649 :                  ENDIF
0650 :              CASE newvalue = 5
0651 :                  IF !(&expression.)
0652 :                      KEYBOARD CHR(24)
```

```
0653 :              ENDIF
0654 :            CASE newvalue = 18
0655 :               IF !(&expression.)
0656 :                  KEYBOARD CHR(3)
0657 :               ENDIF
0658 :            ENDCASE
0659 :          ENDIF
0660 :       ENDIF
0661 :       RETURN(1)
0662 :
0663 : ********************
0664 :
0665 : PROCEDURE Tallyback
0666 :
0667 :    IF SELECT() = 2
0668 :       tally = tally + B->now_due
0669 :       @ 15, 30 SAY " Total => " + ;
0670 :          TRANSFORM(tally, "999,999,999.99") + " "
0671 :    ENDIF
0672 :
0673 : ********************
0674 :
0675 : PROCEDURE Codescr
0676 :
0677 :    PARAMETERS codeway
0678 :
0679 :    @ 12,22 SAY CHR(17) + CHR(32) + codeway + CHR(32) + CHR(16)
0680 :
0681 :    FOR y = 1 TO FCOUNT()
0682 :       ntemp = FIELD(y)
0683 :       @ 12 + y, Right_just(FIELD(y), 37) SAY ;
0684 :          Upperlower(FIELD(y)) + " => " GET &ntemp.
0685 :    NEXT
0686 :
0687 : ********************
0688 :
0689 : PROCEDURE Transscr
0690 :
0691 :    PARAMETERS transway
0692 :
0693 :    @ 14,27 SAY CHR(17) + CHR(32) + transway + CHR(32) + CHR(16)
0694 :
0695 :    FOR y = IF(transway = "Add", 2, 1) TO FCOUNT()
0696 :       ntemp = FIELD(y)
0697 :       @ 15 + y, Right_just(FIELD(y), 38) SAY ;
0698 :          Upperlower(FIELD(y)) + " => " GET &ntemp.
0699 :    NEXT
0700 :
0701 : ********************
0702 :
0703 : FUNCTION Goodcode
0704 :
0705 :    PARAMETERS acode
```

```
0706 :
0707 :     IF LASTKEY() = 27
0708 :        RETURN(.T.)
0709 :     ELSEIF C->(Seekit(acode))
0710 :        @ ROW(), COL()+2 SAY C->descript
0711 :        RETURN(.T.)
0712 :     ELSE
0713 :        Op(C->(Top()))
0714 :        Pushscreen(4,38,14,73,.T.,.T.,.T.,.T.)
0715 :        Op(C->(DBEDIT(5,39,13,72)))
0716 :        IF LASTKEY() = 13
0717 :           REPLACE &newtemp. WITH C->status
0718 :        ENDIF
0719 :        Popscreen(4,38,14,73,.T.)
0720 :        KEYBOARD CHR(13)           && Enter Key
0721 :        RETURN(.F.)
0722 :     ENDIF
0723 :
0724 : ******************
0725 :
0726 : FUNCTION D_or_r
0727 :
0728 :     * This stands for Delete or Recall...
0729 :
0730 :     PARAMETERS do_delete, condition
0731 :
0732 :     IF PCOUNT() = 1
0733 :        condition = ""
0734 :     ENDIF
0735 :
0736 :     IF do_delete
0737 :        IF EMPTY(condition)
0738 :           DELETE
0739 :        ELSE
0740 :           @ 24,00 SAY "Deleting Records...."
0741 :           DELETE ALL FOR &condition. WHILE Show_rec(24,20)
0742 :           @ 24,00
0743 :        ENDIF
0744 :     ELSE
0745 :        IF EMPTY(condition)
0746 :           RECALL
0747 :        ELSE
0748 :           @ 24,00 SAY "Recalling Records...."
0749 :           RECALL ALL FOR &condition. WHILE Show_rec(24,21)
0750 :           @ 24,00
0751 :        ENDIF
0752 :     ENDIF
0753 :     RETURN(.T.)
0754 :
0755 : ******************
0756 :
0757 : FUNCTION Additup
0758 :
0759 :     stuffback = 0
```

```
0760 :
0761 :     @ 24,00 SAY "Adding now..."
0762 :     Op(B->(Sum_it("B->now_due", @stuffback, ;
0763 :            "B->account = A->account")))
0764 :     @ 24,00
0765 :     KEYBOARD Strvalue(stuffback)
0766 :     RETURN(.T.)
0767 :
0768 : *******************
0769 :
0770 : PROCEDURE Sum_it
0771 :
0772 :     PARAMETERS field, variable, condition, row_loc, col_loc
0773 :
0774 :     SUM &field. TO variable FOR &condition. WHILE ;
0775 :         IF(PCOUNT()=3, .T., Show_rec(row_loc, col_loc))
0776 :
0777 : ******************
0778 :
0779 : PROCEDURE Gotoit
0780 :
0781 :     PARAMETERS recordnum
0782 :
0783 :     IF EMPTY(PCOUNT())
0784 :         recordnum = 1
0785 :     ENDIF
0786 :     GOTO recordnum
0787 :
0788 : ******************
0789 :
0790 : PROCEDURE Changeit
0791 :
0792 :     PARAMETER change1, change2, change3, change4
0793 :
0794 :     IF PCOUNT() = 4
0795 :         * this means do to all
0796 :         REPLACE ALL &change1. WITH &change2. FOR ;
0797 :                     &change3 WHILE &change4.
0798 :     ELSEIF PCOUNT() = 3
0799 :         REPLACE &change1. WITH &change2 FOR &change3.
0800 :     ELSE
0801 :         REPLACE &change1. WITH &change2.
0802 :     ENDIF
0803 :
0804 : * *********************************************
0805 : * * The following procedure(s)/function(s) are  *
0806 : * * part of Steve Straley's ToolkiT(tm) -       *
0807 : * * Release 2, published by Four Seasons        *
0808 : * * Publishing Co., Inc.  All Rights Reserved   *
0809 : * * Information: 212-599-2141 / 800-662-2278    *
0810 : * * All Rights Reserved                         *
0811 : * * *********************************************
0812 :
0813 : ******************
```

```
0814 :
0815 : PROCEDURE Op
0816 :
0817 :    PARAMETER _something
0818 :
0819 : ********************
0820 :
0821 : FUNCTION Popscreen
0822 :
0823 :    PARAMETERS _pop1, _pop2, _pop3, _pop4, _popshad, _popstype
0824 :
0825 :    PRIVATE _poptemp
0826 :
0827 :    scr_level = IF(scr_level = 1, scr_level, scr_level - 1)
0828 :
0829 :    IF PCOUNT() = 4
0830 :       _popshad = .F.
0831 :    ELSEIF PCOUNT() = 0
0832 :       _pop1    = IF(EMPTY(SUBSTR(allwindows[scr_level],1,2)),;
0833 :                      0, SUBSTR(allwindows[scr_level], 1, 2))
0834 :       _pop2    =IF(EMPTY(SUBSTR(allwindows[scr_level],4,2)),;
0835 :                      0, SUBSTR(allwindows[scr_level], 4, 2))
0836 :       _pop3    =IF(EMPTY(SUBSTR(allwindows[scr_level],7,2)),;
0837 :                      24, SUBSTR(allwindows[scr_level], 7, 2))
0838 :       _pop4    =IF(EMPTY(SUBSTR(allwindows[scr_level],10,2)),;
0839 :                      79, SUBSTR(allwindows[scr_level],10, 2))
0840 :       _popshad = SUBSTR(allwindows[scr_level],13)
0841 :       IF _popshad $ ".T..F."
0842 :          _popshad = &_popshad.
0843 :       ELSEIF EMPTY(_popshad) .OR. TYPE("_popshad") != "L"
0844 :          _popshad = .F.
0845 :       ENDIF
0846 :       _popstype = 1
0847 :    ELSEIF PCOUNT() = 5
0848 :       _popstype = 1
0849 :    ENDIF
0850 :
0851 :    _poptemp = ""
0852 :
0853 :    _poptemp = allscreens[scr_level]
0854 :    SETCOLOR(allcolor[scr_level])
0855 :
0856 :    IF _popshad
0857 :       DO CASE
0858 :       CASE _popstype = 1
0859 :          RESTSCREEN(_pop1, _pop2, _pop3+1, _pop4+2, _poptemp)
0860 :       CASE _popstype = 2
0861 :          RESTSCREEN(_pop1, _pop2-1, _pop3+1, _pop4, _poptemp)
0862 :       CASE _popstype = 3
0863 :          RESTSCREEN(_pop1-1, _pop2-1, _pop3, _pop4, _poptemp)
0864 :       CASE _popstype = 4
0865 :          RESTSCREEN(_pop1-1, _pop2, _pop3, _pop4+2, _poptemp)
0866 :       ENDCASE
0867 :    ELSE
```

```
0868 :        RESTSCREEN(_pop1, _pop2, _pop3, _pop4, _poptemp)
0869 :    ENDIF
0870 :
0871 :    allwindows[scr_level+1] = ""
0872 :    allscreens[scr_level+1] = ""
0873 :    allcolor[scr_level+1]   = ""
0874 :    RELEASE _poptemp
0875 :    RETURN(scr_level)
0876 :
0877 : *******************
0878 :
0879 : FUNCTION Pushscreen
0880 :
0881 :    PARAMETERS _push1, _push2, _push3, _push4, _pushsave, ;
0882 :               _pushscr, _pushbord, _pushshad
0883 :
0884 :
0885 :    * This is the first function/procedure that is used
0886 :    * to draw a screen and push the screen stack.  The screen
0887 :    * stack is stored in the array "allscreens," the color stack
0888 :    * is stored in the array "allcolor," and the window
0889 :    * logic is housed in the "allwindows" array.  The stack
0890 :    * counter is housed in the "scr_level" variable.
0891 :    *
0892 :    * The return value is the
0893 :
0894 :    IF TYPE("allscreens") != "A"
0895 :       PUBLIC allscreens[20], scr_level, allcolor[20], ;
0896 :                 allwindows[20]
0897 :       scr_level = 2
0898 :       AFILL(allscreens, "")
0899 :       AFILL(allcolor, "")
0900 :       AFILL(allwindows, "")
0901 :    ENDIF
0902 :
0903 :    IF EMPTY(PCOUNT())     && No Parameters!
0904 :       _push1    = 0
0905 :       _push2    = 0
0906 :       _push3    = 24
0907 :       _push4    = 79
0908 :       _pushsave = .T.
0909 :       _pushscr  = .F.
0910 :       _pushbord = .F.
0911 :       _pushshad = .F.
0912 :
0913 :    ELSEIF PCOUNT() = 4  && No border, No Frame, Just save
0914 :       _pushsave = .T.
0915 :       _pushscr  = .T.
0916 :       _pushbord = .F.
0917 :       _pushshad = .F.
0918 :
0919 :    ELSEIF PCOUNT() = 5  && Save area without border logic
0920 :       _pushscr  = .T.
0921 :       _pushbord = .F.
```

```
0922 :          _pushshad = .F.
0923 :
0924 :      ELSEIF PCOUNT() = 6
0925 :          _pushbord = .T.
0926 :          _pushshad = .F.
0927 :
0928 :      ELSEIF PCOUNT() = 7
0929 :          _pushshad = .F.
0930 :
0931 :      ENDIF
0932 :
0933 :      IF _pushsave
0934 :          allscreens[scr_level] = ""
0935 :          IF _pushshad
0936 :             allscreens[scr_level] = SAVESCREEN(_push1, _push2, ;
0937 :                  _push3 + 1, _push4 + 2)
0938 :          ELSE
0939 :             allscreens[scr_level] = SAVESCREEN(_push1, _push2, ;
0940 :                  _push3, _push4)
0941 :          ENDIF
0942 :          allcolor[scr_level] = SETCOLOR()
0943 :          IF _pushshad
0944 :             allwindows[scr_level] = TRANSFORM(_push1, "99") + ;
0945 :                 "/" + TRANSFORM(_push2, "99") + "/" + ;
0946 :                 TRANSFORM(_push3+1, "99") + "/" + ;
0947 :                 TRANSFORM(_push4+2, "99") + "/.T."
0948 :          ELSE
0949 :             allwindows[scr_level] = TRANSFORM(_push1, "99") + ;
0950 :                 "/" + TRANSFORM(_push2, "99") + "/" + ;
0951 :                 TRANSFORM(_push3, "99") + "/" + ;
0952 :                 TRANSFORM(_push4, "99") + "/.F."
0953 :          ENDIF
0954 :          scr_level = IF(scr_level = 20, scr_level, scr_level + 1)
0955 :      ENDIF
0956 :
0957 :      IF _pushbord      && Yes, I want a border!
0958 :          IF !_pushscr  && I just want a frame, hold the filling
0959 :             IF TYPE("scrframe") = "U"
0960 :                 @ _push1, _push2 TO _push3, _push4 DOUBLE
0961 :             ELSE
0962 :                 @ _push1, _push2, _push3, _push4 BOX ;
0963 :                     SUBSTR(scrframe, 1, 8)
0964 :             ENDIF
0965 :          ELSE
0966 :             IF TYPE("scrframe") = "U"
0967 :                 @ _push1, _push2 CLEAR TO _push3, _push4
0968 :                 @ _push1, _push2 TO _push3, _push4 DOUBLE
0969 :             ELSE
0970 :                 @ _push1, _push2, _push3, _push4 BOX scrframe
0971 :             ENDIF
0972 :          ENDIF
0973 :          IF _pushshad
0974 :             SHADOW(_push1, _push2, _push3, _push4, 1)
0975 :          ENDIF
```

```
0976 :        ENDIF
0977 :
0978 :        RETURN(scr_level-1)
0979 :
0980 : ********************
0981 :
0982 : FUNCTION Upperlower
0983 :
0984 :        PARAMETERS _upla
0985 :
0986 :        * Take the parameter string and uppercase the first
0987 :        * letter, lowercasing all other letters
0988 :
0989 :        IF PCOUNT() != 1
0990 :           RETURN("")
0991 :        ENDIF
0992 :        RETURN(UPPER(SUBSTR(_upla, 1, 1)) + LOWER(SUBSTR(_upla,2)))
0993 :
0994 : ********************
0995 :
0996 : FUNCTION Shadow
0997 :
0998 :        PARAMETERS _shada, _shadb, _shadc, _shadd, _shadde, ;
0999 :                   _shaddf, _shaddg
1000 :
1001 :        PRIVATE _shadcolor, _shadx
1002 :
1003 :        IF PCOUNT() = 4
1004 :           _shadde = CHR(177)
1005 :           _shaddf = 1
1006 :           _shaddg = IF ( (TYPE("scrmono") = "U"), .T., !scrmono)
1007 :        ELSEIF PCOUNT() = 5
1008 :           _shaddf = 1
1009 :           _shaddg = IF ( (TYPE("scrmono") = "U"), .T., !scrmono)
1010 :        ELSEIF PCOUNT() = 6
1011 :           _shaddg = IF ( (TYPE("scrmono") = "U"), .T., !scrmono)
1012 :        ENDIF
1013 :
1014 :        IF TYPE("_shadde") = "N"
1015 :           _shaddf = _shadde
1016 :           _shadde = CHR(177)
1017 :           _shaddg = .T.
1018 :        ENDIF
1019 :        _shadde = SUBSTR(IF(EMPTY(_shadde),CHR(177), _shadde),1,1)
1020 :
1021 :        _shadcolor = SETCOLOR()
1022 :        SETCOLOR( STRTRAN( _shadcolor, "+", "" ) )
1023 :
1024 :        DO CASE
1025 :        CASE _shaddf = 1                        && Right side, underneath
1026 :           FOR _shadx = _shada+1 TO _shadc+1
1027 :              @ _shadx, _shadd+1 SAY _shadde + _shadde
1028 :           NEXT
1029 :           @ _shadc+1,_shadb+1 SAY REPLICATE(_shadde, _shadd-_shadb)
```

```
1030 :
1031 :     CASE _shaddf = 2
1032 :        FOR _shadx = _shada+1 TO _shadc+1
1033 :           @ _shadx, _shadb-2 SAY _shadde + _shadde
1034 :        NEXT
1035 :        @ _shadc+1,_shadb SAY REPLICATE(_shadde, _shadd-_shadb)
1036 :
1037 :     CASE _shaddf = 3                    && Left side, on bottom
1038 :        FOR _shadx = _shada-1 TO _shadc-1
1039 :           @ _shadx, _shadb-2 SAY _shadde + _shadde
1040 :        NEXT
1041 :        @ _shada-1,_shadb-1 SAY REPLICATE(_shadde, _shadd-_shadb)
1042 :
1043 :     CASE _shaddf = 4                    && Right side, on top
1044 :        FOR _shadx = _shada-1 TO _shadc-1
1045 :           @ _shadx, _shadd+1 SAY _shadde + _shadde
1046 :        NEXT
1047 :        @ _shada-1,_shadb+2 SAY REPLICATE(_shadde, _shadd-_shadb)
1048 :     ENDCASE
1049 :
1050 :     SETCOLOR( _shadcolor )
1051 :     RETURN("")
1052 :
1053 : ********************
1054 :
1055 : FUNCTION Mess_cent
1056 :
1057 :     PARAMETERS _a1, _a2, _a3
1058 :
1059 :     PRIVATE _d, _e, _f
1060 :
1061 :     * _a1 is the string
1062 :     * _a2 is the line's length
1063 :     * _a3 is the character to center the message with
1064 :     * _d is the length of _a
1065 :     * _e is length of the line minus half of string's length
1066 :     * _f is the total length
1067 :
1068 :     IF PCOUNT() = 1
1069 :        _a2 = 80
1070 :        _a3 = " "
1071 :     ELSEIF PCOUNT() = 2
1072 :        _a3 = " "
1073 :     ENDIF
1074 :
1075 :     IF !EMPTY(_a3)
1076 :        _a1 = " " + _a1 + " "
1077 :     ENDIF
1078 :
1079 :     _a2 = INT(_a2 / 2)
1080 :
1081 :     _d = LEN(_a1)
```

```
1082 :     _e = INT(_a2 - _d / 2)
1083 :     _f = (2 * _a2) - _d - _e
1084 :
1085 :     RETURN( REPLICATE(_a3, _e) + _a1 + REPLICATE(_a3, _f) )
1086 :
1087 : ********************
1088 :
1089 : FUNCTION Sjsread
1090 :
1091 :     PARAMETERS _withoutpg, _update
1092 :
1093 :     IF EMPTY(PCOUNT())
1094 :       _withoutpg = .F.
1095 :       _update = .F.
1096 :     ELSEIF PCOUNT() = 1
1097 :       _update = .F.
1098 :     ENDIF
1099 :
1100 :     IF _withoutpg
1101 :        SET KEY 3 TO Nogo
1102 :        SET KEY 8 TO Nogo
1103 :     ENDIF
1104 :     scrcursor = .T.
1105 :     SET CURSOR ON
1106 :     READ
1107 :     SET CURSOR OFF
1108 :     SET KEY 3 TO
1109 :     SET KEY 18 TO
1110 :     scrcursor = .F.
1111 :     IF !_update
1112 :        RETURN( LASTKEY() != 27 )
1113 :     ELSE
1114 :        RETURN(UPDATED())
1115 :     ENDIF
1116 :
1117 : ******************
1118 :
1119 : PROCEDURE Nogo
1120 :
1121 :     KEYBOARD ""
1122 :
1123 : ********************
1124 :
1125 : FUNCTION Fill_out
1126 :
1127 :     PARAMETERS _filla, _fillb
1128 :
1129 :     * _filla = the string to be filled out
1130 :     * _fillb = the Length to fill out the string to
1131 :
1132 :     IF PCOUNT() = 1
1133 :        _fillb = 80
1134 :     ELSE
```

```
1135 :        IF TYPE("_fillb") = "C"
1136 :           _fillb = VAL(b)
1137 :        ENDIF
1138 :        _fillb = IIF(_fillb <= 1, 80, _fillb)
1139 :     ENDIF
1140 :
1141 :     IF _fillb <= LEN(_filla)
1142 :        RETURN(_filla)
1143 :     ENDIF
1144 :     RETURN(LEFT(_filla + SPACE(_fillb - LEN(_filla)),_fillb))
1145 :
1146 : ********************
1147 :
1148 : FUNCTION Seekit
1149 :
1150 :     PARAMETERS _lookforit, _order
1151 :
1152 :     IF PCOUNT() = 1
1153 :        _order = INDEXORD()
1154 :     ENDIF
1155 :
1156 :     PRIVATE _oorder
1157 :
1158 :     _oorder = INDEXORD()
1159 :
1160 :     SET ORDER TO (_order)
1161 :
1162 :     SEEK _lookforit
1163 :
1164 :     SET ORDER TO (_oorder)
1165 :
1166 :     RETURN(FOUND())
1167 :
1168 : ********************
1169 :
1170 : FUNCTION Verify
1171 :
1172 :     PARAMETERS _comp, _extra
1173 :
1174 :     DO CASE
1175 :     CASE PCOUNT() = 0
1176 :        _comp = "YyNn"
1177 :        _extra = .F.
1178 :     CASE PCOUNT() = 1
1179 :        IF TYPE("_comp") = "L"
1180 :           _extra = _comp
1181 :           _comp = "YyNn"
1182 :        ELSE
1183 :           _extra = .F.
1184 :        ENDIF
1185 :     ENDCASE
1186 :
1187 :     scrpause = IF((TYPE("scrpause") = "U"), 100, scrpause)
1188 :
```

```
1189 :     DO WHILE .T.
1190 :         the_var = ""
1191 :         inside = INKEY(0)
1192 :         DO CASE
1193 :         CASE inside = 4
1194 :             the_var = "Y"
1195 :         CASE inside = 19
1196 :             the_var = "N"
1197 :         OTHERWISE
1198 :             the_var = CHR(inside)
1199 :         ENDCASE
1200 :         IF the_var$_comp .OR. inside = 27
1201 :             EXIT
1202 :         ENDIF
1203 :     ENDDO
1204 :     IF the_var$SUBSTR(_comp,1,2)
1205 :         ?? "Yes"
1206 :         IF _extra
1207 :             INKEY(0)
1208 :         ELSE
1209 :             FOR qaz = 1 TO scrpause
1210 :             NEXT
1211 :         ENDIF
1212 :         RETURN(.T.)
1213 :     ELSE
1214 :         ?? "No "
1215 :         IF _extra
1216 :             INKEY(0)
1217 :         ELSE
1218 :             FOR qaz = 1 TO scrpause
1219 :             NEXT
1220 :         ENDIF
1221 :         RETURN(.F.)
1222 :     ENDIF
1223 :
1224 : ******************
1225 :
1226 : FUNCTION Packit
1227 :
1228 :     PACK
1229 :
1230 :     RETURN( DOSERROR() = 0 )
1231 :
1232 : ******************
1233 :
1234 : FUNCTION Append
1235 :
1236 :     IF !EMPTY(ALIAS())
1237 :         APPEND BLANK
1238 :         RETURN(.T.)
1239 :     ELSE
1240 :         RETURN(.F.)
1241 :     ENDIF
1242 :
```

```
1243 : ********************
1244 :
1245 : FUNCTION Right_just
1246 :
1247 :    PARAMETERS _a, _b
1248 :
1249 :    * _a is the right justified string
1250 :    * _b is the column to right justify to
1251 :
1252 :    IF PCOUNT() = 1
1253 :       _b = 79
1254 :    ENDIF
1255 :    RETURN(IF(LEN(_a) > _b, 0, _b - LEN(_a)))
1256 :
1257 : ********************
1258 :
1259 : FUNCTION Show_rec
1260 :
1261 :    PARAMETERS _showrow, _showcol
1262 :
1263 :    * Show the current record pointer and a set of screen
1264 :    * coordinates, left justified.
1265 :
1266 :    IF PCOUNT() = 0
1267 :       _showrow = ROW()
1268 :       _showcol = COL()
1269 :    ELSE
1270 :       IF PCOUNT() = 1
1271 :          _showcol = COL()
1272 :       ENDIF
1273 :    ENDIF
1274 :
1275 :    @ _showrow, _showcol SAY RECNO() PICT "@B"
1276 :    RETURN((INKEY() != 27))
1277 :
1278 : ********************
1279 :
1280 : PROCEDURE Top
1281 :
1282 :    GO TOP
1283 :
1284 : ********************
1285 :
1286 : FUNCTION Strvalue
1287 :
1288 :    PARAMETERS _showstr
1289 :
1290 :    * This function returns the string representation
1291 :    * of the given parameter.
1292 :
1293 :    IF PCOUNT() != 1
1294 :       RETURN("")
1295 :    ENDIF
1296 :
```

```
1297 :     DO CASE
1298 :     CASE TYPE("_showstr") = "C"
1299 :        RETURN(_showstr)
1300 :
1301 :     CASE TYPE("_showstr") = "N"
1302 :        RETURN(STR(_showstr))
1303 :
1304 :     CASE TYPE("_showstr") = "M"
1305 :        IF LEN(_showstr) > (MEMORY(0) * 1024) * .80
1306 :           RETURN( SUBSTR(_showstr, 1, ;
1307 :                   INT((MEMORY(0) * 1024) * .80)) )
1308 :        ELSE
1309 :           RETURN(_showstr)
1310 :        ENDIF
1311 :
1312 :     CASE TYPE("_showstr") = "D"
1313 :        RETURN(DTOC(_showstr))
1314 :
1315 :     CASE TYPE("_showstr") = "L"
1316 :        RETURN(IF(_showstr, "True", "False"))
1317 :
1318 :     OTHERWISE
1319 :        RETURN("")
1320 :
1321 :     ENDCASE
1322 :
1323 : * End of File
```

Keep in mind that this example puts many of the previously discussed topics together in one routine. For example, it should now be obvious that the first column in the first work area's DBEDIT() should be the value of the RECNO() function (line 57). Also note that the value displayed in the third column in the first DBEDIT() is the value from the **C->dsiscript** field. Now, let's take a look at the flow of the program and how data ties in with other information. First, map out how the files are opened and if there are any relations built. In SELECT area 3, the Statcode database is used; in work area 2, the Trans database is used; and finally, in work area A, the Clients database is used. And on that last database on lines 47 and 48, a RELATION is built; for every time the record pointer in the Clients database is moved, the value from the account field is SEEKed in the Trans work area and the value from the **status** field is SEEKed in the Statcode work area. Relating this to our original point, this means that, instead of a meaningless code appearing on the screen in the first DBEDIT() function, the related information in the Statcode work area is displayed: namely, the description for that code (not the code itself).

The next items to note are the special variables that control the flow of information within the DBEDIT() function. First, the **bottom** variable will hold the last row for the display of the DBEDIT() window, the **expression** variable will hold the value that will simulate the SET FILTER TO command, and the **maincolor** variable will hold the original color of the DBEDIT(). This will become clearer in a few moments. Finally, the call to the DBEDIT() function is made on lines 92 through 94, using the extended parentheses of the Clipper language. This is explained further in the chapter on Function-Oriented Programming. For now, consider this function and the keystroke function named Func1() all working from the A work area.

As with all of the other examples, the heart of DBEDIT()'s versatility is the programming muscle within the keystroke-exception function. So, on lines 106 through 110, the keystroke-exception function is forcing extra right arrow keys into the KEYBOARD buffer. Looking at the code closely we can see that if the column pointer's value (the **p2** variable) is a 1, the KEYBOARD will be stuffed with two right arrow keys; if the value of **p2** is a 2, one right arrow will be stuffed to the KEYBOARD. This means that the first two columns are locked, and the user cannot move to them. If the user is sitting on the third column and presses the left arrow key, the value of **p2** will go from a 3 to a 2 and the KEYBOARD will be stuffed with that value, sending the end user back to the third column.

Lines 112 and following test for the space bar CHR(32) as well as the value of **p1** (the mode of the DBEDIT()) being 4 (an exception key). Within this test, the value of **p2** is tested. The space bar becomes an edit key in this example, and, based on the value of the column pointer, different edit possibilities spring forward. For example, if the space bar is pressed while the user is sitting on the fourth column, and if an adjustment is made to the **account** field in the Clients database (lines 123 through 132), not only is that field so adjusted, but so should the corresponding fields in the Trans database. The Changeit() function accomplishes this task (lines 128 and 129). If the user should sit on the twelfth field, the **due** field, two SET KEY TO commands are activated. These work from either the "C" or the "c" characters and will sum up the values from the associated field in the Trans database and stuff the KEYBOARD with the total. Looking at that routine, which is on lines 755 through 766, the call is eventually made to the Sum_it() procedure, which modifies the value of the **stuffback** variable that was passed by reference on line 762. That value is then converted into a string and the KEYBOARD is stuffed. Even though the value will be a numeric in the **due** field, the KEYBOARD must be stuffed with characters; those characters can be numeric representations of actual numbers.

Finally, the other test condition to note is on lines 113 through 120. Here, if the **status** field is to be changed, this code will take effect. An @...SAY...GET within the user-defined function is made. Looking closer we see that another UDF is called on the VALID clause of the command. This function, Goodcode(), begins on line 701 and concludes on line 722. If the value passed to the function is FOUND() via the Seekit() function (which is part of the ToolkiT), the value for the Goodcode() function will be a logical true (.T.) (line 711). If it is not, the record pointer is placed at the top of the database in the "C" work area (line 713) and another DBEDIT() is called (line 715). Here, the end user can press the Enter key, pick the appropriate value, REPLACE the field in the variable **newtemp** (line 717), force the KEYBOARD with a CHR(13) (the Enter key), and return a logical false (.F.) for the value of Goodcode(). At that point, the Enter key in the KEYBOARD will be executed, calling the Goodcode() function again. This time, the value will be found since it was picked, and all is satisfied. Consider the code that we just walked through; at one point we are in DBEDIT(), called by a user-defined function activated by the VALID command on a GET, called by a user-defined function for keystroke exceptions, coming from the original DBEDIT(). The reality is powerful.

This example is filled with nuances such as the ability to call a MEMOEDIT() within a MEMOEDIT() on lines 256 and 257, calling the Editthis() function beginning on line 410, or the ability to have PROMPTS within the DBEDIT(), or adding records to any one of the three databases, or viewing the information, or altering the color of the picked items in a list box, yet maintaining the color of the system. All of that and much more is within this one example. Indeed, the true power of Clipper is yet to be discovered!

SUMMARY

We need to review several key points. First, let us start by talking about where we were in relationship to the language before we started this chapter. We can look at the manual, take it literally, and be left behind, or we can push ourselves, see what the manual tells us what we cannot do and try everything else. The latter approach brings greater rewards. We will be on the cutting edge of Clipper technology, and we will be programming for the future.

It is interesting to observe that while we did not change the internal workings of the DBEDIT() function (only Nantucket can do that since they have the source code), we were able to alter the data that we passed to it, causing the function to behave in phenomenal ways. We should look at this, and from now on program data rather than functions. This is a basic principle of object-oriented programming, the next generation of Clipper programming. While these small code fragments do not entirely show this new direction for the Clipper language, they give us a flavor for what the future will hold: unlimited possibilities.

CHAPTER THREE

Window and Screen Technology

No matter how a manufacturer tries to implement menu, window, display, and graphical interfaces into a language, some programmers will ignore those implementations. The reasons vary from programmer to programmer; yet, in the end, the truth is simple: Interfacing is the stylistic and personal part of the programmer's trade. In admitting this, we recognize that the philosophies in this book are not going to be accepted by everyone. Nantucket will face the same wall if true relative windowing is ever implemented in Clipper. Therefore this chapter will try to point out the many functions in Clipper that give you the power to create your own unique style of windowing, shadowing, menuing, and error display. This chapter deals with these issues from a pure Clipper point of view.

MAKING A WINDOW

Many of us who have used Clipper since the autumn of '86 release have envisioned the concepts of a window, saving screens to memory variables, and having a system that would automatically handle the row and column positions within the various windows in our application. As a starting block, we began to build procedures that would clear a screen area at specified row and column coordinates. This code looked something like this:

```
********************
* Name      Windowa.prg
* Author    Stephen J. Straley
* Date      July 15, 1989
* Notice    Copyright (c) 1989 Stephen J. Straley & Associates
*           All Rights Reserved
* Compile   Clipper Windowa -m
* Release   Summer 87
* Link      PLINK86 FI Windowa LIB Clipper LIB Extend;
* Note      This is the first window program file
*
********************

option = 1
SET WRAP ON
SET SCOREBOARD OFF
SET MESSAGE TO 24 CENTER
DO WHILE .T.
   DO Wopen WITH 0,0,24,79
   @  5,27 PROMPT " Chart of Account       " ;
      MESSAGE "Enter/Edit COA Information"
   @  7,27 PROMPT " Transactions           " ;
      MESSAGE "Enter/Edit Transactions"
   @  9,27 PROMPT " Balancing and Posting " ;
      MESSAGE "Balance Items/Post to Ledger"
   @ 11,27 PROMPT " Reporting and Lists   " ;
      MESSAGE "Financial Reports and Listings"
   @ 13,27 PROMPT " Utilities              " ;
      MESSAGE "Managerial Utilities"
   @ 15,27 PROMPT " End of Period          " ;
      MESSAGE "End of Period Processing"
```

```
    @ 17,27 PROMPT " Quit                          " ;
       MESSAGE "Quit to DOS"
    MENU TO option
    IF EMPTY(option) .OR. option = 7
       EXIT
    ELSE
       ext = TRANSFORM(option, "9")
       DO Menu&ext.
    ENDIF
 ENDDO

 ********************

 PROCEDURE Menu1

   base = (option * 2)
   DO Wopen WITH 5 + base, 35, 15 + base, 45
   @  7+base, 37 PROMPT "Add   "
   @  9+base, 37 PROMPT "Edit  "
   @ 11+base, 37 PROMPT "Scan  "
   @ 13+base, 37 PROMPT "Delete"
   MENU TO dummy

 ********************

 PROCEDURE Menu2

   base = (option * 2)
   DO Wopen WITH 5 + base, 35, 15 + base, 45
   @  7+base, 37 PROMPT "Add   "
   @  9+base, 37 PROMPT "Edit  "
   @ 11+base, 37 PROMPT "Scan  "
   @ 13+base, 37 PROMPT "Delete"
   MENU TO dummy

 ********************

 PROCEDURE Menu3

   * This is just a stub

 ********************

 PROCEDURE Menu4

   * This is just a stub

 ********************

 PROCEDURE Menu5

   * This is just a stub

 ********************
```

```
PROCEDURE Menu6

  * This is just a stub

********************

PROCEDURE Wopen

   PARAMETERS _w1, _w2, _w3, _w4

   @ _w1, _w2 CLEAR TO _w3, _w4

* End of File
```

From this, we can see that if we expanded the concept, the same procedure could not only clear the screen for us but draw a border as well:

```
********************
* Name      Windowb.prg
* Author    Stephen J. Straley
* Date      July 15, 1989
* Notice    Copyright (c) 1989 Stephen J. Straley & Associates
*           All Rights Reserved
* Compile   Clipper Windowb -m
* Release   Summer 87
* Link      PLINK86 FI Windowb LIB Clipper LIB Extend;
* Note      This is the second window program file, this
*           time with a border!
*
********************

option = 1
SET WRAP ON
SET SCOREBOARD OFF
SET MESSAGE TO 24 CENTER
DO WHILE .T.
   DO Wopen WITH 0,0,24,79
   @  5,27 PROMPT " Chart of Account      " ;
      MESSAGE "Enter/Edit COA Information"
   @  7,27 PROMPT " Transactions          " ;
      MESSAGE "Enter/Edit Transactions"
   @  9,27 PROMPT " Balancing and Posting " ;
      MESSAGE "Balance Items/Post to Ledger"
   @ 11,27 PROMPT " Reporting and Lists   " ;
      MESSAGE "Financial Reports and Listings"
   @ 13,27 PROMPT " Utilities             " ;
      MESSAGE "Managerial Utilities"
   @ 15,27 PROMPT " End of Period         " ;
      MESSAGE "End of Period Processing"
   @ 17,27 PROMPT " Quit                  " ;
      MESSAGE "Quit to DOS"
   MENU TO option
```

```
036 :     IF EMPTY(option) .OR. option = 7
037 :        EXIT
038 :     ELSE
039 :        ext = TRANSFORM(option, "9")
040 :        DO Menu&ext.
041 :     ENDIF
042 : ENDDO
043 : CLEAR SCREEN
044 : *******************
045 :
046 : PROCEDURE Menu1
047 :
048 :     base = (option * 2)
049 :     DO Wopen WITH 5 + base, 35, 15 + base, 45
050 :     @  7+base, 37 PROMPT "Add    "
051 :     @  9+base, 37 PROMPT "Edit   "
052 :     @ 11+base, 37 PROMPT "Scan   "
053 :     @ 13+base, 37 PROMPT "Delete"
054 :     MENU TO dummy
055 :
056 : *******************
057 :
058 : PROCEDURE Menu2
059 :
060 :     base = (option * 2)
061 :     DO Wopen WITH 5 + base, 35, 15 + base, 45
062 :     @  7+base, 37 PROMPT "Add    "
063 :     @  9+base, 37 PROMPT "Edit   "
064 :     @ 11+base, 37 PROMPT "Scan   "
065 :     @ 13+base, 37 PROMPT "Delete"
066 :     MENU TO dummy
067 :
068 : *******************
069 :
070 : PROCEDURE Menu3
071 :
072 :     * This is just a stub
073 :
074 : *******************
075 :
076 : PROCEDURE Menu4
077 :
078 :     * This is just a stub
079 :
080 : *******************
081 :
082 : PROCEDURE Menu5
083 :
084 :     * This is just a stub
085 :
086 : *******************
087 :
088 : PROCEDURE Menu6
089 :
```

```
     * This is just a stub

   ********************

   PROCEDURE Wopen

      PARAMETERS _w1, _w2, _w3, _w4

      @ _w1, _w2 CLEAR TO _w3, _w4
      @ _w1, _w2 TO _w3, _w4 DOUBLE

   * End of File
```

These two pieces are the first steps of building a window system. The concept of using the SAVE TO and RESTORE FROM commands gives more depth to these functions. In the following example, we have added the saving and restoring commands to either the Wopen() or the Wclose() procedures and have created global memory variables to house each screen of information. Consider the following:

```
********************
* Name     Windowc.prg
* Author   Stephen J. Straley
* Date     July 15, 1989
* Notice   Copyright (c) 1989 Stephen J. Straley & Associates
*          All Rights Reserved
* Compile  Clipper Windowc -m
* Release  Summer 87
* Link     PLINK86 FI Windowc LIB Clipper LIB Extend;
* Note     This is the third window program file, this
*          time with a border, saving the previous screen,
*          and closing the prior screen as well.
*
********************

option = 1
SET WRAP ON
SET SCOREBOARD OFF
SET MESSAGE TO 24 CENTER
STORE "" TO ascreen, bscreen, cscreen, dscreen
DO Wopen WITH 0,0,24,79,ascreen
DO WHILE .T.
   @  5,27 PROMPT " Chart of Account      " ;
      MESSAGE "Enter/Edit COA Information"
   @  7,27 PROMPT " Transactions          " ;
      MESSAGE "Enter/Edit Transactions"
   @  9,27 PROMPT " Balancing and Posting " ;
      MESSAGE "Balance Items/Post to Ledger"
   @ 11,27 PROMPT " Reporting and Lists   " ;
      MESSAGE "Financial Reports and Listings"
   @ 13,27 PROMPT " Utilities             " ;
      MESSAGE "Managerial Utilities"
   @ 15,27 PROMPT " End of Period         " ;
```

```
      MESSAGE "End of Period Processing"
   @ 17,27 PROMPT " Quit                    " ;
      MESSAGE "Quit to DOS"
   MENU TO option
   IF EMPTY(option) .OR. option = 7
      EXIT
   ELSE
      ext = TRANSFORM(option, "9")
      DO Menu&ext.
   ENDIF
ENDDO
DO Wclose WITH ascreen

********************

PROCEDURE Menu1

  base = (option * 2)
  DO Wopen WITH 5 + base, 35, 15 + base, 45, bscreen
  @  7+base, 37 PROMPT "Add   "
  @  9+base, 37 PROMPT "Edit  "
  @ 11+base, 37 PROMPT "Scan  "
  @ 13+base, 37 PROMPT "Delete"
  MENU TO dummy
  DO Wclose WITH bscreen

********************

PROCEDURE Menu2

  base = (option * 2)
  DO Wopen WITH 5 + base, 35, 15 + base, 45, bscreen
  @  7+base, 37 PROMPT "Add   "
  @  9+base, 37 PROMPT "Edit  "
  @ 11+base, 37 PROMPT "Scan  "
  @ 13+base, 37 PROMPT "Delete"
  MENU TO dummy
  DO Wclose WITH bscreen

********************

PROCEDURE Menu3

  * This is just a stub

********************

PROCEDURE Menu4

  * This is just a stub

********************

PROCEDURE Menu5
```

```

   * This is just a stub

********************

PROCEDURE Menu6

   * This is just a stub

********************

PROCEDURE Wopen

   PARAMETERS _w1, _w2, _w3, _w4, pointer

   SAVE SCREEN TO pointer
   @ _w1, _w2 CLEAR TO _w3, _w4
   @ _w1, _w2 TO _w3, _w4 DOUBLE

*********************

PROCEDURE Wclose

   PARAMETERS screen

   IF EMPTY(PCOUNT())
      CLEAR SCREEN
   ELSE
      RESTORE SCREEN FROM screen
   ENDIF

* End of File
```

Then came the Summer '87 release and the concept of saving portions of the screen became important. Expanding the previous example, instead of using memory variables to hold the screen, we could potentially save each screen prior to the construction of a window to memory variables. Then, when the window was closed, that previous screen could be quickly brought back up. And from here, the next logical conclusion came: Use a Clipper PUBLIC array to keep the screens in order as the application progressed. Looking at the flow of a program, we could have one procedure not only clear and draw the screen, but also save the previous screen to an element in the PUBLIC array. This procedure would also increment a PUBLIC pointer that would, when incremented, position the application to the next available location in the PUBLIC array. Then we would have another procedure that would decrement the pointer for the screen array, get the previous screen, display the contents of that array subscript value, and clear out the value of that array element. In essence, we would have one procedure "push" the screen stack while another procedure would "pop" it as the program progressed.

Prior to the Summer '87 release, this was a very "memory intensive" technique, since each screen that was saved via the SAVE SCREEN TO <memvar> took 4000 bytes away from the memory pool because we could save only the entire screen to a memory variable or to an array subscript. Now, we can save screen portions to memory variables. Instead of saving the prior screens in our windowing functions, we can now save the portion of the screen that will be drawn or written over. This is very Macintosh-like in attitude and approach. Many times, with pull-down screens, much of the video does not change from one menu to the next. Now, we can think of the screen as just those portions that would be affected by the window that would be eventually drawn. Taking the preceding code, we can change it to the following:

```
********************
* Name      Windowd.prg
* Author    Stephen J. Straley
* Date      July 15, 1989
* Notice    Copyright (c) 1989 Stephen J. Straley & Associates
*           All Rights Reserved
* Compile   Clipper Windowd -m
* Release   Summer 87
* Link      PLINK86 FI Windowd LIB Clipper LIB Extend;
* Note      This is the fourth window program file, this
*           time with a border, saving the previous screen
*           portion by using the SAVESCREEN() and RESTSCREEN()
*           functions.  Additionally, we have built Wopen()
*           and Wclose() which now uses the arrays in Clipper
*           and the concept of pushing and popping the window
*           stack with the variable scr_level.
*
********************

option = 1
SET WRAP ON
SET SCOREBOARD OFF
SET MESSAGE TO 24 CENTER
*
* These are our arrays for the screens/windows
*
PUBLIC allscreens[20], scr_level, allcolor[20], allwindows[20]
AFILL(allscreens, "")
AFILL(allcolor, "")
AFILL(allwindows, "")
scr_level = 1
*
scrframe = CHR(201) + CHR(205) + CHR(187) + CHR(186) + ;
           CHR(188) + CHR(205) + CHR(200) + CHR(186)

Wopen(0,0,24,79)
DO WHILE .T.
   @ 5,27 PROMPT " Chart of Account       " ;
      MESSAGE "Enter/Edit COA Information"
   @ 7,27 PROMPT " Transactions           " ;
      MESSAGE "Enter/Edit Transactions"
   @ 9,27 PROMPT " Balancing and Posting " ;
      MESSAGE "Balance Items/Post to Ledger"
```

```
044 :    @ 11,27 PROMPT " Reporting and Lists   " ;
045 :        MESSAGE "Financial Reports and Listings"
046 :    @ 13,27 PROMPT " Utilities            " ;
047 :        MESSAGE "Managerial Utilities"
048 :    @ 15,27 PROMPT " End of Period        " ;
049 :        MESSAGE "End of Period Processing"
050 :    @ 17,27 PROMPT " Quit                 " ;
051 :        MESSAGE "Quit to DOS"
052 :    MENU TO option
053 :    IF EMPTY(option) .OR. option = 7
054 :        EXIT
055 :    ELSE
056 :        ext = TRANSFORM(option, "9")
057 :        DO Menu&ext.
058 :    ENDIF
059 : ENDDO
060 : Wclose()
061 :
062 : ********************
063 :
064 : PROCEDURE Menu1
065 :
066 :    base = (option * 2)
067 :    Wopen(5 + base, 35, 15 + base, 45)
068 :    @  7+base, 37 PROMPT "Add    "
069 :    @  9+base, 37 PROMPT "Edit   "
070 :    @ 11+base, 37 PROMPT "Scan   "
071 :    @ 13+base, 37 PROMPT "Delete"
072 :    MENU TO dummy
073 :    Wclose()
074 :
075 : ********************
076 :
077 : PROCEDURE Menu2
078 :
079 :    base = (option * 2)
080 :    Wopen(5 + base, 35, 15 + base, 45)
081 :    @  7+base, 37 PROMPT "Add    "
082 :    @  9+base, 37 PROMPT "Edit   "
083 :    @ 11+base, 37 PROMPT "Scan   "
084 :    @ 13+base, 37 PROMPT "Delete"
085 :    MENU TO dummy
086 :    Wclose()
087 :
088 : ********************
089 :
090 : PROCEDURE Menu3
091 :
092 :    * This is just a stub
093 :
094 : ********************
095 :
096 : PROCEDURE Menu4
097 :
```

```
   Wopen(13,17,20,40)
   DO WHILE .T.
      @ 14,20 PROMPT " Balance Sheet     "
      @ 15,20 PROMPT " Income Statement  "
      @ 16,20 PROMPT " Trial Balance     "
      @ 17,20 PROMPT " Transactions      "
      @ 18,20 PROMPT " Standard Entries  "
      @ 19,20 PROMPT " Chart of Accounts "
      MENU TO newoption
      IF EMPTY(newoption)
         EXIT
      ELSE
         Wopen(14+newoption, 25, 16+newoption, 65)
         DO WHILE .T.
            @ 15+newoption, 27 PROMPT " Screen "
            @ 15+newoption, 40 PROMPT " Printer "
            @ 15+newoption, 55 PROMPT " File "
            MENU TO this
            IF EMPTY(this)
               EXIT
            ENDIF
         ENDDO
         Wclose()
      ENDIF
   ENDDO
   Wclose()

********************

PROCEDURE Menu5

  * This is just a stub

********************

PROCEDURE Menu6

  * This is just a stub

********************

FUNCTION Wopen

   PARAMETERS _w1, _w2, _w3, _w4

   allcolor[scr_level]   = SETCOLOR()
   allscreens[scr_level] = SAVESCREEN(_w1, _w2, _w3, _w4)
   allwindows[scr_level] = TRANSFORM(_w1, "99") + "/" + ;
      TRANSFORM(_w2, "99") + "/" + TRANSFORM(_w3, "99") + ;
      "/" + TRANSFORM(_w4, "99")
   scr_level = IF(scr_level = 20, scr_level, scr_level + 1)
   @ _w1, _w2, _w3, _w4 BOX SPACE(9)
   @ _w1, _w2, _w3, _w4 BOX SUBSTR(scrframe, 1, 8)
```

```
151 :     RETURN(scr_level)
152 :
153 : *********************
154 :
155 : FUNCTION Wclose
156 :
157 :     PARAMETERS _w1, _w2, _w3, _w4
158 :
159 :     IF PCOUNT() = 4
160 :        _wcol = SETCOLOR()
161 :     ELSEIF PCOUNT() = 0 .OR. PCOUNT() = 1
162 :        IF PCOUNT() = 1
163 :           * This allows a specific window to be closed
164 :           * if the programmer knows this in advance;
165 :           * otherwise, just let the system guess!
166 :           scr_level = _w1 + 1
167 :        ENDIF
168 :        _w1 = VAL(SUBSTR(allwindows[scr_level - 1], 1,  2))
169 :        _w2 = VAL(SUBSTR(allwindows[scr_level - 1], 4,  2))
170 :        _w3 = VAL(SUBSTR(allwindows[scr_level - 1], 7,  2))
171 :        _w4 = VAL(SUBSTR(allwindows[scr_level - 1], 10, 2))
172 :        IF _w1 = -1
173 :           RESTSCREEN(0,0,24,79, allscreens[scr_level-1] )
174 :           scr_level = IF(scr_level = 1, scr_level, scr_level - 1)
175 :           allscreens[scr_level+1] = ""
176 :           allcolor[scr_level+1] = ""
177 :           allwindows[scr_level] = ""
178 :           RETURN(.T.)
179 :        ENDIF
180 :     ENDIF
181 :
182 :     IF PCOUNT() != 1
183 :        scr_level = IF(scr_level = 1, scr_level, scr_level - 1)
184 :     ENDIF
185 :
186 :
187 :     _temp = allscreens[scr_level]
188 :
189 :     RESTSCREEN(_w1, _w2, _w3, _w4, _temp)
190 :
191 :     allscreens[scr_level+1] = ""
192 :     allcolor[scr_level+1] = ""
193 :     allwindows[scr_level] = ""
194 :     RETURN(.T.)
195 :
196 : * End of File
```

Before going on to the next level of this discussion, let us go through the previous example and highlight a few of the major points. This time, we have initialized three arrays, **allscreens[]**, **allcolor[]**, and **allwindows[]**. In addition, there is a PUBLIC pointer variable named **scr_level**. The concept is simple; as the programmer moves down from menu level to menu level, a call to the Wopen() function is made. In this function, the array pointer named **scr_level** is incremented before values are stored to the three arrays. Next, the current screen color is stored to the **allcolor[]** array at the subscript position on **scr_level**. Along with this, the screen is saved at the four coordinates (line 144) using the SAVESCREEN() function; again, it is saved to the current counter position of **scr_level** in the **allscreens[]** array. Finally, the coordinates are TRANSFORMed into four string pieces (lines 145 through 147) using the "/ " as a delimiter between each value. In other words, if the window began at coordinates 10,23 and continued on to coordinates 20,40, the string in the array **allwindows[]** at subscript position **scr_level** would be "10/23/20/40." As you can probably guess, the Parsing() function described in Chapter 1 will come in handy.

Once the window is opened, closing it is just as easy, if not easier. Since we have previously saved the color of the screen, the portion of the screen that has been written over with information, and the window coordinates to array subscript values, we can simply decrement the **scr_level** counter, evaluate the values of the three array subscripts, and reverse the process.

Now, we are beginning to make a windowing system that could fit our needs. From this point, adding additional "nice-to-haves" is easy. Since we have the video coordinates of the window, it would take little effort to build a shadow line surrounding the frame of the border or to add colors to our windows. Here is an example of this addition:

```
********************
* Name      Windowe.prg
* Author    Stephen J. Straley
* Date      July 15, 1989
* Notice    Copyright (c) 1989 Stephen J. Straley & Associates
*           All Rights Reserved
* Compile   Clipper Windowe -m
* Release   Summer 87
* Link      PLINK86 FI Windowe LIB Clipper LIB Extend;
* Note      This is the fifth window program file, this
*           time with a border, saving the previous screen
*           portion by using the SAVESCREEN() and RESTSCREEN()
*           functions.  Additionally, we have built Wopen()
*           and Wclose() which now uses the arrays in Clipper
*           and the concept of pushing and popping the window
*           stack with the variable scr_level.  This also
*           incorporates different colors for the windows
*           as well as fake shadow lines.
*
********************

option = 1
SET WRAP ON
SET SCOREBOARD OFF
SET MESSAGE TO 24 CENTER
*
* These are our arrays for the screens/windows
*
```

```
029 : PUBLIC allscreens[20], scr_level, allcolor[20], allwindows[20]
030 : AFILL(allscreens, "")
031 : AFILL(allcolor, "")
032 : AFILL(allwindows, "")
033 : scr_level = 1
034 : *
035 : scrframe = CHR(201) + CHR(205) + CHR(187) + CHR(186) + ;
036 :             CHR(188) + CHR(205) + CHR(200) + CHR(186)
037 :
038 : Wopen(0,0,24,79,"7/1, 1/7")
039 : DO WHILE .T.
040 :     @  5,27 PROMPT " Chart of Account      " ;
041 :         MESSAGE "Enter/Edit COA Information"
042 :     @  7,27 PROMPT " Transactions          " ;
043 :         MESSAGE "Enter/Edit Transactions"
044 :     @  9,27 PROMPT " Balancing and Posting " ;
045 :         MESSAGE "Balance Items/Post to Ledger"
046 :     @ 11,27 PROMPT " Reporting and Lists   " ;
047 :         MESSAGE "Financial Reports and Listings"
048 :     @ 13,27 PROMPT " Utilities             " ;
049 :         MESSAGE "Managerial Utilities"
050 :     @ 15,27 PROMPT " End of Period         " ;
051 :         MESSAGE "End of Period Processing"
052 :     @ 17,27 PROMPT " Quit                  " ;
053 :         MESSAGE "Quit to DOS"
054 :     MENU TO option
055 :     IF EMPTY(option) .OR. option = 7
056 :         EXIT
057 :     ELSE
058 :         ext = TRANSFORM(option, "9")
059 :         DO Menu&ext.
060 :     ENDIF
061 : ENDDO
062 : Wclose()
063 :
064 : ********************
065 :
066 : PROCEDURE Menu1
067 :
068 :     base = (option * 2)
069 :     Wopen(5 + base, 35, 15 + base, 45, "7/2, 2/7", 3)
070 :     @  7+base, 37 PROMPT "Add   "
071 :     @  9+base, 37 PROMPT "Edit  "
072 :     @ 11+base, 37 PROMPT "Scan  "
073 :     @ 13+base, 37 PROMPT "Delete"
074 :     MENU TO dummy
075 :     Wclose()
076 :
077 : ********************
078 :
079 : PROCEDURE Menu2
080 :
081 :     base = (option * 2)
082 :     Wopen(5 + base, 35, 15 + base, 45, "7/2, 2/7", 1)
```

```
  @  7+base, 37 PROMPT "Add   "
  @  9+base, 37 PROMPT "Edit  "
  @ 11+base, 37 PROMPT "Scan  "
  @ 13+base, 37 PROMPT "Delete"
  MENU TO dummy
  Wclose()

********************

PROCEDURE Menu3

  * This is just a stub

********************

PROCEDURE Menu4

   Wopen(13,17,20,40, "2+/7, 7/2", 7)
   DO WHILE .T.
      @ 14,20 PROMPT " Balance Sheet      "
      @ 15,20 PROMPT " Income Statement   "
      @ 16,20 PROMPT " Trial Balance      "
      @ 17,20 PROMPT " Transactions       "
      @ 18,20 PROMPT " Standard Entries   "
      @ 19,20 PROMPT " Chart of Accounts "
      MENU TO newoption
      IF EMPTY(newoption)
         EXIT
      ELSE
         Wopen(14+newoption, 25, 16+newoption, 65,"3/0,0/3",9)
         DO WHILE .T.
            @ 15+newoption, 27 PROMPT " Screen "
            @ 15+newoption, 40 PROMPT " Printer "
            @ 15+newoption, 55 PROMPT " File "
            MENU TO this
            IF EMPTY(this)
               EXIT
            ENDIF
         ENDDO
         Wclose()
      ENDIF
   ENDDO
   Wclose()

********************

PROCEDURE Menu5

  * This is just a stub

********************

PROCEDURE Menu6

```

```
137 :    * This is just a stub
138 :
139 : * ***********************************************
140 : * * The following procedure(s)/function(s) are  *
141 : * * part of Steve Straley's ToolkiT(tm) -        *
142 : * * Release 2, published by Four Seasons         *
143 : * * Publishing Co., Inc.  All Rights Reserved    *
144 : * * Information: 212-599-2141 / 800-662-2278     *
145 : * * All Rights Reserved                          *
146 : * ***********************************************
147 :
148 : FUNCTION Wopen
149 :
150 :     PARAMETERS _w1, _w2, _w3, _w4, _w5, _w6
151 :
152 :     IF PCOUNT() = 4
153 :        _w5 = SETCOLOR()
154 :        _w6 = 5
155 :     ELSEIF PCOUNT() = 5
156 :        _w6 = 5
157 :     ENDIF
158 :
159 :     allcolor[scr_level]   = _w5
160 :     *
161 :     * Must now calculate the windowed area including
162 :     * the shadow line, if applicable!
163 :     *
164 :     IF _w6 = 3
165 :        _n1 = _w1
166 :        _n2 = _w2
167 :        _n3 = _w3+1
168 :        _n4 = _w4+2
169 :     ELSEIF _w6 = 1
170 :        _n1 = _w1
171 :        _n2 = _w2-2
172 :        _n3 = _w3+1
173 :        _n4 = _w4
174 :     ELSEIF _w6 = 7
175 :        _n1 = _w1-1
176 :        _n2 = _w2-2
177 :        _n3 = _w3
178 :        _n4 = _w4
179 :     ELSEIF _w6 = 9
180 :        _n1 = _w1-1
181 :        _n2 = _w2
182 :        _n3 = _w3
183 :        _n4 = _w4+2
184 :     ELSE
185 :        _n1 = _w1
186 :        _n2 = _w2
187 :        _n3 = _w3
188 :        _n4 = _w4
189 :     ENDIF
190 :
```

```

   allscreens[scr_level] = SAVESCREEN(_n1, _n2, _n3, _n4)
   allwindows[scr_level] = TRANSFORM(_n1, "99") + "/" + ;
      TRANSFORM(_n2, "99") + "/" + TRANSFORM(_n3, "99") + ;
      "/" + TRANSFORM(_n4, "99")
   allcolor[scr_level] = SETCOLOR()

   SETCOLOR(_w5)
   scr_level = IF(scr_level = 20, scr_level, scr_level + 1)
   @ _w1, _w2, _w3, _w4 BOX SPACE(9)
   @ _w1, _w2, _w3, _w4 BOX SUBSTR(scrframe, 1, 8)
   IF _w6 = 3
      @ _n3,_w2+2,_n3,_n4   BOX REPLICATE(CHR(177), 9)
      @ _w1+1,_n4-1,_n3,_n4 BOX REPLICATE(CHR(177), 9)
   ELSEIF _w6 = 1
      @ _n3,_n2,_n3,_w4-1     BOX REPLICATE(CHR(177), 9)
      @ _n1+1,_n2,_w3+1,_n2+1 BOX REPLICATE(CHR(177), 9)
   ELSEIF _w6 = 7
      @ _n1,_n2,_n1,_w4-2     BOX REPLICATE(CHR(177), 9)
      @ _n1,_n2,_n3-1,_n2+1   BOX REPLICATE(CHR(177), 9)
   ELSEIF _w6 = 9
      @ _n1,_w2+2,_n1,_n4     BOX REPLICATE(CHR(177), 9)
      @ _n1,_n4-1,_n3-1,_n4   BOX REPLICATE(CHR(177), 9)
   ENDIF
   RETURN(scr_level)

********************

FUNCTION Wclose

   PARAMETERS _w1, _w2, _w3, _w4

   IF PCOUNT() = 4
      _wcol = SETCOLOR()
   ELSEIF PCOUNT() = 0 .OR. PCOUNT() = 1
      IF PCOUNT() = 1
         * This allows a specific window to be closed
         * if the programmer knows this in advance;
         * otherwise, just let the system guess!
         scr_level = _w1 + 1
      ENDIF
      _w1 = VAL(SUBSTR(allwindows[scr_level - 1], 1,  2))
      _w2 = VAL(SUBSTR(allwindows[scr_level - 1], 4,  2))
      _w3 = VAL(SUBSTR(allwindows[scr_level - 1], 7,  2))
      _w4 = VAL(SUBSTR(allwindows[scr_level - 1], 10, 2))
      IF _w1 = -1
         RESTSCREEN(0,0,24,79, allscreens[scr_level-1] )
         scr_level = IF(scr_level = 1, scr_level, scr_level - 1)
         allscreens[scr_level+1] = ""
         allcolor[scr_level+1] = ""
         allwindows[scr_level] = ""
```

```
            RETURN(.T.)
         ENDIF
      ENDIF

      IF PCOUNT() != 1
         scr_level = IF(scr_level = 1, scr_level, scr_level - 1)
      ENDIF


      RESTSCREEN(_w1, _w2, _w3, _w4, allscreens[scr_level])
      SETCOLOR(allcolor[scr_level])

      allscreens[scr_level+1] = ""
      allcolor[scr_level+1] = ""
      allwindows[scr_level] = ""
      RETURN(.T.)

   * End of File
```

In this extension of our example windowing program, we have added two additional parameters to our Wopen() function: the color string that is used when opening the window and the style of the window's shadow. The following will clarify the last phrase of that sentence. Several Clipper add-on libraries, including Steve Straley's ToolkiT and Dirk Lesko's FUNCky, have standardized on the parameter format for calling the shadowing routines. Consider the following chart:

7	8	9
4	5	6
1	2	3

This is the outline of a standard numeric keypad on most computers. The shadowing direction for the windows directly correlates with this chart. For example, if the shadow were to originate on the bottom rightmost corner of the window, extending up the right side of the window as well as along the bottom edge, the parameter value used to indicate this would be a 3, since this is the bottom, rightmost number on the keypad. The same pattern holds for the 7, 9, and 1 parameter values. Any other value represents no shadow.

Of course, we could change the parameters slightly to have different styles of shadowing, shadow directions, and even true shadowing. We will go into that concept in a moment. And as for the color string being passed to the function, we could embellish on this to pass words or variables with color-worded strings to the function, such as:

```
Wopen(4,10,20,70,"Blue", "White", "Blue", "Green", 3)
```

This would tell the Wopen() function that the standard colors for the windowed area are a blue background with white letters and an enhanced color set of a blue background with green letters. Of course, the shadowing direction will be a 3, originating from the bottom rightmost corner of the windowed area.

This is a rough overview of the windowing possibilities. In the next few sections of this chapter, we will embellish on some screen and window possibilities that could be added to the above samples. The point of this is simple: Windowing is necessary for an application. And no matter how Nantucket chooses to implement the concepts of windowing, the language is still flexible enough for you to develop your own windowing style and concepts. Because of this, the language becomes an extension of you; your applications are just reflections of this style.

ATTRIBUTES AND SCREEN COLORS

Every screen has text and coordinating video attribute bytes. For example, a 25-row by 80-column screen contains 2000 characters of actual text. However, each text has an associated video attribute byte. This means that a normal, full screen of information is really 4000 bytes of information: 2000 bytes for text and 2000 bytes for the video attributes for each character. The order of the information in this string is simple: first the character for the display, followed by the video attribute byte. For example, if we were to look at the portion of the screen that had the letter "H" displayed on a blue and white screen, the string for this would be "H"+CHR(32). Another good example of this is with black-and-white screens being saved to a text file. Consider this code fragment:

```
********************
* Name      Rawscrn.prg
* Author    Stephen J. Straley
* Date      July 1, 1989
* Notice    Copyright (c) 1989 Stephen J. Straley & Associates
*           All Rights Reserved
* Compile   Clipper Rawscrn -m
* Release   Summer 87
* Link      PLINK86 FI Rawscrn LIB Clipper LIB Extend;
* Note      This program shows the CHR(7) as the video
*           attribute for each character of the DIR
*
********************

SETCOLOR("")     && This makes sure that the screen is
                 && set to 7/0, 0/7
CLEAR SCREEN
RUN DIR /W  && This is just to get a partial screen
MEMOWRIT("RAWSCRN.TXT", SAVESCREEN(0,0,24,79))
CLEAR
variable = SUBSTR(MEMOREAD("RAWSCRN.TXT"), 50, 10)
WAIT "And now to type out a part of the file..."
```

```
? variable

* End of File
```

Notice that the bell goes off every time a letter is displayed. That is caused by the CHR(7) video attribute byte that tells Ctrl-G (or the bell) to sound.

With the Summer '87 release of Clipper and the SAVESCREEN() function we are able to look at specific locations of the screen as well as the video byte for those same locations. Remember, any specific row,column coordinate will yield a 2-byte long string. From this we could begin to consider the possibility of manipulating the screen outside of the normal SET COLOR TO command or SETCOLOR() function. Since we can obtain the actual displayed string from the screen, we could potentially change the contents, including the video attribute byte, and redisplay the information in a different format or even different color. The important perception you must carry into this chapter is the ability to see the screen as a string. The screen is not some mystical address in the computer that controls how characters appear; that's left to Clipper and the assembly programmers in the world who like to get their hands dirty. To us, the screen is nothing more than a long string and as such, we have control over it with functions like SAVESCREEN(), RESTSCREEN(), STUFF(), SUBSTR(), and many more.

To see this point more clearly, let us examine the program listed below:

```
********************
* Name      Text1.prg
* Author    Stephen J. Straley
* Date      July 15, 1989
* Notice    Copyright (c) 1989 Stephen J. Straley & Associates
*           All Rights Reserved
* Compile   Clipper Text1 -m
* Release   Summer 87
* Link      PLINK86 FI Text1 LIB Clipper LIB Extend;
* Note      This shows how we can see items on the screen
*           even after they are displayed...
*
********************

string = "This is a test to see if items in this " + ;
         "string can be plucked off of the screen " + ;
         "by the end user."

CLEAR SCREEN
@ 0,0 SAY "ESC to Quit..."
MEMOEDIT(string, 2,30,8,50,.F.,.F.)
row = 2
col = 30
DO WHILE .T.
   @ 10,10 SAY "Enter a ROW Number " GET row RANGE 2,8
   @ 12,10 SAY "    and COL Number " GET col RANGE 30,50
   READ
```

```
28 :     IF LASTKEY() = 27
29 :        EXIT
30 :     ENDIF
31 :     @ 14,10 SAY "The character at those coordinates is " +;
32 :                 "the letter ... "
33 :     @ 16,40 SAY The_char(row, col)
34 :     var = The_char(row,col)
35 :     @ row,col GET var
36 :     CLEAR GETS
37 :     @ 18,10 SAY "Any key to continue...."
38 :     INKEY(0)
39 :     @ row,col SAY var
40 :     @ 10,00 CLEAR
41 : ENDDO
42 :
43 : * ***********************************************
44 : * * The following procedure(s)/function(s) are  *
45 : * * part of Steve Straley's ToolkiT(tm) -       *
46 : * * Release 2, published by Four Seasons        *
47 : * * Publishing Co., Inc.  All Rights Reserved   *
48 : * * Information: 212-599-2141 / 800-662-2278    *
49 : * * All Rights Reserved                         *
50 : * ***********************************************
51 :
52 : ********************
53 :
54 : FUNCTION The_char
55 :
56 :     * to return a specific character from any screen
57 :     * location already displayed.
58 :
59 :     PARAMETERS _attrow, _attcol
60 :
61 :     IF PCOUNT() != 2
62 :        RETURN("")
63 :     ENDIF
64 :
65 :     RETURN(SUBSTR(SAVESCREEN(_attrow, _attcol, _attrow, ;
66 :                   _attcol), 1, 1))
67 : * End of File
```

In the previous program, the ability to take a portion of the results from the SAVESCREEN() function is important. On line 65, the use of the SUBSTR() function actually yields the character on the screen at the specified row,column coordinates of **_attrow**, **_attcol**. With this, it is obvious that the SAVESCREEN() function will yield a 2-byte string, and that the first byte is the actual character on the screen. Working with the video byte is not as simple because the value that is obtained from the SAVESCREEN() function for that byte is a number ranging from 0 to 127. Therefore, a formula is needed that will convert a video byte with an ASCII value for 32 into something usable such as "0/2."

In the following example, we show how the second byte, the video attribute byte at the specified row,column coordinates can be obtained and converted to a string:

```
001 : ********************
002 : * Name      Text2.prg
003 : * Author    Stephen J. Straley
004 : * Date      July 15, 1989
005 : * Notice    Copyright (c) 1989 Stephen J. Straley & Associates
006 : *           All Rights Reserved
007 : * Compile   Clipper Text2 -m
008 : * Release   Summer 87
009 : * Link      PLINK86 FI Text2 LIB Clipper LIB Extend;
010 : * Note      This shows how we can see colors on the screen
011 : *           even after they are displayed...
012 : *
013 : ********************
014 :
015 : CLEAR SCREEN
016 : @ 0,0 SAY "ESC to Quit..."
017 : DECLARE string[8]
018 : string[1] = " This is a test to see  "
019 : string[2] = " if items in this       "
020 : string[3] = " string can be plucked   "
021 : string[4] = " off of the screen by    "
022 : string[5] = " the end user. Also,     "
023 : string[6] = " the colors will change  "
024 : string[7] = " for each line that is   "
025 : string[8] = " displayed...            "
026 :
027 : FOR x = 1 TO 8
028 :    var = "0/" + TRANSFORM(x, "9")
029 :    SETCOLOR(var)
030 :    @ x,30 SAY string[x]
031 :    @ x,1 SAY "Color = " + var + " | Row = " + ;
032 :                LTRIM(STR(x+1))
033 : NEXT
034 :
035 : row = 2
036 : SETCOLOR("")
037 : DO WHILE .T.
038 :    @ 10,10 SAY "Enter a ROW Number " GET row RANGE 2,8
039 :    READ
040 :    IF LASTKEY() = 27
041 :       EXIT
042 :    ENDIF
043 :    *
044 :    * Remember, row 2 to end-use will be row 3 on the
045 :    * screen!
046 :    *
047 :    @ 14,10 SAY "The ASCII value for the attribute " + ;
048 :                "byte on that row is ... "
049 :    @ 16,40 SAY Attribute(row-1, 30)
050 :    @ 18,10 SAY "And the string for this byte is " +;
```

```
051 :                    Set_color(Attribute(row-1, 30))
052 :      @ 20,10 SAY "Any key to continue...."
053 :      INKEY(0)
054 :      @ 10,00 CLEAR
055 : ENDDO
056 : CLEAR SCREEN
057 :
058 : * ********************************************
059 : * * The following procedure(s)/function(s) are  *
060 : * * part of Steve Straley's ToolkiT(tm) -       *
061 : * * Release 2, published by Four Seasons        *
062 : * * Publishing Co., Inc.  All Rights Reserved   *
063 : * * Information: 212-599-2141 / 800-662-2278    *
064 : * * All Rights Reserved                         *
065 : * ********************************************
066 :
067 : ********************
068 :
069 : FUNCTION Attribute
070 :
071 :      * to return the screen attribute byte for any given row
072 :      * and column position to an already-displayed screen.
073 :
074 :      PARAMETERS _attrow, _attcol
075 :
076 :      IF PCOUNT() != 2
077 :         RETURN(0)
078 :      ENDIF
079 :      IF TYPE("_attrow") + TYPE("_attcol") != "NN"
080 :         RETURN(0)
081 :      ENDIF
082 :
083 :      RETURN(ASC(SUBSTR(SAVESCREEN(_attrow, _attcol, ;
084 :                  _attrow, _attcol), 2, 1)))
085 :
086 : *********************
087 :
088 : FUNCTION Set_color
089 :
090 :      PARAMETERS _setvalue
091 :
092 :      PRIVATE _tval1, _tval2, _retstr
093 :
094 :      * based on the ASCII value of the screen
095 :      * attribute byte as established by the
096 :      * ATTRIBUTE() function, this function
097 :      * returns a string with the appropriate
098 :      * screen colors.
099 :
100 :      _retstr = ""
101 :
102 :      IF PCOUNT() = 1
103 :         IF TYPE("_setvalue") = "N"
104 :            _tval1 = VAL(TRANSFORM(_setvalue % 16, "99"))
```

```
105 :         _tval2 = VAL(TRANSFORM(_setvalue / 16 , "99"))
106 :
107 :         IF _tval1 > 7
108 :            _retstr = LTRIM(TRANSFORM(_tval1 - 8, "99")) + ;
109 :                      "+/" + LTRIM(TRANSFORM(_tval2-1,"99"))
110 :         ELSE
111 :            _retstr = LTRIM(TRANSFORM(_tval1, "99")) +;
112 :                      "/" + LTRIM(TRANSFORM(_tval2, "99"))
113 :         ENDIF
114 :      ENDIF
115 :   ENDIF
116 :   RETURN(_retstr)
117 :
118 : * End of File
```

As you can see on lines 83 and 84, the Attribute() function refers to the second byte of the RETURN value from the SAVESCREEN() function. That then is passed to the Set_color() function, which takes that number and performs a two-pass formula conversion. The video string that we all can recognize is a combination of the ASCII value of the video attribute byte divided by 16 and that same number and the modulus (or remainder) divided by 16. This function is outlined on lines 86 through 118.

Now it should be clear that the screen is nothing more than a string. In the past when an application built on multiple windows with different colors displayed a message outside of the current window, that message would typically be displayed in the wrong color. Consider this:

```
********************
* Name      Windowf.prg
* Author    Stephen J. Straley
* Date      July 15, 1989
* Notice    Copyright (c) 1989 Stephen J. Straley & Associates
*           All Rights Reserved
* Compile   Clipper Windowf -m
* Release   Summer 87
* Link      PLINK86 FI Windowf LIB Clipper LIB Extend;
* Note      This is the sixth window program file, this
*           time with a border, saving the previous screen
*           portion by using the SAVESCREEN() and RESTSCREEN()
*           functions.  Additionally, we have built Wopen()
*           and Wclose() which now uses the arrays in Clipper
*           and the concept of pushing and popping the window
*           stack with the variable scr_level.  This also
*           incorporates different colors for the windows
*           as well as fake shadow lines.
*
*           This program shows how the video byte can be
*           obtained from the screen yet show a different
*           color!
*
********************
```

```

option = 1
SET WRAP ON
SET SCOREBOARD OFF
SET MESSAGE TO 24 CENTER
*
* These are our arrays for the screens/windows
*
PUBLIC allscreens[20], scr_level, allcolor[20], allwindows[20]
AFILL(allscreens, "")
AFILL(allcolor, "")
AFILL(allwindows, "")
scr_level = 1
*
scrframe = CHR(201) + CHR(205) + CHR(187) + CHR(186) + ;
           CHR(188) + CHR(205) + CHR(200) + CHR(186)

KEYBOARD "R" + "B"
Wopen(0,0,24,79,"7/1, 1/7")
DO WHILE .T.
   @  5,27 PROMPT " Chart of Account       " ;
      MESSAGE "Enter/Edit COA Information"
   @  7,27 PROMPT " Transactions           " ;
      MESSAGE "Enter/Edit Transactions"
   @  9,27 PROMPT " Balancing and Posting " ;
      MESSAGE "Balance Items/Post to Ledger"
   @ 11,27 PROMPT " Reporting and Lists    " ;
      MESSAGE "Financial Reports and Listings"
   @ 13,27 PROMPT " Utilities              " ;
      MESSAGE "Managerial Utilities"
   @ 15,27 PROMPT " End of Period          " ;
      MESSAGE "End of Period Processing"
   @ 17,27 PROMPT " Quit                   " ;
      MESSAGE "Quit to DOS"
   MENU TO option
   IF EMPTY(option) .OR. option = 7
      EXIT
   ELSE
      ext = TRANSFORM(option, "9")
      DO Menu&ext.
   ENDIF
ENDDO
Wclose()

********************

PROCEDURE Menu1

  base = (option * 2)
  Wopen(5 + base, 35, 15 + base, 45, "7/2, 2/7", 3)
  @  7+base, 37 PROMPT "Add   "
  @  9+base, 37 PROMPT "Edit  "
  @ 11+base, 37 PROMPT "Scan  "
  @ 13+base, 37 PROMPT "Delete"
```

```
079 :    MENU TO dummy
080 :    Wclose()
081 :
082 : ********************
083 :
084 : PROCEDURE Menu2
085 :
086 :    base = (option * 2)
087 :    Wopen(5 + base, 35, 15 + base, 45, "7/2, 2/7", 1)
088 :    @  7+base, 37 PROMPT "Add    "
089 :    @  9+base, 37 PROMPT "Edit   "
090 :    @ 11+base, 37 PROMPT "Scan   "
091 :    @ 13+base, 37 PROMPT "Delete"
092 :    MENU TO dummy
093 :    Wclose()
094 :
095 : ********************
096 :
097 : PROCEDURE Menu3
098 :
099 :    * This is just a stub
100 :
101 : ********************
102 :
103 : PROCEDURE Menu4
104 :
105 :    Wopen(13,17,20,40, "2+/7, 7/2", 7)
106 :    DO WHILE .T.
107 :       @ 14,20 PROMPT " Balance Sheet     "
108 :       @ 15,20 PROMPT " Income Statement  "
109 :       @ 16,20 PROMPT " Trial Balance     "
110 :       @ 17,20 PROMPT " Transactions      "
111 :       @ 18,20 PROMPT " Standard Entries  "
112 :       @ 19,20 PROMPT " Chart of Accounts "
113 :       MENU TO newoption
114 :       IF EMPTY(newoption)
115 :          EXIT
116 :       ELSE
117 :          Wopen(14+newoption, 25, 16+newoption, 65,"3/0,0/3",9)
118 :          oldcolor = SETCOLOR()
119 :          SETCOLOR(Set_color(Attribute(22,1)))
120 :          @ 22,1 SAY "The current color is &oldcolor. but " + ;
121 :                     "the color of this line is " + ;
122 :                     SET_COLOR(ATTRIBUTE(22,1))
123 :          INKEY(0)
124 :          @ 22,1 SAY SPACE(70)
125 :          SETCOLOR(oldcolor)
126 :          DO WHILE .T.
127 :             @ 15+newoption, 27 PROMPT " Screen "
128 :             @ 15+newoption, 40 PROMPT " Printer "
129 :             @ 15+newoption, 55 PROMPT " File "
130 :             MENU TO this
131 :             IF EMPTY(this)
132 :                EXIT
```

```
133 :              ENDIF
134 :           ENDDO
135 :           Wclose()
136 :        ENDIF
137 :    ENDDO
138 :    Wclose()
139 :
140 : *******************
141 :
142 : PROCEDURE Menu5
143 :
144 :    * This is just a stub
145 :
146 : *******************
147 :
148 : PROCEDURE Menu6
149 :
150 :    * This is just a stub
151 :
152 : * ***********************************************
153 : * * The following procedure(s)/function(s) are  *
154 : * * part of Steve Straley's ToolkiT(tm) -       *
155 : * * Release 2, published by Four Seasons        *
156 : * * Publishing Co., Inc.  All Rights Reserved   *
157 : * * Information: 212-599-2141 / 800-662-2278    *
158 : * * All Rights Reserved                         *
159 : * ***********************************************
160 :
161 : FUNCTION Wopen
162 :
163 :    PARAMETERS _w1, _w2, _w3, _w4, _w5, _w6
164 :
165 :    IF PCOUNT() = 4
166 :       _w5 = SETCOLOR()
167 :       _w6 = 5
168 :    ELSEIF PCOUNT() = 5
169 :       _w6 = 5
170 :    ENDIF
171 :
172 :    allcolor[scr_level]   = _w5
173 :    *
174 :    * Must now calculate the windowed area including
175 :    * the shadow line, if applicable!
176 :    *
177 :    IF _w6 = 3
178 :       _n1 = _w1
179 :       _n2 = _w2
180 :       _n3 = _w3+1
181 :       _n4 = _w4+2
182 :    ELSEIF _w6 = 1
183 :       _n1 = _w1
184 :       _n2 = _w2-2
185 :       _n3 = _w3+1
186 :       _n4 = _w4
```

```
   ELSEIF _w6 = 7
      _n1 = _w1-1
      _n2 = _w2-2
      _n3 = _w3
      _n4 = _w4
   ELSEIF _w6 = 9
      _n1 = _w1-1
      _n2 = _w2
      _n3 = _w3
      _n4 = _w4+2
   ELSE
      _n1 = _w1
      _n2 = _w2
      _n3 = _w3
      _n4 = _w4
   ENDIF
   allscreens[scr_level] = SAVESCREEN(_n1, _n2, _n3, _n4)
   allwindows[scr_level] = TRANSFORM(_n1, "99") + "/" + ;
      TRANSFORM(_n2, "99") + "/" + TRANSFORM(_n3, "99") + ;
      "/" + TRANSFORM(_n4, "99")
   allcolor[scr_level] = SETCOLOR()
   SETCOLOR(_w5)
   scr_level = IF(scr_level = 20, scr_level, scr_level + 1)
   @ _w1, _w2, _w3, _w4 BOX SPACE(9)
   @ _w1, _w2, _w3, _w4 BOX SUBSTR(scrframe, 1, 8)
   IF _w6 = 3
      @ _n3,_w2+2,_n3,_n4   BOX REPLICATE(CHR(177), 9)
      @ _w1+1,_n4-1,_n3,_n4 BOX REPLICATE(CHR(177), 9)
   ELSEIF _w6 = 1
      @ _n3,_n2,_n3,_w4-1     BOX REPLICATE(CHR(177), 9)
      @ _n1+1,_n2,_w3+1,_n2+1 BOX REPLICATE(CHR(177), 9)
   ELSEIF _w6 = 7
      @ _n1,_n2,_n1,_w4-2     BOX REPLICATE(CHR(177), 9)
      @ _n1,_n2,_n3-1,_n2+1   BOX REPLICATE(CHR(177), 9)
   ELSEIF _w6 = 9
      @ _n1,_w2+2,_n1,_n4     BOX REPLICATE(CHR(177), 9)
      @ _n1,_n4-1,_n3-1,_n4   BOX REPLICATE(CHR(177), 9)
   ENDIF
   RETURN(scr_level)
*********************
FUNCTION Wclose
   PARAMETERS _w1, _w2, _w3, _w4
   IF PCOUNT() = 4
      _wcol = SETCOLOR()
   ELSEIF PCOUNT() = 0 .OR. PCOUNT() = 1
      IF PCOUNT() = 1
         * This allows a specific window to be closed
```

```
241 :                * if the programmer knows this in advance;
242 :                * otherwise, just let the system guess!
243 :                scr_level = _w1 + 1
244 :           ENDIF
245 :           _w1 = VAL(SUBSTR(allwindows[scr_level - 1], 1,  2))
246 :           _w2 = VAL(SUBSTR(allwindows[scr_level - 1], 4,  2))
247 :           _w3 = VAL(SUBSTR(allwindows[scr_level - 1], 7,  2))
248 :           _w4 = VAL(SUBSTR(allwindows[scr_level - 1], 10, 2))
249 :           IF _w1 = -1
250 :                RESTSCREEN(0,0,24,79, allscreens[scr_level-1] )
251 :                scr_level = IF(scr_level = 1, scr_level, scr_level - 1)
252 :                allscreens[scr_level+1] = ""
253 :                allcolor[scr_level+1] = ""
254 :                allwindows[scr_level] = ""
255 :                RETURN(.T.)
256 :           ENDIF
257 :      ENDIF
258 :
259 :      IF PCOUNT() != 1
260 :           scr_level = IF(scr_level = 1, scr_level, scr_level - 1)
261 :      ENDIF
262 :
263 :
264 :      RESTSCREEN(_w1, _w2, _w3, _w4, allscreens[scr_level])
265 :      SETCOLOR(allcolor[scr_level])
266 :
267 :      allscreens[scr_level+1] = ""
268 :      allcolor[scr_level+1] = ""
269 :      allwindows[scr_level] = ""
270 :      RETURN(.T.)
271 :
272 : * ***********************************************
273 : * * The following procedure(s)/function(s) are  *
274 : * * part of Steve Straley's ToolkiT(tm) -        *
275 : * * Release 2, published by Four Seasons         *
276 : * * Publishing Co., Inc.  All Rights Reserved    *
277 : * * Information: 212-599-2141 / 800-662-2278     *
278 : * * All Rights Reserved                          *
279 : * ***********************************************
280 :
281 : ********************
282 :
283 : FUNCTION Attribute
284 :
285 :      * to return the screen attribute byte for any given row
286 :      * and column position to an already-displayed screen.
287 :
288 :      PARAMETERS _attrow, _attcol
289 :
290 :      IF PCOUNT() != 2
291 :           RETURN(0)
292 :      ENDIF
293 :      IF TYPE("_attrow") + TYPE("_attcol") != "NN"
```

```
294 :          RETURN(0)
295 :       ENDIF
296 :
297 :       RETURN(ASC(SUBSTR(SAVESCREEN(_attrow, _attcol, ;
298 :                  _attrow, _attcol), 2, 1)))
299 :
300 : *********************
301 :
302 : FUNCTION Set_color
303 :
304 :       PARAMETERS _setvalue
305 :
306 :       PRIVATE _tval1, _tval2, _retstr
307 :
308 :       * based on the ASCII value of the screen
309 :       * attribute byte as established by the
310 :       * ATTRIBUTE() function, this function
311 :       * returns a string with the appropriate
312 :       * screen colors.
313 :
314 :       _retstr = ""
315 :
316 :       IF PCOUNT() = 1
317 :          IF TYPE("_setvalue") = "N"
318 :             _tval1 = VAL(TRANSFORM(_setvalue % 16, "99"))
319 :             _tval2 = VAL(TRANSFORM(_setvalue / 16 , "99"))
320 :
321 :             IF _tval1 > 7
322 :                _retstr = LTRIM(TRANSFORM(_tval1 - 8, "99")) + ;
323 :                          "+/" + LTRIM(TRANSFORM(_tval2-1,"99"))
324 :             ELSE
325 :                _retstr = LTRIM(TRANSFORM(_tval1, "99")) +;
326 :                          "/" + LTRIM(TRANSFORM(_tval2, "99"))
327 :             ENDIF
328 :          ENDIF
329 :       ENDIF
330 :       RETURN(_retstr)
331 :
332 : * End of File
```

When the message on lines 120 through 123 is displayed, it is not displayed in the current screen color. The video attribute byte is picked up at row 22, column 1 and a message is then displayed. After the message, the color is changed back to its original value in order to continue processing normally. We could build into our windowing and ancillary display functions the feature to calculate screen displays and readjust the colors for those areas accordingly, or we could store each color change to different memory variables and manipulate accordingly.

Remember, it is important to have complete control of the screen and there are enough functions in the Clipper language that will allow you to do this.

SHADOWING

Now that we are convinced that we have control over the video bytes as well as the textual bytes, we can begin to apply this technique to our windows as well. In the past, shadow lines added depth to our windows and the extra lines added a more personal quality to our applications. These shadows were easy to attach to the windowing functions because those very functions had the coordinates of the window that are needed to offset the shadowing line. Also, the shadow lines were easy to build because they were nothing more than a REPLICATE() of CHR(177) for the width and length of one corner of the window box. Looking at the Windowd.prg program, the boxes that are drawn for the windows do not have any shadowing feature. Compare those screens with the screens from the Windowe.prg.

As more and more programs implemented this feature, one drawback of shadow lines became obvious: They overwrote information on the background palate. For example, consider a menuing system with overlaying windows. It seemed that the shadow line was always writing over that one piece of information that appeared on a previous menu. Indeed, "popping" off the window to view the information on the back window is possible, but if the shadow line were truly a shadow rather than an overwrite, no menuing change would be needed. From this came the push for true shadowing: the ability to just dull the screen in the area that would have been written over by a solid white line. This would mean developing the ability to take the information at the specific row and column positions and maintain the textual content of that screen, yet alter the video attribute. By now this "what if" should be perceived as reality since the technology to accomplish this is as easy as a FOR...NEXT loop. Here is a sample program that demonstrates this point:

```
********************
* Name      Windowg.prg
* Author    Stephen J. Straley
* Date      July 15, 1989
* Notice    Copyright (c) 1989 Stephen J. Straley & Associates
*           All Rights Reserved
* Compile   Clipper Windowg -m
* Release   Summer 87
* Link      PLINK86 FI Windowg LIB Clipper LIB Extend;
* Note      This is the seventh window program file, and
*           the only difference between this and WINDOWF.PRG
*           is that this file has TRUE shadowing!
*
********************

option = 1
SET WRAP ON
SET SCOREBOARD OFF
SET MESSAGE TO 24 CENTER
*
* These are our arrays for the screens/windows
*
```

```
023 : PUBLIC allscreens[20], scr_level, allcolor[20], allwindows[20]
024 : AFILL(allscreens, "")
025 : AFILL(allcolor, "")
026 : AFILL(allwindows, "")
027 : scr_level = 1
028 : *
029 : scrframe = CHR(201) + CHR(205) + CHR(187) + CHR(186) + ;
030 :           CHR(188) + CHR(205) + CHR(200) + CHR(186)
031 :
032 : Wopen(0,0,24,79,"7/1, 1/7")
033 : DO WHILE .T.
034 :    @  5,27 PROMPT " Chart of Account     " ;
035 :       MESSAGE "Enter/Edit COA Information"
036 :    @  7,27 PROMPT " Transactions         " ;
037 :       MESSAGE "Enter/Edit Transactions"
038 :    @  9,27 PROMPT " Balancing and Posting " ;
039 :       MESSAGE "Balance Items/Post to Ledger"
040 :    @ 11,27 PROMPT " Reporting and Lists   " ;
041 :       MESSAGE "Financial Reports and Listings"
042 :    @ 13,27 PROMPT " Utilities            " ;
043 :       MESSAGE "Managerial Utilities"
044 :    @ 15,27 PROMPT " End of Period        " ;
045 :       MESSAGE "End of Period Processing"
046 :    @ 17,27 PROMPT " Quit                 " ;
047 :       MESSAGE "Quit to DOS"
048 :    MENU TO option
049 :    IF EMPTY(option) .OR. option = 7
050 :       EXIT
051 :    ELSE
052 :       ext = TRANSFORM(option, "9")
053 :       DO Menu&ext.
054 :    ENDIF
055 : ENDDO
056 : Wclose()
057 :
058 : *******************
059 :
060 : PROCEDURE Menu1
061 :
062 :    base = (option * 2)
063 :    Wopen(5 + base, 35, 15 + base, 45, "7/2, 2/7", 3)
064 :    @  7+base, 37 PROMPT "Add    "
065 :    @  9+base, 37 PROMPT "Edit   "
066 :    @ 11+base, 37 PROMPT "Scan   "
067 :    @ 13+base, 37 PROMPT "Delete"
068 :    MENU TO dummy
069 :    Wclose()
070 :
071 : *******************
072 :
073 : PROCEDURE Menu2
074 :
075 :    base = (option * 2)
076 :    Wopen(5 + base, 35, 15 + base, 45, "7/2, 2/7", 1)
```

```
  @  7+base, 37 PROMPT "Add   "
  @  9+base, 37 PROMPT "Edit  "
  @ 11+base, 37 PROMPT "Scan  "
  @ 13+base, 37 PROMPT "Delete"
  MENU TO dummy
  Wclose()

********************

PROCEDURE Menu3

  * This is just a stub

********************

PROCEDURE Menu4

   Wopen(13,17,20,40, "2+/7, 7/2", 7)
   DO WHILE .T.
      @ 14,20 PROMPT " Balance Sheet      "
      @ 15,20 PROMPT " Income Statement   "
      @ 16,20 PROMPT " Trial Balance      "
      @ 17,20 PROMPT " Transactions       "
      @ 18,20 PROMPT " Standard Entries   "
      @ 19,20 PROMPT " Chart of Accounts  "
      MENU TO newoption
      IF EMPTY(newoption)
         EXIT
      ELSE
         Wopen(14+newoption, 25, 16+newoption, 65,"3/0,0/3",9)
         DO WHILE .T.
            @ 15+newoption, 27 PROMPT " Screen "
            @ 15+newoption, 40 PROMPT " Printer "
            @ 15+newoption, 55 PROMPT " File "
            MENU TO this
            IF EMPTY(this)
               EXIT
            ENDIF
         ENDDO
         Wclose()
      ENDIF
   ENDDO
   Wclose()

********************

PROCEDURE Menu5

  * This is just a stub

********************

PROCEDURE Menu6

```

```
131 :    * This is just a stub
132 :
133 : * **********************************************
134 : * * The following procedure(s)/function(s) are  *
135 : * * part of Steve Straley's ToolkiT(tm) -       *
136 : * * Release 2, published by Four Seasons        *
137 : * * Publishing Co., Inc.  All Rights Reserved   *
138 : * * Information: 212-599-2141 / 800-662-2278    *
139 : * * All Rights Reserved                         *
140 : * **********************************************
141 :
142 : FUNCTION Wopen
143 :
144 :    PARAMETERS _w1, _w2, _w3, _w4, _w5, _w6
145 :
146 :    IF PCOUNT() = 4
147 :       _w5 = SETCOLOR()
148 :       _w6 = 5
149 :    ELSEIF PCOUNT() = 5
150 :       _w6 = 5
151 :    ENDIF
152 :
153 :    allcolor[scr_level]   = _w5
154 :    *
155 :    * Must now calculate the windowed area including
156 :    * the shadow line, if applicable!
157 :    *
158 :    IF _w6 = 3
159 :       _n1 = _w1
160 :       _n2 = _w2
161 :       _n3 = _w3+1
162 :       _n4 = _w4+2
163 :    ELSEIF _w6 = 1
164 :       _n1 = _w1
165 :       _n2 = _w2-2
166 :       _n3 = _w3+1
167 :       _n4 = _w4
168 :    ELSEIF _w6 = 7
169 :       _n1 = _w1-1
170 :       _n2 = _w2-2
171 :       _n3 = _w3
172 :       _n4 = _w4
173 :    ELSEIF _w6 = 9
174 :       _n1 = _w1-1
175 :       _n2 = _w2
176 :       _n3 = _w3
177 :       _n4 = _w4+2
178 :    ELSE
179 :       _n1 = _w1
180 :       _n2 = _w2
181 :       _n3 = _w3
182 :       _n4 = _w4
183 :    ENDIF
184 :
```

```

   allscreens[scr_level] = SAVESCREEN(_n1, _n2, _n3, _n4)
   allwindows[scr_level] = TRANSFORM(_n1, "99") + "/" + ;
      TRANSFORM(_n2, "99") + "/" + TRANSFORM(_n3, "99") + ;
      "/" + TRANSFORM(_n4, "99")
   allcolor[scr_level] = SETCOLOR()

   SETCOLOR(_w5)
   scr_level = IF(scr_level = 20, scr_level, scr_level + 1)
   @ _w1, _w2, _w3, _w4 BOX SPACE(9)
   @ _w1, _w2, _w3, _w4 BOX SUBSTR(scrframe, 1, 8)
   IF _w6 = 3
      RESTSCREEN(_n3,_w2+2,_n3,_n4, ;
          DULLING(SAVESCREEN(_n3,_w2+2,_n3,_n4)))
      RESTSCREEN(_w1+1,_n4-1,_n3,_n4, ;
          DULLING(SAVESCREEN(_w1+1,_n4-1,_n3,_n4)))
   ELSEIF _w6 = 1
      RESTSCREEN(_n3,_n2,_n3,_w4-1, ;
          DULLING(SAVESCREEN(_n3,_n2,_n3,_w4-1)))
      RESTSCREEN(_n1+1,_n2,_w3+1,_n2+1, ;
          DULLING(SAVESCREEN(_n1+1,_n2,_w3+1,_n2+1)))
   ELSEIF _w6 = 7
      RESTSCREEN(_n1,_n2,_n1,_w4-2, ;
          DULLING(SAVESCREEN(_n1,_n2,_n1,_w4-2)))
      RESTSCREEN(_n1,_n2,_n3-1,_n2+1, ;
          DULLING(SAVESCREEN(_n1,_n2,_n3-1,_n2+1)))
   ELSEIF _w6 = 9
      RESTSCREEN(_n1,_w2+2,_n1,_n4, ;
          DULLING(SAVESCREEN(_n1,_w2+2,_n1,_n4)))
      RESTSCREEN(_n1,_n4-1,_n3-1,_n4, ;
          DULLING(SAVESCREEN(_n1,_n4-1,_n3-1,_n4)))
   ENDIF
   RETURN(scr_level)

*********************

FUNCTION Wclose

   PARAMETERS _w1, _w2, _w3, _w4

   IF PCOUNT() = 4
      _wcol = SETCOLOR()
   ELSEIF PCOUNT() = 0 .OR. PCOUNT() = 1
      IF PCOUNT() = 1
         * This allows a specific window to be closed
         * if the programmer knows this in advance;
         * otherwise, just let the system guess!
         scr_level = _w1 + 1
      ENDIF
      _w1 = VAL(SUBSTR(allwindows[scr_level - 1], 1,  2))
      _w2 = VAL(SUBSTR(allwindows[scr_level - 1], 4,  2))
      _w3 = VAL(SUBSTR(allwindows[scr_level - 1], 7,  2))
      _w4 = VAL(SUBSTR(allwindows[scr_level - 1], 10, 2))
```

```
238 :       IF _w1 = -1
239 :          RESTSCREEN(0,0,24,79, allscreens[scr_level-1] )
240 :          scr_level = IF(scr_level = 1, scr_level, scr_level - 1)
241 :          allscreens[scr_level+1] = ""
242 :          allcolor[scr_level+1] = ""
243 :          allwindows[scr_level] = ""
244 :          RETURN(.T.)
245 :       ENDIF
246 :    ENDIF
247 :
248 :    IF PCOUNT() != 1
249 :       scr_level = IF(scr_level = 1, scr_level, scr_level - 1)
250 :    ENDIF
251 :
252 :
253 :    RESTSCREEN(_w1, _w2, _w3, _w4, allscreens[scr_level])
254 :    SETCOLOR(allcolor[scr_level])
255 :
256 :    allscreens[scr_level+1] = ""
257 :    allcolor[scr_level+1] = ""
258 :    allwindows[scr_level] = ""
259 :    RETURN(.T.)
260 :
261 : *******************
262 :
263 : FUNCTION Dulling
264 :
265 :    PARAMETERS _astring
266 :
267 :    IF TYPE("_astring") != "C"
268 :       RETURN("")
269 :    ENDIF
270 :
271 :    * This function takes a string and returns it
272 :    * with the attribute byte dulled.
273 :
274 :    PRIVATE _qqq, _gstring    && A lonely nite.
275 :
276 :    _gstring = ""
277 :
278 :    FOR _qqq = 1 TO LEN(_astring) STEP 2
279 :       _gstring = _gstring + SUBSTR(_astring, _qqq, 1) + CHR(8)
280 :    NEXT
281 :
282 :    RETURN( _gstring )
283 :
284 : * End of File
```

In essence, the old fake shadowing technique of using REPLICATE() with the CHR(177) character was replaced with a triple function call. One such example is on lines 197 and 198; the three functions involved are Clipper's RESTSCREEN() and SAVESCREEN(), and ToolkiT's DULLING(). Remember the rules for multiple function calls: You take the innermost function or expression, solve for it, and expand outward. Looking at lines 197 and 198, the SAVESCREEN() function is the innermost of the three. The value of this function is the data that is returned from the function when it is called; in this case, it is a character string. This value is then passed directly to the DULLING() function. Suffice it to say that the DULLING() function will yield a string that is directly passed to the RESTSCREEN() function, using the exact coordinates used by the SAVESCREEN() function on the same line.

Now looking at the DULLING() function, it should be obvious that the video string returned from the SAVESCREEN() function is manipulated on lines 276 through 280. A variable named **_gstring** is initialized to a null byte and concatenated in a FOR...NEXT loop beginning on line 278. This loop goes for the length of the main video string and rebuilds a new video string, replacing the old video attribute byte with that of the ASCII value of CHR(8) (line 279). Since the stepping process of the FOR...NEXT loop is set to 2, beginning with the first byte, and since we know from previous examples that the first byte of every two bytes in a video string is the actual character, this loop skips over the video attribute character in the main video string. And since the color value of CHR(8) is a black background with dull-white letters, the DULLING() function actually rebuilds the video screen by altering the video bytes to CHR(8).

Note that in the past, this technique was used only by assembly and C programmers. But now Clipper can offer more power in pure Clipper code.

EXPLODING WINDOWS

Another feature that some programmers like to add, which is enjoyed by many end users, is the exploding window. Again, this feature can be added to the basic logic of our two main windowing functions, Windowpush() and Windowpop(). The key to this is timing: You must give the illusion of an exploding or contracting window without slowing down the application too much with multiple video calls. Before going into the logical steps that make up this technique, let us look at a piece of sample code:

```
********************
* Name      Windowh.prg
* Author    Stephen J. Straley
* Date      July 15, 1989
* Notice    Copyright (c) 1989 Stephen J. Straley & Associates
*           All Rights Reserved
* Compile   Clipper Windowh -m
* Release   Summer 87
* Link      PLINK86 FI Windowh LIB Clipper LIB Extend;
* Note      This is the eighth window program file, and
*           shows the implementation of the exploding
*           windows.
*
********************
```

```
option = 1
SET WRAP ON
SET SCOREBOARD OFF
SET MESSAGE TO 24 CENTER
*
* These are our arrays for the screens/windows
*
PUBLIC allscreens[20], scr_level, allcolor[20], allwindows[20]
AFILL(allscreens, "")
AFILL(allcolor, "")
AFILL(allwindows, "")
scr_level = 1
*
scrframe = CHR(201) + CHR(205) + CHR(187) + CHR(186) + ;
           CHR(188) + CHR(205) + CHR(200) + CHR(186)

Wopen(0,0,24,79,"7/1, 1/7")
DO WHILE .T.
   @  5,27 PROMPT " Chart of Account       " ;
      MESSAGE "Enter/Edit COA Information"
   @  7,27 PROMPT " Transactions           " ;
      MESSAGE "Enter/Edit Transactions"
   @  9,27 PROMPT " Balancing and Posting " ;
      MESSAGE "Balance Items/Post to Ledger"
   @ 11,27 PROMPT " Reporting and Lists    " ;
      MESSAGE "Financial Reports and Listings"
   @ 13,27 PROMPT " Utilities              " ;
      MESSAGE "Managerial Utilities"
   @ 15,27 PROMPT " End of Period          " ;
      MESSAGE "End of Period Processing"
   @ 17,27 PROMPT " Quit                   " ;
      MESSAGE "Quit to DOS"
   MENU TO option
   IF EMPTY(option) .OR. option = 7
      EXIT
   ELSE
      ext = TRANSFORM(option, "9")
      DO Menu&ext.
   ENDIF
ENDDO
Wclose()

********************

PROCEDURE Menu1

  base = (option * 2)
  Wopen(5 + base, 35, 15 + base, 45, "7/2, 2/7", 3, 1)
  @  7+base, 37 PROMPT "Add   "
  @  9+base, 37 PROMPT "Edit  "
  @ 11+base, 37 PROMPT "Scan  "
  @ 13+base, 37 PROMPT "Delete"
  MENU TO dummy
```

```
069 :    Wclose()
070 :
071 : *******************
072 :
073 : PROCEDURE Menu2
074 :
075 :    base = (option * 2)
076 :    Wopen(5 + base, 35, 15 + base, 45, "7/2, 2/7", 1, 1)
077 :    @  7+base, 37 PROMPT "Add    "
078 :    @  9+base, 37 PROMPT "Edit   "
079 :    @ 11+base, 37 PROMPT "Scan   "
080 :    @ 13+base, 37 PROMPT "Delete"
081 :    MENU TO dummy
082 :    Wclose()
083 :
084 : *******************
085 :
086 : PROCEDURE Menu3
087 :
088 :    * This is just a stub
089 :
090 : *******************
091 :
092 : PROCEDURE Menu4
093 :
094 :    Wopen(13,17,20,40, "2+/7, 7/2", 7, 1)
095 :    DO WHILE .T.
096 :       @ 14,20 PROMPT " Balance Sheet       "
097 :       @ 15,20 PROMPT " Income Statement    "
098 :       @ 16,20 PROMPT " Trial Balance       "
099 :       @ 17,20 PROMPT " Transactions        "
100 :       @ 18,20 PROMPT " Standard Entries    "
101 :       @ 19,20 PROMPT " Chart of Accounts "
102 :       MENU TO newoption
103 :       IF EMPTY(newoption)
104 :          EXIT
105 :       ELSE
106 :          Wopen(14+newoption,25,16+newoption,65,"3/0,0/3",9,0)
107 :          DO WHILE .T.
108 :             @ 15+newoption, 27 PROMPT " Screen "
109 :             @ 15+newoption, 40 PROMPT " Printer "
110 :             @ 15+newoption, 55 PROMPT " File "
111 :             MENU TO this
112 :             IF EMPTY(this)
113 :                EXIT
114 :             ENDIF
115 :          ENDDO
116 :          Wclose()
117 :       ENDIF
118 :    ENDDO
119 :    Wclose()
120 :
121 : *******************
122 :
```

```
123 : PROCEDURE Menu5
124 :
125 :    * This is just a stub
126 :
127 : ********************
128 :
129 : PROCEDURE Menu6
130 :
131 :    * This is just a stub
132 :
133 : * **********************************************
134 : * * The following procedure(s)/function(s) are  *
135 : * * part of Steve Straley's ToolkiT(tm) -        *
136 : * * Release 2, published by Four Seasons         *
137 : * * Publishing Co., Inc.  All Rights Reserved    *
138 : * * Information: 212-599-2141 / 800-662-2278     *
139 : * * All Rights Reserved                          *
140 : * **********************************************
141 :
142 : FUNCTION Wopen
143 :
144 :    PARAMETERS _w1, _w2, _w3, _w4, _w5, _w6, _w7
145 :
146 :    IF PCOUNT() = 4
147 :       _w5 = SETCOLOR()
148 :       _w6 = 5
149 :       _w7 = 0
150 :    ELSEIF PCOUNT() = 5
151 :       _w6 = 5
152 :       _w7 = 0
153 :    ELSEIF PCOUNT() = 6
154 :       _w7 = 0
155 :    ENDIF
156 :
157 :    allcolor[scr_level]  = _w5
158 :    *
159 :    * Must now calculate the windowed area including
160 :    * the shadow line, if applicable!
161 :    *
162 :    IF _w6 = 3
163 :       _n1 = _w1
164 :       _n2 = _w2
165 :       _n3 = _w3+1
166 :       _n4 = _w4+2
167 :    ELSEIF _w6 = 1
168 :       _n1 = _w1
169 :       _n2 = _w2-2
170 :       _n3 = _w3+1
171 :       _n4 = _w4
172 :    ELSEIF _w6 = 7
173 :       _n1 = _w1-1
174 :       _n2 = _w2-2
175 :       _n3 = _w3
176 :       _n4 = _w4
```

```
    ELSEIF _w6 = 9
       _n1 = _w1-1
       _n2 = _w2
       _n3 = _w3
       _n4 = _w4+2
    ELSE
       _n1 = _w1
       _n2 = _w2
       _n3 = _w3
       _n4 = _w4
    ENDIF


    allscreens[scr_level] = SAVESCREEN(_n1, _n2, _n3, _n4)
    allwindows[scr_level] = TRANSFORM(_n1, "99") + "/" + ;
       TRANSFORM(_n2, "99") + "/" + TRANSFORM(_n3, "99") + ;
       "/" + TRANSFORM(_n4, "99") + "/" + TRANSFORM(_w7, "99")
    allcolor[scr_level] = SETCOLOR()

    SETCOLOR(_w5)
    scr_level = IF(scr_level = 20, scr_level, scr_level + 1)

    IF !EMPTY(_w7)  && Exploding Window!
       Blowup(_w1, _w2, _w3, _w4)
    ENDIF

    @ _w1, _w2, _w3, _w4 BOX SPACE(9)
    @ _w1, _w2, _w3, _w4 BOX SUBSTR(scrframe, 1, 8)

    IF _w6 = 3
       RESTSCREEN(_n3,_w2+2,_n3,_n4, ;
           DULLING(SAVESCREEN(_n3,_w2+2,_n3,_n4)))
       RESTSCREEN(_w1+1,_n4-1,_n3,_n4, ;
           DULLING(SAVESCREEN(_w1+1,_n4-1,_n3,_n4)))
    ELSEIF _w6 = 1
       RESTSCREEN(_n3,_n2,_n3,_w4-1, ;
           DULLING(SAVESCREEN(_n3,_n2,_n3,_w4-1)))
       RESTSCREEN(_n1+1,_n2,_w3+1,_n2+1, ;
           DULLING(SAVESCREEN(_n1+1,_n2,_w3+1,_n2+1)))
    ELSEIF _w6 = 7
       RESTSCREEN(_n1,_n2,_n1,_w4-2, ;
           DULLING(SAVESCREEN(_n1,_n2,_n1,_w4-2)))
       RESTSCREEN(_n1,_n2,_n3-1,_n2+1, ;
           DULLING(SAVESCREEN(_n1,_n2,_n3-1,_n2+1)))
    ELSEIF _w6 = 9
       RESTSCREEN(_n1,_w2+2,_n1,_n4, ;
           DULLING(SAVESCREEN(_n1,_w2+2,_n1,_n4)))
       RESTSCREEN(_n1,_n4-1,_n3-1,_n4, ;
           DULLING(SAVESCREEN(_n1,_n4-1,_n3-1,_n4)))
    ENDIF
    RETURN(scr_level)

********************
```

```
231 : FUNCTION Wclose
232 :
233 :     PARAMETERS _w1, _w2, _w3, _w4
234 :
235 :     IF PCOUNT() = 4
236 :         _wcol = SETCOLOR()
237 :     ELSEIF PCOUNT() = 0 .OR. PCOUNT() = 1
238 :         IF PCOUNT() = 1
239 :             * This allows a specific window to be closed
240 :             * if the programmer knows this in advance;
241 :             * otherwise, just let the system guess!
242 :             scr_level = _w1 + 1
243 :         ENDIF
244 :         _w1 = VAL(SUBSTR(allwindows[scr_level - 1], 1,  2))
245 :         _w2 = VAL(SUBSTR(allwindows[scr_level - 1], 4,  2))
246 :         _w3 = VAL(SUBSTR(allwindows[scr_level - 1], 7,  2))
247 :         _w4 = VAL(SUBSTR(allwindows[scr_level - 1], 10, 2))
248 :         _w5 = VAL(SUBSTR(allwindows[scr_level - 1], 13, 2))
249 :         IF _w1 = -1
250 :             RESTSCREEN(0,0,24,79, allscreens[scr_level-1] )
251 :             scr_level = IF(scr_level = 1, scr_level, scr_level - 1)
252 :             allscreens[scr_level+1] = ""
253 :             allcolor[scr_level+1] = ""
254 :             allwindows[scr_level] = ""
255 :             RETURN(.T.)
256 :         ENDIF
257 :     ENDIF
258 :
259 :     IF PCOUNT() != 1
260 :         scr_level = IF(scr_level = 1, scr_level, scr_level - 1)
261 :     ENDIF
262 :
263 :     RESTSCREEN(_w1, _w2, _w3, _w4, allscreens[scr_level])
264 :     SETCOLOR(allcolor[scr_level])
265 :
266 :     allscreens[scr_level+1] = ""
267 :     allcolor[scr_level+1] = ""
268 :     allwindows[scr_level] = ""
269 :     RETURN(.T.)
270 :
271 : *******************
272 :
273 : FUNCTION Dulling
274 :
275 :     PARAMETERS _astring
276 :
277 :     IF TYPE("_astring") != "C"
278 :         RETURN("")
279 :     ENDIF
280 :
281 :     * This function takes a string and returns it
282 :     * with the attribute byte dulled.
283 :
```

```
284 :     PRIVATE _qqq, _gstring    && A lonely nite.
285 :
286 :     _gstring = ""
287 :
288 :     FOR _qqq = 1 TO LEN(_astring) STEP 2
289 :        _gstring = _gstring + SUBSTR(_astring, _qqq, 1) + CHR(8)
290 :     NEXT
291 :
292 :     RETURN( _gstring )
293 :
294 : ********************
295 :
296 : FUNCTION Blowup
297 :
298 :     PARAMETERS _blow1, _blow2, _blow3, _blow4
299 :
300 :     IF EMPTY(PCOUNT())
301 :        RETURN(.F.)
302 :     ELSEIF TYPE("_blow1") + TYPE("_blow2") + ;
303 :            TYPE("_blow3") + TYPE("_blow4") != "NNNN"
304 :        RETURN(.F.)
305 :     ENDIF
306 :
307 :     _seed1  = INT((_blow3 - _blow1) / 2)
308 :     _seed2  = INT((_blow4 - _blow2) / 2)
309 :     _blowt1 = _blow1 + _seed1
310 :     _blowt2 = _blow2 + _seed2
311 :     _blowt3 = _blowt1
312 :     _blowt4 = _blowt2
313 :
314 :     DO WHILE (_blowt1 > _blow1 .AND. _blowt2 > _blow2) ;
315 :        .AND. (_blowt3 < _blow3 .AND. _blowt4 < _blow4)
316 :        @ _blowt1, _blowt2, _blowt3, _blowt4 ;
317 :           BOX SUBSTR(scrframe, 1, 8)
318 :        INKEY(.01)
319 :        SCROLL(_blowt1, _blowt2, _blowt3, _blowt4, 0)
320 :        _blowt1 = _blowt1 - 1
321 :        _blowt2 = _blowt2 - (_seed2 / _seed1)
322 :        _blowt3 = _blowt3 + 1
323 :        _blowt4 = _blowt4 + (_seed2 / _seed1)
324 :     ENDDO
325 :     RETURN(.T.)
326 :
327 : * End of File
```

In this example, the Blowup() function takes the window coordinates passed to it and determines the center row, column position (lines 307 and 308). The DO WHILE loop beginning on line 314 continues until the outer limits of the bordered area match the four coordinates passed to the function. Each time that the loop makes a pass, a smaller box is drawn, wiping out the previous box. Eventually, as the boxes are removed and then drawn with increasing row-column coordinates, the illusion is of an exploding window.

Contracting windows are not impossible to produce but require a considerable amount of programming muscle. The steps for such a feature would slow down the application drastically because the process revolves around viewing each windowed area in smaller strips that will act like a video circumference. Or, if you prefer, it takes the video screen and dissects donut-like squares, each smaller than the next, and displays these video strings to the screen in reverse (or largest first) order.

Of course, the TONE() function could be added to give sound to our exploding and contracting windows. However, like excessive video calls, this, too, will slow down an application and may be scrapped for faster, snappy windows.

PANNING TEXT ONSCREEN

Several other options and programming additions also come to mind. Consider the possibility of panning information from the screen. The SCROLL() function performs this task adequately for text scrolling either to the top or bottom of a particular video region. But what about scrolling information from a video page either to the left or right? Again, using a predefined standard and referring to our table of the numeric keypad, the panning directions are 2 for down, 4 for left, 6 for right, and 8 for up. The parameter value of 0, or any other response, will simply wipe out the screen. First, consider this code, which will be followed by a brief explanation.

```
********************
* Name      Panit.prg
* Author    Stephen J. Straley
* Date      July 15, 1989
* Notice    Copyright (c) 1989 Stephen J. Straley & Associates
*           All Rights Reserved
* Compile   Clipper Panit -m
* Release   Summer 87
* Link      PLINK86 FI Panit LIB Clipper LIB Extend;
* Note      This program shows how one can pan information
*           from the screen using the SAVESCREEN() and
*           RESTSCREEN() functions.
*
********************
string = "This is a test to see if items in this " + ;
         "string can be panned across the screen from " +;
         "four directions: 2, 4, 6, and 8"
SET CURSOR OFF
CLEAR SCREEN
FOR x = 0 TO 8 STEP 2
   @ 10,30 SAY "Press Any key to Pan"
   MEMOEDIT(string, 2,30,8,50,.F.,.F.)
   INKEY(0)
   Pan(2,30,8,50,x)
```

```
027 :    @ 10,00 CLEAR
028 :    @ 10,30 SAY "That was a PAN(" + LTRIM(STR(x)) + ;
029 :              "). Any key..."
030 :    INKEY(0)
031 :    @ 10,00 CLEAR
032 : NEXT
033 : SET CURSOR ON
034 :
035 : * ************************************************
036 : * * The following procedure(s)/function(s) are  *
037 : * * part of Steve Straley's ToolkiT(tm) -        *
038 : * * Release 2, published by Four Seasons         *
039 : * * Publishing Co., Inc.  All Rights Reserved    *
040 : * * Information: 212-599-2141 / 800-662-2278     *
041 : * * All Rights Reserved                          *
042 : * ************************************************
043 :
044 : *******************
045 :
046 : FUNCTION Pan
047 :
048 :    PARAMETERS _clr1, _clr2, _clr3, _clr4, _style
049 :
050 :    * _style = 0 or no parameter = clear screen
051 :    * _stype = 6 fade from left to right
052 :    * _style = 4 fade from right to left
053 :    * _style = 8 fade from bottom to top
054 :    * _style = 2 fade from top to bottom
055 :
056 :    _style = IF( TYPE("_style") != "N", 0, _style)
057 :
058 :    * Some of the calculations for a style of 4 or
059 :    * 6 were originally based on windowing routines
060 :    * in the ToolkiT - Release 2 and have been altered
061 :    * for this publication.
062 :
063 :    IF     _style = 4
064 :       _clr1 = _clr1 - 1
065 :       _clr2 = _clr2 - 1
066 :       _clr3 = _clr3 + 1
067 :       _times = (_clr4 - _clr2)
068 :       FOR _qaz = 1 TO _times + 1
069 :          RESTSCREEN(_clr1 + 1, _clr2 + 1, _clr3 - 1, ;
070 :                     _clr4 - 2, SAVESCREEN(_clr1 + 1, ;
071 :                     _clr2 + 2, _clr3 - 1, _clr4 - 1))
072 :          SCROLL(_clr1+1, _clr4-1, _clr3-1, _clr4-1, 0)
073 :          _clr4 = _clr4 - 1
074 :          INKEY(.1)
075 :       NEXT
076 :
077 :    ELSEIF _style = 6
078 :       * Take the bottom right coordinates, increment
079 :       * by one every time, and move to the right.  Re-
080 :       * adjust the top left coordinate and repeat,
```

```
081 :          * blanking out the strip on the left.
082 :
083 :          _times = (_clr4 - _clr2)
084 :          _clr1 = _clr1 - 1
085 :          _clr2 = _clr2 - 1
086 :          _clr3 = _clr3 + 1
087 :          FOR _qaz = 1 TO _times
088 :              RESTSCREEN(_clr1 + 1, _clr2 + 2, _clr3 - 1, ;
089 :                          _clr4 - 1, SAVESCREEN(_clr1 + 1, ;
090 :                          _clr2 + 1, _clr3 - 1, _clr4 - 2))
091 :              SCROLL(_clr1+1, _clr2+1, _clr3-1, _clr2 + 1, 0)
092 :              _clr2 = _clr2 + 1
093 :              INKEY(.1)
094 :          NEXT
095 :          SCROLL(_clr1, _clr2+1, _clr3, _clr2+1, 0)
096 :
097 :      ELSEIF _style = 2
098 :          FOR _qaz = _clr1 TO _clr3
099 :              SCROLL(_clr1, _clr2, _clr3, _clr4, -1)
100 :              INKEY(.1)
101 :          NEXT
102 :      ELSEIF _style = 8
103 :          FOR _qaz = _clr1 TO _clr3
104 :              SCROLL(_clr1, _clr2, _clr3, _clr4,1)
105 :              INKEY(.1)
106 :          NEXT
107 :      ELSE
108 :          SCROLL(_clr1,_clr2,_clr3, _clr4,0)
109 :      ENDIF
110 :      RETURN(.T.)
111 :
112 : * End of File
```

In this function, we use the SCROLL() function, as expected, to remove the information from the screen and to scroll the information from the top to the bottom and from the bottom to the top. However, a trickier technique is needed to get the same textual information to move either from left to right or from right to left. In essence, a portion of the screen is saved, and a smaller portion of that string is then redisplayed to the screen. When the process repeats, either for the left or the right, the image appears to be moving across the screen in that direction.

Keep this in mind when working with combinations of the SAVESCREEN() and RESTSCREEN() functions. It is no problem for the RESTSCREEN() function to redisplay a smaller video string than was saved via the SAVESCREEN() function. However, if a larger string is required than is returned from the SAVESCREEN() function, Clipper will grab the required number of bytes to satisfy the RESTSCREEN() from the free memory pool. While these additional bytes have nothing to do with the video portion of your application, if this should occur, you will see some interesting video characters, colors, and characteristics.

BUILDING SCREENS FOR DISPLAY

Expanding on the concept of the DULLING() function, and working with the notion that the video attribute bytes on the screen are nothing more than ASCII characters, it should be relatively easy to conceive the notion of building a color screen and displaying it instantly without the use of the SAVESCREEN() function. For a demonstration of this, consider the following:

```
********************
* Name      Buildit.prg
* Author    Stephen J. Straley
* Date      July 15, 1989
* Notice    Copyright (c) 1989 Stephen J. Straley & Associates
*           All Rights Reserved
* Compile   Clipper Buildit -m
* Release   Summer 87
* Link      PLINK86 FI Buildit LIB Clipper LIB Extend;
* Note      This shows how a string can be converted to the
*           proper format for a direction call to the
*           RESTSCREEN() function WITHOUT a call to the
*           SAVESCREEN() function.
*
********************

string = FILL_OUT("This piece of text will be displayed "+;
                  "on the screen without any previous "+;
                  "SAVESCREEN() call", 244)

CLEAR SCREEN
FOR x = 0 TO (16 * 7) STEP 16
   RESTSCREEN(2,10,5,70, Str2scr(string, x))
   @ 20,00 SAY "Press any key..."
   INKEY(0)
   @ 20,00 CLEAR
NEXT

* ***********************************************
* * The following procedure(s)/function(s) are  *
* * part of Steve Straley's ToolkiT(tm) -       *
* * Release 2, published by Four Seasons        *
* * Publishing Co., Inc.  All Rights Reserved   *
* * Information: 212-599-2141 / 800-662-2278    *
* * All Rights Reserved                         *
* ***********************************************

********************

FUNCTION Str2scr

   PARAMETERS _string, _ascii

   _retstr = ""
```

```
45 :    FOR _x = 1 TO LEN(_string)
46 :       _retstr = _retstr + SUBSTR(_string, _x, 1) + CHR(_ascii)
47 :    NEXT
48 :    RETURN(_retstr)
49 :
50 : ******************
51 :
52 : FUNCTION Fill_out
53 :
54 :    PARAMETERS _filla, _fillb
55 :
56 :    * _filla = the string to be filled out
57 :    * _fillb = the Length to fill out the string to
58 :
59 :    IF PCOUNT() = 1
60 :       _fillb = 80
61 :    ELSE
62 :       IF TYPE("_fillb") = "C"
63 :          _fillb = VAL(b)
64 :       ENDIF
65 :       _fillb = IIF(_fillb <= 1, 80, _fillb)
66 :    ENDIF
67 :
68 :    IF _fillb <= LEN(_filla)
69 :       RETURN(_filla)
70 :    ENDIF
71 :    RETURN(LEFT(_filla + SPACE(_fillb - LEN(_filla)),_fillb))
72 :
73 : * End of File
```

As opposed to the use of the CHR(8) in the DULLING() function, this function takes whatever number is passed to the Str2scr() function and yields the CHR() of that parameter: **_ascii**. In this program, the variable **string** is padded with enough blank space to have a LEN() of 244 (lines 17 through 19). This variable is passed to the FILL_OUT() function because we know that the LEN() of a video string covering the screen at 2,10 to 5,70 is 488 bytes. These are the video coordinates passed to the RESTSCREEN() function on line 23. Because we know that 2 bytes are necessary for every row,column screen position, the actual length of the string should be one half of 488, or 244. Then, beginning with a value of 0 and skipping in lots of 16 (line 22), the string and the value of the FOR...NEXT counter **x** is passed to the Str2scr() function. This function builds the string up to 488 bytes, placing the STR() of the ASCII character of **x** between each character string as the passed parameter **_string**. The results are the same screen in different colors, similar to the effect created by the DULLING() function.

RELATIVE WINDOWING — @...SAY...GET

The concept of relative windowing displays the power and scope of the Clipper language. The principle is simple: the @...SAY...GET logic should automatically display to the screen in a position relative to the borders of the window. For example, at the beginning of an application, the relative beginning row and column coordinates are 0,0. However, if the window begins at row,column coordinates 2,5, the actual position for relative coordinates 1,1 should be 3,6. This means that as the window coordinates move, the @...SAY...GET coordinates should follow. If these values are placed in parameters or string or memory variables from a memory file or fields from a database, the amount of physical hard coding to our application should be considerably less. For an example of this, work through the logic of this program:

```
********************
* Name      Windowi.prg
* Author    Stephen J. Straley
* Date      July 15, 1989
* Notice    Copyright (c) 1989 Stephen J. Straley & Associates
*           All Rights Reserved
* Compile   Clipper Windowi -m
* Release   Summer 87
* Link      PLINK86 FI Windowi LIB Clipper LIB Extend;
* Note      This is the ninth window program file, and
*           shows the implementation of the relative
*           windowing.
*
********************

option = 1
SET WRAP ON
SET SCOREBOARD OFF
SET MESSAGE TO 24 CENTER
*
* These are our arrays for the screens/windows
*
PUBLIC allscreens[20], scr_level, allcolor[20], allwindows[20]
AFILL(allscreens, "")
AFILL(allcolor, "")
AFILL(allwindows, "")
scr_level = 1
*
scrframe = CHR(201) + CHR(205) + CHR(187) + CHR(186) + ;
           CHR(188) + CHR(205) + CHR(200) + CHR(186)

KEYBOARD "B"
Wopen(0,0,24,79,"7/1, 1/7")
DO WHILE .T.
   @  5,27 PROMPT " Chart of Account       " ;
      MESSAGE "Enter/Edit COA Information"
   @  7,27 PROMPT " Transactions           " ;
      MESSAGE "Enter/Edit Transactions"
   @  9,27 PROMPT " Balancing and Posting " ;
      MESSAGE "Balance Items/Post to Ledger"
   @ 11,27 PROMPT " Reporting and Lists    " ;
      MESSAGE "Financial Reports and Listings"
   @ 13,27 PROMPT " Utilities              " ;
```

```
044 :        MESSAGE "Managerial Utilities"
045 : a 15,27 PROMPT " End of Period        " ;
046 :        MESSAGE "End of Period Processing"
047 : a 17,27 PROMPT " Quit                 " ;
048 :        MESSAGE "Quit to DOS"
049 : MENU TO option
050 : IF EMPTY(option) .OR. option = 7
051 :    EXIT
052 : ELSE
053 :    ext = TRANSFORM(option, "9")
054 :    DO Menu&ext.
055 : ENDIF
056 : ENDDO
057 : Wclose()
058 :
059 : *******************
060 :
061 : PROCEDURE Menu1
062 :
063 :    base = (option * 2)
064 :    Wopen(5 + base, 35, 15 + base, 45, "7/2, 2/7", 3, 1)
065 :    a  7+base, 37 PROMPT "Add    "
066 :    a  9+base, 37 PROMPT "Edit   "
067 :    a 11+base, 37 PROMPT "Scan   "
068 :    a 13+base, 37 PROMPT "Delete"
069 :    MENU TO dummy
070 :    Wclose()
071 :
072 : *******************
073 :
074 : PROCEDURE Menu2
075 :
076 :    base = (option * 2)
077 :    Wopen(5 + base, 35, 15 + base, 45, "7/2, 2/7", 1, 1)
078 :    a  7+base, 37 PROMPT "Add    "
079 :    a  9+base, 37 PROMPT "Edit   "
080 :    a 11+base, 37 PROMPT "Scan   "
081 :    a 13+base, 37 PROMPT "Delete"
082 :    MENU TO dummy
083 :    Wclose()
084 :
085 : *******************
086 :
087 : PROCEDURE Menu3
088 :
089 :    Wopen(9,15,14,65,"3+/1. 2/3", 1)
090 :    row = 1
091 :    col = 1
092 :    name = SPACE(15)
093 :    age = 10
094 :    DO WHILE .T.
095 :       a 11,20 SAY "Enter beginning Row (1 - 15):" ;
096 :               GET row VALID row >= 1 .AND. row <= 15
097 :       a 12,20 SAY "                   Col (1 - 40):" ;
```

```
098 :               GET col VALID col >= 1 .AND. col <= 40
099 :       READ
100 :       IF LASTKEY() = 27
101 :          EXIT
102 :       ELSE
103 :          Wopen(row,col,row+6,col+35,"4/0, 0/4", 3)
104 :          @ Wrow(2), Wcol(3) SAY "Enter a name " ;
105 :                 GET name
106 :          @ Wrow(4), Wcol(3) SAY "..and an age " ;
107 :                 GET age
108 :          READ
109 :          Wclose()
110 :       ENDIF
111 :    ENDDO
112 :    Wclose()
113 :
114 :
115 : *******************
116 :
117 : PROCEDURE Menu4
118 :
119 :    Wopen(13,17,20,40, "2+/7, 7/2", 7, 1)
120 :    DO WHILE .T.
121 :       @ 14,20 PROMPT " Balance Sheet      "
122 :       @ 15,20 PROMPT " Income Statement   "
123 :       @ 16,20 PROMPT " Trial Balance      "
124 :       @ 17,20 PROMPT " Transactions       "
125 :       @ 18,20 PROMPT " Standard Entries   "
126 :       @ 19,20 PROMPT " Chart of Accounts "
127 :       MENU TO newoption
128 :       IF EMPTY(newoption)
129 :          EXIT
130 :       ELSE
131 :          Wopen(14+newoption,25,16+newoption,65,"3/0,0/3",9,0)
132 :          DO WHILE .T.
133 :             @ 15+newoption, 27 PROMPT " Screen "
134 :             @ 15+newoption, 40 PROMPT " Printer "
135 :             @ 15+newoption, 55 PROMPT " File "
136 :             MENU TO this
137 :             IF EMPTY(this)
138 :                EXIT
139 :             ENDIF
140 :          ENDDO
141 :          Wclose()
142 :       ENDIF
143 :    ENDDO
144 :    Wclose()
145 :
146 : *******************
147 :
148 : PROCEDURE Menu5
149 :
150 :    * This is just a stub
151 :
```

```
152 : ********************
153 :
154 : PROCEDURE Menu6
155 :
156 :    * This is just a stub
157 :
158 : * *************************************************
159 : * * The following procedure(s)/function(s) are  *
160 : * * part of Steve Straley's ToolkiT(tm) -        *
161 : * * Release 2, published by Four Seasons         *
162 : * * Publishing Co., Inc.  All Rights Reserved    *
163 : * * Information: 212-599-2141 / 800-662-2278     *
164 : * * All Rights Reserved                          *
165 : * *************************************************
166 :
167 : FUNCTION Wopen
168 :
169 :    PARAMETERS _w1, _w2, _w3, _w4, _w5, _w6, _w7
170 :
171 :    IF PCOUNT() = 4
172 :       _w5 = SETCOLOR()
173 :       _w6 = 5
174 :       _w7 = 0
175 :    ELSEIF PCOUNT() = 5
176 :       _w6 = 5
177 :       _w7 = 0
178 :    ELSEIF PCOUNT() = 6
179 :       _w7 = 0
180 :    ENDIF
181 :
182 :    allcolor[scr_level]   = _w5
183 :    *
184 :    * Must now calculate the windowed area including
185 :    * the shadow line, if applicable!
186 :    *
187 :    IF _w6 = 3
188 :       _n1 = _w1
189 :       _n2 = _w2
190 :       _n3 = _w3+1
191 :       _n4 = _w4+2
192 :    ELSEIF _w6 = 1
193 :       _n1 = _w1
194 :       _n2 = _w2-2
195 :       _n3 = _w3+1
196 :       _n4 = _w4
197 :    ELSEIF _w6 = 7
198 :       _n1 = _w1-1
199 :       _n2 = _w2-2
200 :       _n3 = _w3
201 :       _n4 = _w4
202 :    ELSEIF _w6 = 9
203 :       _n1 = _w1-1
204 :       _n2 = _w2
205 :       _n3 = _w3
```

```
      _n4 = _w4+2
   ELSE
      _n1 = _w1
      _n2 = _w2
      _n3 = _w3
      _n4 = _w4
   ENDIF


   allscreens[scr_level] = SAVESCREEN(_n1, _n2, _n3, _n4)
   allwindows[scr_level] = TRANSFORM(_n1, "99") + "/" + ;
      TRANSFORM(_n2, "99") + "/" + TRANSFORM(_n3, "99") + ;
      "/" + TRANSFORM(_n4, "99") + "/" + TRANSFORM(_w7, "99")
   allcolor[scr_level] = SETCOLOR()

   SETCOLOR(_w5)
   scr_level = IF(scr_level = 20, scr_level, scr_level + 1)

   IF !EMPTY(_w7)  && Exploding Window!
      Blowup(_w1, _w2, _w3, _w4)
   ENDIF

   @ _w1, _w2, _w3, _w4 BOX SPACE(9)
   @ _w1, _w2, _w3, _w4 BOX SUBSTR(scrframe, 1, 8)

   IF _w6 = 3
      RESTSCREEN(_n3,_w2+2,_n3,_n4, ;
          DULLING(SAVESCREEN(_n3,_w2+2,_n3,_n4)))
      RESTSCREEN(_w1+1,_n4-1,_n3,_n4, ;
          DULLING(SAVESCREEN(_w1+1,_n4-1,_n3,_n4)))
   ELSEIF _w6 = 1
      RESTSCREEN(_n3,_n2,_n3,_w4-1, ;
          DULLING(SAVESCREEN(_n3,_n2,_n3,_w4-1)))
      RESTSCREEN(_n1+1,_n2,_w3+1,_n2+1, ;
          DULLING(SAVESCREEN(_n1+1,_n2,_w3+1,_n2+1)))
   ELSEIF _w6 = 7
      RESTSCREEN(_n1,_n2,_n1,_w4-2, ;
          DULLING(SAVESCREEN(_n1,_n2,_n1,_w4-2)))
      RESTSCREEN(_n1,_n2,_n3-1,_n2+1, ;
          DULLING(SAVESCREEN(_n1,_n2,_n3-1,_n2+1)))
   ELSEIF _w6 = 9
      RESTSCREEN(_n1,_w2+2,_n1,_n4, ;
          DULLING(SAVESCREEN(_n1,_w2+2,_n1,_n4)))
      RESTSCREEN(_n1,_n4-1,_n3-1,_n4, ;
          DULLING(SAVESCREEN(_n1,_n4-1,_n3-1,_n4)))
   ENDIF
   RETURN(scr_level)

********************

FUNCTION Wclose

   PARAMETERS _w1, _w2, _w3, _w4

```

```
260 :     IF PCOUNT() = 4
261 :         _wcol = SETCOLOR()
262 :     ELSEIF PCOUNT() = 0 .OR. PCOUNT() = 1
263 :         IF PCOUNT() = 1
264 :             * This allows a specific window to be closed
265 :             * if the programmer knows this in advance;
266 :             * otherwise, just let the system guess!
267 :             scr_level = _w1 + 1
268 :         ENDIF
269 :         _w1 = VAL(SUBSTR(allwindows[scr_level - 1], 1,  2))
270 :         _w2 = VAL(SUBSTR(allwindows[scr_level - 1], 4,  2))
271 :         _w3 = VAL(SUBSTR(allwindows[scr_level - 1], 7,  2))
272 :         _w4 = VAL(SUBSTR(allwindows[scr_level - 1], 10, 2))
273 :         _w5 = VAL(SUBSTR(allwindows[scr_level - 1], 13, 2))
274 :         IF _w1 = -1
275 :             RESTSCREEN(0,0,24,79, allscreens[scr_level-1] )
276 :             scr_level = IF(scr_level = 1, scr_level, scr_level - 1)
277 :             allscreens[scr_level+1] = ""
278 :             allcolor[scr_level+1] = ""
279 :             allwindows[scr_level] = ""
280 :             RETURN(.T.)
281 :         ENDIF
282 :     ENDIF
283 :
284 :     IF PCOUNT() != 1
285 :         scr_level = IF(scr_level = 1, scr_level, scr_level - 1)
286 :     ENDIF
287 :
288 :     RESTSCREEN(_w1, _w2, _w3, _w4, allscreens[scr_level])
289 :     SETCOLOR(allcolor[scr_level])
290 :
291 :     allscreens[scr_level+1] = ""
292 :     allcolor[scr_level+1] = ""
293 :     allwindows[scr_level] = ""
294 :     RETURN(.T.)
295 :
296 : *******************
297 :
298 : FUNCTION Dulling
299 :
300 :     PARAMETERS _astring
301 :
302 :     IF TYPE("_astring") != "C"
303 :         RETURN("")
304 :     ENDIF
305 :
306 :     * This function takes a string and returns it
307 :     * with the attribute byte dulled.
308 :
309 :     PRIVATE _qqq, _gstring     && A lonely nite.
310 :
311 :     _gstring = ""
312 :
313 :     FOR _qqq = 1 TO LEN(_astring) STEP 2
```

```
314 :         _gstring = _gstring + SUBSTR(_astring, _qqq, 1) + CHR(8)
315 :     NEXT
316 :
317 :     RETURN( _gstring )
318 :
319 : ********************
320 :
321 : FUNCTION Blowup
322 :
323 :     PARAMETERS _blow1, _blow2, _blow3, _blow4
324 :
325 :     IF EMPTY(PCOUNT())
326 :        RETURN(.F.)
327 :     ELSEIF TYPE("_blow1") + TYPE("_blow2") + ;
328 :            TYPE("_blow3") + TYPE("_blow4") != "NNNN"
329 :        RETURN(.F.)
330 :     ENDIF
331 :
332 :     _seed1  = INT((_blow3 - _blow1) / 2)
333 :     _seed2  = INT((_blow4 - _blow2) / 2)
334 :     _blowt1 = _blow1 + _seed1
335 :     _blowt2 = _blow2 + _seed2
336 :     _blowt3 = _blowt1
337 :     _blowt4 = _blowt2
338 :
339 :     DO WHILE (_blowt1 > _blow1 .AND. _blowt2 > _blow2) ;
340 :        .AND. (_blowt3 < _blow3 .AND. _blowt4 < _blow4)
341 :        @ _blowt1, _blowt2, _blowt3, _blowt4 ;
342 :          BOX SUBSTR(scrframe, 1, 8)
343 :        INKEY(.01)
344 :        SCROLL(_blowt1, _blowt2, _blowt3, _blowt4, 0)
345 :        _blowt1 = _blowt1 - 1
346 :        _blowt2 = _blowt2 - (_seed2 / _seed1)
347 :        _blowt3 = _blowt3 + 1
348 :        _blowt4 = _blowt4 + (_seed2 / _seed1)
349 :     ENDDO
350 :     RETURN(.T.)
351 :
352 : ******************
353 :
354 : FUNCTION Wrow
355 :
356 :     PARAMETERS _therow
357 :
358 :     IF scr_level-1 <= 0
359 :        RETURN(0 + IF( PCOUNT()=0, 0, _therow) )
360 :     ELSE
361 :        _base = VAL(SUBSTR(allwindows[scr_level-1],1, 2))+;
362 :                IF( PCOUNT()=0, 0, _therow)
363 :        RETURN( _base )
364 :     ENDIF
365 :
366 : ******************
367 :
```

```
368 : FUNCTION Wcol
369 :
370 :     PARAMETERS _thecol
371 :
372 :     IF scr_level-1 <= 0
373 :        RETURN(0 + IF( PCOUNT()=0, 0, _thecol) )
374 :     ELSE
375 :        _base = VAL(SUBSTR(allwindows[scr_level - 1],4,2))+;
376 :                IF( PCOUNT()=0, 0, _thecol)
377 :        RETURN( _base )
378 :     ENDIF
379 :
380 : * End of File
```

Since the window coordinates for the current windowed array are stored by the Wopen() function to the **allwindows[]** array, it is easy to add the relative positions of any screen to calculate the actual position on the monitor. The two functions called to accomplish this task are Wrow() and Wcol(). Notice that, no matter what values are entered by the user on lines 95 through 98, the window will open and the @...SAY...GET commands on lines 104 through 107 will always appear within the current windowed area as opened by the Wopen() on line 103.

While Wrow() and Wcol() are just two functions, many functions could be built to complement the windowing concepts outlined in this chapter. Possibilities include calculating window depth, width, complete window logic for any @...SAY...GET...PICT...VALID command, and much more.

SUMMARY

The video portion of your application is important. Regardless of the algorithm within the program, if the application does not have a sufficient number of bells and whistles, the end user will not be satisfied. And the fancier the screens, regardless of content, the better chance of getting a higher fee for the time and effort. People like fancy windows; different colors appeal to the end-user's eyes; relative windowing relieves a programmer's constant worry of ROW() and COL() positions; and true shadowing adds spice to a program. Along with these issues, the concept of a mouse and graphical interfaces can also be discussed. Face it, glitz pays and we, as Clipper programmers, must compete with the C programmers who give their clients just that. As end users become more and more educated, their wants and desires will increase. In order to be competitive, we have to understand that Clipper can handle all of these issues (some with a little help), and that we, as Clipper programmers, must cultivate the ideas and designs with each new application we write.

CHAPTER FOUR

Unique Features of Clipper

This chapter deals with several unique features and functions in the Clipper language. Some of the concepts are difficult, while others are obvious. The topics range from conditional indexing to nested GETs. Since this chapter has no specific focus, allow each concept in each section to stand on its own merits, and use them in your applications.

BAR CHARTS ON INDEX

This concept is discussed in greater detail in Chapter 6 under working with the low-level file functions. One of the biggest disadvantages the compiler has when compared with interpreters is the inability to show the progress of an index, a report, or a deletion operation. While it may be argued that the little red light on most computer's hard-disk systems is sufficient to tell the end user that something is happening, a far greater number will argue to the contrary. Clipper can simulate, in the interpreter, the luxury of having the percentage of the index displayed on the screen. Consider this:

```
********************
* Name      Index1.prg
* Author    Stephen J. Straley
* Date      June 1, 1989
* Notice    Copyright (c) 1988 Stephen J. Straley & Associates
* Compile   Clipper Index1 -m
* Release   Summer 87
* Link      PLINK86 FI Index1 LIB Extend LIB Clipper;
* Note      This shows how a simple INDEX ON command can
*           include a BAR GRAPH and a percentage sign.
*
********************

IF !FILE("FILENOS.DBF")
   ? "Data files not present.   Run Startup Program, re-try!"
   QUIT
ENDIF

CLEAR SCREEN
@ 0,0 SAY "Working on the Indexing Technique"
@ 1,0 SAY "Percentage Index: "
USE Filenos
INDEX ON STR(RECNO()) + PERCENTAGE(1,18) TO Per
GO TOP
WAIT
DO WHILE !EOF()
   @ 20,00 SAY RECNO()
   SKIP
ENDDO


********************

FUNCTION Percentage
```

```
35 :
36 :     PARAMETERS a, b
37 :
38 :     IF TYPE("a") = "U" .OR. TYPE("b") = "U"
39 :        RETURN("")
40 :     ENDIF
41 :
42 :     IF RECNO() > LASTREC()
43 :        @ a, b SAY TRANSFORM( 0, "999.99 %")
44 :     ELSE
45 :        @ a, b SAY TRANSFORM((RECNO()/LASTREC())*100, "999.99 %")
46 :     ENDIF
47 :     INKEY(.2)
48 :     RETURN("")
50 :
51 : * End of File
```

The key to this example is in the testing of the data state of the two parameters that, in the INDEX ON command, set the stage for this unique feature. Look at lines 38 through 40; the data type for the two parameter variables **a** and **b** while indexing will both be numeric. However, once the indexing operation has completed, and since the key still contains reference to the Percentage() function, any reference to the database with this index will continue to call the function without values. Since no values are specifically passed to the Percentage() function for a SKIP or a SEEK operation, the data types will be "U" and will cause the function to simply return a null byte, avoiding the displaying feature. Looking further, we can see the logic in this because, at INDEX time, the row and column coordinates passed to the Percentage() function are constants and are not involved in the specific key of the index.

If percentages are not your ideal graphical interface, you take the same concept and display a bar chart. Consider this coding example:

```
********************
* Name      Morentx.prg
* Author    Stephen J. Straley
* Date      June 1, 1989
* Notice    Copyright (c) 1988 Stephen J. Straley & Associates
* Compile   Clipper Morentx -m
* Release   Summer 87
* Link      PLINK86 FI Morentx LIB Extend LIB Clipper;
* Note      This shows how a simple INDEX ON command can
*           include a BAR GRAPH with a SEEK operation.
*
********************

IF !FILE("FILENOS.DBF")
   ? "Data files not present. Run Startup Program, re-try!"
   QUIT
ENDIF

```

```
19 : CLEAR SCREEN
20 : @ 0,0 SAY "Working on the First Indexing Technique"
21 : counter = 0
22 : USE Filenos
23 : INDEX ON STR(RECNO()) + BARCHART(2,01,@counter) TO Bar
24 : @ 20,00 SAY "Any key for a seek..."
25 : INKEY(0)
26 : CLEAR SCREEN
27 : GO TOP
28 : DO WHILE !EOF()
29 :    @ 20,00 SAY RECNO()
30 :    SKIP
31 : ENDDO
32 : WAIT "Next screen!"
33 : SEEK STR(LASTREC()-2)
34 : ? FOUND()
35 : ? EOF()
36 :
37 : *******************
38 :
39 : FUNCTION Barchart
40 :
41 :    PARAMETERS a, b, c
42 :
43 :    * Take the number of columns, the number of records, and
44 :    * find out how many records in the database represent a
45 :    * column.  This is slightly modified for this example for
46 :    * it turns off the display if any of the parameters are
47 :    * missing or void.
48 :
49 :    IF TYPE("c") = "U" .OR. TYPE("a") = "U" .OR. TYPE("b") = "U"
50 :       RETURN("")
51 :    ENDIF
52 :
53 :    columns   = 78 - b
54 :    records   = LASTREC()
55 :    recpercol = columns / records
56 :
57 :    IF EMPTY(counter)
58 :       @ a-1,b-1 TO a+1,80 DOUBLE
59 :       PUBLIC startat, remainder
60 :       startat = b
61 :       remainder = 0
62 :    ENDIF
63 :
64 :    counter   = RECNO()
65 :    @ a, startat SAY REPLICATE(CHR(178), recpercol)
66 :
67 :    remainder = remainder + (recpercol - INT(recpercol))
68 :    startat = startat + INT(recpercol)
69 :    IF remainder >= 1
70 :       @ ROW(),COL() SAY CHR(178)
71 :       startat = startat + 1
72 :       remainder = remainder - 1
```

```
   ENDIF
   RETURN("")
* End of File
```

CONDITIONAL INDEXING

The previous section implies the ability to create conditional indexing. Hypothesize the following scenario: A report is needed of the current subscription base. In the database there are enough fields to contain summer housing information, winter housing information, or both. Surveys have shown that 40 percent of the user base has a summer residence. The report, a "cold-call" sheet for high-volume marketing types, will list only one telephone number: the summer address phone (if there is one) or the winter address phone. The sales representative will not call both. A program is needed to produce this report; however, the program should traverse the database only once. The following is an example of this concept:

```
********************
* Name      Condit.prg
* Author    Stephen J. Straley
* Date      July 15, 1989
* Notice    Copyright (c) 1989 Stephen J. Straley & Associates
*           All Rights Reserved
* Compile   Clipper Condit -m
* Release   Summer 87
* Link      PLINK86 FI Condit LIB Clipper LIB Extend;
* Note      This program shows how a conditional index works.
*
********************
? "Using the Files... and indexing"
USE Filenos
INDEX ON IF( EMPTY(file_size), disk_no, sub_no) TO Condit
GO TOP
DO WHILE !EOF()
   ? RECNO()
   ?? SPACE(5) + IF(EMPTY(Filenos->file_size), ;
      Filenos->disk_no, Filenos->sub_no)
   ?? IF( EMPTY(Filenos->file_size), "  <<-Special", "")
   SKIP
   IF INKEY() = 27
      EXIT
   ENDIF
ENDDO
* End of File
```

This example demonstrates the simple use of Clipper's immediate IF() function. We have substituted the summer and winter addresses with the fields **disk_no** and **sub_no**. The only trouble with simulated conditional indexing is that not only must the index file be properly built, but the same test that built the index must be made for printing out the report as well. In this example, we see the IF() function being called on line 16 to create the INDEX, but the same test is performed on line 22 when the answer is eventually displayed in this simulated report.

Of course, we could carry the idea of unique indexing to another realm: checksum algorithms and multilevel conditional indexing. The latter concept expands on the previous coding extract and allows for not just a simple IF() function but a DO CASE...ENDCASE or IF...ELSEIF...ENDIF construction. Multicased tests can condense an expression down to a simple 1- or 2-byte index key. A good example would be a user-defined function that took the various state fields in a database and a special one-digit code that would convert the zip codes into their proper order.

Along with this notion is the concept of a checksum. A checksum is primarily used for data validation. In many data entry shops, one person is responsible for entering the data while another individual reenters some of the same information. In both cases, the data is converted to a single checksum figure and the record is considered "validated" when the checksum figure derived from the first pass of the record matches the second pass of the record. Consider the following program:

```
********************
* Name      Checkit.prg
* Author    Stephen J. Straley
* Date      July 15, 1989
* Notice    Copyright (c) 1989 Stephen J. Straley & Associates
*           All Rights Reserved
* Compile   Clipper Checkit -m
* Release   Summer 87
* Link      PLINK86 FI Checkit LIB Clipper LIB Extend;
* Note      This shows how the Checksum() function is called.
*
********************

CLEAR SCREEN
? "Using and indexing first time"
USE Filenos
GO (LASTREC() / 2)
search = sub_name
GO TOP
INDEX ON sub_name TO Check1
? "The search item is &search."
SEEK search
? "Item was " + IF(FOUND(), "", "not") + " found!"
USE
? "File size for CHECK1.NTX is " + ;
   TRANSFORM(Filesize("CHECK1.NTX"), "9999999999")
? "Using and indexing second time"
USE Filenos
```

```
29 : INDEX ON STR(Checksum(sub_name)) TO Check2
30 : ? "Search criteria is " + STR(Checksum(sub_name))
31 : SEEK Checksum(search)
32 : ? "Item was " + IF(FOUND(), "", "not") + " found!"
33 : USE
34 : ? "File size for CHECK2.NTX is " + ;
35 :    TRANSFORM(Filesize("CHECK2.NTX"), "9999999999")
36 :
37 : * ***********************************************
38 : * * The following procedure(s)/function(s) are  *
39 : * * part of Steve Straley's ToolkiT(tm) -        *
40 : * * Release 2, published by Four Seasons         *
41 : * * Publishing Co., Inc.  All Rights Reserved    *
42 : * * Information: 212-599-2141 / 800-662-2278     *
43 : * * All Rights Reserved                          *
44 : * ***********************************************
45 :
46 : ********************
47 :
48 : FUNCTION Filesize
49 :
50 :     PARAMETERS _temp
51 :
52 :     _temp = UPPER(LTRIM(TRIM(_temp)))
53 :     IF !FILE(_temp)
54 :        RETURN(0)
55 :     ENDIF
56 :
57 :     DECLARE _fname[1], _fsize[1]
58 :     ADIR(_temp, _fname, _fsize)
59 :     RETURN(_fsize[1])
60 :
61 : ********************
62 :
63 : FUNCTION Checksum
64 :
65 :     * Written and contributed by ESSOR MASO
66 :
67 :     PARAMETERS _astring
68 :
69 :     IF TYPE("_astring") != "C"
70 :        RETURN("")
71 :     ENDIF
72 :
73 :     PRIVATE _sum, _l, _qaz
74 :
75 :     _sum = 0
76 :     _l   = LEN(_astring)
77 :     FOR _qaz =1 TO _l
78 :        _sum = _sum + ASC(SUBSTR(_astring,_qaz,1))
79 :     NEXT
80 :     IF _l = 0
81 :        RETURN(0)
82 :     ELSE
```

```
83 :        * 16777216=2^24, 4294967296=2^32
84 :        RETURN((16777216 * _l - 256 * ASC(SUBSTR(_astring, ;
85 :                1,1)) + _sum * 257)%4294967296)
86 :     ENDIF
87 :
88 : * End of File
```

In this routine, we converted the 45-byte character field **sub_name** to a unique number using the Checksum() function written by Essor Maso. In this algorithm, you can see that the RETURNed number for each character field begins as a summation of the ASCII value of that character in the field. This takes place on lines 77 through 79. A massive mathematical equation (lines 84 and 85) that returns a unique number follows. Now, like many character-based indexes, it is sometimes possible to have two (or more) records with the same key value. The same could be said for the Checksum() function. Checksum is also like working with typical character-based fields, in which the more fields involved with the index, the lower the likelihood of duplicate keys. All that is needed in the above example is a bigger key expression for the second index. However, the point to this should not be lost: This technique assists in reducing the basic file size, which in turn reduces the demand on disk I/O. The index file Check1.ntx is over 108,000 bytes while the index file size for Check2.ntx is a little over 42,000 bytes. This test was based on 1800 records in the Filenos database.

Obviously, with the extension of Clipper user-defined functions and the open architecture of the language, the programmer is virtually left in charge.

VARIABLE SPEED REPORTS

Another added feature of the language is the ability to break out from a report. Better yet would be the ability to alter the speed of the output from the report. Before offering an explanation, here is a program that does just that:

```
********************
* Name      Speed.prg
* Author    Stephen J. Straley
* Date      July 15, 1989
* Notice    Copyright (c) 1989 Stephen J. Straley & Associates
*           All Rights Reserved
* Compile   Clipper Spped -m
* Release   Summer 87
* Link      PLINK86 FI Speed LIB Clipper LIB Extend;
* Note      This shows how the use of the plus, minus, and
*           ESC keys can affect the output from a .FRM
*           file.
*
********************

pause = 100
```

```
17 : USE FIlenos
18 : REPORT FORM Filenos WHILE Brkpoint()
19 :
20 : * *********************************************
21 : * * The following procedure(s)/function(s) are  *
22 : * * part of Steve Straley's ToolkiT(tm) -       *
23 : * * Release 2, published by Four Seasons        *
24 : * * Publishing Co., Inc.  All Rights Reserved   *
25 : * * Information: 212-599-2141 / 800-662-2278    *
26 : * * All Rights Reserved                         *
27 : * *********************************************
28 :
29 : FUNCTION Brkpoint
30 :
31 :    PRIVATE _whatkey, _x
32 :
33 :    _whatkey = INKEY()
34 :
35 :    IF _whatkey = ASC("+")
36 :       pause = pause + 25
37 :    ELSEIF _whatkey = ASC("-")
38 :       pause = pause - 25
39 :       IF pause < 0
40 :          pause = 0
41 :       ENDIF
42 :    ELSEIF _whatkey = 27  && The ESC key
43 :       RETURN(.F.)
44 :    ENDIF
45 :
46 :    FOR _x = 1 TO pause
47 :    NEXT
48 :
49 :    RETURN(.T.)
50 :
51 : * End of File
```

This little program works from a report file named Filenos.frm that simply places two fields on the screen. The two fields are **disk_no** and **sub_no**. On line 16, a PUBLICly implied variable named **pause** is initialized to 100 and is the key to this feature. While the report is printing out from line 18, Clipper will call the Brkpoint() function for each record in the Filenos database. This means that the REPORT FORM command will first call the function, resolve the value it may return, and, if allowed, print the specified fields in the report. Looking at the function that begins its definition on line 29, we see that when the call to the function is made, the ASCII value of the INKEY() function is stored to the variable **_whatkey**. If the plus key was pressed when the call was made, the value of **pause** will increase by 25; if the minus key was pressed when the call was made, the value of **pause** will decrease by 25. Additionally in this test, if the value of **pause** should drop below 0, the value is reset to 0 (lines 39 through 41). Finally, if the Esc key is pressed when the call is made, the function will RETURN a logical false value (.F.) that will complete the value for the WHILE clause on line 18 and will tell the Clipper REPORT FORM command to stop executing.

However, if the Esc key is not pressed and either the plus or the minus key is, lines 46 and 47 will be executed. This is simply a FOR...NEXT loop for the duration of 0 to the value of **pause**. After this loop, the function returns a logical true (.T.) to the WHILE clause and allows the REPORT FORM command to continue to print.

This means that the plus and minus keys can either speed up or slow down the output of the report. Of course, you can add extra hot keys to stop or pause a report or perform any other operation. The important concept here is the user-defined function on the WHILE clause working with a variable initialized at a higher level.

NESTING GETS

While there are many fine products on the market, like Neil Weicher's GET-IT program, that go far beyond simply nesting GETs, pure Clipper code can be written for simple nested GETs. This technique came about from a need, as most techniques do, to let the end user quickly add an item to a code table or to an inventory database while entering information on an invoice. Many times, end users will not realize that a specific inventory item or code is not yet logged in, yet they will proceed to enter information on the invoice. Then, in the middle of the operation, they come to the astonishing discovery (especially when your validation routines tell them) that the item is not yet in the system. There they sit with a screen (or two) full of data that would be lost if they could not simply suspend the current READ, switch to the inventory section of the application, and add the item. This is the heart of nesting GETs: to have a series of GETs at one point in the program suspended while a series of GETs at another data entry point is active. Now that we have described the need, here is the solution to fill it:

```
********************
* Name      Nestget.prg
* Author    Stephen J. Straley
* Date      July 15, 1989
* Notice    Copyright (c) 1989 Stephen J. Straley & Associates
*           All Rights Reserved
* Compile   Clipper Nestget -m
* Release   Summer 87
* Link      PLINK86 FI Nestget LIB Clipper LIB Extend;
* Note      This shows how to work with nesting GETs
*           in pure Clipper code.
*
********************

* Each subscript represents each nested GET level.

PUBLIC counter[4], looping[4]
AFILL(counter, 1)
```

```
019 : AFILL(looping, .T.)
020 : STORE 0 TO a, b, c, d, e, f, g, h, i, j, k, l, m, ;
021 :            n, o, p, q, r, s, t
022 : SET SCOREBOARD OFF
023 :
024 : DO WHILE looping[1]
025 :    level = 1          && This is for the level marker
026 :    CLEAR SCREEN
027 :    @ 0,0 SAY " F10 = next level of GETS | ESC = TO Exit "+;
028 :                " | PgUp = Up a Level "
029 :    SET KEY -9 TO Level1
030 :    @ 2,0 SAY "Enter first value =>" GET a VALID ;
031 :         PROCESS(level)
032 :    @ 3,0 SAY "     second value =>" GET b VALID ;
033 :         PROCESS(level)
034 :    @ 4,0 SAY "      third value =>" GET c VALID ;
035 :         PROCESS(level)
036 :    @ 5,0 SAY "     fourth value =>" GET d VALID ;
037 :         PROCESS(level)
038 :    READ
039 :    IF LASTKEY() = 27
040 :       EXIT
041 :    ENDIF
042 :    counter[level] = 1  && Resets counter to the GET number
043 : ENDDO
044 :
045 : ******************
046 :
047 : PROCEDURE Level1
048 :
049 :    PARAMETERS program, line, variable
050 :
051 :    SET KEY 18 TO Getout
052 :    SET KEY  3 TO Getout
053 :    CLEAR GETS
054 :    DO WHILE looping[2]
055 :       level = 2
056 :       @ 5,40 CLEAR
057 :       @ 6,00 CLEAR
058 :       SET KEY -9 TO Level2
059 :       @ 5,40 SAY "Enter Sixth Value =>" GET e VALID ;
060 :             PROCESS(level)
061 :       @ 6,40 SAY "     Seventh Value =>" GET f VALID ;
062 :             PROCESS(level)
063 :       @ 7,40 SAY "     Eighth Value =>" GET g VALID ;
064 :             PROCESS(level)
065 :       @ 8,40 SAY "      Ninth Value =>" GET h VALID ;
066 :             PROCESS(level)
067 :       @ 9,40 SAY "      Tenth Value =>" GET i VALID ;
068 :             PROCESS(level)
069 :       READ
070 :       IF looping[level]
071 :          counter[level] = 1
072 :       ENDIF
```

```
   ENDDO
   KEYBOARD REPLICATE(CHR(24), (counter[level-1] - 1) )
   counter[level] = 1   && Resets counter to the GET number
   looping[level] = .T.

********************

PROCEDURE Level2

   PARAMETERS program, line, variable

   CLEAR GETS
   DO WHILE looping[3]
      level = 3
      @ 7,00 CLEAR TO 20,39
      @ 11,00 CLEAR
      SET KEY -9 TO Level3
      @  7,0 SAY "Enter 11th Value =>" GET j VALID ;
             PROCESS(level)
      @  8,0 SAY "      12th Value =>" GET k VALID ;
             PROCESS(level)
      @  9,0 SAY "      13th Value =>" GET l VALID ;
             PROCESS(level)
      @ 10,0 SAY "      14th Value =>" GET m VALID ;
             PROCESS(level)
      @ 11,0 SAY "      15th Value =>" GET n VALID ;
             PROCESS(level)
      @ 12,0 SAY "      16th Value =>" GET o VALID ;
             PROCESS(level)
      READ
      IF looping[level]
         counter[level] = 1
      ENDIF
   ENDDO
   KEYBOARD REPLICATE(CHR(24), (counter[level-1] - 1) )
   counter[level] = 1   && Resets counter to the GET number
   looping[level] = .T.

********************

PROCEDURE Level3

   PARAMETERS program, line, variable

   CLEAR GETS
   DO WHILE looping[4]
      level = 4
      SET KEY -9 TO
      @ 11,40 CLEAR TO 20,79
      @ 11,40 SAY "Enter 17th Value =>" GET p VALID ;
              PROCESS(level)
      @ 12,40 SAY "      18th Value =>" GET q VALID ;
              PROCESS(level)
      @ 13,40 SAY "      19th Value =>" GET r VALID ;
```

```
127 :                PROCESS(level)
128 :        @ 14,40 SAY "      20th Value =>" GET s VALID ;
129 :                PROCESS(level)
130 :        @ 15,40 SAY "      21st Value =>" GET t VALID ;
131 :                PROCESS(level)
132 :        READ
133 :        IF looping[level]
134 :           counter[level] = 1
135 :        ENDIF
136 :     ENDDO
137 :     KEYBOARD REPLICATE(CHR(24), (counter[level-1] - 1) )
138 :     counter[level] = 1
139 :     looping[level] = .T.
140 :
141 : *******************
142 :
143 : FUNCTION Process
144 :
145 :     PARAMETERS the_number
146 :
147 :     * This function processes the keystroke which completed
148 :     * the GET and determines how to increment the counter[]
149 :     * subscript value.
150 :
151 :     IF counter[the_number] = 1 .AND. LASTKEY() = 5
152 :        RETURN(.F.)
153 :     ELSE
154 :       counter[the_number] = counter[the_number] + ;
155 :               IF((LASTKEY() = 5), -1, 1)
156 :       RETURN(.T.)
157 :     ENDIF
158 :
159 : *******************
160 :
161 : PROCEDURE Getout
162 :
163 :     PARAMETERS program, line, variable
164 :
165 :     * This sets the proper loop variable and CLEARs the
166 :     * pending GET stack
167 :
168 :     looping[level] = .F.
169 :     CLEAR GETS
170 :
171 : * End of File
```

Look at the lines beginning with the array of counters that is PUBLICly declared on line 17 with the PUBLIC command. The essence of this array is that for each nesting level, there will be an associated counter element that will keep track of which GET was the last pending GET. In theory, as you go from the top level to the Level1 Procedure, the element in **counter[1]** will point to the GET that was pending in the main procedure. As you go from procedure to procedure, the hot key is SET to new procedures; the main module points to Procedure Level1, Procedure Level1 points to the Level2 Procedure, and Level2 Procedure calls Procedure Level3 if the F10 key is pressed. In each procedure, the variable **level** keeps track of which level to point to in the **counter[]** array. The VALID Function Process actually increments the **counter[]** array element, based on the LASTKEY() pressed within the GET. In other words, if the up arrow is pressed (LASTKEY() = 5 is on line 155), the **counter[]** element should be decremented, not incremented. On line 151, the test is to see if the LASTKEY() is equal to the up arrow and if the user is working on the first GET. If so, the function should return a logical false (.F.). In all cases, the Function Process processes this information, stores the proper value in the array based on the value of the **level** variable, and returns a logical true (.T.) to complete the GET. Once that particular level of GETS is completed, the KEYBOARD is stuffed with the proper number of down arrow keys to reposition the end user on the proper GET. Additionally, the **counter[]** element for that particular area is reestablished back to reflect the first GET.

After you've grasped the mutual concepts of the VALID clause with the Function Process, the SET KEY TO logic in conjunction with the F10 key, the **level** variable, and the **counter[]** array, there is one remaining trick. The escape routine is controlled by the Procedure Getout, which is in turn toggled by the SET KEY TO logic on lines 51 and 52. As you can see, the procedure not only CLEARS the GETS, but it sets the **looping[]** element to a logical false (.F.). This causes the loop for that particular nested GET to be terminated and to pop up to the previous GET condition. In all cases, the lower-level procedures reset the **counter[]** element value as well as stuffing the KEYBOARD with the proper number of down arrow keystrokes.

MAKING A MEMOEDIT() LOOK LIKE A READ

Of course, not every programming situation will call for such an extensive measure as the algorithms used to simulated nested GETs. It is possible to fake a GET by making the MEMOEDIT() look and feel like a GET. Indeed, this may be an example of something that looks like a duck, walks like a duck, and talks like a duck, but is not a duck. Consider this coding example:

```
********************
* Name      Notaget.prg
* Author    Stephen J. Straley
* Date      July 15, 1989
* Notice    Copyright (c) 1989 Stephen J. Straley & Associates
*           All Rights Reserved
* Compile   Clipper Notaget -m
* Release   Summer 87
* Link      PLINK86 FI Notaget LIB Clipper LIB Extend;
* Note      This program shows how to fake a GET in Clipper
*           using the MEMOEDIT() function.  Right now, this
*           example will only work with character strings;
*           however, it can be modified with little effort
*           to work with other data types and formats.
```

```
015 : *
016 : ********** **********
017 :
018 : SET SCOREBOARD OFF
019 : STORE SPACE(10) TO a, b, c
020 : SET KEY 9 TO Callit  && The TAB key.
021 : DO WHILE .T.
022 :    CLEAR SCREEN
023 :    @  4,00 SAY "Press the ESC Key to exit "+;
024 :                   "this Test / TAB to Fake a GET"
025 :    @  6,10 SAY "Enter a value " GET a
026 :    @  8,10 SAY "       b value " GET b
027 :    @ 10,10 SAY "       c value " GET c
028 :    READ
029 :    IF LASTKEY() = 27
030 :       EXIT
031 :    ENDIF
032 : ENDDO
033 :
034 : ******************
035 :
036 : PROCEDURE Callit
037 :
038 :    PARAMETERS p, l, v
039 :
040 :    IF v = "A"      && Fakegets 'b'
041 :      _tcolor = SETCOLOR()
042 :      SAVE SCREEN
043 :      @ 6,37 SAY "Enter 'B' value: "
044 :      SETCOLOR(REVERSE())
045 :      b = RESTRICT(b, 6,54)
046 :      SETCOLOR(_tcolor)
047 :      RESTORE SCREEN
048 :    ELSEIF v = "B"  && Fakesgets 'c'
049 :      _tcolor = SETCOLOR()
050 :      SAVE SCREEN
051 :      @ 8,37 SAY "Enter 'C' value: "
052 :      SETCOLOR(REVERSE())
053 :      c = RESTRICT(c, 8,54)
054 :      SETCOLOR(_tcolor)
055 :      RESTORE SCREEN
056 :    ENDIF
057 :
058 : ******************
059 :
060 : FUNCTION Restrict
061 :
062 :    PARAMETERS withwhat, atwhat, andwhat
063 :
064 :    limit = 0
065 :    charcnt = LEN(withwhat)
066 :    oldval  = withwhat
067 :    newval  = withwhat
068 :    RETURN(SUBSTR(STRTRAN(MEMOEDIT(newval, ;
```

```
069 :          atwhat, andwhat, atwhat, andwhat + ;
070 :              LEN(withwhat)+1, .T., "LT"), ;
071 :    CHR(13)+CHR(10)," "),1, LEN(withwhat)))
072 :
073 : *******************
074 :
075 : FUNCTION Lt
076 :
077 :    PARAMETERS the_mode, the_row, the_col
078 :
079 :    IF LASTKEY() = 27
080 :        RETURN(0)
081 :    ELSEIF LASTKEY() = 13
082 :        KEYBOARD CHR(23)
083 :        RETURN(0)
084 :    ELSEIF LASTKEY() = 23
085 :        RETURN(0)
086 :    ELSEIF the_mode = 0
087 :        IF LASTKEY() = 8 .OR. LASTKEY() = 7
088 :            limit = IF(EMPTY(limit), limit, limit - 1)
089 :            RETURN(1)
090 :        ELSEIF LASTKEY() >= 32 .AND. LASTKEY() <= 127
091 :            IF limit = charcnt
092 :                limit = limit + 1
093 :                KEYBOARD CHR(8)
094 :                RETURN(0)
095 :            ELSE
096 :                limit = limit + 1
097 :                RETURN(1)
098 :            ENDIF
099 :        ELSE
100 :            RETURN(1)
101 :        ENDIF
102 :    ENDIF
103 :    RETURN(1)
104 :
105 : * *********************************************
106 : * * The following procedure(s)/function(s) are  *
107 : * * part of Steve Straley's ToolkiT(tm) -        *
108 : * * Release 2, published by Four Seasons         *
109 : * * Publishing Co., Inc.  All Rights Reserved   *
110 : * * Information: 212-599-2141 / 800-662-2278     *
111 : * * All Rights Reserved                          *
112 : * * *********************************************
113 :
114 : FUNCTION Reverse
115 :
116 :    PARAMETERS _a
117 :
118 :    * _a is the color string to reverse
119 :
120 :    IF PCOUNT() = 0
121 :        _a = SETCOLOR()
122 :    ENDIF
```

```
123 :
124 :     PRIVATE _b
125 :
126 :     * _b is the SAY color string
127 :
128 :     _b = STRTRAN(SUBSTR(_a, 1, AT(",", _a)-1), "+", "")
129 :
130 :     RETURN(SUBSTR(_b, AT("/", _b)+1) + "/" + SUBSTR(_b, ;
131 :                   1, AT("/", _b)-1))
132 :
133 : * End of File
```

The key to this example is twofold. First, we have to take one of the natural characteristics of a GET and make it work for a MEMOEDIT(). This is, of course, the reverse video in which most GET fields and/or variables appear. If a MEMOEDIT() is to look like a GET, it must be set to the colors of the GET. In this example, no color is used; therefore, the start-up colors for this program will be "7/0,0/7." The "0/7" is for the GET fields, and the "7/0" is for the SAY and MEMOEDIT() functions. However, by reversing the colors, the SAYs and the MEMOEDIT()s will look like a GET. Indeed, within the Callit procedure that is set to a hot key (the TAB key on line 20), we can see on lines 44 and 52 that the color of the system is reversed with the Reverse() function. Of course, in both cases, this is after a simple SAY instruction is issued (lines 43 and 51).

Finally, we have to restrict the number of characters that will be allowed in the MEMOEDIT(). In a GET, this is specified either by the PICTURE clause or the default length of the field or variable. Here, if the width of the character should be exceeded, the KEYBOARD is stuffed with a CHR(8) (line 93), which will delete the prior key. In addition, if you look closely, you will see that the width of the MEMOEDIT() will be one greater than the value of the LEN() function (line 70). This is to allow the CHR(8) to perform on that line and not down on the next line. Remember, MEMOEDIT() will automatically word-wrap to a new line and in the case of a GET, we do not want that. Therefore, we must make the width of the area for the MEMOEDIT() one character larger so that if a character is typed in, the cursor will not be forced to a new line and all will be visually correct.

GETS FROM RIGHT TO LEFT

One of the ways Clipper shows its muscle over competitive interpreters is that it allows user-defined functions in many places of the command line. Unlike in other packages, with Clipper the concept of a user-defined function is no different from a user-defined procedure or a user-defined command. Since the symbol reference to a variable string is stored in the same place as a function name (or a procedure name), the two may be virtually interchangeable. That location is the symbol table; therefore, it is possible to place a user-defined function directly in the PICTURE clause, and if we are careful, we can now get our GETs to look like this:

```
001 : ********************
002 : * Name      Onapict.prg
003 : * Author    Stephen J. Straley
004 : * Date      July 15, 1989
005 : * Notice    Copyright (c) 1989 Stephen J. Straley & Associates
006 : *           All Rights Reserved
007 : * Compile   Clipper Onapict -m
008 : * Release   Summer 87
009 : * Link      PLINK86 FI Onapict LIB Clipper LIB Extend;
010 : * Note      This shows that user-defined functions are
011 : *           applicable to the string for a PICTURE clause.
012 : *
013 : ********************
014 :
015 : CLEAR
016 : wait_st = SPACE(40)
017 : DO WHILE .T.
018 :    @ 4,10 SAY "BACKSPACE and Left Arrow Keys WORK!!!" + ;
019 :               "  Press ESC to Exit!"
020 :    @ 2, 5 SAY "Enter a File Name => " GET wait_st ;
021 :    PICT EXPLODEC("XXXXXXXXXXXXXXXXXXXXXXXXXXXXXXXXXXXXXXXXXX",;
022 :    @wait_st)
023 :    READ
024 :    IF LASTKEY() = 27
025 :       EXIT
026 :    ENDIF
027 :    totbytes = FILESIZE(wait_st)
028 :    IF EMPTY(totbytes)
029 :       @ 6,10 SAY "That file is NOT on the disk"
030 :    ELSE
031 :       @ 6,10 SAY "That file IS on the disk!!"
032 :       @ 8,10 SAY totbytes
033 :    ENDIF
034 :    @ 10,5 SAY "Press Any Key to Try Again!!!"
035 :    INKEY(0)
036 :    @ 2,0 CLEAR
037 : ENDDO
038 :
039 : * **********************************************
040 : * * The following procedure(s)/function(s) are  *
041 : * * part of Steve Straley's ToolkiT(tm) -       *
042 : * * Release 2, published by Four Seasons        *
043 : * * Publishing Co., Inc.  All Rights Reserved   *
044 : * * Information: 212-599-2141 / 800-662-2278    *
045 : * * All Rights Reserved                         *
046 : * **********************************************
047 :
048 : ********************
049 :
050 : FUNCTION Explodec
051 :
052 :    PARAMETERS _a, _tchar
053 :
054 :    PRIVATE _b, _c, _gfar, _astr, _disp, _awhat, ;
```

```
055 :                 _how, _tchar, _front
056 :
057 :     _b = ROW()
058 :     _c = COL()
059 :     _gfar = LEN("&_a")
060 :     _astr = SPACE(_gfar)
061 :     @ _b,_c GET _astr PICT "&_a."
062 :     CLEAR GETS
063 :     _disp = ""
064 :     _awhat = _c + _gfar - 1
065 :     @ _b,_awhat + 1 SAY ""
066 :     _how = 1
067 :
068 :     DO WHILE INKEY(0) <> 13
069 :        DO CASE
070 :        CASE LASTKEY() = 27
071 :           EXIT
072 :        CASE (LASTKEY() >= 32 .AND. LASTKEY() <= 126)
073 :
074 :           _disp = _disp + CHR(LASTKEY())
075 :           _how = _how + 1
076 :
077 :           @ _b,_awhat GET _disp PICT "&_a."
078 :
079 :           IF _awhat > _c
080 :              _awhat = _awhat - 1
081 :           ENDIF
082 :        CASE LASTKEY() = 19 .OR. LASTKEY() = 8 .OR. ;
083 :                               LASTKEY() = 7
084 :           _disp = SPACE(_gfar - LEN(_disp) + 1) + ;
085 :                   SUBSTR(_disp, 1, LEN(_disp) - 1)
086 :           _how = _how - 1
087 :           @ _b,_c GET _disp PICT "&_a."
088 :           _disp = LTRIM(_disp)
089 :           IF _awhat >= _c + _gfar - 1
090 :              _awhat = _c + _gfar - 1
091 :           ELSE
092 :              _awhat = _awhat + 1
093 :           ENDIF
094 :        ENDCASE
095 :        CLEAR GETS
096 :
097 :     ENDDO
098 :
099 :     IF LASTKEY() = 27
100 :        KEYBOARD CHR(27)
101 :     ELSE
102 :        KEYBOARD CHR(13)
103 :     ENDIF
104 :
105 :     _front = SPACE(_gfar - LEN(_disp))
106 :     _tchar = _front + _disp
107 :     @ _b,_c SAY ""
108 :     RETURN("&_a.")
```

```

********************

FUNCTION Filesize

   PARAMETERS _temp

   _temp = UPPER(LTRIM(TRIM(_temp)))
   IF !FILE(_temp)
      RETURN(0)
   ENDIF

   DECLARE _fname[1], _fsize[1]
   ADIR(_temp, _fname, _fsize)
   RETURN(_fsize[1])

* End of File
```

Be aware of the placement of this example. If it is placed in the middle of a series of GETs, the GETs will be displayed on the screen up to the line with the user-defined function on the PICTURE clause. At that point, the user-defined function will take over. Once that operation is completed, the rest of the GETs will be displayed and the READ command will take effect, starting back at the top of the list and working its way down. Therefore, this trick should be used only in a series of GETs that will be followed by a CLEAR GETS command, at the top of a series of GETS, at the bottom of a series of GETs, or, preferably, by itself.

END OF MEMO AND MEMO RESTRICTIONS

Finally, we will discuss a few unique items pertaining to memos. The two biggest "nice-to-haves" for memo fields are the ability to restrict the cursor from continuously going beyond a predefined limit and the ability to position the cursor at the end of the memo. The first feature was easy to simulate by working with several Clipper features, most importantly, the ability to call another function from the MEMOEDIT() function. This is simulated in the Notaget.prg listed earlier in the chapter. Limiting the number of lines for a MEMOEDIT() is just as easy. By counting the number of times the CHR(13) is entered inside of the user-defined function called by the MEMOEDIT() function, you can stuff the KEYBOARD to get rid of it. Having solved one of the first mysteries of the MEMOEDIT() function, the second point should be simple. There are two ways to get the cursor to sit at the end of a memo. Initially, the cursor will sit at the top leftmost corner of the memo and windowed area unless otherwise specified. This means using almost all of the other parameters available in MEMOEDIT(). The first example uses this technique.

```
********************
* Name      Badmemo.prg
* Author    Stephen J. Straley
* Date      July 15, 1989
```

```
05 : * Notice    Copyright (c) 1989 Stephen J. Straley & Associates
06 : *           All Rights Reserved
07 : * Compile   Clipper Badmemo -m
08 : * Release   Summer 87
09 : * Link      PLINK86 FI Badmemo LIB Clipper LIB Extend;
10 : * Note      This shows that the use of the 7th, 8th, and 9th
11 : *           parameters in MEMOEDIT() function works well
12 : *           in conjunction with functions in the ToolkiT
13 : *
14 : *******************
15 :
16 :
17 : string = "This is a test to see if the delete key will work "+;
18 :          "as I think it really should in order to give a fair "+;
19 :          "and honest test!."
20 : DO WHILE .T.
21 :    CLEAR SCREEN
22 :    @ 0,0 TO 7,41
23 :    string = MEMOEDIT(string, 1,1,6,40,.T.,"Keys", "", "", ;
24 :                      MLDOWN(string, 1, 40), ;
25 :                      MLOVER(string, 1, 40), 6 )
26 :    @ 8,0
27 :    WAIT "Press any key to do again, or ESC to quit!"
28 :    IF LASTKEY() = 27
29 :       EXIT
30 :    ENDIF
31 : ENDDO
32 :
33 : *******************
34 :
35 : FUNCTION Keys
36 :
37 :    PARAMETERS mode, row, col
38 :
39 :    RETURN(0)
40 :
41 : * **********************************************
42 : * * The following procedure(s)/function(s) are   *
43 : * * part of Steve Straley's ToolkiT(tm) -        *
44 : * * Release 2, published by Four Seasons         *
45 : * * Publishing Co., Inc.  All Rights Reserved    *
46 : * * Information: 212-599-2141 / 800-662-2278     *
47 : * * All Rights Reserved                          *
48 : * * **********************************************
49 :
50 : *******************
51 :
52 : FUNCTION Mldown
53 :
54 :    PARAMETER _thething, _begat, _endat
55 :
56 :    RETURN( MLCOUNT(_thething, _endat - _begat) )
57 :
```

```
58 : ********************
59 :
60 : FUNCTION Mlover
61 :
62 :    PARAMETERS _thething, _begat, _endat
63 :
64 :    RETURN(LEN(SUBSTR(_thething, MLPOS(_thething, ;
65 :          (_endat - _begat), MLCOUNT(_thething, ;
66 :          (_endat - _begat)) ) ) ) )
67 :
68 : * End of File
```

Here, the ninth parameter in the MEMOEDIT() function is used to set the row for the last screen position for the MEMOEDIT(). This insures that the screen will be filled with as much text as possible. To complete the process, two additional functions help yield the right values so that MEMOEDIT() knows exactly how many lines down and how many columns across are in the variable string. The extra two parameters passed to the Mldown() and Mlover() functions are the beginning and ending screen positions used within the MEMOEDIT() function. Taking a further look at line 23, the top left row and column coordinates are 1,1 and the bottom right row and column coordinates are 6,40. From this we can see that the beginning column position for the MEMOEDIT() function is 1 and the ending column position for the MEMOEDIT() is 40. These are the two values that are passed to both the Mldown() and Mlover() functions.

However, if you don't want to use all of those extra parameters to get the cursor where you want it, a simpler method may be possible, but it is only feasible with relatively small strings and/or memos. It involves stuffing the KEYBOARD with the proper number of down arrow and right arrow keys to position the cursor at the suitable location:

```
********************
* Name      Endmemo
* Author    Stephen J. Straley
* Date      July 20, 1989
* Notice    Copyright (c) 1989 Stephen J. Straley & Associates
*           All Rights Reserved
* Compile   Clipper Endmemo -m
* Release   Summer 87
* Link      PLINK86 FI Endmemo LIB Clipper LIB Extend;
* Note      This shows how the END OF MEMO can be reached
*           without the use of the extra parameters in
*           MEMOEDIT().
*
********************


string = "This is a test to see if the delete key will work "+;
         "as I think it really should in order to give a fair "+;
         "and honest test!."
DO WHILE .T.
```

```
21 :     CLEAR SCREEN
22 :     @ 0,0 TO 7,41
23 :     KEYBOARD Eomemo(string, 1, 40)
24 :     string = MEMOEDIT(string, 1,1,6,40,.T.,"Keys")
25 :     @ 8,0
26 :     WAIT "Press any key to do again, or ESC to quit!"
27 :     IF LASTKEY() = 27
28 :        EXIT
29 :     ENDIF
30 : ENDDO
31 :
32 : ********************
33 :
34 : FUNCTION Keys
35 :
36 :     PARAMETERS mode, row, col
37 :
38 :     RETURN(0)
39 :
40 : * **********************************************
41 : * * The following procedure(s)/function(s) are  *
42 : * * part of Steve Straley's ToolkiT(tm) -        *
43 : * * Release 2, published by Four Seasons         *
44 : * * Publishing Co., Inc.  All Rights Reserved    *
45 : * * Information: 212-599-2141 / 800-662-2278     *
46 : * * All Rights Reserved                          *
47 : * * **********************************************
48 : ********************
49 :
50 : FUNCTION Eomemo
51 :
52 :     PARAMETER _thething, _begat, _endat
53 :
54 :     PRIVATE _width
55 :
56 :     IF PCOUNT() = 2
57 :        _width = _begat
58 :     ELSEIF PCOUNT() = 3
59 :        _width = _endat - _begat
60 :     ELSE
61 :        _width = 79
62 :     ENDIF
63 :
64 :     _howdown = (MLCOUNT(_thething, _width) - 1)
65 :     _howover = LEN(SUBSTR(_thething, MLPOS(_thething, ;
66 :                         _width, _howdown + 1) ))
67 :
68 :     SET TYPEAHEAD TO _howdown + _howover
69 :
70 :     RETURN( REPLICATE(CHR(24), _howdown) + ;
71 :             REPLICATE(CHR(4), _howover) )
72 :
73 : * End of File
```

We could not use the KEYBOARD with the End key or with Ctrl-PgDn (for end of the memo) because of internal key conflicts that could not be resolved. Consider the End key for a moment. The ASCII value for this key is a 6, which is the same as Ctrl-F, or one-word-over-right. If the KEYBOARD was stuffed with CHR(6), instead of getting to the end of the line, the cursor would sit at the beginning of the first-word-right from the beginning of the line: Ctrl-F. However, when doing a test of LASTKEY() or INKEY(0), the value for the End key is a 6. Obviously, there is a key conflict here, and after a couple of calls and looking at the manual, we determined that there is no resolution to this situation. However, the Eomemo() function calculates the exact number of down arrow and right arrow keys needed to get the cursor to the proper location. Additionally, the TYPEAHEAD buffer is set to the number of bytes that will be eventually in the string that will be stuffed to the KEYBOARD (line 23).

SUMMARY

The entire focus of this chapter was to provide additional insight into the capabilities of the native Clipper language. Again, the key to good Clipper programming is to constantly look at the combinations of the commands and functions, at the architecture of the language, and at your own ingenuity to push the language even further. Constantly ask yourself "what if" and soon the nice-to-haves will be reality.

CHAPTER FIVE

Function-Oriented Programming

What is function-oriented programming and how can it benefit the programmer, the programming staff, and ultimately, the application? In simple terms, function-oriented programming is nothing new and is no different from the commonly used procedure-oriented programming as established by the basic dBASE and how-many-columns-across dialect. However, if we can alter our thinking patterns to accept this new approach, many corporate programming departments will run more smoothly because of a common base of style between C and Clipper programmers. You will begin to see this point as we look at specific Clipper code. Before we do that, we will define some terms.

Without going into the concept of parameter passing between the two ideas, a procedure can be loosely defined as a routine of code that "does" something. A function can be loosely defined as a routine of code that has "value." This does not mean that functions do not do anything; generally they do. However, it is the idea of functions having value that differentiates them from procedures. In other words, all functions are procedures, but not all procedures are functions.

In this sample piece of code, let's look at a generic function that takes the parameters passed to it and adds their values to the fields in a STRUCTURE EXTENDED database.

```
********************
* **********************************************
* * The following procedure(s)/function(s) are  *
* * part of Steve Straley's ToolkiT(tm) -        *
* * Release 2, published by Four Seasons         *
* * Publishing Co., Inc.  All Rights Reserved    *
* * Information: 212-599-2141 / 800-662-2278     *
* * All Rights Reserved                          *
* **********************************************

PROCEDURE Ap_it

   PARAMETERS _apa, _apb, _apc, _apd
   * _apa = the field name
   * _apb = the field data type
   * _apc = the field length
   * _apd = the field decimal

   * This function call is to replace the REPLACE field_name WITH
   * Now: AP_IT("Lastname","C",1)

   * This function replaces the parameters into a STRUCTURE EXTENDED
   * database that is previously created and open.

   IF PCOUNT() = 3
      _apd = 0
   ENDIF
   IF EMPTY(ALIAS())
      RETURN
   ELSEIF TYPE("field_name") = "U"
      RETURN
```

```
   ELSEIF TYPE("_apa") + TYPE("_apb") + TYPE("_apc") + ;
          TYPE("_apd") != "CCNN"
      RETURN
   ENDIF

   LOCATE ALL FOR UPPER(field_name) == UPPER(_apa)
   IF FOUND()
      RETURN(0)
   ELSE
      APPEND BLANK
      IF _apc > 255
         REPLACE field_name WITH _apa, field_type WITH _apb, ;
                 field_len WITH INT(_apc % 256), ;
                 field_dec WITH INT(_apc / 256)
      ELSE
         REPLACE field_name WITH _apa, field_type WITH _apb, ;
                 field_len WITH _apc, field_dec WITH _apd
      ENDIF
   ENDIF

* End of File
```

In Clipper, the RETURN statement is implied. That is to say that if the end of file marker for the .PRG file is tested for and experienced, or if the word FUNCTION or PROCEDURE is encountered, the preceding line will contain an implied RETURN command. In dBASE, the RETURN command is vital; in Clipper, it is just an extra piece of code that the compiler takes care of. But looking at this further, we should be able to see that this routine has no value: It simply performs a task. To call it (activate it), we would have this code:

```
CREATE Template
Do Ap_it WITH "LASTNAME", "C", 10
```

Even in the coding convention, we can only expect the **Ap_it** procedure to work on the STRUCTURE EXTENDED database named Template.

Clipper has one more concept that needs to be understood. The implied RETURN command is actually a return of a null byte. And as we go further into this chapter, you will see that this slight alteration to the fundamental concept will open up new avenues approaching the Clipper language. But before that, let's look at the concept of a function.

Remember, a function has a value. Often, functions have to do several things before returning a value, but the end result is the same: A specific value is returned. We work with functions every day. For example, we do not necessarily know precisely what operations are being performed on a database whenever the EOF() function is called, but we do know that its value is either a logical true (.T.) or a logical false (.F.). Look at this piece of code:

```
DO WHILE !EOF()
   * commands
ENDDO
```

If we were to isolate the EOF() function, we could see that this entity has a unique value. If you want to, you can look at functions as begin like memory variables. With memory variables, values are looked at, expressed, and even evaluated. The same can be said for functions. The only real difference between a function and a variable is that (a) the function will perform some action in order to obtain the value, and (b) the value is not maintained past the initial call. In other words, variables hold their values; functions only have value the one time they are called. This obviously means that functions need to be repeatedly called in order to continuously get a value, or their values need to be stored to memory variables.

Now, let's consider a function of our own: a user-defined function. Consider the following function:

```
********************
* ***********************************************
* * The following procedure(s)/function(s) are  *
* * part of Steve Straley's ToolkiT(tm) -       *
* * Release 2, published by Four Seasons        *
* * Publishing Co., Inc.  All Rights Reserved   *
* * Information: 212-599-2141 / 800-662-2278    *
* * All Rights Reserved                         *
* ***********************************************

FUNCTION Asciisum

   PARAMETERS _tstring

   IF EMPTY(PCOUNT())
      RETURN(0)
   ELSEIF TYPE("_tstring") != "C"
      RETURN(0)
   ENDIF

   PRIVATE _qaz, _ttot

   _ttot = 0

   FOR _qaz = 1 TO LEN(_tstring)
      _ttot = _ttot + ASC(SUBSTR(_tstring, _qaz, 1))
   NEXT

   RETURN(_ttot)

* End of File
```

When used in the program, it may look something like this:

```
? Asciisum("Hello")
```

Or something like this:

```
STORE Asciisum("Hello") TO variable
```

Or even something on this order:

```
IF Asciisum("Hello") > 100
   * do something
ENDIF
```

In all three cases, we took the value of the function ASCIISUM() and did something with it: expressed it, stored it, or evaluated it. One cannot do this to a procedure. Therefore, we should know our functions more than we should know our procedures or commands. They are the keys to good structured programming.

PROCEDURES HAVE VALUE

Earlier in this chapter we said that an implied RETURN command is given to every Clipper procedure and that the RETURN actually returns a null byte to the calling application. Let us expand on this. Looking to the internals of Clipper, let's break apart the structure of a typical Clipper command. There are three elements, or tokens, that make up the command line: a code token, a constant token, and a symbol token. The code and constant tokens are fairly easy to understand: constants are literal strings and code tokens are those elements of a command line that are part of the Clipper base language (for example, mathematical operations, commands). Variables, expressions, and even procedure and function names are kept in the symbol table. Both the procedure and the function are symbol tokens and there is no difference between the two. To test this theory, consider the following code extract:

```
*******************
* Name      Example.prg
* Author    Stephen J. Straley
* Date      July 4, 1989
* Notice    Copyright (c) 1989 Stephen J. Straley & Associates
* Compile   Clipper Example -m
* Release   Summer 87
* Link      PLINK86 FI Example LIB Clipper LIB Extend;
* Note      This shows how a procedure and a user defined
*           function cannot have the same name!
*
*******************

CLEAR SCREEN
DO Pop_up
? Pop()

*******************

PROCEDURE Pop_up
```

```

   ? "Hello there"

******************

FUNCTION Pop_up

   RETURN("Hello there")

* End of File
```

If we tried to compile this, we would get the following screen:

```
E>clipper example -m
The Clipper Compiler, Summer '87
Copyright (c) Nantucket Corp 1985-1987.  All Rights Reserved.
Microsoft C Runtime Library Routines,
Copyright (c) Microsoft Corp 1984-1987.  All Rights Reserved.

Compiling EXAMPLE.PRG
line 26:  symbol redefinition error
FUNCTION Pop_up
          ^
1 error
Code Pass 1
FATAL at 0 - invalid procedure mode
```

A duplicate symbol message means that Clipper tried to assign the token the name of the function but found that it had previously assigned a token with that name to the procedure. Therefore, it would be safe to say that, in Clipper, there is no difference between a procedure and a function. Basically, a procedure does have a value: a null byte. It is interesting to note that one of the perceived major accomplishments of the Clipper language is the user-defined function. However, by considering all procedures with the same fundamentals as functions, this accomplishment becomes staggering. To some, the idea of a user-defined function is hard to grasp even though the idea of a user-defined procedure is as second nature as riding a bike; one of the very first things we programmed in dBASE was a procedure. By turning our focus away from the procedure and toward the function, Clipper became what it is today. It is this difference that sets it apart from all of the other would-be compilers.

CODING FOR THE FUTURE

Talking about this in theory is one thing, but seeing the code on paper is a different matter. By altering our coding technique, we can see new potential and new horizons that can be tackled by the Clipper compiler. Let's keep in mind the emphasis of this book: introducing the C language. Along with this must be the conventions used by many C programmers and the method Clipper programmers can use to make their coding techniques look and act like their C counterparts. While we do not subscribe to the notion of mixing the two languages for haphazard reasons, the fundamental belief is to still code in Clipper up to the point where Clipper cannot perform the desired operation. At that point, and that point only, should the concept of a C subroutine be brought into the Clipper application. We will explain why this is important at a later time. However, although we believe this, we do not stand steadfast to the dBASE way of coding. If Clipper code can look similar to good C code, many C programmers will become more receptive to accepting Clipper as a legitimate language. Additionally, the communication level between Clipper and C programmers will be heightened. With this in mind, let us start to look at the concept of putting most of the Clipper commands in user-defined functions.

COMMANDS IN FUNCTIONS

Why have commands in functions? As an advanced concept, it is appropriate for several reasons. We want to stress control, structure, and purpose in our code and in our style. The ability to look at a piece of code and quickly deduce the operation is paramount. Since we have established the concept that procedures and functions are, in reality, identical in Clipper, we should expand that concept to the issue surrounding the Clipper commands. For example, what is a command? It is nothing more than a series of instructions within the Clipper library that will perform a specific operation. But, in many ways, this is similar to a procedure: a series of routines programmed to perform a specific operation. Additionally, the ability to place commands in functions and to rework the Clipper library into a function-oriented coding techniques will give our personal libraries more flexibility over the basic set of Clipper commands. Finally, sometimes when commands are placed in functions, corporate programming houses, accustomed to a C stylistic convention, will adapt quickly to the Clipper language. Let's take a look at some of the potential of this concept. The old way is:

```
READ
```

The new way is:

```
********************
* ************************************************
* * The following procedure(s)/function(s) are   *
* * part of Steve Straley's ToolkiT(tm) -        *
* * Release 2, published by Four Seasons         *
* * Publishing Co., Inc.  All Rights Reserved    *
* * Information: 212-599-2141 / 800-662-2278     *
* * All Rights Reserved                          *
* ************************************************

FUNCTION Sjsread

   PARAMETERS _withoutpg, _update

   IF EMPTY(PCOUNT())
      _withoutpg = .F.
      _update = .F.
```

```
   ELSEIF PCOUNT() = 1
      _update = .F.
   ENDIF

   IF _withoutpg
      SET KEY 3 TO Nogo
      SET KEY 18 TO Nogo
   ENDIF
   scrcursor = .T.
   SET CURSOR ON
   READ
   SET CURSOR OFF
   SET KEY 3 TO
   SET KEY 18 TO
   scrcursor = .F.
   IF !_update
      RETURN( LASTKEY() != 27 )
   ELSE
      RETURN(UPDATED())
   ENDIF

*******************

PROCEDURE Nogo

   KEYBOARD ""

* End of file
```

Here, we have taken the simple command READ, placed it in a user-defined function, surrounded the READ command with other commands, and allowed for multiple parameters to alter how the function works. In a piece of code, using this technique, the end result would look something like this:

```
SELECT C
@  6,02 SAY "Journal:" GET mjournal PICT "!!"   ;
        VALID Goodtype(@mjournal,06,11, 6, 15)
@  7,02 SAY "Ref No.:"
@  6,45 SAY "Date..:"  GET mdate      ;
        VALID Setperiod(mdate,@mperiod,@myear)
@  7,45 SAY "Period:"  GET mperiod  PICT "99"    ;
        VALID mperiod > 0 .and. mperiod <= glperiods
@  7,57 SAY "Year:"    GET myear    PICT "9999" ;
        VALID myear <= YEAR( xdate )
Sjsread()
```

Or, expanding on the potential return value from the Sjsread() function, we could have the following:

```
Windowpush(13,35,19,75,"RED","WHITE","WHITE","RED")
@ WROW(1),WCOL(1) SAY "What level of detail (1-99): "       ;
                  GET whatlevel  PICT "99" ;
```

```
                      VALID whatlevel >=1 .AND. whatlevel<=99
@ WROW(2),WCOL(1) SAY "What periods (1-"+STR(glperiods,2)+")....:" ;
                      GET whatperiod PICT "99" ;
                      VALID (whatperiod<=glperiods .AND. ;
                      whatperiod>=0) .OR. LASTKEY() =5
@ WROW(3),WCOL(1) SAY "What fiscal year....:"  ;
                      GET whatyear PICT "9999"
@ WROW(4),WCOL(1) SAY "Leave at zero to get current period"
IF Sjsread()
   IF whatyear > 0 .AND. !Compare(whatyear,xfiscyear)
      mmfile = "DETL"+STR(whatyear,4)
      IF !FILE(scrdata+scrpath+mmfile+".DBF")
         Errmsg("No history for "+STR(whatyear,4))
         Windowpop()
         RETURN(.F.)
      ELSE
         SELECT E
         USE (scrdata+scrpath+mmfile)
         SET INDEX TO (scrdata+scrpath+mmfile)
         new_det = .T.
      ENDIF
   ENDIF
ENDIF
Windowpop()
RETURN (LASTKEY() <> 27)
```

Now, we could expand every Clipper command into separate Clipper functions. Below is a sample subset of some of the Clipper commands in functions:

```
PACK
DELETE
SUM
TOTAL
CREATE
INDEX
ZAP
APPEND BLANK
COPY STRUCTURE
```

THE EXTENDED USE OF PARENTHESES

In the Summer '87 version of Clipper, the concept of the parenthesis was expanded. On the surface, it was noted that the use of parentheses in some areas of the code could replace the conventional macro substitution, and in doing this, the speed of the application could be greatly enhanced. For example, normally, if a file name is placed in a memory variable and that file needs to be opened, the conventional way of approaching this would be:

```
file = "CHART.DBF"
USE &file.
```

In Clipper and in dBASE, the macro is expanded on the USE command line. However, the new way this can be achieved would be through the following code extract:

```
file = "CHART.DBF"
USE (file)
```

This is approximately 33 percent faster than the code extract that uses the macro expansion symbol. This is partly because of Clipper's knowledge of the command line and the fact that the use of the left and right parentheses delineate a macro during the compilation. If the "&" symbol is used in place of the "()," Clipper's run-time macro library would have to expand the macro out to its fullest length before the USE command is executed. In other words, using the above example, let's expand out the potential command line to be the following:

```
file = "CHART.DBF"
scrdata = "C:"
scrpath = "\SSAP\"
USE &scrdata.&scrpath.&file.
```

In the USE command above, Clipper would see the first macro, find its value, and expand. In doing so, it would have to find the length of the variable **scrdata** (2 bytes), read each character until it could read no more, then come back to the original command line (the USE), and proceed onto the next macro. This involves processor time that, over the course of a complete application, could slow down its speed. By altering our code, we could issue a command line that looked like this:

```
USE (scrdata + scrpath + file)
```

The concatenation of the three strings occurs first, then the macro is expanded through the extended use of parentheses. This is obviously faster and easier to read.

Parentheses may also come in handy with the SET commands. For example, if we had global variables that could toggle the SET commands, we would have, in the past, programmed the following:

```
intense = .T.
IF intense
   SET INTENSE ON
ELSE
   SET INTENSE OFF
ENDIF
```

This would be much easier to read and to code if we used the extended parentheses for the SET logic as well, which would look like the following:

```
intense = .T.
SET INTENSE (intense)
```

If the variable **intense** is set to a logical true (.T.), the SET INTENSITY flag would be SET to true as well. The same holds true for the value of logical false (.F.) for the **intense** variable.

Of course, there are some cases where the use of the parentheses cannot replace the use of the macro substitution symbol. Nantucket will provide a list of them upon request.

EXTENDING THE USE OF THE PARENTHESES

One of the side issues involved with the use of the parentheses is the ability to get information in unselected work areas. Clipper gives us the ability to "point" to the areas we want information from. Each work area has its own unique set of pointer logic. For example, the RECNO() function works across all 250 work areas; each work area has a unique RECNO() value. The same could be said for the EOF(), BOF(), FOUND(), and DBFILTER() functions, just to name a few. As a matter of fact, all of the Clipper functions can be "sent" to or "pointed" to work in another work area. For example, let's take a look at the old way to acquire the record number from a secondary work area:

```
SELECT B
USE People
GO 5
SELECT A
USE Chart
GO 10
* additional programming lines
SELECT B
variable = RECNO()
SELECT A
? "The active record number in the B area is " + ;
  STR(variable)
```

Now, with this new way of looking at Clipper, we have the following:

```
SELECT B
USE People
GO 5
SELECT A
USE Chart
GO 10
* additional programming lines
? "The active record number in the B area is " + ;
   STR(B->(RECNO()))
```

There are two fundamental principles here. First is the ability to select the needed area and assign the information to a variable; reselecting the original area is no longer needed. This is extremely important when we begin to talk about list-box technology and the conventional way of remembering the current work area: Select the list-box database work area, get the information, then reselect the original work area before proceeding onto the next GET. We will take a look at this type of coding construct again. However, the second thing we should note is the use of the parentheses in conjunction with the area pointer. The last line of the above coding example is simple and clear. Basically, after the string is displayed, Clipper's internal logic will get the value of RECNO() for the B-> work area, and that value is then passed to the STR() function. The parentheses surround the function in question, with the area pointer in front. In other words, we are telling Clipper "get me the value of this function from that work area." Clipper maintains the current work area position as it is sent off to perform the function's operation in the designated work area. Once the function returns with a value for the parentheses expression, Clipper automatically logs onto the original work area. The work area alias letter is used in this case, followed by the -> symbol (the pointing symbol), followed by the encasing (), surrounding the RECNO() function. Remember, since functions have value, they have the same meaning as storing the RECNO() value to a variable. This variable would then be passed to the string function. In this case the value of the function in the B-> work area is passed to the STR() function. It would be even easier if we used the database's ALIAS() name. Again, using the above example, the coded extract would look something like this:

```
SELECT B
USE People
GO 5
SELECT A
USE Chart
GO 10
* additional programming lines
? "The active record number in the B area is " + ;
   STR(People->(RECNO()))
```

Extending this new development in the Clipper language, we can see how the FOUND() function takes on new meaning when it is put inside the extended parentheses. Of course, the same could be said for the LASTREC(), EOF(), BOF(), DBRELATE(), ALIAS(), and DBFILTER() functions as well. And to expand on a previously discussed topic, we could also apply this new technology to the DBEDIT() function, which will perform all of the features in unselected work areas.

THE NEXT STEP

The next step is the most logical. Since we have demonstrated the ability to send Clipper functions off to other, unselected work areas, we should be able to apply this to our functions as well. For example, inside of a VALID clause, if we were to write a list-box function that would work in another work area, the code might look like this:

```
********************
* Name      Findit.prg
* Author    Stephen J. Straley
* Date      July 1, 1989
```

```
005 : * Notice    Copyright (c) 1989 Stephen J. Straley & Associates
006 : * Compile   Clipper Findit -m
007 : * Release   Summer 87
008 : * Link      PLINK86 FI Findit LIB Clipper LIB Extend;
009 : * Note      This shows how a user-defined function in a VALID
010 : *           command/clause can redirect the work area of the GET
011 : *           without the assistance of the SELECT command or
012 : *           function.
013 : *
014 : ********************
015 :
016 : SELECT B
017 : USE Filenos
018 : INDEX ON File_name TO Tempname
019 : SELECT A
020 : USE Disknos INDEX Disknos
021 : CLEAR SCREEN
022 : mfile = SPACE(10)
023 : mmore = SPACE(20)
024 : SET KEY 9 TO Inquire
025 : @  8,10 SAY "Press ESC to quit, TAB for Listing"
026 : @ 10,10 SAY "What file do you want? " GET mfile ;
027 :         VALID Filenos->(Lookup(@mfile, "5", "5/6/7/8/9/20", .T.))
028 : @ 12,10 SAY "Just an extra GET for display" GET mmore
029 : READ
030 : WAIT ALIAS()
031 : CLEAR SCREEN
032 :
033 : ********************
034 :
035 : PROCEDURE Inquire
036 :
037 :     KEYBOARD "?" + CHR(13)
038 :
039 : * **********************************************
040 : * * The following procedure(s)/function(s) are  *
041 : * * part of Steve Straley's ToolkiT(tm) -        *
042 : * * Release 2, published by Four Seasons         *
043 : * * Publishing Co., Inc.  All Rights Reserved   *
044 : * * Information: 212-599-2141 / 800-662-2278     *
045 : * * All Rights Reserved                          *
046 : * * **********************************************
047 :
048 : FUNCTION Lookup
049 :
050 :     * make sure that the type of the variable and the
051 :     *       type of the data field are the same
052 :     * make sure that the fields in the field list are available
053 :     * make sure that the field in the get list is available
054 :     * verify window coordinates
055 :     * make sure that the database is available
056 :     * verify all parameters
057 :
058 :     PARAMETER _var, _gets, _says, _stuff
```

```
059 :
060 :    IF PCOUNT() < 3
061 :       RETURN(.F.)
062 :    ELSEIF EMPTY(ALIAS())
063 :       RETURN(.F.)
064 :    ELSEIF TYPE("_gets") + TYPE("_says") != "CC"
065 :       RETURN(.F.)
066 :    ENDIF
067 :
068 :    PRIVATE _gname, _old, _qaz
069 :
070 :    _gname = FIELD(VAL(_gets))
071 :
072 :    && Get field is not there
073 :
074 :    IF EMPTY(_gname)
075 :       RETURN(.F.)
076 :    ENDIF
077 :
078 :    && The data types do not match
079 :
080 :    IF TYPE("_var") != TYPE(_gname)
081 :       RETURN(.F.)
082 :    ENDIF
083 :
084 :    && Seek to see if it is there...
085 :
086 :    SEEK _var
087 :    IF FOUND()
088 :       RETURN(.T.)
089 :    ELSE
090 :       GO TOP
091 :    ENDIF
092 :
093 :    _stuff = IF(TYPE("_stuff") != "L", .F., _stuff)
094 :
095 :    _old = _says
096 :    _cnt = 0
097 :    _tot = 0
098 :    DO WHILE !EMPTY(_old)
099 :       _tot = _tot + 1
100 :       _sname = FIELD(VAL(Parsing(@_old)))
101 :
102 :       && the SAY is not there
103 :
104 :       _cnt = _cnt + IF((EMPTY(_sname)), 1, 0)
105 :
106 :    ENDDO
107 :
108 :    DECLARE _show[_tot - _cnt]
109 :    _old = _says
110 :    _cnt = 1
111 :    DO WHILE !EMPTY(_old)
112 :       _sname = FIELD(VAL(Parsing(@_old)))
```

```
113 :        IF !EMPTY(_sname)
114 :           _show[_cnt] = Upperlower(_sname)
115 :           _cnt = _cnt + 1
116 :        ENDIF
117 :     ENDDO
118 :
119 :     _lookrow = ROW()
120 :     IF _lookrow > 16
121 :        _lookrow = 4
122 :     ENDIF
123 :
124 :     _lookcol = COL()
125 :     IF _lookcol > 60
126 :        _lookcol = 60
127 :        _lookrow = _lookrow + 1
128 :     ENDIF
129 :
130 :     _lookscr = SAVESCREEN(_lookrow-1,_lookcol-1,_lookrow + 7, ;
131 :              _lookcol + (79 - _lookcol))
132 :     @ _lookrow - 1, _lookcol - 1 CLEAR TO _lookrow + 7, ;
133 :              _lookcol + (79 - _lookcol)
134 :     @ _lookrow - 1, _lookcol - 1 TO _lookrow + 7, ;
135 :              _lookcol + (79 - _lookcol) DOUBLE
136 :
137 :     DBEDIT(_lookrow, _lookcol, _lookrow + 6, _lookcol + ;
138 :         (78 - _lookcol), _show)
139 :     IF LASTKEY() = 13
140 :        _var = &_gname.
141 :        IF _stuff
142 :           KEYBOARD CHR(13)
143 :        ENDIF
144 :     ENDIF
145 :     RESTSCREEN(_lookrow - 1, _lookcol - 1, _lookrow + 7, ;
146 :              _lookcol + (79 - _lookcol), _lookscr)
147 :     RETURN(.F.)
148 :
149 : ********************
150 :
151 : FUNCTION Upperlower
152 :
153 :     PARAMETERS _upla
154 :
155 :     * Take the parameter string and uppercase the first
156 :     * letter, lowercasing all other letters
157 :
158 :     IF PCOUNT() != 1
159 :        RETURN("")
160 :     ENDIF
161 :     RETURN(UPPER(SUBSTR(_upla, 1, 1)) + LOWER(SUBSTR(_upla,2)))
162 :
163 : ********************
164 :
165 : FUNCTION Parsing
166 :
```

```
167 :      PARAMETERS _getstr
168 :
169 :      PRIVATE _location, _tempback
170 :
171 :      _location    = IF(EMPTY(AT("+", _getstr)), ;
172 :                       AT("/", _getstr), AT("+", _getstr))
173 :      _tempback = IF(!EMPTY(_location), ;
174 :                       SUBSTR(_getstr, 1, _location - 1), _getstr)
175 :      _getstr = IF(!EMPTY(_location), ;
176 :                       SUBSTR(_getstr, _location + 1), "")
177 :      RETURN(_tempback)
178 :
179 :  * End of File
```

Note on lines 16 through 20 the changing of the SELECT work areas in order to open two files: Filenos.dbf and Disknos.dbf. Starting with the second, or B, work area, the files are opened along with any necessary index file associated with that database. In the case of the Filenos.dbf file, a special index file using just the field **field_name** is created. By the time we reach the READ command on line 29, we should be in work area 1 associated with the Disknos database. On line 27, the VALID clause is in operation with the extended use of the parentheses. In essence, this piece of code is telling Clipper to make a call to the Lookup() function and to perform all operations within that function in the Filenos work area. Once the function returns a value to the VALID clause, Clipper will automatically return to the work area it was in before the call was made. Executing this program would show that the DBEDIT() call on line 137 works on the database in the Filenos work area, even though no SELECT command (outside the first two at the beginning of the program) is included. After the READ command finishes executing on line 29, the results of the WAIT command on line 30 would yield the string "DISKNOS" showing that the first work area is selected and not the second.

But the power does not stop here. Your ability to push Clipper rests mainly in your ability to push yourself to try out new ideas. To be a good programmer means finding out answers on one's own initiative, reading the fine print about many Clipper features and using those features interactively to make something new and powerful. So it is with this next step. We have demonstrated the power of the parenthesis extension to the Clipper language; we have demonstrated the concept of viewing procedures as functions, and vice versa; and we have demonstrated the concept of embedding Clipper commands in user-defined functions. What would be the results of all three issues combined? Consider the following command:

```
SEEK value
```

If this were to appear in a user-defined function — call it SEEKIT() — we would have the following:

```
***************

FUNCTION Seekit
```

```
PARAMETERS _search

_search = IF(TYPE("_search") = "U", "", _search)
* If no parameter is passed to the function, then
* seek a NULL byte, which should position the pointer
* to the top of the file yet set the FOUND() function
* to a logical true (.T.)

SEEK _search

RETURN(FOUND())
```

In our code, we do the following:

```
@ 10,10 GET value
READ
IF B->(Seekit(value))
   * perform a task since condition was found
ELSE
   @ 24,00 SAY "Value NOT found!"
ENDIF
```

Notice that we do not care what work area we are in, only what work area we are pointing to. Too much time is wasted in remembering the current work area position and status. The above type of coding allows our programs to point to our information. In many ways, object-oriented programming behaves the same way. In essence, we are passing the work area for the function to operate in and that can be said to be inferred.

Another interesting side issue is the command syntax. In this example, there is no SEEK command. While it is in the SEEKIT() function, it is not in the piece of code calling that function. Entire applications could be now programmed without multiple command lines; one SEEK is sufficient for the entire application.

Extending our base from this point, we may look at some additional issues. For example, because there is no real difference between functions and procedures, we could ponder performing a function as though it were a procedure. In other words, what if, in the above example, we were not concerned with the value of the function SEEKIT(); we simply want the function to perform the operation in the designated work area. In Clipper, if no value is desired from a function or a procedure, the value simply falls off the internal stack. Clipper maintains the integrity. We would know this to be true if we were to look at procedures once again. Since we know that there is an implied RETURN("") at the end of every procedure, we also know we never had a problem with corrupted stacks and never concerned ourselves with assigning procedures to variables. We simply called them with a DO command. The same could be said for functions if we turned the logic around. If we just "did" or "called" the function without expressing it, assigning it to a variable, or performing any operation from it, would Clipper handle this? Many of us have had experience with this concept. For example, Clipper's ADIR() function returns a value, based on the skeleton value of the first parameter. A coding extract using this function would look something like this:

```
DECLARE file[ADIR("*.prg")]
```

The value of ADIR() is used by the DECLARE command when portioning enough memory to create the array called files[]. However, the documented (in the Clipper manual as well as in *Programming in Clipper, 2nd Edition* [Addison-Wesley]) method for putting the names of the files into the array would be the following:

```
ADIR("*.prg", files)
```

Since arrays are passed by reference, the individual names of the arrays are placed in the designated array. However, the value from the ADIR() function is not needed in this example, especially since we previously acquired the value when establishing the array. Note that this value simply drops off of Clipper's memory stack and all is well. We could easily carry this concept to any of our functions as well. To test the theory, let's modify the above coding example and see:

```
@ 10,10 GET value
READ
B->(Seekit(value))
* do some operation
```

This is telling Clipper to perform the function SEEKIT() in work area B, returning a value to the original work area. Since that value is not being stored anywhere, nor is it expressed, the value will simply fall off of Clipper's internal stack. However, these lines of code will not compile properly. If we were to try this, we would get the following error message:

```
E>clipper try -m
The Clipper Compiler, Summer '87
Copyright (c) Nantucket Corp 1985-1987.  All Rights Reserved.
Microsoft C Runtime Library Routines,
Copyright (c) Microsoft Corp 1984-1987.  All Rights Reserved.

Compiling TRY.PRG
line 3:  invalid variable
   B->(Seekit(value))
      ^
line 3:  ASSIGNMENT error
   B->
      ^
2 errors
Code Pass 1
Code Pass 2
Code size 60, Symbols 64, Constants 4
```

However, the solution is simple. All we would need is a simple procedure that will perform the designated operation. In my ToolkiT–Release 2, I have written such a simple procedure called Op(). It looks like this:

```
***************

PROCEDURE Op

   PARAMETERS _why_not

* End of Procedure
```

Now, to bring back our previous example, the coded extract would look something like this:

```
@ 10,10 GET value
READ
Op(B->(Seekit(value)))
* do some operation
```

This way there will no longer be any compilation error and all is satisfied. The Op() function (passed as a parameter) instructs Clipper to perform the designated operation as expected and to return a null byte to the calling procedure or function. With this, and taking the sum of the topics we have previously touched upon, the Clipper code of the past may now look like Clipper code (or C code) of the future. For example, the old way would be:

```
CLEAR SCREEN
@ 1,  2 SAY "First, generate the file structures"
DO Filestru

@ 2,  2 SAY "Now, create the first database"
SELECT A

DO Dbfmake WITH "Ontap", file1      && File1 is an array
DO Dbfindex WITH "Ontap", "files"
DO Dbfindex WITH "Ontap", "Ontap"

@ 3,  2 SAY "Now, create the second database"
SELECT B
DO Dbfmake WITH "Clients", file2

USE Clients

@ 4, 2 SAY "Now create the third database"
SELECT C
DO Dbfmake WITH "Filenos", file6

DO Dbfindex WITH "Filenos", "sub_no + file_name", "Filenos"
DO Dbfindex WITH "Filenos", "sub_no + sub_name",  "Filesub"
DO Dbfindex WITH "Filenos", "sub_no + file_type", "Filetype"
```

```
USE Filenos INDEX Filenos, Filesub, Filetype
```

The new way to code this would be:

```
Clear_area()
Windowpush(5,20,18,60)
Wsayget(1,2, "First, generate the file structures")
Filestru()
Wsayget(2,2, "Now, create the first database")
Op(A->(Dbfmake("Ontap", file1)))
Op(A->(Dbfindex("Ontap", "files")))
Op(A->(Selecting("Ontap", "Ontap")))
Wsayget(3,2, "Now, create the second database")
Op(B->(Dbfmake("Clients", file2)))
Op(B->(Selecting("Clients")))
Wsayget(4,2, "Now, create the third database")
Op(C->(Dbfmake("Filenos", file6)))
Op(C->(Dbfindex("Filenos", "sub_no + file_name", "Filenos")))
Op(C->(Dbfindex("Filenos", "sub_no + sub_name",  "Filesub")))
Op(C->(Dbfindex("Filenos", "sub_no + file_type", "Filetype")))
Op(C->(Selecting("Filenos", "Filenos/Filesub/Filetype")))
Windowpop()
```

As you can see, the concept of the command and a command (or verb intensive) language is eliminated. Though future versions of Clipper may support a command-driven syntax dialect (that is, user-defined commands), the above method provides the most convenient way to get programmers inside and outside of the Clipper world to talk together.

THE ULTIMATE CHALLENGE

We have now expanded and stretched our previously held ideas of functions and procedures and added a new dimension to the Clipper mind-set. It is no longer necessary to remember work areas; we can work in unselected work areas. This frees us of the troublesome and cumbersome necessity of keeping many pointers in memory variables. As a result, our memory allocation and load requirements should decrease dramatically. In addition, our code will perform more efficiently and many C programmers will be able to read our Clipper code as if it were their own C code. Consider the following program:

```
********************
* Name      Unselect.prg
* Author    Stephen J. Straley
* Date      July 4, 1989
* Notice    Copyright (c) 1989 Stephen J. Straley & Associates
* Compile   Clipper Unselect -m
* Release   Summer 87
* Link      PLINK86 FI Unselect LIB Clipper LIB Extend;
* Note      This shows some of the possibilities using the
*           extended macro system in the newest Clipper.
```

```
011 : *
012 : ********************
013 :
014 : CLEAR SCREEN
015 : Op(B->(Selecting("FILENOS","FILENOS")))
016 : Op(A->(Selecting("DISKNOS", "DISKNOS")))
017 : DO WHILE !( Disknos->(EOF()) )
018 :     ? Disknos->sub_no, Disknos->(RECNO())
019 :     IF Filenos->( SEEKIT(Disknos->sub_no) )
020 :         ?? "==>"
021 :         ?? Filenos->sub_no, Filenos->sub_name, ;
022 :             Filenos->(RECNO())
023 :     ELSE
024 :         ?? "==>"
025 :         ?? " Not Found!"
026 :     ENDIF
027 :     Op( Disknos->( SKIPIT() ) )
028 :     INKEY(.6)
029 :     IF ROW() > 20
030 :         CLEAR SCREEN
031 :     ENDIF
032 : ENDDO
033 : WAIT
034 :
035 : * ************************************************
036 : * * The following procedure(s)/function(s) are   *
037 : * * part of Steve Straley's ToolkiT(tm) -         *
038 : * * Release 2, published by Four Seasons          *
039 : * * Publishing Co., Inc.  All Rights Reserved     *
040 : * * Information: 212-599-2141 / 800-662-2278      *
041 : * * All Rights Reserved                           *
042 : * ************************************************
043 :
044 : ********************
045 :
046 : FUNCTION Skipit
047 :
048 :     PARAMETERS _thismany
049 :
050 :     _thismany = IF( EMPTY(PCOUNT()), 1, _thismany)
051 :     SKIP _thismany
052 :     RETURN("")
053 :
054 : ********************
055 :
056 : FUNCTION Seekit
057 :
058 :     PARAMETERS _lookforit, _order
059 :
060 :     IF PCOUNT() = 1
061 :         _order = INDEXORD()
062 :     ENDIF
063 :
064 :     SET ORDER TO (_order)
```

```
065 :
066 :    SEEK _lookforit
067 :
068 :    RETURN(FOUND())
069 :
070 : ********************
071 :
072 : FUNCTION Selecting
073 :
074 :    PARAMETERS _thefile, _theindexes
075 :
076 :    IF PCOUNT() < 1
077 :       RETURN(.F.)
078 :    ENDIF
079 :    _withindex = (PCOUNT() = 2)
080 :    USE (_thefile)
081 :    IF _withindex
082 :       SET INDEX TO (_theindexes)
083 :    ENDIF
084 :    RETURN( DOSERROR() = 0 )
085 :
086 : ********************
087 :
088 : FUNCTION Parsing
089 :
090 :    PARAMETERS _getstr
091 :
092 :    PRIVATE _location, _temp
093 :
094 :    _location    = IF(EMPTY(AT("+", _getstr)), ;
095 :                   AT("/", _getstr), AT("+", _getstr))
096 :    _temp = IF(!EMPTY(_location), SUBSTR(_getstr, 1, ;
097 :            _location - 1), _getstr)
098 :    _getstr = IF(!EMPTY(_location), SUBSTR(_getstr, ;
099 :            _location + 1), "")
100 :    RETURN(_temp)
101 :
102 : *******************
103 :
104 : PROCEDURE Op
105 :
106 :    PARAMETERS _nothing
107 :
108 : * End of File
```

Go through lines 14 through 33 and try to find a SELECT command. In addition, scan through the functions starting on line 35; no SELECTs will be found. Pushing the limits of working in unselected work area means just that: you never will have to remember what work area you are currently in before going to the work area you want. Even the typical DO WHILE !EOF() command has been altered to point to the work area we want. As you can see, we now have the control over all of the work areas. Conceptually, you should now think about pointing to the areas where you need information, where you want a task performed, or where an expression needs to be evaluated. You should not have to concern yourself with changing work areas: the code and Clipper should do it automatically for you. On another level, you should note that the procedures and functions within this example are coded only once even through they may act differently depending on the work area they have been assigned to. In other words, it would not take too much effort to create generic ADD, EDIT, and DELETE data routines that perform differently based on the work area pointed to prior to the call to the procedure. Following this logic, the object — the ADD, EDIT, or DELETE routine — needs only to be coded once. Modifications to the routine only require one program location; all others should fall in place. And if program modification and change can be simplified, if functions and procedures are looked at as objects, and if work areas are "pointed" to by the programmer, we have taken a giant leap out of the dBASE mind-set and prepared ourselves for the object-oriented work of Nantucket Future Technology.

But this is not all: Databases can be created and indexed, relations properly established and information obtained and assigned to work areas, all in unselected work areas. Our programming will reflect this change in perspective. No longer will we be concerned with where we are and how to get back to it. All we will have to do is point to the designated areas. This freedom is subtle yet powerful. We no longer look at an application from the perspective of the currently selected database; rather, our applications will reflect all of the databases available in the system. Our base point, or base work area, is not important and as such, we will not be concerned with it. Generic procedures can work by simply pointing to them with the appropriate work area. Consider the following example:

```
********************
* Name      Genadd.prg
* Author    Stephen J. Straley
* Date      July 4, 1989
* Notice    Copyright (c) 1989 Stephen J. Straley & Associates
* Compile   Clipper Genadd -m
* Release   Summer 87
* Link      PLINK86 FI Genadd LIB Clipper LIB Extend;
* Note      This program shows how a generic ADD routine can
*           be created to perform on different databases.
*
********************

SET SCOREBOARD OFF
SELECT 2
USE Filenos INDEX Filenos, Filesub, Filetype
SELECT 1
USE Disknos INDEX Disknos
CLEAR SCREEN
@ 0,0 SAY "The number of records in work area 2 is " + ;
      LTRIM(STR(Filenos->( LASTREC() ) ))
@ 1,0 SAY "The number of records in work area 1 is " + ;
      LTRIM(STR(Disknos->( LASTREC() ) ))
?
WAIT "Press any key for adding...."
```

```
026 : SAVE SCREEN
027 : CLEAR SCREEN
028 : Op( Filenos->( Add(1, .T.) ) )
029 : a 24,00 SAY "Press ANY key for next one...."
030 : INKEY(0)
031 : CLEAR SCREEN
032 : Op( Disknos->( Add(1, .T.) ) )
033 : a 24,00 SAY "Press ANY key for final screen...."
034 : INKEY(0)
035 : RESTORE SCREEN
036 : a 5,0 SAY "The number of records in work area 2 is " + ;
037 :        LTRIM(STR(Filenos->( LASTREC() ) ))
038 : a 6,0 SAY "The number of records in work area 1 is " + ;
039 :        LTRIM(STR(Disknos->( LASTREC() ) ))
040 : ?
041 : ? "One moment...."
042 : Op( Disknos->(Delete()) )
043 : Op( Filenos->(Delete()) )
044 : Op( Disknos->(Packit()) )
045 : Op( Filenos->(Packit()) )
046 : ? "Finished!"
047 :
048 : ********************
049 :
050 : PROCEDURE Delete
051 :
052 :    DELETE
053 :
054 : * *********************************************
055 : * * The following procedure(s)/function(s) are  *
056 : * * part of Steve Straley's ToolkiT(tm) -        *
057 : * * Release 2, published by Four Seasons         *
058 : * * Publishing Co., Inc.  All Rights Reserved    *
059 : * * Information: 212-599-2141 / 800-662-2278     *
060 : * * All Rights Reserved                          *
061 : * *********************************************
062 :
063 : ********************
064 :
065 : FUNCTION Add
066 :
067 :    PARAMETER _method, _append, _array
068 :
069 :    * 1 for WITH READ
070 :    * 2 for CLEAR GETS
071 :    * 3 for NO READ/NO CLEAR GETS
072 :
073 :    _method = IF(TYPE("_method") != "N", 1, _method)
074 :
075 :    * .T. for APPEND BLANK
076 :    * .F. for no APPEND BLANK
077 :
078 :    _append = IF(TYPE("_append") != "L", .F., _append)
```

```
079 :
080 :    * This should be altered so that any memo field should
081 :    * only appear and if there is a READ instruction, then
082 :    * the MEMOEDIT() functions should be individually called
083 :
084 :    IF _append
085 :       APPEND BLANK
086 :    ENDIF
087 :
088 :    IF TYPE("_array") = "A"
089 :       * This will be compatible with ToolkiT's and
090 :       * FUNCky's text file processing functions and
091 :       * facilities.
092 :    ELSE
093 :       * all of this must be done by hand!
094 :       _row = 0
095 :       _col = 0
096 :       _len = 0
097 :       FOR _qaz = 1 TO FCOUNT()
098 :          _pict = ""
099 :          _fname = FIELD(_qaz)
100 :          IF TYPE(_fname) = "C"
101 :             IF LEN(&_fname) > 15
102 :                _pict = "@S15"
103 :             ENDIF
104 :          ENDIF
105 :          IF TYPE(_fname) = "M"  && Memo fields are different!
106 :             @ _row, _col SAY Flushright(Upperlower(_fname), ;
107 :                      _col + 10 )
108 :             _here = COL() + 1
109 :             _ocolor = SETCOLOR()
110 :             SETCOLOR(Reverse())
111 :             REPLACE &_fname. WITH ;
112 :                MEMOEDIT(&_fname.,_row,_here,_row,_here + 20,;
113 :                IF((_method = 2), .F., .T. ),"Likegets()", 80)
114 :             SETCOLOR(_ocolor)
115 :             IF _len < _col + 20 + LEN(Upperlower(_fname)) + 2
116 :                _len = _col + 20 + LEN(Upperlower(_fname))   2
117 :             ENDIF
118 :          ELSE
119 :             IF EMPTY(_pict)   && No picture clause
120 :                @ _row, _col SAY Flushright(Upperlower(_fname), ;
121 :                      _col + 10) GET &_fname.
122 :             ELSE
123 :                @ _row, _col SAY Flushright(Upperlower(_fname), ;
124 :                      _col + 10) GET &_fname. PICT _pict
125 :             ENDIF
126 :             IF _len < COL() + 2
127 :                _len = COL() + 2
128 :             ENDIF
129 :          ENDIF
130 :          IF _row > 23
131 :             _col = _len
```

```
132 :                 _row = 0
133 :                 IF _col > 65
134 :                     EXIT
135 :                 ENDIF
136 :             ELSE
137 :                 _row = _row + 1
138 :             ENDIF
139 :         NEXT
140 :     ENDIF
141 :
142 :     IF _method = 1
143 :         READ
144 :     ELSEIF _method = 2
145 :         CLEAR GETS
146 :     ELSE
147 :         * do nothing
148 :     ENDIF
149 :
150 :     RETURN(.T.)
151 :
152 : *******************
153 :
154 : FUNCTION Likegets
155 :
156 :     PARAMETERS _mode
157 :
158 :     IF (_mode = 1 .OR. _mode = 2) .AND. LASTKEY() = 13
159 :         KEYBOARD CHR(23)
160 :     ENDIF
161 :     RETURN(0)
162 :
163 : *******************
164 :
165 : PROCEDURE Op
166 :
167 :     PARAMETERS _nothing
168 :
169 : *******************
170 :
171 : FUNCTION Packit
172 :
173 :     PACK
174 :
175 :     RETURN( DOSERROR() = 0 )
176 :
177 : *******************
178 :
179 : FUNCTION Flushright
180 :
181 :     PARAMETERS _string, _size, _padding
182 :
183 :     IF EMPTY(PCOUNT())
184 :         RETURN("")
```

```
185 :     ELSEIF PCOUNT() = 2
186 :        _padding = " "
187 :     ENDIF
188 :
189 :     IF TYPE("_string")+TYPE("_size")+TYPE("_padding") != "CNC"
190 :        RETURN("")
191 :     ENDIF
192 :
193 :     IF LEN(_string) >= _size
194 :        RETURN(RIGHT(_string, _size))
195 :     ELSE
196 :        RETURN( REPLICATE(SUBSTR(_padding, 1, 1), ;
197 :                _size - LEN(_string)) + _string)
198 :     ENDIF
199 :
200 : *******************
201 :
202 : FUNCTION Upperlower
203 :
204 :     PARAMETERS _upla
205 :
206 :     * Take the parameter string and uppercase the first
207 :     * letter, lowercasing all other letters
208 :
209 :     IF PCOUNT() != 1
210 :        RETURN("")
211 :     ENDIF
212 :     RETURN(UPPER(SUBSTR(_upla, 1, 1)) + ;
213 :            LOWER(SUBSTR(_upla,2)))
214 :
215 :
216 : *******************
217 :
218 : FUNCTION Reverse
219 :     .
220 :     PARAMETERS _a
221 :
222 :     * _a is the color string to reverse
223 :
224 :     IF PCOUNT() = 0
225 :        _a = SETCOLOR()
226 :     ENDIF
227 :
228 :     PRIVATE _b
229 :
230 :     * _b is the SAY color string
231 :
232 :     _b = STRTRAN(SUBSTR(_a, 1, ;
233 :          AT(",", _a)-1), "+", "")
234 :
235 :     RETURN(SUBSTR(_b, AT("/", _b)+1) + ;
236 :            "/" + SUBSTR(_b, 1, AT("/", _b)-1))
237 :
238 : * End of File
```

While much could be added to the Add() function, the main concept is clear; the function reacts and acts differently based upon the work area that the function was directed to. Again, this object-like style of programming can open up new avenues of programming.

PUSHING THE LIMITS

While it should now be easy to perceive commonality between a procedure and a function, knowing when to call a procedure rather than a function becomes important, as does knowing when to mix and match, and where these new limits can be safely reached without causing havoc in our applications. Earlier, we said that any routine should still be called a function whenever a value is expected from that routine. Conversely, a procedure should be coded whenever the routine simply does something. However, a problem arises in the code section of our application; the calling conventions for a procedure and for a function look the same. For example, consider the following:

```
Op(A->(Packit()))
```

If we were to search through our personal library of routines that support our applications, how would we look up this routine, as "PROCEDURE Packit" or as "FUNCTION Packit"? From the code within the application, we could not tell and this brings confusion into our system. To avoid this, two possible conventions may be adapted. If a returned value is guaranteed, the routine should be called a function, and the only way to know this is to memorize the routine. This is not a bad idea under normal circumstances; those routines that would fall into this category are those routines that make up your personal library, and they should be memorized. Of course, we would continue to have those items that just "do" something and would therefore code those routines as procedures. Another option is to code everything as a function, procedure and function alike: to either have a function assume a RETURN of a null byte or to convert all procedures to return a specific value, other than a null byte. For those routines where no value is required, either a RETURN("") may be used or no RETURN() issued at all. Again, Clipper will automatically issue a RETURN of a null byte when it encounters the end of file marker for the .PRG file or when it encounters either the PROCEDURE or FUNCTION command statement. Since it is agreed that, to Clipper, functions are procedures, we can carry the same understanding across the language: No RETURN is required for the FUNCTION command. Consider the following coding extract:

```
Op(A->(Packit()))

********************

FUNCTION Op

   PARAMETERS _nothing

*******************
```

```
FUNCTION Packit

   PACK

   RETURN( DOSERROR() = 0 )
```

This code compiles and executes without trouble. And while it may not be considered a function in the strictest sense of the word, searching for the beginning of this routine becomes simple (especially for those case-sensitive text editors). By adhering to a rule, even though the Op() routine is more like a procedure, we can find the code more readily if we treat it like a function rather than a procedure.

We suggested calling a procedure as though it were a function, but at times calling a function as though it were a procedure is even more beneficial. For example, let us explore the SET KEY TO command. This command allows us to tag a hot key to a routine (normally this would be a procedure) that will be called if Clipper is in a "wait" state. Basically, a wait state is anything other than the INKEY(0) function: WAIT "" is an acceptable wait state as are the READ, INPUT, ACCEPT, and MENU TO commands. Now, if we alter our thinking slightly and incorporate the possibility of a function being called via the SET KEY TO command, we would see some interesting results. For example, here is a function that returns the name of the assigned alias:

```
? Whatname(20)
```

And the function would look something like this:

```
***************

FUNCTION Whatname

   PARAMETERS _area

   _retto = SELECT()

     SELECT (_area)
   _name = ALIAS()
   SELECT (_retto)
   RETURN(_name)

* End of Function
```

Now, what if this function was called via the SET KEY TO command? One possibility would be to allow the function to display all of the alias names in the all of the work areas, while maintaining the original functionality. In order to achieve this, we could use the PCOUNT() function to toggle between the potential ways this function could be called. Consider the following programming example, using the PCOUNT() function in conjunction with a routine designed to display all of the memory variables in an application:

```
001 : ********************
002 : * Name       Moremem.prg
003 : * Author     Essor Maso / Stephen J. Straley
004 : * Date       June 1, 1989
005 : * Notice     Copyright (c) 1989 Stephen J. Straley & Associates
006 : * Compile    Clipper Moremem -m
007 : * Release    Summer 87
008 : * Link       PLINK86 FI Morememmem LIB Clipper LIB Extend;
009 : * Note       A diagnostic tool to view memory variables easily.
010 : *
011 : *            It is assumed that F7 is set to Disp_mem:
012 : *
013 : *            Call:   SET KEY -6 TO Disp_mem
014 : *
015 : ********************
016 :
017 : CLEAR SCREEN
018 : SET KEY -6 TO Disp_mem
019 : variable = SPACE(10)
020 : adate    = DATE()
021 : anumber  = 10
022 : alogic   = .T.
023 : @ 10,10 SAY "Enter Variable or F7 for DISP MEMO: " ;
024 :         GET variable
025 : READ
026 : Disp_mem("AD")
027 :
028 : * **********************************************
029 : * * The following procedure(s)/function(s) are  *
030 : * * part of Steve Straley's ToolkiT(tm) -       *
031 : * * Release 2, published by Four Seasons        *
032 : * * Publishing Co., Inc.  All Rights Reserved   *
033 : * * Information: 212-599-2141 / 800-662-2278    *
034 : * * All Rights Reserved                         *
035 : * **********************************************
036 :
037 : ********************
038 :
039 : FUNCTION Disp_mem
040 :
041 :    SAVE SCREEN
042 :
043 :    PARAMETERS _tdum, _tdum1, _tdum2
044 :
045 :    _tdum = IF((TYPE("_tdum") != "C"), "", ;
046 :            UPPER(LTRIM(TRIM(_tdum))))
047 :
048 :    IF PCOUNT() = 3    && This came from the SET KEY TO
049 :       _tdum = ""
050 :    ENDIF
051 :
052 :    && Save memory variables
053 :    SAVE TO S_____ ALL EXCEPT _tdum*
054 :
```

```
055 :    PRIVATE _1vn,_1vt,_1vr,_1mc,_1sc,_1fh,_1fl
056 :
057 :    _1fh=FOPEN('S_____.MEM')
058 :    _1fl=FSEEK(_1fh,0,2)
059 :
060 :    FSEEK(_1fh,0)    && Top of file
061 :
062 :    CLEAR SCREEN
063 :
064 :    IF _1fl < 2
065 :
066 :        && File contains EOF marker.
067 :        @ 0,0 SAY "There are no memory variables present."
068 :
069 :    ELSE
070 :        _count = 1
071 :        _vars  = 0
072 :        _bytes = 0
073 :        DO WHILE FSEEK(_1fh,0,1)+1<_1fl
074 :            *
075 :            * Variable specific information is contained in the
076 :            * first 18 bytes of the variable packet. The value
077 :            * of the variable is contained from position 33 on.
078 :            *
079 :            _1mw = SPACE(18)
080 :            *
081 :            * Get the variable specific information.
082 :            *
083 :            FREAD(_1fh,@_1mw,18)
084 :            *
085 :            * The variable name is in the first 10 positions
086 :            * with a CHR(0) terminator.
087 :            *
088 :            _1vn = LEFT(_1mw,AT(CHR(0),_1mw)-1)
089 :            *
090 :            * The variable type is in position 12 of the packet.
091 :            * C3h is character or memo, CCh is logical,
092 :            * CEh is numeric, C4h is date.
093 :            *
094 :            _1vt=SUBSTR(_1mw,12,1)
095 :            *
096 :            * For character and logical variables, positions 17
097 :            * and 18 contain the hex value for the range of the
098 :            * data. For numeric and date variables, the range
099 :            * is 8. This points to the end of the variable packet.
100 :            *
101 :            _1vr=BIN2W(RIGHT(_1mw,2))
102 :            IF _1vt $ CHR(195) + CHR(204)
103 :                _1mc=14+_1vr
104 :            ELSE
105 :                _1mc=22
106 :            ENDIF
107 :            FSEEK(_1fh,_1mc,1)    && Go to next packet.
```

```
108 :        IF _1vr>51.AND._1vt $ CHR(195) + CHR(204)
109 :           _1r=STRTRAN(LEFT(&_1vn,50), CHR(7), CHR(1))
110 :           _ttemp = LEFT(_1vn+SPACE(10),10) + ;
111 :                    "  TYPE " + TYPE(_1vn) + ["] + ;
112 :                    _1r + ["]
113 :        ELSE
114 :           _1r=STRTRAN(&_1vn, CHR(7), CHR(1))
115 :           _ttemp = LEFT(_1vn+SPACE(10),10) + ;
116 :                    "  TYPE " + TYPE(_1vn) + "  " + ;
117 :                    IF(TYPE(_1vn) = "C", ["]+_1r+["], ;
118 :                    Strvalue(&_1vn))
119 :        ENDIF
120 :        IF    TYPE(_1vn) = "C"
121 :           _bytes = _bytes + LEN(&_1vn.)
122 :           _a = LEN(&_1vn.)
123 :        ELSEIF TYPE(_1vn) = "N"
124 :           _bytes = _bytes + 9
125 :           _a = 9
126 :        ELSEIF TYPE(_1vn) = "L"
127 :           _bytes = _bytes + 2
128 :           _a = 2
129 :        ELSEIF TYPE(_1vn) = "D"
130 :           _bytes = _bytes + 9
131 :           _a = 9
132 :        ENDIF
133 :
134 :        IF EMPTY(_tdum)
135 :           @ _count, 1 SAY IF( LEN(_ttemp) > 51, ;
136 :              SUBSTR(_ttemp, 1, 50), _ttemp)
137 :           @ _count, 49 SAY TRIM(TRANSFORM(_a, "9999999")) + ;
138 :              " bytes"
139 :           _count = _count + 1
140 :           _vars = _vars + 1
141 :        ELSE
142 :           IF _tdum $ _1vn
143 :              @ _count, 1 SAY IF( LEN(_ttemp) > 51, ;
144 :                 SUBSTR(_ttemp, 1, 50), _ttemp)
145 :              @ _count, 49 SAY TRIM(TRANSFORM(_a, "9999999"))+;
146 :                 " bytes"
147 :              _count = _count + 1
148 :              _vars = _vars + 1
149 :           ENDIF
150 :        ENDIF
151 :
152 :        IF ROW() > 14
153 :           @ 24,00 SAY 'Press Q TO Quit...'
154 :           INKEY(0)
155 :           IF CHR(LASTKEY())$"Qq"
156 :              End_disp()
157 :              RETURN
158 :           ELSE
159 :              CLEAR SCREEN
160 :              _count = 1
```

```
161 :            ENDIF
162 :          ENDIF
163 :        ENDDO
164 :      ENDIF
165 :      End_disp()
166 :
167 : *******************
168 :
169 : PROCEDURE End_disp
170 :
171 :    ERASE S_____.MEM
172 :    IF _count > 0
173 :       @ _count+1, 1 SAY SPACE(50)
174 :       @ _count+2, 1 SAY SPACE(50)
175 :       @ _count+2, 1 SAY "Memory Variables Displayed " + ;
176 :                    LTRIM(STR(_vars)) + " with " + ;
177 :                    LTRIM(STR(_bytes)) + " bytes used "
178 :       @ _count+3,1 SAY "Any Key to Continue...."
179 :       INKEY(0)
180 :    ENDIF
181 :    FCLOSE(_1fh)
182 :    RESTORE SCREEN
183 :
184 : *******************
185 :
186 : FUNCTION Strvalue
187 :
188 :    PARAMETERS _showstr
189 :
190 :    * This function returns the string representation
191 :    * of the given parameter.
192 :
193 :    IF PCOUNT() != 1
194 :       RETURN("")
195 :    ENDIF
196 :
197 :    DO CASE
198 :    CASE TYPE("_showstr") = "C"
199 :       RETURN(_showstr)
200 :    CASE TYPE("_showstr") = "N"
201 :       RETURN(STR(_showstr))
202 :    CASE TYPE("_showstr") = "M"
203 :       IF LEN(_showstr) > (MEMORY(0) * 1024) * .80
204 :          RETURN( SUBSTR(_showstr, 1, ;
205 :                  INT((MEMORY(0) * 1024) * .80)) )
206 :       ELSE
207 :          RETURN(_showstr)
208 :       ENDIF
209 :    CASE TYPE("_showstr") = "D"
210 :       RETURN(DTOC(_showstr))
211 :    CASE TYPE("_showstr") = "L"
212 :       RETURN(IF(_showstr, "True", "False"))
213 :    OTHERWISE
214 :       RETURN("")
```

```
215 :     ENDCASE
216 :
217 : * End of File
```

However, in this case, there is a twist: The function will yield different results if the function Disp_mem() was called via the SET KEY TO command or if a direct call as made on line 26. For example, if the F7 key is pressed while in the READ command, the SET KEY TO logic has been coded to make a call to the Disp_mem() routine, as seen on line 18. In the actual function, the Disp_mem() routine tests for the number of parameters passed to the function, and if PCOUNT() is equal to 3, it may be considered as a SET KEY TO call. In this case, the variable **_tdum** is set to a null byte to prevent the filtering-out effect that the function allows for. On the other hand, if a parameter is passed to the Disp_mem() routine, the string of the function is tested against every memory variable and allows a filtering condition to exist. Executing this program, the first call to the Disp_mem() routine with the SET KEY TO logic shows all of the variables in the system, excluding those beginning with the letters **_tdum** (which are the names of the three parameter variables in the Disp_mem() function). On the second call to the function, the Disp_mem() routine would only show the **adate** variable since it is the only variable with the "AD" substring as part of its name.

The point to this is to show you that functions can take on multiple meanings, operations, and potential values if the SET KEY TO command is involved. If a RETURNed value was needed from a function called via the SET KEY TO command, that RETURN value would have to be stored to a PUBLIC variable to be analyzed at a later time. This is because the RETURN stack inside of Clipper cannot be looked at immediately after the use of the SET KEY TO command. Other than this, the range of possibilities for functions grows astronomically.

TESTING FOR A SYMBOL'S EXISTENCE

Many times, especially when building a function or procedural library, we want to know if a particular function or procedure symbol is present in a system before the call is actually made. An example is the following code:

```
SET KEY 28 TO Inhelp
```

Here, if we fail to link in the INHELP() function or procedure, we will get an error "MISSING EXTERNAL" whenever the key is pressed or shortly thereafter. Since Clipper will not automatically resolve these types of external symbols, we must make sure they are resolved before the program is executed. Otherwise, there is an increasing likelihood that the end user will press the one key that will terminate the application. One way to avoid this is through the use of the EXTERNAL command. We will talk at length about this when we begin to talk about data-driven programming, but for now let us look at the following code extract:

```
EXTERNAL Mustfill

Windowpush(6,11,20,69,"GREEN","WHITE","BLACK", "", .T.)
Wsayget(Wdepth()/2, Wwidth()/2, "Opening Files")

Op(A->(Selecting("Notap", "Notap")))
Clear_area()
Op(A->(Append()))
Wsayget( 1, 2, A->(ALIAS()))
Wsayget( 1,35, A->(RECNO()))
Wsayget( Wdepth(), 2, left)
Wsayget( 4, 5,"  Files =>", "A->files", "@X", "Mustfill(A->files)")
Wsayget( 5, 5,"  Sizes =>", "A->sizes")
Wsayget( 6, 5,"   Date =>", "A->datestamp")
Wsayget( 7, 5,"   Time =>", "A->times")
Wsayget( 8, 5,"Commnet =>", "A->file_use", "@S20")
Wsayget( 9, 5,"  Drive =>", "A->subdrive", "@S25")
Wsayget(10, 5,"Percent =>", "A->per_used")
IF Sjsread()
   IF Looknum("Demo2.exe")
      left = left - 1
      Writenum("Demo2.exe", left)
   ENDIF
ELSE
   Op(A->(Delete_it()))
   Op(A->(Packit()))
   EXIT
ENDIF
Op(A->(Selecting("")))   && Close the file
Windowpop()
```

As you can probably predict, the MUSTFILL() function will be called in completion of a VALID clause; however, it is within quotation marks, which means that Clipper will not automatically pull the reference to the MUSTFILL() function out of the ToolkiT Library. To ensure that this reference is present (that is, part of the symbol table) within the application, we must use the EXTERNAL command, forcing Clipper to generate an appropriate token that would in turn tell the linker to pull in the reference for the external function or procedure. On the other hand, it would be more advantageous to be able to test for the existence of a procedure or function's symbol within the application before it is actually called, as shown in the following:

```
******************
* ***********************************************
* * The following procedure(s)/function(s) are   *
* * part of Steve Straley's ToolkiT(tm) -        *
* * Release 2, published by Four Seasons         *
* * Publishing Co., Inc.  All Rights Reserved    *
* * Information: 212-599-2141 / 800-662-2278     *
* * All Rights Reserved                          *
* ***********************************************
```

```
FUNCTION Wsayget

   PARAMETERS _row, _col, _say, _get, _pict, ;
              _valid, _withread

   IF PCOUNT() = 1
      IF TYPE("_row") = "L"
         scrcursor = .T.
         SET CURSOR ON
         IF _row
            READ
         ELSE
            CLEAR GETS
         ENDIF
         SET CURSOR OFF
         RETURN( IF( (LASTKEY() = 27), .F., UPDATED() ) )
      ENDIF
   ENDIF

   IF TYPE("_row") = "L"
      IF TYPE("_col") != "U"
         _row = _col
      ENDIF
      IF TYPE("_say") != "U"
         _col = _say
         _say = ""
      ENDIF
      IF TYPE("_get") != "U"
         _say = _get
         _get = ""
      ENDIF
      IF TYPE("_pict") != "U"
         _get = _pict
         _pict = ""
      ENDIF
      IF TYPE("_valid") != "U"
         _pict = _valid
         _valid = ".T."
      ENDIF
      IF TYPE("_withread") != "U"
         _valid = _withread
      ELSE
         _valid = ".T."
      ENDIF
      _withread = .T.
   ELSE
      _withread = .F.
   ENDIF


   IF PCOUNT() < 3
      RETURN(.F.)
   ELSE
```

```
064 :        IF scr_level - 1 <= 0
065 :           _therow = _row + 0
066 :           _thecol = _col + 0
067 :        ELSE
068 :           _therow = _row + VAL(SUBSTR(allwindows[scr_level-1], ;
069 :                       1, 2))
070 :           _thecol = _col + VAL(SUBSTR(allwindows[scr_level-1], ;
071 :                       4, 2))
072 :        ENDIF
073 :     ENDIF
074 :
075 :     IF TYPE("_pict") != "U"
076 :
077 :        && if no at sign in picture and data type of
078 :
079 :        IF !("@"$_pict) .AND. TYPE(_get) = "C"
080 :           *
081 :           *    the GET is of character type, then...
082 :           *
083 :           _difference = ( LEN(Strvalue(_say)) + ;
084 :                           IF( (TYPE("_pict") = "U" ), ;
085 :                           LEN(Strvalue(_get)), ;
086 :                           LEN(_pict) ) + 2 ) - Wwidth()
087 :
088 :           * If empty(difference), o.k. or if difference is
089 :           * a negative number, it's o.k. too.  But if positive,
090 :           * take the number, LTRIM(STR()) it and add an "@" to
091 :           * the pict of the GET so that it will fit in the
092 :           * window area...
093 :
094 :           IF _difference > 0
095 :              _pict = "@S"
096 :              IF TYPE("_pict") = "U"
097 :                 _pict = _pict + LTRIM(STR(_difference - ;
098 :                              LEN(Strvalue(_get)) ))
099 :              ELSE
100 :                 _pict = _pict + LTRIM(STR(_difference - ;
101 :                              LEN(_pict) ))
102 :              ENDIF
103 :           ENDIF
104 :        ENDIF
105 :     ELSE
106 :        IF TYPE("_get") != "U"
107 :           IF TYPE(_get) = "C"
108 :              _difference = ( LEN(Strvalue(_say)) + ;
109 :                              IF( (TYPE("_pict") = "U" ), ;
110 :                              LEN(Strvalue(_get)), ;
111 :                              LEN(_pict) ) + 2 ) - Wwidth()
112 :
113 :              * If empty(difference), o.k. or if difference is
114 :              * a negative number, it's o.k. too.  But if positive,
115 :              * take the number, LTRIM(STR()) it, add an "@" to
116 :              * the pict of the GET so that it will fit in the
117 :              * window area...
```

```
118 :
119 :                  IF _difference > 0
120 :                     _pict = "@S" + LTRIM(STR(_difference)) + ;
121 :                             IF( (TYPE("_pict") = "U" ), ;
122 :                             LEN(Strvalue(_get)), LEN(_pict) )
123 :                  ENDIF
124 :               ENDIF
125 :            ENDIF
126 :      ENDIF
127 :
128 :      IF TYPE("_pict") = "U"
129 :         IF TYPE("_get") != "U"
130 :            IF TYPE(_get) = "D"
131 :               _pict = "99/99/99"
132 :            ELSEIF TYPE(_get) = "M"
133 :               _pict = "@S10"
134 :            ELSEIF TYPE(_get) = "L"
135 :               _pict = "@!"
136 :            ENDIF
137 :         ENDIF
138 :      ENDIF
139 :
140 :      IF TYPE("_get") = "U"
141 :         @ _therow, _thecol SAY _say
142 :
143 :      ELSEIF TYPE("_get") != "U" .AND. TYPE("_valid") = "U"
144 :
145 :         && No Say
146 :         IF EMPTY(_say)
147 :
148 :            && With Picture
149 :            IF TYPE("_pict") != "U"
150 :               IF TYPE(_get) = "U"
151 :               ELSE
152 :                  @ _therow, _thecol GET &_get. PICT _pict
153 :               ENDIF
154 :            ELSE          && Without Picture
155 :               IF TYPE(_get) = "U"
156 :               ELSE
157 :                  @ _therow, _thecol GET &_get.
158 :               ENDIF
159 :            ENDIF
160 :         ELSE                        && With SAY
161 :            IF TYPE("_pict") != "U" && With Picture
162 :               IF EMPTY(_get)
163 :                  @ _therow, _thecol SAY _say PICT _pict
164 :               ELSE
165 :                  IF TYPE(_get) = "U"
166 :                     @ _therow, _thecol SAY _say
167 :                  ELSE
168 :                     @ _therow, _thecol SAY _say ;
169 :                        GET &_get. PICT _pict
170 :                  ENDIF
171 :               ENDIF
```

```
172 :          ELSE         && Without Picture
173 :             IF EMPTY(_get)
174 :                @ _therow, _thecol SAY _say
175 :             ELSE
176 :                IF TYPE(_get) = "U"
177 :                   @ _therow, _thecol SAY _say
178 :                ELSE
179 :                   @ _therow, _thecol SAY _say GET &_get.
180 :                ENDIF
181 :             ENDIF
182 :          ENDIF
183 :       ENDIF
184 :
185 :    ELSEIF TYPE("_valid") != "U"
186 :       IF TYPE(_valid) == "U" && This tests unresolved externals
187 :          _valid = ".T."
188 :       ENDIF
189 :       IF EMPTY(_say)
190 :          IF TYPE(_get) = "U"
191 :          ELSE
192 :             @ _therow, _thecol GET &_get. ;
193 :               PICT _pict VALID &_valid.
194 :          ENDIF
195 :       ELSE
196 :          IF EMPTY(_get)
197 :             @ _therow, _thecol SAY _say PICT _pict
198 :          ELSE
199 :             IF TYPE(_get) = "U"
200 :                @ _therow, _thecol SAY _say
201 :             ELSE
202 :                @ _therow, _thecol SAY _say ;
203 :                  GET &_get. PICT _pict VALID &_valid.
204 :             ENDIF
205 :          ENDIF
206 :       ENDIF
207 :    ENDIF
208 :
209 :    IF _withread
210 :       scrcursor = .T.
211 :       SET CURSOR ON
212 :       READ
213 :       SET CURSOR OFF
214 :       scrcursor = .F.
215 :       RETURN( IF( (LASTKEY() = 27), .F., UPDATED() ) )
216 :    ELSE
217 :       RETURN(.T.)
218 :    ENDIF
219 :
220 : * End of File
```

The key is on lines 185 and 186. If the string or parameter that contains the name of a function that is to be processed in conjunction with any of the VALID clauses is present, the test of line 186 fails. This line tests to see if the function, as specified in the string, is actually in the symbol table. If it is present, because the EXTERNAL command is literally made in the previous example, the IF condition would yield a value and the string may then be expanded in conjunction with the VALID clauses as in lines 193 and 203. If, on the other hand, the function is not in the system, the string is quickly converted to a ".T.," which would satisfy the expansion on the VALID clause. Under most conditions, the TYPE() of a variable that contains the name of a function that is present in a Clipper application should yield a "UI," not a "UE" or a "U." Knowing this, one can build AI-like applications that can test themselves and the validity of the function statements before the actual call to those functions or procedures is made.

To get a better feel for more of the Clipper language and its ability to take on chameleon-like effects, take a look at some of the function-oriented code and some of the C code provided in Chapters 8 and 9. Following are a few functions and a piece of sample code that demonstrate the look and feel of the function-oriented approach to programming:

```
Cls()
Publics()
Setup(.F.)
Savesys()
Setscore(.F.)  && SETS scoreboard OFF
Palate(2)
Windowpush(5,20,18,60)
Wsayget(1,2, "First, generate the file structures")
Filestru()
Wsayget(2,2, "Now, create the first database")
Op(A->(Dbfmake("Ontap", file1)))
Op(A->(Dbfindex("Ontap", "files")))
Op(A->(Selecting("Ontap", "Ontap")))

Wsayget(3,2, "Now, create the second database")
Op(B->(Dbfmake("Clients", file2)))
Op(B->(Selecting("Clients")))

Wsayget(4,2, "Now, create the third database")
Op(C->(Dbfmake("Trans", file3)))
Op(C->(Selecting("Trans")))

Wsayget(5,2, "Now, create the fourth database")
Op(D->(Dbfmake("Statcode", file4)))
Op(D->(Selecting("Statcode")))

Wsayget(6,2, "Now, create the fifth database")
Op(E->(Dbfmake("Disknos", file5)))
Op(E->(Dbfindex("Disknos", "disk_no")))
Op(E->(Selecting("Disknos", "Disknos")))

Wsayget(7,2, "Now, create the sixth database")
Op(F->(Dbfmake("Filenos", file6)))
Op(F->(Dbfindex("Filenos", "sub_no + file_name", "Filenos")))
```

```
Op(F->(Dbfindex("Filenos", "sub_no + sub_name",  "Filesub")))
Op(F->(Dbfindex("Filenos", "sub_no + file_type", "Filetype")))
Op(F->(Selecting("Filenos", "Filenos/Filesub/Filetype")))

Wsayget(8,2, "Now, create the seventh database")
Op(G->(Dbfmake("Statbase", file7)))
Op(G->(Selecting("Statbase")))

Wsayget(9,2, "Now, create the eighth database")
Op(H->(Dbfmake("Notap", file8)))
Op(H->(Dbfindex("Notap", "files")))
Op(H->(Selecting("Notap", "Notap")))

Wsayget(Wdepth(), 2, "Ready for next phase? ")
Prompt()
Pan(8)

Wsayget(1, 2, "Adding Information to first file")
Op(A->(Withone()))

Wsayget(2, 2, "Working with second file")
Op(B->(Withtwo()))

Wsayget(3, 2, "Adding Transactions to file")
Op(C->(Withthree()))

Wsayget(4, 2, "Storing Code information...")
Op(D->(Withfour()))

Wsayget(5, 2, "Making the Help Files....")
Mhelp()

Wsayget(6, 2, "Searching through the drive")

* a DECLARE command is made
Declare(Nosubdr("C:"), "array")
Drnames(array, "C:")

Wsayget(7, 2, "Obtaining File Information!")
Wsayget(8, 2, "          Secondary File ...")
Op(E->(Obtain()))

Wsayget(9, 2, "Adding State Information.")
Op(G->(Statbase()))

Wsayget(10,2, "Now adding the final piece.")
Op(H->(Final()))

Wsayget(Wdepth(), 2, "Any key for final screen ")
INKEY(0)
Pan(4)
Windowpop()
Stats()
IF LASTKEY() = 27 .OR. LASTKEY() = 13
```

```
    Sjs_hello()
ENDIF
Cls()
```

SUMMARY

The avocation of programming in C over Clipper would be, for most data-based applications, a foolish notion. Equally shortsighted would be the concept of programming as we have since the days of dBASE II and CP/M. Clipper has evolved into a unique language. It can have the look and feel of a dBASE compiler, or it can have the power and elegance of a C or Pascal compiler or language. We advocate the latter.

Programming in a function-oriented way will give us the ability to look at C code and learn; give C programmers room to view our code and appreciate it; and give the corporate stratosphere time to ponder the new-found harmony between the two camps. No longer can it be said with scorn and disdain that Clipper is just a dBASE compiler; it is a language that can look and feel like C just as much as it can look and feel like dBASE. In many ways, it is superior to C and the numerous libraries that are available to that language; in Clipper, screen, low-level, error handling, memory management, database management libraries are all handled by one incorporated library, CLIPPER.LIB. This chapter should shed some new light on the new ways in which we can code and approach our database management problems of the future.

CHAPTER SIX

Low-Level File Functions

We have shown how using advanced Clipper tricks and tips can improve the speed of your application and shorten both its development cycle and the amount of time required to make changes to it. The latter concept is the thrust behind object-oriented programming. The Clipper language has evolved away from the verb-oriented construct of the dBASE world and has embraced a C- and Pascal-like world. We intend to demonstrate the power of these functions and the concepts within them. In this chapter, we will take an in-depth look at the low-level file functions in Clipper and will show some unique features these functions now offer.

IN THE BEGINNING

Before we go any further, there are two major rules to understand. First, when using the low-level file functions, everything is referred to as a DOS file handle. This means that the concept of a name or a work area is foreign; each file that is opened is represented by a unique integer. We will discuss these values in a moment. The second thing to keep in mind is that nothing is taken for granted; you want to have total control, and you can have it. This type of power is not only attractive, but it is potentially hazardous, especially to the inexperienced programmer. On the other side of the issue, the only way to gain experience with these functions is through active use.

The Fundamentals and Hazardous Roads

As mentioned above, everything is referred to as a file handle. In Clipper, when we normally USE a file, we refer to the database name or the work area by the alias of that file. In DOS, that name is referred to by number, and Clipper handles the conversion for us. In DOS, there are five default files that are opened by the operating system. They are as follows:

File Handle Number	Standard Device Name
0	Input
1	Output
2	Error
3	Auxiliary
4	Printer

There are two items in this table that should appear obvious: No file handle is lower than 0 (which means no negative numbers), and the first file opened by a program (other than the operating system files) begins with 5. Before DOS version 3.3, the maximum number of files one could open in a Clipper program was 15; 20 allowed by DOS minus 5 for DOS operating procedures. To circumvent this, many add-on libraries, like FUNCky by dLESKO and Associates, have patches to the application to allow Clipper (Summer '87 or later) to open more than this limit. For machines running on DOS 3.3 or greater, the maximum number of files that can be opened by a Clipper application is 250.

It is important to understand that a database, an index, a memory variable file, and a report file are all referred to by DOS numeric values rather than by their names. Therefore, for this chapter, each low-level file function either requires the DOS file handle for the file you want to work with or returns the DOS file handle that you want to work with. For example, the functions FOPEN() and FCREATE() require a file name passed to them, but they in turn return a number. This number is either an error code (a negative number that signifies that the appointed file cannot be either opened or created, depending upon which function is called) or a DOS file handle. In the latter case, this DOS file handle should be stored to a memory variable and referred to when calling the following functions: FCLOSE(), FREAD(), FREADSTR(), FSEEK(), and FWRITE(). In conventional Clipper code, a file is opened and closed in the following fashion:

```
USE Clients
USE && or CLOSE DATABASES
```

Using the low-level file functions, the same effect is programmed this way:

```
fhandle = FOPEN("Clients.dbf")
FCLOSE(fhandle)
```

The value of the function FOPEN() is passed to the variable **fhandle**. We could test this value to see if it is other than a negative number, or we could test the value of the FERROR() function to see if the file is indeed open and no error condition exists. Once the file is opened and the DOS file handle is assigned to the variable, the FCLOSE() function closes the file assigned by the numeric value in the variable. Also note that the file extension of the database file must be given and must be in quotes. Normally, we can safely assume the database file extension when working with the USE commands, but, our first rule when working with the low-level file functions is never assume anything. A good idea to maintain when using these functions is that while the low-level file functions give the Clipper programmer absolute power, it also gives inexperienced programmers a greater ability to corrupt data. For example, it is not uncommon to accidentally FOPEN() a file in READ ONLY mode, attempt to make a low-level file change to that file, only to find out that the attempt failed. Many hours of frustration could be avoided if the programmer knew that assumptions (like opening a file to be read and written to) are not valid when using these functions. But some justice must be given to these functions, since with them, additional tools can be built to add more power and flexibility to your applications.

One last topic that must be discussed before moving on is the difference between a file handle and a file pointer. The file handle is the variable that contains the DOS file handle, as described above. The file pointer is the actual byte pointer within the file, as specified by the value of the file handle. While this may sound confusing, it is important to maintain the difference in your mind. Again, looking at the internals of Clipper, consider the following command:

```
USE Clients
GO TOP
SKIP
```

Using the low-level file functions, those three commands would be equal to the following:

```
* pretend we know the length, in bytes,
* of each record and it is stored to a
* variable named 'length'

fhandle = FOPEN("Clients.dbf")
FSEEK(fhandle, 0, 0)
FSEEK(fhandle, 1 * length, 1)
```

In the next section we will look at obtaining the length of a .DBF record; however, the point should be clear: Much more effort is involved when using the low-level file functions.

ADDITIONAL LOW-LEVEL FILE FUNCTIONS

With the concept of a user-defined function, we can build our own set of additional low-level file functions. While many of these functions appear in Steve Straley's ToolkiT–Release 2, they are needed for the following educational programs and are provided here.

FBOF()	Tests for Beginning of File
FEOF()	Tests for End of File
FEND()	Returns the number of bytes to the FEOF()
FPOSIT()	Returns the byte position in the file
FTOP()	Rewinds file to top of the file

Low-Level Function 1

```
* ****************************************
* * The following function is part of    *
* * Steve Straley's ToolkiT(tm) -  Rel.  *
* * 2, published by Four Seasons Pub.    *
* * Co., Inc.  All Rights Reserved       *
* * Information: 212-599-2141            *
* ****************************************

FUNCTION Fbof

   PARAMETER _fp1
```

```
   IF EMPTY(PCOUNT())
      RETURN(.F.)
   ELSEIF TYPE("_fp1") != "N"
      RETURN(.F.)
   ENDIF

   PRIVATE _original
   _original = FSEEK(_fp1, 0, 1)
   IF _original = 0
      RETURN(.T.)
   ELSE
      FSEEK(_fp1, _original, 0)
      RETURN(.F.)
   ENDIF

* End of File
```

Low-Level Function 2

```
********************
* **************************************
* * The following function is part of    *
* * Steve Straley's ToolkiT(tm) -  Rel.  *
* * 2, published by Four Seasons Pub.    *
* * Co., Inc.  All Rights Reserved       *
* * Information: 212-599-2141            *
* **************************************

FUNCTION Feof

   PARAMETER _fp1

   IF EMPTY(PCOUNT())
      RETURN(.F.)
   ELSEIF TYPE("_fp1") != "N"
      RETURN(.F.)
   ENDIF

   PRIVATE _original

   _original = FSEEK(_fp1, 0, 1)
   FSEEK(_fp1, 0, 2)
   IF _original = FSEEK(_fp1, 0, 1)  && At the end
      FSEEK(_fp1, _original, 0)
      RETURN(.T.)
   ELSE
      FSEEK(_fp1, _original, 0)
      RETURN(.F.)
   ENDIF

* End of File
```

Low-Level Function 3

```
**********************
* ****************************************
* * The following function is part of    *
* * Steve Straley's ToolkiT(tm) -  Rel.  *
* * 2, published by Four Seasons Pub.    *
* * Co., Inc.  All Rights Reserved       *
* * Information: 212-599-2141            *
* ****************************************

FUNCTION Fend

   PARAMETERS _thefile

   IF EMPTY(PCOUNT())
      RETURN(-1)
   ELSEIF TYPE("_thefile") != "N"
      RETURN(-1)
   ENDIF

   PRIVATE _current, _thelength

   _current = FSEEK(_thefile, 0, 1)        && current position
   _thelength = FSEEK(_thefile, 0, 2)      && the file length
   FSEEK(_thefile, _current, 0)            && reset position (safety)
   RETURN( (_thelength - _current) )

* End of File
```

Low-Level Function 4

```
***********************
* ****************************************
* * The following function is part of    *
* * Steve Straley's ToolkiT(tm) -  Rel.  *
* * 2, published by Four Seasons Pub.    *
* * Co., Inc.  All Rights Reserved       *
* * Information: 212-599-2141            *
* ****************************************

FUNCTION Fposit

   PARAMETER _fp1

   IF EMPTY(PCOUNT())
      RETURN(0)
   ELSEIF TYPE("_fp1") != "N"
      RETURN(0)
   ENDIF
```

```
   RETURN( FSEEK(_fp1, 0, 1))

* End of File
```

Low-Level Function 5

```
********************
* ***************************************
* * The following function is part of    *
* * Steve Straley's ToolkiT(tm) -  Rel.  *
* * 2, published by Four Seasons Pub.    *
* * Co., Inc.  All Rights Reserved       *
* * Information: 212-599-2141            *
* ***************************************

FUNCTION Ftop

   PARAMETERS _rhand

   IF EMPTY(PCOUNT())
      RETURN(.F.)
   ELSEIF TYPE("_rhand") != "N"
      RETURN(.F.)
   ENDIF

   * _rhand is the DOS file handle you want to rewind!

   FSEEK(_rhand, 0)
   RETURN(.T.)

* End of File
```

SCANNING A DATABASE AND MULTIPLE FIELDS

One of the first things that can help a programmer understand the power and potential of the low-level file functions is to write a program that will scan a database, such as the following Clipper code:

```
USE Clients
? LASTREC()
? RECSIZE()
? HEADER()
DO WHILE !EOF()
   ? RECNO()
   ?? SPACE(10)
   name = FIELD(1)
   ?? &name.
   INKEY(.2)
```

```
        SKIP
    ENDDO
```

Using the low-level file functions, we would have the following program:

```
001 : ********************
002 : * Name      Contents.prg
003 : * Author    Stephen J. Straley
004 : * Date      June 1, 1989
005 : * Notice    Copyright (c) 1989 Stephen J. Straley & Associates
006 : * Compile   Clipper Contents -m
007 : * Release   Summer 87
008 : * Link      PLINK86 FI Contents LIB Extend LIB Clipper;
009 : * Note      This program shows how to use the low-level file
010 : *           functions and the binary-based functions in
011 : *           order to look at a .DBF file.
012 : *
013 : ********************
014 :
015 : PARAMETERS thefile
016 :
017 : IF PCOUNT() = 0
018 :     ? "Contents <filename>"
019 :     ?
020 :     QUIT
021 : ENDIF
022 :
023 : DECLARE bytes[8]
024 : AFILL(bytes, "")
025 : bytes[5] = 0
026 : CLEAR SCREEN
027 : fhandle = FOPEN(thefile)
028 : IF fhandle = -1
029 :     *
030 :     * This is an error situation since the DOS file
031 :     * handle is not above a 4.
032 :     *
033 :     ? "Can't Open File!"
034 :     ?
035 :     QUIT
036 : ENDIF
037 :
038 : * The beginning structure of the .DBF file is:
039 : *
040 : *  Bytes 0       /  The dBASE Identifier
041 : *  Bytes 1       /  The Year of the Last Update
042 : *  Bytes 2       /  The Month of the Last Update
043 : *  Bytes 3       /  The Day of the Last Update
044 : *  Bytes 4  - 7  /  Number of records in the database
045 : *  Bytes 8  - 9  /  Length of Header in bytes
046 : *  Bytes 10 - 11 /  Length of each record
047 : *  Bytes 12 - 31 /  Reserved bytes...
048 :
```

```
049 :
050 :
051 : bytes[1] = BIN2I(Getbyte(" "))      && Bytes 0
052 : bytes[2] = BIN2I(Getbyte(" "))      && Bytes 1
053 : bytes[3] = BIN2I(Getbyte(" "))      && Bytes 2
054 : bytes[4] = BIN2I(Getbyte(" "))      && Bytes 3
055 : bytes[5] = BIN2L(Getbyte("    "))   && Bytes 4 - 7
056 : bytes[6] = BIN2W(Getbyte("  "))     && Bytes 8 - 9
057 : bytes[7] = BIN2W(Getbyte("  "))     && Bytes 10 - 11
058 : bytes[8] = FREADSTR(fhandle,20)     && Bytes 12 - 31
059 :
060 : FOR x = 1 to 7
061 :     ? bytes[x]
062 : NEXT
063 :
064 : ?
065 : ? "The Date of the last update was " + ;
066 :    TRIM(LTRIM(STR(bytes[3]))) + ;
067 :    "/" + LTRIM(STR(bytes[4])) + "/" + ;
068 :    TRIM(LTRIM(STR(bytes[2])))
069 : ?
070 : ? "The number of records in the database is " + ;
071 :    TRIM(LTRIM(STR(bytes[5])))
072 : ?
073 : ? "The length of each record is " + ;
074 :    TRIM(LTRIM(STR(bytes[7]))) + ;
075 :    " bytes "
076 : ?
077 : WAIT
078 :
079 : CLEAR SCREEN
080 : fieldnumb = 1
081 : frow = 1
082 : fcol = 1
083 : DO WHILE ( FSEEK(fhandle, 0, 1) < bytes[6]-31 )
084 :     IF fcol > 70
085 :         frow = frow + 7
086 :         fcol = 5
087 :     ENDIF
088 :     IF frow > 20
089 :         @ 1,0 CLEAR
090 :         frow = 1
091 :         fcol = 1
092 :     ENDIF
093 :     @ frow+1, fcol SAY "Field Number " + ;
094 :                 TRIM(LTRIM(STR(fieldnumb)))
095 :     && Name of field
096 :     @ frow+2, fcol SAY "     Name is " + ;
097 :                 FREADSTR(fhandle, 11)
098 :     @ frow+3, fcol SAY "     Type = " + ;
099 :                 FREADSTR(fhandle, 1)  && type
100 :
```

```
101 :     BIN2L(FREADSTR(fhandle, 4))   && Address
102 :     *
103 :     * field length
104 :     *
105 :     @ frow+4, fcol SAY "    Length = " + ;
106 :     LTRIM(TRIM(STR(BIN2I(FREADSTR(fhandle, 1)))))
107 :     *
108 :     * dec. length
109 :     *
110 :     decimals = BIN2I(FREADSTR(fhandle, 1))
111 :     IF decimals > 20 .OR. decimals < 0
112 :        @ frow+5, fcol SAY "  Decimals = 0"
113 :     ELSE
114 :        @ frow+5, fcol SAY "  Decimals = " + ;
115 :                    TRIM(LTRIM(STR(decimals)))
116 :     ENDIF
117 :
118 :     FREADSTR(fhandle, 14)
119 :     fieldnumb = fieldnumb + 1
120 :     INKEY(1)
121 :     fcol = fcol + 25
122 : ENDDO
123 : @ 23,00 SAY ""
124 : WAIT "Press Any Key for display of Records..."
125 : CLEAR SCREEN
126 : @ 0,0 SAY "\" + CURDIR() + "\" + UPPER(thefile)
127 : @ 0,45 SAY "Press ESC to Abort while listing!"
128 : ?
129 : FSEEK( fhandle, 0 )
130 : FSEEK( fhandle, bytes[6], 1)
131 : recno = 1
132 : FOR x = 1 TO bytes[5]
133 :    disp = FREADSTR(fhandle, bytes[7])
134 :    IF !EMPTY(AT(CHR(26), disp))
135 :       EXIT
136 :    ENDIF
137 :    ? TRANSFORM(recno, "9999") + "    " + SUBSTR(disp, 1, 69)
138 :    IF ROW() = 21
139 :       SCROLL(2,0,22,79,1)
140 :       @ 20, 00 SAY ""
141 :    ENDIF
142 :    INKEY(.1)
143 :    IF LASTKEY() = 27
144 :       EXIT
145 :    ENDIF
146 :    IF LASTKEY() = 27
147 :       EXIT
148 :    ENDIF
149 :    recno = recno + 1
150 : NEXT
151 : FCLOSE(fhandle)
152 :
```

```
153 : *********************
154 :
155 : FUNCTION Getbyte
156 :
157 :    PARAMETER blank_var
158 :
159 :    * originally, this was set up like this
160 :    * for each and every byte in the header
161 :
162 :    * www = " "
163 :    * FREAD(fhandle, @www, 1)
164 :    * bytes[2] = BIN2I( www )
165 :
166 :    * 'fhandle' is assumed to contain the file
167 :    * handle for this program.
168 :
169 :    FREAD(fhandle, @blank_var, LEN(blank_var))
170 :    RETURN(blank_var)
171 :
172 : * End of file
```

Lines 40 through 47 contain the rough outline of the Clipper database header (.DBF file). Remember is that the detailed record information exists in bytes 32 and following. Before executing this program, try writing a simple program, using the same file, and displaying the RECSIZE() and the LASTREC() values. They will be the same values as generated by this program. In this version of the program, it is important to note the value of the parameter passed to the Getbyte() function, as called on lines 51 through 58. Referring to the actual function beginning on lines 155, the parameter **blank_var** can vary in size, ranging from 1 to 4 bytes. This is important to remember because the number of bytes read using the low-level file functions is related to the LEN() of the string (line 169). In essence, if only 1 byte is desired, a blank space is passed to the function; if 4 bytes must be read, four blank spaces are passed to the function.

Starting with line 27, the FOPEN() function attempts to open the file as specified by the PARAMETER statement on line 15. It should be clear by now that Clipper applications can accept parameters from the DOS command line; this program uses that feature. If the file cannot be opened, the value of the variable **fhandle** will be equal to -1. However, if it can be opened, the program will use the value of the **fhandle** variable throughout in conjunction with FREADSTR() (lines 58, 97, 99, 106, 110, 118), FSEEK() (line 83), FCLOSE() (line 151), and FREAD() (line 169). In each of these calls, the DOS file handle for the assigned file is used, not the actual name.

As you can see, it is very easy to get every piece of information within the .DBF file. In a utility program that packs a .DBT file, you must find out how many memo fields are in a given .DBF file, at what positions. This can be easily accomplished with the low-level file functions.

TOUCHING A FILE

One of the simplest stand-alone utilities uses the low-level file functions. This utility "touches" the specified file so that the DOS date and time stamps are updated. This feature is very handy when working with either Nantucket's or Microsoft's MAKE utility (although we recommend the Microsoft utility over the Nantucket utility, both function similarly but have internal differences). The concept is simple: to update all, or a specified range of, files so that the MAKE script file will be forced to recompile and relink an application. Simply updating the DOS date and time stamp of any given *.PRG file forces the MAKE utility to generate a new .OBJ file with a later DOS date and time stamp. This concept of touching the file is common on many BBS systems throughout the country. While most are written in C and/or ASM, our version is written in 100 percent Clipper code.

```
********************
* Name      Touch.prg
* Author    Stephen J. Straley
* Date      May 28, 1989
* Notice    Copyright (c) 1989 Stephen J. Straley & Associates
* Compile   Clipper Touch -m
* Release   Summer 87
* Link      PLINK86 FI Touch LIB Extend LIB Clipper;
* Note      This program will "touch" the specified file(s)
*           from DOS and update their date and time stamps.
*
*           This is a utility program to help out with the MAKE
*           file for the ToolkiT - Release 2 by Four Seasons
*           Publishing - 212-599-2141 / 800-662-2278
*
* Syntax    TOUCH <file skeleton/file name>
*
********************


PARAMETERS skeleton

   IF EMPTY(PCOUNT())
      ? "A file name or skeleton is required for this program"
   ELSEIF !FILE(skeleton)
      ? "File(s) do not exist."
   ELSE
      DECLARE files[ADIR(skeleton)]
      ADIR(skeleton, files)
      ? "There are " + LTRIM(STR(LEN(files))) + " to be touched."
      ?
      ? "Updating Files..."
      count = 0
      FOR x = 1 TO LEN(files)
         Updates(files[x])
      NEXT
```

```
37 :        ? CHR(13) + SPACE(70)
38 :        ? IF( count = LEN(files), "All files have be TOUCHED", ;
39 :          "Error in Touch")
40 :     ENDIF
41 :
42 : *******************
43 :
44 : PROCEDURE Updatets
45 :
46 :     PARAMETER thefile
47 :
48 :     ?? CHR(13) + SPACE(70)
49 :     ?? CHR(13) + "Working on ... " + thefile
50 :     count = count + 1
51 :     * open the file in READ/WRITE mode
52 :     fhandle =  FOPEN(thefile, 2)
53 :
54 :     * move to the end of the file
55 :     FSEEK(fhandle, 0, 2)
56 :
57 :     * update the date and time stamp
58 :     FWRITE(fhandle, "")
59 :
60 :     * close the file
61 :     FCLOSE(fhandle)
62 :
63 : * End of File
```

Looking at this routine, you can see that the use of the low-level functions is simple. As with the previous coding example, the use of the DOS parameter in a Clipper application is required. This parameter is a DOS file skeleton; in many cases it will be equivalent to "*.*." This parameter is then used in conjunction with the ADIR() function of Clipper. It will create an array with the names of all of the files that match the specified file skeleton (lines 28 and 29). The heart of the program is in lines 34 through 36. The FOR command will scan through the array named **files[]**, which contains the names of the desired files. Each name is then passed to the procedure **Updatets()**. After reading Chapter 5, you should be familiar with the concept of calling procedures in the same fashion as functions so your coding and thinking are more C-like. Remember, both procedures and functions are the same type of token in Clipper's symbol table. Except for the default and potential values that each could return (a procedure defaults to return a null byte while a function may return any data type), the calling conventions can be interchanged. Skeptics should take a look at the use of the ADIR() function on line 28 and 29. As shown in many Nantucket examples, the first call to the ADIR() function is made to obtain a length for the DECLARE command. In the second use of the ADIR() function, a call is made to fill the array with values; the value of the function is not needed, since it was previously obtained. In this case, the function is treated like a procedure since it simply does something.

The Updatets() procedure takes the individual names in the **files[]** array and does something with them. The decision to call Updatets a procedure was made in order to not force a

RETURN statement at the conclusion of the routine. In the Updatets() procedure, four simple steps take place. First, the file is opened in READ/WRITE mode. A key assumption can be made about this file: We do not need to test the value of the variable **fhandle** (line 52). We know the file exists since it was obtained via the ADIR() function. Looking at line 52 specifically, the second parameter passed to the FOPEN() function tells the function to open the file up in READ/WRITE mode. This means that the file can be read from or written to. The other values for this parameter are as follows:

0	Read Only (the default)
1	Write Only
2	Read/Write

Once the file is opened, we have to move the file pointer to the end of the file. This is accomplished with the FSEEK() function. The command in the function call on line 55 says "move the file pointer for file handle **fhandle** 0 bytes from the end of the file (2)." (To get a better understanding of the different combinations the last two parameters can take on, you can consult your favorite reference guide.) Once the file pointer is positioned at the end of the file, a NULL byte is written to the file using the FWRITE() function. Since it is a NULL byte, no information is actually written to the file; however, since a FWRITE() call was made and the write would be successful because the file was FOPEN()ed in READ/WRITE mode, the DOS date and time stamps are updated. This is the essence of this entire program. Finally, once the DOS date and time stamps are updated, the file is closed with the FCLOSE() function.

PACKING A .DBT

One of the worst design flaws of the dBASE database file concerns the memo field. Since memo fields are nothing more than contiguous strings, the methodology used to keep track of them allows the size of the .DBT file to grow enormously. A memo is determined in 512 contiguous byte blocks, and the 10-byte field pointer in the database is no more than a numeric pointer, pointing to the 512-byte block at which the record's associated memo begins. Each memo is in turn terminated by an end of file marker as well: CHR(26) or 1A hex. Let's take this a little more slowly and look at what it means. First, inside of the database file, when creating a database for the first time, we must have a memo field length of 10 bytes. In addition, the default byte size for a numeric (take the STR() of a number and find its length) is also 10 bytes. This similarity is not by chance; inside of each record, for those 10 bytes reserved for the memo field, there is a number. This number points to the location of the associated memo in the memo field.

Now, the problem with growing .DBT files is simple and stems from the way dBASE (and Clipper) handles each 512-byte block. A memo must be a contiguous string of information. The size of the memo in the memo file is determined by the number of 512-byte blocks that would be required to store the memo. If this length should change and cause the number bytes in the file to either go into the next 512-byte block or go back to the previous 512-byte block, the entire memo is moved to the next contiguous area in the file. In other words, let us say you have two records, each with an associated memo 480 bytes long. The file pointer in the .DBF file for the first record reports that its memo begins in the first 512-byte block, and the second record begins in the second 512-byte block. Now, let us say that the end user, through the MEMOEDIT() function, alters the size of the memo in the first record to be 602 bytes. What then takes place is simple: because the memo's length involves two 512-byte blocks, it will try to adjust. However, the first block has another record's memo blocking the way. So, Clipper looks through the file for next two contiguous blocks of 512 bytes, counts the number of blocks it is away from the header of the .DBT file, places that number into the .DBF file as a pointer, and rewrites the entire memo beginning at this new block position. The original memo is left at the original location.

Carrying this to the environment of an application, memos will constantly be shuffling around and moving away from their original positions. In the end, the .DBT file may look like Norton's picture of a fragmented disk through the SpeedDisk program: a block of Swiss cheese.

So when we PACK a file, only the records in the database get rewritten, not the .DBT file. In the past, the only way to shrink the size of a .DBT file was to use the COPY FILE command to force Clipper to go through each record and make a new .DBT file, realigning the 512-byte blocks into contiguous streams, beginning with the first block past the header. In some cases, this may be an acceptable answer to the problem; however, in most circumstances in which there are many records or fields involved with the database, this is not a workable solution because of disk I/O. For example, after a PACK operation, the data file has already been stripped of the unnecessary information. A COPY FILE command will copy all of the fields across to the new file when in essence, the only thing we need to do is write out a new .DBT file with the blocks properly aligned and to adjust the file pointer in the parent database. This happens automatically in a COPY FILE command, but all of the additional fields get copied as well and for some databases with plenty of fields and/or plenty of records, this is not a viable solution.

What is workable is use of low-level functions to PACK the .DBT file, only adjusting the file pointer in the parent database, leaving all of the other fields alone. Consider the following demonstration program:

```
********************
* Name      Packdbts.prg
* Author    Stephen J. Straley
* Date      June 1, 1989
* Notice    Copyright (c) 1989 Stephen J. Straley & Associates
* Compile   Clipper Packdbts -m
* Release   Summer 87
* Link      PLINK86 FI Packdbts LIB Extend LIB Clipper;
* Note      This is a modified routine previously written by
*           SJS & Associates and now works with multiple memo
*           fields.
*
```

```
013 : *            This routine first appeared in FROM D.O.S.S
014 : *            published by Four Seasons Publishing.
015 : *
016 : ********************
017 :
018 : DO WHILE .T.
019 :    CLEAR SCREEN
020 :    file = SPACE(8)
021 :    @ 10,10 SAY "Enter File Name to PACK the .DBT => " GET file
022 :    READ
023 :    IF LASTKEY() = 27
024 :       EXIT
025 :    ELSE
026 :       IF !Packdbt(TRIM(file))
027 :          ?
028 :          ? "An error has occured.  Please check spelling of the"
029 :          ? "root file name or space to see if there is enough"
030 :          ? "room for the operation..."
031 :       ELSE
032 :          ? "Operation Completed.  Any Key to Continue..."
033 :       ENDIF
034 :       WAIT
035 :    ENDIF
036 : ENDDO
037 :
038 : * **********************************************
039 : * * The following procedure(s)/function(s) are  *
040 : * * part of Steve Straley's ToolkiT(tm) -       *
041 : * * Release 2, published by Four Seasons        *
042 : * * Publishing Co., Inc.  All Rights Reserved   *
043 : * * Information: 212-599-2141 / 800-662-2278    *
044 : * * All Rights Reserved                         *
045 : * **********************************************
046 :
047 : ********************
048 :
049 : FUNCTION Packdbt
050 :
051 :    PARAMETERS tfile
052 :
053 :    * This function has two ancillary functions
054 :    * that are part of this main routine.  They
055 :    * are MAKEDBTHEAD() and COPYDBT()
056 :
057 :    IF PCOUNT() = 0
058 :       RETURN(.F.)
059 :    ELSE
060 :       IF !FILE(tfile + ".DBF")
061 :          RETURN(.F.)
062 :       ENDIF
063 :    ENDIF
064 :
065 :    USE (tfile)
066 :    _thehead = HEADER()
```

```
_theleng = RECSIZE()
_thenumb = LASTREC()
USE

* Now get the number of memos in the file
* and their beginning byte position.
* The 'whereat' variable is a string which
* needs to be parsed in order to determine
* the position of the .DBT.
_whereat = ""
memos = FTYPECNT(tfile + ".DBF", "M", @_whereat)

&& Original Database  <-- IN READ/WRITE MODE
_fhandle = FOPEN(tfile + ".DBF", 2)

&& New .DBT file
_newdbt   = FCREATE("SJSTEMP.$$$")

&& Original .DBT file
_olddbt   = FOPEN(tfile + ".DBT")

&& Creates the header
IF !MAKEDBTHEAD(_newdbt, _olddbt)
   RETURN(.F.)        && An error has occurred
ENDIF

* if the _dbhandle is o.k., continue, otherwise, quit
written = 1

FSEEK(_fhandle, _thehead, 0)
FOR x = 1 TO _thenumb
   string = SPACE(_theleng)

   && Gets the file pointer
   _justok = FSEEK(_fhandle, 0, 1)

   && Get the record
   FREAD(_fhandle, @string, _theleng)

   && Store the parse to a temp
   STORE _whereat TO tempparse
   FOR y = 1 TO memos
      _z = GETNUM(@tempparse)
      _dbtpoint = VAL(SUBSTR(string, VAL(_z), 10))
      IF !EMPTY(_dbtpoint)
         writeback = TRANSFORM(written, "9999999999")
         string = SUBSTR(string,1,VAL(_z)-1) + writeback + ;
                  SUBSTR(string, VAL(_z)+10)
         numblocks=COPYDBT(_olddbt,_newdbt,_dbtpoint,written)
         IF EMPTY(numblocks)   && An error has occured.
            RETURN(.F.)
         ENDIF
         written = written + numblocks
```

```
120 :          ENDIF
121 :       NEXT
122 :       * Reposition the file pointer to the
123 :       * beginning of the record
124 :       FSEEK(_fhandle, _justok, 0)
125 :
126 :       * Write out the new string which in turn
127 :       * points to the next record
128 :       FWRITE(_fhandle, string)
129 :       IF FERROR() != 0
130 :          RETURN(.F.)
131 :       ENDIF
132 :    NEXT
133 :    FWRITE(_newdbt, I2BIN(26), 1)
134 :    FCLOSE(_fhandle)
135 :    FCLOSE(_newdbt)
136 :    FCLOSE(_olddbt)
137 :    ERASE &tfile..dbt
138 :    COPY FILE SJSTEMP.$$$ TO &tfile..dbt
139 :    ERASE Sjstemp.$$$
140 :    RETURN(.T.)
141 :
142 : ********************
143 :
144 : FUNCTION Makedbthead
145 :
146 :    PARAMETERS handle1, handle2
147 :
148 :    * handle1 is the file handle to the temp DBT
149 :    * handle2 is the file handle to the good DBT file
150 :
151 :    FSEEK(handle2, 0, 0)
152 :    FWRITE(handle1, I2BIN(3), 1)
153 :    FOR x = 2 TO 100
154 :       FWRITE(handle1, I2BIN(0), 1)
155 :    NEXT
156 :    FWRITE(handle1, "Packed by Steve Straley's ToolkiT(tm) ")
157 :    FWRITE(handle1, ;
158 :       "Published by Four Season's Publishing - 212-599-2141")
159 :    IF FERROR() != 0
160 :       RETURN(.F.)
161 :    ENDIF
162 :    DO WHILE FSEEK(handle1, 0, 1) != 512
163 :       FWRITE(handle1, I2BIN(0), 1)
164 :    ENDDO
165 :    RETURN((FERROR() = 0))
166 :
167 : ****************
168 :
169 : FUNCTION Copydbt
170 :
171 :    PARAMETERS _filepoint, _farpoint, _filestart, _farstart
172 :
```

```
173 :    *            old dbt    , new dbt,   old point,  new point
174 :
175 :    * Take the file pointer for the old dbt file '_farpoint'
176 :    * and write out the contents to the new dbt file in the
177 :    * file pointer '_filepoint'.  The position in the old dbt
178 :    * file to start looking at is in '_filestart' and the return
179 :    * value will be the block pointer in the new dbt file.
180 :
181 :    * _seedpoint is the original file position in the old
182 :    * DBT file.
183 :
184 :    _seedpoint = FSEEK(_filepoint, 1, 0)
185 :
186 :    * Set the file pointer in the NEW dbt to the end
187 :    * of the last block written to it.
188 :
189 :    bytecount = 0
190 :
191 :    * Go to the beginning block pointer in the old dbt.
192 :
193 :    FSEEK(_filepoint, (512 * _filestart), 0)
194 :
195 :    * Read the file and find the end of memo counter
196 :    * and if the byte is not 1A, then write out the
197 :    * byte to the new DBT file.
198 :
199 :    _www = " "
200 :    DO WHILE .T.
201 :       FREAD(_filepoint, @_www, 1)
202 :       IF BIN2I(_www) != 26
203 :          bytecount = bytecount + 1
204 :          FWRITE(_farpoint, _www)
205 :          IF FERROR() != 0
206 :             RETURN(0)
207 :          ENDIF
208 :       ELSE
209 :          EXIT
210 :       ENDIF
211 :    ENDDO
212 :
213 :    * Find out how many blocks were written out
214 :    * to the new file.
215 :
216 :    blckcount = (INT(bytecount / 512)) + 1
217 :
218 :    * Figure out how many bytes until the end of the
219 :    * next memo file, reposition the files, and return
220 :    * the number of blocks written.
221 :
222 :    remaining = (blckcount * 512) - bytecount - 1
223 :    FWRITE(_farpoint, I2BIN(32), remaining)
224 :    FWRITE(_farpoint, I2BIN(26), 1)
225 :    IF FERROR() != 0
226 :       RETURN(0)
```

```
   ENDIF

   && Original dbt
   FSEEK(_filepoint, _seedpoint, 0)
   RETURN(blckcount)

*****************

FUNCTION Ftypecnt

   PARAMETERS _thefile, _thetype, _position

   PRIVATE _location

   _location = 0

   _return = LTRIM(STR(SELECT()))
   SELECT 0
   USE (_thefile)
   _header = HEADER()
   USE
   SELECT &_return.
   _f1 = FOPEN(_thefile)
   FSEEK(_f1, 32, 0)   && Past the basic header stuff
   _count = 0
   DO WHILE FSEEK(_f1, 0, 1) < (_header - 31)
      _fname = SPACE(11)
      _ftype = SPACE(1)
      _fwhy  = SPACE(4)
      _flen  = SPACE(1)
      _fdec  = SPACE(1)
      FREAD(_f1, @_fname, 11)
      FREAD(_f1, @_ftype, 1)
      FREAD(_f1, @_fwhy, 4)
      FREAD(_f1, @_flen, 1)
      FREAD(_f1, @_fdec, 1)
      _location = _location + BIN2I(_flen)
      IF _ftype = UPPER(_thetype)
         IF PCOUNT() = 3
            _position = _position + "/" + ;
                    LTRIM(STR(_location - 8))
         ENDIF
         _count = _count + 1
      ENDIF
      FSEEK(_f1, 14, 1)
   ENDDO
   FCLOSE(_f1)
   IF PCOUNT() = 3
      IF SUBSTR(_position, 1, 1) = "/"
         _position = SUBSTR(_position, 2)
      ENDIF
   ENDIF
   RETURN(_count)
```

```
281 : ********************
282 :
283 : FUNCTION Getnum
284 :
285 :    PARAMETERS getstring
286 :
287 :    whereat   = IF(EMPTY(AT("+", getstring)), ;
288 :                AT("/", getstring), AT("+", getstring))
289 :    newstring = IF(!EMPTY(whereat), ;
290 :                SUBSTR(getstring, 1, whereat - 1), getstring)
291 :    getstring = IF(!EMPTY(whereat), ;
292 :                SUBSTR(getstring, whereat + 1), "")
293 :    RETURN(newstring)
294 :
295 : * End of File
```

Several things are taking place in this demonstration, so let's take each step, one by one. First, without writing out our own routines, we have to get some vital pieces of information pertaining to the database file: the size of the header, the length of each record in the database, and finally, how many records are in the database. These variables are defined in lines 66 through 68. Next, we have to find out how many memo fields are in the database, which is determined by the FTYPECNT() function searching the field type field for "m's" and counting them. We have modified this function in the ToolkiT to yield not only the byte count but the actual field position in the database as well. This function was designed to tell how many fields of a certain type are in a database. Additionally, if used and passed by reference, a string will be built that points to the positions of these fields. This variable is **_whereat** and is passed by reference by the "@" symbol in the call of the function on line 77. So, for example, let's say the FTYPECNT() function reports that there are two memo fields in the database, one beginning at byte 42 and the other at byte 68. The **_whereat** variable will look like this: 42/68. This variable is built this way to allow the ToolkiT's **GETNUM()** [renamed in later versions to Parsing()] function to parse out the proper values. This is far easier than building an array because all that needs to happen is that the string is built as the field positions are determined. Otherwise, with an array, the array would have to be DECLAREd first to the proper size and then the value proper filled.

The next step is vital. When the files are opened using the low-level file functions, make sure to open the .DBF file in READ/WRITE mode and do not take the default mode of READ ONLY. This takes place on line 80 and is properly set by the 2 that is passed to the FOPEN() function. After all of the files are either opened or created, the header of the new .DBT file is built. This takes place in the function MAKEDBTHEAD() and is defined on lines 142 through 165. From this point on, the fun begins.

The flow of the operation is simple. First look at the original database file for the block pointer, go to that byte in the .DBT file, and begin to read in characters of the memo. As this happens, write out those characters to the newly created .DBT file (temporarily called SJSTEMP.$$$) and report back the new block position in the new .DBT file, which in turn will get written back into the original .DBF file. After this is finished, the original .DBT file is erased, and the new .DBT file is copied over with the name of the original .DBT file and is then erased as well. All of this may sound complicated and can be if the file pointers for all of these files and the block and byte positions are not well kept.

The first FSEEK() function (line 96) positions the file pointer in the original .DBF file to just past the header of the file. From here, the records are read in like strings (dates, numbers, and logicals all look like their string representations when viewed in this manner). This READ is performed with the FREAD() function on line 104. The next line, "STORE _whereat to tempparse," is necessary because of the operation performed by the GETNUM() function. Notice on line 109 that the call to this function is passing the variable by reference. It will be modified every time the function is called, and it will also return a value. This means that the variable **tempparse** needs to be reset to the original value of **_whereat**; otherwise, this entire operation will only work for the first record. Now, the value of **_z** is simple: It is the byte position of the memo in the record. Remember, this variable will change based on the number of memo fields in the database, and this FOR loop is controlled by the return value from the FTYPECNT() function. Once we have the byte position, we know that the size of a number and the size of the memo field are each 10 bytes; therefore, if we take a SUBSTR() of 10 bytes, beginning at the value of **_z**, we then have the beginning block pointer in the .DBT file. The COPYDBT() function actually performs the read/write operation from the old .DBT file to the new .DBT file and will report the number of blocks written. Keep in mind that a block is distinguished as a 512-byte segment. So long as this return value is not a 0, the operation goes smoothly. The beginning block counter is kept in the variable **written** and the number of blocks written is then stored to this variable. From here, the record of the database, kept in the variable **string** is modified to reflect the new position. This takes place on lines 114 and 115. Once the .DBT is read and the new one has been written to, the record containing the new block pointers are then written back to the database (line 128). One thing to keep in mind when writing out the new .DBT file is if the memo falls short of a full block, the file pointer needs to be filled and moved so that it is properly sitting at the beginning of the next available 512-byte block marker.

Once all of this takes place, the files are closed and properly erased and/or copied. You can take this routine and add many speed enhancements to improve the performance. The thrust of this program is to take each byte in the memo file and analyze it and act on it by either closing the file, moving onto the next memo and filling up the previous memo, or simply copying it to the temporary file. One of the tricky things to maintain is the multiple FOPEN()s or FCREATE()s. As you can see on lines 134 through 136, there are three files being worked over with the low-level file functions: the original .DBF and .DBT and the newly created .DBT. Additionally, this operation can be turbo-charged by programming the routine to look at blocks of 512 bytes since that is the smallest block size for a memo. Once 512 bytes are read in, scan through the string for the end of memo marker and act accordingly. This is a good practice drill to better familiarize yourself with the power and use of the low-level file functions.

TESTING FOR DRIVE AND PATH

The power of the low-level functions is really based on your perceptions of the language. If all you can see in these functions are a few ways to gather information within files other than just .DBF files, you are still wearing your dBlinders; you still are not converted to the Clipper way of thinking. For example, one of the subtle features of the low-level file functions is in their disconnection. Normally, whenever an error is encountered in Clipper, a message is displayed at the top of the screen. The information presented at this point will, with any luck, give some indication of the nature of the problem. Using the error system, we can even program our own error message. But the low-level file functions are different: They are "outside" of the standard error-handling interface. For example, if we tried to USE a file that did not exist, we could expect to receive an OPEN ERROR from the Clipper run-time error system. On the other hand, if we tried to open that same file with the low-level file functions, we would not get an error message. What we would get would either be an invalid DOS file pointer or a value from the FERROR() function other than a 0.

Given this, here is a program that uses the low-level file functions that test for the existence of a path:

```
********************
* Name      Testdrve.prg
* Author    Stephen J. Straley
* Date      June 1, 1989
* Notice    Copyright (c) 1989 Stephen J. Straley & Associates
* Compile   Clipper Testdrve -m
* Release   Summer 87
* Link      PLINK86 FI Testdrve LIB Extend LIB Clipper;
* Note      This sample shows how low-level functions can test
*           the existence of a drive/path without C or ASM.
*
********************

DO WHILE .T.
   CLEAR SCREEN
   path = SPACE(50)
   @ 10, 5 SAY "Enter Sub-Directory: " GET path PICT "@!@S20"
   READ
   IF LASTKEY() = 27
      EXIT
   ENDIF
   IF Valid_path(LTRIM(TRIM(path)))
      @ 12, 10 SAY "That's o.k.  It's here."
   ELSE
      @ 12,10 SAY "That is not available, shall I create?"
      IF Verify(.T.)
         path = LTRIM(TRIM(path))
         RUN MD &path.
      ENDIF
   ENDIF
```

```
031 : ENDDO
032 :
033 : * ************************************************
034 : * * The following procedure(s)/function(s) are   *
035 : * * part of Steve Straley's ToolkiT(tm) -        *
036 : * * Release 2, published by Four Seasons         *
037 : * * Publishing Co., Inc.  All Rights Reserved    *
038 : * * Information: 212-599-2141 / 800-662-2278     *
039 : * * All Rights Reserved                          *
040 : * ************************************************
041 :
042 : ********************
043 :
044 : FUNCTION Valid_path
045 :
046 :     PARAMETERS pathname
047 :
048 :     PRIVATE _new, _errway, _file
049 :
050 :     _file = pathname + "\SST$$$.TXT"
051 :
052 :     _file = LTRIM(TRIM(STRTRAN(_file, "\\", "\")))
053 :
054 :     _new = FCREATE(_file, 0)
055 :
056 :     _errway = FERROR()
057 :
058 :     IF EMPTY(_errway)
059 :        FCLOSE(_new)
060 :        IF FILE(_file)
061 :           ERASE (_file)
062 :        ENDIF
063 :     ENDIF
064 :     RETURN( (_errway = 0) )
065 :
066 : ********************
067 :
068 : FUNCTION Verify
069 :
070 :     PARAMETERS _comp, _extra
071 :
072 :     DO CASE
073 :     CASE PCOUNT() = 0
074 :        _comp = "YyNn"
075 :        _extra = .F.
076 :     CASE PCOUNT() = 1
077 :        IF TYPE("_comp") = "L"
078 :           _extra = _comp
079 :           _comp = "YyNn"
080 :        ELSE
081 :           _extra = .F.
082 :        ENDIF
083 :     ENDCASE
084 :
```

```
085 :    scrpause = IF((TYPE("scrpause") = "U"), 100, scrpause)
086 :
087 :    DO WHILE .T.
088 :       the_var = ""
089 :       inside = INKEY(0)
090 :       DO CASE
091 :       CASE inside = 4
092 :          the_var = "Y"
093 :       CASE inside = 19
094 :          the_var = "N"
095 :       OTHERWISE
096 :          the_var = CHR(inside)
097 :       ENDCASE
098 :       IF the_var$_comp .OR. inside = 27
099 :          EXIT
100 :       ENDIF
101 :    ENDDO
102 :    IF the_var$SUBSTR(_comp,1,2)
103 :       ?? "Yes"
104 :       IF _extra
105 :          INKEY(0)
106 :       ELSE
107 :          FOR qaz = 1 TO scrpause
108 :          NEXT
109 :       ENDIF
110 :       RETURN(.T.)
111 :    ELSE
112 :       ?? "No "
113 :       IF _extra
114 :          INKEY(0)
115 :       ELSE
116 :          FOR qaz = 1 TO scrpause
117 :          NEXT
118 :       ENDIF
119 :       RETURN(.F.)
120 :    ENDIF
121 :
122 : * End of File
```

Once the user types in the name of a subdirectory on line 17, the READ is completed. Provided that the Esc key was not the last key pressed, the call to the Valid_path() function will be made. Inside of that function beginning on line 42 and following, the name of the path is joined with the string "\SST$$$.TXT." This will only work if there is not a file named "SST$$$.TXT" anywhere on the designated drive. If there is, change the value of this string to any other esoteric value. After the assignment on line 50, a call to the STRTRAN() function is made that eliminates any double "\\" characters and replaces them with single "\" characters. After this step, an attempt to create the file is made (line 54). The theory is that if the path exists, the FCREATE() function will yield a valid DOS file handle to the variable named **_new**. If there is no such directory on the drive, as prescribed in the variable **pathname**, a -1 will be assigned to the variable **_new**, a nonzero number will be assigned to the variable **_errway** [as returned from the FERROR() function], and no error message will be displayed from Clipper error-handling system because the low-level file functions act outside of those internal routines. If by chance the file is created, the **_errway** will have a value of 0 and, thus, will be EMPTY(). The file is then closed using the FCLOSE() function and erased. The function will return a logical value, based on whether the file "SST$$$.TXT" was or was not created on the assigned drive.

LOOKING AT THE .MEM FILE

Another viable use of the low-level file functions is looking at and analyzing the contents of the .MEM file. This has many ramifications, including the ability to display all current memory variables present in an application and the ability to convert the .MEM file to a text file. The latter is useful when converting an application over to a data-driven application as discussed in Chapter 7. Normally, independent debugging routines are just as handy as commercial routines and using the low-level functions to strip a .MEM file, thus showing all of the memory variables, their values, and their sizes, adds to the potential power of debugging an application. If we were to simply SET a KEY to a procedure that displayed the contents of the memory variable file, we could simulate the DISPLAY MEMORY command in dBASE. Consider the following:

```
********************
* Name      Dispmem.prg
* Author    Essor Maso
* Date      June 1, 1989
* Notice    Copyright (c) 1989 Stephen J. Straley & Associates
* Compile   Clipper Dispmem -m
* Release   Summer 87
* Link      PLINK86 FI Dispmem LIB Clipper LIB Extend;
* Note      A diagnostic tool to view memory variables easily.
*
*           It is assumed that F7 is set to Disp_mem:
*
*           Call:   SET KEY -6 TO Disp_mem
*
********************

CLEAR SCREEN
SET KEY -6 TO Disp_mem
variable = SPACE(10)
adate    = DATE()
anumber  = 10
alogic   = .T.
@ 10,10 SAY "Enter Variable or F7 for DISP MEMO: " ;
        GET variable
READ

********************

PROCEDURE Disp_mem

```

```
031 :    SAVE SCREEN
032 :
033 :    SAVE TO S_____         && Save memory variables
034 :
035 :    PRIVATE _1vn,_1vt,_1vr,_1mc,_1sc,_1fh,_1fl
036 :
037 :    _1fh=FOPEN('S_____.MEM')
038 :    _1fl=FSEEK(_1fh,0,2)
039 :
040 :    FSEEK(_1fh,0)   && Top of file
041 :
042 :    CLEAR SCREEN
043 :
044 :    IF _1fl < 2
045 :
046 :       && File contains EOF marker.
047 :       @ 0,0 SAY "There are no memory variables present."
048 :
049 :    ELSE
050 :       _count = 1
051 :       _vars  = 0
052 :       _bytes = 0
053 :       DO WHILE FSEEK(_1fh,0,1)+1<_1fl
054 :          *
055 :          * Variable specific information is contained in the
056 :          * first 18 bytes of the variable packet. The value
057 :          * of the variable is contained from positon 33 on.
058 :          *
059 :          _1mw = SPACE(18)
060 :          *
061 :          * Get the variable specific information.
062 :          *
063 :          FREAD(_1fh,@_1mw,18)
064 :          *
065 :          * The variable name is in the first 10 positions
066 :          * with a CHR(0) terminator.
067 :          *
068 :          _1vn = LEFT(_1mw,AT(CHR(0),_1mw)-1)
069 :          *
070 :          * The variable type is in position 12 of the packet.
071 :          * C3h is character or memo, CCh is logical,
072 :          * CEh is numeric, C4h is date.
073 :          *
074 :          _1vt=SUBSTR(_1mw,12,1)
075 :          *
076 :          * For character and logical variables, position 17
077 :          * and 18 contain the hex value for the range of the
078 :          * data. For numeric and date variables, the range
079 :          * is 8. This points to the end of the variable packet.
080 :          *
081 :          _1vr=BIN2W(RIGHT(_1mw,2))
082 :          IF _1vt $ CHR(195) + CHR(204)
083 :             _1mc=14+_1vr
084 :          ELSE
```

```
085 :                  _1mc=22
086 :             ENDIF
087 :             FSEEK(_1fh,_1mc,1)    && Go to next packet.
088 :             IF _1vr>51.AND._1vt $ CHR(195) + CHR(204)
089 :                 _1r=STRTRAN(LEFT(&_1vn,50), CHR(7), CHR(1))
090 :                 _ttemp = LEFT(_1vn+SPACE(10),10) + ;
091 :                         "  TYPE " + TYPE(_1vn) + ["] + ;
092 :                         _1r + ["]
093 :             ELSE
094 :                 _1r=STRTRAN(&_1vn, CHR(7), CHR(1))
095 :                 _ttemp = LEFT(_1vn+SPACE(10),10) + ;
096 :                         "  TYPE " + TYPE(_1vn) + "  " + ;
097 :                         IF(TYPE(_1vn) = "C", ["]+_1r+["], ;
098 :                         Strvalue(&_1vn))
099 :             ENDIF
100 :             IF    TYPE(_1vn) = "C"
101 :                 _bytes = _bytes + LEN(&_1vn.)
102 :                 _a = LEN(&_1vn.)
103 :             ELSEIF TYPE(_1vn) = "N"
104 :                 _bytes = _bytes + 9
105 :                 _a = 9
106 :             ELSEIF TYPE(_1vn) = "L"
107 :                 _bytes = _bytes + 2
108 :                 _a = 2
109 :             ELSEIF TYPE(_1vn) = "D"
110 :                 _bytes = _bytes + 9
111 :                 _a = 9
112 :             ENDIF
113 :
114 :             @ _count, 1 SAY IF( LEN(_ttemp) > 51, ;
115 :                 SUBSTR(_ttemp, 1, 50), _ttemp)
116 :             @ _count, 49 SAY TRIM(TRANSFORM(_a, "9999999")) + ;
117 :                 " bytes"
118 :             _count = _count + 1
119 :
120 :             _vars = _vars + 1
121 :             IF ROW() > 14
122 :                 @ 24,00 SAY 'Press Q TO Quit...'
123 :                 INKEY(0)
124 :                 IF CHR(LASTKEY())$"Qq"
125 :                     End_disp()
126 :                     RETURN
127 :                 ELSE
128 :                     CLEAR SCREEN
129 :                     _count = 1
130 :                 ENDIF
131 :             ENDIF
132 :         ENDDO
133 :     ENDIF
134 :     End_disp()
135 :
136 : ******************
137 :
138 : PROCEDURE End_disp
```

```
139 :
140 :     ERASE S_____.MEM
141 :     IF _count > 0
142 :        @ _count+1, 1 SAY SPACE(50)
143 :        @ _count+2, 1 SAY SPACE(50)
144 :        @ _count+2, 1 SAY "Memory Variables Displayed " + ;
145 :                        LTRIM(STR(_vars)) + " with " + ;
146 :                        LTRIM(STR(_bytes)) + " bytes used "
147 :        @ _count+3,1 SAY "Any Key to Continue...."
148 :        INKEY(0)
149 :     ENDIF
150 :     FCLOSE(_1fh)
151 :     RESTORE SCREEN
152 :
153 : * **********************************************
154 : * * The following procedure(s)/function(s) are  *
155 : * * part of Steve Straley's ToolkiT(tm) -       *
156 : * * Release 2, published by Four Seasons        *
157 : * * Publishing Co., Inc.  All Rights Reserved   *
158 : * * Information: 212-599-2141 / 800-662-2278    *
159 : * * All Rights Reserved                         *
160 : * **********************************************
161 :
162 : ********************
163 :
164 : FUNCTION Strvalue
165 :
166 :     PARAMETERS _showstr
167 :
168 :     * This function returns the string representation
169 :     * of the given parameter.
170 :
171 :     IF PCOUNT() != 1
172 :        RETURN("")
173 :     ENDIF
174 :
175 :     DO CASE
176 :     CASE TYPE("_showstr") = "C"
177 :        RETURN(_showstr)
178 :     CASE TYPE("_showstr") = "N"
179 :        RETURN(STR(_showstr))
180 :     CASE TYPE("_showstr") = "M"
181 :        IF LEN(_showstr) > (MEMORY(0) * 1024) * .80
182 :           RETURN( SUBSTR(_showstr, 1, ;
183 :                   INT((MEMORY(0) * 1024) * .80)) )
184 :        ELSE
185 :           RETURN(_showstr)
186 :        ENDIF
187 :     CASE TYPE("_showstr") = "D"
188 :        RETURN(DTOC(_showstr))
189 :     CASE TYPE("_showstr") = "L"
190 :        RETURN(IF(_showstr, "True", "False"))
191 :     OTHERWISE
192 :        RETURN("")
```

```
193 :     ENDCASE
194 :
195 : * End of File
```

Since the F7 key has been SET to the Disp_mem procedure, you need only to press the hot key while in the READ/GET command to test this program. Once the special key is pressed, the Disp_mem procedure is called. The key to this is to store all of the memory variables in the system to a temporary .MEM file, S_______. Using the low-level function, this file is then opened as shown on line 38. Line 39 gets the length of the file, only to be followed by the file pointer repositioned to the top of the file in line 40. Line 53 is simple: Continue skipping through the file so long as the end of the file has not been reached. Actually, the line of code instructs Clipper to continue processing so long as the value returned from the FSEEK() function plus 1 is less than the actual size of the file as obtained in the variable **_lf1** on line 38.

While the code is heavily documented, one fact must be pointed out: Much of the information on the variables is obtained from combining the data in the .MEM file and the data within the system. For example, numeric and date information is stored to a .MEM file using a MANTISSA as a base. While it is simple to get the actual information on data that is either logical or character in nature, it is far more difficult to get the same data for numbers and/or dates. The above routine just takes the name of the variable as listed in the .MEM file (line 68) and gets the actual value (which should be in the system since all variables were saved to the file to begin with) by macro expanding this variable named **_lvn**. On line 94 we can see the STRTRAN() function taking the contents of **_lvn** with the macro expansion sign in front rather than the actual value of **_lvn**. This translation is then stored to the variable **_lr**. Again, you can see the macro implications by referring to lines 100 and following. Rather than make a call to the TYPE() function with the customary quotation marks surrounding the variable's name, they are omitted because we want to get the TYPE() of the macro of the variable, not the actual variable. Since the macro of the variable is the actual variable name stored in the .MEM file, which is sitting in the memory pool of the system, this call should yield a normal response.

As stated earlier, converting a .MEM file to a .TXT file is just as easy, except the actual value for the numbers and dates contained within the .MEM file must be expanded and obtained. This means some heavy number-crunching tactics are involved. Following is a sample program that takes the same concept as the preceding example and generates a text file instead:

```
********************
* Name      Dispmem2.prg
* Author    Essor Maso
* Date      June 1, 1989
* Notice    Copyright (c) 1989 Stephen J. Straley & Associates
* Compile   Clipper Dispmem2 -m
* Release   Summer 87
* Link      PLINK86 FI Dispmem2 LIB Clipper LIB Extend;
* Note      A diagnostic tool to view memory variables easily.
```

```
010 : *
011 : *            It is assumed that F7 is set to Disp_mem:
012 : *
013 : *            Call:   SET KEY -6 TO Disp_mem
014 : *
015 : *            This also writes out a text file and shows how the
016 : *            numeric and date information in a .MEM file can be
017 : *            obtained!
018 : *
019 : ********************
020 :
021 : CLEAR SCREEN
022 : SET KEY -6 TO Disp_mem
023 : variable = SPACE(10)
024 : adate    = DATE()
025 : anumber  = 10
026 : alogic   = .T.
027 : @ 10,10 SAY "Enter Variable or F7 for DISP MEMO: " ;
028 :           GET variable
029 : READ
030 : CLEAR SCREEN
031 : TYPE SYSTEM.TXT
032 : ?
033 : WAIT "That's the contents of the TEXT file.  Any key...."
034 :
035 : ********************
036 :
037 : PROCEDURE Disp_mem
038 :
039 :    SAVE SCREEN
040 :
041 :    SAVE TO S_____         && Save memory variables
042 :
043 :    PRIVATE _1vn,_1vt,_1vr,_1mc,_1sc,_1fh,_1fl
044 :
045 :    _1fh=FOPEN('S_____.MEM')
046 :    _1fl=FSEEK(_1fh,0,2)
047 :
048 :    FSEEK(_1fh,0)   && Top of file
049 :
050 :    CLEAR SCREEN
051 :
052 :    IF _1fl < 2
053 :
054 :        && File contains EOF marker.
055 :        @ 0,0 SAY "There are no memory variables present."
056 :
057 :    ELSE
058 :        _count = 1
059 :        _vars  = 0
060 :        _bytes = 0
061 :        DO WHILE FSEEK(_1fh,0,1)+1<_1fl
062 :            *
063 :            * Variable specific information is contained in the
```

```
064 :        * first 18 bytes of the variable packet. The value
065 :        * of the variable is contained from position 33 on.
066 :        *
067 :        _1mw = SPACE(18)
068 :        *
069 :        * Get the variable specific information.
070 :        *
071 :        FREAD(_1fh,@_1mw,18)
072 :        *
073 :        * The variable name is in the first 10 positions
074 :        * with a CHR(0) terminator.
075 :        *
076 :        _1vn = LEFT(_1mw,AT(CHR(0),_1mw)-1)
077 :        *
078 :        * The variable type is in position 12 of the packet.
079 :        * C3h is character or memo, CCh is logical,
080 :        * CEh is numeric, C4h is date.
081 :        *
082 :        _1vt=SUBSTR(_1mw,12,1)
083 :        *
084 :        * For character and logical variables, position 17
085 :        * and 18 contain the hex value for the range of the
086 :        * data. For numeric and date variables, the range
087 :        * is 8. This points to the end of the variable packet.
088 :        *
089 :        _1vr=BIN2W(RIGHT(_1mw,2))
090 :        IF _1vt $ CHR(195) + CHR(204)
091 :            _1mc=14+_1vr
092 :        ELSE
093 :            _1mc=22
094 :        ENDIF
095 :        FSEEK(_1fh,_1mc,1)    && Go to next packet.
096 :        IF _1vr>51.AND._1vt $ CHR(195) + CHR(204)
097 :            _1r=STRTRAN(LEFT(&_1vn,50), CHR(7), CHR(1))
098 :            _ttemp = LEFT(_1vn+SPACE(10),10) + ;
099 :                     " TYPE " + TYPE(_1vn) + ["] + ;
100 :                     _1r + ["]
101 :        ELSE
102 :            _1r=STRTRAN(&_1vn, CHR(7), CHR(1))
103 :            _ttemp = LEFT(_1vn+SPACE(10),10) + ;
104 :                     " TYPE " + TYPE(_1vn) + "  " + ;
105 :                     IF(TYPE(_1vn) = "C", ["]+_1r+["], ;
106 :                     Strvalue(&_1vn))
107 :        ENDIF
108 :        IF     TYPE(_1vn) = "C"
109 :            _bytes = _bytes + LEN(&_1vn.)
110 :            _a = LEN(&_1vn.)
111 :        ELSEIF TYPE(_1vn) = "N"
112 :            _bytes = _bytes + 9
113 :            _a = 9
114 :        ELSEIF TYPE(_1vn) = "L"
115 :            _bytes = _bytes + 2
116 :            _a = 2
117 :        ELSEIF TYPE(_1vn) = "D"
```

```
118 :              _bytes = _bytes + 9
119 :               _a = 9
120 :          ENDIF
121 :
122 :          @ _count, 1 SAY IF( LEN(_ttemp) > 51, ;
123 :               SUBSTR(_ttemp, 1, 50), _ttemp)
124 :          @ _count, 49 SAY TRIM(TRANSFORM(_a, "9999999")) + ;
125 :             " bytes"
126 :          _count = _count + 1
127 :
128 :          _vars = _vars + 1
129 :          IF ROW() > 14
130 :             @ 24,00 SAY 'Press Q TO Quit...'
131 :             INKEY(0)
132 :             IF CHR(LASTKEY())$"Qq"
133 :                End_disp()
134 :                RETURN
135 :             ELSE
136 :                CLEAR SCREEN
137 :                _count = 1
138 :             ENDIF
139 :          ENDIF
140 :       ENDDO
141 :    ENDIF
142 :    End_disp()
143 :
144 : ******************
145 :
146 : PROCEDURE End_disp
147 :
148 :    IF _count > 0
149 :       @ _count+1, 1 SAY SPACE(50)
150 :       @ _count+2, 1 SAY SPACE(50)
151 :       @ _count+2, 1 SAY "Memory Variables Displayed " + ;
152 :                       LTRIM(STR(_vars)) + " with " + ;
153 :                       LTRIM(STR(_bytes)) + " bytes used "
154 :       @ _count+3,1 SAY "Any Key to Continue...."
155 :       INKEY(0)
156 :    ENDIF
157 :    FCLOSE(_1fh)
158 :    O_memtext("S_____.MEM", "SYSTEM.TXT")
159 :    ERASE S_____.MEM
160 :    RESTORE SCREEN
161 :
162 : * ********************************************
163 : * * The following procedure(s)/function(s) are  *
164 : * * part of Steve Straley's ToolkiT(tm) -       *
165 : * * Release 2, published by Four Seasons        *
166 : * * Publishing Co., Inc.  All Rights Reserved   *
167 : * * Information: 212-599-2141 / 800-662-2278    *
168 : * * All Rights Reserved                         *
169 : * ********************************************
170 :
```

```
********************

FUNCTION Strvalue

   PARAMETERS _showstr

   * This function returns the string representation
   * of the given parameter.

   IF PCOUNT() != 1
      RETURN("")
   ENDIF

   DO CASE
   CASE TYPE("_showstr") = "C"
      RETURN(_showstr)
   CASE TYPE("_showstr") = "N"
      RETURN(STR(_showstr))
   CASE TYPE("_showstr") = "M"
      IF LEN(_showstr) > (MEMORY(0) * 1024) * .80
         RETURN( SUBSTR(_showstr, 1, ;
                 INT((MEMORY(0) * 1024) * .80)) )
      ELSE
         RETURN(_showstr)
      ENDIF
   CASE TYPE("_showstr") = "D"
      RETURN(DTOC(_showstr))
   CASE TYPE("_showstr") = "L"
      RETURN(IF(_showstr, "True", "False"))
   OTHERWISE
      RETURN("")
   ENDCASE

*******************

FUNCTION O_memtext

   PARAMETERS _mem, _txt

   * The numeric and date-writing portion of this function
   * was written by the Wizard: Essor Maso...

   IF PCOUNT() != 2     && Not enough parameters
      RETURN(.F.)
   ELSEIF !FILE(_mem)   && FIle NOT file
      RETURN(.F.)
   ELSEIF FILE(_txt)    && File is there
      RETURN(.F.)
   ENDIF

   _fh1 = FOPEN(_mem)             && File handle for the mem file
   _fp1 = FSEEK(_fh1, 0, 2)       && Gets ID for the file.
   FSEEK(_fh1, 0)                 && Repositions the pointer.
```

```
IF _fp1 < 2
   FCLOSE(_fh1)
   RETURN(.F.)
ENDIF
_fh2 = FCREATE(_txt)     && File handle for the txt file
DO WHILE FSEEK(_fh1, 0, 1) + 1 < _fp1
   _realvar = SPACE(18)
   FREAD(_fh1, @_realvar, 18)
   _name = LEFT(_realvar, AT(CHR(0), _realvar) - 1 )
   _data = SUBSTR(_realvar, 12, 1)
   _dtyp = BIN2W(RIGHT(_realvar, 2))
   IF _data $ ""
      _drng = 14 + _dtyp
   ELSE
      _drng = 22
   ENDIF
   _dval = SPACE(_drng)
   FREAD(_fh1, @_dval, _drng)       && String of value
   _nval = SUBSTR(_dval, 15)
   FWRITE(_fh2, _name, LEN(_name))
   FWRITE(_fh2, SPACE(12 - LEN(_name)), 12 - LEN(_name))
   FWRITE(_fh2, "  =  ", 5)
   IF     _data = CHR(195) && character
      FWRITE(_fh2, _nval, LEN(_nval))

   ELSEIF _data = CHR(204) && logical
      FWRITE(_fh2, IF((ASC(_nval) = 1), ".T.", ".F."))

   ELSEIF _data = CHR(206) && numeric
      _dval = SUBSTR(_dval, 15)
      _pad1 = MOD(ASC(SUBSTR(_dval, 8, 1)), 128) * 16
      _pad2 = INT(ASC(SUBSTR(_dval, 7, 1)) / 16)
      _powr = _pad1 + _pad2 - 1023
      _mins = INT(ASC(SUBSTR(_dval, 8, 1)) / 16) >= 8
      _man0 = MOD(ASC(SUBSTR(_dval, 7, 1)), 16) / 16
      _man1 = BIN2W(SUBSTR(_dval, 5, 2)) / ;
              (65536*16)
      _man2 = BIN2W(SUBSTR(_dval, 3, 2)) / ;
              (65536 * 65536 * 16)
      _man3 = BIN2W(SUBSTR(_dval, 1, 2)) / ;
              (65536 * 65536 * 65536 * 16)
      _mant = _man0 + _man1 + _man2 + _man3
      _numb = IF(_mins, -(1 + _mant) * ;
              (2 ^ _powr), (1 + _mant) * (2 ^ _powr))
      _sdec = ASC(RIGHT(_realvar, 1))

       FWRITE(_fh2, TRANSFORM(_numb, "@B"))

   ELSEIF _data = CHR(196) && date
      _dval = SUBSTR(_dval, 15)
      _pad1 = MOD(ASC(SUBSTR(_dval, 8, 1)), 128) * 16
      _pad2 = INT(ASC(SUBSTR(_dval, 7, 1)) / 16)
      _powr = _pad1 + _pad2 - 1023
      _mins = INT(ASC(SUBSTR(_dval, 8, 1)) / 16) >= 8
```

```
            _man0 = MOD(ASC(SUBSTR(_dval, 7, 1)), 16) / 16
            _man1 = BIN2W(SUBSTR(_dval, 5, 2)) / ;
                    (65536*16)
            _man2 = BIN2W(SUBSTR(_dval, 3, 2)) / ;
                    (65536 * 65536 * 16)
            _man3 = BIN2W(SUBSTR(_dval, 1, 2)) / ;
                    (65536 * 65536 * 65536 * 16)
            _mant = _man0 + _man1 + _man2 + _man3
            _numb = IF(_mins, -(1 + _mant) * ;
                    (2 ^ _powr), (1 + _mant) * (2 ^ _powr))
            _sdec = ASC(RIGHT(_realvar, 1))
             FWRITE(_fh2, DTOC(CTOD("01/01/0100") + ;
                    _numb - 1757585))

        ELSE
           FWRITE(_fh2, "error", 5)
        ENDIF
        FWRITE(_fh2, CHR(13)+CHR(10), 2)
     ENDDO
     FCLOSE(_fh1)
     FCLOSE(_fh2)
     RETURN(.T.)

  * End of File
```

Remember, using the FREAD() function, character and logical data are easy to handle because they are essentially in the same format as a variable in the file. This is not the case for dates and numbers; in Clipper, dates are handled as numbers and both are stored on the disk in IEEE format as follows. The number is broken down into two parts, the characteristic and the mantissa, which is a fancy way of saying scientific notation. The mantissa is a number between 1 and 2, or 0, while the characteristic is the power of 2 by which to multiply the mantissa to get the original number. To avoid the possibility of having a negative exponent, 1023 must be added to the power in order to get the characteristic. Now, when the actual number is stored on the disk, we can eliminate the 1 to the left of the radix point (binary point) and store only the fraction. To display the number, we must convert the number to fixed point form as just described. When dealing with a date data type, one additional step is required. First, there is a known problem in Clipper with dates prior to January 1, 0100. To circumvent this, that date is used as the beginning point for all dates; therefore, when a number that is a date is found on the disk and converted from floating point to fixed, the difference between the number for the date and the number of 1/1/100 is added to the date variable for 1/1/100. So you can see, Clipper is capable of handling a variety of complex situations and calculations.

STRIPPING THE CONTENTS OF THE INDEX

An added feature of the Clipper language is the ability to either display a message telling the user the percentage of the INDEX file as it is being created (much like the interpreter's) or to be creative and fancy and display a gas-gauge-like screen showing the same information. Both are vital when dealing with large files and subsequent large indexes; the little red light on the hard drive is barely enough indication to the end user that something is happening and that the machine should not be turned off. For this, the ability to display user-friendly messages is both essential and possible in Clipper.

To accomplish this, add a user-defined function to the KEY for the index file so that while the file is being created and indexed, the call to the function will be made for each record. This function in turn will take the information passed to it and display the desired message to the screen. Now, the only trouble with this is that the name of the function is part of the KEY in the index file's header. And while the function in the key may only return a NULL byte, the mere fact that it is in the header of the file indicates that any operation involving the index file will make a subsequent call to the function. The trick is to remove the function's name from the index file's header. Before going any further, let's look at an example:

```
********************
* Name      Index1.prg
* Author    Stephen J. Straley
* Date      June 1, 1989
* Notice    Copyright (c) 1988 Stephen J. Straley & Associates
* Compile   Clipper Index1 -m
* Release   Summer '87
* Link      PLINK86 FI Index1 LIB Extend LIB Clipper;
* Note      This shows how a simple INDEX ON command can
*           include a BAR GRAPH and a percentage sign.
*
********************

IF !FILE("FILENOS.DBF")
   ? "Data files not present.  Run Startup Program, re-try!"
   QUIT
ENDIF

CLEAR SCREEN
@ 0,0 SAY "Working on the First Indexing Technique"
counter = 0
USE Filenos
INDEX ON STR(RECNO()) + BARCHART(2,01,@counter) TO Bar
@ 6,0
WAIT
@ 7,0
@ 7,0 SAY "Percentage Index: "
GO TOP
INDEX ON STR(RECNO()) + PERCENTAGE(7,18) TO Per

********************

FUNCTION Percentage

   PARAMETERS a, b
```

```
36 :
37 :    IF TYPE("a") = "U" .OR. TYPE("b") = "U"
38 :       RETURN("")
39 :    ENDIF
40 :
41 :    IF RECNO() > LASTREC()
42 :       @ a, b SAY TRANSFORM( 0, "999.99 %")
43 :    ELSE
44 :       @ a, b SAY TRANSFORM((RECNO()/LASTREC())*100, "999.99 %")
45 :    ENDIF
46 :    INKEY(.2)
47 :    RETURN("")
48 :
49 : ********************
50 :
51 : FUNCTION Barchart
52 :
53 :    PARAMETERS a, b, c
54 :
55 :    * Take the number of columns, the number of records, and
56 :    * find out how many records in the database represent a
57 :    * column.
58 :
59 :    IF TYPE("c") = "U" .OR. TYPE("a") = "U" .OR. TYPE("b") = "U"
60 :       RETURN("")
61 :    ENDIF
62 :
63 :    columns   = 78 - b
64 :    records   = LASTREC()
65 :    recpercol = columns / records
66 :
67 :    IF EMPTY(counter)
68 :       @ a-1,b-1 TO a+1,80 DOUBLE
69 :       PUBLIC startat, remainder
70 :       startat = b
71 :       remainder = 0
72 :    ENDIF
73 :
74 :    counter   = RECNO()
75 :    @ a, startat SAY REPLICATE(CHR(178), recpercol)
76 :
77 :    remainder = remainder + (recpercol - INT(recpercol))
78 :    startat = startat + INT(recpercol)
79 :    IF remainder >= 1
80 :       @ ROW(),COL() SAY CHR(178)
81 :       startat = startat + 1
82 :       remainder = remainder - 1
83 :    ENDIF
84 :    INKEY(.2)
85 :    RETURN("")
86 :
87 : * End of File
```

Now, let's take a look at the contents of the index file as seen from DEBUG.COM. First, here's the output from BAR.NTX:

```
E>debug bar.ntx
-d
157C:0100  06 00 01 00 00 80 00 00-00 00 00 00 0F 00 07 00   ................
157C:0110  00 00 3A 00 1D 00 53 54-52 28 52 45 43 4E 4F 28   ..:...STR(RECNO(
157C:0120  29 29 2B 42 41 52 43 48-41 52 54 28 32 2C 30 31   ))+BARCHART(2,01
157C:0130  2C 40 63 6F 75 6E 74 65-72 29 00 00 00 00 00 00   ,@counter)......
157C:0140  00 00 00 00 00 00 00 00-00 00 00 00 00 00 00 00   ................
157C:0150  00 00 00 00 00 00 00 00-00 00 00 00 00 00 00 00   ................
157C:0160  00 00 00 00 00 00 00 00-00 00 00 00 00 00 00 00   ................
157C:0170  00 00 00 00 00 00 00 00-00 00 00 00 00 00 00 00   ................
-
```

Second, here's the output from PER.NTX:

```
E>debug per.ntx
-d
157C:0100  06 00 01 00 00 80 00 00-00 00 00 00 0F 00 07 00   ................
157C:0110  00 00 3A 00 1D 00 53 54-52 28 52 45 43 4E 4F 28   ..:...STR(RECNO(
157C:0120  29 29 2B 50 45 52 43 45-4E 54 41 47 45 28 37 2C   ))+PERCENTAGE(7,
157C:0130  31 38 29 00 00 00 00 00-00 00 00 00 00 00 00 00   18).............
157C:0140  00 00 00 00 00 00 00 00-00 00 00 00 00 00 00 00   ................
157C:0150  00 00 00 00 00 00 00 00-00 00 00 00 00 00 00 00   ................
157C:0160  00 00 00 00 00 00 00 00-00 00 00 00 00 00 00 00   ................
157C:0170  00 00 00 00 00 00 00 00-00 00 00 00 00 00 00 00   ................
-
```

The trick is to write a routine, using the low-level file functions, that will open up the index file after the cute display screen is finished and remove the reference to the user-defined function. Since the function returns a NULL byte, the actual contents of the key are not altered, just the key's expression.

```
********************
* Name       Index2.prg
* Author     Stephen J. Straley
* Date       June 1, 1989
* Notice     Copyright (c) 1988 Stephen J. Straley & Associates
* Compile    Clipper Index2 -m
* Release    Summer '87
* Link       PLINK86 FI Index2 LIB Extend LIB Clipper;
* Note       This shows how a simple INDEX ON command can
*            include a BAR GRAPH and a percentage sign.
*
*            This routine also shows how to remove the
*            PERCENTAGE() and BARCHART() calls in the
*            header of the .NTX file.
*
********************

```

```
018 : IF !FILE("FILENOS.DBF")
019 :    ? "Data files not present.   Run Startup Program, re-try!"
020 :    QUIT
021 : ENDIF
022 :
023 : CLEAR SCREEN
024 : @ 0,0 SAY "Working on the First Indexing Technique"
025 : counter = 0
026 : USE Filenos
027 : INDEX ON STR(RECNO()) + BARCHART(2,01,@counter) TO Bar
028 : @ 6,0
029 : WAIT
030 : @ 7,0
031 : @ 7,0 SAY "Percentage Index: "
032 : GO TOP
033 : INDEX ON STR(RECNO()) + PERCENTAGE(7,18) TO Per
034 : USE    && This closes the index file to be written!
035 : WAIT
036 : Keyremove(" + BARCHART(2,01,@counter)", "BAR" + INDEXEXT() )
037 : WAIT "Press any key for next file .... "
038 : Keyremove(" + PERCENTAGE(7,18)", "PER" + INDEXEXT() )
039 : ? "All finished!"
040 :
041 : *******************
042 :
043 : FUNCTION Percentage
044 :
045 :    PARAMETERS a, b
046 :
047 :    IF TYPE("a") = "U" .OR. TYPE("b") = "U"
048 :       RETURN("")
049 :    ENDIF
050 :
051 :    IF RECNO() > LASTREC()
052 :       @ a, b SAY TRANSFORM( 0, "999.99 %")
053 :    ELSE
054 :       @ a, b SAY TRANSFORM((RECNO()/LASTREC())*100, "999.99 %")
055 :    ENDIF
056 :    RETURN("")
057 :
058 : ******************
059 :
060 : FUNCTION Barchart
061 :
062 :    PARAMETERS a, b, c
063 :
064 :    * Take the number of columns, the number of records, and
065 :    * find out how many records in the database represent a
066 :    * column.
067 :
068 :    IF TYPE("c") = "U" .OR. TYPE("a") = "U" .OR. TYPE("b") = "U"
069 :       RETURN("")
070 :    ENDIF
071 :
```

```
072 :       columns   = 78 - b
073 :       records   = LASTREC()
074 :       recpercol = columns / records
075 :
076 :       IF EMPTY(counter)
077 :          @ a-1,b-1 TO a+1,80 DOUBLE
078 :          PUBLIC startat, remainder
079 :          startat = b
080 :          remainder = 0
081 :       ENDIF
082 :
083 :       counter   = RECNO()
084 :       @ a, startat SAY REPLICATE(CHR(178), recpercol)
085 :
086 :       remainder = remainder + (recpercol - INT(recpercol))
087 :       startat = startat + INT(recpercol)
088 :       IF remainder >= 1
089 :          @ ROW(),COL() SAY CHR(178)
090 :          startat = startat + 1
091 :          remainder = remainder - 1
092 :       ENDIF
093 :       RETURN("")
094 :
095 : * ***********************************************
096 : * * The following procedure(s)/function(s) are  *
097 : * * part of Steve Straley's ToolkiT(tm) -        *
098 : * * Release 2, published by Four Seasons         *
099 : * * Publishing Co., Inc.  All Rights Reserved    *
100 : * * Information: 212-599-2141 / 800-662-2278     *
101 : * * All Rights Reserved                          *
102 : * ***********************************************
103 :
104 : *******************
105 :
106 : FUNCTION Keyremove
107 :
108 :       PARAMETERS _thekey, _thefile
109 :
110 :       * Be sure to open the file in read/write
111 :       * mode; otherwise, nothing will be written.
112 :
113 :       fhandle = FOPEN(_thefile, 2)
114 :
115 :       IF fhandle < 4    && An error has taken place
116 :          RETURN(.F.)
117 :       ENDIF
118 :
119 :       _thekey = STRTRAN(_thekey, " ", "")
120 :
121 :       * First build the string with the expression
122 :       * from the index file.
123 :
124 :       FSEEK(fhandle, 22, 0)
125 :       string = SPACE(255)
```

```

   FREAD(fhandle, @string, 255)

   string = TRIM(string)

   * Next, find the position in the string where
   * the removed key starts

   where = AT(_thekey, string) - 1  && This offsets it

   * Reposition the file pointer to the beginning
   * of the key plus the number of bytes into the
   * key to get to the unwanted expression.

   FSEEK(fhandle, 22 + where, 0)

   * Now, write null bytes into the header where
   * the index expression used to be.

   FOR qaz = 1 TO LEN(_thekey)
      FWRITE(fhandle, CHR(0), 1)
   NEXT
   FCLOSE(fhandle)
   RETURN(.T.)

* End of File
```

Looking at the output from DEBUG.COM, we can see the following:

```
E>debug bar.ntx
-d
157C:0100  06 00 01 00 00 80 00 00-00 00 00 00 0F 00 07 00   ................
157C:0110  00 00 3A 00 1D 00 53 54-52 28 52 45 43 4E 4F 28   ..:...STR(RECNO(
157C:0120  29 29 00 00 00 00 00 00-00 00 00 00 00 00 00 00   ))..............
157C:0130  00 00 00 00 00 00 00 00-00 00 00 00 00 00 00 00   ................
157C:0140  00 00 00 00 00 00 00 00-00 00 00 00 00 00 00 00   ................
157C:0150  00 00 00 00 00 00 00 00-00 00 00 00 00 00 00 00   ................
157C:0160  00 00 00 00 00 00 00 00-00 00 00 00 00 00 00 00   ................
157C:0170  00 00 00 00 00 00 00 00-00 00 00 00 00 00 00 00   ................
-
```

And now, here is the new structure for PER.NTX:

```
E>debug per.ntx
-d
157C:0100  06 00 01 00 00 80 00 00-00 00 00 00 0F 00 07 00   ................
157C:0110  00 00 3A 00 1D 00 53 54-52 28 52 45 43 4E 4F 28   ..:...STR(RECNO(
157C:0120  29 29 00 00 00 00 00 00-00 00 00 00 00 00 00 00   ))..............
157C:0130  00 00 00 00 00 00 00 00-00 00 00 00 00 00 00 00   ................
157C:0140  00 00 00 00 00 00 00 00-00 00 00 00 00 00 00 00   ................
157C:0150  00 00 00 00 00 00 00 00-00 00 00 00 00 00 00 00   ................
157C:0160  00 00 00 00 00 00 00 00-00 00 00 00 00 00 00 00   ................
157C:0170  00 00 00 00 00 00 00 00-00 00 00 00 00 00 00 00   ................
-
```

It may be interesting to note that in this second example, calls to the INKEY(.2) were removed (refer to INDEX1.PRG on lines 46 and 84). Additionally, it is important to note the command on line 34. If the file is not closed, the header to the index file is not completely written and if the file is then opened with the low-level file routines, the length of the file will be 0. It is important to note that the low-level file functions work on the DOS level and not on the Clipper level. If line 34 is omitted, the call to the Keyremove() function would be erroneous.

SAVING ARRAYS TO DISK

Before the low-level file functions came into the Clipper dialect, the trick of using the MEMOWRITE() and MEMOREAD() functions for saving an array to the disk ruled. While this concept provided new insights and perspectives into the Clipper language, it also limited the size of the array that could be saved. Using the low-level file functions, array elements could be individually written and decoded for the array file. In addition, the file format for the array file need not be in the .MEM format; programmers can choose their own formats. Consider the following program that stores several pieces of information to several arrays and then stores them to the disk:

```
********************
* Name      Arrays.prg
* Author    Stephen J. Straley
* Date      July 2, 1989
* Notice    Copyright (c) 1989 Stephen J. Straley & Associates
* Compile   Clipper Arrays -m
* Release   Summer '87
* Link      PLINK86 FI Arrays LIB Clipper  LIB Extend;
* Note      This routine shows how four arrays, created with the
*           assistance of the ADIR(),  can be saved to the
*           disk.  Following this, the memory of the system is
*           cleared out and the arrays are restored.
*
********************

CLEAR SCREEN
DECLARE names[ADIR("*.*")], dates[ADIR("*.*")], ;
        sizes[ADIR("*.*")], times[ADIR("*.*")]

ADIR("*.*", names, dates, sizes, times)
@ 24,00 SAY "ESC when finished and ready for next step!"
ACHOICE(0,0,22,12, names)
Arraysave(names, "anames")
Arraysave(dates, "adates")
Arraysave(sizes, "asizes")
Arraysave(times, "atimes")
CLEAR SCREEN
```

```
028 : ? "Before the arrays are wiped out, the TYPE('names') is " + ;
029 :     TYPE("names")
030 : CLEAR ALL
031 : ?
032 : ? "And now, the TYPE('names') is " + TYPE("names")
033 : ?
034 : WAIT
035 : DECLARE newname[ADECLARE("Anames")]
036 : DECLARE newdate[ADECLARE("Adates")]
037 : DECLARE newsize[ADECLARE("Asizes")]
038 : DECLARE newtime[ADECLARE("Atimes")]
039 : Arrayrest(newname, "Anames")
040 : Arrayrest(newdate, "Adates")
041 : Arrayrest(newsize, "Asizes")
042 : Arrayrest(newtime, "Atimes")
043 : ASORT(newname)
044 : CLEAR SCREEN
045 : KEYBOARD "A"
046 : @ 24,00 SAY "Press ESC when finished or search for 'ANAMES'!"
047 : ACHOICE(0,0,22,12, newname)
048 : CLEAR SCREEN
049 : @ 0,0 SAY "Here are the contents of the array on disk.  " + ;
050 :           "ESC when finished!"
051 : MEMOEDIT(MEMOREAD("Anames"), 2, 0, 23, 79)
052 : CLEAR SCREEN
053 :
054 : * ********************************************
055 : * * The following procedure(s)/function(s) are  *
056 : * * part of Steve Straley's ToolkiT(tm) -       *
057 : * * Release 2, published by Four Seasons        *
058 : * * Publishing Co., Inc.  All Rights Reserved   *
059 : * * Information: 212-599-2141 / 800-662-2278    *
060 : * * All Rights Reserved                         *
061 : * ********************************************
062 :
063 : ********************
064 :
065 : FUNCTION Arraysave
066 :
067 :     PARAMETER _warray, _fname
068 :
069 :     IF PCOUNT() != 2
070 :        RETURN(.F.)
071 :     ELSEIF TYPE("_warray") + TYPE("_fname") != "AC"
072 :        RETURN(.F.)
073 :     ENDIF
074 :
075 :     PRIVATE _retval, _tmp, _qaz, _wtype, _addme, _fn, _tmp, _hw
076 :
077 :     _retval = .F.
078 :     _tmp1 = ""
```

```
079 :     _tmp2 = ""
080 :     FOR _qaz = 1 TO LEN(_warray)
081 :       _wtype= TYPE("_warray[_qaz]")
082 :       _addme = ""
083 :       DO CASE
084 :       CASE _wtype = "C"
085 :           _addme = _warray[_qaz]
086 :       CASE _wtype = "D"
087 :           _addme = DTOC(_warray[_qaz])
088 :       CASE _wtype = "N"
089 :           _addme = STR(_warray[_qaz])
090 :       CASE _wtype = "L"
091 :           _addme = IF(_warray[_qaz],"T","F")
092 :       ENDCASE
093 :       _tmp1 = _tmp1+_wtype+STR( LEN(_addme),5)
094 :       _tmp2 = _tmp2+_addme
095 :     NEXT
096 :     _fn = FCREATE(_fname,0) && Normal READ/WRITE mode!
097 :     IF _fn >= 0
098 :       _tmp = "SJS"+STR( LEN(_warray), 10) + ;
099 :              STR( LEN(_tmp1),10)+STR(LEN(_tmp2),10) + ;
100 :              _tmp1 + _tmp2
101 :       _hw = FWRITE(_fn,_tmp)
102 :       _retval =  (_hw = LEN(_tmp))
103 :       FCLOSE(_fn)
104 :     ENDIF
105 :     RETURN(_retval)
106 :
107 : ********************
108 :
109 : FUNCTION Adeclare
110 :
111 :     PARAMETERS _fname
112 :
113 :     IF EMPTY(PCOUNT())
114 :        RETURN(0)
115 :     ELSEIF TYPE("_fname") != "C"
116 :        RETURN(0)
117 :     ENDIF
118 :
119 :     PRIVATE _fhandle, _fileid
120 :
121 :     _fhandle = FOPEN(_fname)
122 :     _fileid  = SPACE(33)
123 :     FREAD(_fhandle, @_fileid, 33)
124 :     FCLOSE(_fhandle)
125 :     RETURN(VAL(SUBSTR(_fileid, 4, 10)))
126 :
127 : ******************
128 :
129 : FUNCTION Arrayrest
130 :
131 :     PARAMETER _warray, _fname
```

```
132 :
133 :      IF PCOUNT() != 2
134 :         RETURN(.F.)
135 :      ELSEIF TYPE("_warray") + TYPE("_fname") != "AC"
136 :         RETURN(.F.)
137 :      ENDIF
138 :
139 :      PRIVATE _retval, _fn, _hw, _fid, _t1, _t2, _tmp1, ;
140 :              _tmp2, _k, _tmp3, _t0, _wtype, _wsize
141 :
142 :      _retval = .F.
143 :      IF FILE(_fname)
144 :         _fn = FOPEN(_fname,0)
145 :         IF _fn >=0
146 :            _fid = SPACE(33)
147 :            _hw = FREAD(_fn,@_fid,33)
148 :            IF _hw = 33
149 :               * read rest of file
150 :               IF LEFT(_fid,3) = "SJS"
151 :                  _t0 = VAL(SUBSTR(_fid,4,10))
152 :                  _t1 = VAL(SUBSTR(_fid,14,10))
153 :                  _t2 = VAL(SUBSTR(_fid,24,10))
154 :                  _tmp1 = SPACE(_t1)
155 :                  _tmp2 = SPACE(_t2)
156 :                  _hw = FREAD(_fn,@_tmp1,_t1)
157 :                  IF _hw = _t1
158 :                     _hw = FREAD(_fn,@_tmp2,_t2)
159 :                     IF _t2 = _hw
160 :                        _retval = .T.
161 :                        _hw = LEN(_tmp1)/6
162 :                        FOR _k = 1 TO MIN( _hw,LEN(_warray) )
163 :                           _wtype = LEFT(_tmp1,1)
164 :                           _wsize = VAL( SUBSTR(_tmp1,2,5) )
165 :                           _tmp1 = SUBSTR(_tmp1,7)
166 :                           _tmp3 = LEFT(_tmp2,_wsize)
167 :                           _tmp2 = SUBSTR(_tmp2,_wsize+1)
168 :                           DO CASE
169 :                           CASE _wtype = "C"
170 :                              _warray[_k]=_tmp3
171 :                           CASE _wtype = "N"
172 :                              _warray[_k]=VAL(_tmp3)
173 :                           CASE _wtype = "D"
174 :                              _warray[_k]=CTOD(_tmp3)
175 :                           CASE _wtype = "L"
176 :                              _warray[_k]=IF(_tmp3="T",.T.,.F.)
177 :                           ENDCASE
178 :                        NEXT
179 :                     ENDIF
180 :                  ENDIF
181 :               ENDIF
182 :            ENDIF
183 :            FCLOSE(_fn)
184 :      ENDIF
```

```
185 :      ENDIF
186 :      RETURN(_retval)
187 :
188 :  * End of File
```

As you can see on lines 96, 101, 103, 121, 123, 124, 144, 147, 156, 158, and 183, the use of the low-level file functions is critical in saving the array to disk, obtaining the size of the array that is saved on the disk, and in restoring the array to the system. One critical item to note is on line 96: The use of the FCREATE() function. Note the second parameter passed to the function; this value should not be confused with the value passed to the FOPEN() function. With the FCREATE() function, the file will be created in normal READ/WRITE attributes provided that the second parameter passed to the function is set to 0 (or if this parameter is not passed, the function will automatically assign the file to this mode). However, if the file is simply opened with the FOPEN() function, the value of the parameter in the second position must be a 2 in order to achieve the same READ/WRITE effect. If a 2 is accidentally used with the FCREATE() function, the designated file will be created as a hidden file. Conversely, using the 0 value as the second parameter for the FOPEN() function will open the file in READ ONLY mode and changes to the file cannot be made. It is critical that you have a firm understanding of the value and implications of all of the parameters involved with the low-level file functions. Otherwise, some results will be unforeseen and many hours of programming (and perceived "bug" hunting) may be wasted.

In using the ADIR() function to create the arrays in lines 17 through 18, a simple ACHOICE() is used in order to show the elements contained within the **names[]** array. Four calls are made to the Arraysave() function, which uses the low-level file functions to create a file that will contain the individual array subscripted elements. While the function is defined on lines 65 and following, note that the file format of the array file specifies that the beginning characters of the file must be "SJS." This can be seen on line 97 through 104. In these lines, if the file in the variable **_fname** can be created, the first 10 bytes of the file will begin with the letters "SJS" followed by the string representation of the length of the array. Keep in mind that this entire operation is possible not only with the low-level file functions but with the fundamental concept of arrays being passed by reference rather than by value. Additionally, it should be noted that modifications, as provided for in the ToolkiT, can adjust the order in which the array file and subsequent header is created. The header of the file could be created first before the individual array elements are converted to string format. Inside of the FOR...NEXT command, the low-level file function to save the subscript contents could be made. Again, the decision of when to create and write to a file is purely up to the programmer.

The purpose of this routine is to show you new possibilities, including embellishing on an old concept: data-driven technology. Now, arrays, which are naturally fast since they reside in memory, can be created from one program, which in turn can drive another program. Data entry screens could be designed from one program, the coordinates saved to the disk for another program to use; the possibilities are endless.

EMBEDDING INFORMATION IN AN .EXE

We can even use Clipper's low-level file functions to tag the back end of a Clipper-compiled application. Since the header of the executable file contains information on how many bytes to read from the disk in order for the application to run properly, we can go beyond that position and write information to the file without creating havoc in the compiled program. It must be noted that the information added to the file must not alter any of the information within the original contents of the executable file; otherwise, the machine may hang up during execution. However, this feature allows the programmer to program in advance, within the application itself, the ability to look beyond its own end of file marker and obtain vital and pertinent information. Consider the following program:

```
001 : ********************
002 : * Name     Tagged.prg
003 : * Author   Stephen J. Straley
004 : * Notice   Copyright (c) 1989 Stephen J.
005 : *          Straley & Associates
006 : *          All Rights Reserved.
007 : * Date     July 2, 1989
008 : * Compile  Clipper Tagged -m
009 : * Release  Summer '87
010 : * Link     Plink86 Fi Tagged LIB Clipper, Extend
011 : * Note     This program shows how the low-level
012 : *          file functions can be used for a demo counter
013 : *          as well as a date-stamp encrypter which may
014 : *          help facilitate the concept of being paid
015 : *          on time by the client/customer.
016 : *
017 : ********************
018 :
019 : CLEAR SCREEN
020 : IF !FILE("NOTAP.*")
021 :    ? "Data Files are not present.  Please create and retry!"
022 :    QUIT
023 : ENDIF
024 : Fordata()
025 : Adddata()
026 : Fordata()
027 : CLEAR SCREEN
028 : WAIT "Press any key to try to add more data again!"
029 : Fordata()
030 : CLEAR SCREEN
031 :
032 : **********************
033 :
034 : PROCEDURE Fordata
035 :
036 :    @ 0,0 SAY "Opening Files"
037 :    USE Notap INDEX Notap
038 :    IF Looknum("Tagged.exe")
039 :       left = Readnum("Tagged.exe")
```

```
040 :     ELSE
041 :        left = 9999999999999999999
042 :     ENDIF
043 :
044 :     CLEAR SCREEN
045 :
046 :     DO WHILE !EMPTY(left)
047 :        APPEND BLANK
048 :        @  1, 2 SAY  A->(ALIAS())
049 :        @  1,35 SAY  A->(RECNO())
050 :        @  4, 5 SAY "  Files =>" GET A->files PICT "@X"
051 :        @  5, 5 SAY "  Sizes =>" GET A->sizes
052 :        @  6, 5 SAY "   Date =>" GET A->datestamp
053 :        @  7, 5 SAY "   Time =>" GET A->times
054 :        @  8, 5 SAY "Commnet =>" GET A->file_use PICT  "@S20"
055 :        @  9, 5 SAY "  Drive =>" GET A->subdrive PICT "@S25"
056 :        @ 10, 5 SAY "Percent =>" GET A->per_used
057 :        @ 23, 0 SAY "Press ESC when finished"
058 :        @ 24, 0 SAY "Records left to add: " + ;
059 :                    TRANSFORM(left, "@B")
060 :        READ
061 :        IF LASTKEY() != 27
062 :           IF Looknum("Tagged.exe")
063 :              left = left - 1
064 :              Writenum("Tagged.exe", left)
065 :           ENDIF
066 :        ELSE
067 :           EXIT
068 :        ENDIF
069 :     ENDDO
070 :     IF EMPTY(left)
071 :        @ 10,10 CLEAR TO 12, 60
072 :        @ 10,10 TO 12, 60
073 :        @ 11,12 SAY "Your Demo Period is OVER!  Any key"
074 :        INKEY(0)
075 :     ENDIF
076 :     USE
077 :
078 : ********************
079 :
080 : PROCEDURE Adddata
081 :
082 :     CLEAR SCREEN
083 :     value = 0
084 :     @ 12, 8 SAY "Enter APPENDING amont =>" GET value PICT "@X" ;
085 :             VALID value >= 1 .AND. value <= 10
086 :     READ
087 :     IF Writenum("Tagged.exe", value)
088 :        @ 14, 8 SAY "Value Written.  Any Key to Continue"
089 :     ELSE
090 :        @ 14, 8 SAY "Error in file.  Any key..."
091 :     ENDIF
092 :     INKEY(0)
093 :
```

```
094 : * *********************************************
095 : * * The following procedure(s)/function(s) are  *
096 : * * part of Steve Straley's ToolkiT(tm) -       *
097 : * * Release 2, published by Four Seasons        *
098 : * * Publishing Co., Inc.  All Rights Reserved   *
099 : * * Information: 212-599-2141 / 800-662-2278    *
100 : * * All Rights Reserved                         *
101 : * *********************************************
102 :
103 : ********************
104 :
105 : FUNCTION Readnum
106 :
107 :     PARAMETERS _file
108 :
109 :     IF PCOUNT() != 1
110 :         RETURN(0)
111 :     ELSEIF TYPE("_file") != "C"
112 :         RETURN(0)
113 :     ELSEIF !FILE(_file)
114 :         RETURN(0)
115 :     ENDIF
116 :
117 :     PRIVATE _fhandle, _temp, _length
118 :
119 :     _fhandle = FOPEN(_file, 2)
120 :
121 :     FSEEK(_fhandle, -6, 2)
122 :     _temp = FREADSTR(_fhandle, 4)
123 :     IF _temp != "SJSN"
124 :         RETURN(0)
125 :     ENDIF
126 :     *
127 :     * To get back to the original position
128 :     *
129 :     FSEEK(_fhandle, -4, 1)
130 :     *
131 :     * Get the length of the character string to read
132 :     *
133 :     FSEEK(_fhandle, -10,1)
134 :     _length = VAL(FREADSTR(_fhandle, 10))
135 :     *
136 :     * Get the length of the character string to read
137 :     *
138 :     FSEEK(_fhandle, -10, 1)
139 :     FSEEK(_fhandle, _length * -1, 1)
140 :     _temp = VAL(FREADSTR(_fhandle, _length))
141 :     FCLOSE(_fhandle)
142 :     RETURN(_temp)
143 :
144 : ********************
145 :
146 : FUNCTION Looknum
147 :
```

```
148 :     PARAMETERS _file
149 :
150 :     IF PCOUNT() != 1
151 :        RETURN(0)
152 :     ELSEIF TYPE("_file") != "C"
153 :        RETURN(0)
154 :     ELSEIF !FILE(_file)
155 :        RETURN(0)
156 :     ENDIF
157 :
158 :     PRIVATE _fhandle, _temp
159 :
160 :     _fhandle = FOPEN(_file, 2)
161 :
162 :     FSEEK(_fhandle, -6, 2)
163 :     _temp = FREADSTR(_fhandle, 4)
164 :     FCLOSE(_fhandle)
165 :
166 :     RETURN( (_temp = "SJSN") )
167 :
168 : ********************
169 :
170 : FUNCTION Writenum
171 :
172 :     PARAMETERS _file, _temp
173 :
174 :     * Take the _file and the _temp and write the _temp
175 :     * to the back end of the _file, marking the file with
176 :     * the _temp and a special code: dddddddxxxxxSJSN
177 :
178 :     IF PCOUNT() != 2
179 :        RETURN(.F.)
180 :     ENDIF
181 :
182 :     IF TYPE("_file") + TYPE("_temp") != "CN"
183 :        RETURN(.F.)
184 :     ENDIF
185 :
186 :     IF !FILE(_file)
187 :        RETURN(.F.)
188 :     ENDIF
189 :
190 :     PRIVATE _length, _fhandle, _string
191 :
192 :     _length = LEN(STR(_temp))
193 :     _string = TRIM(I2BIN(26) + STR(_temp) + ;
194 :               TRANSFORM(_length, "9999999999") + ;
195 :               "SJSN" + I2BIN(26))
196 :     _fhandle = FOPEN(_file, 2)
197 :     FSEEK(_fhandle, FSEEK(_fhandle, 0, 2))
```

```
198 :     FWRITE(_fhandle, _string)
199 :     FCLOSE(_fhandle)
200 :     RETURN( (FERROR() = 0) )
201 :
202 : * End of File
```

In this program, there are three functions that make the entire concept of using the low-level file functions of Clipper work: LOOKNUM(), READNUM(), and WRITENUM(). On line 24, the call to the Fordata() procedure allows you to enter as many records as you like because the value from the Looknum() function will be a logical false (.F.). This is because the file has not been appropriately tagged by the Writenum() function. Looking at the function Looknum() more closely (lines 144 and following), we can see that if the specified file does not have the letters "SJSN" tagged embedded within the file, the function will return a logical false (.F.). The Writenum() function obviously not only writes a number to the end of the specified file but the letters "SJSN" (signifying a numeric value) as well. The FSEEK() function on line 162 moves the file pointer in the specified file (as pointed to by the value of the **_fhandle** variable) 6 bytes backward, beginning from the end of the file. The third parameter in the FSEEK() function tells the function at what point to move the file pointer; a 0 is beginning of the file, 1 is the current file pointer position, and a 2 is from the end of the file. At that point, the next 4 bytes are read and passed to the string **_temp** as seen on line 163.

Once the function notes that the specified file is not encrypted, the value of the variable **left** is set to many 9s. Again, on this first pass through the procedure Fordata(), this is what that variable should be set to. After the Esc key is pressed and the flow of the program now moves on to the Adddata() procedure, a specified number of records is called for. This is the number that will be tagged to the back end of the executable file. For this, a call to the Writenum() function is eventually made and in that function, not only is the desired number placed at the end of the file but so are the letters "SJSN." After this, the program once again calls the Fordata() procedure and the number of records that are allowed to be added to the database is now determined by the number embedded at the end of the executable file, as written by the actual executable file itself. As you can see, this should open up an entire new set of parameters by which you, the programmer, can create demonstration packages without effort or worry.

You can carry this to many new levels. One example would be to tag the back end of an application with a DOS date stamp. As the end user gets closer to that date and as the bill for services rendered has not been paid, a warning and potential lock-out message may be continuously displayed. Or, entire screens could be tagged to the back end of the executable file rather than to disk or saved in memory. This means that the memory typically used for a system to manage the menuing structure could be then freed to handle other tasks. Again, with the low-level file functions, the choice is purely up to you.

SUMMARY

This chapter has introduced you to the power and use of the functions and shown how you, as the programmer, can be in control. You should use these functions and begin to test the potential of breaking other file formats, including work sheets from a spreadsheet program, extracting information from a data file created by another database management package, and even creating your own file format in which data will be stored. The possibilities are endless.

CHAPTER SEVEN

Data-Driven Technology

The title of this chapter gives a sense of innovation on old technology. However, what we are really talking about is “text file data processing.” This terminology may give you a better indication of the direction, focus, and emphasis of the philosophy that follows.

With Clipper, the concept of many text files driving an application is not only viable, but practical as well. Although we do not view the .DBF file format as impractical, it is cumbersome to make quick changes in the early stages of development if the system information resides in a .DBF file. To make a change to the data, which in turn would alter the application, a copy of a Clipper interpreter would have to be resident on the machine. With the concept of text file processing, memory variables can be initialized outside of the program and database structures, database and index names, index expression, windowing colors and positions, menus, pointers to procedures, and even VALID expressions on a READ can be easily altered, even with EDLIN or COPY CON. While neither method is suggested, the point is clear; you can control the file format and the method in which information can be stored and processed. Before exploring this further, let us start at the beginning with a few fundamental concepts.

INITIALIZING VARIABLES OUTSIDE THE .EXE

What would the ramifications be if all memory variables that were required to run a system were initialized outside of the compiled application? It would obviously give the Clipper programmer more memory, more flexibility, and more maneuverability within the 640K environment than ever before. This is a radical new way of thinking and in many ways it combines the philosophy of object-oriented programming and data-driven programming.

First, let's start with the two driving concepts behind this technology. The first concept comes to us from dBASE; it is the use of macros and macro substitution. In Clipper, the macro library is practically everywhere and we, and our applications, are subject to it. Up until now, the macro parser, being involved with practically everything within the Clipper library, got in the way. This was especially true if the code was literal information. Where is the need for a parser if the data is literal and available at compile time? Now, if we take this negative, and turn it into a positive by using it in our favor, interesting results will occur. This minor alteration in the way we use Clipper can be extremely advantageous.

The second part of this trick involves our parsing function, discussed in Chapter 1. In previous examples, we had the parser look at information on the left and right sides of the “/ ”; the “+” sign has also been used, as has the “ \” character. Now, we must stretch our perceptions to involve the way we code. For example, consider the following typical code extract:

```
scrprog = "C:"
scrcolor = "7/0, 0/7"
```

If we were to interpret those lines, we could say that Clipper will take everything on the right and assign it to the variable on the left. But how can that variable on the right get assigned if it is not compiled? Simple. We use the macro library in Clipper to do the work. Consider this piece of standard Clipper code:

```
variable = SPACE(10)
x = "variable"
@ 1,1 GET &x.
```

In essence, we would be GETting the value for the variable named **variable**. The same thing can be applied to this concept. If we move the initial variable assignment outside, while keeping a user-defined function in our program as the second variable assignment, and we make that variable PUBLIC in nature, the trick will work. In other words, move the line variable = SPACE(10) to an outside text file and have a user-defined function perform the x = "variable" operation (however, instead of the literal **variable**, the function would macro the name of the variable listed to the left of the equal sign inside of the text file). Consider the following coding extract:

```
CLEAR SCREEN
GETVARS("SETUP.TXT")
SCRCOLOR(scrcolor)
@ 10,10 SAY "Hello"
```

Inside of the text file named Setup.txt, we have one line of text:

```
scrcolor = "7/1,1/7"
```

When the test program ran, the word "Hello" was displayed on a blue background with white letters.

Now let's take it one step further. Let's make a variable assignment in our text file based on another variable assigned in that same file. The trick is to make the variable assignment after the primary assignment. This should not be too difficult to see since we have to do that anyway; a variable cannot be assigned a value of a variable that has yet to be defined (we would get an UNDEFINED IDENTIFIER error message if we did). Therefore, using the above example, we could change the text file to the following:

```
maincolor = "7/1,1/7"
scrcolor  = maincolor
```

If this principle holds true, we should be able to set the screen to the color in the variable **scrcolor**. Taking this approach to its conclusion, we could do the following:

```
startdate = DATE()
enddate   = DATE() + 40
```

Here, we are making a calculation. We are asking Clipper to macro expand the element on the right side of the equal sign and assign it to the variable on the left that will also be macro expanded. Finally, we can add user defined functions inside of our text file. Consider this text fragment:

```
myname = Upperlower("steve")
```

If we were able to resolve this, we could program the text file, or have the data programmed in advance. This concept is a fundamental principle of object-oriented programming. The following test example requires a text file named "SETUP.TXT" with a variable named **color** assigned to a screen color. This function, named **GETVARS()**, is a preliminary and simplified version of the **O_VARS()** function found in the ToolkiT — Release 2.

```
********************
* Name      Textread.prg
* Author    Stephen J. Straley
* Date      July 15, 1989
* Notice    Copyright (c) 1989 Stephen J.
*           Straley & Associates
* Compile   Clipper Textread -m
* Release   Summer '87
* Link      PLINK86 FI Textread LIB Clipper, Extend;
* Note      The function GETVARS() is a simplified
*           version of the O_VARS() function found in
*           Steve Straley's ToolkiT - Release 2
*
********************

Maketext()
Dotext()

*******************

PROCEDURE Maketext

   MEMOWRIT("SETUP.TXT", [color = "0/7, 7/0"])
   CLEAR SCREEN
   WAIT "File created.  Any key...."

*******************

PROCEDURE Dotext

   Getvars("Setup.txt")
   SETCOLOR(color) && This is the variable declared!
   CLEAR SCREEN
   @ 10,10 SAY "Hello"

   * GETVARS() is a simplified and rudimentary version
   * of the O_VARS() function found in the ToolkiT -
   * Release 2.  All Rights Reserved.
```

```
039 :
040 : ********************
041 :
042 : FUNCTION Getvars
043 :
044 :     PARAMETERS _file
045 :
046 :     PRIVATE _fhandle, _line, _end, _char, _thevar, _theval
047 :
048 :     _fhandle = FOPEN(_file)
049 :     _line = ""
050 :     _end = FSEEK(_fhandle, 0, 2)    && POINT 1
051 :     FSEEK(_fhandle, 0, 0)
052 :     DO WHILE .T.
053 :        _char = " "
054 :        _exit = ( FSEEK(_fhandle, 0, 1) = _end - 1 )
055 :        IF FREADSTR(_fhandle, 1) + FREADSTR(_fhandle, 1) = ;
056 :           CHR(13)+CHR(10) .OR. _exit
057 :           _thevar = LTRIM(TRIM(Parsing(@_line, "=")))
058 :           _theval = LTRIM(TRIM(_line))
059 :           IF EMPTY(_thevar) .OR. EMPTY(_line)
060 :           ELSE
061 :              IF TYPE(_theval) == "U" .OR. TYPE(_theval) == "UE"
062 :              ELSE    && POINT #2
063 :                 PUBLIC &_thevar.
064 :                 &_thevar. = &_theval.
065 :              ENDIF
066 :           ENDIF
067 :           _line = ""
068 :           * this is the end of the line
069 :        ELSE
070 :           FSEEK(_fhandle, -2, 1)
071 :           FREAD(_fhandle, @_char, 1)
072 :           _line = _line + _char
073 :        ENDIF
074 :        IF _exit
075 :           EXIT
076 :        ENDIF
077 :     ENDDO
078 :     FCLOSE(_fhandle)
079 :     RETURN(.T.)
080 :
081 : * ************************************************
082 : * * The following procedure(s)/function(s) are   *
083 : * * part of Steve Straley's ToolkiT(tm) -         *
084 : * * Release 2, published by Four Seasons          *
085 : * * Publishing Co., Inc.  All Rights Reserved     *
086 : * * Information: 212-599-2141                      *
087 : * * 212-599-2141 - All Rights Reserved            *
088 : * ************************************************
089 :
090 : ********************
091 :
092 : FUNCTION Parsing
```

```
093 :
094 :     PARAMETERS _getstr, _forcode
095 :
096 :     PRIVATE _forcode, _location, _temp
097 :
098 :     IF PCOUNT() = 2
099 :        IF TYPE("_forcode") = "L"
100 :           _thechar = "|"
101 :        ELSE
102 :           _thechar = _forcode
103 :        ENDIF
104 :        _forcode = .T.
105 :     ELSE
106 :        _forcode = .F.
107 :     ENDIF
108 :
109 :     IF _forcode
110 :        _location    = AT(_thechar, _getstr)
111 :     ELSE
112 :        _location    = IF(EMPTY(AT("+", _getstr)), ;
113 :                    AT("/", _getstr), AT("+", _getstr))
114 :     ENDIF
115 :
116 :     _temp = IF(!EMPTY(_location), SUBSTR(_getstr, ;
117 :             1, _location - 1), _getstr)
118 :     _getstr = IF(!EMPTY(_location), SUBSTR(_getstr, ;
119 :             _location + 1), "")
120 :     RETURN(_temp)
121 :
122 : * End of File
```

As you can see, the PARSING() function, also found in the ToolkiT, is instrumental in parsing out the information on either side of the equal sign inside of the text file. In addition, you can see the low-level file functions in Clipper being used to their fullest. Every line in the file is looked at individually. Each element on the left side of the equal sign is assigned to a private variable named **_thevar**; the value is kept in another variable named **_theval**. The idea is to make the variable **_thevar** a PUBLIC variable and to macro-expand it into the run-time variable table. We need to do this in order to have the variable available to the rest of the program after the call to the GETVARS() function is complete. Otherwise, all of the variables would be released as soon as program control returned from the GETVARS() function. Finally, there is one thing to keep in mind if you opt to expand this technology to involve your user-defined functions, like the UPPERLOWER() example. The function used in the text file must be present in the system in order for the variable assignment to be resolved. To accomplish this, the EXTERNAL command is necessary.

Also, there are two additional points that must be made. The first issue involves line 50. Prior to the publication of this book, the original versions of this function did not have this line. The expression on line 50 actually appeared on line 74. The problem was that on line 55 and 56, the file pointer would skip two places and compare that byte with the string

CHR(13)+CHR(10). What if the last item in the text file did not have a carriage return, line feed combination? Well, the variable on that line would not get assigned; therefore, a variable testing the validity of the end of file marker needs to be tested on line 56 and again on line 74.

The second point involves the possibility of this item appearing in your test file:

```
color = "7/0, 0/7
```

It is obvious to us that the second quotation mark is missing. Indeed, if this were to be compiled, Clipper would flag the error as well. But we are circumventing the compiler with these text file concepts, so our functions must be intelligent enough to see the potential problems in advance, much like the compiler. On lines 61 and 62, there is a comparison to the status of the variable **_theval**. If the concluding quotation mark had been in place, the value for TYPE(_theval) would equal a "C" and the value of TYPE("_theval") would also equal a "C." At that point, we know we have a legitimate expression that can be assigned to the variable to the left of our delimiting equal sign. If we assign the **&_thevar.** PUBLIC prior to this test, the results could be fatal. In this example, it could potentially hang the machine. Therefore the lesson to learn is that if you are going to take control, you have to take it completely; otherwise, the results may be difficult to resolve.

READING A TEXT FILE TO AN ARRAY

The remaining topics in this chapter revolve around the concept of reading text files from the disk and storing each line into an array. For example, if we had a text file that contained the following:

```
   STORE 1 TO steve
"Mary had a little lamb"
x = 3
```

And if we were to create an array that would contain each line, that array would be DECLARed to three elements: DECLARE file[3]. Now, using our low-level file function knowledge, we can read in each line of the file, storing the contents of each line to a position in the array where eventually we would get the following in memory:

```
   file[1] <-> STORE 1 TO steve
file[2] <-> "Mary had a little lamb"
file[3] <-> x = 3
```

Obviously, we need to create a couple of functions that would serve this purpose. To illustrate this point, here is a sample program:

```
********************
* Name      Showarry.prg
* Author    Stephen J. Straley
```

```
* Date      July 15, 1989
* Notice    Copyright (c) 1989 Stephen J. Straley & Associates
*           All Rights Reserved,
* Compile   Clipper Showarry -m
* Release   Summer '87
* Link      PLINK86 FI Showarry LIB Clipper LIB Extend;
* Note      This shows the concept of reading in information
*           from a text file similiar to the Getvars() function.
*
********************

cr = CHR(13) + CHR(10)
string =             [STORE 1 TO Steve] + cr
string = string + ["Mary had a little lamb"] + cr
string = string + [x = 3]
MEMOWRIT("NEWFILE.TXT", string)
O_arrays("data", "newfile.txt")
FOR x = 1 TO LEN(data)
  ? "data[" + LTRIM(STR(x)) + "] = " + data[x]
NEXT
WAIT
CLEAR SCREEN
IF FILE(PROCFILE() + ".PRG")
   O_arrays("data", PROCFILE() + ".PRG")
   FOR x = 1 TO LEN(data)
     ? "data[" + LTRIM(STR(x)) + "] = " + data[x]
   NEXT
ENDIF

* ***********************************************
* * The following procedure(s)/function(s) are   *
* * part of Steve Straley's ToolkiT(tm) -        *
* * Release 2, published by Four Seasons         *
* * Publishing Co., Inc.  All Rights Reserved    *
* * Information: 212-599-2141 / 800-662-2278     *
* * All Rights Reserved                          *
* ***********************************************

********************

FUNCTION Parsing

   PARAMETERS _getstr, _forcode

   * _getstr is the string to be parsed
   * _forcode is the code that parses.

   * This function is the string parser.  Basically, return the
   * beginning fragment of a string, adjust the string, and if
   * passed by reference, alter the contents of the original
   * string.

   PRIVATE _forcode, _location, _tempback, _width

```

```
058 :    IF PCOUNT() = 2
059 :       IF TYPE("_forcode") = "L"
060 :          _thechar = "|"
061 :       ELSE
062 :          _thechar = _forcode
063 :       ENDIF
064 :       _forcode = .T.
065 :    ELSE
066 :       _forcode = .F.
067 :    ENDIF
068 :
069 :    IF _forcode
070 :       _location   = AT(_thechar, _getstr)
071 :       _width      = LEN(_thechar)
072 :    ELSE
073 :       _location   = IF(EMPTY(AT("+", _getstr)), ;
074 :                        AT("/", _getstr), AT("+", _getstr))
075 :       _width      = 1
076 :    ENDIF
077 :
078 :    _tempback = IF(!EMPTY(_location), SUBSTR(_getstr, 1, ;
079 :                        _location - 1), _getstr)
080 :    _getstr   = IF(!EMPTY(_location), SUBSTR(_getstr, ;
081 :                        _location + _width), "")
082 :    RETURN(_tempback)
083 :
084 : ******************
085 :
086 : FUNCTION O_arrays
087 :
088 :    * This has been modified to NOT allow a master
089 :    * condition as discussed in the ToolkiT -
090 :    * Release 2
091 :
092 :    PARAMETERS _mastar, _thefile, _ismast
093 :
094 :    IF PCOUNT() < 1
095 :       RETURN(.F.)
096 :    ELSEIF PCOUNT() = 1
097 :       IF TYPE("_mastar") != "A"
098 :          RETURN(.F.)
099 :       ENDIF
100 :       _thefile = ""
101 :       _ismast = .F.
102 :    ELSEIF PCOUNT() = 2
103 :       IF TYPE("_mastar") + TYPE("_thefile") != "CC"
104 :          RETURN(.F.)
105 :       ENDIF
106 :       IF !FILE(_thefile)
107 :          RETURN(.F.)
108 :       ENDIF
109 :       _ismast = .F.
110 :    ELSE
111 :       IF TYPE("_mastar") + TYPE("_thefile") + ;
```

```
112 :           TYPE("_ismast") != "CCL"
113 :             RETURN(.F.)
114 :         ENDIF
115 :         IF !FILE(_thefile)
116 :             RETURN(.F.)
117 :         ENDIF
118 :     ENDIF
119 :
120 :     PRIVATE _fhandle, _line, _end, _char, _vals, ;
121 :             _count, _elemn
122 :
123 :     IF TYPE("_thefile") != "C"
124 :         RETURN(.F.)
125 :     ELSEIF !FILE(_thefile)
126 :         RETURN(.F.)
127 :     ENDIF
128 :     _size = O_asize(_thefile)
129 :     IF !EMPTY(_size)
130 :         _name = Parsing(_mastar, ";")
131 :         PUBLIC &_name.[_size]
132 :         AFILL(&_name., "")
133 :         * now fill the array with the elements
134 :         O_asize(_thefile, &_name.)
135 :     ELSE
136 :         RETURN(.F.)
137 :     ENDIF
138 :     RETURN(.T.)
139 :
140 : ********************
141 :
142 : FUNCTION O_asize
143 :
144 :     PARAMETERS _ofile, _array
145 :
146 :     PRIVATE _cnt, _fh
147 :
148 :     IF EMPTY(PCOUNT())
149 :         RETURN(0)
150 :     ELSEIF PCOUNT() = 1
151 :         IF !FILE(_ofile)
152 :             RETURN(0)
153 :         ENDIF
154 :     ELSEIF PCOUNT() = 2
155 :         IF !FILE(_ofile)
156 :             RETURN(0)
157 :         ENDIF
158 :         IF TYPE("_array") != "A"
159 :             RETURN(0)
160 :         ENDIF
161 :     ENDIF
162 :
163 :     _fh = FOPEN(_ofile)
164 :     _end = FSEEK(_fh, 0, 2)
165 :     _line = ""
```

```
166 :     _count = 0
167 :     FSEEK(_fh, 0, 0)
168 :     * Originally, this was set to read in only one
169 :     * byte at a time, similiar to Getvars/O_vars()
170 :     * Now we are going to speed this up by reading
171 :     * in 1K at a time and work that way!
172 :
173 :     _bytes = 1024   && This can be modified to speed it up
174 :
175 :     DO WHILE .T.
176 :        _char = SPACE(_bytes)
177 :        _exit = FREAD(_fh, @_char, _bytes ) != _bytes
178 :
179 :        *
180 :        * now add the residue if this has passed through
181 :        * previously
182 :        *
183 :
184 :        _char = _line + _char
185 :        DO WHILE !EMPTY(_char)
186 :           _line = Parsing(@_char, CHR(13)+CHR(10) )
187 :           IF LEFT(LTRIM(TRIM(_line)), 1) = "*"
188 :              _line = ""
189 :
190 :           ELSEIF "NOTE" = SUBSTR(UPPER(LTRIM(_line)),1,4)
191 :              _line = ""
192 :
193 :           ELSEIF "&&" = SUBSTR(LTRIM(_line), 2, 4)
194 :              _line = ""
195 :
196 :           ELSEIF EMPTY(_line)
197 :              _line = ""
198 :           ELSE
199 :              IF !EMPTY(_char)
200 :                 _count = _count + 1
201 :                 IF PCOUNT() = 2
202 :                    _array[_count] = _line
203 :                 ENDIF
204 :              ENDIF
205 :           ENDIF
206 :        ENDDO
207 :        *
208 :        * if _char is empty and _line is NOT, then _line
209 :        * must be added to char at the top of the loop
210 :        *
211 :        IF _exit
212 :           * replace EOF marker with null byte
213 :           _line = STRTRAN(_line, CHR(26), "")
214 :           * if there are still characters, write it out.
215 :           IF !EMPTY(_line)
216 :              _count = _count + 1
217 :              IF PCOUNT() = 2
218 :                 _array[_count] = _line
219 :              ENDIF
```

```
220 :             ENDIF
221 :             EXIT
222 :          ENDIF
223 :       ENDDO
224 :       FCLOSE(_fh)
225 :       RETURN(_count)
226 :
227 : * End of File
```

Reading in a text file and storing it to an array is a two-step process. First, you must determine the number of lines that will be read, and second, you must actually read in the line. The main focus should be in keeping the same function for both operations — it would be foolish to have one function initialize the array to a wrong value, causing an error when the other function tries to store values to that same array.

To start with, the text file Newfile.txt is built on line 19 via the MEMOWRIT() function. Next comes the call to the one function that initializes and stores information to an array: O_arrays() (line 20). Here, the name of an array that will be created is called **data** and the correlating file that will be associated with that array is the very text file we created on line 19. You can quickly see that on line 21, not only is the array built because it is being called by the LEN() function, but the individual elements will be displayed by line 22. And as good measure, the program file itself will be read in an array and then displayed as well (lines 26 through 31).

So, the key to this is the O_arrays() function, which begins on line 86. The third parameter **_ismast** coincides with having an array of pointers to other arrays, thus keeping the programmer focused on just one text file at a time. That technology will be saved for another time. For now, let us concern ourselves with having only two parameters involved with this function. Remember, the variable **_mastar** contains the name of the array that will be created, and **_thefile** contains the name of the text file that will be read. After a bit of data verification and type checking, a call is made to the O_asize() function (line 128), which counts the number of lines in the array (if only 1 parameter is passed to it) and stores individual line elements from the text file to the array (if two parameters are passed to it). If there is any error experienced by the O_asize() function, its value will be 0. If this should happen, 0 will be the value of **_size** (line 128) and cause the program flow to skip over the IF condition on line 129. This will cause the value of the O_arrays() function to be false. For now, let us imagine a possible size for the text file and thus, a value for the variable named **_size**. Eventually, the array is now in a variable named **_name**, which is made PUBLIC (line 131) and is set to contain **_size** number of elements. The array is then filled with NULL bytes via the AFILL() function and another call is then made to the O_asize function, this time, with the file and the array. Look at line 134. It is important to remember that the name of the array is contained in the variable **_name**. It is equally important to recall one fundamental principle in Clipper: Arrays are passed by reference, allowing subprocedures to alter the values of their subscripts. In order to get the array passed to the O_asize() function and not the name of the array, the variable **_name** must be macro-expanded.

This time, in the O_asize() function, the individual elements are stored to the array. Looking closely at this function we can see that the low-level file functions are used in reading the file and that this function allows for several possibilities. After the variables are passed to the function, the text file is opened using the FOPEN() function on line 163 and the DOS file handle is stored to the **_fh** variable. Two important variables are then initialized to their beginning values: **_line** (the actual contents of the lines) and **_count** (the positioner for the subscripts). Now, rather than reading in 1 byte at a time, a faster method can be programmed by reading in chunks of text, then parsing out the individual lines. This process should continue through the string containing the chunk of data obtained, each time stripping out analyzed lines, eventually coming to the end of the string. At that time, the remainder of the string should be attached to the front of the next chunk of data from the disk. This should continue until the end-of-file marker is reached.

The amount of information to be read in at one time will be 1024 bytes (line 173) and the string that will contain the read information will be a variable named **_char** (line 176). The next step is tricky; we want to do two operations at the same time. First, we want to pick up as much information as we can and store it to the variable **_char** and we want to test for the end-of-file marker. We know that the FREAD() function will return the number of bytes actually read from the disk and if this value does not match the number of attempted bytes as set by the variable named **_bytes**, we will know that the end-of-file marker has been reached. In this event, the variable named **_exit** will be set to logical true (.T.); otherwise, a logical false (.F.) will be set. At the same time, we passed the variable **_char** to the FREAD() function by reference, causing those bytes that were read to be stored to the variable.

The next step is one that plans for the future. If this is the second pass through the loop, we can assume that information is remaining in the variable named **_line**. You see, there is no guarantee that the remainder of information from the variable **_char** will be a full line. More likely only partial lines will remain. In that event, they should be added to the front of the data that will be read in. Seeing that this is the first time through the loop, we do not have to worry about this, especially since the variable **_line** is set to a NULL byte. From here, we come to yet another loop that will continue processing as long as information is in the variable **_char**. Stopping here for a moment, we have to ask ourselves what differentiates one line of text from another. It is obvious: the carriage return and line feed character combination.

Like so many other examples, here is another case for our Parsing() function. This time, the function is going to look for a two-character delimiter combination rather than a single one. Because of this, the Parsing() function has been modified to look at the width of the character parameter rather than assuming a single character (lines 71, 76, and 81). If those characters are found, the line is stored to the variable **_line** and that information, plus the CHR(13)+CHR(10) combination, is removed from the original string **_char** (line 186). We then test to see if any of the common Clipper notation characters appear in any of the lines and if so, no count is given. However, if the line read in is not a comment line nor is it blank, the subscript pointer is incremented (**_count** on line 200) and the value of the **_line** is stored to the **_array[]** at line 202. Notice on line 201 that if only one parameter is passed to this function, PCOUNT() will not equal 2. This means that only a simple count will be taken; otherwise, the actual item is stored. This is how we can get the same function to do two operations.

Eventually, the file will be completely read in and parsed, causing the value of .T. to be stored to the variable **_exit**. At that point, the end-of-file character needs to be removed from the **_line** string. If there is information remaining in the variable, the counter needs to be incremented one more time (line 216). Then a final test is made of the PCOUNT() function, and if applicable, the item is so stored to the **_array[]**. In the end, the value of the variable **_count** is passed back to the calling routine or function.

Once we understand this concept, we can use it for the remaining four topics. With this idea, we will be able to build and maintain databases and indexes, windows, menus, and data screens from text files.

DATABASE GENERATION

Before we begin talking about this new way of looking at the Clipper language, there are a couple of rules that we must follow. While these rules are not set in stone, they are standards that a few of us have agreed to accept and abide by. The others are Dirk Lesko of dLESKO & Associates, Corey Schwartz of HJS Research, Neil Weicher of Communication Horizons, and John Halovanic of Silverware. The file format we have agreed to is simple: Asterisks denote a comment line, blank lines are ignored, lines must end with CHR(13)+CHR(10) character combinations, and the semicolon is the delimiter within the line. The last point will become obvious in a few moments. These rules make it easy for other people to read, understand, and use code not only with Clipper, but with the products of each of these vendors (including SJS & Associates' ToolkiT).

In the case of the delimiter rule, let's first take a look at a file that will contain a database structure and related information.

```
********************
* Name      In.txt
* Author    Stephen J. Straley
* Date      July 15, 1989
* Notice    Copyright (c) 1989 Stephen J. Straley & Associates
*           All Rights Reserved
* Compile   n/a
* Release   Summer 87
* Link      n/a
* Note      This is the partial structure to Steve Straley's
*           Accounting Package published by Four Seasons Publishing Co.
*
********************
```

```
chart
internal; n; 8
account; c; 16
desc; c; 28
normal; c; 1
balance; n; 12; 2
cons_acct; n; 8
rpt_level; n; 2
posting; c; 1
mast_cons; c; 16
acct_type; c; 1
category; c; 2
cash; l; 1
history; l; 1

CHT_ACCT
Fill_out(Stripfrom(account,"-. "),16)

CHT_DESC
UPPER(desc)

CHT_KEY
internal

* End of File
```

Look at the lines of text pertaining to the field information; each field has a name, a data type, a length, and if applicable, a decimal length. All of the other lines contain single-tiered information, that is, the complete line has only one item in it. The lines with index expressions contain an entire expression, even though it may appear to have many. If we were to parse this line, looking for the semicolon, we could store a complete set of information about a field on a single line. Let us now take a look at this technique in action:

```
********************
* Name      Makedata.prg
* Author    Stephen J. Straley
* Date      July 15, 1989
* Notice    Copyright (c) 1989 Stephen J. Straley & Associates
*           All Rights Reserved
* Compile   Clipper Makedata -m
* Release   Summer '87
* Link      PLINK86 FI Makedata LIB Clipper LIB Extend;
* Note      This shows how a database and index files can be
*           made from a text file and USED from a text file.
*
*           The file formats are created in conjunction by:
*           Dirk Lesko - FUNCky Library
*           Steve Straley - ToolkiT Library
*
********************

CLEAR SCREEN
```

```
020 : ? "Making File..."
021 : Makeit()
022 : ? "Reading Information.."
023 : Doit()
024 : CLEAR SCREEN
025 :
026 : ********************
027 :
028 : PROCEDURE Doit
029 :
030 :     EXTERNAL Stripfrom
031 :
032 :     EXTERNAL Fill_out
033 :
034 :     IF O_arrays("Data", "THEDATA.TXT")
035 :        IF O_file(data, .T.) > 0
036 :           *
037 :           * use the file
038 :           pointer = STR(O_file(data))
039 :           *
040 :           ? &pointer.->(ALIAS())
041 :           ? &pointer.->(FCOUNT())
042 :           ? &pointer.->(LASTREC())
043 :           ? &pointer.->(INDEXKEY(INDEXORD()))
044 :           ? &pointer.->(HEADER())
045 :           WAIT
046 :           Op(&pointer.->(DBEDIT()))
047 :        ENDIF
048 :     ENDIF
049 :
050 : ********************
051 :
052 : PROCEDURE Makeit
053 :
054 :     cr = CHR(13)+CHR(10)
055 :     string =          "chart" + cr
056 :     string = string + "internal; n; 8" + cr + ;
057 :             "account; c; 16" + cr + "desc; c; 28" + cr
058 :     string = string + "normal; c; 1" + cr +;
059 :             "balance; n; 12; 2" + cr + "cons_acct; n; 8" + cr
060 :     string = string + "rpt_level; n; 2" + cr + ;
061 :             "posting; c; 1" + cr + "mast_cons; c; 16" + cr
062 :     string = string + "acct_type; c; 1" + cr + ;
063 :             "category; c; 2" + cr + "cash; l; 1" + cr
064 :     string = string + "history; l; 1" + cr + cr + "CHT_ACCT" + ;
065 :             cr + "Fill_out(Stripfrom(account,'-. '),16)" + cr
066 :     string = string + cr + "CHT_DESC" + cr + "UPPER(desc)" + ;
067 :             cr + cr + "CHT_KEY" + cr + "internal" + cr + cr + ;
068 :             "* End of File"
069 :     MEMOWRIT("Thedata.txt", string)
070 :
071 : * *********************************************
072 : * * The following procedure(s)/function(s) are   *
073 : * * part of Steve Straley's ToolkiT(tm) -        *
```

```
074 : * * Release 2, published by Four Seasons      *
075 : * * Publishing Co., Inc.  All Rights Reserved *
076 : * * Information: 212-599-2141 / 800-662-2278   *
077 : * * All Rights Reserved                        *
078 : * *********************************************
079 :
080 :
081 : ********************
082 :
083 : FUNCTION O_file
084 :
085 :    PARAMETERS _f, _ftog
086 :
087 :    IF EMPTY(PCOUNT())
088 :       RETURN(-1)
089 :    ELSEIF TYPE("_f") != "A"
090 :       WAIT
091 :       RETURN(-1)
092 :    ENDIF
093 :
094 :    _ftog = IF((TYPE("_ftog") != "L"), .F., _ftog)
095 :
096 :    IF _ftog
097 :       _area = SELECT()
098 :       SELECT 0
099 :       CREATE Template
100 :       USE Template
101 :       FOR _qaz = 2 TO LEN(_f)
102 :          && I'm at the index file, stop
103 :          && creating field information
104 :          IF EMPTY(AT(";", _f[_qaz]))
105 :             EXIT
106 :          ENDIF
107 :          _t = _f[_qaz]
108 :          _t1 = Parsing(@_t, ";")
109 :          _t2 = UPPER(LTRIM(TRIM(Parsing(@_t, ";"))))
110 :          _t3 = VAL(LTRIM(TRIM(Parsing(@_t, ";"))))
111 :          _t4 = IF(EMPTY(_t), 0, _t)
112 :          Ap_it(_t1, _t2, _t3, _t4)
113 :       NEXT
114 :       USE
115 :       CREATE (_f[1]) FROM Template
116 :       ERASE Template.dbf
117 :       USE (_f[1])
118 :       FOR _qwert = _qaz TO LEN(_f) STEP 2
119 :          _express = _f[_qwert + 1]
120 :          IF TYPE(_express) $ "CLDN"
121 :             INDEX ON &_express. TO (_f[_qwert])
122 :          ENDIF
123 :       NEXT
124 :       USE
125 :       SELECT (_area)
126 :       RETURN (1)
127 :    ELSE
```

```
128 :        && This means that the database has not
129 :        && been created yet.
130 :        IF !FILE(Extention(_f[1], "DBF"))
131 :            RETURN(0)     && means file NOT opened
132 :        ENDIF
133 :        && Find the select work area to open this in
134 :        _area = SELECT()
135 :        SELECT 0
136 :        USE (_f[1])
137 :        FOR _qaz = 2 TO LEN(_f)
138 :            IF EMPTY(AT(";", _f[_qaz])) && Find the index file
139 :                EXIT
140 :            ENDIF
141 :        NEXT
142 :        IF _qaz < LEN(_f)
143 :            _wsx = 0            && count the number of indexes....
144 :            FOR _qwert = _qaz TO LEN(_f) STEP 2
145 :                && means that the index file has not
146 :                && been created yet
147 :                IF !FILE(Extention(_f[_qwert], "NTX"))
148 :                    EXIT
149 :                ENDIF
150 :                _wsx = _wsx + 1
151 :            NEXT
152 :            * now open up the proper number of indexes
153 :            * to the file
154 :            IF EMPTY(_wsx)
155 :                * no index
156 :            ELSEIF _wsx = 1
157 :                SET INDEX TO (_f[_qaz])
158 :            ELSEIF _wsx = 2
159 :                SET INDEX TO (_f[_qaz]), (_f[_qaz + 2])
160 :            ELSEIF _wsx = 3
161 :                SET INDEX TO (_f[_qaz]), (_f[_qaz + 2]), ;
162 :                             (_f[_qaz + 4])
163 :            ELSEIF _wsx = 4
164 :                SET INDEX TO (_f[_qaz]), (_f[_qaz + 2]), ;
165 :                             (_f[_qaz + 4]), (_f[_qaz + 6])
166 :            ELSEIF _wsx = 5
167 :                SET INDEX TO (_f[_qaz]), (_f[_qaz + 2]), ;
168 :                             (_f[_qaz + 4]), (_f[_qaz + 6]), ;
169 :                             (_f[_qaz + 8])
170 :            ELSEIF _wsx = 6
171 :                SET INDEX TO (_f[_qaz]), (_f[_qaz + 2]), ;
172 :                             (_f[_qaz + 4]), (_f[_qaz + 6]), ;
173 :                             (_f[_qaz + 8]), (_f[_qaz + 10])
174 :            ELSEIF _wsx = 7
175 :                SET INDEX TO (_f[_qaz]), (_f[_qaz + 2]), ;
176 :                             (_f[_qaz + 4]), (_f[_qaz + 6]), ;
177 :                             (_f[_qaz + 8]), (_f[_qaz + 10]), ;
178 :                             (_f[_qaz + 12])
179 :            ELSEIF _wsx = 8
180 :                SET INDEX TO (_f[_qaz]), (_f[_qaz + 2]), ;
181 :                             (_f[_qaz + 4]), (_f[_qaz + 6]), ;
```

```
                        (_f[_qaz + 8]), (_f[_qaz + 10]), ;
                        (_f[_qaz + 12]), (_f[_qaz + 14])
        ELSEIF _wsx = 9
           SET INDEX TO (_f[_qaz]), (_f[_qaz + 2]), ;
                        (_f[_qaz + 4]), (_f[_qaz + 6]), ;
                        (_f[_qaz + 8]), (_f[_qaz + 10]), ;
                        (_f[_qaz + 12]), (_f[_qaz + 14]), ;
                        (_f[_qaz + 16])
        ELSEIF _wsx = 10
           SET INDEX TO (_f[_qaz]), (_f[_qaz + 2]), ;
                        (_f[_qaz + 4]), (_f[_qaz + 6]), ;
                        (_f[_qaz + 8]), (_f[_qaz + 10]), ;
                        (_f[_qaz + 12]), (_f[_qaz + 14]), ;
                        (_f[_qaz + 16]), (_f[_qaz + 18])
        ELSEIF _wsx = 11
           SET INDEX TO (_f[_qaz]), (_f[_qaz + 2]), ;
                        (_f[_qaz + 4]), (_f[_qaz + 6]), ;
                        (_f[_qaz + 8]), (_f[_qaz + 10]), ;
                        (_f[_qaz + 12]), (_f[_qaz + 14]), ;
                        (_f[_qaz + 16]), (_f[_qaz + 18]), ;
                        (_f[_qaz + 20])
        ELSEIF _wsx = 12
           SET INDEX TO (_f[_qaz]), (_f[_qaz + 2]), ;
                        (_f[_qaz + 4]), (_f[_qaz + 6]), ;
                        (_f[_qaz + 8]), (_f[_qaz + 10]), ;
                        (_f[_qaz + 12]), (_f[_qaz + 14]), ;
                        (_f[_qaz + 16]), (_f[_qaz + 18]), ;
                        (_f[_qaz + 20]), (_f[_qaz + 22])
        ELSEIF _wsx = 13
           SET INDEX TO (_f[_qaz]), (_f[_qaz + 2]), ;
                        (_f[_qaz + 4]), (_f[_qaz + 6]), ;
                        (_f[_qaz + 8]), (_f[_qaz + 10]), ;
                        (_f[_qaz + 12]), (_f[_qaz + 14]), ;
                        (_f[_qaz + 16]), (_f[_qaz + 18]), ;
                        (_f[_qaz + 20]), (_f[_qaz + 22]), ;
                        (_f[_qaz + 24])
        ELSEIF _wsx = 14
           SET INDEX TO (_f[_qaz]), (_f[_qaz + 2]), ;
                        (_f[_qaz + 4]), (_f[_qaz + 6]), ;
                        (_f[_qaz + 8]), (_f[_qaz + 10]), ;
                        (_f[_qaz + 12]), (_f[_qaz + 14]), ;
                        (_f[_qaz + 16]), (_f[_qaz + 18]), ;
                        (_f[_qaz + 20]), (_f[_qaz + 22]), ;
                        (_f[_qaz + 24]), (_f[_qaz + 26])
        ELSEIF _wsx = 15
           SET INDEX TO (_f[_qaz]), (_f[_qaz + 2]), ;
                        (_f[_qaz + 4]), (_f[_qaz + 6]), ;
                        (_f[_qaz + 8]), (_f[_qaz + 10]), ;
                        (_f[_qaz + 12]), (_f[_qaz + 14]), ;
                        (_f[_qaz + 16]), (_f[_qaz + 18]), ;
                        (_f[_qaz + 20]), (_f[_qaz + 22]), ;
                        (_f[_qaz + 24]), (_f[_qaz + 26]), ;
                        (_f[_qaz + 28])
        ENDIF
```

```
236 :        ENDIF
237 :        SELECT (_area)
238 :        RETURN (_area) && means file is open in this work area.
239 :     ENDIF
240 :
241 : ********************
242 :
243 : FUNCTION Ap_it
244 :
245 :     PARAMETERS _apa, _apb, _apc, _apd
246 :
247 :     * _apa = the field name
248 :     * _apb = the field data type
249 :     * _apc = the field length
250 :     * _apd = the field decimal
251 :
252 :     * This function replaces the parameters
253 :     * into a STRUCTURE EXTENDED database this is
254 :     * previously created and open.
255 :
256 :     IF PCOUNT() = 3
257 :        _apd = 0
258 :     ENDIF
259 :
260 :     IF EMPTY(ALIAS())
261 :        RETURN(-1)
262 :     ELSEIF TYPE("field_name") = "U"
263 :        RETURN(-3)
264 :     ELSEIF TYPE("_apa") + TYPE("_apb") + TYPE("_apc") + ;
265 :             TYPE("_apd") != "CCNN"
266 :        RETURN(-2)
267 :     ENDIF
268 :
269 :     LOCATE ALL FOR UPPER(field_name) == UPPER(_apa)
270 :
271 :     IF FOUND()
272 :        RETURN(0)
273 :     ELSE
274 :        APPEND BLANK
275 :        IF _apc > 255
276 :           REPLACE field_name WITH _apa, field_type WITH _apb,;
277 :                   field_len WITH INT(_apc % 256), ;
278 :                   field_dec WITH INT(_apc / 256)
279 :        ELSE
280 :           REPLACE field_name WITH _apa, field_type WITH _apb,;
281 :                   field_len WITH _apc, field_dec WITH _apd
282 :        ENDIF
283 :     ENDIF
284 :     RETURN(RECNO())
285 :
286 : ******************
287 :
288 : FUNCTION O_arrays
289 :
```

```
290 :     * This has been modified to NOT allow a master
291 :     * condition as discussed in the ToolkiT -
292 :     * Release 2
293 :
294 :     PARAMETERS _mastar, _thefile, _ismast
295 :
296 :     IF PCOUNT() < 1
297 :        RETURN(.F.)
298 :     ELSEIF PCOUNT() = 1
299 :        IF TYPE("_mastar") != "A"
300 :           RETURN(.F.)
301 :        ENDIF
302 :        _thefile = ""
303 :        _ismast = .F.
304 :     ELSEIF PCOUNT() = 2
305 :        IF TYPE("_mastar") + TYPE("_thefile") != "CC"
306 :           RETURN(.F.)
307 :        ENDIF
308 :        IF !FILE(_thefile)
309 :           RETURN(.F.)
310 :        ENDIF
311 :        _ismast = .F.
312 :     ELSE
313 :        IF TYPE("_mastar") + TYPE("_thefile") + ;
314 :           TYPE("_ismast") != "CCL"
315 :           RETURN(.F.)
316 :        ENDIF
317 :        IF !FILE(_thefile)
318 :           RETURN(.F.)
319 :        ENDIF
320 :     ENDIF
321 :
322 :     PRIVATE _fhandle, _line, _end, _char, _vals, ;
323 :             _count, _elemn
324 :
325 :     IF TYPE("_thefile") != "C"
326 :        RETURN(.F.)
327 :     ELSEIF !FILE(_thefile)
328 :        RETURN(.F.)
329 :     ENDIF
330 :     _size = O_asize(_thefile)
331 :     IF !EMPTY(_size)
332 :        _name = Parsing(_mastar, ";")
333 :        PUBLIC &_name.[_size]
334 :        AFILL(&_name., "")
335 :        * now fill the array with the elements
336 :        O_asize(_thefile, &_name.)
337 :     ELSE
338 :        RETURN(.F.)
339 :     ENDIF
340 :     RETURN(.T.)
341 :
342 : ********************
343 :
```

```
344 :  FUNCTION O_asize
345 :
346 :      PARAMETERS _ofile, _array
347 :
348 :      PRIVATE _cnt, _fh
349 :
350 :      IF EMPTY(PCOUNT())
351 :          RETURN(0)
352 :      ELSEIF PCOUNT() = 1
353 :          IF !FILE(_ofile)
354 :              RETURN(0)
355 :          ENDIF
356 :      ELSEIF PCOUNT() = 2
357 :          IF !FILE(_ofile)
358 :              RETURN(0)
359 :          ENDIF
360 :          IF TYPE("_array") != "A"
361 :              RETURN(0)
362 :          ENDIF
363 :      ENDIF
364 :
365 :      _fh = FOPEN(_ofile)
366 :      _end = FSEEK(_fh, 0, 2)
367 :      _line = ""
368 :      _count = 0
369 :      FSEEK(_fh, 0, 0)
370 :      * Originally, this was set to read in only one
371 :      * byte at a time, similar to Getvars/O_vars().
372 :      * Now, we are going to speed this up by reading
373 :      * in 1K at a time and work that way!
374 :
375 :      _bytes = 1024  && This can be modified to speed it up
376 :
377 :      DO WHILE .T.
378 :         _char = SPACE(_bytes)
379 :         _exit = FREAD(_fh, @_char, _bytes ) != _bytes
380 :
381 :         *
382 :         * now add the residue if this has passed through
383 :         * previously
384 :         *
385 :
386 :         _char = _line + _char
387 :         DO WHILE !EMPTY(_char)
388 :            _line = Parsing(@_char, CHR(13)+CHR(10) )
389 :            IF LEFT(LTRIM(TRIM(_line)), 1) = "*"
390 :                _line = ""
391 :
392 :            ELSEIF "NOTE" = SUBSTR(UPPER(LTRIM(_line)),1,4)
393 :                _line = ""
394 :
395 :            ELSEIF "&&" = SUBSTR(LTRIM(_line), 2, 4)
396 :                _line = ""
397 :
```

```
398 :            ELSEIF EMPTY(_line)
399 :               _line = ""
400 :            ELSE
401 :               IF !EMPTY(_char)
402 :                  _count = _count + 1
403 :                  IF PCOUNT() = 2
404 :                     _array[_count] = _line
405 :                  ENDIF
406 :               ENDIF
407 :            ENDIF
408 :         ENDDO
409 :         *
410 :         * if _char is empty and _line is NOT, then _line
411 :         * must be added to char at the top of the loop
412 :         *
413 :         IF _exit
414 :            * replace EOF marker with null byte
415 :            _line = STRTRAN(_line, CHR(26), "")
416 :            * if there are still characters, write it out.
417 :            IF !EMPTY(_line)
418 :               _count = _count + 1
419 :               IF PCOUNT() = 2
420 :                  _array[_count] = _line
421 :               ENDIF
422 :            ENDIF
423 :            EXIT
424 :         ENDIF
425 :      ENDDO
426 :      FCLOSE(_fh)
427 :      RETURN(_count)
428 :
429 : ********************
430 :
431 : FUNCTION Extention
432 :
433 :      PARAMETERS _afile, _aext
434 :
435 :      IF PCOUNT() < 2
436 :         RETURN("")
437 :      ELSEIF TYPE("_afile") + TYPE("_aext") != "CC"
438 :         RETURN("")
439 :      ELSEIF LEN(_aext) > 3
440 :         IF LEN(_aext) = 4 .AND. !EMPTY(AT(".", _aext))
441 :            _aext = STRTRAN(_aext, ".", "")
442 :         ELSE
443 :            RETURN("")
444 :         ENDIF
445 :      ENDIF
446 :
447 :      IF EMPTY(AT(".", _afile))
448 :         RETURN(LTRIM(TRIM(_afile)) + "." + ;
449 :                LTRIM(TRIM(_aext)))
450 :      ELSE
```

```
451 :        RETURN(LTRIM(TRIM(_afile)))
452 :     ENDIF
453 :
454 : ********************
455 :
456 : FUNCTION Parsing
457 :
458 :     PARAMETERS _getstr, _forcode
459 :
460 :     * _getstr is the string to be parsed
461 :     * _forcode is the code that parses.
462 :
463 :     * This function is the string parser.  Basically, return
464 :     * the beginning fragment of a string, adjust the string,
465 :     * and if passed by reference, alter the contents of the
466 :     * original string.
467 :
468 :     PRIVATE _forcode, _location, _tempback, _width
469 :
470 :     IF PCOUNT() = 2
471 :        IF TYPE("_forcode") = "L"
472 :           _thechar = "|"
473 :        ELSE
474 :           _thechar = _forcode
475 :        ENDIF
476 :        _forcode = .T.
477 :     ELSE
478 :        _forcode = .F.
479 :     ENDIF
480 :
481 :     IF _forcode
482 :        _location  = AT(_thechar, _getstr)
483 :        _width     = LEN(_thechar)
484 :     ELSE
485 :        _location  = IF(EMPTY(AT("+", _getstr)), ;
486 :                       AT("/", _getstr), AT("+", _getstr))
487 :        _width     = 1
488 :     ENDIF
489 :
490 :     _tempback = IF(!EMPTY(_location), SUBSTR(_getstr, 1, ;
491 :                        _location - 1), _getstr)
492 :     _getstr = IF(!EMPTY(_location), SUBSTR(_getstr, ;
493 :                        _location + _width), "")
494 :     RETURN(_tempback)
495 :
496 : ******************
497 :
498 : PROCEDURE Op
499 :
500 :     PARAMETER _something
501 :
502 : ********************
503 :
```

```
504 :  FUNCTION Fill_out
505 :
506 :      PARAMETERS _filla, _fillb
507 :
508 :      * _filla = the string to be filled out
509 :      * _fillb = the Length to fill out the string to
510 :
511 :      IF PCOUNT() = 1
512 :          _fillb = 80
513 :      ELSE
514 :         IF TYPE("_fillb") = "C"
515 :            _fillb = VAL(b)
516 :         ENDIF
517 :         _fillb = IIF(_fillb <= 1, 80, _fillb)
518 :      ENDIF
519 :
520 :      IF _fillb <= LEN(_filla)
521 :         RETURN(_filla)
522 :      ENDIF
523 :      RETURN(LEFT(_filla + SPACE(_fillb - ;
524 :            LEN(_filla)),_fillb))
525 :
526 :  ********************
527 :
528 :  FUNCTION Stripfrom
529 :
530 :      PARAMETERS _stripstr, _what_strp
531 :
532 :      PRIVATE _qaz, _retstr
533 :
534 :      IF PCOUNT() != 2
535 :         RETURN ("")
536 :      ENDIF
537 :
538 :      * _what_strp may be longer than one element
539 :      * for one element, STRTRAN() is as effective
540 :
541 :      _retstr = ""
542 :
543 :      FOR _qaz = 1 TO LEN(_stripstr)
544 :         IF (SUBSTR(_stripstr, _qaz, 1)) $ _what_strp
545 :         ELSE
546 :            _retstr = _retstr + SUBSTR(_stripstr, _qaz, 1)
547 :         ENDIF
548 :      NEXT
549 :      RETURN(_retstr)
550 :
551 :  * End of File
```

We can apply the principles used in counting and reading information from a text file to database generation as well. Here, the format is more stringent and a few rules must be obeyed. First, we have the name of the database that will be created. Next, we will have the individual field items. Eventually, we will have the name of an index followed by an index expression. But how do we know when the field information stops and the indexing information begins? We know because as soon as we start reading in field information, we will begin to see the semicolon. As soon as we stop seeing that special character, we know that the information we have pertains to the index name. After that, the index information will always be paired off until the end-of-file marker is reached.

Looking at the Doit procedure, we can see that the array **data**[] will be created from the THEDATA.TXT text file. If the O_arrays() function returns a logical true (.T.), the array can then be passed to the O_file() function. We will explain the two EXTERNAL commands on lines 30 and 32 in a moment. First let us examine the O_file() function. Notice on line 35 the number of parameters passed to the function, as opposed to the function call, on line 38. As in the previous coding example, we can get two operations out of the same function by testing the value of PCOUNT(); vary the number of parameters to a function and get different results. This is not a bad programming habit since these operations are so similar and cause only a couple of extra lines of code in order to test for each possible condition. It would be bad practice if the same function performed radically different operations based solely on the number and data type of the parameters.

The O_file() function begins on line 83. In essence, the array passed to this function will be read. The name of the file that always appears at the top of the array will be created (line 115) from a structure extended database. This is created (line 99) in the next available work area (line 98). When that database is USEd, the individual field items are looked at. We know that the field elements begin in the second subscript position of the array **_f**[]; therefore, we either continue this FOR...NEXT loop from 2 to the end of the array, or we test to see if the semicolon is missing from the line and immediately jump out of the loop if it is (lines 104 to 106). If we have field information, the line in the array **_f**[] at subscript position **_qaz** is stored to a temporary variable named **_t**. This way we are parsing a temporary variable and not the array. Again looking over the code on lines 108 through 110, the special delimiter that is looked for is the semicolon. Eventually, the name of the field, the data type of the field, the length of the field, and, if applicable, the number of decimal places in the field are all passed to the Ap_it() procedure. This procedure, lines 243 and following, simply appends a blank record to the currently open structure extended database, and REPLACEs the field information in the database.

After the database is created (line 115) from the template, the file is used. From here, we then traverse through the **_f**[] array to potentially create the applicable indexes. Starting at the last position of the **_qaz** variable, we stored the next subscript's value to a variable named **_express**. This should be our index expression. If the data type of the expression is either character, logical, date, or numeric (line 120), we know we have a good index key. At that point, we simply index on the macro of the variable **_express** to the index file specified at the current position in the array **_f**[]. If all is well, we skip two elements to the next potential index name and continue. Now, at this point we must refer to the EXTERNAL commands. Notice in the text file, one of the index keys is built on a call to two functions: Fill_out() and Stripfrom(). Since this was originally in ToolkiT.Lib and since the compiler does not see any reference to these two functions in the actual code, we must make sure that they are brought into the executable file at link time. The way to do this, without making a direct call or with the actual code in the .PRG file (which it is in this case), is to make an EXTERNAL call. This way, when the TYPE() on the variable **_express** is made, one of the expected values will be returned. If either of the functions is not in the compiled application when the TYPE() test is made, the value will be a "UE" for undefined expression or a "U" for simply undefined.

The above program flow is for a call to the function should two parameters be passed to the O_file() function. In the second call, only one parameter is passed. This tells the function to USE the file and not just build it. Looking at this ELSE branch (line 127 and following), we have a similar scenario where the next available work area is selected (line 135) and the file in the first subscript position is then USEd. This time, the field information is skipped and we proceed to the index information. Since Clipper now supports commas in a complex SET INDEX TO expression, we must count the number of potential indexes defined in the array, see if they are all present on the disk, and jump to the ELSEIF branch that matches the number of index files so specified. Taking a look at any of these conditions, notice the complex SET INDEX TO structure from the **_f[]** array that jumps every two subscript positions. This is how the common problem of complex indexing scenarios can be tackled. Eventually, all of the indexes are properly set and the O_file() function will return the numeric value for the work area in which the file is opened.

If we take the STR() of that value and use it like a pointer (lines 38 through 46), we can perform many Clipper operations and functions from the newly created database without ever having to directly USE it, SET INDEX TO it, or SELECT it.

WINDOW GENERATION

The next step, window generation, is slightly different from the previous section. As a matter of fact, the rest of the sections in this chapter relate to this section. Window generation is the simplest, yet the most powerful process. From this point, windows may be created and colors and window definitions may be quickly established for other routines to work from. For example, in Chapter 3 we discussed the concept of relative windowing, in which the text on the screen moves in conjunction with the row and column coordinates of the active window. Here, if we properly create a window, our text files for our menus and reads will work from these text files. First, let's take a look at a typical window text file:

```
********************
* Name      WIN1.TXT
* Author    Stephen J. Straley
* Date      July 15, 1989
* Notice    Copyright (c) 1989 Stephen J. Straley & Associates
*           All Rights Reserved
* Compile   N/A
* Release   Summer '87
* Link      N/A
```

```
* Note     This is the windowing file
*
********************

* this is the format for the windowing file.
* the row; the column; the bottom row; the bottom column;
*     menu type; exploding toggle; color or window; color
*     of letter; color of prompt; color to others;
*     intensity on

 5; 5; 15; 65; COLOR; 3; 1

* End of File
```

Based on the final program example in Chapter 3, it should be obvious that the window will begin at row and column coordinates 5,5 and continue to 15,65. The color of the window will be determined by the value of the variable named **color**, and the type of shadowing will be a 3. Stretch the shadow line beginning at the lower-left corner of the windowed area, and the window will explode. If we were to include the technique of initializing variables outside of the compiler application, we could potentially see another text file with this assignment in it:

```
color = "7/1, 1/7"
```

Looking at this in action, we would get the following:

```
********************
* Name      Makewin.prg
* Author    Stephen J. Straley
* Date      July 15, 1989
* Notice    Copyright (c) 1989 Stephen J. Straley & Associates
*           All Rights Reserved
* Compile   Clipper Makewin -m
* Release   Summer '87
* Link      PLINK86 FI Makewin LIB Clipper LIB Extend;
* Note      This shows the continuation of text file
*           processing which includes variable initialization
*           and window processing.
*
********************

Makevars()
Maketext()
Doit()

*******************

PROCEDURE Doit

CLEAR SCREEN
Getvars("Vars.txt")
```

```
026 : ? color
027 : WAIT "That's the value of color....  any key for window..."
028 : CLEAR SCREEN
029 : SET SCOREBOARD OFF
030 :
031 : O_arrays("DATA", "WINDOW.TXT")
032 : O_window(data)
033 :
034 : @ ROW()+1, COL() + 2 SAY SETCOLOR() GET color
035 : READ
036 :
037 : O_window()
038 :
039 : ******************
040 :
041 : PROCEDURE Makevars
042 :
043 :     EXTERNAL AFILL    && Just to make sure!
044 :
045 :     IF !FILE("VARS.TXT")
046 :        string =          "color = [7/1, 1/7]" + CHR(13)+CHR(10)
047 :        string = string + "scrmono = .F." + CHR(13)+CHR(10)
048 :        string = string + "scr_level = 1" + CHR(13)+CHR(10)
049 :        string = string + "allscreens[20]" + CHR(13)+CHR(10)
050 :        string = string + "allcolor[20]" + CHR(13)+CHR(10)
051 :        string = string + "allwindows[20]" + CHR(13)+CHR(10)
052 :        string = string + "AFILL(allscreens, '')"+CHR(13)+CHR(10)
053 :        string = string + "AFILL(allcolor, '')" + CHR(13)+CHR(10)
054 :        string = string + "AFILL(allwindows, '')"+CHR(13)+CHR(10)
055 :        string = string + "scrframe = CHR(201) + CHR(205) + "
056 :        string = string + "CHR(187) + CHR(186) + CHR(188) + "
057 :        string = string + "CHR(205) + CHR(200) + CHR(186)"
058 :        MEMOWRIT("VARS.TXT", string)
059 :     ENDIF
060 :
061 : ******************
062 :
063 : PROCEDURE Maketext
064 :
065 :     IF !FILE("WINDOW.TXT")
066 :        MEMOWRIT("WINDOW.TXT", "5;5;15;65;COLOR;3;1")
067 :     ENDIF
068 :
069 : * ********************************************
070 : * * The following procedure(s)/function(s) are  *
071 : * * part of Steve Straley's ToolkiT(tm) -       *
072 : * * Release 2, published by Four Seasons       *
073 : * * Publishing Co., Inc.  All Rights Reserved  *
074 : * * Information: 212-599-2141 / 800-662-2278   *
075 : * * All Rights Reserved                        *
076 : * ********************************************
077 :
078 : FUNCTION Wopen
079 :
080 :     PARAMETERS _w1, _w2, _w3, _w4, _w5, _w6, _w7
```

```
081 :
082 :     IF PCOUNT() = 4
083 :         _w5 = SETCOLOR()
084 :         _w6 = 5
085 :         _w7 = 0
086 :     ELSEIF PCOUNT() = 5
087 :         _w6 = 5
088 :         _w7 = 0
089 :     ELSEIF PCOUNT() = 6
090 :         _w7 = 0
091 :     ENDIF
092 :
093 :     allcolor[scr_level]   = _w5
094 :     *
095 :     * Must now calculate the windowed area including
096 :     * the shadow line, if applicable!
097 :     *
098 :     IF _w6 = 3
099 :         _n1 = _w1
100 :         _n2 = _w2
101 :         _n3 = _w3+1
102 :         _n4 = _w4+2
103 :     ELSEIF _w6 = 1
104 :         _n1 = _w1
105 :         _n2 = _w2-2
106 :         _n3 = _w3+1
107 :         _n4 = _w4
108 :     ELSEIF _w6 = 7
109 :         _n1 = _w1-1
110 :         _n2 = _w2-2
111 :         _n3 = _w3
112 :         _n4 = _w4
113 :     ELSEIF _w6 = 9
114 :         _n1 = _w1-1
115 :         _n2 = _w2
116 :         _n3 = _w3
117 :         _n4 = _w4+2
118 :     ELSE
119 :         _n1 = _w1
120 :         _n2 = _w2
121 :         _n3 = _w3
122 :         _n4 = _w4
123 :     ENDIF
124 :
125 :     allscreens[scr_level] = SAVESCREEN(_n1, _n2, _n3, _n4)
126 :     allwindows[scr_level] = TRANSFORM(_n1, "99") + "/" + ;
127 :         TRANSFORM(_n2, "99") + "/" + TRANSFORM(_n3, "99") + ;
128 :         "/" + TRANSFORM(_n4, "99") + "/" + TRANSFORM(_w7, "99")
129 :     allcolor[scr_level] = SETCOLOR()
130 :
131 :     SETCOLOR(_w5)
132 :     scr_level = IF(scr_level = 20, scr_level, scr_level + 1)
133 :
134 :     IF !EMPTY(_w7)  && Exploding Window!
```

```
      Blowup(_w1, _w2, _w3, _w4)
   ENDIF

   @ _w1, _w2, _w3, _w4 BOX SPACE(9)
   @ _w1, _w2, _w3, _w4 BOX SUBSTR(scrframe, 1, 8)

   IF _w6 = 3
      RESTSCREEN(_n3,_w2+2,_n3,_n4, ;
          DULLING(SAVESCREEN(_n3,_w2+2,_n3,_n4)))
      RESTSCREEN(_w1+1,_n4-1,_n3,_n4, ;
          DULLING(SAVESCREEN(_w1+1,_n4-1,_n3,_n4)))
   ELSEIF _w6 = 1
      RESTSCREEN(_n3,_n2,_n3,_w4-1, ;
          DULLING(SAVESCREEN(_n3,_n2,_n3,_w4-1)))
      RESTSCREEN(_n1+1,_n2,_w3+1,_n2+1, ;
          DULLING(SAVESCREEN(_n1+1,_n2,_w3+1,_n2+1)))
   ELSEIF _w6 = 7
      RESTSCREEN(_n1,_n2,_n1,_w4-2, ;
          DULLING(SAVESCREEN(_n1,_n2,_n1,_w4-2)))
      RESTSCREEN(_n1,_n2,_n3-1,_n2+1, ;
          DULLING(SAVESCREEN(_n1,_n2,_n3-1,_n2+1)))
   ELSEIF _w6 = 9
      RESTSCREEN(_n1,_w2+2,_n1,_n4, ;
          DULLING(SAVESCREEN(_n1,_w2+2,_n1,_n4)))
      RESTSCREEN(_n1,_n4-1,_n3-1,_n4, ;
          DULLING(SAVESCREEN(_n1,_n4-1,_n3-1,_n4)))
   ENDIF
   RETURN(scr_level)

*********************

FUNCTION Wclose

   PARAMETERS _w1, _w2, _w3, _w4

   IF PCOUNT() = 4
      _wcol = SETCOLOR()
   ELSEIF PCOUNT() = 0 .OR. PCOUNT() = 1
      IF PCOUNT() = 1
         * This allows a specific window to be closed
         * if the programmer knows this in advance;
         * otherwise, just let the system guess!
         scr_level = _w1 + 1
      ENDIF
      _w1 = VAL(SUBSTR(allwindows[scr_level - 1], 1,  2))
      _w2 = VAL(SUBSTR(allwindows[scr_level - 1], 4,  2))
      _w3 = VAL(SUBSTR(allwindows[scr_level - 1], 7,  2))
      _w4 = VAL(SUBSTR(allwindows[scr_level - 1], 10, 2))
      _w5 = VAL(SUBSTR(allwindows[scr_level - 1], 13, 2))
      IF _w1 = -1
         RESTSCREEN(0,0,24,79, allscreens[scr_level-1] )
         scr_level = IF(scr_level = 1, scr_level, scr_level - 1)
         allscreens[scr_level+1] = ""
```

```
188 :                allcolor[scr_level+1] = ""
189 :                allwindows[scr_level] = ""
190 :                RETURN(.T.)
191 :           ENDIF
192 :       ENDIF
193 :
194 :       IF PCOUNT() != 1
195 :           scr_level = IF(scr_level = 1, scr_level, scr_level - 1)
196 :       ENDIF
197 :
198 :       RESTSCREEN(_w1, _w2, _w3, _w4, allscreens[scr_level])
199 :       SETCOLOR(allcolor[scr_level])
200 :
201 :       allscreens[scr_level+1] = ""
202 :       allcolor[scr_level+1] = ""
203 :       allwindows[scr_level] = ""
204 :       RETURN(.T.)
205 :
206 : *******************
207 :
208 : FUNCTION Dulling
209 :
210 :       PARAMETERS _astring
211 :
212 :       IF TYPE("_astring") != "C"
213 :           RETURN("")
214 :       ENDIF
215 :
216 :       * This function takes a string and returns it
217 :       * with the attribute byte dulled.
218 :
219 :       PRIVATE _qqq, _gstring      && A lonely nite.
220 :
221 :       _gstring = ""
222 :
223 :       FOR _qqq = 1 TO LEN(_astring) STEP 2
224 :           _gstring = _gstring + SUBSTR(_astring, _qqq, 1) + CHR(8)
225 :       NEXT
226 :
227 :       RETURN( _gstring )
228 :
229 : *******************
230 :
231 : FUNCTION Blowup
232 :
233 :       PARAMETERS _blow1, _blow2, _blow3, _blow4
234 :
235 :       IF EMPTY(PCOUNT())
236 :           RETURN(.F.)
237 :       ELSEIF TYPE("_blow1") + TYPE("_blow2") + ;
238 :               TYPE("_blow3") + TYPE("_blow4") != "NNNN"
239 :           RETURN(.F.)
240 :       ENDIF
```

```
241 :
242 :      _seed1  = INT((_blow3 - _blow1) / 2)
243 :      _seed2  = INT((_blow4 - _blow2) / 2)
244 :      _blowt1 = _blow1 + _seed1
245 :      _blowt2 = _blow2 + _seed2
246 :      _blowt3 = _blowt1
247 :      _blowt4 = _blowt2
248 :
249 :      DO WHILE (_blowt1 > _blow1 .AND. _blowt2 > _blow2) ;
250 :         .AND. (_blowt3 < _blow3 .AND. _blowt4 < _blow4)
251 :         @ _blowt1, _blowt2, _blowt3, _blowt4 ;
252 :            BOX SUBSTR(scrframe, 1, 8)
253 :         INKEY(.01)
254 :         SCROLL(_blowt1, _blowt2, _blowt3, _blowt4, 0)
255 :         _blowt1 = _blowt1 - 1
256 :         _blowt2 = _blowt2 - (_seed2 / _seed1)
257 :         _blowt3 = _blowt3 + 1
258 :         _blowt4 = _blowt4 + (_seed2 / _seed1)
259 :      ENDDO
260 :      RETURN(.T.)
261 :
262 : *******************
263 :
264 : FUNCTION O_arrays
265 :
266 :      * This has been modified to NOT allow a master
267 :      * condition as discussed in the ToolkiT -
268 :      * Release 2
269 :
270 :      PARAMETERS _mastar, _thefile, _ismast
271 :
272 :      IF PCOUNT() < 1
273 :         RETURN(.F.)
274 :      ELSEIF PCOUNT() = 1
275 :         IF TYPE("_mastar") != "A"
276 :            RETURN(.F.)
277 :         ENDIF
278 :         _thefile = ""
279 :         _ismast = .F.
280 :      ELSEIF PCOUNT() = 2
281 :         IF TYPE("_mastar") + TYPE("_thefile") != "CC"
282 :            RETURN(.F.)
283 :         ENDIF
284 :         IF !FILE(_thefile)
285 :            RETURN(.F.)
286 :         ENDIF
287 :         _ismast = .F.
288 :      ELSE
289 :         IF TYPE("_mastar") + TYPE("_thefile") + ;
290 :            TYPE("_ismast") != "CCL"
291 :            RETURN(.F.)
292 :         ENDIF
293 :         IF !FILE(_thefile)
294 :            RETURN(.F.)
```

```
295 :          ENDIF
296 :       ENDIF
297 :
298 :       PRIVATE _fhandle, _line, _end, _char, _vals, ;
299 :              _count, _elemn
300 :
301 :       IF TYPE("_thefile") != "C"
302 :          RETURN(.F.)
303 :       ELSEIF !FILE(_thefile)
304 :          RETURN(.F.)
305 :       ENDIF
306 :       _size = O_asize(_thefile)
307 :       IF !EMPTY(_size)
308 :          _name = Parsing(_mastar, ";")
309 :          PUBLIC &_name.[_size]
310 :          AFILL(&_name., "")
311 :          * now fill the array with the elements
312 :          O_asize(_thefile, &_name.)
313 :       ELSE
314 :          RETURN(.F.)
315 :       ENDIF
316 :       RETURN(.T.)
317 :
318 : ********************
319 :
320 : FUNCTION O_asize
321 :
322 :       PARAMETERS _ofile, _array
323 :
324 :       PRIVATE _cnt, _fh
325 :
326 :       IF EMPTY(PCOUNT())
327 :          RETURN(0)
328 :       ELSEIF PCOUNT() = 1
329 :          IF !FILE(_ofile)
330 :             RETURN(0)
331 :          ENDIF
332 :       ELSEIF PCOUNT() = 2
333 :          IF !FILE(_ofile)
334 :             RETURN(0)
335 :          ENDIF
336 :          IF TYPE("_array") != "A"
337 :             RETURN(0)
338 :          ENDIF
339 :       ENDIF
340 :
341 :       _fh = FOPEN(_ofile)
342 :       _end = FSEEK(_fh, 0, 2)
343 :       _line = ""
344 :       _count = 0
345 :       FSEEK(_fh, 0, 0)
346 :       * Originally, this was set to read in only one
347 :       * byte at a time, similar to Getvars/O_vars().
348 :       * Now, we are going to speed this up by reading
```

```
349 :      * in 1K at a time and work that way!
350 :
351 :      _bytes = 1024  && This can be modified to speed it up.
352 :
353 :      DO WHILE .T.
354 :         _char = SPACE(_bytes)
355 :         _exit = FREAD(_fh, @_char, _bytes ) != _bytes
356 :
357 :         *
358 :         * Now add the residue if this has passed through
359 :         * previously.
360 :         *
361 :
362 :         _char = _line + _char
363 :         DO WHILE !EMPTY(_char)
364 :            _line = Parsing(@_char, CHR(13)+CHR(10) )
365 :            IF LEFT(LTRIM(TRIM(_line)), 1) = "*"
366 :               _line = ""
367 :
368 :            ELSEIF "NOTE" = SUBSTR(UPPER(LTRIM(_line)),1,4)
369 :               _line = ""
370 :
371 :            ELSEIF "&&" = SUBSTR(LTRIM(_line), 2, 4)
372 :               _line = ""
373 :
374 :            ELSEIF EMPTY(_line)
375 :               _line = ""
376 :            ELSE
377 :               IF !EMPTY(_char)
378 :                  _count = _count + 1
379 :                  IF PCOUNT() = 2
380 :                     _array[_count] = _line
381 :                  ENDIF
382 :               ENDIF
383 :            ENDIF
384 :         ENDDO
385 :         *
386 :         * If _char is empty and _line is NOT, then _line
387 :         * must be added to char at the top of the loop.
388 :         *
389 :         IF _exit
390 :            * replace EOF marker with null byte
391 :            _line = STRTRAN(_line, CHR(26), "")
392 :            * if there are still characters, write it out.
393 :            IF !EMPTY(_line)
394 :               _count = _count + 1
395 :               IF PCOUNT() = 2
396 :                  _array[_count] = _line
397 :               ENDIF
398 :            ENDIF
399 :            EXIT
400 :         ENDIF
401 :      ENDDO
```

```
402 :    FCLOSE(_fh)
403 :    RETURN(_count)
404 :
405 : ********************
406 :
407 : FUNCTION Parsing
408 :
409 :    PARAMETERS _getstr, _forcode
410 :
411 :    * _getstr is the string to be parsed
412 :    * _forcode is the code that parses.
413 :
414 :    * This function is the string parser.  Basically, return the
415 :    * beginning fragment of a string, adjust the string, and if
416 :    * passed by reference, alter the contents of the original
417 :    * string.
418 :
419 :    PRIVATE _forcode, _location, _tempback, _width
420 :
421 :    IF PCOUNT() = 2
422 :       IF TYPE("_forcode") = "L"
423 :          _thechar = "|"
424 :       ELSE
425 :          _thechar = _forcode
426 :       ENDIF
427 :       _forcode = .T.
428 :    ELSE
429 :       _forcode = .F.
430 :    ENDIF
431 :
432 :    IF _forcode
433 :       _location  = AT(_thechar, _getstr)
434 :       _width     = LEN(_thechar)
435 :    ELSE
436 :       _location  = IF(EMPTY(AT("+", _getstr)), ;
437 :                      AT("/", _getstr), AT("+", _getstr))
438 :       _width     = 1
439 :    ENDIF
440 :
441 :    _tempback = IF(!EMPTY(_location), SUBSTR(_getstr, 1, ;
442 :                          _location - 1), _getstr)
443 :    _getstr   = IF(!EMPTY(_location), SUBSTR(_getstr, ;
444 :                          _location + _width), "")
445 :    RETURN(_tempback)
446 :
447 : ******************
448 :
449 : FUNCTION Getvars
450 :
451 :    PARAMETERS _file
452 :
453 :    PRIVATE _fhandle, _line, _end, _char, _thevar, _theval, ;
454 :            _bytes
```

```
455 :
456 :      _fhandle = FOPEN(_file)
457 :      _line = ""
458 :      _end = FSEEK(_fhandle, 0, 2)
459 :      FSEEK(_fhandle, 0, 0)
460 :      _bytes = 1024
461 :      DO WHILE .T.
462 :        _char = SPACE(_bytes)
463 :        _exit = FREAD(_fhandle, @_char, _bytes) != _bytes
464 :        _char = _line + _char
465 :        DO WHILE !EMPTY(_char)
466 :          _line  = Parsing(@_char, CHR(13)+CHR(10) )
467 :          IF LEFT(LTRIM(TRIM(_line)), 1) = "*"
468 :            _line = ""
469 :
470 :          ELSEIF "NOTE" = SUBSTR(UPPER(LTRIM(_line)),1,4)
471 :            _line = ""
472 :
473 :          ELSEIF "&&" = SUBSTR(LTRIM(_line), 2, 4)
474 :            _line = ""
475 :
476 :          ELSEIF EMPTY(_line)
477 :            _line = ""
478 :
479 :          ELSE
480 :
481 :            O_line(_line)
482 :
483 :          ENDIF
484 :        ENDDO
485 :
486 :        IF _exit
487 :          _line = STRTRAN(_line, CHR(26), "")
488 :          IF !EMPTY(_line)
489 :            O_line(_line)
490 :          ENDIF
491 :          EXIT
492 :        ENDIF
493 :      ENDDO
494 :      FCLOSE(_fhandle)
495 :      RETURN(.T.)
496 :
497 : *******************
498 :
499 : PROCEDURE O_line
500 :
501 :      PARAMETERS _line
502 :
503 :      _thevar = LTRIM(TRIM(Parsing(@_line, "=")))
504 :      _theval = LTRIM(TRIM(_line))
505 :      IF EMPTY(_theval) .AND. !EMPTY(_thevar)
506 :        *
507 :        * test to see if an array
508 :        *
```

```
509 :          IF "["$_thevar .AND. "]"$_thevar
510 :             _tempvar = _thevar
511 :             Parsing(@_tempvar, "[")
512 :             _subscr = VAL(Parsing(@_tempvar, "]"))
513 :             IF !EMPTY(_subscr)
514 :                _isarray = Parsing(@_thevar, "[")
515 :                PUBLIC &_isarray[_subscr]
516 :             ENDIF
517 :          *
518 :          * See if it is a function
519 :          *
520 :          ELSEIF "("$_thevar .AND. ")"$_thevar
521 :             IF TYPE(_thevar) == "UI"
522 :                * Perform function
523 :                OP(&_thevar.)
524 :             ENDIF
525 :          ENDIF
526 :       ELSEIF EMPTY(_thevar) .OR. EMPTY(_line)
527 :          * either side is empty...
528 :       ELSEIF (TYPE(_theval) == "U") .OR. ;
529 :             (TYPE(_theval) == "UE")
530 :          * Missing second quote or bad format
531 :       ELSE
532 :          *
533 :          * Assign the variable
534 :          *
535 :          PUBLIC &_thevar.
536 :          &_thevar. = &_theval.
537 :       ENDIF
538 :
539 : ******************
540 :
541 : FUNCTION O_window
542 :
543 :    PARAMETERS _t
544 :
545 :    IF EMPTY(PCOUNT())
546 :       Wclose()
547 :       RETURN(.T.)
548 :    ENDIF
549 :
550 :    IF TYPE("_t") != "A"
551 :       RETURN(.F.)
552 :    ELSEIF TYPE("_t[1]") != "C"
553 :       RETURN(.F.)
554 :    ENDIF
555 :
556 :    PRIVATE  _tt, _t1, _t2, _t3, _t4, _t5, _t6, _t7
557 :
558 :    _tt = _t[1]
559 :
560 :    * top, left row
561 :    _t1  = VAL(LTRIM(TRIM(Parsing(@_tt, ";"))))
562 :    * top, left column
```

```
563 :      _t2  = VAL(LTRIM(TRIM(Parsing(@_tt, ";"))))
564 :      * bottom, right row
565 :      _t3  = VAL(LTRIM(TRIM(Parsing(@_tt, ";"))))
566 :      * bottom, right column
567 :      _t4  = VAL(LTRIM(TRIM(Parsing(@_tt, ";"))))
568 :      * color
569 :      _t5  = LTRIM(TRIM(Parsing(@_tt, ";")))
570 :      * shadow type
571 :      _t6  = VAL(LTRIM(TRIM(Parsing(@_tt, ";"))))
572 :      * exploding toggle
573 :      _t7  = VAL(LTRIM(TRIM(Parsing(@_tt, ";"))))
574 :
575 :      Wopen(_t1, _t2, _t3, _t4, IF( (TYPE(_t5) != "U"), ;
576 :           &_t5., _t5 ), _t6, _t7)
577 :
578 :      RETURN(.T.)
579 :
580 :   ******************
581 :
582 :   PROCEDURE Op
583 :
584 :      PARAMETERS _dummy
585 :
586 :   * End of File
```

As you can see, not only is the window definition outside of the application, but the variables it refers to it as well. We should also point out that the Getvars() function has been greatly expanded in this example.

Before tackling the function, let us look at the text file that this program will create. On lines 49 through 51, the name of an array with the number of elements is listed, followed by three more lines with direct function calls. Now, looking at the Getvars() function (line 449 and following), we see a new addition. If the variable **_line** is neither a comment nor a blank line, a new call to the O_line() function is made. Skipping to line 499, we can see what this new function entails. The new test being performed on the variable **_line** is to see if the value of the expression is EMPTY(), while the name of the variable is not. Remember, normally an assignment line entails a variable and a value, separated by an equal sign. Parsing out the equal sign, we have two new variables. If there is no equal sign, the element containing the variable information will have something in it (**_thevar**) while the element for the value information will not (**_theval**). If this is true, we then test to see if both the left and right hard brackets are in the string (line 509). If this is true, we then try to determine the VAL() of the contents between the two brackets. If the brackets are for strings, it would be logical to assume that those would appear in the **_theval** and not the **_thevar** variable, and it would be logical to assume that the value of such a string would be 0. Only if an array is being initialized will the VAL() of such a substring be something greater than 0. If this is true, we then take that value, add it to a name of the array, and initialize the array (line 512 through 516).

Now, if the "(" and ")" characters are the contents of the variable **_thevar** and **_theval** is empty, we can also begin to conclude that this is making a call to a function. If that is so, we can try to macro-expand that variable (line 521) and see what TYPE() it yields. If it is equal to a "UI," we can assume that the function's symbol is within the confines of the compiled application, in which case we can simply call it (line 523). Looking back to the text file procedure for this array, we can see on line 43 that we are ensuring that the function AFILL() is in the compiled application because an EXTERNAL call is being made.

Eventually, the window information is parsed and the information is passed to the Wopen() and Wclose() functions. It should be noted at this point that a window will be opened if an array is passed to the O_window() function (line 32) and the pointer for the window is incremented. That window will then be closed when a call to the O_window() function is made without a parameter. Further information on the logistics of the windowing techniques used in this example is given in Chapter 3.

MENU GENERATION

Here we are going to add to the discussion in Chapter 3 involving windowing and window concepts. Before we go any further, you may wish to reread that section before tackling this next step. We use the concept of an array to hold the window information that was read in via the text file processing outlined in the previous few paragraphs. Since the text was read in and the window was established, we have a sense of relevance: future screen positions will be based on the actual screen position of the current and active window. In essence, move a window from one location to another and the associated GETs and PROMPTs will tag along. Using the previous window file as our base, let's look at a possible text file for a menu:

```
********************
* Name      Menu1.txt
* Author    Stephen J. Straley
* Date      July 15, 1989
* Notice    Copyright (c) 1989 Stephen J. Straley & Associates
*           All Rights Reserved
* Compile   N/A
* Release   Summer '87
* Link      N/A
* Note      This is the text file and format for the menu
*           information for text file processing.
*
********************

* Relative row, column coordinates,
* message, display string, and procedure to run.

 2; 3; Chart of Accounts ; Enter COA Information; Chart
 4; 3; Transactions      ; Enter a Transaction ; Trans
 6; 3; Reconciliation    ; Reconcile Transactions ; Recon
```

```
8; 3; End of Period     ; Close a Period ; Close

* End of File
```

Again, notice that the semicolons are the delimiters between the critical information. The screen positions for each prompt are based on the current window position. For example, the first actual menu item that will be displayed occurs at row 2, column 3. However, this is a relative position based on a window that started at coordinates 5,5 to 15,65. This means that the actual screen position for the first PROMPT will be 17,18. However, you need not worry about this because the functions have been properly built to take care of this adjustment for you.

As you can see it is now easy to change the relative position of a menu prompt, the contents of the prompt, and even the message that the prompt will display. There is one additional feature: a pointer to a procedure. With this technology, it is possible to have the same function that displays the prompts call the associated procedure or function. In the above example, the first menu item will, if selected, make a call to the Chart procedure or function. This has dramatic implications as well because extensive DO CASE...ENDCASE statements can be eliminated and menu items quickly reassigned to other procedures or functions. Remember, the existence of a procedure or a function can be tested by simply placing the name of the procedure or function in a TYPE() function. If the results are “UI,” the function exists; any other response should be ignored.

Let’s expand on the previous programming example to reflect our working knowledge of menu text files by looking at a practical example.

```
********************
* Name       Makemens.prg
* Author     Stephen J. Straley
* Date       July 15, 1989
* Notice     Copyright (c) 1989 Stephen J. Straley & Associates
*            All Rights Reserved
* Compile    Clipper Makemens -m
* Release    Summer '87
* Link       PLINK86 FI Makemens LIB Clipper LIB Extend;
* Note       This shows how the menuing system works from
*            the windowing system.  Also, this shows how
*            no CASE statement for the menus and how procedures are
*            called from menus
*
********************

Makevars()
Maketext()
Makemenu()
Doit()

*******************
```

```
023 :
024 : PROCEDURE Doit
025 :
026 : CLEAR SCREEN
027 : Getvars("Vars.txt")
028 : CLEAR SCREEN
029 :
030 : SET SCOREBOARD (scrboard)
031 : SET WRAP (scrwrap)
032 :
033 : O_arrays("DATA", "WINDOW.TXT")
034 : O_arrays("MENU", "MENUS.TXT")
035 : O_window(data)     && Push a window
036 : DO WHILE .T.
037 :     IF EMPTY(O_menu(menu, .T.))
038 :         IF LASTKEY() = 27
039 :             EXIT
040 :         ENDIF
041 :     ENDIF
042 : ENDDO
043 : O_window()          && Pop a window
044 :
045 : *******************
046 :
047 : PROCEDURE Chart
048 :
049 :     @ Wrow(1), Wcol(1) CLEAR TO Wrow(4), Wcol(35)
050 :     @ Wrow(2), Wcol(2) SAY "You picked the item for this"
051 :     @ Wrow(3), Wcol(2) SAY "  Procedure... any key..."
052 :     INKEY(0)
053 :     @ Wrow(1), Wcol(1) CLEAR TO Wrow(4), Wcol(35)
054 :
055 : *******************
056 :
057 : PROCEDURE Makemenu
058 :
059 :     cr = CHR(13) + CHR(10)
060 :     string =            " 2; 3; Chart of Accounts ; " +;
061 :                         "Enter COA Information; Chart" + cr
062 :     string = string + " 4; 3; Transactions       ; " +;
063 :                         "Enter a Transaction ; Trans" + cr
064 :     string = string + " 6; 3; Reconciliation     ; " +;
065 :                         "Reconcile Transactions ; Recon" + cr
066 :     string = string + " 8; 3; End of Period     ; " + ;
067 :                         "Close a Period ; Close"
068 :     MEMOWRIT("MENUS.TXT", string)
069 :
070 : *******************
071 :
072 : PROCEDURE Makevars
073 :
074 :     EXTERNAL AFILL   && Just to make sure!
075 :
076 :     string =              "color = [7/1, 1/7]" + CHR(13)+CHR(10)
```

```
077 :    string = string + "scrmono = .F." + CHR(13)+CHR(10)
078 :    string = string + "scr_level = 1" + CHR(13)+CHR(10)
079 :    string = string + "scrboard = .F." + CHR(13)+CHR(10)
080 :    string = string + "scrwrap = .T." + CHR(13)+CHR(10)
081 :    string = string + "allscreens[20]" + CHR(13)+CHR(10)
082 :    string = string + "allcolor[20]" + CHR(13)+CHR(10)
083 :    string = string + "allwindows[20]" + CHR(13)+CHR(10)
084 :    string = string + "AFILL(allscreens, '')" + CHR(13)+CHR(10)
085 :    string = string + "AFILL(allcolor, '')" + CHR(13)+CHR(10)
086 :    string = string + "AFILL(allwindows, '')" + CHR(13)+CHR(10)
087 :    string = string + "scrframe = CHR(201) + CHR(205) + "
088 :    string = string + "CHR(187) + CHR(186) + CHR(188) + "
089 :    string = string + "CHR(205) + CHR(200) + CHR(186)"
090 :    MEMOWRIT("VARS.TXT", string)
091 :
092 : ********************
093 :
094 : PROCEDURE Maketext
095 :
096 :    IF !FILE("WINDOW.TXT")
097 :       MEMOWRIT("WINDOW.TXT", "5;5;15;65;COLOR;3;1")
098 :    ENDIF
099 :
100 : * ***********************************************
101 : * * The following procedure(s)/function(s) are  *
102 : * * part of Steve Straley's ToolkiT(tm) -        *
103 : * * Release 2, published by Four Seasons         *
104 : * * Publishing Co., Inc.  All Rights Reserved    *
105 : * * Information: 212-599-2141 / 800-662-2278     *
106 : * * All Rights Reserved                          *
107 : * ***********************************************
108 :
109 : FUNCTION Wopen
110 :
111 :    PARAMETERS _w1, _w2, _w3, _w4, _w5, _w6, _w7
112 :
113 :    IF PCOUNT() = 4
114 :       _w5 = SETCOLOR()
115 :       _w6 = 5
116 :       _w7 = 0
117 :    ELSEIF PCOUNT() = 5
118 :       _w6 = 5
119 :       _w7 = 0
120 :    ELSEIF PCOUNT() = 6
121 :       _w7 = 0
122 :    ENDIF
123 :
124 :    allcolor[scr_level]   = _w5
125 :    *
126 :    * Must now calculate the windowed area including
127 :    * the shadow line, if applicable!
128 :    *
129 :    IF _w6 = 3
130 :       _n1 = _w1
```

```
      _n2 = _w2
      _n3 = _w3+1
      _n4 = _w4+2
   ELSEIF _w6 = 1
      _n1 = _w1
      _n2 = _w2-2
      _n3 = _w3+1
      _n4 = _w4
   ELSEIF _w6 = 7
      _n1 = _w1-1
      _n2 = _w2-2
      _n3 = _w3
      _n4 = _w4
   ELSEIF _w6 = 9
      _n1 = _w1-1
      _n2 = _w2
      _n3 = _w3
      _n4 = _w4+2
   ELSE
      _n1 = _w1
      _n2 = _w2
      _n3 = _w3
      _n4 = _w4
   ENDIF

   allscreens[scr_level] = SAVESCREEN(_n1, _n2, _n3, _n4)
   allwindows[scr_level] = TRANSFORM(_n1, "99") + "/" + ;
      TRANSFORM(_n2, "99") + "/" + TRANSFORM(_n3, "99") + ;
      "/" + TRANSFORM(_n4, "99") + "/" + TRANSFORM(_w7, "99")
   allcolor[scr_level] = SETCOLOR()

   SETCOLOR(_w5)
   scr_level = IF(scr_level = 20, scr_level, scr_level + 1)

   IF !EMPTY(_w7)  && Exploding Window!
      Blowup(_w1, _w2, _w3, _w4)
   ENDIF

   @ _w1, _w2, _w3, _w4 BOX SPACE(9)
   @ _w1, _w2, _w3, _w4 BOX SUBSTR(scrframe, 1, 8)

   IF _w6 = 3
      RESTSCREEN(_n3,_w2+2,_n3,_n4, ;
          DULLING(SAVESCREEN(_n3,_w2+2,_n3,_n4)))
      RESTSCREEN(_w1+1,_n4-1,_n3,_n4, ;
          DULLING(SAVESCREEN(_w1+1,_n4-1,_n3,_n4)))
   ELSEIF _w6 = 1
      RESTSCREEN(_n3,_n2,_n3,_w4-1, ;
          DULLING(SAVESCREEN(_n3,_n2,_n3,_w4-1)))
      RESTSCREEN(_n1+1,_n2,_w3+1,_n2+1, ;
          DULLING(SAVESCREEN(_n1+1,_n2,_w3+1,_n2+1)))
   ELSEIF _w6 = 7
      RESTSCREEN(_n1,_n2,_n1,_w4-2, ;
          DULLING(SAVESCREEN(_n1,_n2,_n1,_w4-2)))
```

```
185 :        RESTSCREEN(_n1,_n2,_n3-1,_n2+1, ;
186 :              DULLING(SAVESCREEN(_n1,_n2,_n3-1,_n2+1)))
187 :     ELSEIF _w6 = 9
188 :        RESTSCREEN(_n1,_w2+2,_n1,_n4, ;
189 :              DULLING(SAVESCREEN(_n1,_w2+2,_n1,_n4)))
190 :        RESTSCREEN(_n1,_n4-1,_n3-1,_n4, ;
191 :              DULLING(SAVESCREEN(_n1,_n4-1,_n3-1,_n4)))
192 :     ENDIF
193 :     RETURN(scr_level)
194 :
195 : ********************
196 :
197 : FUNCTION Wclose
198 :
199 :     PARAMETERS _w1, _w2, _w3, _w4
200 :
201 :     IF PCOUNT() = 4
202 :        _wcol = SETCOLOR()
203 :     ELSEIF PCOUNT() = 0 .OR. PCOUNT() = 1
204 :        IF PCOUNT() = 1
205 :           * This allows a specific window to be closed
206 :           * if the programmer knows this in advance;
207 :           * otherwise, just let the system guess!
208 :           scr_level = _w1 + 1
209 :        ENDIF
210 :        _w1 = VAL(SUBSTR(allwindows[scr_level - 1], 1,  2))
211 :        _w2 = VAL(SUBSTR(allwindows[scr_level - 1], 4,  2))
212 :        _w3 = VAL(SUBSTR(allwindows[scr_level - 1], 7,  2))
213 :        _w4 = VAL(SUBSTR(allwindows[scr_level - 1], 10, 2))
214 :        _w5 = VAL(SUBSTR(allwindows[scr_level - 1], 13, 2))
215 :        IF _w1 = -1
216 :           RESTSCREEN(0,0,24,79, allscreens[scr_level-1] )
217 :           scr_level = IF(scr_level = 1, scr_level, ;
218 :                          scr_level - 1)
219 :           allscreens[scr_level+1] = ""
220 :           allcolor[scr_level+1] = ""
221 :           allwindows[scr_level] = ""
222 :           RETURN(.T.)
223 :        ENDIF
224 :     ENDIF
225 :
226 :     IF PCOUNT() != 1
227 :        scr_level = IF(scr_level = 1, scr_level, ;
228 :                       scr_level - 1)
229 :     ENDIF
230 :
231 :     RESTSCREEN(_w1, _w2, _w3, _w4, allscreens[scr_level])
232 :     SETCOLOR(allcolor[scr_level])
233 :
234 :     allscreens[scr_level+1] = ""
235 :     allcolor[scr_level+1] = ""
236 :     allwindows[scr_level] = ""
237 :     RETURN(.T.)
238 :
```

```
239 : ******************
240 :
241 : FUNCTION Dulling
242 :
243 :     PARAMETERS _astring
244 :
245 :     IF TYPE("_astring") != "C"
246 :        RETURN("")
247 :     ENDIF
248 :
249 :     * This function takes a string and returns it
250 :     * with the attribute byte dulled.
251 :
252 :     PRIVATE _qqq, _gstring     && A lonely nite.
253 :
254 :     _gstring = ""
255 :
256 :     FOR _qqq = 1 TO LEN(_astring) STEP 2
257 :        _gstring = _gstring + SUBSTR(_astring, ;
258 :                      _qqq, 1) + CHR(8)
259 :     NEXT
260 :
261 :     RETURN( _gstring )
262 :
263 : ********************
264 :
265 : FUNCTION Blowup
266 :
267 :     PARAMETERS _blow1, _blow2, _blow3, _blow4
268 :
269 :     IF EMPTY(PCOUNT())
270 :        RETURN(.F.)
271 :     ELSEIF TYPE("_blow1") + TYPE("_blow2") + ;
272 :            TYPE("_blow3") + TYPE("_blow4") != "NNNN"
273 :        RETURN(.F.)
274 :     ENDIF
275 :
276 :     _seed1  = INT((_blow3 - _blow1) / 2)
277 :     _seed2  = INT((_blow4 - _blow2) / 2)
278 :     _blowt1 = _blow1 + _seed1
279 :     _blowt2 = _blow2 + _seed2
280 :     _blowt3 = _blowt1
281 :     _blowt4 = _blowt2
282 :
283 :     DO WHILE (_blowt1 > _blow1 .AND. _blowt2 > _blow2) ;
284 :        .AND. (_blowt3 < _blow3 .AND. _blowt4 < _blow4)
285 :        @ _blowt1, _blowt2, _blowt3, _blowt4 ;
286 :           BOX SUBSTR(scrframe, 1, 8)
287 :        INKEY(.01)
288 :        SCROLL(_blowt1, _blowt2, _blowt3, _blowt4, 0)
289 :        _blowt1 = _blowt1 - 1
290 :        _blowt2 = _blowt2 - (_seed2 / _seed1)
291 :        _blowt3 = _blowt3 + 1
292 :        _blowt4 = _blowt4 + (_seed2 / _seed1)
```

```
293 :    ENDDO
294 :    RETURN(.T.)
295 :
296 : *******************
297 :
298 : FUNCTION O_arrays
299 :
300 :    * This has been modified to NOT allow a master
301 :    * condition as discussed in the ToolkiT -
302 :    * Release 2
303 :
304 :    PARAMETERS _mastar, _thefile, _ismast
305 :
306 :    IF PCOUNT() < 1
307 :       RETURN(.F.)
308 :    ELSEIF PCOUNT() = 1
309 :       IF TYPE("_mastar") != "A"
310 :          RETURN(.F.)
311 :       ENDIF
312 :       _thefile = ""
313 :       _ismast = .F.
314 :    ELSEIF PCOUNT() = 2
315 :       IF TYPE("_mastar") + TYPE("_thefile") != "CC"
316 :          RETURN(.F.)
317 :       ENDIF
318 :       IF !FILE(_thefile)
319 :          RETURN(.F.)
320 :       ENDIF
321 :       _ismast = .F.
322 :    ELSE
323 :       IF TYPE("_mastar") + TYPE("_thefile") + ;
324 :          TYPE("_ismast") != "CCL"
325 :          RETURN(.F.)
326 :       ENDIF
327 :       IF !FILE(_thefile)
328 :          RETURN(.F.)
329 :       ENDIF
330 :    ENDIF
331 :
332 :    PRIVATE _fhandle, _line, _end, _char, _vals, ;
333 :            _count, _elemn
334 :
335 :    IF TYPE("_thefile") != "C"
336 :       RETURN(.F.)
337 :    ELSEIF !FILE(_thefile)
338 :       RETURN(.F.)
339 :    ENDIF
340 :    _size = O_asize(_thefile)
341 :    IF !EMPTY(_size)
342 :       _name = Parsing(_mastar, ";")
343 :       PUBLIC &_name.[_size]
344 :       AFILL(&_name., "")
345 :       * now fill the array with the elements
346 :       O_asize(_thefile, &_name.)
```

```
347 :     ELSE
348 :         RETURN(.F.)
349 :     ENDIF
350 :     RETURN(.T.)
351 :
352 : ********************
353 :
354 : FUNCTION O_asize
355 :
356 :     PARAMETERS _ofile, _array
357 :
358 :     PRIVATE _cnt, _fh
359 :
360 :     IF EMPTY(PCOUNT())
361 :         RETURN(0)
362 :     ELSEIF PCOUNT() = 1
363 :         IF !FILE(_ofile)
364 :             RETURN(0)
365 :         ENDIF
366 :     ELSEIF PCOUNT() = 2
367 :         IF !FILE(_ofile)
368 :             RETURN(0)
369 :         ENDIF
370 :         IF TYPE("_array") != "A"
371 :             RETURN(0)
372 :         ENDIF
373 :     ENDIF
374 :
375 :     _fh = FOPEN(_ofile)
376 :     _end = FSEEK(_fh, 0, 2)
377 :     _line = ""
378 :     _count = 0
379 :     FSEEK(_fh, 0, 0)
380 :     * Originally, this was set to read in only one
381 :     * byte at a time, similar to Getvars/O_vars().
382 :     * Now, we are going to speed this up by reading
383 :     * in 1K at a time and work that way!
384 :
385 :     _bytes = 1024   && This can be modified to speed it up
386 :
387 :     DO WHILE .T.
388 :         _char = SPACE(_bytes)
389 :         _exit = FREAD(_fh, @_char, _bytes ) != _bytes
390 :
391 :         *
392 :         * Now add the residue if this has passed through
393 :         * previously.
394 :         *
395 :
396 :         _char = _line + _char
397 :         DO WHILE !EMPTY(_char)
398 :             _line = Parsing(@_char, CHR(13)+CHR(10) )
399 :             IF LEFT(LTRIM(TRIM(_line)), 1) = "*"
400 :                 _line = ""
```

```
401 :
402 :            ELSEIF "NOTE" = SUBSTR(UPPER(LTRIM(_line)),1,4)
403 :                _line = ""
404 :
405 :            ELSEIF "&&" = SUBSTR(LTRIM(_line), 2, 4)
406 :                _line = ""
407 :
408 :            ELSEIF EMPTY(_line)
409 :                _line = ""
410 :            ELSE
411 :                IF !EMPTY(_char)
412 :                    _count = _count + 1
413 :                    IF PCOUNT() = 2
414 :                        _array[_count] = _line
415 :                    ENDIF
416 :                ENDIF
417 :            ENDIF
418 :        ENDDO
419 :        *
420 :        * If _char is empty and _line is NOT, then _line
421 :        * must be added to char at the top of the loop.
422 :        *
423 :        IF _exit
424 :            * replace EOF marker with null byte
425 :            _line = STRTRAN(_line, CHR(26), "")
426 :            * if there are still characters, write it out.
427 :            IF !EMPTY(_line)
428 :                _count = _count + 1
429 :                IF PCOUNT() = 2
430 :                    _array[_count] = _line
431 :                ENDIF
432 :            ENDIF
433 :            EXIT
434 :        ENDIF
435 :    ENDDO
436 :    FCLOSE(_fh)
437 :    RETURN(_count)
438 :
439 : ********************
440 :
441 : FUNCTION Parsing
442 :
443 :    PARAMETERS _getstr, _forcode
444 :
445 :    * _getstr is the string to be parsed
446 :    * _forcode is the code that parses.
447 :
448 :    * This function is the string parser.  Basically,
449 :    * return the beginning fragment of a string, adjust
450 :    * the string, and if passed by reference, alter the
451 :    * contents of the original string.
452 :
453 :    PRIVATE _forcode, _location, _tempback, _width
454 :
```

```
455 :    IF PCOUNT() = 2
456 :       IF TYPE("_forcode") = "L"
457 :          _thechar = "|"
458 :       ELSE
459 :          _thechar = _forcode
460 :       ENDIF
461 :       _forcode = .T.
462 :    ELSE
463 :       _forcode = .F.
464 :    ENDIF
465 :
466 :    IF _forcode
467 :       _location   = AT(_thechar, _getstr)
468 :       _width      = LEN(_thechar)
469 :    ELSE
470 :       _location   = IF(EMPTY(AT("+", _getstr)), ;
471 :                       AT("/", _getstr), AT("+", _getstr))
472 :       _width      = 1
473 :    ENDIF
474 :
475 :    _tempback = IF(!EMPTY(_location), SUBSTR(_getstr, 1, ;
476 :                           _location - 1), _getstr)
477 :    _getstr   = IF(!EMPTY(_location), SUBSTR(_getstr, ;
478 :                           _location + _width), "")
479 :    RETURN(_tempback)
480 :
481 : *******************
482 :
483 : FUNCTION Getvars
484 :
485 :    PARAMETERS _file
486 :
487 :    PRIVATE _fhandle, _line, _end, _char, _thevar, _theval, ;
488 :            _bytes
489 :
490 :    _fhandle = FOPEN(_file)
491 :    _line = ""
492 :    _end = FSEEK(_fhandle, 0, 2)
493 :    FSEEK(_fhandle, 0, 0)
494 :    _bytes = 1024
495 :    DO WHILE .T.
496 :       _char = SPACE(_bytes)
497 :       _exit = FREAD(_fhandle, @_char, _bytes) != _bytes
498 :       _char = _line + _char
499 :       DO WHILE !EMPTY(_char)
500 :          _line   = Parsing(@_char, CHR(13)+CHR(10) )
501 :          IF LEFT(LTRIM(TRIM(_line)), 1) = "*"
502 :             _line = ""
503 :
504 :          ELSEIF "NOTE" = SUBSTR(UPPER(LTRIM(_line)),1,4)
505 :             _line = ""
506 :
507 :          ELSEIF "&&" = SUBSTR(LTRIM(_line), 2, 4)
508 :             _line = ""
```

```
509 :
510 :            ELSEIF EMPTY(_line)
511 :               _line = ""
512 :
513 :            ELSE
514 :
515 :               O_line(_line)
516 :
517 :            ENDIF
518 :         ENDDO
519 :
520 :         IF _exit
521 :            _line = STRTRAN(_line, CHR(26), "")
522 :            IF !EMPTY(_line)
523 :               O_line(_line)
524 :            ENDIF
525 :            EXIT
526 :         ENDIF
527 :      ENDDO
528 :      FCLOSE(_fhandle)
529 :      RETURN(.T.)
530 :
531 : ******************
532 :
533 : PROCEDURE O_line
534 :
535 :      PARAMETERS _line
536 :
537 :      _thevar = LTRIM(TRIM(Parsing(@_line, "=")))
538 :      _theval = LTRIM(TRIM(_line))
539 :      IF EMPTY(_theval) .AND. !EMPTY(_thevar)
540 :         *
541 :         * test to see if an array
542 :         *
543 :         IF "["$_thevar .AND. "]"$_thevar
544 :            _tempvar = _thevar
545 :            Parsing(@_tempvar, "[")
546 :            _subscr = VAL(Parsing(@_tempvar, "]"))
547 :            IF !EMPTY(_subscr)
548 :               _isarray = Parsing(@_thevar, "[")
549 :               PUBLIC &_isarray[_subscr]
550 :            ENDIF
551 :         *
552 :         * See if it is a function
553 :         *
554 :         ELSEIF "("$_thevar .AND. ")"$_thevar
555 :            IF TYPE(_thevar) == "UI"
556 :               * Perform function
557 :               OP(&_thevar.)
558 :            ENDIF
559 :         ENDIF
560 :      ELSEIF EMPTY(_thevar) .OR. EMPTY(_line)
561 :         * either side is empty...
562 :      ELSEIF (TYPE(_theval) == "U") .OR. ;
```

```
563 :             (TYPE(_theval) == "UE")
564 :          * Missing second quote or bad format
565 :       ELSE
566 :          *
567 :          * Assign the variable
568 :          *
569 :          PUBLIC &_thevar.
570 :          &_thevar. = &_theval.
571 :       ENDIF
572 :
573 : ******************
574 :
575 : FUNCTION O_window
576 :
577 :       PARAMETERS _t
578 :
579 :       IF EMPTY(PCOUNT())
580 :          Wclose()
581 :          RETURN(.T.)
582 :       ENDIF
583 :
584 :       IF TYPE("_t") != "A"
585 :          RETURN(.F.)
586 :       ELSEIF TYPE("_t[1]") != "C"
587 :          RETURN(.F.)
588 :       ENDIF
589 :
590 :       PRIVATE  _tt, _t1, _t2, _t3, _t4, _t5, _t6, _t7
591 :
592 :       _tt = _t[1]
593 :
594 :       * top, left row
595 :       _t1  = VAL(LTRIM(TRIM(Parsing(@_tt, ";"))))
596 :       * top, left column
597 :       _t2  = VAL(LTRIM(TRIM(Parsing(@_tt, ";"))))
598 :       * bottom, right row
599 :       _t3  = VAL(LTRIM(TRIM(Parsing(@_tt, ";"))))
600 :       * bottom, right column
601 :       _t4  = VAL(LTRIM(TRIM(Parsing(@_tt, ";"))))
602 :       * color
603 :       _t5  = LTRIM(TRIM(Parsing(@_tt, ";")))
604 :       * shadow type
605 :       _t6  = VAL(LTRIM(TRIM(Parsing(@_tt, ";"))))
606 :       * exploding toggle
607 :       _t7  = VAL(LTRIM(TRIM(Parsing(@_tt, ";"))))
608 :
609 :       Wopen(_t1, _t2, _t3, _t4, IF( (TYPE(_t5) != "U"), ;
610 :             &_t5., _t5 ), _t6, _t7)
611 :
612 :       RETURN(.T.)
613 :
614 : ******************
615 :
616 : PROCEDURE Op
```

```
617 :
618 :    PARAMETERS _dummy
619 :
620 : *******************
621 :
622 : FUNCTION O_menu
623 :
624 :    PARAMETERS _t, _doit
625 :
626 :    IF EMPTY(PCOUNT())
627 :       RETURN("")
628 :    ELSEIF TYPE("_t") != "A"
629 :       RETURN("")
630 :    ENDIF
631 :
632 :    _doit = IF((TYPE("_doit") != "L"), .F., _doit)
633 :
634 :    * If the LEN() of the array is larger than 10, then
635 :    * the for LOOP will be used, otherwise, the hard-coded
636 :    * approach will be toggled.
637 :
638 :    IF LEN(_t) > 10
639 :       FOR _qaz = 1 TO LEN(_t)
640 :          _tt = _t[_qaz]
641 :          _pit()
642 :       NEXT
643 :    ELSE
644 :       _tt = _t[1]
645 :       _pit()
646 :       IF LEN(_t) > 1
647 :          _tt = _t[2]
648 :          _pit()
649 :       ENDIF
650 :       IF LEN(_t) > 2
651 :          _tt = _t[3]
652 :          _pit()
653 :       ENDIF
654 :       IF LEN(_t) > 3
655 :          _tt = _t[4]
656 :          _pit()
657 :       ENDIF
658 :       IF LEN(_t) > 4
659 :          _tt = _t[5]
660 :          _pit()
661 :       ENDIF
662 :       IF LEN(_t) > 5
663 :          _tt = _t[6]
664 :          _pit()
665 :       ENDIF
666 :       IF LEN(_t) > 6
667 :          _tt = _t[7]
668 :          _pit()
669 :       ENDIF
670 :       IF LEN(_t) > 7
```

```
            _tt = _t[8]
            _pit()
         ENDIF
         IF LEN(_t) > 8
            _tt = _t[9]
            _pit()
         ENDIF
         IF LEN(_t) > 9
            _tt = _t[10]
            _pit()
         ENDIF
      ENDIF
      scrcursor = .F.
      SET CURSOR OFF
      MENU TO _tempopt
      SET CURSOR ON
      scrcursor = .T.
      IF EMPTY(_tempopt)
         RETURN("")
      ELSE
         _proc = LTRIM(TRIM(SUBSTR(_t[_tempopt], RAT(";", ;
                    _t[_tempopt])+1)))
         IF _doit
            IF TYPE("&_proc.()") = "UI"
               DO &_proc.
            ELSE
               _proc = ""
            ENDIF
         ELSE
            IF TYPE("&_proc.()") = "UI"
            ELSE
               _proc = ""
            ENDIF
         ENDIF
         RETURN(_proc)
      ENDIF

   ********************

   PROCEDURE _pit

      IF TYPE("allwindows") != "A"
         _trow = 0
         _tcol = 0
      ELSEIF TYPE("scr_level") != "N"
         _trow = 0
         _tcol = 0
      ELSEIF TYPE("allwindows[scr_level]") != "C"
         _trow = 0
         _tcol = 0
      ELSE
         _trow = VAL(LTRIM(SUBSTR(allwindows[scr_level-1],;
                        1, 2)))
         _tcol = VAL(LTRIM(SUBSTR(allwindows[scr_level-1],;
```

```
725 :                       4, 2)))
726 :     ENDIF
727 :
728 :     @ VAL(LTRIM(TRIM(Parsing(@_tt, ";")))) + _trow, ;
729 :       VAL(LTRIM(TRIM(Parsing(@_tt, ";")))) + _tcol ;
730 :       PROMPT Parsing(@_tt, ";") MESSAGE Parsing(_tt, ";")
731 :
732 : ******************
733 :
734 : FUNCTION Wrow
735 :
736 :     PARAMETERS _therow
737 :
738 :     IF scr_level-1 <= 0
739 :        RETURN(0 + IF( PCOUNT()=0, 0, _therow) )
740 :     ELSE
741 :        _base =  VAL(SUBSTR(allwindows[scr_level-1],1, 2))+;
742 :                 IF( PCOUNT()=0, 0, _therow)
743 :        RETURN( _base )
744 :     ENDIF
745 :
746 : ******************
747 :
748 : FUNCTION Wcol
749 :
750 :     PARAMETERS _thecol
751 :
752 :     IF scr_level-1 <= 0
753 :        RETURN(0 + IF( PCOUNT()=0, 0, _thecol) )
754 :     ELSE
755 :        _base = VAL(SUBSTR(allwindows[scr_level - 1],4,2))+;
756 :                IF( PCOUNT()=0, 0, _thecol)
757 :        RETURN( _base )
758 :     ENDIF
759 :
760 : * End of File
```

The only thing that should be noted is that the menuing system is based on the windowing system and that in six lines of code (lines 36 through 42), any number of menu items can be displayed and tested and execution branches can be performed.

DATA ENTRY SCREENS

The final step in this journey involves working with data entry screens. The concepts here are similar to those discussed for menu files: everything may be based on relative windowing. Here is an example of a data entry text file:

```
********************
* Name     Read1.txt
* Author   Stephen J. Straley
```

```
     * Date       July 15, 1989
     * Notice     Copyright (c) 1989 Stephen J. Straley & Associates
     *            All Rights Reserved
     * Compile    N/A
     * Release    Summer '87
     * Link       N/A
     * Note       This is the contents of the data entry file for a
     *            READ command.  It works with the menu and window
     *            system of the text file processing chapter.
     *
     ********************

     * this is the file format for the READ file

     3; 1; Last Name => ; last_name; @!; MUSTFILL(last_name)
     5; 1;      Age => ; age
     7; 1; Birthdate => ; bdate ; ; (bdate < DATE())

     * End of File
```

By now, you should be able to figure out what each of these elements are. The first two pertain to the relative position within the current window for the @...SAY...GET, followed by the SAY expression, the GET expression, the PICTURE string, and the VALID expression.

And again, using the same programming file, we now can expand that procedure called by the menu text file to point to a series of GETs:

```
0001 : ********************
0002 : * Name       Makeall.prg
0003 : * Author     Stephen J. Straley
0004 : * Date       July 15, 1989
0005 : * Notice     Copyright (c) 1989 Stephen J. Straley & Associates
0006 : *            All Rights Reserved
0007 : * Compile    Clipper Makeall -m
0008 : * Release    Summer '87
0009 : * Link       PLINK86 FI Makeall LIB Clipper LIB Extend;
0010 : * Note       This puts it all together except the O_file()
0011 : *            function and database generation.
0012 : *
0013 : ********************
0014 :
0015 : Makevars()
0016 : Maketext()
0017 : Makemenu()
0018 : Makeread()
0019 : Doit()
0020 :
0021 : ********************
0022 :
0023 : PROCEDURE Doit
0024 :
```

```
0025 : CLEAR SCREEN
0026 : Getvars("Vars.txt")
0027 : CLEAR SCREEN
0028 :
0029 : SET SCOREBOARD (scrboard)
0030 : SET WRAP (scrwrap)
0031 :
0032 : O_arrays("DATA", "WINDOW.TXT")
0033 : O_arrays("MENU", "MENUS.TXT")
0034 : O_arrays("READS", "READS.TXT")
0035 : O_window(data)    && Push a window
0036 : DO WHILE .T.
0037 :    IF EMPTY(O_menu(menu, .T.))
0038 :       IF LASTKEY() = 27
0039 :          EXIT
0040 :       ENDIF
0041 :    ENDIF
0042 : ENDDO
0043 : O_window()        && Pop a window
0044 :
0045 : ******************
0046 :
0047 : PROCEDURE Recon
0048 :
0049 :    @ Wrow(1), Wcol(1) CLEAR TO Wrow(8), Wcol(55)
0050 :    O_read(reads)
0051 :    @ Wrow(1), Wcol(1) CLEAR TO Wrow(8), Wcol(55)
0052 :
0053 : ******************
0054 :
0055 : PROCEDURE Chart
0056 :
0057 :    @ Wrow(1), Wcol(1) CLEAR TO Wrow(4), Wcol(35)
0058 :    @ Wrow(2), Wcol(2) SAY "You picked the item for this"
0059 :    @ Wrow(3), Wcol(2) SAY "  Procedure... any key..."
0060 :    INKEY(0)
0061 :    @ Wrow(1), Wcol(1) CLEAR TO Wrow(4), Wcol(35)
0062 :
0063 : ******************
0064 :
0065 : PROCEDURE Makemenu
0066 :
0067 :    cr = CHR(13) + CHR(10)
0068 :    string =          " 2; 3; Chart of Accounts ; " +;
0069 :                      "Enter COA Information; Chart" + cr
0070 :    string = string + " 4; 3; Transactions        ; " +;
0071 :                      "Enter a Transaction ; Trans" + cr
0072 :    string = string + " 6; 3; Reconciliation     ; " +;
0073 :                      "Reconcile Transactions ; Recon" + cr
0074 :    string = string + " 8; 3; End of Period      ; " + ;
0075 :                      "Close a Period ; Close"
0076 :    MEMOWRIT("MENUS.TXT", string)
0077 :
0078 : ******************
```

```

PROCEDURE Makeread

   cr = CHR(13)+CHR(10)
   string =             "4; 1; Last Name => ; last_name; " +;
                        "@!; MUSTFILL(last_name)" + cr
   string = string + "6; 1;        Age => ; age" + cr
   string = string + "8; 1; Birthdate => ; bdate ; ; " +;
                        "(bdate < DATE())"
   MEMOWRIT("READS.TXT", string)

*******************

PROCEDURE Makevars

   EXTERNAL AFILL   && Just to make sure!

   cr = CHR(13)+CHR(10)
   *
   * regular variables
   *
   string =             "color      = [7/1, 1/7]" + cr
   string = string + "scrmono    = .F." + cr
   string = string + "scr_level  = 1" + cr
   string = string + "scrboard   = .F." + cr
   string = string + "scrwrap    = .T." + cr
   string = string + "last_name  = SPACE(20)" + cr
   string = string + "age        = 0" + cr
   string = string + "bdate      = DATE()" + cr
   *
   * array variables
   *
   string = string + "allscreens[20]" + cr
   string = string + "allcolor[20]" + cr
   string = string + "allwindows[20]" + cr
   *
   * functions to perform
   *
   string = string + "AFILL(allscreens, '')" + cr
   string = string + "AFILL(allcolor, '')" + cr
   string = string + "AFILL(allwindows, '')" + cr
   *
   * frames
   *
   string = string + "scrframe = CHR(201) + CHR(205) + "
   string = string + "CHR(187) + CHR(186) + CHR(188) + "
   string = string + "CHR(205) + CHR(200) + CHR(186)"
   MEMOWRIT("VARS.TXT", string)

*******************

PROCEDURE Maketext

   IF !FILE("WINDOW.TXT")
```

```
0133 :        MEMOWRIT("WINDOW.TXT", "5;5;15;65;COLOR;3;1")
0134 :     ENDIF
0135 :
0136 : * ************************************************
0137 : * * The following procedure(s)/function(s) are   *
0138 : * * part of Steve Straley's ToolkiT(tm) -         *
0139 : * * Release 2, published by Four Seasons          *
0140 : * * Publishing Co., Inc.  All Rights Reserved     *
0141 : * * Information: 212-599-2141 / 800-662-2278      *
0142 : * * All Rights Reserved                           *
0143 : * ************************************************
0144 :
0145 : FUNCTION Wopen
0146 :
0147 :     PARAMETERS _w1, _w2, _w3, _w4, _w5, _w6, _w7
0148 :
0149 :     IF PCOUNT() = 4
0150 :         _w5 = SETCOLOR()
0151 :         _w6 = 5
0152 :         _w7 = 0
0153 :     ELSEIF PCOUNT() = 5
0154 :         _w6 = 5
0155 :         _w7 = 0
0156 :     ELSEIF PCOUNT() = 6
0157 :         _w7 = 0
0158 :     ENDIF
0159 :
0160 :     allcolor[scr_level]   = _w5
0161 :     *
0162 :     * Must now calculate the windowed area including
0163 :     * the shadow line, if applicable!
0164 :     *
0165 :     IF _w6 = 3
0166 :         _n1 = _w1
0167 :         _n2 = _w2
0168 :         _n3 = _w3+1
0169 :         _n4 = _w4+2
0170 :     ELSEIF _w6 = 1
0171 :         _n1 = _w1
0172 :         _n2 = _w2-2
0173 :         _n3 = _w3+1
0174 :         _n4 = _w4
0175 :     ELSEIF _w6 = 7
0176 :         _n1 = _w1-1
0177 :         _n2 = _w2-2
0178 :         _n3 = _w3
0179 :         _n4 = _w4
0180 :     ELSEIF _w6 = 9
0181 :         _n1 = _w1-1
0182 :         _n2 = _w2
0183 :         _n3 = _w3
0184 :         _n4 = _w4+2
0185 :     ELSE
0186 :         _n1 = _w1
```

```
0187 :        _n2 = _w2
0188 :        _n3 = _w3
0189 :        _n4 = _w4
0190 :     ENDIF
0191 :
0192 :     allscreens[scr_level] = SAVESCREEN(_n1, _n2, _n3, _n4)
0193 :     allwindows[scr_level] = TRANSFORM(_n1, "99") + "/" + ;
0194 :        TRANSFORM(_n2, "99") + "/" + TRANSFORM(_n3, "99") + ;
0195 :        "/" + TRANSFORM(_n4, "99") + "/" + TRANSFORM(_w7, "99")
0196 :     allcolor[scr_level] = SETCOLOR()
0197 :
0198 :     SETCOLOR(_w5)
0199 :     scr_level = IF(scr_level = 20, scr_level, scr_level + 1)
0200 :
0201 :     IF !EMPTY(_w7)   && Exploding Window!
0202 :        Blowup(_w1, _w2, _w3, _w4)
0203 :     ENDIF
0204 :
0205 :     @ _w1, _w2, _w3, _w4 BOX SPACE(9)
0206 :     @ _w1, _w2, _w3, _w4 BOX SUBSTR(scrframe, 1, 8)
0207 :
0208 :     IF _w6 = 3
0209 :        RESTSCREEN(_n3,_w2+2,_n3,_n4, ;
0210 :            DULLING(SAVESCREEN(_n3,_w2+2,_n3,_n4)))
0211 :        RESTSCREEN(_w1+1,_n4-1,_n3,_n4, ;
0212 :            DULLING(SAVESCREEN(_w1+1,_n4-1,_n3,_n4)))
0213 :     ELSEIF _w6 = 1
0214 :        RESTSCREEN(_n3,_n2,_n3,_w4-1, ;
0215 :            DULLING(SAVESCREEN(_n3,_n2,_n3,_w4-1)))
0216 :        RESTSCREEN(_n1+1,_n2,_w3+1,_n2+1, ;
0217 :            DULLING(SAVESCREEN(_n1+1,_n2,_w3+1,_n2+1)))
0218 :     ELSEIF _w6 = 7
0219 :        RESTSCREEN(_n1,_n2,_n1,_w4-2, ;
0220 :            DULLING(SAVESCREEN(_n1,_n2,_n1,_w4-2)))
0221 :        RESTSCREEN(_n1,_n2,_n3-1,_n2+1, ;
0222 :            DULLING(SAVESCREEN(_n1,_n2,_n3-1,_n2+1)))
0223 :     ELSEIF _w6 = 9
0224 :        RESTSCREEN(_n1,_w2+2,_n1,_n4, ;
0225 :            DULLING(SAVESCREEN(_n1,_w2+2,_n1,_n4)))
0226 :        RESTSCREEN(_n1,_n4-1,_n3-1,_n4, ;
0227 :            DULLING(SAVESCREEN(_n1,_n4-1,_n3-1,_n4)))
0228 :     ENDIF
0229 :     RETURN(scr_level)
0230 :
0231 : ********************
0232 :
0233 : FUNCTION Wclose
0234 :
0235 :     PARAMETERS _w1, _w2, _w3, _w4
0236 :
0237 :     IF PCOUNT() = 4
0238 :        _wcol = SETCOLOR()
0239 :     ELSEIF PCOUNT() = 0 .OR. PCOUNT() = 1
0240 :        IF PCOUNT() = 1
```

```
0241 :              * This allows a specific window to be closed
0242 :              * if the programmer knows this in advance;
0243 :              * otherwise, just let the system guess!
0244 :              scr_level = _w1 + 1
0245 :           ENDIF
0246 :           _w1 = VAL(SUBSTR(allwindows[scr_level - 1], 1,  2))
0247 :           _w2 = VAL(SUBSTR(allwindows[scr_level - 1], 4,  2))
0248 :           _w3 = VAL(SUBSTR(allwindows[scr_level - 1], 7,  2))
0249 :           _w4 = VAL(SUBSTR(allwindows[scr_level - 1], 10, 2))
0250 :           _w5 = VAL(SUBSTR(allwindows[scr_level - 1], 13, 2))
0251 :           IF _w1 = -1
0252 :              RESTSCREEN(0,0,24,79, allscreens[scr_level-1] )
0253 :              scr_level = IF(scr_level = 1, scr_level, ;
0254 :                             scr_level - 1)
0255 :              allscreens[scr_level+1] = ""
0256 :              allcolor[scr_level+1] = ""
0257 :              allwindows[scr_level] = ""
0258 :              RETURN(.T.)
0259 :           ENDIF
0260 :        ENDIF
0261 :
0262 :        IF PCOUNT() != 1
0263 :           scr_level = IF(scr_level = 1, scr_level, ;
0264 :                          scr_level - 1)
0265 :        ENDIF
0266 :
0267 :        RESTSCREEN(_w1, _w2, _w3, _w4, allscreens[scr_level])
0268 :        SETCOLOR(allcolor[scr_level])
0269 :
0270 :        allscreens[scr_level+1] = ""
0271 :        allcolor[scr_level+1] = ""
0272 :        allwindows[scr_level] = ""
0273 :        RETURN(.T.)
0274 :
0275 : ********************
0276 :
0277 : FUNCTION Dulling
0278 :
0279 :        PARAMETERS _astring
0280 :
0281 :        IF TYPE("_astring") != "C"
0282 :           RETURN("")
0283 :        ENDIF
0284 :
0285 :        * This function takes a string and returns it
0286 :        * with the attribute byte dulled.
0287 :
0288 :        PRIVATE _qqq, _gstring     && A lonely nite.
0289 :
0290 :        _gstring = ""
0291 :
0292 :        FOR _qqq = 1 TO LEN(_astring) STEP 2
0293 :           _gstring = _gstring + SUBSTR(_astring, ;
0294 :                      _qqq, 1) + CHR(8)
```

```
0295 :    NEXT
0296 :
0297 :    RETURN( _gstring )
0298 :
0299 : ********************
0300 :
0301 : FUNCTION Blowup
0302 :
0303 :    PARAMETERS _blow1, _blow2, _blow3, _blow4
0304 :
0305 :    IF EMPTY(PCOUNT())
0306 :       RETURN(.F.)
0307 :    ELSEIF TYPE("_blow1") + TYPE("_blow2") + ;
0308 :          TYPE("_blow3") + TYPE("_blow4") != "NNNN"
0309 :       RETURN(.F.)
0310 :    ENDIF
0311 :
0312 :    _seed1  = INT((_blow3 - _blow1) / 2)
0313 :    _seed2  = INT((_blow4 - _blow2) / 2)
0314 :    _blowt1 = _blow1 + _seed1
0315 :    _blowt2 = _blow2 + _seed2
0316 :    _blowt3 = _blowt1
0317 :    _blowt4 = _blowt2
0318 :
0319 :    DO WHILE (_blowt1 > _blow1 .AND. _blowt2 > _blow2) ;
0320 :       .AND. (_blowt3 < _blow3 .AND. _blowt4 < _blow4)
0321 :       @ _blowt1, _blowt2, _blowt3, _blowt4 ;
0322 :          BOX SUBSTR(scrframe, 1, 8)
0323 :       INKEY(.01)
0324 :       SCROLL(_blowt1, _blowt2, _blowt3, _blowt4, 0)
0325 :       _blowt1 = _blowt1 - 1
0326 :       _blowt2 = _blowt2 - (_seed2 / _seed1)
0327 :       _blowt3 = _blowt3 + 1
0328 :       _blowt4 = _blowt4 + (_seed2 / _seed1)
0329 :    ENDDO
0330 :    RETURN(.T.)
0331 :
0332 : ******************
0333 :
0334 : FUNCTION O_arrays
0335 :
0336 :    * This has been modified to NOT allow a master
0337 :    * condition as discussed in the ToolkiT -
0338 :    * Release 2
0339 :
0340 :    PARAMETERS _mastar, _thefile, _ismast
0341 :
0342 :    IF PCOUNT() < 1
0343 :       RETURN(.F.)
0344 :    ELSEIF PCOUNT() = 1
0345 :       IF TYPE("_mastar") != "A"
0346 :          RETURN(.F.)
0347 :       ENDIF
0348 :       _thefile = ""
```

```
0349 :        _ismast = .F.
0350 :     ELSEIF PCOUNT() = 2
0351 :        IF TYPE("_mastar") + TYPE("_thefile") != "CC"
0352 :           RETURN(.F.)
0353 :        ENDIF
0354 :        IF !FILE(_thefile)
0355 :           RETURN(.F.)
0356 :        ENDIF
0357 :        _ismast = .F.
0358 :     ELSE
0359 :        IF TYPE("_mastar") + TYPE("_thefile") + ;
0360 :           TYPE("_ismast") != "CCL"
0361 :           RETURN(.F.)
0362 :        ENDIF
0363 :        IF !FILE(_thefile)
0364 :           RETURN(.F.)
0365 :        ENDIF
0366 :     ENDIF
0367 :
0368 :     PRIVATE _fhandle, _line, _end, _char, _vals, ;
0369 :             _count, _elemn
0370 :
0371 :     IF TYPE("_thefile") != "C"
0372 :        RETURN(.F.)
0373 :     ELSEIF !FILE(_thefile)
0374 :        RETURN(.F.)
0375 :     ENDIF
0376 :     _size = O_asize(_thefile)
0377 :     IF !EMPTY(_size)
0378 :        _name = Parsing(_mastar, ";")
0379 :        PUBLIC &_name.[_size]
0380 :        AFILL(&_name., "")
0381 :        * now fill the array with the elements
0382 :        O_asize(_thefile, &_name.)
0383 :     ELSE
0384 :        RETURN(.F.)
0385 :     ENDIF
0386 :     RETURN(.T.)
0387 :
0388 : ********************
0389 :
0390 : FUNCTION O_asize
0391 :
0392 :     PARAMETERS _ofile, _array
0393 :
0394 :     PRIVATE _cnt, _fh
0395 :
0396 :     IF EMPTY(PCOUNT())
0397 :        RETURN(0)
0398 :     ELSEIF PCOUNT() = 1
0399 :        IF !FILE(_ofile)
0400 :           RETURN(0)
0401 :        ENDIF
0402 :     ELSEIF PCOUNT() = 2
```

```
0403 :        IF !FILE(_ofile)
0404 :            RETURN(0)
0405 :        ENDIF
0406 :        IF TYPE("_array") != "A"
0407 :            RETURN(0)
0408 :        ENDIF
0409 :    ENDIF
0410 :
0411 :    _fh = FOPEN(_ofile)
0412 :    _end = FSEEK(_fh, 0, 2)
0413 :    _line = ""
0414 :    _count = 0
0415 :    FSEEK(_fh, 0, 0)
0416 :    * Originally, this was set to read in only one
0417 :    * byte at a time, similar to Getvars/O_vars().
0418 :    * Now, we are going to speed this up by reading
0419 :    * in 1K at a time and work that way!
0420 :
0421 :    _bytes = 1024   && This can be modified to speed it up
0422 :
0423 :    DO WHILE .T.
0424 :        _char = SPACE(_bytes)
0425 :        _exit = FREAD(_fh, @_char, _bytes ) != _bytes
0426 :
0427 :        *
0428 :        * Now add the residue if this has passed through
0429 :        * previously.
0430 :        *
0431 :
0432 :        _char = _line + _char
0433 :        DO WHILE !EMPTY(_char)
0434 :            _line = Parsing(@_char, CHR(13)+CHR(10) )
0435 :            IF LEFT(LTRIM(TRIM(_line)), 1) = "*"
0436 :                _line = ""
0437 :
0438 :            ELSEIF "NOTE" = SUBSTR(UPPER(LTRIM(_line)),1,4)
0439 :                _line = ""
0440 :
0441 :            ELSEIF "&&" = SUBSTR(LTRIM(_line), 2, 4)
0442 :                _line = ""
0443 :
0444 :            ELSEIF EMPTY(_line)
0445 :                _line = ""
0446 :            ELSE
0447 :                IF !EMPTY(_char)
0448 :                    _count = _count + 1
0449 :                    IF PCOUNT() = 2
0450 :                        _array[_count] = _line
0451 :                    ENDIF
0452 :                ENDIF
0453 :            ENDIF
0454 :        ENDDO
0455 :        *
0456 :        * if _char is empty and _line is NOT, then _line
```

```
0457 :          * must be added to char at the top of the loop
0458 :          *
0459 :          IF _exit
0460 :             * replace EOF marker with null byte
0461 :             _line = STRTRAN(_line, CHR(26), "")
0462 :             * if there are still characters, write it out.
0463 :             IF !EMPTY(_line)
0464 :                _count = _count + 1
0465 :                IF PCOUNT() = 2
0466 :                   _array[_count] = _line
0467 :                ENDIF
0468 :             ENDIF
0469 :             EXIT
0470 :          ENDIF
0471 :       ENDDO
0472 :       FCLOSE(_fh)
0473 :       RETURN(_count)
0474 :
0475 : ********************
0476 :
0477 : FUNCTION Parsing
0478 :
0479 :       PARAMETERS _getstr, _forcode
0480 :
0481 :       * _getstr is the string to be parsed
0482 :       * _forcode is the code that parses.
0483 :
0484 :       * This function is the string parser.  Basically,
0485 :       * return the beginning fragment of a string, adjust
0486 :       * the string, and if passed by reference, alter the
0487 :       * contents of the original string.
0488 :
0489 :       PRIVATE _forcode, _location, _tempback, _width
0490 :
0491 :       IF PCOUNT() = 2
0492 :          IF TYPE("_forcode") = "L"
0493 :             _thechar = "|"
0494 :          ELSE
0495 :             _thechar = _forcode
0496 :          ENDIF
0497 :          _forcode = .T.
0498 :       ELSE
0499 :          _forcode = .F.
0500 :       ENDIF
0501 :
0502 :       IF _forcode
0503 :          _location   = AT(_thechar, _getstr)
0504 :          _width      = LEN(_thechar)
0505 :       ELSE
0506 :          _location   = IF(EMPTY(AT("+", _getstr)), ;
0507 :                          AT("/", _getstr), AT("+", _getstr))
0508 :          _width      = 1
0509 :       ENDIF
0510 :
```

```
0511 :    _tempback = IF(!EMPTY(_location), SUBSTR(_getstr, 1, ;
0512 :                         _location - 1), _getstr)
0513 :    _getstr   = IF(!EMPTY(_location), SUBSTR(_getstr, ;
0514 :                         _location + _width), "")
0515 :    RETURN(_tempback)
0516 :
0517 : ********************
0518 :
0519 : FUNCTION Getvars
0520 :
0521 :    PARAMETERS _file
0522 :
0523 :    PRIVATE _fhandle, _line, _end, _char, _thevar, _theval, ;
0524 :            _bytes
0525 :
0526 :    _fhandle = FOPEN(_file)
0527 :    _line = ""
0528 :    _end = FSEEK(_fhandle, 0, 2)
0529 :    FSEEK(_fhandle, 0, 0)
0530 :    _bytes = 1024
0531 :    DO WHILE .T.
0532 :       _char = SPACE(_bytes)
0533 :       _exit = FREAD(_fhandle, @_char, _bytes) != _bytes
0534 :       _char = _line + _char
0535 :       DO WHILE !EMPTY(_char)
0536 :          _line  = Parsing(@_char, CHR(13)+CHR(10) )
0537 :          IF LEFT(LTRIM(TRIM(_line)), 1) = "*"
0538 :             _line = ""
0539 :
0540 :          ELSEIF "NOTE" = SUBSTR(UPPER(LTRIM(_line)),1,4)
0541 :             _line = ""
0542 :
0543 :          ELSEIF "&&" = SUBSTR(LTRIM(_line), 2, 4)
0544 :             _line = ""
0545 :
0546 :          ELSEIF EMPTY(_line)
0547 :             _line = ""
0548 :
0549 :          ELSE
0550 :
0551 :             O_line(_line)
0552 :
0553 :          ENDIF
0554 :       ENDDO
0555 :
0556 :       IF _exit
0557 :          _line = STRTRAN(_line, CHR(26), "")
0558 :          IF !EMPTY(_line)
0559 :             O_line(_line)
0560 :          ENDIF
0561 :          EXIT
0562 :       ENDIF
0563 :    ENDDO
0564 :    FCLOSE(_fhandle)
```

```
0565 :    RETURN(.T.)
0566 :
0567 : ******************
0568 :
0569 : PROCEDURE O_line
0570 :
0571 :    PARAMETERS _line
0572 :
0573 :    _thevar = LTRIM(TRIM(Parsing(@_line, "=")))
0574 :    _theval = LTRIM(TRIM(_line))
0575 :    IF EMPTY(_theval) .AND. !EMPTY(_thevar)
0576 :       *
0577 :       * test to see if an array
0578 :       *
0579 :       IF "["$_thevar .AND. "]"$_thevar
0580 :          _tempvar = _thevar
0581 :          Parsing(@_tempvar, "[")
0582 :          _subscr = VAL(Parsing(@_tempvar, "]"))
0583 :          IF !EMPTY(_subscr)
0584 :             _isarray = Parsing(@_thevar, "[")
0585 :             PUBLIC &_isarray[_subscr]
0586 :          ENDIF
0587 :       *
0588 :       * See if it is a function
0589 :       *
0590 :       ELSEIF "("$_thevar .AND. ")"$_thevar
0591 :          IF TYPE(_thevar) == "UI"
0592 :             * Perform function
0593 :             OP(&_thevar.)
0594 :          ENDIF
0595 :       ENDIF
0596 :    ELSEIF EMPTY(_thevar) .OR. EMPTY(_line)
0597 :       * either side is empty...
0598 :    ELSEIF (TYPE(_theval) == "U") .OR. ;
0599 :           (TYPE(_theval) == "UE")
0600 :       * Missing second quote or bad format
0601 :    ELSE
0602 :       *
0603 :       * Assign the variable
0604 :       *
0605 :       PUBLIC &_thevar.
0606 :       &_thevar. = &_theval.
0607 :    ENDIF
0608 :
0609 : ******************
0610 :
0611 : FUNCTION O_window
0612 :
0613 :    PARAMETERS _t
0614 :
0615 :    IF EMPTY(PCOUNT())
0616 :       Wclose()
0617 :       RETURN(.T.)
0618 :    ENDIF
```

```
0619 :
0620 :     IF TYPE("_t") != "A"
0621 :        RETURN(.F.)
0622 :     ELSEIF TYPE("_t[1]") != "C"
0623 :        RETURN(.F.)
0624 :     ENDIF
0625 :
0626 :     PRIVATE  _tt, _t1, _t2, _t3, _t4, _t5, _t6, _t7
0627 :
0628 :     _tt = _t[1]
0629 :
0630 :     * top, left row
0631 :     _t1  = VAL(LTRIM(TRIM(Parsing(@_tt, ";"))))
0632 :     * top, left column
0633 :     _t2  = VAL(LTRIM(TRIM(Parsing(@_tt, ";"))))
0634 :     * bottom, right row
0635 :     _t3  = VAL(LTRIM(TRIM(Parsing(@_tt, ";"))))
0636 :     * bottom, right column
0637 :     _t4  = VAL(LTRIM(TRIM(Parsing(@_tt, ";"))))
0638 :     * color
0639 :     _t5  = LTRIM(TRIM(Parsing(@_tt, ";")))
0640 :     * shadow type
0641 :     _t6  = VAL(LTRIM(TRIM(Parsing(@_tt, ";"))))
0642 :     * exploding toggle
0643 :     _t7  = VAL(LTRIM(TRIM(Parsing(@_tt, ";"))))
0644 :
0645 :     Wopen(_t1, _t2, _t3, _t4, IF( (TYPE(_t5) != "U"), ;
0646 :          &_t5., _t5 ), _t6, _t7)
0647 :
0648 :     RETURN(.T.)
0649 :
0650 : ******************
0651 :
0652 : PROCEDURE Op
0653 :
0654 :     PARAMETERS _dummy
0655 :
0656 : ******************
0657 :
0658 : FUNCTION O_menu
0659 :
0660 :     PARAMETERS _t, _doit
0661 :
0662 :     IF EMPTY(PCOUNT())
0663 :        RETURN("")
0664 :     ELSEIF TYPE("_t") != "A"
0665 :        RETURN("")
0666 :     ENDIF
0667 :
0668 :     _doit = IF((TYPE("_doit") != "L"), .F., _doit)
0669 :
0670 :     * If the LEN() of the array is larger than 10, then
0671 :     * the for LOOP will be used, otherwise, the hard-coded
0672 :     * approach will be toggled.
```

```

   IF LEN(_t) > 10
      FOR _qaz = 1 TO LEN(_t)
         _tt = _t[_qaz]
         _pit()
      NEXT
   ELSE
      _tt = _t[1]
      _pit()
      IF LEN(_t) > 1
         _tt = _t[2]
         _pit()
      ENDIF
      IF LEN(_t) > 2
         _tt = _t[3]
         _pit()
      ENDIF
      IF LEN(_t) > 3
         _tt = _t[4]
         _pit()
      ENDIF
      IF LEN(_t) > 4
         _tt = _t[5]
         _pit()
      ENDIF
      IF LEN(_t) > 5
         _tt = _t[6]
         _pit()
      ENDIF
      IF LEN(_t) > 6
         _tt = _t[7]
         _pit()
      ENDIF
      IF LEN(_t) > 7
         _tt = _t[8]
         _pit()
      ENDIF
      IF LEN(_t) > 8
         _tt = _t[9]
         _pit()
      ENDIF
      IF LEN(_t) > 9
         _tt = _t[10]
         _pit()
      ENDIF
   ENDIF
   scrcursor = .F.
   SET CURSOR OFF
   MENU TO _tempopt
   SET CURSOR ON
   scrcursor = .T.
   IF EMPTY(_tempopt)
      RETURN("")
   ELSE
```

```
0727 :          _proc = LTRIM(TRIM(SUBSTR(_t[_tempopt], RAT(";", ;
0728 :                  _t[_tempopt])+1)))
0729 :       IF _doit
0730 :          IF TYPE("&_proc.()") = "UI"
0731 :             DO &_proc.
0732 :          ELSE
0733 :             _proc = ""
0734 :          ENDIF
0735 :       ELSE
0736 :          IF TYPE("&_proc.()") = "UI"
0737 :          ELSE
0738 :             _proc = ""
0739 :          ENDIF
0740 :       ENDIF
0741 :       RETURN(_proc)
0742 :    ENDIF
0743 :
0744 : *******************
0745 :
0746 : PROCEDURE _pit
0747 :
0748 :    IF TYPE("allwindows") != "A"
0749 :       _trow = 0
0750 :       _tcol = 0
0751 :    ELSEIF TYPE("scr_level") != "N"
0752 :       _trow = 0
0753 :       _tcol = 0
0754 :    ELSEIF TYPE("allwindows[scr_level]") != "C"
0755 :       _trow = 0
0756 :       _tcol = 0
0757 :    ELSE
0758 :       _trow = VAL(LTRIM(SUBSTR(allwindows[scr_level-1],;
0759 :                  1, 2)))
0760 :       _tcol = VAL(LTRIM(SUBSTR(allwindows[scr_level-1],;
0761 :                  4, 2)))
0762 :    ENDIF
0763 :
0764 :    @ VAL(LTRIM(TRIM(Parsing(@_tt, ";")))) + _trow, ;
0765 :      VAL(LTRIM(TRIM(Parsing(@_tt, ";")))) + _tcol ;
0766 :      PROMPT Parsing(@_tt, ";") MESSAGE Parsing(_tt, ";")
0767 :
0768 : *******************
0769 :
0770 : FUNCTION Wrow
0771 :
0772 :    PARAMETERS _therow
0773 :
0774 :    IF scr_level-1 <= 0
0775 :       RETURN(0 + IF( PCOUNT()=0, 0, _therow) )
0776 :    ELSE
0777 :       _base = VAL(SUBSTR(allwindows[scr_level-1],1, 2))+;
0778 :                  IF( PCOUNT()=0, 0, _therow)
0779 :       RETURN( _base )
0780 :    ENDIF
```

```
0781 :
0782 : *******************
0783 :
0784 : FUNCTION Wcol
0785 :
0786 :     PARAMETERS _thecol
0787 :
0788 :     IF scr_level-1 <= 0
0789 :         RETURN(0 + IF( PCOUNT()=0, 0, _thecol) )
0790 :     ELSE
0791 :         _base = VAL(SUBSTR(allwindows[scr_level - 1],4,2))+;
0792 :                 IF( PCOUNT()=0, 0, _thecol)
0793 :         RETURN( _base )
0794 :     ENDIF
0795 :
0796 : ******************
0797 :
0798 : FUNCTION O_read
0799 :
0800 :     PARAMETERS _t, _read
0801 :
0802 :     IF EMPTY(PCOUNT())
0803 :         RETURN (.F.)
0804 :     ELSE
0805 :         IF !(TYPE("_t") $ "AC")
0806 :             RETURN(.F.)
0807 :         ENDIF
0808 :     ENDIF
0809 :
0810 :     IF TYPE("_t") = "C"
0811 :         _temp = _t
0812 :         DECLARE _t[Occurence(";", _temp)]
0813 :         FOR _qaz = 1 TO LEN(_t)
0814 :             _t[_qaz] = Parsing(_temp, ";")
0815 :         NEXT
0816 :     ENDIF
0817 :     _read = IF((TYPE("_read") != "N"), 1, _read)
0818 :     IF LEN(_t) >= 30
0819 :         FOR _qaz = 1 TO LEN(_t)
0820 :             _in_the(_t[_qaz])
0821 :         NEXT
0822 :     ELSE
0823 :         _in_the(_t[1])
0824 :         IF LEN(_t) > 1
0825 :             _in_the(_t[2])
0826 :         ENDIF
0827 :         IF LEN(_t) > 2
0828 :             _in_the(_t[3])
0829 :         ENDIF
0830 :         IF LEN(_t) > 3
0831 :             _in_the(_t[4])
0832 :         ENDIF
0833 :         IF LEN(_t) > 4
0834 :             _in_the(_t[5])
```

```
0835 :        ENDIF
0836 :        IF LEN(_t) > 5
0837 :            _in_the(_t[6])
0838 :        ENDIF
0839 :        IF LEN(_t) > 6
0840 :            _in_the(_t[7])
0841 :        ENDIF
0842 :        IF LEN(_t) > 7
0843 :            _in_the(_t[8])
0844 :        ENDIF
0845 :        IF LEN(_t) > 8
0846 :            _in_the(_t[9])
0847 :        ENDIF
0848 :        IF LEN(_t) > 9
0849 :            _in_the(_t[10])
0850 :        ENDIF
0851 :        IF LEN(_t) > 10
0852 :            _in_the(_t[11])
0853 :        ENDIF
0854 :        IF LEN(_t) > 11
0855 :            _in_the(_t[12])
0856 :        ENDIF
0857 :        IF LEN(_t) > 12
0858 :            _in_the(_t[13])
0859 :        ENDIF
0860 :        IF LEN(_t) > 13
0861 :            _in_the(_t[14])
0862 :        ENDIF
0863 :        IF LEN(_t) > 14
0864 :            _in_the(_t[15])
0865 :        ENDIF
0866 :        IF LEN(_t) > 15
0867 :            _in_the(_t[16])
0868 :        ENDIF
0869 :        IF LEN(_t) > 16
0870 :            _in_the(_t[17])
0871 :        ENDIF
0872 :        IF LEN(_t) > 17
0873 :            _in_the(_t[18])
0874 :        ENDIF
0875 :        IF LEN(_t) > 18
0876 :            _in_the(_t[19])
0877 :        ENDIF
0878 :        IF LEN(_t) > 19
0879 :            _in_the(_t[20])
0880 :        ENDIF
0881 :        IF LEN(_t) > 20
0882 :            _in_the(_t[21])
0883 :        ENDIF
0884 :        IF LEN(_t) > 21
0885 :            _in_the(_t[22])
0886 :        ENDIF
0887 :        IF LEN(_t) > 22
0888 :            _in_the(_t[23])
```

```
0889 :          ENDIF
0890 :          IF LEN(_t) > 23
0891 :              _in_the(_t[24])
0892 :          ENDIF
0893 :          IF LEN(_t) > 24
0894 :              _in_the(_t[25])
0895 :          ENDIF
0896 :          IF LEN(_t) > 25
0897 :              _in_the(_t[26])
0898 :          ENDIF
0899 :          IF LEN(_t) > 26
0900 :              _in_the(_t[27])
0901 :          ENDIF
0902 :          IF LEN(_t) > 27
0903 :              _in_the(_t[28])
0904 :          ENDIF
0905 :          IF LEN(_t) > 28
0906 :              _in_the(_t[29])
0907 :          ENDIF
0908 :          IF LEN(_t) > 29
0909 :              _in_the(_t[30])
0910 :          ENDIF
0911 :      ENDIF
0912 :      SET KEY 3 TO Nopage
0913 :      SET KEY 18 TO Nopage
0914 :      scrcursor = .T.
0915 :      SET CURSOR ON
0916 :      IF _read = 1
0917 :          READ
0918 :      ELSEIF _read = 2
0919 :          CLEAR GETS
0920 :      ENDIF
0921 :      SET CURSOR OFF
0922 :      SET KEY 3 TO
0923 :      SET KEY 18 TO
0924 :      scrcursor = .F.
0925 :      IF LASTKEY() = 27
0926 :          RETURN(.F.)
0927 :      ELSE
0928 :          RETURN(UPDATED())
0929 :      ENDIF
0930 :
0931 : ********************
0932 :
0933 : PROCEDURE _in_the
0934 :
0935 :      PARAMETERS _tt
0936 :
0937 :      IF TYPE("allwindows") != "A"
0938 :          _trow = 0
0939 :          _tcol = 0
0940 :      ELSEIF TYPE("scr_level") != "N"
0941 :          _trow = 0
```

```
0942 :         _tcol = 0
0943 :     ELSEIF TYPE("allwindows[scr_level]") != "C"
0944 :         _trow = 0
0945 :         _tcol = 0
0946 :     ELSE
0947 :         _trow = VAL(LTRIM(SUBSTR(allwindows[scr_level-1], 1, 2)))
0948 :         _tcol = VAL(LTRIM(SUBSTR(allwindows[scr_level-1], 4, 2)))
0949 :     ENDIF
0950 :
0951 :     _row = VAL(TRIM(LTRIM(Parsing(@_tt, ";")))) + _trow
0952 :     _col = VAL(TRIM(LTRIM(Parsing(@_tt, ";")))) + _tcol
0953 :     _say = Parsing(@_tt, ";")
0954 :     _get = LTRIM(TRIM(Parsing(@_tt, ";")))
0955 :     _pic = LTRIM(TRIM(Parsing(@_tt, ";")))
0956 :     _val = LTRIM(TRIM(Parsing(@_tt, ";")))
0957 :
0958 :     IF EMPTY(_val)
0959 :         _val = ".T."
0960 :     ENDIF
0961 :
0962 :     IF TYPE(_val) == "U" .OR. TYPE(_val) == "UE"
0963 :         _val = ".T."
0964 :     ENDIF
0965 :
0966 :     IF !EMPTY(_get)
0967 :         IF EMPTY(_pic)
0968 :             @ _row, _col SAY _say GET &_get. VALID &_val.
0969 :         ELSE
0970 :             @ _row, _col SAY _say GET &_get. ;
0971 :                          PICT _pic VALID &_val.
0972 :         ENDIF
0973 :     ELSE
0974 :         IF EMPTY(_pic)
0975 :             @ _row, _col SAY _say
0976 :         ELSE
0977 :             @ _row, _col SAY _say PICT _pic
0978 :         ENDIF
0979 :     ENDIF
0980 :
0981 : ******************
0982 :
0983 : PROCEDURE Nopage
0984 :
0985 :     KEYBOARD ""
0986 :
0987 : *******************
0988 :
0989 : FUNCTION Mustfill
0990 :
0991 :     PARAMETERS _mustfa, _mustfb, _mustfc, _mustfd, _mustfe
0992 :
0993 :     * This is a drastically modified version of this
0994 :     * function from the one in the ToolkiT - Release 2
```

```
0995 :
0996 :     IF EMPTY(PCOUNT())
0997 :        RETURN(.F.)
0998 :     ELSEIF PCOUNT() = 1
0999 :        _mustfb = ROW()
1000 :        _mustfc = COL()+1
1001 :        _mustfd = "This field MUST be filled"
1002 :        _mustfe = .T.
1003 :     ENDIF
1004 :
1005 :     PRIVATE _mustcol
1006 :
1007 :     IF LASTKEY() = 5 .OR. !EMPTY(_mustfa)
1008 :        IF !EMPTY(_mustfd)
1009 :           @ _mustfb, _mustfc SAY SPACE(LEN(_mustfd))
1010 :        ENDIF
1011 :        RETURN(.T.)
1012 :     ELSE
1013 :        IF _mustfe
1014 :           TONE(168.00, 4)
1015 :           TONE(140,00, 1)
1016 :        ENDIF
1017 :        IF !EMPTY(_mustfd)
1018 :           @ _mustfb, _mustfc SAY _mustfd
1019 :        ENDIF
1020 :        RETURN(.F.)
1021 :     ENDIF
1022 :
1023 : ********************
1024 :
1025 : FUNCTION Occurence
1026 :
1027 :     PARAMETERS _astring, _bstring
1028 :
1029 :     PRIVATE _clipper_bug
1030 :
1031 :     _clipper_bug = LEN(_bstring) - ;
1032 :             LEN(STRTRAN(_bstring, _astring,"") )
1033 :     RETURN( INT(_clipper_bug / LEN(_astring)) )
1034 :
1035 : * End of File
```

Before we look at the core sections of the example above, this may appear to require a considerable amount of programming effort to get just one menu, one window, and one data entry screen. It is. However, the same amount of code can handle 10 menus, 20 windows, and even 40 data entry screens. We have built small engines that can handle the various pieces of information that we feed them.

Now let's look at the key points in the example program. As we have demonstrated in the past, user-defined functions can be specified in a text file so long as the definitions for those functions are in the symbol table and, thus, in the compiled application. In this data-entry routine, the text file shows reference to the Mustfill() function, which is defined on lines 989 and following. In addition, the variables that are used in the GET portion of the data entry text file are defined outside the compiled application and are brought in via the Getvars() function. As with the menuing system, the locations for the @...SAY...GET commands are relative to the windowing system and the contents of the SAY portion, or any other portion of the command, can be easily altered. Looking at the menu file, the third prompt points to the Recon procedure, which in turn makes a call to the O_read() function and passes the contents of the data entry array **reads[]** (line 50). The only major point that is new within the O_read() function is the huge IF condition starting on line 824 and concluding on line 910. This was built to circumvent the sluggish behavior of the FOR...NEXT loop. Because of this, if there are over 30 GETS to any one particular data entry screen, the O_read() function will process the array through a conventional FOR...NEXT loop. However, if there are not, the number of elements in the **_t[]** array is then tested for each conditional branch. Keep this in mind: not only will your users dislike the sluggish nature of the data entry screen if the FOR...NEXT loop is performed, but they will be very disgruntled if there are that many data entry items on one screen. Finally, it should be noted that the READ is within the O_read() function and not within the main program.

SUMMARY

There are several conclusions that can be drawn here. First, demonstration packages can be easily created. Second, engines can be built that look at these text files. Third, a preprocessor in Clipper, for Clipper, can now be easily created. Fourth, and perhaps the most important, you will have the beginning steps of the next generation of Clipper programs. Fifth, it is possible to build a complex application with one READ, USE, SELECT, INDEX ON, SET INDEX TO, PROMPT, GET, SAY, and MENU TO command. In this chapter we have given some degree of intelligence to the data. As with DBEDIT(), we can program our usual way, or we can expand our ideas to program in a different fashion. The results are exceptional. Some other issues may enter into the discussion, such as the load time for the text files and the possibility that the end user may ruin them or delete them. Both of these objections are easily overcome. First, there are commercial packages that speed up the time in which files are read into arrays: the FUNCky Library and ToolkiT–Release 2 to name a couple of them. Second, we demonstrated the ability to tag an executable file with information; why not apply the same concepts to text files for this technology as well? Remember, the key to good Clipper programming is a simple five-letter word: think. Consider it a challenge to place code fragments in text files and variable definitions and assignments in text files as well. Invent your own database structure to handle these files. All of this is possible because Clipper has this power.

CHAPTER EIGHT

A C Tutorial for Clipper Users

INTRODUCTION

The C programming language always seems to become part of Clipper discussion, in part because Clipper and the other dBASE compilers are written in C. C is very popular. It is especially popular in the current IBM PC and PC-compatible marketplace, where most commercial software products are written in C, PC Assembler, or a combination of the two.

C has become so popular that many high-level programming products, including Clipper, provide an interface to it. Clipper's own interface to C is called the Extend System, which is discussed in Chapter 10.

Clipper is, however, a stand-alone language that does not require us to know C. Furthermore, Clipper developers keep finding ways to do things in Clipper that C and PC Assembler programmers say can only be done in C or PC Assembler. This is because of the flexibility of Clipper, with its large toolbox and provisions for adding one's own tools.

Given these capabilities, is it really important to know C if you are a Clipper programmer? We believe it is. Since most PC products, including dBASE and Clipper, are based in C, much can be learned about these products, about the fundamentals of PCs, and about computers in general by understanding C.

Furthermore, while a skilled programmer can do an enormous amount with Clipper and user-defined functions in Clipper, there are instances where interfaces to lower-level languages, such as C or PC Assembler, are required. For example, SJS & Associates found it necessary to write C functions callable from Clipper that would allow Clipper programmers to use a popular PC–mainframe communications board.

With C one can go a step further and break away from Clipper to write independent C programs. Programs we might wish to write in C without Clipper are those that must run in a small amount of memory. Such a C program can give you better performance in memory handling because it does not have the overhead of Clipper.

One may also need or wish to write an entire database-handling application in C. We've written such applications for corporate clients who want their programs written in C. In these applications, we have accessed dBASE or Clipper database, index, and memo files in C. Later, we'll introduce C tools, such as Sequiter Software's Code Base, that allow us this access from C to the dBASE and Clipper file formats.

So far we have not mentioned the biggest advantage of C — and current disadvantage of Clipper — which is portability to other computer environments. C is the most portable programming language; dBASE and/or Clipper code, on the other hand, will now only work on a handful of computers. As we go to press, however, Nantucket promises more portable products soon as part of Nantucket Future Technologies.

Not only is the C language itself portable, but so are many C add-on function libraries and other C software tools. With revisions to the low-level routines that interface with particular computer hardware, one can adapt a C application to run on any computer with a C compiler. There are also commercial libraries that provide these low-level interfaces to a particular machine so that we do not have to write them ourselves. For screen management on a VAX, for example, we can use Vermont Creative Software's Windows for C and Windows for Data.

A dBASE and Clipper Learning Bridge to C

The flip side of learning more about dBASE and Clipper from C is that we can use our knowledge of dBASE and Clipper to learn C. Sorting through the components of the C language can be easier for programmers who already know the parallels for these components in dBASE or Clipper. Wading through C's data storage types and classes, program flow control statements, mathematical operators, and function calls is much easier for the dBASE or Clipper swimmer. In addition, we can more easily dive into the deeper parts of the C language: pointers and data structures.

Therefore, our chapters on Clipper and C serve a dual purpose. If a dBASE or Clipper user wants to understand C, it is easier to learn C through a comparative approach, where we show the relationships between Clipper and C. Otherwise, a Clipper software developer can use this part of the text to learn more about Clipper's foundations by viewing its C construction.

Historical Background

The C language was created in 1972, at Bell Laboratories, by Dennis Ritchie. C became immediately popular as a language that could do many programming tasks previously only possible by using Assembler language.

Assembler has the advantage of being "close to the machine" — it allows us to manipulate the hardware of the computer directly, without intermediate steps. It has the disadvantage, however, of being machine dependent — each computer environment must have its own Assembler language. Assembler on an IBM PC, for example, is quite different from Assembler on an IBM mainframe.

C, however, can both be ported to different machines and allows direct access to a computer's hardware. C, like Assembler, addresses the hardware at the most fundamental low level of the machine. Unlike Assembler, however, we can take our C source file to another machine with a C compiler and compile a working program for that other computer.

C's first major role was in a portable operating system at Bell Labs, called UNIX. Before C, operating systems were always coded in Assembler, which meant that they were not portable. C and UNIX both became popular within Bell Labs and at universities, running on a larger and larger variety of machines.

Widespread use of C and UNIX, however, did not occur until nearly a decade after C's invention. In 1978 Brian Kernighan and Dennis Ritchie published the definitive text on the language, *The C Programming Language*, which popularized C outside of Bell Labs and research and academic environments then running UNIX.

It was the advent of microcomputers that really put C in demand. On a microcomputer such as an Apple or IBM PC, memory and disk storage space have been limited as compared to a mainframe. On micros, conserving bytes, whether in memory or disk storage, has been necessary because there haven't been that many bytes to work with.

Since C uses memory and disk storage conservatively, it became a valuable language in the micro environment. Many early PC programs could only be written in Assembler because both memory and disk storage were extremely limited and because C compilers did not yet exist on PCs. Today, most commercial applications on PCs are coded in either C, Assembler, or some combination of both.

All versions of Clipper were created using commercial PC C compilers. Clipper, up until the Summer '87 release, was coded using Lattice C. Lattice C was the standard PC C compiler for several years, until the advent of Microsoft's C compiler. Now Microsoft C, version 5.1, is the standard PC C compiler, with many users also working with Borland's Turbo C compiler, version 2.0. The current Summer '87 version of Clipper is written in Microsoft C version 5.1.

In addition to the technological advances in C compilers, the C language itself has undergone a formal evolution. The American National Standards Institute, or ANSI, created a committee to make the evolution of C a formal one, where changes to the language would be universally accepted. The result is ANSI C, which is the version of C adapted by most compiler manufacturers both on PCs and mainframes. Both Microsoft C 5.1 and Turbo C 2.0 are ANSI C compilers.

Organization of Our Discussion of Clipper and C

Our discussion of Clipper and C is organized into four chapters. Chapter 8 is a tutorial on C for Clipper users. It is meant to complement, not replace, a good book on the C language. Along with our tutorial, there are two books we highly recommend for beginners in C. These are Kernighan and Ritchie's *The C Programming Language, 2d Ed.* (Prentice-Hall), and Hancock's *The C Primer*. The latter is written by English teachers and has many clear, step-by-step examples. Kernighan and Ritchie's book is the classic, revised to include the ANSI changes to the C language.

Chapter 9 is titled "Hands-On C for Clipper Users." Here we've written four sections on how to build a database application. These sections cover four components of such an application: file handling, screen handling, get handling, and full screen, dbedit()-like field editing.

Chapter 10 is called "Interfacing Clipper and C" and has two main sections. The first is on the Extend System, where we show how to call C functions from Clipper. The second explains how to write C functions to access the BIOS to perform many low-level activities in C.

Chapter 11 is "A Cross-Reference Between C and Clipper." Here we go through every Clipper command and function and show how to mimic its functionality in C. We had the most fun writing this chapter.

"HELLO WORLD"

Almost all C books begin with a program that displays the words "Hello World."

In Clipper, a complete program to display the phrase above would be coded:

```
? "Hello World"
```

In C, a complete program to display the phrase above would be coded:

```
#include <stdio.h>

int main()
{
        printf ( "Hello World" ) ;
        return ( 0 ) ;
}
```

To create the dBASE or Clipper display of "Hello World" only one line of code is needed. The code line contains the ? dBASE display command and a text string literal.

To create the C display of "Hello World" six lines of code were used. The C program begins with the C preprocessor statement containing the directive #include. This directive tells the C compiler to include a separate file of instructions when it compiles our source file. After the preprocessor statement, a user-defined function called main() forms the remainder of our C program.

Curly braces are used to mark the beginning and end of all user defined C functions, including this example of main(). Within the curly braces are C statements, each one ending with a semicolon. There are two statements in main(): a function call and a return statement. The function call references printf(), a C standard library function. The library function printf() accomplishes in C what the ? command does in Clipper. In this case it displays the text "Hello World."

The second statement in main is a return() statement. Every C function returns a value, unless we tell it explicitly not to. The function main() returns an integer value. Since main() is always the first function called in a C program, the value is returned to the operating system. In MS-DOS, the return value from main() becomes the value of the ERRORLEVEL environment variable. This value is generally set to 0 when no error occurs.

Certainly the code to create the screen output "Hello World" is more complex in C than in Clipper. The run-time results of the program in terms of memory usage, however, should make the extra effort worthwhile. The Clipper "Hello World" program, using the Summer '87 version of Clipper, requires 150K to run; the C version, using Microsoft C, version 5.1, requires only 11K.

At the time this book went to press, Nantucket had not released Clipper 5.0. With Clipper 5.0, simple programs such as the Clipper "Hello World" program will run in significantly less memory when linked with the Rtlink linker. The size of the Clipper executable program, however, will still not be nearly as small as C executable code for the "Hello World" program.

Compiling in C

The compilers needed to create our C and Clipper run-time versions of "Hello World" are also quite different. To compile the Clipper program, the source module is named hello.prg and the Clipper compiler is installed so that it can be accessed from our current working directory. Then, at the DOS command line, we type

```
Clipper hello.prg
```

If there are no errors in the hello.prg source file, the Clipper compiler will output a file called hello.obj, also referred to as an object or object file.

To compile the C program, the source module is named hello.c and the C compiler is installed so that it can be accessed from our current working directory. Then, at the DOS command line, we enter:

```
cl -c hello.prg
```

The -c command line parameter tells the C compiler not to link the program yet. If there are no compile errors in the hello.c source file, the C compiler will output an object file called hello.obj.

Linking in C

Once the Clipper and C compilers have produced their respective hello.obj files, we need to create a program with these object files. A run-time program is created from a single object file or set of object files through the use of a linker.

To link either our Clipper or C program, we can use a variety of linkers. Because of its flexibility and speed, we are using Microsoft Link version 3.51 in this book for all Clipper and C linking. This is the linker shipped with Microsoft C version 5.1. Readers may wish to use this or some other ANSI C-compatible linker.

To link our Clipper object file, hello.obj, with Microsoft Link, we make the Clipper library, Clipper.lib, accessible to our current working directory. Then, at the DOS command line, we enter:

```
Link hello ,,, Clipper ;
```

To link our C program with Microsoft Link, we need to make the Microsoft C standard library, SLIB*.LIB, accessible to our current working directory. Then, at the DOS command line, we enter:

```
Link /CP:1 hello ,,, ;
```

In both link examples, we specified the name of our object, hello.obj. We left out the filename extension, .obj, because the linker assumes that the object filename will have a .obj extension. In the first link example, we are specifying the hello.obj created by the Clipper compiler. In the second, we are specifying the hello.obj created by the C compiler.

Creating a Program with Another Name

With Microsoft Link we can specify the name of the run-time or executable program if its root filename is different from the root filename of our source code and object files. In this case, we want the name of our executable program to be hello.exe. This is the same root filename as hello.c, our source file, and hello.obj, our object file. If we wanted to specify a different name, we would insert it between the first two commas on the link line. For example:

```
Link hello, hello ,, Clipper ;
```

would create an executable file named **hello.exe**.

```
Link hello, hi ,, Clipper ;
```

would create an executable file named **hi.exe**.

Link Listing Files

With Microsoft Link we can produce an optional list file that gives us details of the linking process. Usually we do not need these details, so we leave out the list file parameter. If, however, we wanted the listing file, we would insert its name between the second and third comma on the link line. For example:

```
Link hello, hi, hi.lst , Clipper ;
```

would create from an object named **hello.obj** an executable file named **hi.exe** and a list file named **hi.lst**.

Linking Libraries

In both cases, we are linking in a library of functions, which is a collection of object files placed in a single file called a *library file*, with a filename extension .lib. The librarian program shipped with Microsoft C and Microsoft's other language products, called lib.exe, allows us to add, subtract, and replace objects in any library file. Borland provides a librarian called tlib.exe with its Turbo language products, such as Turbo C. There are other PC librarians as well, and there are librarians for other operating systems and computers.

When to Supply a Library's Name When Linking

In our first link example, where we are linking a Clipper program, we must explicitly name the Clipper library when linking. This is because our Clipper object file depends on the objects in the Clipper library to create a working program. If the Clipper hello.obj is linked without Clipper.lib, the linker will give us a long list of "unresolved externals." These are the functions referenced in hello.obj for which the linker can't find any source.

The C Standard Library

In the second link example, when linking a Microsoft C program, we do not need to explicitly name the C standard library. This is because the Microsoft C compiler expects that we are going to need to use functions in the standard library and embeds calls to the library into our object file hello.obj. Again, our C object file depends on objects in the C standard library to create a working program. If the linker cannot find the C standard library, it will also display an error list of "unresolved externals."

C's Floating Point Libraries

Another behind-the-scenes library automatically linked to our C program is a machine implementation dependent library called a floating point library. Intel machines optionally use a coprocessor to process large numbers either to the left or right of the decimal point. With the Microsoft C compiler, and most other popular C compilers, we can use the coprocessor if it is in our computer or else emulate what it does if it isn't there. At the time we install the Microsoft C compiler, we are given various default library options. One of these options asks us which floating point math library to use by default. At this time, we can set up the library defaults to use the floating point coprocessor library or the emulator library.

Library Function Management

A library also has the added benefit of controlling the number of objects used by an application. In our "Hello World" program we have a single call to a function or nested set of functions to display "Hello World" on the screen. The linker will pull from the library only those objects that include the screen display function(s) needed. This means that any functions in the library not needed aren't used if the screen display functions are compiled separately from the other, unneeded functions into separate objects placed separately into the library.

Clipper.lib, for proprietary reasons, does not follow the standard rule of placing each function in a library into a separate object file. Clipper.lib is instead a library with hundreds of functions but only a few objects. When we create the run-time program **Hello.exe** using Clipper, we are therefore including a large chunk of the Clipper functions in Clipper.lib, which is why our "Hello World" Clipper program, along with any other Clipper program, requires a minimum of 150K to run.

Microsoft C's libraries do follow the separate function per object rule. When we reference the C function printf() to display "Hello World," we are referencing an object file in the Microsoft C library SLIB*.LIB that contains the printf() function and any functions in turn called by printf(). That is why our "Hello World" C program, linked with the minimum memory allocation option, requires only 11K to run.

Memory

The link option /CP:1 tells the linker to allocate the minimum amount of run-time memory to the run-time C program. Without this option, any C program compiled in a small memory model, such as our "Hello World" program, will use a memory block of 64K at run-time. With /CP:1, we are allocating only the minimum memory the program needs: 11K.

We need to be aware of memory models when working with C on Intel machines using 8086, 8286, or 8386 processors. These machines all run IBM DOS or MS-DOS whether they are compiling and linking stand-alone C programs or using Clipper's Extend System for combining C code with Clipper code. Memory models are used by the compiler and linker to tell the computer where to look for the components of a computer program: code and data. The following table lists memory models used with Microsoft's C 5.1 compiler:

Memory Model	Code	Data	Comments
Small	< 64K	< 64K	
Medium	< 64K	> 64K	
Compact	> 64K	< 64K	
Large	> 64K		Supports arrays of < 64K
Huge	> 64K		Supports arrays of > 64K

Our small "Hello World" program, which is compiled with the small memory model, looks for both code and data within one 64K area, or segment. When a program created on a PC or compatible uses more than 64K of code or data, the computer must know to look outside of the 64K segment for part of the information. Clipper uses more than 64K of both code and data, so we need to use the large memory model when using the Extend System with Clipper.

Clipper programs always use the large model. Clipper code and data must always be assumed to be larger than 64K. The Clipper compiler only creates large model output.

The C Function main()

Every C program must have a function called main(). If we create a C program by creating and compiling a dependent C function with a function or library of functions that already has a main(), we don't need a main(). Clipper already provides us with a main() when we use the Extend System, so we can write Extend System functions without writing another main().

The function main() can appear in the form

```
main()
```

or in the form

```
main ( argc, argv )
int argc ;
char *argv[] ;
```

or in the form

```
main ( argc, argv, env )
int argc#;
char *argv[] ;
char *env[] ;
```

In the second case, there are two variables in parentheses used to process command line arguments to a C program. In the first case, there is nothing in (), and when main() is used in this form, no command line arguments are processed.

In the third case, main() may optionally access the environment variables set at the operating system level. In MS-DOS, these variables are set with the SET command or PATH statements. Later in this chapter there is a detailed discussion on how to parse command line arguments and environmental variables through arguments to main().

Every C function uses curly braces to delimit the beginning and the end. Inside the curly braces, the function does all or part of the program's task. Therefore, in our "Hello World" example, the body of our function main() is set off by curly braces. Within the braces we do the only task of the program, which is to call another function whose job it is to display "Hello World" on the terminal.

In C, we have a built-in function called printf() that seems to work the same way as the dBASE ? command. It is probable that the ? command calls printf() internally. Printf() is provided for us as part of the C standard library and is used by all C compilers on all machines. The above C program will therefore compile and run on any computer.

As a parameter, or argument, to printf(), we pass the literal string "Hello World." As in a Clipper, parameters to C functions are placed inside parentheses, where multiple parameters are comma delimited.

After the printf() function call, there is a semicolon. Every C statement in a C program must end with a semicolon. C is not a line-oriented language; one C statement can span several lines. The following, for example, is perfectly legal, although terrible style:

```
int main()
{
        printf
        ( "Hello World" )
        ;
        return ( 0 ) ;
}
```

Summary of "Hello World"

As we have seen from our "Hello World" example, the language syntax for C is quite different from dBASE or Clipper, even though both dBASE and Clipper are written in C.

However, we will see more of a relationship between Clipper and C subsequently, particularly in our discussions of data types, operators, and control flow statements.

DATA TYPES, VARIABLES, DECLARATIONS, FLOATING POINT, AND DOUBLE PRECISION FLOATING POINT VARIABLES

What Are Data Types?

If the C function printf() can be used in the same way as the Clipper ? command to display a literal string, can we also use it to display a literal number? For example, if we want to display the number 65 on the screen, we write the following Clipper code

```
? 65
```

This works. In C, however, the following will not work:

```
printf ( 65 ) ;   /* will cause compiler barfing */
```

But the following will work:

```
printf ( "%d", 65 ) ; /* the compiler likes this */
```

The added parameter, or argument, in printf(), shown here as "%d", is called a format control string. The control string contains information about what type of C variable we wish to display and how to display it. In this case, the literal number 65 is interpreted by the control string "%d", to mean the decimal value 65. If we had coded the following, the capital letter A would be displayed:

```
printf ( "%c", 65 ) ;
```

The control string "%c", forces the ASCII character value of the literal number 65 to be displayed. This has the same effect on the display of the value 65 as the following Clipper code:

```
? CHR(65)
```

In addition to being picky about how we display our numbers, C demands that we know how big we expect them to be. In Clipper, there is only one data type for numbers of which we are aware: the dBASE standard type numeric. The same Clipper memory variable can be used to handle either the number 65 or the number 65,1234,8766.12. In C, however, this is not the case. In C there are different numeric data types for different types and sizes of numbers. All of these types can be used in our C program.

The C data types on a machine using an Intel processor (PC/XT/AT/386,PS2) are shown in the following table.

Name of Data Type	Alternate Names	Range of Values that Type Can Store	Storage in Bytes
char	signed char	-128 to 127	1 byte
unsigned char	None	0 to 255	1 byte
int	signed signed int	-32,768 to 32,767	2 bytes
unsigned int	unsigned	0 to 65,535	2 bytes
short	short int signed short signed short int	-32,768 to 32,767	2 bytes
unsigned short	unsigned short unsigned short int	0 to 65,535	2 bytes
long	long int signed long signed long int	-2,147,483,648 to 2,147,483,647	4 bytes
unsigned long	unsigned long int	0 to 4,294,967,295	4 bytes
enum	None	0 to 65,535	2 bytes
float	None	Approximately 1.7E-308 to 1.7E+308 (7-digit precision)	4 bytes
double	None	Approximately 1.7E-308 to 1.7E+308 (15-digit precision)	4 bytes
long double	None	Approximately 1.7E-308 to 1.7E+308 (15-digit precision)	4 bytes

Since Clipper is written in C, Clipper's numeric data type is really one or more of the types from the table. This means that when we write an application using Clipper's numeric data type, we are working with one or more of C's numeric types.

Which C numeric type Clipper uses is transparent to us. In Clipper, we only worry about numeric precision when we do operations with real numbers. Clipper then gives us commands such as SET DECIMALS and functions such as ROUND and PICTURE for achieving the precision we desire in an application.

In C, however, the programmer is responsible for what data type is used and how to present it. From the available types, the programmer determines what C data type is best suited for a particular task.

For example, suppose we need to create the smallest possible program. It is a given that the largest calculated number in this program will be 300. What data type should be used? From among the available numeric types in C, we find that the data will not fit into a char or an unsigned char but will fit into an integer. In another program, it is a given that the largest calculated value a variable will hold will be 9,000,000.99. In this case, we will not be able to use anything smaller than a double.

Working with Variables

There are many flexible ways in C to manipulate and present data once you figure out what data type to use. Usually, when working with numeric expressions in Clipper, a literal numeric expression or database numeric field is STOREd to a memory variable. Later, the memory variable may be manipulated and displayed. A basic Clipper example might look something like this:

```
CodeName = 65
? CodeName
```

In a C program, you can similarly store literal numeric expressions in a variable. The C code that gives us the same output as our Clipper example above looks like this:

```
#include <stdio.h>

main()
{
      char CodeName = 65 ;
      printf ( "%d", CodeName ) ;
}
```

The previous C code could also be written:

```
#include <stdio.h>

main()
{
      char CodeName ;
      CodeName = 65 ;
      printf ( "%d", CodeName ) ;
}
```

Declaring Variables

The two previous examples in C assign numbers to a variable, illustrating an important point. In Clipper, variables appear to be available on the fly. They can be created and assigned a value anywhere in an application with the STORE or = commands.

In C, variables must all be made known to the compiler first and then assigned a value. The process of making the variable known to the compiler is called *declaring* the variable. All C variables must be declared. After the variables are declared, they may be assigned a value and used in C statements. In Clipper, the following is a perfectly legal program:

```
? CodeName  = 65
```

In C, the following is quite wrong:

```
#include <stdio.h>

int main()
{
printf ( "%d", int codename = 65 ) ;
}
```

In C the legal ways to write this are:

```
#include <stdio.h>

int main()
{
int codename ;

printf ( "%d", codename = 65 ) ; /* value assigned in statement */
}
```

or:

```
#include <stdio.h>

int main()
{
int codename = 65 ; /* variable initialized with a value */

printf ( "%d", codename ) ;
}
```

In the last case the variable appears to be given a value as it is declared. What really occurs, however, is that the variable is declared first and then given a value immediately afterward.

The following C code is also not legal:

```
#include <stdio.h>

int main()
{
char codename1 = 65 ; /* variable initialized with a value */
printf ( "%d", codename1 ) ;
char codename2 = 66 ;
printf ( "%d", codename2 ) ;
}
```

The following Clipper code will compile cleanly, however:

```
codename1 = 65
? codename1
codename2 = 66
? codename2
```

The C code would need to look as follows, with all the declarations at the start of the function:

```
int main()
{
char codename1 = 65 ;
char codename2 = 66 ; /* all variables local to a function are
                         declared at the beginning of the
                         function */

printf ( "%d", codename1 ) ;
printf ( "%d", codename2 ) ;
}
```

The Clipper STORE Command, C Declarations, and Dynamic Allocation of Space

Why do we need to set up variables in a different way in C then in Clipper? The answer lies in understanding why variables need to be declared in C and what Clipper does when we use a new memory variable with the STORE or = commands.

Declaring variables in C tells the compiler how much room to give each one. The variables codename1 and codename2 were each declared to be of type char, which makes them 1 byte long, with a signed bit. According to our table above, the variables codename1 and codename2 can hold numeric values of -128 to 127.

Suppose we know we'll need a lot of variables in our program but don't know how many. These variables may need to hold strings or arrays of data, but we don't know right away how big the strings or arrays will need to be.

C provides an alternative to fixed declarations of variables with a technique called dynamic allocation of space. With it, we can declare a pointer — a variable representing an address — to hold a block of memory. We can then use this memory for different purposes as our application is running.

The technique of dynamic space allocation is used by Clipper in its STORE OR = commands. Clipper declares pointers and allocates memory to them behind the scenes. These pointers are then made to point to memory variables as we need them. The appearance is that we are declaring memory variables in Clipper on the fly. In reality they have already been declared as pointers and allocated storage.

Later in this chapter we discuss dynamic allocation of space. We mention it here to introduce the relationship of Clipper and C declared variables. To understand how dynamic allocation of space works requires a solid knowledge of C pointers.

Working with Floating Point and Double Precision Floating Point Variables

When working with types float and double in C on a PC or PC-compatible, we have to take into account the way the Intel processor handles floating point numbers. In addition to linking with the proper floating point library to calculate these numbers, we also must set up our C source file to handle these numbers in a special way. C provides us with a convention for doing this, which is to include the following preprocessor statement at the top of our source file:

```
# include <math.h>
```

Math.h, like stdio.h, is a standard include file provided by every C compiler manufacturer. Math.h contains instructions, in the form of proprecessor definitions and macros, to handle the overhead involved when working with floating point numbers in C.

Here is a typical C source file that uses floating point numbers:

```
#include <stdio.h>  /* standard input and output header file */
#include <math.h>   /* math floating point header file */

main()
{
     double SkysTheLimit, HowMuchIsALot = 100000000.00 ;

     SkysTheLimit = pow ( HowMuchIsALot, 2.00 ) ;
     printf ( "Money not from this book= $%.2lf",SkysTheLimit) ;
}
```

In the above example, we declared two variables on one line with the use of a comma to separate them. Our first variable, **HowMuchIsALot**, is declared and assigned a value. Our second variable, **SkysTheLimit**, is declared without having a value assigned to it. Its value will be assigned in the next C statement.

As in Clipper, we can assign a value to a variable in C with the return value from a function. The double **SkysTheLimit** is assigned the return value of the standard C library function **pow()**, which returns a number raised to a power.

The number to be raised, **HowMuchIsALot**, is the first argument used in pow(), and the power to raise it to, our literal 2.00, is the second argument. We used the literal 2.00 and not 2 because the function expects the second argument to be a double, which is a floating point type.

Note the use of the control string "%.2lf" in the above example of the function printf(). "lf" (ell eff) indicates that the number is a double, sometimes referred to as a **l**ong **f**loat. ".2" is the number of decimal places we wish to display, also called the precision specifier. We could have also used "%2.2lf," which would have displayed two whole numbers and two decimal places. The number of specified whole places in the printf() statement is termed the width specifier.

Printf() Function Syntax

The above example follows the general form of the printf() control string for display of a number, which is:

```
"%[<width>][.][<precision>]<control type>,<argument list>"
```

The printf() control type is derived from the following table:

Name of Data Type	Possible Printf Control Type	Output
signed char	d	Decimal Value
	x	Hex Value
	c	Character Value*
unsigned char	ud	Decimal Value
	ux	Hex Value
	uc	Character Value*
signed int	d	Decimal Value
	x	Hex Value
	c	Character Value*

Name of Data Type	Possible Printf Control Type	Output
unsigned int	ud	Decimal Value
	ux	Hex Value
	uc	Character Value*
signed long	ld	Decimal Value
	lx	Hex Value
float	f.<dec places>	Floating Point Value
double	lf.<dec places>	Double Precision Floating Point Value

The asterisks (*) indicate that on an IBM PC or compatible ASCII characters meant for display range from decimal 32 to decimal 255. Values greater than 127 comprise graphic or special character symbols in the PC's Extended Character Set. On machines other than IBM PCs and compatibles, characters displayed with ASCII values greater than 127 may be undefined or defined differently. However, ASCII values less than or equal to 127 will have the same character display on any computer using the ASCII character set.

Mathematical Operators

To manipulate the numeric data we have discussed, there are a host of C mathematical operators. dBASE III and Clipper share the following fundamental operators with C:

Operator	Meaning
=	assignment
+	addition
-	subtraction
/	division
()	grouping

The dBASE and Clipper exponent operators, ** and ^, do not exist in C as operators. To calculate exponents in C, we multiply two of the same numbers together or use the standard library raise-to-power-of function pow(), of which we saw an example earlier.

Clipper, in the August '86 release, included the following popular C operator:

```
% modulus
```

The modulus operator is used to calculate remainders such as

```
5 % 2
```

which yields a remainder of 1.

C's Increment and Decrement Operators

In addition to the mathematical operators above, C also provides some other interesting operators. These operators are not included with Clipper, nor do they exist in dBASE. Most valuable among them are the increment and decrement operators where ++ increments and – – decrements a variable. Using the increment operator, instead of writing:

```
count = count+1 ;
```

to increment a variable, we can write

```
count++ ;
```

Similarly, instead of writing

```
count = count-1 ;
```

to decrement a variable, we can write

```
count--;
```

The increment operator can be nicely nested in function calls as well, as in the following source file:

```
#include <stdio.h>

main()
{
      int count = 0 ;
      printf ( "%d" , count++ ) ;
      printf ( "%d" , count++ ) ;
      printf ( "%d" , count++ ) ;
      printf ( "%d" , count++ ) ;
      printf ( "%d" , count++ ) ;
      printf ( "%d" , count++ ) ;
}
```

If we compile, link, and run this sample, we get the output:

```
01235
```

Note: Care should be taken when nesting increment or decrement operations because side effects can occur when a C expression is evaluated by different C compilers.

A more common use of nested increment and decrement operations using the C increment or decrement operators is in loops. For now, we'll introduce a C while loop as being analogous to a Clipper DO WHILE loop, although there are differences in syntax. Using a DO WHILE, the following code might be used in Clipper to decrement a variable in a loop:

```
count = 5
DO WHILE (count != 0 )
     count = count -1
ENDDO
```

Using a C while loop, the code could be written:

```
#include <stdio.h>
main()
{
     int count = 5 ;
     while (count--) ;
}
```

In the C example, the loop could be simplified by taking advantage of the C decrement operator. The decrement operator subtracts 1 from the variable count each subsequent time through the loop. The initial value of count is 5, and each subsequent time through the loop, count is decremented by 1.

Not only does the while loop look simpler, but it executes faster. The execution is speeded because the decrement instruction count– – takes fewer machine steps to process than does count = count –1, which assigns a variable to the same variable minus 1.

In C we can also use the increment and decrement operators to preincrement and predecrement a number. To do this, instead of writing count– –, we would write – –count. Our C, example would then be rewritten:

```
#include <stdio.h>
main()
{
     int count = 5 ;
     while (--count) ;
}
```

By predecrementing count, the while loop executes one less time. This is because the value of **count** is 4, not 5, when the loop is started.

Assignment Operators

What if we wanted to decrement the variable **count** by 5, instead of 1, each time through the loop? No problem. With one of C's assignment operators, we would rewrite our example as follows:

```
#include <stdio.h>
main()
{
      int count = 5 ;
      while (count-=5) ; /* this loop will only execute once */
}
```

The assignment operator –= is used to decrement count by 5. Instead of writing count = count–5, we can more simply and efficiently write count–=5. We may wish to use C's other assignment operators as well. They are:

Operator	Meaning
=	Equality
+=	Addition equality
–=	Subtraction equality
*=	Multiplication equality
/=	Division equality
%=	Modulus equality

Bitwise Operators

C also provides us with a handsome set of bitwise operators. These operators allow us to change the value of a variable by adjusting its individual bits. Bitwise operations on variables are not something we can presently do in Clipper. Bitwise operations are often used, however, in C. C's bitwise operators are explained in the following list:

One's Complement Operator. This operator changes the bit pattern of a variable so that all binary 0s are changed to binary 1s and all binary 1s are change to binary 0s. In the following code, the original value of num is 0, where all bits in num are off:

```
unsigned char num = 0 ;
printf ( "%d\n", num ) ;
```

The displayed value will be –1, where all bits in num are on.

Bit Shift Operators << and >>. These operators shift bits in a binary string. << shifts bits to the left and >> shifts bits to the right.

Bitwise AND Operator &. This operator is used to find the logical product of operands. When 2 bits are ANDed, the result is 0 unless both bits are 1s.

Bitwise OR Operator |. This operator is used to find the logical sum of operands. When 2 bits are ORed, the result is 0 unless one or both of the original bits are 1s.

Bitwise XOR Operator ^. This operator is also called the EXCLUSIVE-OR operator. When a bit is XORed with a 1, its value is inverted.

Bitwise Equality Operators. C provides the following variations on the above operators so that we can do bitwise equality operations:

Operator	Meaning
&=	Bitwise and equality
^=	Bitwise equality
|=	Bitwise or equality
<<=	Bitwise left shift equality
>>=	Bitwise right shift equality

Summary on the Subject of Operators

So far we've toured a wide range of operators. All of the Clipper and C operators have been covered except for the logical operators in both languages. These will be explored at length in the section "Control Flow Statements."

Clipper has a mathematical operator that is not available in C, the exponent operator **. The other form of the exponent operator, ^, is also a C operator, but the C ^ operator performs an EXCLUSIVE-OR, not exponentiation.

C has a host of mathematical operators that are not available, at least yet, in Clipper. It's fair to say not yet because with each new release of Clipper, more C operators appear in the language.

Now that we have discussed the operators available to us in both languages, it's time to move on to see how they are used in mathematical expressions.

Order of Precedence

In expressions involving operations with variables, it is vital to know the order of precedence. This is the order in which variables in the expression are evaluated. What, for instance, is the run-time result of this C program?

```
#include <stdio.h>

int main()
{
int a = 1, b = 2, c = 3 ;
```

```
a = b+= 5 * c + a ;
printf ( "%d\n", a ) ;
}
```

The answer is ascertained from fixed rules followed by every C compiler. These rules cover the order of precedence and associativity of operators and are listed in the following table:

<table>
<tr><th>Operators</th><th>Associativity</th></tr>
<tr><td>() [] -> .</td><td>Left to right</td></tr>
<tr><td>! ++ -- + - * & (type) sizeof</td><td>Right to left</td></tr>
<tr><td>* / %</td><td>Left to right</td></tr>
<tr><td>+ -</td><td>Left to right</td></tr>
<tr><td><< >></td><td>Left to right</td></tr>
<tr><td>< <= > >=</td><td>Left to right</td></tr>
<tr><td>== !=</td><td>Left to right</td></tr>
<tr><td>&</td><td>Left to right</td></tr>
<tr><td>^</td><td>Left to right</td></tr>
<tr><td>|</td><td>Left to right</td></tr>
<tr><td>&&</td><td>Left to right</td></tr>
<tr><td>||</td><td>Left to right</td></tr>
<tr><td>?:</td><td>Right to left</td></tr>
<tr><td>= += -= *= /= %= &= ^= |= <<= >>=</td><td>Right to left</td></tr>
<tr><td>,</td><td>Left to right</td></tr>
</table>

In the table, operators at the top of the list have higher precedence than operators at the bottom of the list. Note that in the table + and – are listed twice. This is because in some cases + and – are unary, used in the form +<variable> or –<variable>. In other cases + or – is binary, used in the form <variable1> + <variable2> or <variable1> – <variable2>. The unary form of + or – has higher precedence.

Combining the rules of precedence with the rules of associativity, our expression above would evaluate as follows:

```
a = b+= 5 * c + a ;
a = b+= 15 + a ;
a = b+= 16 ;
a = 18 ;
```

Owing to the rules of precedence, multiplication has higher precedence in an expression than addition, just as in algebra. Assignment operators such as += also have a lower precedence than multiplication or addition, so they are evaluated last in our example. Also because assignment operators evaluate from right to left, the assignment operator += is evaluated before the assignment operator =.

Clipper also has fixed rules of precedence and associativity. Given that there are currently fewer operators in Clipper than C, there are not nearly as many rules and they are not as complex as those in C.

Mixed Type Expressions — Type Conversion and Casting

It is easy enough to figure out the result of an assignment or calculation between numbers of the same C data type. For example:

```
short n, m = 7 ;
n = m ;
```

will store the number 7 in the variable **n** as a 2-byte entity. But what would happen in the following situation?

```
char n
short m = 7 ;
n=7 ;
```

or in this next example?

```
short n
char m = 7 ;
n=7 ;
```

The answer lies in type conversion rules built into the C compiler. The table below shows the type of the result of an arithmetic operation between C operands of different types:

	char	short	int	unsigned	long	float	double
char	int	int	int	unsigned	long	double	double
short	int	int	int	unsigned	long	double	double
int	int	int	int	unsigned	long	double	double
unsigned	unsigned	unsigned	unsigned	unsigned	long	double	double
long	long	long	long	long	long	double	double
float	double	double	double	double	double	double	double
double	double	double	double	double	double	double	double

Casting — Overriding Default Conversion Rules

The designers of the C language understood that these conversion rules might need to be overridden. Therefore there is the facility to alter the data type conversion rules with a cast. A cast has a variety of uses. One of the simplest applications is an alternative way to initialize a variable. Without a cast, when initializing a long integer, we would have to postfix an L to the initializing constant:

```
long record_count = 1L ;
```

With a cast, we can initialize the long variable this way:

```
long record_count = (long) 1 ;
```

Similarly, without a cast, we would initialize a double this way:

```
double amount = 0.00 ;
```

With a cast, the double floating point variable can also be initialized this way:

```
double = (double) 0 ;
```

With a cast, we can also modify the results of an expression such as the inches to feet conversion in the following sample:

```
#include <stdio.h>
#include <math.h>

main()
{
        int inches = 13 ;
        double feet ;

        feet = inches/12 ;
        printf ( "%d = inches, %2.2f = feet", inches, feet ) ;

}
```

The preceding example will display the following at run-time:

```
13 = inches, 1.00 = feet
```

Here, the decimal value of feet is incorrect. Following the conversion rules, the use of the constant integer value 12 in the division truncated our result. To correct this, we could rewrite the inches to feet expression as follows:

```
feet = inches/12.00 ;
```

or we could use a cast in either one of two ways:

```
feet = inches/(double) 12 ;
feet = (double) (inches/12) ;
```

Classes and Scope, Strings and Arrays

Storage Classes and Scope

In Clipper, casting between numeric variables and expressions is handled behind the scenes. Casting between Clipper numeric variables or expressions and other Clipper types cannot occur; there is no way to cast in Clipper. Mixed type conversions, however, are easily handled through the many Clipper functions set up for this purpose.

Since Clipper uses one numeric type, mixed type conversions are not nearly as prevalent in Clipper as they are in C. For certain specialized operations, however, such as constructing an integer value for a binary file, Clipper provides a set of functions.

In Clipper, memory variables may be assigned so that they have a specified scope in an application. The scope of a variable is determined by its storage class. In the **IMPLIED** storage class, which is the Clipper default, the scope of a variable is the source file that uses it. In the **PUBLIC** storage class, a variable's scope is the entire application, regardless of how many sources and corresponding objects are used in the application. In the **PRIVATE** storage class, a variable's scope should be an individual procedure or UDF in which it is assigned. This means that when the PRIVATE variable is assigned outside of a procedure or UDF in a source file, the procedure or UDF does not recognize it.

In C, when a variable is declared, we can assign the scope of a variable, as in Clipper. To do this there are four storage classes available. These four storage classes set up three variable scopes. Here is a table of how this works:

C scope	Clipper scope	Effect
Local, or automatic	PRIVATE	Known only to the individual function or procedure.
Extern	PUBLIC	Known throughout the application.
Static	IMPLIED	Known to a particular source file.
Register	---	The same as automatic, but the variable is stored in a hardware register rather than RAM, so it executes faster. Note: Use sparingly and with caution.

In C the default scope is not static, as would be assumed from the above table, which compares static to Clipper's IMPLIED. Instead the default storage class within a function is automatic, like a Clipper PRIVATE. This means that by default a variable declared inside a C function is known only to that function. Consider the following:

```
#include <stdio.h>

int main()
{
  int num = 5, calculate(void), display(void) ;

  calculate() ;
  display() ;

    return (0) ;
}
int calculate (void)
{
num++ ;
}

int display (void)
{
printf ("the value of num is %d\n", num ) ;
}
```

The source file above has three user-defined C functions: main(), calculate(), and display(). For now, let's assume that the function shells and the function declarations in main() are correct. Will the above source file compile? The answer is no, because of the scope of the variable **num**. This code assumes that the scope of **num** is global to the application or to the source file, while in fact the scope is local to one function, main(), where it was declared.

A C variable declared outside of a function, however, is by default **extern**. This means that it is known throughout an application.

Therefore if we had initialized num outside of main() and any other C function, the source would have compiled, as follows:

```
#include <stdio.h>

int num = 5 ;

int main()
{
  int calculate(void), display(void) ;

  calculate() ;
  display() ;

    return (0) ;
}
```

```
int calculate (void)
{
num++ ;
}

int display (void)
{
printf ("the value of num is %d\n", num ) ;
}
```

We could have also declared the variable num as follows:

```
static int num = 5 ;
```

and the source would have compiled.

Sharing Variables in Different Source Files

We said that variables declared outside of a C function, or explicitly declared as extern, are known throughout an application. There is, however, one wrinkle in this rule. The problem is this: When a source file is compiled separately, how does one source file know about the variables declared in the other?

C does not compile like Clipper, where a DO <procedure> command will force the compiler to compile separate .PRG source files. In C every source file is compiled separately, like using the -m switch in the Clipper compiler.

Therefore when a C source file is compiled, it does not know about extern, or global, variables declared in another source file. In order for a source file in C to know about a global variable declared in a different source file, it must be pseudo-redeclared. In this pseudo-redeclaration the name of the global variable is prefixed with the extern keyword. Following this rule the first source file's general declaration syntax is:

```
<data type> <variable>[<array subscripts>] [= initializers] ;
```

And the second source file's general pseudo-redeclaration syntax is:

```
<extern> <data type> [<empty brackets if it's an array>] ;
```

If we rewrote our last example so that the function display is in a separate source file, the code could be modified as follows:

Source file 1:

```
int num = 5 ;
```

```
  int main()
{
   int calculate(void), display(void) ;

   calculate() ;
   display() ;
     return (0) ;
}

  int calculate (void)
  {
  num++ ;
  }
```

Source file 2:

```
#include <stdio.h>

extern int num ;

int display (void)
{
printf ("the value of num is %d\n", num ) ;
}
```

More examples of separate compilation and variable storage classes and scopes will be given as we move along. Now that we have a fundamental knowledge of Clipper and C numeric data types, it's time to go on to explore more complex data types.

Character Expressions and Strings

Usually, when working with character expressions in Clipper, a literal text expression or database character field is assigned to a memory variable using the STORE or = command. Later, the memory variable is displayed. Clipper code to do this might look something like this:

```
MenuDriven = "loser friendly"
? "I cannot stand " + MenuDriven + " Programs."
```

The output looks like this:

```
I cannot stand loser friendly programs.
```

In a C program, you can similarly store literal text expressions or other character expressions in a variable. The C code that gives us the same output as our Clipper example above would look like this:

```
#include <stdio.h>

main()
{
      static char MenuDriven[] = "loser friendly" ;
      printf ( "I Cannot stand %s programs", MenuDriven ) ;
}
```

In C the declaration static char Menudriven[]= “loser friendly” creates a data entity called a character string. The string, as its name suggests, consists of individual characters strung together. The end of the string is marked by an ASCII 0, often referred to as a null character. If we were to look at a character string grid of our string MenuDriven, above, this is what it would look like.

ASCII Char	l	o	s	e	r		f	r	i	e	n	d	l	y	\0
ASCII Val	108	111	115	101	114	32	102	114	105	101	110	100	108	121	0

The actual display characters that make up the string are shown on the first line of the grid. “ \0” is the C control character for the terminating null character. The corresponding ASCII values are displayed on the second line of the grid. In order to display the entire string in C, along with the other literal information, we use the following printf() control string:

```
printf ( "I Cannot stand %s programs", MenuDriven ) ;
```

“%s” is used when we want to display a string, which in this case is represented by the variable MenuDriven.

A Character String Is a Character Array

A character string, because it is a collection of characters, is also called an array of characters, or a character array. Each character in the array is referred to as an element in the array. We can look at any character in our string by referencing it as an array element. To do this, we take the character’s offset from the beginning of the array and place it in square brackets next to the array’s name. Some sample C code to do this might look like this:

```
#include <stdio.h>

main()
{
      static char HelloStr[]= "Hello World" ;
```

```
        printf ("%c", HelloStr[6] ) ;
    }
```

The output of this program is the letter "W."

Note that "W" has an **offset** of 6 bytes from the beginning of the array HelloStr. Of course, the letter "W" has a **position** of 7 bytes into the string. When referencing array elements in C, always remember to take the offset and not the position. The letter "H" in our string, following this rule, is referenced as HelloStr[0]. The first element in any C string always has an offset of 0.

This rule differs from the dBASE and Clipper convention, where character string positions are always measured by position. Our previous example in C might be written in Clipper as follows:

```
HelloStr = "Hello World"
? substr( HelloStr,7,1)
```

In the Clipper example, the substr() function references the seventh character from the memory variable HelloStr, not the sixth as in our C example.

More on Assigning Literals to Strings in C Functions

In our previous two C source examples, the static storage class was used to declare a character array and then assign it a literal expression. Simultaneously declaring and assigning a literal expression to an array is also called initializing the array. C requires us to declare all arrays with the static storage class if the array is initialized within a C function. The following version of "Hello World" will therefore produce an error:

```
#include <stdio.h>

main()
{
        char HelloStr[]= "Hello World" ; /* static missing */
        printf ("%s", HelloStr ) ;
}
```

This version, where HelloStr is static, will compile cleanly:

```
#include <stdio.h>

main()
{
        static char HelloStr[]= "Hello World" ;
        printf ("%s", HelloStr ) ;
}
```

This version, where HelloStr is global, will also compile cleanly:

```
#include <stdio.h>
char HelloStr[]= "Hello World"
main()
{
        printf ("%s", HelloStr ) ;
}
```

If a character array in C must be automatic, its array elements must be assigned values after it is initialized. One way to do this is to use the C standard library strcpy() function, which copies a Null terminated character array or literal to a character array. The source string is the second argument and the target string is the first argument of strcpy() as follows:

```
#include <stdio.h>
#include <string.h>
main()
{
        char HelloStr[12] ;

        strcpy ( HelloStr, "Hello World" ) ;
        printf ("%s", HelloStr ) ;
}
```

Declaring Space for Uninitialized Arrays

All uninitialized C arrays must be declared with a constant number in square brackets. Otherwise, the array has no storage in memory. The constant number in brackets indicates how much storage is needed for the array.

If the maximum size of HelloStr will be the size of the array "Hello World," HelloStr will need to be declared with 12 bytes of storage.

While the phrase "Hello World" is 11 characters long, an extra byte of storage must be allocated for the terminating Null character of a C character string.

We could also declare an array with more than the required amount of storage:

```
char HelloStr [80] ;
```

When there is enough memory to work with, it is safest to declare arrays with additional storage. We can also declare additional storage for an initialized array:

```
static char HelloStr[80] = "Hello World" ;
```

This provides storage to add to HelloStr later in a program. We can do this with another C standard library function strcat():

```
#include <stdio.h>
#include <string.h>
main()
{
        static char HelloStr[80] = "Hello World" ;
        char HelloStr[12] ;

        strcat ( HelloStr, " and Other Planets" ) ;
        printf ("%s", HelloStr ) ;
}
```

C Arrays of Other Types

In C, we can have arrays other than character arrays. There can be, for example, an array of integers. An example of a program using such an array is:

```
/* a program to print team averages */

main()
{
        static int TeamAverage[] = { 621, 351, 342, 331, 222, 111 } ;
        printf ( "First  Place team average is .%d\n", TeamAverage[0] ) ;
        printf ( "Second Place team average is .%d\n", TeamAverage[1] ) ;
        printf ( "Third  Place team average is .%d\n", TeamAverage[2] ) ;
        printf ( "Fourth Place team average is .%d\n", TeamAverage[3] ) ;
        printf ( "Fifth  Place team average is .%d\n", TeamAverage[4] ) ;
        printf ( "Sixth  Place team average is .%d\n", TeamAverage[5] ) ;
}
```

The initialization of an array containing literal numbers differs from the initialization of a character array. Opening and closing curly braces mark the beginning and end of the array, initializing literal numbers. Commas separate the array elements. The braces and commas are only part of the initialization statement; they do not become part of the array itself, which only includes literal numbers.

The amount of space used by each element in the array depends upon the size of the data type. In the above array of integers, each element in the array takes up 2 bytes. If this were an array of long integers, each element in the array would take up 4 bytes.

In the previous example, each element in the array of integers is displayed. To do this each of the six array elements is referenced, starting with the first element, TeamAverage[0], and ending with the last element, TeamAverage[5]. Even though each element in an array of integers uses 2 bytes, each element is referenced consecutively, just as in an array of characters.

When we reference the next consecutive element in an array of integers, the C compiler knows to skip an extra byte. It determines the number of bytes to skip based on the data type of the array. The team averages array is composed of integers, so the compiler skips 2 bytes each time we reference the next consecutive element in the array.

Clipper and C Arrays

Arrays in Clipper are more complex than the C arrays we have so far introduced. They are really arrays of C unions. A union is a type of C data structure, which is a complex data type that can contain or reference one or more C variables.

Dates in Clipper and C

In a .DBF file, dates are not stored as numbers but as a sequence of characters in the form YYYYMMDD. This character sequence is converted by Clipper into a number of the same form, YYYYMMDD. This number is then referenced by the Clipper type DATE, which follows the dBASE standard.

In C there is no type date. By convention, C date and time information are stored in numeric variables of type long. In C both the date and time are stored in one long integer that stores the amount of seconds from January 1, 1970. In Clipper, a date variable contains only date and not time information.

The C standard library gives us several functions with which to get date and time information from the operating system. The use of these functions requires a knowledge of C data structures. Therefore we will leave further discussion of date and time functions in C to later in this chapter.

Logical Types and Expressions

In dBASE and Clipper there is a logical data type. This type is used in control flow statements, the subject of our next section. The logical type is either logically true, tested with .T., or logically false, tested with .F.. In a dBASE or Clipper database, a logical field is marked with a "T" for true, or "F" for false.

In C no logical type exists. How then does C handle logical processing? In C any numeric type serves as a logical type, and any numeric expression serves as a logical expression. Here's how it works: Any C numeric expression is a logical true when it returns a nonzero value, and it is a logical false when it returns a zero value. We used Clipper and C logical expressions before when the increment and decrement C operators were introduced. For Clipper it is:

```
count = 5
DO WHILE (count <> 0 )
     count = count -1
ENDDO
```

For C it is:

```
#include <stdio.h>
main()
{
     int count = 5 ;
     while (count--) ;
}
```

Now let us see how the logical conditions work in the above code fragments. In Clipper, a logical condition is formed from a numeric expression through a logical comparison:

```
DO WHILE (count <> 0 )
```

where the value of count is compared to 0.

In Clipper, the numeric expression is already a logical condition:

```
while (count--) ;
```

where the value of count becomes a logical false when it is decremented to 0. The while loop then terminates when count becomes equal to 0.

The same process applies to a C IF statement where

```
if (<non-zero numeric expression>)
```

equates to Clipper's

```
IF (<logical comparison is TRUE>)
```

Summary of Data Types

We have compared the uses of memory variables and data types for C and Clipper. Data declarations and storage classes, mathematical operators, assignment operators, and character arrays were among the topics covered.

It has often been said that understanding C's data types is the most critical part of learning C. Familiarity with C's data types also helps us know more about how computers work because they deal with the machine on the bits and bytes level. This fundamental view of data types provides a foundation on which to build, whether we are working with Clipper or C.

CONTROL FLOW STATEMENTS

The previous discussion of logical types and expressions leads us into the next logical topic: control flow statements. Both Clipper and C have two types of control flow statements. Branch statements, such as if and case statements, allow for conditional processing, and loop statements, such as WHILE and FOR loops, allow iterative processing to take place.

In this chapter, we will compare in detail the syntax and use of branch and loop control flow statements in Clipper and C. First, we'll compare those control flow statements used in branching, and then we'll look at those used in processing loops.

Clipper's IF Command

The most general branch statement in Clipper is the IF command. Its syntax is as follows:

```
IF <logical expression is true>
     execute statements...
[ELSEIF <logical expression is true>
     execute statements...]
[ELSE
     execute statements...]
ENDIF
```

With the IF command we can branch execution of our program via a logical expression. When the IF expression evaluates to a logical true (.T.), Clipper evaluates the statements on the lines below the IF command until it reaches an ELSEIF, ELSE, or ENDIF command.

When the IF expression evaluates to a logical false (.F.), Clipper does not evaluate the statements on the lines below the IF command until it reaches an ELSEIF, ELSE, or ENDIF command. When Clipper reads an ELSEIF command after an IF command, it evaluates the statements on the lines below the ELSEIF command as it did with those below the IF command.

Clipper may also read an ELSE command after an IF command or an ELSE command after an ELSEIF command. When Clipper encounters an ELSE command, it evaluates any statements on the lines below the ELSE command until it reaches an ENDIF command. The statements on the lines below a Clipper ELSE command are evaluated if the logical expression or expressions in the previous IF or ELSEIF commands return a logical false (.F.).

C's If Statement

The most general branch statement in C is the if statement. C's if statement is functionally analogous to Clipper's IF command. The syntax of the C if statement is as follows:

```
    if ( <logical expression is true> )
         {
         execute statements
         }
    else if ( <logical expression is true> )
         {
         execute statements
         }
else
         {
         execute statements
         }
```

From the above, it appears that the general form of the IF command in Clipper and the if statement in C are the same. In Clipper as in C we have an if, else if, and else component of the if branch control structure. The logical evaluation of the IF command in Clipper and the if statement in C are also the same.

We notice, however, that the syntax for the C if statement is different from the Clipper IF command. In particular, there is no equivalent in C to Clipper's ENDIF. In C there is no END<anything> command or keyword. The execution of multiple statements in C's control flow statements is handled, as it is in the body of a function, with curly brace delimiters.

When the logical expression in the if statement in C evaluates to a logical true (a nonzero value), C evaluates the statements below the if statement when they are enclosed in curly braces. When there are no curly braces, C only evaluates, as part of the if statement, the single statement following the if statement. For example, the following two statements both evaluate the same way, since there is a single statement in the if statement:

```
if ( more eggs )
     start_new_dozen() ;
```

and

```
if ( more eggs )
     {
     start_new dozen() ;
     }
```

When there are multiple statements, however, this will not work. For example, the following will only call the function make_half_dozen() once, not twice, within the if statement;

```
if ( more_eggs )
     make_half_dozen() ;
     make_half_dozen() ;
```

On the other hand, this will call make_half_dozen() twice within the if statement if more_eggs evaluates to a logical true:

```
if ( more_eggs )
     {
     make_half_dozen() ;
     make_half_dozen() ;
     }
```

In the if statement, as with any C program flow statement, we can also do nothing at all. For example, the following does nothing:

```
if ( more_eggs ) ;
```

And if we had coded the following, no calls to make_half_dozen() would have occurred:

```
if ( more_eggs ) ;
     {
     make_half_dozen() ;
     make_half_dozen() ;
     }
```

Note that in C a statement is not defined as a line as in Clipper. In C, the end of a statement, other than an if statement or other control structure statement, is marked by a semicolon. Therefore, in a C if statement, everything following the if statement is evaluated until the first semicolon.

General Rules Governing C If Statements

When the logical expression in the if statement evaluates to a logical false (a zero value), C does not evaluate the statements below the if statement if these statements are enclosed in curly braces. When these statements are not enclosed in curly braces, C does not evaluate the first statement below the if statement. Any statements after the first statement, however, would be evaluated.

When C reads an else if statement after an if statement, it evaluates the statement or statements below the else if statement as it did those below the if statement. If the logical expression in the previous if statement evaluates to a logical false, the logical expression in the else if statement evaluates to a logical true.

C may also read an else statement after an if statement or an else statement after an else if statement. When C encounters an else statement, it evaluates the statements delimited with curly braces or a single statement below the else statement.

The statements on the lines below a C else statement are evaluated if the logical expression or expressions in the previous if evaluates to a logical false. The logical expression or expressions in any previous else if statements evaluate to a logical false (.F.).

Below is a sample comparison between Clipper's IF command and C's if; they both produce the same result. In Clipper we would write:

```
year = 1988

IF ( year % 4 == 0 )
     ?? "It's a "
     ?  "leap year!"
ENDIF
```

In C we would write:

```
#include <stdio.h>

main()
{
     int year = 1988 ;
     if ( (year % 4) )
     {
          printf ( "It's a " ) ;
          printf (  "leap year!\n" ) ;
     }
     }
```

As we noted above, we could also write the above example as follows:

```
#include <stdio.h>

main()
{
     int year = 1988 ;
     if ( !(year % 4) )
          printf ( "It's a leap year!\n" ) ;
}
```

Evaluation of Logical Statements in C and Clipper

Another clear difference between Clipper and C in the above comparison is in the coding of the logical expression. In Clipper we needed to compare the result of the numeric expression year % 4 with 0 to create a logical expression. The logical expression is then written in Clipper as year % 4 == 0.

The same logical expression is written in C as !(year % 4). Here the logical not operator (!) is used. It converts the evaluation of a logical expression that returns a logical true to one that returns a logical false.

In Clipper we needed to compare the result of a numeric expression with a value to achieve a logical expression, as in:

```
IF ( year % 4 == 0 )
```

In C a numeric expression is already a logical expression. There, we detailed the following rule for logical expression evaluation in C: Any C numeric expression is a logical TRUE when it returns a nonzero value; any C numeric expression is a logical FALSE when it returns a zero value.

Because we wanted to evaluate the logical expression year % 4 in C as being FALSE, we used the C logical not operator. We then used parentheses so that the logical not operator would operate on the full expression **year % 4** and not just the variable **year**.

The C Ternary Operator and Clipper's IF() Function

In Clipper we can evaluate a branch logical expression on one line using the Clipper IF() function. The general syntax of the Clipper IF() function is

```
IF ( <condition > ) <expression1>,<expression2>
```

where the IF() function processes <expression1> if <condition> is logically true or <expression2> if condition is logically false.

In C the functionality of the if command is accomplished with an operator. The operator is the ternary operator, and its syntax is as follows:

```
<condition> ? <expression1> : <expression2>
```

The ternary operator works similarly to the IF() command. Here the ternary operator processes <expression1> if <condition> is logically true or <expression2> if condition is logically false.

A Clipper IF() function might be coded:

```
IF ( eggs > 12 ) new_dozen(), fill_same_dozen()
```

The same statement in C might be coded:

```
eggs > 12 ? new_dozen() : fill_same_dozen() ;
```

Clipper's DO CASE Command and C Switch Case Statements

In Clipper, when we need to branch execution of a program based on more than two conditions, we can, as an alternative to the IF ELSE command, use the DO CASE and CASE commands. The general syntax for the Clipper DO CASE and CASE commands are as follows:

```
DO CASE
CASE <logical expression is true>
     <commands>
CASE <logical expression is true>
     <commands>
CASE <logical expression is true>
     <commands>
OTHERWISE
     <commands>
ENDCASE
```

The C language provides a case control structure, but it works in a different way than in Clipper. In C the case control structure is called a switch case statement, and it allows us to branch program execution based on multiple evaluation of one numeric expression, as follows:

```
switch ( < numeric expression > )
     {
     case < matching numeric expression >:
          statements
     case < matching numeric expression >:
          statements
     case < matching numeric expression >:
          statements
     default:
          statements
     }
```

Based on what the numeric expression evaluates to, we can branch execution of our program. The best way to illustrate how this works is by way of a comparative example. A common use of a Clipper DO CASE command or C switch case statement is in branching execution of a program based on a key pressed by a program's user. In Clipper, we might code a low-level input key testing function as follows:

```
escape = 27

key = INKEY(0)
```

```
DO CASE
     CASE key == ASC('A') .OR. key == ASC('a')
          ?? "You have pressed a big or little A."
     CASE key == ASC('B') .OR. key == ASC('b')
          ?? "You have pressed a big or little B."
     CASE key == ASC(C)
          ?? "You have pressed a big C."
     CASE key == ASC(C)
          ?? "You have pressed a little c."
     OTHERWISE
          ? "You have pressed "
          ?? "an undefined key."
ENDCASE
```

A similar program could be written in C using the function getchar() from the C standard function library. The function getchar() requires that you press the Enter key to confirm the keystroke. We'll look at more INKEY(0)-like C key functions in the next section. For now, we'll code our C case switch sample as follows:

```
#include <stdio.h>

main()
     {
     int key = getchar() ;

     switch ( key )
          {
          case 'A':
          case 'a':
               printf( "You have pressed a big or little A.\n" ) ;
               break ;
          case 'B':
          case 'b':
               printf( "You have pressed a big or little C.\n" ) ;
               break ;
          case C:
               printf( "You have pressed a big C.\n" ) ;
               break ;
          case C:
               printf( "You have pressed a little c.\n" ) ;
               break ;
          default:
               printf ( "You have pressed " ) ;
               printf ( "an undefined key.\n" ) ;
          }
```

Based on the value of the key, we branched to a particular statement or statements. In the Clipper sample, once one CASE command was evaluated as true, the statements on the lines below that CASE were executed until the next CASE command, and then program control moved to the ENDCASE command.

In the C sample, each **case** numeric expression was matched to the numeric expression in the switch. When a match occurred, the statements below the case were executed, including any subsequent case commands.

Since we did not want to evaluate any subsequent case commands, we broke out of the switch case command with a C break statement. We will discuss the C break statement in complete detail at the end of this section.

It is optional, but wise, to include a default statement when coding a C switch case, to handle any unpredicted results of the numeric expression in the switch. In the absence of a default, the switch case statement will terminate after the last case statement before the closing curly brace in the switch.

To see what happens in the switch case statement in our preceding C example, try coding the sample without the break and/or default statements. Then compile and run the sample, testing for how the switch case statement will branch process on a key pressed.

Goto

The C language also provides a goto statement whose general syntax is:

```
goto <label> ;

<label>:
     C statements
```

When goto is encountered, processing jumps from the goto to the label and resumes from there. Goto is very rarely used in C. There are, however, instances where a goto is valuable. Nested situations like the following are a plausible example:

```
while (..)
     {
     for (..)
          {
          while (..)
               {
               switch ( var )
                    {
                    HORRIBLE_ERROR:
                    default
                         goto ejector_seat;
                    }
               }
          }
     }
ejector_seat:
```

```
          detoxify() ;
          go_home() ;
```

Loops

In addition to branching control in a program, control flow statements are used in processing repetitive instructions in loops.

While Loops

The most commonly used loop is a while loop, which allows us to execute statements until a condition is met. The form of this loop, which Clipper inherits from dBASE, is the DO WHILE LOOP. The general syntax of Clipper's DO WHILE command is as follows:

```
DO WHILE (logical expression is true)
     execute statements...
ENDDO
```

The C language provides two types of while loops. The first evaluates expression in the loop:

```
while ( logical expression is true )
     {
     execute statements
     }
```

The second C while loop, the do..while, allows for a statement to be presented first and then evaluated in a loop.

```
do
     {
     execute statements
     }
while ( logical expression is true ) ;
```

Clipper's DO WHILE command works like our first C while loop, where expressions are evaluated within the loop until a logical condition is satisfied. Consider the following Clipper code, where we display each character in a character expression:

```
string = "Hello"
length = len ( string )

count = 1
DO WHILE ( count <= length )
     ?? substr ( string, count, 1 )
     count = count+1
ENDDO
```

Now look at the following C code, where we do the same:

```
#include <stdio.h>
#include  <string.h>

main()
{
     static char string[] = "hello" ;
     unsigned int count, length = strlen (string) ;

     count = 0 ;
     while ( count <= length )
          {
          printf ("%c", string[count] ) ;
          count++ ;
          }
}
```

Where in Clipper we used the substr() function to print out a single character from the character expression "hello," in C we referenced the character in the character string "hello" by its array element.

In Clipper, the first character in the character expression is referenced as position 1, and therefore the Clipper memory variable count is initialized to 1. In C, the first character in the character string is offset 0, and therefore the C variable count is initialized to 0.

In Clipper, we used the statement count = count+1 to increment the memory variable count by 1. In C we used the statement count++ to increment the memory variable count by 1. The rules of syntax in the while loop follow from what we saw previously with the if statement: use curly braces to surround multiple statements to be executed in a C control structure.

Using a C do while loop, we could recode the previous example as follows:

```
#include <stdio.h>
#include  <string.h>

main()
{
     static char string[] = "hello" ;
     unsigned int count, length = strlen (string) ;

     count = 0 ;

     do
          {
          printf ("%c", string[count] ) ;
          count++ ;
          }
     while ( count <= length ) ;
}
```

And we could streamline this code as follows:

```
#include <stdio.h>
#include <string.h>

main()
{
	static char string[] = "hello" ;
	unsigned int count, length = strlen (string) ;

	count = 0 ;

	do
		printf ("%c", string[count] ) ;
	while ( count++ <= length ) ;
}
```

As with Clipper, C has many ways to get to the same result. The streamlined code above is probably a little faster because we could evaluate and increment the variable count in one statement.

In general practice, the C while loop is far more commonplace than the do while loop.

For Loops

The other processing loop we will look at is the for loop. For loops do not exist in dBASE but have existed in Clipper since the Autumn '86 release. In Clipper, the for loop is known as the FOR NEXT command. The general syntax of the FOR NEXT command is:

```
FOR <initial value> TO <termination value> [STEP]
	statements...
NEXT
```

For initial value we supply the value we want a variable to contain when we start the loop. For termination value we supply the value we want a variable to contain when we end the loop. For STEP we supply the incremental or decremental change to the variable with each pass through the loop.

C provides us with a for loop as well. C's for loop, similarly, allows for initial values to be processed in the loop and values to be modified with each iteration of the loop. The general syntax of the C for loop is:

```
for (initial statements ;logical expression ;modifying statements )
	{
	statements ;
	}
```

For example:

```
#include <stdio.h>

main()
{
        int i ;
        static char HelloStr = "Hello World" ;

        for ( i = 11 ; i > 0 ; i-- )
                {
                HelloStr[i] = '\0' ;
                printf ( "%s\n", HelloStr ) ;
                }
```

The previous sample is an example of a countdown loop. It will shorten the string by one character each time through the loop and then display the string with C's printf() function. To do this, we look at the string as an array. We then start at the last character in the array and count down to the first. With each count we shorten the string by changing the character at that array offset to a null.

We could code the above example in Clipper as follows:

```
HelloStr = "Hello World"

FOR i = 11 TO 1 STEP -1
        HelloStr = substr ( HelloStr, 1, i) + CHR(0)
        ? HelloStr
NEXT
```

First in the loop is our initialization of routine HelloStr[i] as a character in the string at offset i, which we change to a null in a loop that counts down. Offset i is initialized as the value 10, the length of the string.

dBASE III and Clipper also allow for logical parsing in several commands. These commands have the following general syntax:

```
<COMMAND NAME>...[FOR (logical expression)] [WHILE (logical
expression]
```

Control Structure Control

Like Clipper, C provides us with a way to get out of or go to the top of a loop. We break out of a loop as follows:

Clipper	EXIT
C	break

We go to the top of a loop this way:

Clipper	LOOP
C	continue

C, like Clipper, also provides us with a way to terminating a program:

Clipper	QUIT
C	exit (<termination code>)

Note that the EXIT command in C is very different from the exit statement in C.

Summary of Control Flow Statements

In this section we examined control flow statements in Clipper and C. We compared similarities and showed differences between branch processing control flow statements, such as IF and CASE, and loop processing control flow statements, such as WHILE and FOR. We also compared the use of logical variables and expressions in control flow statements.

For the remainder of this chapter, we will illustrate many other examples of control flow statements. The power and flexibility of these statements in both Clipper and C allow us to use either language in a fully structured way. We are thereby afforded what the names of these statements denote: control of our applications.

PASSING BY REFERENCE OR VALUE, FUNCTION VALUES

What Are Functions?

In Clipper or C, a function is a processing box. We might stuff something into the box, as input to the process, and hope to get something useful out of the box. Using a function is like sending out a letter with instructions for its recipient to do something. Whoever gets the letter might mail us back a response and/or perform another task or tasks requested in the letter.

In Clipper we use functions provided by Nantucket, which are part of Clipper.lib and are included at link time. We understand what they do and how to use them by reading a Clipper manual and/or a book such as *Programming in Clipper*.

We might also use, with Clipper, third-party function libraries that allow us to perform tasks Clipper.lib does not. Steve Straley's ToolkiT, Neil Weicker's NetLib and dLESKO Associates' FUNCky are examples of third-party Clipper libraries that are useful in a wide variety of applications.

In C, we also use some functions provided by the compiler manufacturer. Most of these are part of a portable C standard library. Functions in the C standard library are designed to take the same input and provide the same output on any computer with a C compiler. An example is the C standard library function strlen(), which returns the length of a string.

Almost always, there are some functions provided by the C compiler manufacturer that are not part of the C standard library. These are dedicated to perform a particular task or tasks on a given machine. An example is the Microsoft and TurboC function int86(), which is provided only on PCs and compatibles to access the ROM BIOS.

We might also use third-party function libraries. These allow us to perform tasks the C compiler manufacturer's library or libraries do not.

Creating and Using Your Own Functions

While both Clipper and C give us premade functions, we can also create and use our own functions in either language. Nantucket calls these functions user-defined functions, or UDFs, to distinguish functions written by Clipper users/developers from functions in Clipper.lib. In C, our own homegrown functions are created and called just like other C functions in the standard library.

The Anatomy of Clipper UDFs

Although many readers have worked with them in the past, we'll go through the anatomy of Clipper UDFs again. In this way, we can better compare the UDF building process with creating C functions.

When we create a Clipper UDF, the following general syntax is used:

```
FUNCTION <name>
PARAMETERS <parameter list>
     statements
     RETURN <variable>
```

Here FUNCTION is a keyword followed by <name>, the name with which the function will be called.

PARAMETERS is another keyword, and it is followed by a list of parameter variables, or arguments. We expect these parameters to be passed to the function when it is called. The line containing the keyword PARAMETERS and the parameter list is optional; it is omitted if the function takes no parameters.

The RETURN keyword is used to return a variable. The variable is explicitly returned to wherever we called the function from. We may have called the function from another function, a procedure, or our main program.

An example of a UDF might be a function named welcome, which displays n characters of "Hello World" and returns the full string length of the character expression "Hello World":

```
FUNCTION welcome
PARAMETERS size
     ? substr ( "Hello World", 1, size )
     RETURN ( LEN ("Hello World") )
```

The function might be called as follows:

```
? (welcome ( 5 )
```

and the output would look like this:

```
Hello     11
```

The Anatomy of C Functions

A C function, like a Clipper function, has a unique name and an argument list. The general syntax for a C function is as follows:

```
<data type returned> <name> ( <arguments> )
<data type and corresponding name of each argument in list> ;
     {
     <statements}
     }
```

An example is the following not-very-useful but illustrative function called **multiply()**, which only handles integer values:

```
    int multiply ( val1, val2 )
    int val1 ;
int val2 ;
     {
     return ( val1*val2 ) ;
     }
```

Here <name> is the name of the C function, which is case-specific in most compilers. In our example, the function name is multiply.

Function Parameters, or Arguments

C <arguments> are the same as Clipper parameters; what C lingo terms an argument Clipper users refer to as a parameter. As in Clipper, C function arguments can have different names in the called function than in the calling function or procedure. For example, the above multiply() function might be called with:

```
#include <stdio.h>

main()
{
        int value1 = 2, value2 = 4 ;

        printf ( "%d", multiply ( value1, value2 ) ) ;
}
```

The calling function variables value1 and value2 are not the same as the called function variables val1 or val2.

Passing Literal Values to Functions

We may also write the calling function to pass the called function literal values:

```
#include <stdio.h>

main()
{
        printf ( "%d", multiply ( 2, 4 ) ) ;
}
```

In this example the constants 2 and 4, respectively, are passed to the variables val1 or val2 declared inside the called function.

Multiple Arguments Passed to Functions

If there is more than one argument to a C function, like multiple parameters in Clipper, they are separated by commas inside parentheses. As in Clipper, they are passed to the function when it is called. In our example, these arguments are val1 and val2.

Unlike Clipper, every C function must know the data type of each argument being sent to it. The <data type> is specified for each <argument name> after the <argument list>. In our example, we specify the data types as follows:

```
     int multiply ( val1, val2 )
     int val1 ;
int val2 ;
```

We could have also written:

```
int multiply ( val1, val2 )
int val1 , val2 ;
```

Here, just as in a variable declaration list, the same data type is assigned to the variable after each comma. The rules for specifying the data types for each argument to a function are the same as those used for declaring variables inside a function.

How Functions Work with Arguments

In effect, we redeclare the arguments to a function when we specify names and data types for them. The called function makes separate copies of each one of these arguments, giving the copies the variable names we specify and assigning them space in memory according to the data type we specify.

Within the called function, the storage class for these copies of parameters passed as arguments to a function are automatic, or PRIVATE. Once we return from the called function, these copies of the function arguments are not known. If we changed the values of val1 or val2 inside of the function multiply(), the function main() would not be aware of the changes. For example, the following will not change the value of the calling function argument, value1:

```
#include <stdio.h>

main()
{
     int value1 = 2, value2 = 4 ;
     printf ( "%d", multiply ( value1, value2 ) ) ;
}

int multiply ( val1, val2 )
int val1 , val2 ;
     {
     val1+=2 ;
     return ( val1*val2 ) ;
     }
```

However, the return value of the called function, displayed by the calling function main(), will be different. Our original version of multiply() returns 2 times 4, or 8. Our revised version would return 4 times 4, or 16, since we incremented 2 by 2 in the multiply().

Data "Types" of Return Values from Functions

In our examples, the single returned value of the function is the only information transferred from the called function to the calling function. The function return value also has a specific data type. In our example, this is type int.

C functions return type int by default. This means that the called function and calling function expect that this is the data type a function will return. If we want a function to have a returned type other than int, we need to specify what that data type is. This must be done both with the called and the calling function.

If we want our multiply() example to return a double precision floating point value back to main(), we must rewrite multiply() to work with numbers larger than the size of an integer. This would be accomplished as follows:

```
#include <stdio.h>
#include <math.h>

main()
{
      double value1 = 2.0, value2 = 4.0 ;
      double multiply() ;

      printf ( "%lf", multiply ( value1, value2 ) ) ;
}

double multiply ( val1, val2 )
double val1 , val2 ;
      {
      val1+=2 ;
      return ( val1*val2 ) ;
      }
```

Here we specify in the called function that we want it to return a double by preceding its name with the data type it will return. Therefore we write:

```
double multiply ( val1, val2 )
double val1 , val2 ;
{
val1+=2 ;
return ( val1*val2 ) ;
}
```

Declaring Functions

In addition to modifying the called function, we must modify the calling function. This is because the calling function must know how to treat the data the called function will return. We do this with a called function declaration, in which the return type of the called function is made known to the calling function. To do this in our example, we added the following statement to the function main():

```
main()
{
        double value1 = 2.0, value2 = 4.0 ;
        double multiply() ;
        printf ( "%lf", multiply ( value1, value2 ) ) ;
}
```

Any called function that returns a type other than **int** must be declared in the calling function. Otherwise, a warning or error message is generated by the compiler, and unexpected run-time results may occur.

Function Prototypes

A recent addition to the C language is the use of function prototypes. All compilers that follow the ANSI C standard, such as Microsoft C 5.x and Turbo C 1.5 or 2.0, allow us to use function prototypes. A function prototype is the same as a function declaration, with one difference. In a function prototype we can specify not only a function's return type but also the types of the arguments. The function declaration:

```
double multiply () ;
```

would therefore be rewritten:

```
double multiply ( double value1, double value2 ) ;
```

It would appear in our main source file, in place of the function declaration, as follows:

```
main()
{
        double value1 = 2.0, value2 = 4.0 ;
        double multiply ( double value1, double value2 ) ;
        printf ( "%lf", multiply ( value1, value2 ) ) ;
}
```

We could also place the function prototype outside of main(), as follows:

```
double multiply ( double value1, double value2 ) ;
```

```
main()
{
        double value1 = 2.0, value2 = 4.0 ;
        printf ( "%lf", multiply ( value1, value2 ) ) ;
}
```

In a function prototype the name of an argument in parenthesis is not a declaration of a variable. In the welcome() prototype, therefore, the variables value1 and value2 are not declared. Also note, again, that the use of a function prototype replaces the need for a function declaration.

Include Files for Function Prototypes

Because we can place function prototypes outside of the calling function, we can put them in include files. This is because include files can contain any instructions placed in a C source file outside of a function. Include files will be discussed in detail in the next section, which is devoted to the C preprocessor.

ANSI C compilers, such as Microsoft C version 5.1, use function prototypes, placed in include files, for the whole standard C library of functions. For example, the function prototype for printf() is in the standard I/O include file stdio.h.

By including stdio.h in every source file that uses printf(), we do not need our own function declaration or prototype for printf(). By including the appropriate .h include file, we do not have to worry about function declarations or prototypes for the other C standard library functions either.

Which Include File to Use for a Particular Function Prototype

All C functions in the C standard library should document the return type of a function and what standard include file is used in place of our own function declaration or prototype for that function. Any third-party C function library worth using will also provide this documentation. In Microsoft C, refer to the C Library Reference Manual, which is very well written.

After using C for a while, you get to know which include file or files are used for a particular function or functions or set of purposes. For example, the include file time.h contains the function prototypes and data structure templates for working with standard C library date and time functions and calculations.

Order of Functions in a Source File

C functions can appear in any order in a source file. Main() could appear first among a group of functions in a source file, or it could appear last. It could also be in a separate source file. The linker only requires that main() is somewhere in one of the compiled objects that is linked at link-time. Otherwise the linker will give us an error.

In Clipper, there is a function called main(), but we never create or call it. It is part of the Clipper library that we do not have normal access to. Instead, in Clipper we always have an initial source file that begins with an initial, or master, procedure. This procedure in turn calls other procedures or functions, which may be in any order in the same or any other source file.

If we are using C without Clipper, we need to create our own main(), which we could put anywhere. Our preceding example could look like this:

```
#include <stdio.h>
#include <math.h>

double multiply ( val1, val2 )
double val1 , val2 ;
     {
     return ( val1*val2 ) ;
     }

main()
{
     double value1 = 2.0, value2 = 4.0 ;
     double multiply() ;

     printf ( "%lf", multiply ( value1, value2 ) ) ;
}
```

We can also have a source file that look like this, which is the content of a file called multiply.c:

```
#include <stdio.h>
#include <math.h>

double multiply ( val1, val2 )
double val1 , val2 ;
     {
     return ( val1*val2 ) ;
     }
```

This is the content of a file called main.c:

```
#include <stdio.h>
#include <math.h>
```

```
main()
{
        double value1 = 2.0, value2 = 4.0 ;
        double multiply() ;

        printf ( "%lf", multiply ( value1, value2 ) ) ;
}
```

Just as when compiling two Clipper modules to be explicitly linked separately, C source files must be compiled without invoking the linker. To accomplish this, the no-link compile option is used:

```
cl -c multiply.c
cl -c main.c
```

The -c flag is used by most C compilers to suppress automatic linking.

Once we have compiled without errors, we can then enter the link line in order to link more than one source file. Using Microsoft Link, this would be:

```
link main multiply, multiply.exe , , ;
```

The list of objects compiled from the source files are listed first, then the name we wish to give the .exe file is specified as the next link parameter. The remaining parameters may be left blank.

Once the multiply program is successfully linked, it will run just as it did when we used one source file.

Functions with No Arguments

In C, as in Clipper, we can also have functions with no arguments. For example, we may want to create a function called newline() that causes the cursor to jump to the next line when displaying text on the screen. The function would look like this:

```
#include <stdio.h>

void newline (void )
{
printf ( "\n" ) ;
}
```

The function newline() could be called from a calling C function as follows:

```
#include <stdio.h>
void newline (void) ;
```

```
main()
{
printf ( "hello" ) ;
newline() ;
}
```

What is new here is a data type called void. Void is another ANSI enhancement to the C language. We use void when we want to specify, either in a function header or prototype, that we don't want to pass an argument to a function or return a value from a function.

If we don't want to pass an argument to a function, we place the data type void in parentheses when creating the function header. In our example we have the function header:

```
void newline (void )
```

and the function prototype, which looks the same, except for the semicolon needed to end a C statement:

```
void newline (void ) ;
```

Since we also don't want to return a value from a function, we place the data type void in front of the function name as well. In the function header we have:

```
void newline (void )
```

In the function prototype we have:

```
void newline (void ) ;
```

Pass by Reference

The C language provides a technique for passing arguments to functions where the arguments themselves are changed by the called function. This technique is commonly called pass by reference. Summer '87 Clipper provides pass by reference for UDFs when the parameter is a character expression. Clipper 5.0 may allow any data type to be passed by reference, as C currently permits.

Setting up a pass by reference Clipper function involves calling a function with special parameters. These parameters are the addresses of the variables rather than the variables themselves. Inside the called function, either the data at a passed address is altered or new data may be placed at the address.

The following important tasks may be performed with pass by reference:

Returning multiple values from functions. With C functions we may want to return more than one value in the called function; however, we cannot. The only way to do this is to change the values of the parameters passed from the calling function within the called function.

Passing and returning arrays and character strings by reference. Most C functions involving character strings use pass by reference with the string parameter(s). Virtually all the standard C library string functions that change the contents of a string use pass by reference.

The name of a C character string is already the name of an address. Strings are therefore always set up for pass by reference in C functions. The called function controls whether or not the string passed is altered by the function.

Clipper functions using character expressions, for the same reason, may use pass by reference. Clipper character expressions are really C character strings or character buffers. A character buffer is a C string, but the Null byte is not used to mark the end of the buffer. The name of a Clipper character buffer is therefore an address, as it is in C.

Passing Functions to Functions

In C, as in Clipper, functions are passed to functions using pass by reference. This allows the called function to call a function passed to it. To do this in Summer '87 Clipper requires macroing the function name to a string name. In C, the address of a function may be passed without conversion to another type.

Since working with pass by reference in C requires knowing more about addresses, we'll pick up this topic again later in this chapter.

The C Standard Library

In our introduction to this chapter, we introduced the C standard library. C standard library documentation is provided with every C compiler. Microsoft C and Turbo C both provide excellent documentation. The library is generally organized alphabetically, but functions fall into logical categories of use. These categories are:

Category	Description
Data Conversion	Convert data from one type to another where an assignment or cast and assignment won't work. For example, atof() converts a character string containing a string formatted as a number to a double.

Category	Description
Character Classification and Conversion	1. Test characters for belonging to a particular group in the character set. For example isalnum(c) tests to see if c is an alphanumeric character. 2. Convert a character from one group in the character set to another. For example, tolower(c) converts c from uppercase to lowercase. These functions are generally coded as macros.
Math Support	Provide floating point support and include functions for trigonometry, exponentials, and more.
Time Support	Access or set the operating system date and time in C and manipulate the date and time from C.
String Manipulation	Manipulate character strings, which are Null (ASCII 0) terminated C character arrays.
Buffer Manipulation	Manipulate character buffers, which are non-Null (not ASCII 0) terminated C character arrays.
File and Stream Handling	Manipulate files and data streams.
Console I/O	Specifically access the keyboard and the display.
Directory Control	Manage file directories on machines that use them, such as MS-DOS- and UNIX-based machines.
Process Control	Allow a program to interact with other programs and the operating system environment. Include functions to call other programs as child processes and run operating system commands.
Memory Allocation	Allow dynamic memory allocation in C.

Microsoft and Turbo C also provide the following MS-DOS specific functions categories:

S-DOS Interface	Allows access to DOS internals.
BIOS Interface	Allows access to the ROM BIOS.

Summary of Functions

We have dealt with the fundamental construction and use of C functions. We covered passing arguments to functions and return values from functions. The technique of pass by value was also detailed. In pass by value functions, parameters are passed as ordinary values and the function optionally returns an explicit value.

The technique of pass by reference was introduced. In pass by reference functions, parameters are passed by address, and the data stored at the address is interpreted and/or altered by the called function. We did not detail this technique in this section because working with pass by reference in C requires knowing more about addresses.

While Clipper is driven by commands, functions, and global, e.g., SET <command>, parameters, C historically is driven by functions. The fact that Clipper is written in C, however, shows that C is very adaptable to different programming methodologies.

Since functions play such a large role in C, the remaining discussion of C in this chapter will rely heavily on the topics presented in this section.

INTRODUCTION TO PREPROCESSORS

What is the C Preprocessor?

In the C language we have something we have not had in Clipper — a language preprocessor, which will be introduced with Clipper 5.0. A preprocessor gets its name from what it does: It processes macros and other programming instructions prior to actual compilation.

At the time we go to press Clipper version 5.0 has not been released. Therefore this section, with this edition of the book, will not include Clipper's preprocessor. We can assume, however, since Clipper is written in C, that it will "look and feel" much the same as the C preprocessor.

What can a language preprocessor do for us? Below we detail the components of the C preprocessor, which exemplify the many features of this tool.

#define

Virtually every computer program contains constants that are made known to the program at the beginning of execution. In Clipper we would normally assign these constants to memory variables at the beginning of our initial procedure in our initial .PRG source file. For example:

```
* top of sample.prg
public pi = 3.14141414
public yes = .T.
```

```
public no   = .F.
< Clipper statements >
```

In C we could declare global variables to do the same as follows:

```
* top of sample.c
double pi = 3.14141414
yes = 1 ;  /* a non-zero value evaluates to TRUE in C */
no =  0 ;  /* a zero value evaluates to FALSE in C */

main()
     {
          < c statements >
     }
```

In C, however, constants are, by convention, never set up as global variables. Instead, they are set up using the preprocessor statement #define whose general syntax is:

```
#define <macro name> <constant or macro expression>
```

If we rewrite the C sample using #define preprocessor statements, we have:

```
#define PI  3.14141414
#define YES 1 /* a non-zero value evaluates to TRUE in C */
#define NO  0 /* a zero value evaluates to FALSE in C */

main()
     {
          < c statements >
     }
```

So what advantage does the C preprocessor give us over assigning memory variables to constants in Clipper or declaring variables to hold constants in C? The answer lies in the fact that preprocessor instructions are preprocessed. This means that, at compile time, the program already knows what the constant values are.

In other words, instead of having our program evaluate a variable at run-time to find out what value the variable represents, by using a #define, our program already knows what the value is. This is because when we use a #define, our executable file does not contain a variable named PI but the value 3.14141414. The preprocessor converted the #define macro name into a value.

Using #define preprocessor statements we therefore have (a) no memory overhead for constant expressions and (b) use no run-time processing resources. While the former saves on the memory size of our program, the latter can significantly increase the speed of program execution.

Use Uppercase for Preprocessor #define Constants

Notice that we used lowercase **pi** when we created a C function called pi and an uppercase **PI** when we defined PI as a C preprocessor #define constant. By convention, all #define constants are uppercase. This allows us to distinguish between preprocessor references and other nonpreprocessor references in our source code.

Macro Expressions in C

In C we can also use a #define as a macro expression. Simple mathematical operations can be performed neatly, with no memory or processing overhead. For example, the multiply function in the previous section could be written as a #define macro, as follows:

```
#define multiply(x,y)  (x*y)
```

When the preprocessor step is completed at compile time, any code containing the expression

```
multiply (<constant value1>,<constant value2>)
```

will be replaced by

```
(<constant value1>*<constant value2>)
```

The use of parentheses around a numeric expression in a macro is important since the expression might be part of a more complex expression after the macro is parsed by the preprocessor.

Another popular use of C macros is in character conversions, which must be done rapidly and are thereby best done with macros rather than function calls. Consider the following macro, found in various forms in the preprocessor file ctype.h. Here the preprocessor processes a variable that we use as an argument in toupper(). The process converts the variable to uppercase, using the expression in bold:

```
#define toupper(c)     ((c)-'a'+'A')
```

The expression says subtract the value of the character "a" and add the value of the character "A" to the variable. In the ASCII character set, this has the net effect of subtracting 32 from the variable. In another character set, however, the values might be different. Since the macro does not rely on fixed values, it should still work with a character set other than ASCII.

We might want to test the macro toupper() in code such as:

```
#include <stdio.h>
#define toupper(c)      ((c)-'a'+'A')

main()
{
        key = 'a' ;
        if ( toupper(key) == 'A' )
                printf ( "Yikes! The macro works!\n" ) ;
        else
                printf ( "Uh Oh!\n" ) ;
}
```

For this reason, we surround the toupper() equation with parentheses:

```
#define toupper(c)      ((c)-'a'+'A')
```

To be safe, we also surround the letter variable identifier **c** with parentheses:

```
#define toupper(c)      ((c)-'a'+'A')
```

The toupper() macro is a part of the C standard library and is #defined in a C standard include file called ctypes.h.

Comparing Clipper Macros and C Macros

In Clipper, we use macros as well, but the syntax, function, and use of a Clipper macro is somewhat different. The major use for a Clipper macro is to create a variable Clipper command, such as:

```
dir = "dir"
RUN &dir
```

Since C is not a command-driven language, we would not need this sort of functionality in C. C code that does what this Clipper code does looks like this:

```
#include <process.h>

main()
        {
        static dir = "dir" ;
        system ( dir ) ;
        }
```

Here dir is a character string.

Using a C macro, we could have also written the code this way:

```
#include <process.h>
#define DIR "dir"

main()
     {
     system ( DIR ) ;
     }
```

Removing #defines

In some situations we may find ourselves with a macro we want to get rid of. We can easily accomplish this with the #undefine preprocessor directive, whose general syntax is:

```
#undefine <macro name>
```

The #undefine preprocessor directive is usually used in conjunction with conditional preprocessor directives, which we'll discuss and give examples of next.

Conditional Operations in the Preprocessor

We can also perform conditional operations in the preprocessor with the #ifdef, #ifndef, and #elsedefine preprocessor directives. In this way we can test to see if a macro name already exists and, if it does, replace its representation with something else. For example:

```
#ifdef TRUE
     #undefine TRUE
     #define TRUE 1
#endif
```

Or we can test to see if a macro name does not exist and, if it doesn't, #define it:

```
#ifndef
     #define TRUE 1
#endif
```

With the #if preprocessor directive, we can also test a constant expression that returns a logical true or false:

```
#if TRUE
     #define YES  1
#endif
```

With the revised ANSI standard, we also now have a #elif directive as well:

```
#if TRUE
     #define YES  1
```

```
#elif
     #undefine TRUE
     #define TRUE 1
     #define YES  1
#endif
```

Include Files

We have used and talked about the #include preprocessor directive. The directive tells the C preprocessor that we wish to include a header file whose name follows the directive. For example, #include <stdio.h> tells the preprocessor to evaluate a header file called stdio.h.

Include files can contain any information contained in a source file, except for the contents of functions. The contents of the function main(), for example, cannot be placed in a header file. Another way of saying this is that anything outside of a function can be placed in a header file.

When the #include directive is preprocessed, the information in the header file becomes part of the source file, as if the information in the header file had been part of the source file.

Files that are included with #include have, by convention, a .h filename extension. Following the UNIX convention, include files are normally kept in a separate subdirectory that is called the INCLUDE subdirectory. The C preprocessor knows where to find them with an environment variable. On IBM PCs and compatibles running DOS, this environment variable is set up with:

```
SET INCLUDE=\INCLUDE
```

Once we have entered this SET instruction, the C compiler references include files in the \INCLUDE subdirectory, regardless of what our source file subdirectory is. How? To instruct the C preprocessor to look for an include file in the \INCLUDE subdirectory, we surround the include filename in angle braces:

```
#include <stdio.h>
```

By convention, header files used by most C applications are stored in the \INCLUDE subdirectory.

If the include file is in the same directory as our source file, we only need to surround the include filename in double quotation marks:

```
#include "stdio.h"
```

Header files specific to one application, stored in the current working directory, are invoked with the quotation mark syntax.

Including #defines in #include Files

Groups of #define and conditional directives that are used by a number of source files are normally placed in header files. For example, the standard C library header file ctype.h contains many macros that deal with character conversion and grouping.

We could include a header file called logic.h, which contains the following:

```
#ifndef TRUE
     #define TRUE 1
#endif
#ifndef FALSE
     #define FALSE 0
#endif

#ifndef YES
     #define YES 1
#endif
#ifndef NO
     #define NO 0
#endif
```

Including #function Prototypes in #include Files

Functions that are invoked by a number of applications should have their function prototypes placed in a header file. In C standard library header files, these header files are usually placed at the end of a header file.

Summary of the C Preprocessor

In this section we looked at the C preprocessor, a powerful component of the C language not (yet) available in Clipper. We saw the following uses for the preprocessor:

Macros. The #define preprocessor directive is particularly useful for transforming repetitive constants and expressions into simple macro names that take no overhead to process. With a little thought, using macro names for constants and expressions adds tremendous readability to a program. In addition, using macros in place of declared variables can save on program overhead.

Conditional preprocessing. The #ifdefine and #elsedefine preprocessor directives allow us to do conditional preprocessing of applications, which means we can write code that is more flexible and portable.

Header files. The #include preprocessor directive allows us to create header files. Header files serve as a common reference point or points for declarations of global constants, variables, data structures, and function prototypes. We have looked at specific examples of include files containing global constants, variables, and function prototypes. Later in this chapter we will see how include files work in conjunction with data structures.

As we said, we can only assume that the Clipper preprocessor, to come with Clipper 5.0, will provide most, if not all — and perhaps more — of the features of the native C preprocessor.

ADDRESSES AND POINTERS

Most Clipper users have seen the address operator &. In Clipper, a major use of the & operator is to perform macro substitution in commands. Look at the following code:

```
dir = "dir"
RUN &dir
```

Here the & operator is used to list a directory with the Clipper RUN command.

In C, we can similarly do macro substitution, as we have seen with the preprocessor:

```
#include <process.h>
#define DIR "dir"

main()
     {
     system ( DIR ) ;
     }
```

Here system is a C function that uses a character string argument to run a system or a DOS command.

In C, the address operator is used for a different purpose. To understand this use, we need to examine the full role of a variable address in C; it is a major one. An address is a location. On a computer, this location is somewhere in the computer's memory. When a variable is declared in C or a memory variable in Clipper is assigned, this variable uses a particular address or sequence of contiguous addresses. In C we can examine an address by use of the address operator, as follows:

```
#include <stdio.h>

main()
     {
     char c = 1 ;
     printf ( "%d,%d\n", c, &c ) ;
     }
```

At run-time, this code will display:

```
1, <address>
```

Where <address> is a numeric assigned at run-time.

In C we also have an operator to look at an unknown variable stored at an address, called the indirection operator. The indirection operator is an * (asterisk). Expanding the above source code, we could use the indirection operator as follows:

```
#include <stdio.h>

main()
     {
     char c = '1' ;
     printf ( "%d,%d,%d\n", c, &c, *&c ) ;
     }
```

At run-time, this code will display:

```
1, <address>, 1
```

Here we use the indirection operator in the third argument of the printf() function call. It serves as an indirect way to display the value of the variable c; it looks at the contents of the address of variable c.

Pointers

In C terminology, another way of saying "the contents of the address of variable c" is to say "the thing pointed to by the address of c." In C any variable identifying an address is called a *pointer*, and the variable stored at that address is the thing pointed to by the pointer.

In C we can declare explicit pointer variables. Reworking our previous example, we would declare and use a pointer as follows:

```
#include <stdio.h>

main()
     {
     char c = 1 ;
     char *cptr = &c ;

     printf ( "%d,%d,%d\n", c, cptr, *cptr ) ;
     }
```

Here we declare a character pointer variable named cptr. To do this we preface the variable name, cptr, with the indirection symbol, *. In the pointer declaration, *cptr does not refer to "the thing pointed to by cptr." Instead, it is an instruction to the compiler to create a pointer variable that can represent an address in memory.

When a pointer is declared, it must also be declared with a particular pointer data type. The pointer data type corresponds to the data type of the variable it points to. In our case, we want to assign our pointer the address of a variable of type char, &c. Therefore we declare the pointer to be of type pointer to character.

In the same way that we can initialize other variables with a value as we declare them, we can initialize a pointer with an address or another pointer. In our example we initialized the pointer to contain the address of c, declared on the previous line.

Now, throughout the rest of the program, we can substitute the pointer variable, cptr, for &c. We can prove that this works by comparing the output of the printf() statement in the above pointer example with the output of the printf() statement in the address operator example.

Pass By Reference Functions

Having explained C addresses and pointers, we can now detail their use in pass by reference functions. Earlier in this chapter we introduced pass by reference functions in general terms. In pass by reference functions, parameters are passed by address, and the data stored at the address is interpreted and/or altered by the called function. In this section we described what a C address is and does, so we can now detail pass by reference explicitly.

Pass By Reference Functions Returning More Than One Value

The following is an example of a function, circle_stats, that uses pass by reference to return more than one value:

```
#include <stdio.h>
#include <math.h>
#define PI 3.141414

main()
{
     void circle_stats(double radius,double *diamptr,double *circumptr);
     double radius = 1, diameter, circumference ;

     circle_stats ( radius, &diameter, &circumference ) ;
     printf ("circle stats are:\n" ) ;
     printf ("radius = %.2f, diameter = %.2f, circumference = %.2f\n",
             radius, diameter, circumference );
}
```

```
double circle_stats ( radius, diamptr, circumptr )
double radius, *diamptr, *circumptr ;
{
     *diamptr   = 2*radius ;
     *circumptr = 2*radius*PI ;
}
```

The function works by receiving the addresses of the diameter and circumference and changing the values stored at these addresses.

In the calling function main() we passed three arguments to the called function circle_stats(). The first argument is a double, while the second and third arguments are each the address of a double. A function is passed the address of a double by preceding the variable name with the address of the operator.

In the header of the function circle_stats(), we declare the three variables to be used in the called function. The first argument, **radius,** is a double, corresponding to the type of the first argument used for circle_stats() in the calling function.

The second and third arguments, diamptr and circumptr, are each of type pointer to double. The pointer is used to represent the address of the second and third arguments to circle_stats(), which were passed as addresses.

When the function is called at run-time, radius contains a value for the radius, while diamptr and circumptr contain the addresses of the variable's diameter and circumference, which were passed from the main().

In the body of circle_stats(), we have our first statement, which uses the formula for the diameter of a circle. We assign the result of the diameter formula to "the thing pointed to by diamptr" using the indirection operator. This assignment changes the contents of the variable diameter, whose address was passed to circle_stats().

The same process is used in the second statement in circle_stats() to compute and assign the circumference of a circle. This next assignment changes the contents of the variable circumference, whose address was passed to circle_stats().

Pass By Reference and Character Strings

Earlier in this chapter we introduced pass by reference with character strings. Now we show how it works. The name of a string is also the name of an address. The first, or zero, element in the character string array is stored at that address. This means that our string named hello could also be written as &hello[0] and *hello is the same as hello[0]. For example, the statements printf ("%s",hello) ; and printf ("%s",&hello[0]) ; have the same meaning to the compiler. The statements printf ("%c",*hello) ; and printf ("%c",hello[0]) ; also have the same meaning to the compiler.

Passing Character Expressions and Character Strings to Functions

Because the name of a character string is an address, a character string is always passed to a function as an address. The same holds true for a Clipper character expression. The name of a Clipper character expression is the name of a C character string. Therefore a Clipper character expression is passed to a function as an address.

In the called function, the address is received and manipulated with a pointer. Consider the following pair of calling and called string functions. The called function is a version of the C standard library function, strlen(), which determines a string's length.

```
/* the calling function is main() */

main()
{
      /* declarations */
      unsigned strlen (char *hello), length ;
      static char hello[] = "hello" ;

      /* function call */
      strlen (hello) ;

      printf ( "the length of string %s is %u\n", hello, length ) ;
}

/* the called function is strlen() */

unsigned strlen (strptr)
char *strptr ;
{
      unsigned i = 0 ;
      while (*strptr++)
            i++ ;
      return (i) ;
}
```

When we use the string's name to call the strlen() function, strlen (hello) ;, we are really passing the called function strlen (&hello[0]) ;. &hello[0] is the address of the first character in the character string.

In the called function, the address must now be interpreted. To do this, we set up the header of any C function that is passed the name of a string as follows:

```
<return type> <function name> ( <string pointer name> )
char *<string pointer name>
```

In the strlen() sample, the header is:

```
unsigned strlen (strptr)
char *strptr ;
```

Here the declaration **char *strptr** declares **strptr** as a pointer of type **pointer to char.**

Arrays and Pointers

Arrays and pointers have an entwined relationship. This is because the name of an array is a pointer to the array. When we declare an array such as:

```
static char hello[] = Hello World ;
```

and display it with:

```
printf ( "%s", hello ) ;
```

we are sending printf() the initial address of the array named hello.

Another way of saying this is that the first address position in the array is represented by the name of the array, so that hello means the same thing as &hello[0]. Following from this rule, *hello means the same thing as hello[0], which in the above example is the character "H."

Function Parameter Pointers

A pointer declared in a function header is a variable that stores a copy of the parameter address passed to the function. Because we are working with a copy, and not the original, we can manipulate the pointer without the function losing track of the original parameter address.

Pointer Arithmetic

Function pointers are commonly manipulated in C with pointer arithmetic. A pointer or an address is a numeric entity. On a PC or compatible, the pointer is 4 bytes (32 bits) in a large model, and 2 bytes (16 bits) in a small model. Since a pointer is a numeric entity, we can change it in a numeric expression with numeric operators. This process is known as pointer arithmetic.

Since hello is a pointer pointing to the first position in the array, how would we point to the second position in the array? We have already seen that this position can be referenced with the address of operator &hello[1]. Now we can use a combination of pointers and arithmetic to say this: hello+1. The string name hello, we recall, represents the initial position of the array in memory, or its initial address. By adding 1 to the pointer hello, we are now pointing to the next offset position or the next address in the array.

Using pointer arithmetic, we can assess the second character in the string with the code *(hello+1). Here we are accessing "the thing pointed to" by the string address hello+1, or the second character in the array, the letter "e."

Moving Pointers

We can also move the pointer itself, by incrementing it, since it is an address. This was done in the strlen() function example:

```
unsigned strlen (strptr)
char *strptr ;
{
        unsigned i = 0 ;
        while (*strptr++)
                i++ ;
        return (i) ;
}
```

Here a while loop is used to determine where the null byte in a string is. After each pass through the loop, strptr is incremented by 1. Recall that *strptr refers to "the thing pointed to by strptr," which is a character in the string. We start out with strptr pointing to the first character in the string. When strptr is incremented the first time, it points to the second character in the string. When it is incremented again, it points to the third, and so on.

The while loop executes until the logical expression in parentheses is a logical false (when it evaluates to 0). Therefore the while loop in strlen() will terminate when "the thing pointed to by strptr" has a 0 value. This occurs when the null byte terminating the string, whose ASCII value is 0, is reached. At that point the unsigned integer **i**, which we incremented along with strptr, will contain a value that is the length of the string. This value is then explicitly returned by the function using a return statement.

Changing Strings Using Function Call By Reference

As we illustrated, string names are passed to functions as addresses. This means that the contents of the string passed to the function may be changed within the function and returned by reference. This works in the same way as our previous example of a call by reference function, where we used doubles.

As an example, here is a program that includes a function to convert a string to uppercase. It is a version of a C standard library function, strupper(). This version of strupper(), however, does not return any explicit value.

```
#include <stdio.h>
#include <ctype.h>

main()
{
     void strupper (char *string) ;

     static char hello[] = "hello" ;
     printf ( "the string in lowercase is: %s\n", hello ) ;
     strupper ( hello ) ;
printf ( "the string in uppercase is: %s\n", hello ) ;
}
void strupper ( strptr )
char *strptr ;
     {
          while (*strptr)
               {
               if ( islower (*strptr) )
                    *strptr++ = toupper (*strptr) ;
               }
     }
```

The pass by reference code in strupper() is similar to our previous strlen() code. The increment operator is used to increment the pointer so that it points to consecutive addresses in the string, where each character in the string is stored.

In this case, however, the characters in the string are altered. This was done with the C standard library macros islower() and toupper(). The macro islower() returns a TRUE (nonzero) value when the character passed to it is a lowercase character. The macro toupper() returns the lowercase letter passed to it as an uppercase character.

Changing Strings Using Pass By Reference and Pass By Value

Most C library string functions used to alter strings employ pass by reference to alter the string parameter. In addition, they return an explicit pointer to the converted string using pass by value. The following version of the strupper() function uses both pass by reference and pass by value:

```
#include <stdio.h>
#include <ctype.h>

main()
{
     char *strupper (char *string) ;

     static char hello[] = "hello" ;
     printf ( "the string in lowercase is: %s\n", hello ) ;
     strupper ( hello ) ;
     printf ( "the string in uppercase is: %s\n",
```

```
                strupper ( hello ) ) ;
}

char *strupper ( strptr )
char *strptr ;
     {
          static char *return_strptr ;

          while (*strptr)
               {
               if ( islower (*strptr) )
                    *strptr++ = toupper (*strptr) ;
               }
     return ( return_strptr ) ;
     }
```

In the calling function the called function is declared with the type pointer to character (char *) to show that it will return an explicit pointer to the converted string.

In the called function a second pointer is declared. The pointer is declared as:

```
static char *return_strptr ;
```

The pointer must be declared with the static storage class because the storage class of a C variable declared within a function is automatic. The scope of an automatic pointer variable declared in the body of the called function is only the function itself.

Since we wish to return a pointer variable to a function outside of the called function, the storage class static is used. The scope of a static variable declared within a called function includes the calling function it is passed to.

Multidimensional Arrays and Pointers to Arrays

In C we can also have multidimensional arrays and pointers to arrays. Using a two-dimensional array, we can code a list of names as follows:

```
#include <stdio.h>

char names[3][25] =
     {
     "Steve",
     "Dave",
     "Joe",
     } ;
main ()
{
     int count ;
```

```
        for ( count = 0 ; count < 3 ; count++ )
            printf ( "%s\n", names[count] ) ;
}
```

In a two-dimensional array such as this, the first subscript refers to the number of items in the list, while the second subscript refers to the size required to store each item on the list. In the declaration of the two-dimensional array, we could have also omitted the subscript constant for the number of items on the list. If we did this, we would have:

```
#include <stdio.h>

char names[3][25] =
        {
        "Steve",
        "Dave",
        "Joe",
        } ;
main ()
{
        int count ;

        for ( count = 0 ; count < 3 ; count++ )
            printf ( "%s\n", names[count] ) ;
}
```

While the facility for coding lists with multidimensional arrays exists in C, it is not used very often because there are easier approaches to coding a list in C. One of these approaches uses an array of pointers to type **char**. This way, we can code the same list as follows:

```
#include <stdio.h>

char *names[] =
        {
        "Steve",
        "Dave",
        "Joe",
        } ;
main ()
{
        int count ;

        for ( count = 0 ; count < 3 ; count++ )
            printf ( "%s\n", names[count] ) ;
}
```

Here the initialized array of pointers does not require subscripts declaring the size of the array. This works the same way as the initialization of a one-dimensional character array, where we have:

```
char hello[] = "hello world" ; /* declared globally */
```

In the declaration of the one-dimensional character array, we did not need to explicitly declare space for the array since we initialized the array as we declared it.

Similarly, an array of pointers can be declared and initialized without an explicit declaration of storage size for the array. In the case of a multidimensional array, however, only the first subscript may be left out when the array is declared and initialized. In this situation and others, pointers are easier to work with for more complex data objects, such as lists. In C, a list such as the one we have seen is much more commonly declared as an array of type pointer to char.

Arguments to main()

Later in this chapter, we will look at the most common use of arrays of type pointers to char. These are command line arguments, or arguments to the function main().

Passing Functions to Functions

In C functions may be passed to functions using their address. A function is commonly passed to a function in C when using the C standard library function signal(). The function signal() allows a user-defined function activity to be performed when a program abort key, such as Ctrl-Break or Ctrl-C, is hit. As example of this in C is:

```
#include <stdio.h>
#include <signal.h>

/* the user defined function */
void trap (int sig)
{
printf ( "Program terminated with user signal.\n" ) ;
exit(1) ;
}

main()
{
     /* the call to signal */
     signal ( SIGINT, trap );
     for ( ; ; )
          printf ( "Stop me...\n" ) ;
}
```

The Names of C Functions are Addresses

As in the case of a character string, the name of a C function is the name of an address. The second argument to trap, therefore, is the name of the user-defined function trap(). The function name is passed to the called function without parentheses. The called function then, as in the case of a string, uses a pointer to reference the function.

Summary of Addresses and Pointers

In this section we introduced one of the more powerful features of the C language, the manipulation of addresses and the use of pointer variables to addresses.

Using addresses and pointers, we detailed the technique of function pass by reference. Included were examples of pass by reference for multiple return values from a function. There were also examples of string functions and passing functions to functions.

We also showed how the name of a character string in C is an address, how strings are passed to functions, and how to manipulate strings inside functions using pointers.

This section also introduced the topic of passing functions to functions via call by reference. We purposely kept our discussion of this fairly simple, to be at least partly digestible by C newcomers.

In the following sections, we will show how addresses and pointers can do useful things.

COMMAND LINE ARGUMENTS

Command line arguments are those arguments with which we invoke a program from the operating system command line. For example, the DOS COPY command often is called with the following syntax:

```
copy <source filename> <target filename>
```

<source filename> and <target filename> are command line arguments that MS-DOS documentation refers to as command parameters.

Within a program, we may want to interpret command line arguments. Certainly the authors of the DOS COPY command needed to in order to allow us to copy files in MS-DOS. Many readers are familiar with the way command line arguments may be interpreted within a Clipper application. In the initial procedure we write:

```
/* beginning of procedure, e.g. initial source file */
PARAMETERS argument1, argument2
```

```
? argument 1
? argument 2
```

All the command line arguments must be read with the PARAMETERS command in character expression format. If one of the command line arguments needs to be interpreted as a number, we would have to convert it from a numeric string to a number using the Clipper function VAL() or the equivalent.

In C, command line arguments are read into an application via optional arguments to the function main(). The remainder of this section details how this is done.

The Function main()

The C function main() has optional arguments to read a program's command line. In this tutorial, we have so far declared main() without any arguments in our examples. This was to simplify the tutorial prior to this formal discussion of command line arguments. Now we move forward to the discussion.

The general syntax for the function main() is:

```
/* preprocessor statements */
/* global statements */

int main ([[[<argument count>],<argument list>],<environ list>])
int    <argument count> ;
char *<argument list>[] ;
char *<environ list>[] ;
{
     /* body of main function */
}
```

In the current ANSI standard, there are three optional arguments to the function main(). By convention, the arguments to main() have the following names:

Name	Description
argv	Argument count integer
argc	Argument string list
env	Environment string list

These naming conventions are an ipso facto standard. Therefore we can substitute these names in the general syntax of main():

```
int main ( [ [ [ argc ] , argv ] , env ] )
int    argc    ;
char *argv[] ;
```

```
char *env[]  ;
{
        /* body of main function */
}
```

This general syntax of main() is now easier to read and easier to compare with C source code that you will see in this book and elsewhere.

In the original K&R standard, and in most C programs, the function main() usually has the following syntax:

```
int main ( argc, argv )
int argc ;
char *argv[] ;
{
/* body of main function */
}
```

Here two of the optional arguments are used. In the current ANSI standard, however, the function main() may appear in any of the four following ways:

1. Without any arguments:

```
main ( void )
{
/* body of main function */
}
```

2. With one argument (this is rarely used):

```
main ( argc )
int argc ;
{
/* body of main function */
}
```

3. With two arguments (this is most commonly used):

```
main ( argc, argv )
int argc ;
char *argv[] ;
{
/* body of main function */
}
```

4. With three arguments:

```
main ( argc, argv, env )
int argc ;
```

```
char *argv[] ;
char *env[] ;
{
/* body of main function */
}
```

The First Argument to main(), argc

The first argument to main(), argc, is an int that holds the number of command line arguments the C program was called with. To test this we compile and link the following source in a file called argc.c and create a program called argc.exe. Argc.exe will display the number of arguments arc.exe was called with:

```
/* contents of argc.c */
#include <stdio.h>

main (argc)
int argc ;
{
      printf ( "%d\n", argc ) ;
}
```

In this case, to compile and link using Microsoft C version 5 or greater, simply type, on the DOS command line:

```
cl argc.c ;
```

Once argc.exe has been created by successfully compiling and linking argc.c, we can use it to test the number of command line arguments given to a C program. For the first test, type `argc` on the DOS command line without any other command line arguments. What happens? The value 1 is displayed. But we used no command line arguments, or did we? As we just found out, by C convention we did enter a command line argument. This is because the name of our program is counted as a command line argument in C.

For the second test, type `argc argument`on the DOS command line. Now the value 2 is displayed. For the third test, type `argcargumentanother`. Now the value 3 is displayed. And the value of argc will be increased by 1 for each additional string typed on the command line.

Reading Command Line Arguments in C

To read command line arguments in C we use the first two optional arguments to the function main(). Here we introduce the second argument and the variable argv. Argv is declared in the function main() to be of type array of pointer to char:

```
char *argv[] ;
```

Earlier in this chapter, we introduced arrays of pointers as means to store a list. An array of pointers is used here for exactly this purpose, where the list is our list of command line arguments. Each member string in the list is one of the arguments.

To test the use of argv in reading command line arguments let us compile and link the following source from a file called argv.c and create a program called argv.exe. Argv.exe will echo the arguments argv.exe was called with:

```
/* contents of argv.c */
#include <stdio.h>

main (argc, argv)
int argc ;
char *argv[] ;
{
        int count = 0;
        void newline ( void ) ;

        for ( count = 0 ; count < argc ; count++ )
             printf ( "%s ", argv[count] ) ;
        newline() ;
}

void newline ( void )
{
        printf ("\n" ) ;
}
```

In this case, to compile and link using Microsoft C version 5 or greater, simply type `cl argv.c;` on the DOS command line. Once argv.exe has been created by successfully compiling and linking argv.c, we can use it to echo the command line arguments given to a C program. Note that the first argument is the name of the program and is represented by argv[0] ;, which displays the full path name of the program under MS-DOS.

Reading the Operating System Environment in C

With the revised ANSI standard we have a third argument to main(), which allows us to read a list of all environmental variables. In MS-DOS, these variables are displayed with the command set. We can create our own environmental variables with the command set <variable name>=<contents>, where <variable name> is the name of the environmental variable and <contents> is a character string or character expression.

To test the use of env in reading a list of all environment variables, let us compile and link the following source from a file called env.c and create a program called env.exe. Env.exe will display environment variables, just as the set command does.

```
/* contents of env.c */
#include <stdio.h>

main (argc, argv, env)
int argc ;
char *argv[] ;
char *env[] ;
{
     int count = 0;
     void newline ( void ) ;

     for ( count = 0 ;  env[count] != NULL ; count++ )
          printf ( "%s\n", env[count] ) ;
     newline() ;
}

void newline ( void )
{
     printf ("\n" ) ;
}
```

Summary of Command Line Arguments

This section covered the subject of reading command line arguments and environmental variables with Clipper and C. From now on in this text, we will often use command line arguments and make use of the optional arguments to the function main() in reading the command line.

CLIPPER ARRAYS AND C STRUCTURES

In this section we will look at C data structures and Clipper arrays. Clipper arrays are really C data structures. A C data structure allows us access to several variables of the same and/or different types under one umbrella name. Because of this ability to access variables of different types using a common reference, we can access any type of data with a Clipper array element.

What is a C Data Structure?

The common example almost always cited to describe a C data structure involves a customer mailing. Here we group the variables used for the mailing in a data structure as follows:

```
#include <stdio.h>
#include <string.h>
#include <math.h>
```

```
struct SUBSCRIBER {
     char lastname [25] ;
     char firstname [15] ;
     char title [25] ;
     char street [60] ;
     char city [30] ;
     char state [2] ;
     char zip [9] ;
     float postage ;
     int term ;
} ;

struct SUBSCRIBER mailing ;

main()
     {
     int get_captain_info() ;
     get_captain_info() ;
     printf ( "Name = %s %s\n",
              mailing.firstname,
               mailing.lastname ) ;
     printf ( "Cost to Send = $%02.2f\n", mailing.postage  ) ;
     printf ( "Subcription Term = $%d\n", mailing.term     ) ;
     }

void get_captain_info()
     {
     strcpy ( mailing.lastname , "Straley" ) ;
     strcpy ( mailing.firstname, "Stephen J." ) ;
     strcpy ( mailing.title    , "Captain" ) ;
     strcpy ( mailing.street   , "Barrow Street" ) ;
     strcpy ( mailing.city     , "Jersey City" ) ;
     strcpy ( mailing.state    , "NJ" ) ;
     strcpy ( mailing.zip      , "0XXXX" ;
     mailing.postage           = .24 ;
     mailing.term              = 1 ;
     }
```

In this example, the data structure was templated and declared globally, outside of a C function. In practice, however, the structure could be templated and/or declared anywhere, within a C function or outside of it.

Syntax and Terminology — The Struct Keyword

To begin coding a C structure, we have the C keyword struct. Struct is a C type, like char, int, or double. Like the other C data type keywords, it lets the compiler know about how much room in memory will be required for data in the program. Unlike the other C data type keywords, however, struct is a conglomerate data type. This means that it is a data type composed of other data types. In order for the compiler to know how much space a structure will require, it needs to know about all the data types used in the structure, which means that the keyword struct needs to be tied to a map of the data types in the structure. This map is called a structure template. The general syntax of a structure template is:

```
struct <structure tag>
     {
     <structure member variable declarations>
     } ;
```

The structure template portion from our mailing sample is:

```
struct SUBSCRIBER
     {
     char lastname [25] ;
     char firstname [15] ;
     char title [25] ;
     char street [60] ;
     char city [30] ;
     char state [2] ;
     char zip [9] ;
     float postage ;
     int term ;
     } ;
```

Here the C type identifier struct is followed by an optional structure tag. Our structure tag is the word SUBSCRIBER. The tag merely identifies the structure template; the tag does not actually declare the structure or its contents.

The contents of a structure template, enclosed in curly braces, are declarations of variables. These declarations, like the declarations we have seen before, tell the compiler the type of each variable and how much room we will need for each one. Our SUBSCRIBER structure template includes declarations for several character arrays, a float, and an integer.

The structure template acts to describe the structure to the compiler. The structure template is, however, a cookie cutter and not the cookie itself. In other words, a C structure template does not declare a C structure. With the structure template alone, our program would not be able to use a data structure.

Declaring a Data Structure

In order to use a structure, it must be specifically declared, just as batter is poured into the cookie cutter to make a cookie. We declare a structure with a structure name, which is not the same as the structure tag. Once we declare the structure, we can then use the variables we declared inside the structure template.

In our mailing sample, we declared the structure with the following line:

```
struct SUBSCRIBER mailing ;
```

Typedefs

Very commonly a C data structure will be declared using a C typedef. A typedef sets up a name we can use for a C data type. Tyedefs are generally set up in a #include file. The following is an example of a simple typedef:

```
typedef int VANILLA ;
```

Every occurrence of VANILLA will now refer to the type int.

We reserved the topic of typedefs until now because they are most commonly used in conjunction with data structure templates and declarations. We can recode our previous structure samples with a typedef as follows. First, the template:

```
typedef struct
     {
     char lastname [25] ;
     char firstname [15] ;
     char title [25] ;
     char street [60] ;
     char city [30] ;
     char state [2] ;
     char zip [9] ;
     float postage ;
     int term ;
     } SUBSCRIBER ;
```

Then, the declaration:

```
SUBSCRIBER mailing ;
```

Typedefs used in this way make repeated structure references easier.

Structure and Storage Classes

Declared C structures have different storage classes, like other C data types. Our mailing structure sample was declared with a global storage class, outside of any C structure. The structure is, like any other C data type declared globally, known to the entire program. We could also declare a structure within a function, where it would have an automatic storage class. An automatic structure would be known only within the function, as with the other automatic data types. We could also declare a structure as **static**. For example, we could modify the mailing declaration as follows:

```
static struct SUBSCRIBER mailing ;
```

In this case, the mailing structure would only be known within the source file where it is declared. Avoid using the C storage class register for declaring data structures.

Declaring Structures in the Structure Template

We can code a structure template and declare it simultaneously, as follows:

```
struct SUBSCRIBER
     {
     char lastname [25] ;
     char firstname [15] ;
     char title [25] ;
     char street [60] ;
     char city [30] ;
     char state [2] ;
     char zip [9] ;
     float postage ;
     int term ;
     } mailing ;
```

The general syntax for declaring a structure as part of the template is:

```
struct <optional structure tag>
     {
     <structure member variable declarations>
     } <structure name> ;
```

We provide here a structure name that acts to declare the structure with that name. The structure name is placed after the closing brace that follows the structure member variable declarations. Remember that the compiler needs to read the semicolon after the structure name.

In the case where we declare the structure within the template, the structure tag has no purpose and can optionally be omitted. We can therefore code the mailing structure declaration as follows:

```
struct
     {
     char lastname [25] ;
     char firstname [15] ;
     char title [25] ;
     char street [60] ;
     char city [30] ;
```

```
char state [2] ;
char zip [9] ;
float postage ;
int term ;
} mailing ;
```

How Structure Data is Stored

Each variable in a structure is stored contiguously, one right after the other. This means that each member variable in the structure exists, in the computer's memory, next to the variable before it. If we look at the storage of the state and zip code members in the SUBSCRIBER structure, we would see:

member type	member name	offset positions in structure	size of datatype
char	lastname	0 - 24	sizeof(char) = 1
char	firstname	25 - 39	sizeof(char) = 1
char	title	40 - 64	sizeof(char) = 1
char	street	65 - 124	sizeof(char) = 1
char	city	125 - 154	sizeof(char) = 1
char	state	155 - 156	sizeof(char) = 1
char	zip	157 - 165	sizeof(char) = 1
float	postage	166 - 171*	sizeof(float) = 6*
int	term	172 - 173*	sizeof(int) = 2*
struct SUBSCRIBER	mailing	0 - 174	sizeof(mailing) = 174

*Sizes marked with an asterisk are Intel (IBM PC and compatible) specific. These may differ on other computer architectures.

Using Structure Member Variables

Now that we have defined C data structures and illustrated how to template and declare them, it's time to access their member variable contents. The simplest way of doing this is with the C dot operator where

```
<structure name>.<structure member variable name>
```

gives us access to a member variable. In our mailing sample we coded our functions main() and get_captain_info() as follows:

```
main()
     {
     int get_captain_info() ;
     get_captain_info() ;
     printf ( "Name = %s %s\n",
              mailing.firstname,
              mailing.lastname ) ;
     printf ( "Cost to Send = $%02.2f\n", mailing.postage  ) ;
     printf ( "Subcription Term = $%d\n", mailing.term     ) ;
     }
void get_captain_info()
     {
     strcpy ( mailing.lastname , "Straley" ) ;
     strcpy ( mailing.firstname, "Stephen J." ) ;
     strcpy ( mailing.title    , "Captain" ) ;
     strcpy ( mailing.street   , "Barrow Street" ) ;
     strcpy ( mailing.city     , "Jersey City" ) ;
     strcpy ( mailing.state    , "NJ" ) ;
     strcpy ( mailing.zip      , "0XXXX" ;
     mailing.postage           = .24 ;
     mailing.term              = 1 ;
     }
```

Structure Addresses and Pointers

As with other data types, we can use structure addresses and pointers. Using structure pointers, we could rewrite our mailing sample as follows:

```
#include <stdio.h>
#include <string.h>
#include <math.h>

     struct SUBSCRIBER {
          char lastname [25] ;
          char firstname [15] ;
          char title [25] ;
          char street [60] ;
          char city [30] ;
          char state [2] ;
          char zip [9] ;
          float postage ;
          int term ;
     } ;
     struct SUBSCRIBER mailing ;
     struct SUBSCRIBER *mailptr = &mailing ;

     main()
          {
          int get_captain_info() ;
          get_captain_info() ;
```

```
          printf ( "Name = %s %s\n",
                   mailptr->firstname,
                    mailptr->lastname ) ;
          printf ( "Cost to Send = $%02.2f\n", mailptr->postage  ) ;
          printf ( "Subcription Term = $%d\n", mailptr->term     ) ;
          }

     void get_captain_info()
          {
          strcpy ( mailptr->lastname , "Straley" ) ;
          strcpy ( mailptr->firstname, "Stephen J." ) ;
          strcpy ( mailptr->title    , "Captain" ) ;
          strcpy ( mailptr->street   , "Barrow Street" ) ;
          strcpy ( mailptr->city     , "Jersey City" ) ;
          strcpy ( mailptr->state    , "NJ" ) ;
          strcpy ( mailptr->zip      , "0XXXX" ;
          mailptr->postage           = .24 ;
          mailptr->term              = 1 ;
          }
```

A structure pointer, like the other pointers we have seen, is declared using the asterisk (*) operator. In the case of structures, however, the asterisk is placed after the tag, to identify the template.

In our sample we have a structure declaration for the structure variable itself, called mailing. Then there is a separate structure declaration for the structure pointer, called mailptr. The structure pointer mailptr is then assigned the address of the structure mailing.

Remember that a pointer declaration does not declare memory storage for the data at the address the pointer represents. Therefore the storage for the data assigned to the pointer must be previously allocated.

The Arrow Operator

In referencing member variables via a structure pointer, we replace the dot operator with an arrow. Therefore, mailptr->firstname and mailing.firstname represent the same data.

Clipper uses the arrow operator to associate a database name or alias with a field in the database:

```
Select 1
USE mail

Select 2
Use inventory
     ? mail->firstname
```

C Structures and Clipper Databases

This Clipper sample displays the contents of the firstname field in the first record from mail.dbf. The relationship of the arrow operator for Clipper aliases and C data structure members is not coincidental, since C data structures are used by Clipper and virtually every professional C application for I/O operations involving databases.

The Clipper/dBASE .DBF file format is easily used in conjunction with C data structures since the data in a .DBF file is stream-of-character data that is parsed within an application program. If our mailing sample were in a record of a .DBF file, the Clipper database file structure of the .DBF file would look like this:

```
Database file structure for database: mail.dbf
Number of Data Records: 9
Date of Last Update: 12/12/88
Field  Field Name  Type  Width  Dec  Offset
    1    LASTNAME  'C'      15    0       1
    2   FIRSTNAME  'C'      25    0      16
    3       TITLE  'C'      25    0      41
    4      STREET  'C'      60    0      66
    5        CITY  'C'      30    0     126
    6       STATE  'C'       2    0     156
    7         ZIP  'C'       9    0     158
    8     POSTAGE  'N'       6    2     167
    9        TERM  'N'       3    0     173
 ** Total **               176
```

The C data structure template for a record in mail.dbf would look like this:

```
struct DBFMAIL {
     char deleteflag[1];
     char lastname[15];
     char firstname[25];
     char title[25];
     char street[60];
     char city[30];
     char state[2];
     char zip[9];
     char postage[6];
     char term[3];
};
```

This template matches, byte for byte, the layout of the .DBF file record.

Recall that the first byte in the record is a flag that tells us whether a record has been marked for deletion.

Also note that although our .DBF file record contains numeric fields, the numeric data is stored in character format. For example, the value .24 is stored in the postage field as three blanks, followed by a decimal point character (.), followed by a character 2, followed by a character 4. The ASCII decimal values for the six characters in the postage field would read as:

```
32 32 32 46 50 52
```

Clipper, dBASE, and other database software tools that work with .DBF files read a given record in a .DBF file into such a C variable or variables representing the record.

Instead of reading the record into the C data structure byte by byte, we can simply dump the entire record into the structure at once because data in member variables within a C structure are stored contiguously. We then force the compiler to think of the structure as a character array. In C we can force the compiler to think of any data type as some other data type by means of a cast. For example:

```
(char *) &mail
```

will cause the compiler to think that the address where the mail structure begins will contain character data. We could also have used:

```
(char *) mailptr
```

which will cause the compiler to think that the structure pointer mailptr is a character pointer.

To code the expression to read the .DBF buffer into a C structure, we use an ANSI C standard library function called memcpy(). The function memcpy() works just like strcpy(), except that memcpy requires a third function parameter, or argument, requesting the length of the character array we wish to copy. Because we can specify a length and because memcpy() does not place a null at the end of the target string after it is copied, we can use it to work with character buffers that are not null terminated.

Here is working C code to read a .DBF buffer directly into a C structure MAILDBF, displaying the results. This code uses a commercial library of C functions by Sequiter Software, called Code Base.

```
< read record sample >
```

Clipper Arrays Are C Unions

Now that we've explained how a regular C structure works and how .DBF files can be read into C structures, we can talk a little about Clipper arrays. A Clipper array is a specialized type of C structure called a union, which differs from the C structures we have seen before. A union, which is a structure of type union, differs from a structure of type struct. In a structure each member variable references a piece of data stored contiguously, where each member of the structure is stored right after the other. In a union each member variable references the same piece of data. The union is used to reference this piece of data in different ways, for example:

```
union INT_OR_CHARS
     {
     unsigned int integer ;
     unsigned char characters[2] ;
     } int_or_chars ;
```

A union such as the one above gives us a choice of how we want to look at the data. Our reference options are the variable types we declared in the union. In this instance we can break an integer value into its high- and low-order byte:

High-order byte	Low-order byte
15 14 13 12 11 10 9	8 7 6 5 4 3 2 1 0

We could also create a union to access some other data types as well. This feature allows Clipper arrays to work with any of the Clipper variable types.

The workings of Clipper arrays and database strategies to represent multiple records in memory leads us into more advanced topics. The first of these topics is arrays of structures and the second is linked lists.

Arrays of Structures in C

Just as we can have arrays in C of type **char** or type int or any of the other data types, we can also have arrays of type struct. What does this mean? In our above mailing example, we simultaneously templated and declared the structure globally as follows:

```
struct
     {
     char lastname [25] ;
     char firstname [15] ;
     char title [25] ;
     char street [60] ;
     char city [30] ;
     char state [2] ;
     char zip [9] ;
     float postage ;
     int term ;
     } mailing ;
```

ookie metaphor again, this declaration gives us one cookie from the cookie
hat if we wanted many cookies and wanted to group them together somehow.

One way to do this is to use an array of structures. The declaration of an array of structures is like the other array declarations we have seen already.

Converting our example into an array of structures, we would therefore have:

```
#define SIZE 100

     struct
          {
          char lastname [25] ;
          char firstname [15] ;
          char title [25] ;
          char street [60] ;
          char city [30] ;
          char state [2] ;
          char zip [9] ;
          float postage ;
          int term ;
          } mailing [SIZE] ;
```

This array of structures will give us 100 cookies.

Using Arrays of Structures

To use an array of structures, we combine the use of array subscripts with the dot operator. The general syntax is:

```
<structure name>[<subscript>].<member variable>
```

If, therefore, we wanted to reference the lastname member variable in the first element in our example array of structures, we would use:

```
mailing[0].lastname
```

Like the other C arrays we have seen, the subscript numbers of an array begin with 0, so that to reference the first element in an array of structures we use <structure name>[0], not <structure name>[1].

Uses for Arrays of Structures

If we had enough memory, we could represent an entire database in an array of structures. Since this is usually not the case, particularly with microcomputers, we use arrays of structures more sparingly, where we may put some fields of some records from a database into an array of structures. This is particularly useful for BROWSE or listbox activities, such as creating a list box.

Linked Lists

Linked lists are an advanced C topic. However, we introduce them here in general terms because Clipper and Code Base store databases and index files in memory using linked lists. The general syntax for a database linked list data structure is:

```
struct REC
     {
     char *record_buffer ;
     struct REC *next_record ;
     };
```

The pointer record_buffer is set by other code to point to a character buffer containing a .DBF file record. The second member points to another copy of the structure, which will contain the next record in the database. When there are no other records to read, an end of list indicator, such as a NULL, can be assigned.

The previous struct REC template is a singly linked list. Another form of linked list is the doubly linked list. It is used for indexing algorithms. A template for a doubly linked list is as follows:

```
struct REC
     {
     char *record_buffer ;
     struct REC *next, *previous ;
     };
```

Using a doubly linked list, a search routine can begin searching from the middle of a database and look either to the previous or next record until a find is made.

Since this is meant to be a C tutorial, we conclude our discussion of linked lists here. For a detailed discussion of linked lists and advanced sorting techniques, we highly recommend *Advanced C*, by Herbert Shilte. There are many excellent "how to" examples of linked lists in his book.

Date and Time Functions in C

Earlier in this chapter, we discussed the Clipper date type and compared the way dates work in Clipper to the way they work in C. We stated that in C both date and time information are stored in a single variable of type long, which counts the number of seconds since January 1, 1900.

C's standard library date and time functions read dates and times into a datestamp of type long and then allow us to parse the datestamp, via a C structure, into separate year, day, minute, and second information. The standard C header file time.h contains this structure, as follows:

```
    struct tm {
      int tm_sec;        /* seconds after the minute - [0,59] */
      int tm_min;        /* minutes after the hour - [0,59] */
      int tm_hour;       /* hours since midnight - [0,23] */
      int tm_mday;       /* day of the month - [1,31] */
  int tm_mon;            /* months since January - [0,11] */
  int tm_year;           /* years since 1900 */
  int tm_wday;           /* days since Sunday - [0,6] */
  int tm_yday;           /* days since January 1 - [0,365] */
  int tm_isdst;          /* daylight savings time flag */
  };
```

Using the C standard library date functions, here is an example that gets the current date and time from the operating system and displays it:

```
#include <stdio.h>
#include <time.h>
#define TRUE  1
#define FALSE 0

int main()
{
struct tm *ourtime ;
int afternoon = TRUE ;
long ticktock ;

time ( &ticktock ) ;
ourtime = localtime (&ticktock) ;

if ( ourtime->tm_hour < 12 )     afternoon = FALSE ;
if ( ourtime->tm_hour > 12 )     ourtime->tm_hour -=12 ;

if ( afternoon )
   printf ( "%.19s %s\n", asctime(ourtime), "PM" ) ;
else
   printf ( "%.19s %s\n", asctime(ourtime), "AM" ) ;
```

In the example, the standard library C function time() sets the long integer ticktock with the date and time measured in seconds from January 1, 1970. The standard library C function localtime() then adjusts this value to a local time zone. Then the structure pointer ourtime is assigned the return value of localtime(), which returns a pointer to tm, which has been filled in with specific date and time information.

The structure member ourtime->tm_hour is then modified to allow for a formatted display of morning or afternoon. Then the function asctime() is passed ourtime, and asctime() creates a date and time string from the contents of the tm structure pointed to by ourtime.

The string is then displayed using printf(). More specific examples of how Clipper date and time commands and functions can be mapped in C are given in Chapter 11.

Summary of Clipper Arrays and C Structures

In this section we introduced the widely used conglomerate data types of the C language, structures, and unions. In ANSI C, there are now other conglomerate data types, such as enumerated lists. We limited our discussion to structures and unions because these are the most widely used, and they relate to our understanding of Clipper.

We also cross-referenced our discussion of structures and unions with Clipper arrays. Clipper arrays may be unions of arrays of structures whose member variables are array elements. They may also be linked lists to array elements, where the data member of each element data structure is a union.

In this section we also introduced strategies, involving structures and unions, for working with databases and index files.

DYNAMIC ALLOCATION OF SPACE

In Clipper memory variables are created using one of the following syntaxes:

```
STORE <expression> TO <memory variable> / < memory variable list>
```

or

```
<memory variable> = <expression>
```

In C, the variables we've seen so far have all been explicitly declared, with the necessary storage allocated to arrays using subscripts and/or initializers.

Now, however, we'll introduce another way of creating variables in C, which is the way Clipper creates its variables with the STORE or = command. This is using a technique called dynamic allocation of space.

The C standard library has a set of functions for dynamic space allocation. The major function in this set is malloc(). Its function header is as follows:

```
#include <stdlib.h> or #include <malloc.h>

void *malloc (size)
size_t size ;
```

The general usage of this function is:

```
<variable pointer> = malloc ( space to allocate ) ;
```

For example, so far we have declared character string arrays as follows:

```
char hello[5] ;
```

Using malloc(), we could instead set up a character buffer this way:

```
char *hello = malloc ((size_t) 5 ) ;
```

What's the difference? There's a big difference, and it has to do with memory. Storage for arrays and other variables declared within a C function is allocated to stack memory. Stack memory is temporary; it is reused when the C function completes its processing.

Dynamically allocated variable space, however, is allocated to heap memory. Heap memory in a program includes all memory except stack memory (and a safety buffer around the stack). The amount of memory that can be used in a program depends on the memory model used. A small memory model program must use a combined heap and stack space of 64K. In a large model, we can use all the available RAM on our machine for heap memory.

Allocated heap memory does not go away until the program terminates or until one intentionally frees up this memory from within the application. In simplest terms this means that whenever we have a statement such as:

```
char *hello = malloc ((size_t) 5 ) ;
```

we must also have a statement somewhere else in our program that contains the C function free(). To complement the statement above, free might be called this way:

```
free ( hello ) ;
```

The C function header for free() is as follows:

```
#include <stdlib.h> or #include <malloc.h>

free ( ptr )
void *ptr ;
```

Because dynamically allocated space remains in our application, great care should be taken when using dynamic space allocation functions in C. In practice, when using straight C, it is safer to avoid using dynamic space allocation functions when explicit declarations of arrays and other data types will work just as well.

C functions that are to be linked in with the Clipper Extend System, however, almost require using dynamically allocated space because of Clipper's small 2K stack. If we blow this stack by declaring a variable or combination of variables bigger than it, we are certainly more likely to lose our minds than if we had malloc()ed our variables.

Size_t

Size_t is a typedef that may be different types on different machines or in different situations. In Microsoft C, size_t is an unsigned integer value in a small model and a unsigned long in a large model. The function malloc() will map size_t and the return pointer automatically according to the memory model used. In a small model, 16-bit (2-byte) addresses are used, and size_t is therefore an unsigned int. This means that in a small model we can allocate up to 65,535 bytes at one time to a 2-byte pointer.

In a large model, 32-bit (4-byte) addresses are used, and size_t is therefore an unsigned long. This means that in a large model we can allocate up to 64K bytes. These memory model and size limitations are Intel architecture/IBM PC or compatible specific.

_fmalloc()

We can override malloc() and explicitly allocate memory to far pointers on a PC with a Microsoft C specific function called _fmalloc(). The function header for _fmalloc() is as follows:

```
void far *_fmalloc (nbytes)
unsigned long nbytes ;
```

We can override malloc() and explicitly allocate memory to near pointers on a PC with a Microsoft C specific function called _nmalloc(). The function header for _nmalloc() is as follows:

```
void far *_nmalloc (nbytes)
unsigned int nbytes ;
```

To free memory allocated with _fmalloc(), we need to use the corresponding function _ffree() whose header is:

```
void _ffree (block)
void far *block ;
```

To free memory allocated with _fmalloc(), we need to use the corresponding function _ffree() whose header is:

```
void _nfree (block)
void far *block ;
```

In Turbo C, malloc() always uses the small model. Therefore size_t will be an unsigned int and a near pointer will be allocated.

The following name differences exist for the near and far versions of malloc:

Microsoft C	Turbo C
_fmalloc()	farmalloc()
_nmalloc()	nearmalloc()
_ffree()	farfree()
_nfree()	nearfree()

The arguments and return values for these functions are the same.

The Far and Near Keyword

Because of the segmented architecture of the IBM PC/compatible, pointers on the PC are addressed in different sizes, depending on the memory model used. In small and medium memory models, where our code must be less than 64K, pointer sizes are of type unsigned integer. In large, compact, or huge memory models, where code may be greater than 64K, pointer sizes are of type unsigned long.

The ANSI standard helps with this problem with two C keywords — far and near. In a small memory model, all pointer sizes are by default unsigned integers. This can be overridden, however, by supplying the far keyword when referring to a pointer. With the far keyword, the compiler will be forced to interpret the pointer as having a long 32-bit size.

In large memory models, all pointer sizes are by default unsigned long integers. This can be overridden, however, by supplying the near keyword when referring to a pointer. With the near keyword, the compiler will be forced to interpret the pointer as having a short 16-bit size.

Summary of Dynamic Allocation of Space

This section covered C's dynamic allocation functions. The discussion was brief because, except for the segmented architecture peculiarities of the PC, the functions are straightforward to use.

We stated that dynamic allocation functions have the following uses:

- Allocating space to a variable on the fly. This is particularly useful when we don't know how much space we'll require for a variable when we declare it.

- Using heap rather than stack space for temporary data storage. This will prove very useful for C functions we build for Clipper's Extend System.

SUMMARY

This chapter introduced you to the C language from a Clipper perspective. Initially, we took the common "Hello World" and went on to broaden your perspective by showing the similarities between the two languages. Starting with the compiling and linking syntax, we then took on the concept of memory and memory allocation. With C, you have all of the control of the application and of the environment. With that much absolute power, you can corrupt your memory, absolutely; therefore, we looked at a few memory models. From here, we took a tour with arrays, #include, header files, shift operators, order of precedence, and the various data types.

By using Clipper as the common base from which to compare things, the fear of the C language should slowly erode. Indeed, there may come a day where applications are prototyped in Clipper to be converted and partially written in C. Though that day may be somewhat far away, the concept of that idea is not that far fetched.

CHAPTER NINE

Hands-On For Clipper Users

FILES, STREAMS, AND ERROR HANDLING

What About Files

Both Clipper and C can be used to open, close, read, write, and otherwise manipulate any computer file. This is possible only if the operating system gives the rights to a given file.

In dBASE or Clipper, the programmer begins from a very high-level view of files. Commands such as USE and INDEX provide ready and easy access to relational databases. At this high level we can code sophisticated end-user applications easily and quickly.

With the C programming language, the programmer begins from a very low-level view of files. The standard C way of file handling is similar to Clipper's low-level file functions. At this level, the programmer deals with what a file is: a sequence of bytes. The file may not even be a real file, in the sense of stored data. It may be one of several types of data streams: from the keyboard, from another process, to the printer, or to another process.

A C programmer can read, write, or access Clipper files or any other complex file, as well as create straightforward ASCII text files. However, for more complex operations such as working with relational database index files, the C programmer almost always relies on a specialized file function library. Such a database library is often a third-party product, meaning that it is provided by a manufacturer other than the manufacturer of the C compiler.

Why do we need a database library in C? The C standard library contains no canned functions to work with relational database files or their associated indexes. Why? Relational database file formats have historically been specific to a particular machine. On the other hand, the C standard library is portable to different computers. This means that in the absence of high-level relational database file functions in the C standard library, we would either have to construct our own or use a third-party product.

If we built our own functions to work with the Clipper file formats, we would have to create a group of C functions to read the header of the .DBF file, access the record data, and parse the records into fields. To work with Clipper or dBASE indexes, we would have to build binary tree routines. But very few people have the time for such endeavors.

It is far easier to leave the database engine to Clipper and use Clipper's Extend System for other tasks or, if we choose to code an application completely in C, to use a third-party commercial database library. This library would contain the entire relational database engine, as Clipper does, and high-level functions to run it.

An excellent example of a dBASE- and Clipper-compatible database library (which we'll be discussing a great deal in the remainder of this text) is Code Base. Code Base is written by Sequiter Software of Edmonton, Alberta, Canada. It allows programmers to work with all of the Clipper and dBASE file formats using C functions, which are very Clipper-like. The product is new, but solid.

Some readers may be familiar with the database library called dBCIII, from Lattice, which affords similar access to Clipper and dBASE file formats. However, Lattice dBCIII does not work with Clipper index files or share Clipper's network record-locking strategy, while Code Base does. dBCIII function calls are also not like Clipper. Code Base also has the advantage over dBC of having a database engine that is purely ANSI C. This means that Code Base's database component can be ported to other types of computers if needed.

Any C function that works with complex files is a superset of C's low-level file functions. Beneath Clipper commands or Code Base functions that work with complex databases are C's standard library stream I/O functions. These functions do the fundamental work of reading, writing, and appending to files. Code Base actually provides us with its source code, so we can see how this works.

To use C at the high level, with Code Base or a similar product, one needs to understand how file handling works in C. Therefore let us start our discussion of files at the foundation of computer file I/O, where C standard library file functions are.

Streams

In C terminology, a file is often referred to as a *stream*. For example, in C library reference materials, functions that work with files often use the term stream in place of the term file. This is because a file is considered to be only one of several possible data input sources and data output targets. These various sources and targets store or process data as a sequence, or stream, of bytes.

Keyboard Streams

An example of an input stream, other than data from a file, is the stream of characters entered from the keyboard. Historically, keys pressed on the keyboard have been the standard way information is entered into a computer. Therefore C, UNIX, and MS-DOS refer to the keyboard as the standard input device.

Display Streams

An example of an output stream, other than data to a file, is a stream of characters displayed on the display monitor. Historically, data displayed on the monitor has been the standard way information is output from a computer. Therefore C, UNIX, and MS-DOS refer to the monitor as the standard output device.

Print Streams

An example of another output stream is the stream of characters sent to a printer. The stream passes from the CPU to a printer connection through one of a series of ports. These ports allow for serial processing of data, where one bit follows another to the printer, or parallel processing, where several bits are sent to the printer at once. Therefore C refers to the currently available print device as the standard printer.

Auxiliary Output Streams

Very often there is more than one output device on a particular computer. One of these devices, such as a second printer port or a communications port, can be established as a standard auxiliary output device.

Error Handling

Fatal errors in an application program in C can be processed through the device standard error. The output device standard error may be the same as one already mentioned. While output to an output device may be redirected to another output device, standard error output may not be redirected. For example, in MS-DOS the output of a program normally sent to the display may be redirected to the printer using

```
program > prn
```

Information output to standard error, however, would not be redirected to the printer. If standard error is set to be the display, which is generally the case, errors will always appear on the display.

Working with Streams in C

To work with these standard streams MS-DOS and the C language establish the following predefined streams:

Stream name	Stdio.h #define	Handle
Standard Input	stdin	0
Standard Output	stdout	1
Standard Error	stderr	2
Standard Auxiliary	stdaux	3
Standard Printer	stdprn	4

C Standard Library Stream I/O Functions

The C standard library stream I/O functions are broken into two categories: buffered and unbuffered. The buffered stream I/O functions are more high level. With them, we can do things with files and streams a little more easily than we can with the unbuffered stream I/O functions. For example, the C buffered stream I/O function fprintf() can format printf()-style data and output it to a file or to the printer. The C unbuffered stream I/O function write() also can output data to a file, but it performs no formatting.

Many experienced C programmers use the unbuffered stream I/O functions almost exclusively. They are faster and afford support for file sharing in a multiuser or network environment. Clipper itself uses the unbuffered low-level C functions when handling files. For example, write() in C works like fwrite() in Clipper. Clipper's low-level file functions therefore provide access from Clipper to unbuffered file I/O functions in C.

OPENING FILES AND FILE HANDLES

At the high level, when the Clipper command USE is invoked, an operation is performed on the database file the programmer wishes to use. Behind the scenes, the database file is opened so that its dǎta is accessible to the Clipper application. A C function named open() makes this happen. The open() function, if it successfully opens the file, returns a reference variable to the file on disk. Each subsequent call to open() returns a unique reference variable value for each file.

In C terminology, this file reference variable is known as a *file handle*. When working with Clipper low-level file functions or with C functions, file handles are used to identify each file. When working with dBASE or Clipper high-level file commands, programmers don't deal directly with file handles. With Clipper high-level commands the file handles are there as well; Clipper does all the dirty laundry for you.

Clipper can hide the details of file handles because of SELECT work areas. Work area values, or aliases, are virtual file handles in Clipper. They allow the programmer to specify which file is current without specifying the file by a handle. From the C perspective, file handles are work area values. Each file handle is used to manipulate a particular file.

To open a file in C and get a file handle for it, one of several C functions may be called. Below are function headers and brief descriptions of them.

```
FOPEN()

#include <stdio.h>

FILE *fopen ( path, access_string )
char *path, access_string ;
```

The function fopen() is the buffered file I/O routine to open files in C; it returns a high-level file handle. The typedef *FILE, from stdio.h, is the type of this high-level file handle. FILE is a pointer to a data structure used to buffer stream I/O. In the data structure, information pertaining to the file is set once the file is opened.

The first parameter of the function fopen() is the pathname of the file. The parameter path can therefore be any valid MS-DOS pathname. The second parameter access_string can be set to any of the following:

Parameter	Meaning
"r"	Open file for reading.
"w"	Create file for writing; erase previous contents, if any.
"a"	Open file for appending to the end of the file. This may append to an existing file or create a new file if the file doesn't exist.
"r+"	Open file for reading and writing.
"w+"	Create file for reading and writing; position file pointer at end of file.
"a+"	Open file for reading or appending to the end of the file.

By default, files opened with fopen() are opened in text mode; therefore any occurrence of a \n will really mean \r\n. Binary mode can be forced instead by using a "b" after the first letter in the access_strings above. Therefore "rb" will open a file for reading in binary mode. For example:

```
#include <stdio.h>

int main(argc, argv)
int argc ;
char *argv[] ;
{
     FILE *fileptr ;

     if ( ( fileptr = fopen ( argv[1], "rb" ) ) == NULL )
          {
          printf ( "The file %s doesn't exist\n", argv[1] ) ;
          return (1) ;
          }
     else
          printf ( "%s successfully opened\n", argv[1] ) ;

fclose ( fileptr ) ;
return (0) ;
}
```

```
OPEN()

#include <fcntl.h>
#include <sys\stat.h>
#include <io.h>

int open ( <path>, access_int, mode_int )
char *path, access_int [, mode_int] )
```

The function open() is the unbuffered file I/O routine to open files in C; it returns a file handle that is a unique integer value. This value will be 1 greater than the last file opened. In C, the five standard data streams, detailed previously in this chapter, are already opened. Therefore the first file in an application opened with open() will have a handle number of 5.

The first argument, path, is any valid MS-DOS pathname. The second argument, access_int, is a value. The value is constructed by using ORed bit values with the following #defined names:

Name	Meaning
Read/Write Flags	
O_RDONLY	Open for reading only.
O_WRONLY	Open for writing only.
O_RDWR	Open for reading and writing.
Other Flags	
O_NDELAY	Not used; for UNIX compatibility.
O_APPEND	Sets the file to be opened for appending.
O_CREAT	Creates the file if it doesn't exist.
O_TRUNC	An existing file is truncated to 0 bytes in length.
O_EXCL	Used with O_CREAT. If the file exists, an error is returned.
O_BINARY	Open the file in binary mode.
O_TEXT	Open the file in text mode.

The third optional argument, mode_int, is also constructed of ORed bit values with the following #defined names:

<table>
<tr><th>Name</th><th>Meaning</th></tr>
<tr><td>S_IREAD</td><td>Permission to read.</td></tr>
<tr><td>S_IWRITE</td><td>Permission to write.</td></tr>
<tr><td>S_IREAD|S_IWRITE</td><td>Permission to read and write.</td></tr>
</table>

An example is:

```
#include <fcntl.h>
#include <io.h>

int main(argc, argv)
int argc ;
char *argv[] ;
{
     int file_handle ;

     if ( (file_handle = open ( argv[1], O_RDWR|O_BINARY ) ) == -1)
          {
          printf ( "Error opening file %s\n", argv[1] ) ;
          return (1) ;
          }
     else
          printf ( "%s successfully opened\n", argv[1] ) ;

close ( file_handle ) ;
return (0) ;
}
```

```
sopen()

#include <fcntl.h>
#include <sys\stat.h>
#include <share.h>
#include <io.h>

int sopen ( <path>, access_int, mode_int )
char *path, access_int, mode_int )
```

The C standard library macro sopen() is really a call to open(), to which the following ORed #defines may be added for shared file support. This support is for multiuser or local area network applications:

Name	Meaning
SH_COMPAT	Sets compatibility mode.
SH_DENYRW	Denies read and write access.
SH_DENYWR	Denies write access.
SH_DENYRD	Denies read access.
SH_DENYNONE	Permits read/write access.
SH_DENYNO	Permits read/write access.

The complexity of these C functions is readily apparent to any Clipper user, where even the low-level file Clipper function FOPEN() is simpler to use. With Clipper's FOPEN() we similarly pass it the path of the file to open, and one of three values: 0 to open the file for read only, 1 for write only, and 2 for reading and writing. What we get back from Clipper's FOPEN() is an integer file handle that is used to identify the file to Clipper's other low-level file functions.

A Clipper example is:

```
file_name="test"
     file_hdle=fopen(file_name,0)

     IF(file_hdle<1)
          ? "Could not open the file "+filename
     ELSE
          ? "The file "+filename+ "successfully opened"
     ENDIF

     FCLOSE(file_hdle)
```

Beyond the particulars of the file opening functions, it is plain that Clipper's low-level file functions are a superset of C's unbuffered file I/O functions. For example, the Clipper function FSEEK() and the C function lseek() work almost the same way. The following C and Clipper examples both position the file pointer to the beginning of the file:

C:

```
#include <fcntl.h>
#include <io.h>

int main()
{
     static char file_name[] = "test" ;
     int file_hdle ;
     long file_offset ;

     if ((file_hdle = open (file_name, O_RDWR|O_BINARY)) == -1)
          {
          printf ( "Could not open the file %s\n", file_name ) ;
          return (1) ;
          }
     file_offset = lseek ( file_handle, 0L, SEEK_SET ) ;
     printf ( "Position in the file %s is %ld\n",
                file_name, file_offset ) ;
     close(file_hdle) ;
}
```

Clipper:

```
file_name = "test"

file_hdle=FOPEN(file_name,0)

IF(file_hdle<1)
     ? "Could not open the file "+file_name
offset = FSEEK(file_hdle,0,0)
? "Position in the file "+file_name+" is "+STR(offset)
FCLOSE (file_hdle)
```

The following table compares Clipper's low-level file functions and the C unbuffered file I/O functions on which they are based.

Clipper Function	C Function(s)	Description
fcreat()	creat()	Creates a file
fclose()	close()	Closes a file
fopen()	open()	Opens a file
fseek()	lseek()	Repositions the file pointer
fread()	read()	Reads a block of data into a file
freadstr()	read()	Reads a string to a file
fwrite()	write()	Writes data to a file

The above functions are completely cross-referenced in Chapter 11.

Having introduced how files and streams work in C at the fundamental level, let us go back to work with relational databases in C. We will work with them in C in a similar way to how they are worked with in Clipper. For this discussion, we will focus on the C library Code Base.

Opening and Selecting Files in Code Base

The following source, spyvsspy.prg, can be compiled in Clipper to open two .DBF files and to switch between them to get the record count of each file. For now, we're working with a single-user environment.

```
SELECT 1
USE spy1
SELECT 2
USE spy2
SELECT 1
```

```
? RECCOUNT()
SELECT 2
? RECCOUNT()
CLOSE ALL
```

The following source file, spyvsspy.c, can be compiled in C to open the same .DBF files and to switch between them to get the record count of each file. As in our Clipper sample, we're working with a single-user environment

```
#include <stdio.h>        /* standard C */
#include <d4base.h>       /* Code Base header file */
#include <d4main.h>       /* Code Base header file - use only in the
                             source file containing the function
                             main () */

main ( argc, argv )
int argc ;
char *argv[] ;
{
      int workarea1, workarea2 ;

      workarea1 = d4use ( "Spy1" ) ;
      workarea2 = d4use ( "Spy2" ) ;

      d4select ( workarea1 ) ;
      printf ( "%ld", d4reccount() ) ;
      d4select ( workarea2 ) ;
      printf ( "%ld", d4reccount() ) ;

      d4close_all () ;
}
```

Both the Clipper and Code Base examples accomplished the same tasks, providing the same output. In both cases, the functionality was the same, except for one clear difference: In the C example the specific work area was given to us as a return value of the .dbf file opening function, d4use(). d4use therefore performs similarly to Clipper's low-level FOPEN() function or C's open() function, which provide us with a numeric file handle that we then use to reference the file. In Code Base, the file handle is termed the *base reference*. In truth, the base reference is a file handle and work area indicator rolled into one.

The function d4use(), upon opening the first file (which in our example is spy1.dbf) will return a base reference value of 0. This is unlike Clipper, which begins with a work area value of 1.

For our purpose, we don't need to be overly concerned about what the exact Code Base base reference value is, since we can use variable aliases such as workarea1 and workarea2 to indicate what we want to think of as work areas 1 and 2. We only need to test to make sure that d4use() does not return a value of -1, which indicates an error condition. In this case, we should recode our file opening C sample above as follows:

```
#include <stdio.h>      /* standard C */
#include <d4base.h>     /* Code Base header file */
#include <d4main.h>     /* Code Base header file - use only in the
                           source file containing the function
                           main () */

#define OPEN_ERROR -1

main ( argc, argv )
int argc ;
char *argv[] ;
{
     int workarea1, workarea2 ;

     if ( ( workarea1 = d4use ( "Spy1" ) ) == OPEN_ERROR )
          {
          printf ( "Error opening Spy1 database" ) ;
          exit(1) ;
          }
     if ( ( workarea1 = d4use ( "Spy2" ) ) == OPEN_ERROR )
          {
          printf ( "Error opening Spy2 database" ) ;
          exit(1) ;
          }

     d4select ( workarea1 ) ;
     printf ( "%ld", d4reccount() ) ;
     d4select ( workarea2 ) ;
     printf ( "%ld", d4reccount() ) ;

     d4close_all () ;
}
```

Code Base Error Handling

Even without the error checking sample shown above, Code Base would have flagged the error with its own error-checking module. This module is a source file called u4error.c. We are free to use u4error.c as is, and get Clipper-like run-time error messages in our program, or to change it as we wish. Changing this particular module is not difficult. A fairly novice C programmer could modify u4error.c without difficulty.

One of the changes we made to u4error.c was to override index error messages so that indexes could automatically be rebuilt when an index error was generated. This alleviated the chronic problem of index files being missing or indexes being at odds with a database. Of course, just taking the error message out of u4error.c doesn't fix the problem. The error must still be flagged, and the program must fix the problem internally in order for the user not to be notified. In this case, the fix is to have the program automatically rebuild a missing or corrupted index. If it takes too long to build it, the user must still be notified of an error condition.

Does Code Base Replace Clipper?

Code Base must improve before it is functionally similar to Clipper. For example, there is no real MEMOEDIT in Code Base. Code Base simply allows us to call our favorite word processor to edit memo fields. Some of Code Base's other limitations will become apparent.

Code Base provides an excellent alternative to Clipper for certain kinds of applications that must be written to accommodate a small amount of memory. Code Base is also useful for programmers who have a favorite C library for windowing or graphics and would like to have Clipper database compatibility.

VIDEO AND SCREEN I/O ISSUES

Screen I/O Libraries

We have seen that the standard library in C does not provide functions for working with relational databases. Similarly, the C standard library does not provide, as Clipper.lib does, optimized video display functionality for a particular machine. There are no windowing functions, for example, in the C standard library. There are functions in the C standard library for displaying text. We have already visited **printf()** and have seen some of the uses and syntaxes for this C function.

Optimized display I/O functionality is provided in C in the same way that relational database support is offered: through additional function libraries linked with the C standard library. There are many of these libraries that allow us to perform the same or similar programming feats with screens. However, there is no C language standard for the names or parameters of functions in these libraries.

Compiler Screen I/O Library Packages

Some compiler manufacturers ship, along with the C standard library, a nonportable and proprietary screen I/O library. Microsoft, for example, ships a graphics function library with Microsoft C version 5.1. Ironically, this product is incompatible with Microsoft Windows.

Turbo C has the best compiler distributed screen I/O library for the PC. It includes both text and graphics screen I/O functions, and it allows us to direct the video output of standard library functions, such as printf, either to direct screen output or to filtered output through the BIOS. Turbo C also includes fontware and high-level graphics functions, such as pie and bar chart functions.

The drawback for Clipper users is that Turbo C graphics functions will not work with the Extend System for calling C functions from Clipper. This is discussed further later in the chapter.

Third-Party Screen I/O Library Packages

There are many third-party screen I/O library packages. These range from the simple and easy-to-use to the very complex. Some of these have gained wide popularity among C programmers. The best of the lot is Vermont Creative Software's Vermont Views, formerly Windows for C/Windows for Data. This acceptance in the C community is because of View's screen I/O speed, versatility, and relative portability to other computer environments.

Portability Problems

Screen I/O code is the most nonportable code because different systems have different monitors, video controller boards, and varying ways to connect to the monitors and boards. Even in a single-computer environment, as with a stand-alone IBM PC or compatible, it is impossible to automatically configure a program to work with any monitor and video card combination. Programs that will run on any monitor and card combination require an installation procedure to determine which monitor and card combination to work with and configure the system accordingly.

For this reason, a product such as VCS's Views can only be relatively portable because the underlying video interface code for each computer is different. For example, if we purchase the PC MS-DOS source code for Views, we cannot recompile this source on a Digital Vax running VMS and expect it to work. We need a different Views function library on the VAX where the code is specifically optimized for the VAX environment.

Code Base SCREEN I/O

Code Base comes with a set of excellent screen I/O and windowing functions. Unlike Code Base database functions, the usage and naming conventions of these functions are not like those in Clipper. Learning them requires a steep learning curve for Clipper users. Consider the following code, which is based on the sample provided in the Code Base manual:

```
#include <w4.h> /* code base window function header file */

main()
{
     /* set up a window to display */

     int window_ref = w4define (10,30,14,50) ; /* sizes */
```

```
    w4attribute ( B_BLINK | F_WHITE ) ;         /* colors */
    w4border ( DOUBLE, F_BLUE ) ;               /* border */
    /* display it as a pop-up */
    w4activate ( window_ref ) ;
    /* display some text in it using dimensions from w4define() */
    w4centre (1, "Hello World") ;
    /* wait for a key */
    getch() ;
    /* make the window disappear */
    w4deactivate ( window_ref ) ;
    /* free up the window memory, which was dynamically allocated */
    w4close ( window_ref ) ;
    /* exit the window system */
    w4exit() ;
}
```

Now consider the following Clipper code to perform the same activity:

```
SET COLOR TO B/N
@10,30 TO 14,50 DOUBLE
SET COLOR TO W*/N
    @11, 34, SAY "Hello World"
INKEY(0)
CLEAR
```

In the Code Base windowing code, there is an additional task that is not required in Clipper: allocating and deallocating memory for the window. Clipper allocates screen I/O memory for us, which makes screen coding in Clipper simpler than coding in Code Base. To give the programmer control over memory used in an application, Code Base elects to have the programmer allocate space in RAM for screens as it is needed.

As with the Code Base database functions, there is also the use of a handle that describes the window to other functions. The window handle is returned by the w4define() function so that the window can be used or reused. This facilitates window overlays and tiled windows.

The screen I/O functionality on a PC is a very personal choice. Every PC user has a favorite word processor and every C programmer has a favorite screen package; many have written their own. Code Base designers therefore make it possible to use the Code Base database system and use a separate screen I/O library. Therefore we could use Code Base's database functions and another C screen I/O library such as Vermont Views, or code our own, Clipper-like, screen I/O functions.

Coding Screen I/O Functions in C

For developing applications on a PC or compatible, it is not too difficult to create one's own library of text-based screen I/O functions. In the remainder of this section, in order to learn more about how screen I/O works in C, this will be our strategy. To begin with, it will be necessary to examine how video output works on the PC or compatible.

Methods of Display on a PC

There are various methods to display text and graphics on a PC. One is to include the ANSI.SYS driver in your config.sys file and to issue the DOS commands that, when filtered through that driver, control the screen. We will not discuss this method here since we want to focus our attention on screen I/O in C and because the ANSI.SYS driver is the least preferred means of working with the screen from any programming point of view. For a complete discussion of ANSI.SYS and the ANSI.SYS commands, we highly recommend Van Wolverton's *Supercharging MS-DOS* (Microsoft Press).

We said that the ANSI.SYS driver is the least preferred method of working with the screen. This is because it is relatively slow in performing screen updates. It is the most time-consuming way of sending information to the screen. To display a few lines of text, speed makes little difference. But for applications that involve pop-up windows, interchanging whole screens, and animated graphics, speed is important.

ROM BIOS

A faster way of working with the screen is by accessing the PC's ROM BIOS. We have devoted a section to interfacing with the BIOS in Chapter 10. There we illustrate how the BIOS works in C. If you are unfamiliar with the BIOS, it would be useful to read that chapter first and then return to this discussion.

The ROM BIOS interrupt accessed most for performing screen I/O in C is Interrupt 10, which governs Video Services.

Direct Video Hardware Control

The fastest way to write to the display is to write directly to the video display hardware. Many commercial software packages do this, as does Clipper. On a PC or compatible, we write directly to the display by writing to the correct address in video memory.

Video addresses differ on PC monitors. On a monochrome display with a monochrome video board, we write to B0000000 hex. If a color video board and color screen are used, we write to B8000000 hex. If a color video board and monochrome screen are used, we use B8000000 hex, which we also use for color. If a monochrome board and monochrome screen are used, but the monochrome screen allows for gray-scaling of colors, as does the monochrome board for the PS/2 series, we still use B8000000 hex, which we would otherwise use for color.

The EGA (Enhanced Graphics Adapter) complicates things more by using yet another video address for some of its video modes: A8000000. If we are using an EGA in one of these modes, we need to write to this video address.

The second, small problem we encounter is that we must use far pointers to the far region of memory we are writing to when doing direct screen writes. This means that when using small or compact memory models, we must explicitly use the keyword far. In Microsoft C we can make our code transportable between memory models by using Microsoft's internal M_I86?M constants, which are defined at compile time, and do the following:

```
#if (defined(M_I86SM) || defined(M_I86MM))
   char far* ColorScreenPtr = (char far*)0xB8000000 ;
   char far* MonoScreenPtr  = (char far*)0xB0000000 ;
#elif (defined(M_I86CM) || defined(M_I86LM) || defined(M_I86HM))
   char ColorScreenPtr = (char) 0xB8000000 ;
   char MonoScreenPtr  = (char) 0xB0000000 ;
#endif
```

Mapping the Screen Memory

After the screen address has been defined, we can map text to the screen memory. In text mode, each screen is mapped to 4000 bytes, with the full screen memory taking 4K bytes. Every even offset byte in the map, starting from offset 0, will contain a character to be displayed. Every odd offset byte in the map, starting from offset 1, will contain an attribute code for the color, color intensity, and blink toggle of the character preceding it.

To see how this direct screen write works, let's look at how the at_say() function might be coded in C:

```
/* at_say() copyright (c) 1989 SJS & Associates -
   write string to display memory at a given position */

extern say_color_attrib ;

void at_say ( row, col, string )
int row , col ;
unsigned char *string ;
{
    int count = 0, offset = (row*80 + col)*2 ;

    while ( *(string+count) )
    {
         *(ScreenPtr+offset)   = *(string+count) ;
         *(ScreenPtr+offset+1) = say_color_attrib ;
         offset+=2 ;
         count++ ;
    }
}
```

Like Clipper's @..SAY command, this function requires a row and column position and a text string. It also uses a color that has been set elsewhere, as with Clipper's SET COLOR TO command. In Clipper, initialization functions are run each time a Clipper.exe is loaded into memory; they cause the color attribute used for the SAY to default to white on a black background, regardless of the display. In Clipper, we use the command SET COLOR TO to change the color. Likewise, in C we can build a function or macro to change the color and use an external or static variable to let our at_say() C function know what the color is. In the preceding example, the color attribute is a single variable called say_color_attrib.

The simplest way we can code colors on a PC is as follows. First, we create a #include file, called colors.h with the following #defines:

```
#define BLACK 0
#define BLUE 1
#define GREEN 2
#define CYAN 3
#define RED 4
#define MAGENTA 5
#define BROWN 6
#define WHITE 7
#define GRAY 8
#define LT_BLUE 9
#define LT_GREEN 10
#define LT_CYAN 11
#define ORANGE 12
#define LT_MAGENTA 13
#define YELLOW 14
#define LT_WHITE 15
```

In addition to these, we will need the following numbers, which we will use as masks for the attribute byte:

```
#define BLINK 128
#define NORMAL 0
```

Then we can use a C preprocessor macro to code the attribute byte:

```
#define color (fore,back,blink) (fore|(back<<4)|blink)
```

We then add the above macro to our colors.h file. This macro will mask the appropriate bit positions in the attribute byte with the foreground, background, and blink states specified from the table above. Then we can code the following, self-contained C source file:

```
#include <colors.h>
unsigned char say_color_attribute ;

main()
     {
     say_color_attribute = color ( BLUE, WHITE, NORMAL ) ;
```

```
        at_say ( 10, 20, "Hello World" ) ;
        }
```

Note that we have so far given the colors simple names, like BLACK, YELLOW, and GREEN. We could have also used Clipper color names but we felt that in this case it made sense to depart from the standard.

Using at_say() to Display Data of Different Types

Our at_say() function is limited to displaying strings. How would we display other data types? The strategy Clipper's @..SAY command uses to display numeric as well as character string and expression data is similar to the strategy of the C standard library function printf(), where a C union is used to pick the proper type.

Rather than doing something similar, we can simply use the function sprintf() to convert data of various types to a string and then use our at_say() to display it. Sprintf() also has the advantage of formatting a string with various pieces of data. For example:

```
#include <colors.h>
unsigned char say_color_attribute ;

main()
     {
     say_color_attribute = color ( BLUE, WHITE, NORMAL ) ;
     int enough = 50 ;
     char say_string[80] ;
     sprintf ( say_string,
               "We've probably used Hello World %d times in this text.",
               enough ) ;

   at_say ( 10, 0, say_string ) ;
     }
```

Windowing Functions

An advantage of Code Base's and Vermont Views' windowing functions is window support. First-rate windowing support in Clipper is available through third-party products such as Steve Straley's ToolkiT and dLesko's FUNCky library. These products allow the Clipper programmer to use virtual screen coordinates and to create windows with many different border possibilities, including shadow effects. For example:

```
Windowpush(5,15,20,65,3,.T.,"BLUE", "WHITE")
Windowpop()
```

The following is a source code listing for a virtual windowing system in C. It consists of a C header file named at_say.h, a windowing function named window(), and a modified at_say() function.

```
/*******************************************************************
s_say.h
Window and Video system header file
SJS & Associates.  Copyright (c) 1989.  SJSC library
partially reprinted for Advanced Clipper with C
*/
/*******************************************************************
   constants for Windows Border types
*/
#define NO_BDR 0
#define SINGLE 1
#define DOUBLE 2
#define NO_BDR_SHADOW 4
#define SINGLE_SHADOW 5
#define DOUBLE_SHADOW 6

/*******************************************************************
struct S_WIN
   {
   int startrow ;  /* Relative starting row for display */
   int startcol ;  /* Relative starting column for display */
   int rows     ;  /* Relative number of rows for display */
   int cols     ;  /* Relative number of columns for display */
   int border   ;  /* Border type of Window */
   unsigned char saycolor ; /* color attribute for at_say() */
   unsigned char bdrcolor ; /* color attribute for window border */
   } s_win ;

/*******************************************************************
   function prototypes
*/
extern  void at_say(int row,int col,unsigned char *string);
extern  void at_say_at (int row,int col);
extern  int window(int minrow,int mincol,int maxrow,int maxcol,
                   unsigned char fill, unsigned char type);

/*****
end of s_say.h header file
*******************************************************************/

/*******************************************************************
s_say.c
Window and Video system source file
SJS & Associates.  Copyright (c) 1989.  SJSC library
partially reprinted for Advanced Clipper with C
*/

extern char *ScreenPtr ; /* this should be initialized to the
                            proper Screen Address */
```

```
int window ( startrow, startcol, endrow, encol, FillChar, bordertype )
int startrow, startcol, endrow, endcol ;
unsigned char FillChar, bordertype ;
{
int cols = endcol-startcol+1 ;
int rows = endrow-startrow+1 ;
int midcol   = startcol+(cols/2) ;
int midrow   = startrow+(rows/2) ;
int col, leftcol , rightcol, offset ;
int row, uprow, downrow ;
unsigned char tempcolor = s_win.saycolor ;
* default bordertype is DOUBLE */

unsigned char left_upper = '' ;
unsigned char left_lower = '' ;
unsigned char right_upper= '' ;
unsigned char right_lower= '' ;
unsigned char horizontal = '' ;
unsigned char vertical   = '' ;

s_win.border = DOUBLE ;

if ( bordertype == SINGLE || bordertype == SINGLE_SHADOW )
   {
   left_upper  = '' ;
   left_lower  = '' ;
   right_upper = '' ;
   right_lower = '' ;
   horizontal  = '' ;
   vertical    = '' ;
       s_win.border = SINGLE ;
   }

s_win.startrow = startrow ;
s_win.startcol = startcol ;
s_win.rows = rows ;
s_win.cols = cols ;

if ( bordertype != NO_BDR && bordertype != NO_BDR_SHADOW )
   {
     for ( leftcol = midcol-1 , rightcol = midcol ;
       leftcol >= startcol ;
       rightcol++, leftcol-- )
          {
          *(ScreenPtr+(offset=((startrow*80)+rightcol)*2))=right_upper;
          *(ScreenPtr+offset+1) = s_win.saycolor ;
          *(ScreenPtr+(offset=((startrow*80)+rightcol)*2)) = horizontal ;
          *(ScreenPtr+offset+1) = s_win.saycolor ;

          *(ScreenPtr+(offset=((endrow * 80)+rightcol)*2))=right_lower ;
          *(ScreenPtr+offset+1) = s_win.saycolor ;
          *(ScreenPtr+(offset  =((endrow*80)+rightcol)*2)) = horizontal ;
          *(ScreenPtr+offset+1)    = s_win.saycolor ;
```

```
        *(ScreenPtr+(offset = ((endrow * 80)+leftcol )*2))=left_upper ;
        *(ScreenPtr+offset+1) = s_win.saycolor ;
        *(ScreenPtr+(offset=((startrow*80)+leftcol)*2))  = horizontal ;
        *(ScreenPtr+offset+1) = s_win.saycolor ;

        *(ScreenPtr+(offset = ((endrow * 80)+ leftcol )*2))=left_lower;
        *(ScreenPtr+offset+1) = s_win.saycolor ;
        *(ScreenPtr+(offset  =((endrow*80)+leftcol)*2))  = horizontal ;
        *(ScreenPtr+offset+1)   = s_win.saycolor ;

        for ( row = startrow+1 ; row < endrow   ; row++ )
        {
             *(ScreenPtr+(offset=((row*80)+rightcol)*2)) = FillChar ;
             *(ScreenPtr+offset+1) = s_win.saycolor ;
             *(ScreenPtr+(offset=((row*80)+leftcol)*2)) = FillChar ;
             *(ScreenPtr+offset+1) = s_win.saycolor ;
        }
        }

  for ( row = startrow+1 ; row < endrow   ; row++ )
        {
        *(ScreenPtr+(offset=((row*80)+startcol)*2)) = vertical ;
        *(ScreenPtr+offset+1) = s_win.saycolor ;
        *(ScreenPtr+(offset=((row*80)+endcol)*2))   = vertical ;
        *(ScreenPtr+offset+1)   = s_win.saycolor ;
        }

   *(ScreenPtr+(offset=((startrow * 80) + startcol)*2))=left_upper ;
   *(ScreenPtr+offset+1) = s_win.saycolor ;
   *(ScreenPtr+(offset=((startrow * 80) + endcol)  *2))=right_upper ;
   *(ScreenPtr+offset+1) = s_win.saycolor ;
   *(ScreenPtr+(offset=((endrow   * 80) + endcol  )*2))=right_lower ;
   *(ScreenPtr+offset+1)   = s_win.saycolor ;
   *(ScreenPtr+(offset=((endrow   * 80) + startcol)*2))=left_lower ;
   *(ScreenPtr+offset+1)   = s_win.saycolor ;

  at_say_at (startrow+1,startcol+1) ;
   s_win.rows-=2 ;
   s_win.cols-=2 ;
  }

else /* paint a borderless window */
  {
   s_win.border = NO_BDR ;

   for ( leftcol = midcol-1 , rightcol = midcol ;
     leftcol >= startcol ;
     rightcol++, leftcol-- )
        {
   for ( row = startrow ; row <= endrow ; row++ )
        {
             *(ScreenPtr+(offset=((row*80)+rightcol)*2)) = FillChar ;
             *(ScreenPtr+offset+1) = s_win.saycolor ;
```

```
                *(ScreenPtr+(offset=((row*80)+leftcol)*2))  = FillChar ;
                *(ScreenPtr+offset+1) = s_win.saycolor ;
           }
      }
      at_say_at (startrow,startcol) ;
   }

/* shadow logic */

if ( ( bordertype == NO_BDR_SHADOW
    || bordertype == SINGLE_SHADOW
    || bordertype == DOUBLE_SHADOW )
    && startcol >= 2 && endrow <=23 )
       {
       s_win.saycolor = s_win.bdrcolor ;

    for ( col = startcol-2 ; col < startcol ; col++ )
           {
    for ( row = startrow+1 ; row <= endrow+1 ; row++ )
              {
                 *(ScreenPtr+( (row*80+col)*2 +1)) = s_win.saycolor ;
               }
       }

   for ( col = startcol-2 ; col <= endcol-2 ; col++ )
         {
            *(ScreenPtr+ ((row=endrow+1)*80 +col)*2 +1) = s_win.saycolor ;
       }
       s_win.saycolor = tempcolor ;
       }

return (0) ;
}
```

To make the at_say() function work with the window() function, using relative window coordinates and window colors, the at_say() code is modified as follows:

```
/* This function is in the s_say.c SJSC.lib source file */

   void at_say ( row, col, string )
   int row, col ;
   unsigned char *string ;
   {
       int count = 0, offset = (row*80 + col)*2 ;
          /* use virtual cursor position */
          row += s_win.startrow ;
          col += s_win.startcol ;
       while ( *(string+count) )
          {
          *(ScreenPtr+offset)   = *(string+count) ;
          *(ScreenPtr+offset+1) = s_win.saycolor ;
          offset+=2 ;
```

```
            count++ ;
        }
    }
```

To override the window() coordinates, we create an additional function, at_say_at():

```
/* This function is in the s_say.c SJSC.lib source file */

     void at_say_at ( row, col )
     int row, col ;
     {
          s_win.startrow = row ;
          s_win.startcol = col ;
     }
```

To make window coloring more like Clipper, we add one more function to s_say.c:

```
/* This function from SJSC.lib, s_say.c */

     void set_color_to ( foreground, background, blink_state )
     unsigned char foreground, background, blink_state ;
     {
     s_win.saycolor = color ( foreground, background, blink_state ) ;
     }
```

How the SJSC Windowing Functions are Called

Using the "Hello World" example at the beginning of this section, where we compared Code Base and Clipper, we can show how our SJSC windowing code is more Clipper-like:

```
char *ScreenPtr ;

main()
{
     init_win() /* this is a User Defined Function to
                   set the proper address for ScreenPtr */

     set_color_to ( BLACK,WHITE,NORMAL ) ;
     window ( 10,30,15,50, ' ', DOUBLE ) ;
     set_color_to ( WHITE,BLACK,BLINK ) ;
     at_say ( 1,34, "Hello World" ) ;
}
```

GETS

Next we will discuss getting information from a user within a program, using a process that Clipper and dBASE refers to as a "GET." A GET takes its name from the function in dBASE and Clipper called @SAY..GET.

What Does a Get Involve?

Getting information from a user generally involves an interactive process between an input device and an output device. Historically the input device has been a keyboard and the output device a monitor. For this reason, in C and other languages, the keyboard is called the standard input device while the monitor is the standard output device. Currently, however, a growing number of computer environments get user input from other input devices, such as a mouse, and employ other output devices, such as a speaker whose sounds emulate human speech.

In the keyboard/screen user input scenario, the process of collecting user information often works the following way:

1. The screen displays a prompt to the user, which may be some form of character expression or string. The prompt may also be a whole list of choices, a pictorial graphic image, or some other visual display on the screen.

2. The computer may then:

   a. Suspend processing until a key is hit, or

   b. Continue processing while polling the user for a key.

3. Optionally, a screen cursor may appear on the screen. The cursor is a blinking underscore or box character on the screen that identifies a screen location.

4. In response to the prompt, the user presses a key or sequence of keys. Each key pressed may be echoed back to the user. The key is usually echoed on the screen at the current cursor location, and the cursor location is updated to a new position after the echoed key is displayed.

Special keys are used for special activities. For example, the Enter key is normally used to confirm entry of a key or sequence of keys. The F1 key is usually used to display a help screen. Special keys on a PC or compatible keyboard are often not able to be displayed or have display images that have no particular meaning to a user. Therefore, for the most part, these special keys are not echoed on the screen.

As we noted above, usually keys are input in a sequence, as in inputting a character expression or a dollar amount. This sequence is then echoed back, character by character, as it is typed. Here the key sequence is usually called an input field, and the portion of the screen displaying the key sequence is called a screen field. Often the input field relates to a database field, and the input field is stored in a database field as it is collected.

In its most thorough form, the process of collecting user information, or what Clipper users refer to as a GET, would look like this:

1. Display an input field in a picture format. The picture format will be according to the format of the data. For example, a date would probably be formatted MM/DD/YY.

2. Optionally, perform an initial function before going on. An example of this might be displaying a choice list as soon as a user enters a field.

3. Display the cursor at the first input position in the field. Normally this would be at the leftmost position in the field. However, if one were building a calculator-like numeric input function, this might be the rightmost position.

4. Collect a key from the user.

5. Filter and/or validate the key, performing key conversions, or disregard the key.

6. Echo or do not echo the key to the screen, at a particular field location, based on the picture format. Or modify a key or keys already there. For example, the backspace key might be used to erase a previously displayed character in the field. Optionally, update the screen cursor position.

7. Optionally, display a list of input choices if a special key is hit. Many applications use F2 for this.

8. Optionally, display a help screen or window if a special key is pressed. Many applications use F1 for this.

9. Repeat steps 4 through 8 until a field validation key, such as the Enter key, and/or a position in the field is reached, such as a position beyond the end of the field.

10. Perform field validation activities on the set of data collected in the field. For example, make sure that a date is a proper date.

11. Perform end-of-field activity, such as changing an element on the screen or copying the received data to a database.

In Clipper.lib and the C standard library, there are functions and commands to collect user information from the keyboard, echo it to the screen, and store it in a variable. We can collect user information either keystroke by keystroke or via an input field.

In Clipper, the lowest-level, fundamental input function is:

```
INKEY(<exp>)
```

where <exp> is a time to wait, in seconds, before processing a key. The function INKEY() with no arguments can also be used to poll the keyboard for a key, without waiting.

In Clipper, the highest-level command for field input is the command @, whose syntax is:

```
@ <row>, <column>     [SAY <exp> [PICTURE <clause]]
                      [GET <exp> [PICTURE <clause>]
                      [RANGE <exp,exp>]
                      [VALID <exp]]
                      [CLEAR]
```

Now let's look at how we can find or create the above functions in C. For starters, there are some functions that are part of the Microsoft and Turbo C versions of the C standard library for PC GETs in C. In particular, there are the DOS-specific functions getch(), and getche() for getting individual key values from the keyboard. The function getch() does not echo a key pressed on the display, while getche() does.

Coding a C INKEY(0) function using getch() or getche() is almost a straightforward task, except for reading special PC key values, such as the F1 key or arrow key. PC keystrokes are stored internally as 2-byte unsigned integer values.

If a typewriter key is pressed, the low-order byte contains the ASCII value of a key. If a special key is pressed, the low-order byte contains an ASCII 0 and the high-order byte contains a code for the special key. This special key code is termed a scan code by MS-DOS.

When getch() or getche() is called initially, the low-order byte is returned by the function. If the byte is 0, the next call to either function will return the special key scan code. Using this knowledge and the function getch(), we can build a more programmer-friendly key-getting function that, like the INKEY() function, returns a unique value for any key:

```
#include <conio.h>

int getkey(void)
{
        int key ;

        if ((key = getch()) )
              return ( key ) ;
        return ( key= (getch() + 300) ) ;
}
```

The getkey() function above tests for the value of the low-order byte in its first call to getch(). If the value returned by getch() is nonzero, the key is immediately returned. Otherwise, the getkey() function calls getch() again and adds the magic constant 300 to the key. Adding this magic constant ensures that the scan code value of the special key does not conflict with any ASCII value of keys other than special. For example, the scan code value of the F7 function key, decimal 65, is the same as the ASCII value of the capital letter "A." In order to distinguish an "A" from an F7 in the return value of the getkey() function, the ASCII value of "A" is returned as the value 65, while the scan code value of F7 is returned as 365.

Other commercial libraries, such as Vermont Views, simply return a negative for a special key value. In this scenario, the F1 key value becomes -59 decimal.

What Clipper has done with INKEY() is to map key values for special keys to other values that are not in conflict with typeable keys. For instance, the Delete key is marked to an ASCII decimal 7, which is normally used to sound the system speaker. But an ASCII 7 cannot be entered at the keyboard, so this value can safely be used to represent a special key.

A header file, such as the SJSC header file s_keys.h, can be used to give macro names to all special keys returned by getkey():

```
/* S_KEYS.H  SJSC Library, Copyright 1989 SJS & Associates

NOTE1- for all special keys except ESC, BACKSPACE, and TABKEY,
       add 300 to BIOS special key values
       to get the special key values #defined below.

     #define SPECIAL        300

     #define ESCAPE          27
     #define BACKSPACE        8
     #define TABKEY           9
     #define RETURN          13
     #define SPACEBAR        32
     #define QUOTE           34
     #define COMMA           44
     #define PERIOD          46
     #define SLASH           47

     #define SHIFTTAB       315

     #define UP             372
     #define DOWN           380
     #define LEFT           375
     #define RIGHT          377

     #define HOME           371
     #define END            379
     #define PGUP           373
     #define PGDN           381

     #define INSERT         382
     #define DELETE         383
```

```
#define CTRL_LEFT     415
#define CTRL_RIGHT    416
#define CTRL_HOME     419
#define CTRL_END      417
#define CTRL_PGUP     432
#define CTRL_PGDN     418

#define F1            359
#define F2            360
#define F3            361
#define F4            362
#define F5            363
#define F6            364
#define F7            365
#define F8            366
#define F9            367
#define F10           368

#define SHIFT_F1      384
#define SHIFT_F2      385
#define SHIFT_F3      386
#define SHIFT_F4      387
#define SHIFT_F5      388
#define SHIFT_F6      389
#define SHIFT_F7      390
#define SHIFT_F8      391
#define SHIFT_F9      392
#define SHIFT_F10     393

#define CTRL_F1       394
#define CTRL_F2       395
#define CTRL_F3       396
#define CTRL_F4       397
#define CTRL_F5       398
#define CTRL_F6       399
#define CTRL_F7       400
#define CTRL_F8       401
#define CTRL_F9       402
#define CTRL_F10      403

#define ALT_F1        404
#define ALT_F2        405
#define ALT_F3        406
#define ALT_F4        407
#define ALT_F5        408
#define ALT_F6        409
#define ALT_F7        410
#define ALT_F8        411
#define ALT_F9        412
#define ALT_F10       413

#define ALT_1         420
#define ALT_2         421
```

```
#define ALT_3        422
#define ALT_4        423
#define ALT_5        424
#define ALT_6        425
#define ALT_7        426
#define ALT_8        427
#define ALT_9        428
#define ALT_10       429

#define ALT_HYPHEN   430
#define ALT_EQUAL    431
#define ALT_Q        316
#define ALT_W        317
#define ALT_E        318
#define ALT_R        319
#define ALT_T        320
#define ALT_Y        321
#define ALT_U        322
#define ALT_I        323
#define ALT_O        324
#define ALT_P        325
#define ALT_A        330
#define ALT_S        331
#define ALT_D        332
#define ALT_F        333
#define ALT_G        334
#define ALT_H        335
#define ALT_J        336
#define ALT_K        337
#define ALT_L        338
#define ALT_Z        344
#define ALT_X        345
#define ALT_C        346
#define ALT_V        347
#define ALT_B        348
#define ALT_N        349
#define ALT_M        350
```

Once a unique key value can be determined for any key, we can proceed to use its value in a GET function.

A Field Input Function in C

What would a comprehensive GET function look like? Earlier we generalized the components of a data collection function. More specifically, the steps may be as follows:

1. Determine row, column, field size, field type, and field display attribute.

2. Perform an optional field initializing activity.

3. Until the user completes the GET, repeat these steps:

   a. Use a picture string or perform a user-defined function to picture format the field.

   b. Position the cursor in the field in accordance with the picture format chosen.

   c. Display information in the field stored in the variable passed to the function.

   d. Get a valid keystroke. While the key is not a field confirmation key, do the following steps to process the keystroke.

      (1) Perform a field-editing activity if an edit key is pressed, such as backspacing in the field if Backspace is pressed.
      (2) Or perform an action if an action key is pressed, such as getting information from a list-box, or getting a help screen.
      (3) Or write to the field if a write key is pressed.
      (4) Display the field if its contents have been altered by the previous three steps, and move the cursor in the field.

   e. Perform an optional end of GET activity, which includes determining whether or not to allow the user to leave the GET.

4. Copy the contents of the field into the GET field variable. Leave the GET and continue processing.

In a Clipper GET, whether as a direct part of the @..SAY..GET command or in conjunction with it, many of the above field formatting and data collection activities can be accomplished. For more complex activities, the Clipper programmer can pass a user-defined function as part of the VALID clause, which, in addition to performing field validation activities, can perform other activities within a GET. For example,

```
@ 2,3 SAY "Enter Name" GET name PICT "@!" ;
     VALID Mustfill(name, 3,20)
```

What if we could, in addition to passing a user-defined function to a GET in a VALID clause, allow the user to redefine all the steps outlined above? How would such a GET function be coded? Below we show a working GET function in C that accomplishes this.

Similar to the s_say header file and function in the previous section, the GET function below works in conjunction with a header file. The header file is s_get.h, the contents of which we'll explore later. First we look at the way the GET function is set up.

```
/*********************************************************************
SJSC functions Copyright (c) 1989 Steve Straley & Associates
get.c */

#include <stdio.h>
#include <stdlib.h>
#include <string.h>
#include <s_say.h>   /* header file for display functions          */
```

```
#include <s_get.h>    /* header file for get functions              */

get ( row, col, string )
int row, col ;
char *string ;
{
int repeat = 1 ;
while ( s_get.repeat )
     {
   do_picture ( row, col, string ) ;      /* picture format field
                                             contents and
                                             initialize get data
                                             structure  */
   do_display () ; /* display the field and set
                      current cursor position        */

   /* get a valid key.  While the key is not a field confirmation key,
      do functions to process the keystroke                         */
   while ( ( s_get.key = do_valid() ) && !do_confirm() ) /*get loop */
        {
        if ( do_edit () ) ;/* process on edit keys (Backspace, etc. */
        else if ( do_action () ) ; /* optional action function, such
                                      as listbox function           */
        else if ( do_help () ) ;  /* what help to display, if any   */
        else if ( do_write () );  /* how to write keys to field     */

        do_display()              /* redisplay field and
                                     optionally move the cursor     */

        }
     repeat = !do_end() ; /* field validation function.
                             If do_end returns FALSE (0) the get
                             is repeated. */
     }

strcpy ( string, s_get.array) ; /* replace the string passed       */
s_win.saycolor = tempcolor ;    /* restore the color               */
return (0) ;
}
```

The above get() function calls a series of user-defined functions to do all the work. These C UDFs perform as follows:

C UDF	Description
do_picture()	Picture formats the string for the GET and initializes the GET's data structure for the following do_<action>() C UDFs.
do_start()	Performs initial field activities.
do_valid()	Validates each keystroke. Returns TRUE (nonzero) for a valid keystroke and FALSE for an invalid one.

C UDF	Description
do_edit()	Performs an optional edit action on any key. Returns TRUE (nonzero) if an edit action is performed or FALSE if no edit action is performed.
do_action()	Performs a general action on any key. For example, a list-box can be displayed if a ? key is pressed. Returns TRUE (nonzero) if an action is performed or FALSE if no action is performed.
do_help()	Performs an optional help action on any key. Returns TRUE (nonzero) if a help action is performed or FALSE if no help action is performed.
do_write()	Performs an optional write on any key. Returns TRUE (nonzero) if a key is written to the display or FALSE if no write is performed.
do_end()	Performs optional field validation activities, like a Clipper VALID clause. It is also used to unformat any field picture set up with do_picture(). Returns TRUE (nonzero) if the field is validated or FALSE (0) if the field is invalid. If the do_end is false, the GET is repeated.
do_display()	(1) Displays the field, using a call to the at_say() function in the previous section or to a Code Base display function or to some other C display function. (2) Moves the cursor, usually using a call to the BIOS.

Note that none of the do_<action> functions, with the exception of do_picture(), are passed any parameters. How then do we gain access to the GET internals to write the do_<action> functions? The answer is by placing all the component variables in a GET into a global data structure:

```
/* SJSC() library Copyright() 1989, SJS & Associates
   partial extract from the headerfile s_get.h */

struct S_GET          /* current field information -
                         variables set by store_all()
                         and get functions                   */
{
/* These members hold field data: */
int handle ;          /* handle of the GET                   */
unsigned int key ;    /* current key pressed in a 'get'      */
char fieldname [15] ; /* holds current field name            */
char array [255] ;    /* holds field char contents           */
```

```
double value ;          /* holds field numeric contents             */
char clear [255] ;      /* replaces 'array' when field is cleared   */
int type ;              /* field's type 'C','N', 'D', 'L' or 'M'    */
int width ;             /* field's length                           */
int dec ;               /* field's number of decimal places, if any */
int index ;             /* current offset into the 'get'            */
int insert ;            /* TRUE if field is in insert mode          */
unsigned int key ;      /* current key pressed in a 'get'           */
int row ;               /* the screen row of the get                */
int col ;               /* the screen column of the get             */

/* These members are flags for each do_<action> function
   listed below.  The flags are set before entering the
   GET and are interpreted by the corresponding do_action
   function. */

int picture ;           /* do_picture() */
int start   ;           /* do_start()   */
int valid   ;           /* do_valid()   */
int edit    ;           /* do_edit()    */
int action  ;           /* do_action()  */
int help    ;           /* do_help()    */
int display ;           /* do_display() */
int end     ;           /* do_end()     */
/* these members are flags for full screen editing */
int skip    ;           /* the get is skipped when TRUE */
int fld     ;           /* the field number in a full screen mode  */
int move    ;           /* the next field number to move to        */
int rec     ;           /* the record number in a full screen mode */
int quit    ;           /* the full screen mode is quit when TRUE  */
int save    ;           /* the get is saved to .dbf file when TRUE
                           and the field is a database field       */

} s_get ;
```

The global S_GET data structure becomes accessible to each file that #includes the header file s_get.h. The following macros, also in s_get.h, are used to set the flags outside the GET function:

Macro Name	#define
set_picture()	#define set_picture(value) (s_get.picture=value)
set_start	#define set_start(value) (s_get.start=value)
set_valid	#define set_valid(value) (s_get.valid=value)
set_edit	#define set_edit(value) (s_get.edit=value)
set_action	#define set_action(value) (s_get.action=value)
set_help	#define set_help(value) (s_get.help=value)
set_display	#define set_display(value) (s_get.display=value)
set_end	#define set_end(value) (s_get.end=value)

The calling sequence in pseudocode is then:

```
Optionally call the above set_<action> macros
Call the GET function
Perform the user-defined do_<action> functions within the GET.
Each do_<action> function can be set to perform alternative tasks
by branch processing on the set_<action>flag
```

The calling sequence in actual code is:

```
main calling function

     #include <stdio.h>
     #include <s_get.h>

     main()
     {
          static char str[] = "Hello world", numstr[] = "50.00" ;

          set_picture(1) ;
          get ( 10,1, str ) ;
          set_picture(2) ;
          get ( 12,1, numstr ) ;
     }
```

The do_picture function is coded as follows:

```
do_picture ( row, col, array )
int row, col ;
char *array ;
int handle ;
{
s_get.row = row ;
s_get.col = col ;

switch ( s_get.handle = handle )
     {
     case 2:
          strcpy ( s_get.array, array ) ;
          strcpy ( s_get.clear, array ) ;
          s_get.offset = 0 ;
          s_get.type = 'N' ;
          s_get.width = strlen (s_get.array) ;
          s_get.dec = find_dec_places (s_get.array) ;
          s_get.offset = s_get.width-s_get.dec-2 ;
          atof ( s_get.value, s_get.array ) ;
          break ;
     case 1:
     default:
          strcpy ( s_get.array, array ) ;
          strcpy ( s_get.clear, array ) ;
          s_get.type = 'C' ;
```

```
            s_get.width = strlen (s_get.array) ;
            s_get.offset = 0 ;
            break ;
        }
    }
```

The example above branches on the value of s_get.picture with a switch statement. It then sets up the S_GET structure with the appropriate data for a character or numeric type. The s_get.picture value 2 sets up the GET for numeric data, while any other s_get.picture value will set up the GET for character data.

The other set_<action> and do_<action> function pairs work similarly. A full set of ready-made do_<action> S_GET functions, with predefined set_<action> flags for various data types, is included with the SJSC library.

GETs in Other Commercial C Function Libraries

Vermont Creative Software Vermont Views. Our attempt to get functionality in C is only one of many possible approaches. Some commercial C function libraries, such as Vermont Views, offer an even more comprehensive system of data collection in C. The more comprehensive the library is, however, the more complex it is to use. To use Vermont Views, you must read the manual. Because it cannot be picked up casually, it would not be a fair treatment of the product to introduce Views code in this section. With Views, however, one can do all the tasks we presented as part of the SJSC GET system, including list-boxes. Views also provides mouse support and is portable to the Unix and VAX environments.

Sequiter Software Code Base. Code Base also provides a set of GET functions. These functions can perform fairly sophisticated activities, such as collecting data from a list-box. However, the use of the Code Base GET system is not easy. This is particularly true when working with list-boxes and performing customized validation tasks. These tasks can be done in Code Base, but the functionality is not yet programmer-friendly, especially to the novice C programmer. The Code Base product overall is very young, however, and its designers are very talented. Code Base's focus up until now has been to produce a solid, portable, database engine. In the future the product may very well provide an equally substantial and programmer-friendly data collection system.

FULL SCREEN EDITING

We now carry our data collection discussion into another territory known generically as full screen editing. This involves working with multiple fields and/or records in a database. In dBASE, there have been two ways of accomplishing full screen editing. One way is to EDIT one record's fields at a time, and another way is to BROWSE the database as a two-dimensional list of fields across the screen and records down the screen, like a Lotus 1-2-3 spreadsheet.

Clipper users are familiar with Clipper's version of BROWSE, the function DBEDIT(). We have already visited DBEDIT() in our other discussions in this and other texts on Clipper. Here we have seen the merits of DBEDIT() and ways in it can be customized.

There are some limitations with both DBEDIT() and BROWSE. For example, what would we do if we wished to view a database with fields going down the screen, as rows in the spreadsheet, and records going across the screen, as columns? At present, neither the Clipper DBEDIT() function or dBASE BROWSE command can handle this. Achieving this functionality would require building a customized spreadsheet.

Clipper users have also found that DBEDIT() cannot be nested in too many levels. In other words, calling a full edit screen from within another full edit screen in Clipper recursively will cause Clipper to crash after a certain point.

In C we have built a browse system based upon the SJSC get routines. This browse system also is built with, and therefore requires, Code Base for its database engine. The remainder of this section shows the source code for the SJSC browse system.

First, we have the s_browse.h header file, which looks like this:

```
/*------------------------------------
Header file: s_browse.h
Contents:    structures and constants for s_browse functions.
Copyright (c) 1987, 1988, 1989 Steve Straley & Associates

-------------------------------------*/
#define MAX_BROWSE_COLS 80
#define MAX_BROWSE_RECS 25
#define MAX_BROWSE_FLDS 20
#define SIZE_BROWSE_BUF (MAX_BROWSE_COLS+1)

struct S_BROWSE_RECS
   {
   char buf [ SIZE_BROWSE_BUF ] ;
   double sum ;
   } ;

struct S_BROWSE_FLDS

   {
   char fieldname [15] ; /* holds field name                          */
   long ref ;            /* code base reference number for field      */
   int type ;            /* field's type 'C','N','D, 'L' or 'M'       */
   int width ;           /* field's length                            */
   int dec ;             /* field's number of decimal places          */
```

```
    int total ;          /* set to TRUE if field is to be totaled         */
    double value ;       /* holds a numeric fields  value                 */
    double sum ;         /* holds numeric fields  sum                     */
    int offset ;         /* field pos in dbf file record  buffer          */
    int row ;            /* vertical field pos on browse  screen          */
    int col ;            /* horizontal field pos on browse screen         */
    int valid ;          /* get validation,  see do_valid()  ,get_valid()  */
    int confirm ;        /* get confirm,     see do_confirm(),get_confirm()*/
    int listbox ;        /* get listbox,     see do_list()   ,get_list()   */
    int start ;          /* get start rules, see do_start    ,get_start()  */
    int end ;            /* get end rules,   see do_end      ,get_end()    */
    int edit ;           /* get edit rules,  see do_edit()   ,get_edit()   */
    int help ;           /* get help,      ,  see do_help()   ,get_help()   */
    int picture ;        /* get picture,     see do_picture(),get_picture()*/
    int insert ;         /* get ins state,   see do_insert() ,get_insert() */
    } ;

struct S_BROWSE
    {
    int maxfld ;
    int maxrec ;
    int grand_total ;
    int width ;
    int dec ;
    int row ;
    int col ;
    struct S_BROWSE_FLDS flds [ MAX_BROWSE_FLDS ] ;
    struct S_BROWSE_RECS recs [ MAX_BROWSE_RECS ] ;
    } s_br[3] ;

int s_brno ; /* the current array element in the above
               array of structures, representing the current
               browse being worked with */

long s_choice ; /* the record number chosen from a listbox */

#define S_HORIZONTAL 0 /* browse fields horizontally, records listed down */
#define S_VERTICAL   1 /* browse fields vertically, records listed across */
#define S_LISTBOX    2 /* browse list, first field is choice field       */
#define S_MENU       3 /* menu list, returns choice integer              */

#ifndef S_NONE
#define S_NONE         0
#endif

#ifndef S_PICTURE
#define S_PICTURE      1
#endif

#ifndef S_UPPER
#define S_UPPER        2
#endif
```

```
#ifndef S_LOWER
#define S_LOWER        3
#endif

#ifndef S_ALPHA
#define S_ALPHA        4
#endif

#ifndef S_DIGIT
#define S_DIGIT        5
#endif

#ifndef S_DISPLAYABLE
#define S_DISPLAYABLE  6
#endif

#ifndef S_ENCRPYT
#define S_ENCRPYT      7
#endif

#ifndef S_SCROLL
#define S_SCROLL       8
#endif

#ifndef S_SHELF
#define S_SHELF       15
#endif

#ifndef S_CUSTOM
#define S_CUSTOM      16
#endif

#define H_BUF      ( s_br[s_brno].recs [rec].buf )
#define H_COL      ( s_br[s_brno].flds [fld] .col )
#define H_FLD      ( H_BUF + H_COL )
#define H_NEXT_COL ( s_br[s_brno].flds [fld+1] .col )
#define H_NEXT_FLD ( H_BUF + H_NEXT_COL )

#define V_BUF      ( s_br[s_brno].recs [fld].buf )
#define V_COL      ( rec* (s_br[s_brno].flds[fld].width+1) )
#define V_FLD      ( V_BUF + V_COL )
#define V_NEXT_COL ( rec * (s_br[s_brno].flds[fld].width+1) )
#define V_NEXT_BUF ( s_br[s_brno].recs [fld+1].buf )
#define V_NEXT_FLD ( V_NEXT_BUF + V_NEXT_COL )
```

Next, we have the main browse source file itself, named s_browse.c:

```
/*------------------------------------

s_browse functions.
Copyright (c) 1987, 1988, 1989 Steve Straley & Associates
```

```
Description:

These functions allow for flexible, two-dimensional views of a database,
just like dBASE's browse, or Clipper's DBedit.  Here, however, the pro-
grammer has complete control over the view of the database and the way
information is received from the user.
-------------------------------------*/

#include <stdio.h>       /* standard 'C' */
#include <stdlib.h>      /* standard 'C' */
#include <string.h>      /* standard 'C' */
#include <math.h>        /* standard 'C' */
#include <d3base.h>      /* Code base header file */
#include <s_get.h>       /* Starbase get    system header file */
#include <s_say.h>       /* Starbase video  system header file */
#include <s_browse.h>    /* Starbase browse system header file */

double grand_total = 0.00 ;

/*--------------------------
function: browse()

description:

   main browse function.
   browse_set must be called before this function to set up the
   fields of the database to be browsed.

parameters:

int  row    the starting screen row for the browse

int  col    the starting screen col for the browse

int nrecs   the number of records to browse, starting with the
            current record number or position in the index

int view    S_HORIZONTAL will browse fields horizontally across the
            screen and records down the screen. The maximum number
            of fields is set by the #define MAX_BROWSE_FLDS in
            do_browse.h. The maximum number of records is the number
            of rows the screen can display.

            S_VERTICAL will browse fields vertically down the screen
            and records across the screen. The maximum number of
            records is determined by the number of columns the
            screen can display, which is generally 80.

--------------------------*/

int browse ( row, col, nrecs, view )
int row, col, nrecs, view ;
```

```
{
s_br [s_brno].row = row ;
s_br [s_brno].col = col ;
s_br [s_brno].maxrec = nrecs ;

   switch ( view )
      {
      case S_VERTICAL:
         browse_vform    ( 0, nrecs ) ;
         browse_vtotals ( row, col, nrecs ) ;
         while ( !s_get.quit && !s_get.skip )
            {
            browse_vsay ( row, col, nrecs ) ;
            browse_vget ( row, col, nrecs ) ;
            }
         browse_vsave ( 0, nrecs ) ;
         break ;
      case S_LISTBOX:
         browse_hform ( 0, nrecs ) ;
         browse_hsay   ( row, col, nrecs ) ;
         browse_lget   ( row, col, nrecs ) ;
         break ;
      case S_MENU:
         browse_hform ( 0, nrecs ) ;
         browse_hsay   ( row, col, nrecs ) ;
         browse_mget   ( row, col, nrecs ) ;
         break ;
      case S_HORIZONTAL:
         browse_hform ( 0, nrecs ) ;
         browse_htotals ( row, col, nrecs ) ;
         while ( !s_get.quit && !s_get.skip )
            {
            browse_hsay   ( row, col, nrecs ) ;
            browse_hget   ( row, col, nrecs ) ;
            }
         browse_hsave ( 0, nrecs ) ;
      }
}

/*---------------------------
function: browse_set()

description:

   browse setup function.
   browse_set must be called for each field to be browsed.

parameters:

int row:    the row for the field in a vertical browse.
            Use NEXT_BR_POS for the next, contiguous row.
```

```
int col:    the starting column position for the field in a
            horizontal browse.
            Use NEXT_BR_POS for the next, contiguous col.

int order: a number representing the order in which the field
            will be displayed.
            Use NEXT_BR_FLD for the next consecutive order number
            following a previous call to browse_set().

char *fieldname: the name of the field as a null terminated character
                 string.
char *ldfld:     a prompt string, or field separation string,
                 null terminated.

---------------------------*/

int browse_which ( browse_no )
int browse_no ;
{
   if ( browse_no >= 2 )
   return ( 1 ) ;

   s_brno = browse_no ;
   return ( SUCCESS ) ;
}

int browse_set ( row, column, order, fieldname )
int row, column, order ;
char *fieldname ;
{
   long fieldno ;
   int n = s_brno ;

   strcpy ( s_br[n].flds[order].fieldname, fieldname ) ;
   if ( ( fieldno = f3ref ( fieldname ) ) == -1 )
        return ( (int) s_br[n].flds[order].ref) ;
   s_br[n].flds[order].ref    = fieldno ;
   s_br[n].flds[order].offset = f3offset   ( fieldno ) ;
   s_br[n].flds[order].type   = f3type     ( fieldno ) ;
   s_br[n].flds[order].width  = f3width    ( fieldno ) ;
   s_br[n].flds[order].total  = TRUE ;
   s_br[n].width = s_br[n].flds[order].width ;

   s_br[n].flds[order].dec    = f3decimals ( fieldno ) ;
   s_br[n].dec = s_br[n].flds[order].dec ;
   s_br[n].flds[order].row    = row ;
   s_br[n].flds[order].col    = column ;
   s_br[n].maxfld = order ;
   return ( (int) fieldno ) ;
}
```

```
int browse_next_fld ()
{
   return ( s_br[s_brno].maxfld+1 ) ;
}

int browse_next_pos ()
{
   return ( s_br[s_brno].flds[s_br[s_brno].maxfld].col+
            s_br[s_brno].flds[s_br[s_brno].maxfld].width + 1 ) ;
}

int browse_setopts ( valid, confirm, listbox, end, help, edit,
                     picture, insert, total )

int valid, confirm, listbox, end, help, edit, picture, insert, total ;
{
   int fld ;
   int n = s_brno ;

   for ( fld = 0 ; fld <= s_br[n].maxfld ; fld++ )
      {
      s_br[n].flds[fld].valid    = valid ;
      s_br[n].flds[fld].confirm  = confirm ;
      s_br[n].flds[fld].listbox  = listbox ;
      s_br[n].flds[fld].end      = end ;
      s_br[n].flds[fld].help     = help   ;
      s_br[n].flds[fld].edit     = edit   ;
      s_br[n].flds[fld].picture  = picture ;
      s_br[n].flds[fld].insert   = insert ;
      s_br[n].flds[fld].total    = total ;
      }
}

/*------------------------------------------
the functions below are called internally by browse()
------------------------------------------*/

/*------------------------------------------
function: browse_hform()

description:

   initialize the horizontal browse form
   by transferring information from the database
   into the s_br[n].recs array of structures

parameters:

   int nrecs    The number of records to browse.

------------------------------------------*/
```

```
int browse_hform ( rec, nrecs )
int rec, nrecs ;
{
   int fld, end_of_file ;
   int n = s_brno ;
   char *recbuf ;

   for ( end_of_file = FALSE ;
         rec < nrecs && !end_of_file ;
         rec++, end_of_file = d3skip( 1L ) )
      {

      /* get the data */
      recbuf = f3record() ;

      /* transfer to browse array of structures */
      memset ( s_br[n].recs [rec].buf, '\0', SIZE_BROWSE_BUF ) ;
      for ( fld = 0 ; fld <= s_br[n].maxfld ; fld++ )
         {
         memcpy ( s_br[n].recs [rec].buf + s_br[n].flds [fld] .col,
         recbuf + s_br[n].flds [fld] .offset,
                  s_br[n].flds [fld] .width )   ;

         if ( s_br[n].flds [fld].type == 'D' )
            {
            memcpy ( s_br[n].recs [rec].buf + s_br[n].flds [fld] .col,
                     c3dt_format (
                     s_br[n].recs [rec].buf + s_br[n].flds [fld] .col,
                     "MM/DD/YY" ),
                     s_br[n].flds [fld] .width )   ;
            }
         }
      }
   d3skip ( (long) -nrecs ) ;
}

/*--------------------------------------------
function: browse_vform()

description:

   initialize the vertical browse form
   by transferring information from the database
   into the s_br[n].recs array of structures

parameters:

   long nrecs   The number of records to browse.

--------------------------------------------*/
```

```
int browse_vform ( rec, nrecs )
int rec, nrecs ;
{
   int fld , end_of_file ;
   int n = s_brno ;
   char *recbuf ;

   for ( end_of_file = FALSE ;
         rec < nrecs && !end_of_file ;
   rec++, end_of_file = d3skip( 1L ) )
      {
      /* get the data */
      recbuf = f3record() ;

      s_br[n].recs[rec].sum = 0.00 ;
      for ( fld = 0 ; fld <= s_br[n].maxfld ; fld++ )
         {
         if ( rec == 0 )
            {
            memset ( s_br[n].recs [fld].buf, '\0', SIZE_BROWSE_BUF ) ;

            }
         s_br[n].flds[fld].sum = 0.00 ;
         grand_total= 0.00 ;

         memcpy ( s_br[n].recs [fld].buf+ rec*(s_br[n].flds[fld].width+1),
         recbuf + s_br[n].flds [fld] .offset,
                  s_br[n].flds [fld] .width )    ;

         if ( s_br[n].flds [fld].type == 'D' )
            {
            memcpy ( s_br[n].recs [fld].buf+
            rec*(s_br[n].flds[fld].width+1),
                   c3dt_format (
                   s_br[n].recs [fld].buf+
            rec*(s_br[n].flds[fld].width+1),
                   "MM/DD/YY" ),
                   s_br[n].flds [fld] .width )    ;
            }
         }
      }
   d3skip ( (long) -nrecs ) ;
}

/*-------------------------------------------
function: browse_hsay ( )

description: display the browse screen array of structures
3            for a horizontal browse.

-------------------------------------------*/
```

```
int browse_hsay ( row, col, nrecs )
int row, col, nrecs ;
{
    int rec ;
    int fld ;
    int n = s_brno ;

    for ( rec = 0; rec < nrecs ; rec++ )
       {
       for ( fld = 0 ; fld <= s_br[n].maxfld ; fld++ )
          {
          at_say ( row+rec,
                   col+s_br[n].flds[fld].col,
                   H_FLD ) ;
          }
       }
}

/*---------------------------------------------
function: browse_vsay ( )

description: display the browse screen array of structures
             for a vertical browse.

---------------------------------------------*/

int browse_vsay ( row, col, nrecs )
int row, col, nrecs ;
{
   unsigned char tempcolor = video.saycolor ;
   int rec, fld ;
   int n = s_brno ;

   for ( rec = 0; rec < nrecs ; rec++ )
      {
      for ( fld = 0 ; fld <= s_br[n].maxfld ; fld++ )
         {
         if ( ( fld % 2 ) ) video.saycolor = tempcolor ;
         else video.saycolor = video.oddcolor ;

         if ( s_br[n].flds[fld].type == 'N' &&
              ( s_br[n].flds[fld].value = atof (
                s_br[n].recs[fld].buf+ rec* (s_br[n].flds[fld].width+1) ) )
              == 0.00 )
            {
            at_say ( row+fld,
                     col+ rec* (s_br[n].flds[fld].width+1),
                     replicate ( " " , s_br[n].flds[fld].width ) ) ;
            }
         else
```

```
            {
            at_say ( row+fld,
                     col+ rec* (s_br[n].flds[fld].width+1),
                     V_FLD ) ;
            }
         }
      video.saycolor = tempcolor ;
      }
}

int br_hdisplay_rec ( row, col, rec )
int row, col, rec ;
{
   int fld ;
   int n = s_brno ;

   for ( fld = 0 ; fld <= s_br[n].maxfld ; fld++ )
      {
      at_say ( row+rec,
               col+s_br[n].flds[fld].col,
               s_br[n].recs[rec].buf+s_br[n].flds[fld].col ) ;
       }
}

int br_vdisplay_rec ( row, col, rec )
int row, col, rec ;
{
   unsigned char tempcolor = video.saycolor ;
   int fld ;
   int n = s_brno ;

   for ( fld = 0 ; fld <= s_br[n].maxfld ; fld++ )
      {
      if ( ( fld % 2 ) ) video.saycolor = tempcolor ;
      else video.saycolor = video.oddcolor ;

      if ( s_br[n].flds[fld].type == 'N' &&
           ( s_br[n].flds[fld].value = atof (
             s_br[n].recs[fld].buf+ rec* (s_br[n].flds[fld].width+1) ) )
           == 0.00 )
         {
         at_say ( row+fld,
                  col+ rec* (s_br[n].flds[fld].width+1),
                  replicate ( " " , s_br[n].flds[fld].width ) ) ;
         }
      else
         {
         at_say ( row+fld,
                  col+ rec* (s_br[n].flds[fld].width+1),
                  s_br[n].recs[fld].buf+ rec* (s_br[n].flds[fld].width+1) ) ;
         }
      }
   video.saycolor = tempcolor ;
}
```

```
int browse_hget ( row, col, nrecs )
int row, col, nrecs ;
{
   unsigned char tempcolor ;
   int rec, fld = 0, end_of_file ;
   int n = s_brno ;
   s_get.key = 0 ;
   for ( rec = 0 ; rec < nrecs && s_get.skip == FALSE ; )
      {
      tempcolor = video.saycolor ;
      video.saycolor = video.brcolor ;
      br_hdisplay_rec ( row, col, rec ) ;
      for ( ; fld <= s_br[n].maxfld && s_get.skip == FALSE ; )
         {
         s_get.valid    = s_br[n].flds[fld].valid ;
         s_get.confirm  = s_br[n].flds[fld].confirm ;
         s_get.listbox  = s_br[n].flds[fld].listbox ;
         s_get.end      = s_br[n].flds[fld].end ;
         s_get.help     = s_br[n].flds[fld].help ;
         s_get.edit     = s_br[n].flds[fld].edit ;
         s_get.picture  = s_br[n].flds[fld].picture ;
         s_get.insert   = s_br[n].flds[fld].insert ;
         s_get.fld      = fld ;
         s_get.rec      = rec ;
         s_get.startrow = row+rec ;
         s_get.startcol = col+s_br[n].flds[fld].col ;

         video.saycolor = video.getcolor ;
         if ( s_br[n].flds [fld].type == 'N' )
            {
            s_br[n].flds[fld].value = atof (
            s_br[n].recs[rec].buf+s_br[n].flds[fld].col ) ;
            s_br[n].recs[rec].sum -= s_br[n].flds[fld].value ;
            s_br[n].flds[fld].sum -= s_br[n].flds[fld].value ;
            grand_total-= s_br[n].flds[fld].value ;
            getnum ( row+rec,
                     col+s_br[n].flds[fld].col,
                    &s_br[n].flds[fld].value,
                     s_br[n].flds [fld].width,
                     s_br[n].flds [fld].dec )   ;
            s_br[n].recs[rec].sum += s_br[n].flds[fld].value ;
            s_br[n].flds[fld].sum += s_br[n].flds[fld].value ;
            grand_total+= s_br[n].flds[fld].value ;
               br_htotal_say ( row, col, fld, rec, nrecs )   ;
            memcpy ( s_br[n].recs[rec].buf+s_br[n].flds[fld].col,
                     s_get.array,
                     s_br[n].flds [fld].width )   ;
            }
         else if ( s_br[n].flds [fld].type == 'D' )
            {
             getdate ( row+rec,
                       col+s_br[n].flds[fld].col,
                       s_br[n].recs[rec].buf+s_br[n].flds[fld].col ) ;
            }
```

```
         else
            {
             getstr ( row+rec,
                      col+s_br[n].flds[fld].col,
                      s_br[n].recs[rec].buf+s_br[n].flds[fld].col ) ;
            }
         video.saycolor = video.brcolor ;
         at_say ( row+rec,
                  col+s_br[n].flds[fld].col ,
                  s_br[n].recs[rec].buf+s_br[n].flds[fld].col ) ;
         if ( s_get.key == UP ||
              s_get.key == DOWN ||
              s_get.key == PGDN ||
              s_get.key == PGUP ||
              s_get.key == HOME ||
              s_get.key == END )
            break ;
         else if ( ( s_get.key == SHIFTTAB || s_get.key == LEFT )
                  && fld > 0 )
            fld-- ;
         else if ( ( s_get.key == SHIFTTAB || s_get.key == LEFT )
                  && fld == 0 )
            fld = s_br[n].maxfld ;
         else if ( fld < s_br[n].maxfld && s_get.skip == FALSE )
            fld++ ;
         else if ( fld == s_br[n].maxfld && s_get.skip == FALSE )
            {
            fld = 0 ;
            }
         }
      if ( s_get.skip == TRUE )   break ;
      video.saycolor = tempcolor ;
      br_hdisplay_rec ( row, col, rec ) ;
      if      ( s_get.key == UP && rec > 0 )
         rec-- ;
      else if ( s_get.key == DOWN && rec < (nrecs-1) )
         rec++ ;
      else if ( s_get.key == RETURN && s_brno == S_LISTBOX )
         break ;
      else if ( s_get.key == RETURN || s_get.key == TABKEY )
         {
          if ( rec < (nrecs-1) )
            rec++ ;
         else if ( rec == (nrecs-1 )    )
            {
            rec = 0 ;
            fld = 0 ;
            }
         }
      else rec = browse_hscroll ( row, col, nrecs, s_get.key ) ;
      }
}
```

```
int browse_vget ( row, col, nrecs )
int row, col, nrecs ;
{
   unsigned char tempcolor ;
   int rec, fld = 0 ;
   int n = s_brno ;
   s_get.key = 0 ;
   for ( rec = 0; rec < nrecs && s_get.skip == FALSE ; )
      {
      tempcolor = video.saycolor ;
      video.saycolor = video.brcolor ;
      br_vdisplay_rec ( row, col, rec ) ;
      for ( ; fld <= s_br[n].maxfld && s_get.skip == FALSE ; )
         {
         s_get.valid    = s_br[n].flds[fld].valid ;
         s_get.confirm  = s_br[n].flds[fld].confirm ;
         s_get.listbox  = s_br[n].flds[fld].listbox ;
         s_get.end      = s_br[n].flds[fld].end ;
         s_get.help     = s_br[n].flds[fld].help ;
         s_get.edit     = s_br[n].flds[fld].edit ;
         s_get.picture  = s_br[n].flds[fld].picture ;
         s_get.insert   = s_br[n].flds[fld].insert ;
         s_get.fld      = fld ;
         s_get.rec      = rec ;
         s_get.startrow = row+fld ;
         s_get.startcol = col+ rec* (s_br[n].flds[fld].width+1) ;

         video.saycolor = video.getcolor ;
         if ( s_br[n].flds [fld].type == 'N' &&
              s_br[n].flds [fld].total == TRUE )
            {
            s_br[n].flds[fld].value = atof (
            s_br[n].recs[fld].buf+ rec* (s_br[n].flds[fld].width+1) ) ;
            s_br[n].recs[rec].sum -= s_br[n].flds[fld].value ;
            s_br[n].flds[fld].sum -= s_br[n].flds[fld].value ;
            grand_total-= s_br[n].flds[fld].value ;
            getnum ( row+fld,
                     col+ rec* (s_br[n].flds[fld].width+1),
                    &s_br[n].flds[fld].value,
                     s_br[n].flds [fld].width,
                     s_br[n].flds [fld].dec )   ;
            s_br[n].recs[rec].sum += s_br[n].flds[fld].value ;
            s_br[n].flds[fld].sum += s_br[n].flds[fld].value ;
            grand_total+= s_br[n].flds[fld].value ;
            br_vtotal_say ( row, col, fld, rec, nrecs )   ;
            memcpy ( s_br[n].recs [fld].buf+ rec*(s_br[n].flds[fld].width+1),
                     s_get.array,
                     s_br[n].flds [fld].width )   ;
            }
         else if ( s_br[n].flds [fld].type == 'N' )
            {
            s_br[n].flds[fld].value = atof (
            s_br[n].recs[fld].buf+ rec* (s_br[n].flds[fld].width+1) ) ;
            getnum ( row+fld,
```

```
                col+ rec* (s_br[n].flds[fld].width+1),
               &s_br[n].flds[fld].value,
                s_br[n].flds [fld].width,
                s_br[n].flds [fld].dec )   ;
       memcpy ( s_br[n].recs [fld].buf+ rec*(s_br[n].flds[fld].width+1),
                s_get.array,
                s_br[n].flds [fld].width )   ;
       }
    else if ( s_br[n].flds [fld].type == 'D' )
       {
        getdate( row+fld,
                 col+ rec* (s_br[n].flds[fld].width+1),
                 s_br[n].recs[fld].buf+ rec* (s_br[n].flds[fld].width+1) ) ;

       }
    else
       {
        getstr ( row+fld,
                 col+ rec* (s_br[n].flds[fld].width+1),
                 s_br[n].recs[fld].buf+ rec* (s_br[n].flds[fld].width+1) ) ;
       }

    if ( ( fld % 2 ) ) video.saycolor = video.brcolor ;
    else video.saycolor = video.oddcolor ;

    if ( s_br[n].flds[fld].type == 'N' &&
       ( s_br[n].flds[fld].value = atof (
         s_br[n].recs[fld].buf+
             rec* (s_br[n].flds[fld].width+1) ) )
          == 0.00 )
       {
       at_say ( row+fld,
                col+ rec* (s_br[n].flds[fld].width+1),
              replicate ( " " , s_br[n].flds[fld].width ) ) ;
       }
    else
       {
       at_say ( row+fld,
                col+ rec* (s_br[n].flds[fld].width+1),
                s_br[n].recs[fld].buf+
                rec* (s_br[n].flds[fld].width+1) ) ;
       }
    if ( s_get.key ==  SHIFTTAB ||
         s_get.key ==  LEFT ||
         s_get.key ==  TABKEY ||
         s_get.key ==  RIGHT ||
         s_get.key ==  PGDN ||
         s_get.key ==  PGUP ||
         s_get.key ==  HOME ||
         s_get.key ==  END ) break ;
    else if ( s_get.key == UP && fld > 0 )
       fld-- ;
    else if ( s_get.key == UP && fld == 0 )
       fld = s_br[n].maxfld ;
```

```
          else if ( fld < s_br[n].maxfld && s_get.skip == FALSE )
             fld++ ;
          else if ( fld == s_br[n].maxfld && s_get.skip == FALSE )
             {
             fld = 0 ;
             }
          }
       if ( s_get.skip == TRUE )   break ;
       video.saycolor = tempcolor ;
       br_vdisplay_rec ( row, col, rec ) ;
       if ( ( s_get.key == LEFT || s_get.key == SHIFTTAB ) && rec > 0 )
          rec-- ;
       else if ( ( s_get.key == RIGHT || s_get.key == TABKEY ) && rec < (nrecs-1) )
          rec++ ;
       else if ( s_get.key == RETURN && s_brno == S_LISTBOX )
          break ;
       else if ( s_get.key == RETURN )
          {
           if ( rec < (nrecs-1) )
             rec++ ;
          else if ( rec == (nrecs-1 )    )
             {
             rec = 0 ;
             fld = 0 ;
             }
          }
       else rec = browse_vscroll ( row, col, nrecs, s_get.key ) ;
       }
}


int browse_lget ( row, col, nrecs )
int row, col, nrecs ;
{
   unsigned char tempcolor ;
   int rec, fld = 0, end_of_file ;
   int n = s_brno ;
   s_get.key = 0 ;
   strcpy ( s_get.clear, s_get.array ) ;
   for ( rec = 0 ; rec < nrecs && s_get.skip == FALSE ; )
      {
      tempcolor = video.saycolor ;
      video.saycolor = video.brcolor ;
      br_hdisplay_rec ( row, col, rec ) ;
      while ( s_get.skip == FALSE &&
              s_get.key != RETURN && s_get.key != ESCAPE )
         {
         s_get.valid     = s_br[n].flds[fld].valid ;
         s_get.confirm   = s_br[n].flds[fld].confirm ;
         s_get.listbox   = s_br[n].flds[fld].listbox ;
         s_get.end       = s_br[n].flds[fld].end ;
         s_get.help      = s_br[n].flds[fld].help ;
         s_get.edit      = s_br[n].flds[fld].edit ;
         s_get.picture   = s_br[n].flds[fld].picture ;
```

```
         s_get.insert   = s_br[n].flds[fld].insert ;

         video.saycolor = video.getcolor ;
         getstr ( row+rec,
                  col+s_br[n].flds[fld].col,
                  s_br[n].recs[rec].buf+s_br[n].flds[fld].col ) ;
         video.saycolor = video.brcolor ;
           if ( s_get.key == ESCAPE )
            {
            strcpy ( s_get.array, s_get.clear ) ;
            strcpy ( s_br[n].recs[rec].buf+s_br[n].flds[fld].col,
                     s_get.clear ) ;
            }
           if ( s_get.key == RETURN )
            {
            rpad ( s_get.array+s_br[n].flds[fld].col,
                      s_br[n].flds [fld].width, ' ' ) ;
            rpad ( s_br[n].recs[rec].buf+s_br[n].flds[fld].col,
                      s_br[n].flds [fld].width, ' ' ) ;

            }
          at_say ( row+rec,
                   col+s_br[n].flds[fld].col ,
                   s_br[n].recs[rec].buf+s_br[n].flds[fld].col ) ;
         if ( s_get.key == UP ||
              s_get.key == DOWN ||
              s_get.key == PGDN ||
              s_get.key == PGUP ||
              s_get.key == HOME ||
              s_get.key == END )
            break ;
         }
      if ( s_get.skip == TRUE )   break ;
      video.saycolor = tempcolor ;
      br_hdisplay_rec ( row, col, rec ) ;
      if      ( s_get.key == UP && rec > 0 )
         rec-- ;
      else if ( s_get.key == DOWN && rec < (nrecs-1) )
         rec++ ;
      else if ( ( s_get.key == RETURN || s_get.key == ESCAPE )
           && s_brno == S_LISTBOX )
         break ;
      else rec = browse_hscroll ( row, col, nrecs, s_get.key ) ;

      }
   s_choice = (long) rec+ d3recno() ;
}


int browse_mget ( row, col, nrecs )
int row, col, nrecs ;
{
   unsigned char tempcolor ;
   int rec, fld = 0, end_of_file ;
```

```
int n = s_brno ;
s_get.key = 0 ;
strcpy ( s_get.clear, s_get.array ) ;
for ( rec = 0 ; rec < nrecs && s_get.skip == FALSE ; )
   {
   tempcolor = video.saycolor ;
   video.saycolor = video.brcolor ;
   br_hdisplay_rec ( row, col, rec ) ;
   while ( s_get.skip == FALSE &&
            s_get.key != RETURN && s_get.key != ESCAPE )
      {
      s_get.valid    = s_br[n].flds[fld].valid ;
      s_get.confirm  = s_br[n].flds[fld].confirm ;
      s_get.listbox  = s_br[n].flds[fld].listbox ;
      s_get.end      = s_br[n].flds[fld].end ;
      s_get.help     = s_br[n].flds[fld].help ;
      s_get.edit     = s_br[n].flds[fld].edit ;
      s_get.picture  = s_br[n].flds[fld].picture ;
      s_get.insert   = s_br[n].flds[fld].insert ;

      video.saycolor = video.getcolor ;
      getstr ( row+rec,
               col+s_br[n].flds[fld].col,
               s_br[n].recs[rec].buf+s_br[n].flds[fld].col ) ;
      video.saycolor = video.brcolor ;
        if ( s_get.key == RETURN || s_get.key == ESCAPE )
         {
         strcpy ( s_get.array, s_get.clear ) ;
         strcpy ( s_br[n].recs[rec].buf+s_br[n].flds[fld].col,
                s_get.clear ) ;
         }
       at_say ( row+rec,
                col+s_br[n].flds[fld].col ,
                s_br[n].recs[rec].buf+s_br[n].flds[fld].col ) ;
      if ( s_get.key == UP ||
           s_get.key == DOWN ||
           s_get.key == PGDN ||
           s_get.key == PGUP ||
           s_get.key == HOME ||
           s_get.key == END )
         break ;
      }
   if ( s_get.skip == TRUE )   break ;
   video.saycolor = tempcolor ;
   br_hdisplay_rec ( row, col, rec ) ;
   if      ( s_get.key == UP && rec > 0 )
      rec-- ;
   else if ( s_get.key == DOWN && rec < (nrecs-1) )
      rec++ ;
   else if ( ( s_get.key == RETURN || s_get.key == ESCAPE )
        && s_brno == S_LISTBOX )
      break ;
   else rec = browse_hscroll ( row, col, nrecs, s_get.key ) ;
   }
```

```
   s_choice = (long) rec+ d3recno() ;
}

/* save the horizontal browse form */

int browse_hsave ( rec, nrecs )
int rec, nrecs ;
{
   int fld, end_of_file, startrec ;
   int n = s_brno ;
   char *recbuf ;
   for ( end_of_file = FALSE, startrec = rec ;
         rec < nrecs && !end_of_file ;
         rec++, end_of_file = d3skip( 1L ) )
      {
      recbuf = f3record() ;

      /* transfer from browse array of structures */
      for ( fld = 0L ; fld <= s_br[n].maxfld ; fld++ )
         {
         if ( s_br[n].flds [fld].type == 'D' )
            {
            memcpy ( s_br[n].recs [rec].buf + s_br[n].flds [fld] .col,
                     c3dt_unformat (
                     s_br[n].recs [rec].buf + s_br[n].flds [fld] .col,
                     "MM/DD/YY" ),
                     s_br[n].flds [fld] .width )    ;
            }
         memcpy ( recbuf + s_br[n].flds [fld] .offset,
                  s_br[n].recs [rec].buf + s_br[n].flds [fld] .col,
                  s_br[n].flds [fld] .width )    ;
         }
        d3write ( d3recno() ) ;
      }
   d3skip ( (long) - ( rec - startrec ) ) ;
}

/* save the vertical browse form */

int browse_vsave ( rec, nrecs )
int rec, nrecs ;
{
   int fld, end_of_file, startrec ;
   int n = s_brno ;
   char *recbuf ;
   long recno ;

   for ( end_of_file = FALSE, startrec = rec ;
         rec < nrecs && !end_of_file ;
         rec++, end_of_file = d3skip( 1L ) )
      {
      recbuf = f3record() ;
```

```
      /* transfer data from browse array of structures
         to the record buffer */
      for ( fld = 0 ; fld <= s_br[n].maxfld ; fld++ )
         {
         if ( s_br[n].flds [fld].type == 'D' )
            {
            memcpy ( s_br[n].recs [fld].buf+ rec*(s_br[n].flds[fld].width+1),
                     c3dt_unformat (
                     s_br[n].recs [fld].buf+ rec*(s_br[n].flds[fld].width+1),
                     "MM/DD/YY" ),
                     s_br[n].flds [fld] .width )    ;
            }
         memcpy ( recbuf + s_br[n].flds [fld] .offset,
                  s_br[n].recs [fld].buf+ rec*(s_br[n].flds[fld].width+1),
                  s_br[n].flds [fld] .width )    ;
         }
        d3write ( recno = d3recno() ) ;
      }
   d3skip ( (long) - ( rec - startrec ) ) ;
}

/* These functions are called in conjunction with
   browse_set() to preset customized individual field conditions
   within the browse.  The reference number passed as a second
   argument to these functions is referenced by a corresponding
   function in do_get.c.  Do_get.c contains user-redefinable
   source for get activities.

*/

int browse_valid ( order, valid_refno )
int order, valid_refno ;
   {
   int n = s_brno ;
   s_br[n].flds[order].valid = valid_refno ;
   }

int browse_confirm ( order, confirm_refno )
int order, confirm_refno ;
   {
   int n = s_brno ;
   s_br[n].flds[order].confirm = confirm_refno ;
   }

int browse_listbox ( order, listbox_refno )
int order, listbox_refno ;
   {
   int n = s_brno ;
   s_br[n].flds[order].listbox = listbox_refno ;
   }

int browse_start ( order, start_refno )
int order, start_refno ;
```

```
   {
   int n = s_brno ;
   s_br[n].flds[order].start = start_refno ;
   }

int browse_end ( order, end_refno )
int order, end_refno ;
   {
   int n = s_brno ;
   s_br[n].flds[order].end = end_refno ;
   }

int browse_edit ( order, edit_refno )
int order, edit_refno ;
   {
   int n = s_brno ;
   s_br[n].flds[order].edit = edit_refno ;
   }

int browse_help ( order, help_refno )
int order, help_refno ;
   {
   int n = s_brno ;
   s_br[n].flds[order].help = help_refno ;
   }

int browse_picture ( order, picture_refno )
int order, picture_refno ;
   {
   int n = s_brno ;
   s_br[n].flds[order].picture = picture_refno ;
   }

int browse_insert ( order, insert_refno )
int order, insert_refno ;
   {
   int n = s_brno ;
   s_br[n].flds[order].insert = insert_refno ;
   }

int browse_sum_opts ( width, dec )
int width, dec ;
   {
   int n = s_brno ;
   s_br[n].width = width ;
   s_br[n].dec = dec ;
   }

int browse_total ( order, total )
int order, total ;
   {
   int n = s_brno ;
   s_br[n].flds[order].total = total ;
   }
```

```
int browse_htotals (row, col, nrecs )
int row, col, nrecs ;
{
   unsigned char tempcolor = video.saycolor ;

   char saybuf [25] ;
   int rec, fld ;
   int n = s_brno ;
   long recno       = d3recno() ;
   long temprecno   = recno ;
   long reccount    = d3reccount() ;

   for ( rec = 0; rec < nrecs ; rec++ )
      {
      for ( fld = 0 ; fld <= s_br[n].maxfld ; fld++ )
         {
         if ( ( fld % 2 ) ) video.saycolor = color ( BLACK,GREEN,NORMAL) ;
         else video.saycolor = video.oddcolor ;

         if ( s_br[n].flds[fld].type == 'N' )
            {
            s_br[n].recs[rec].sum +=
            ( s_br[n].flds[fld].value = atof (
            s_br[n].recs [rec].buf+s_br[n].flds [fld] .col ) ) ;

            if ( rec == 0 )   /* calculate sums */
               {
               d3top () ;
              grand_total+=
            ( s_br[n].flds[fld].sum = x3sum ( s_br[n].flds[fld].ref ) ) ;
               }

            /* display sums - do this after sum calculations */
            if ( rec == 1 )
               {
            br_htotal_say ( row, col, fld, rec, nrecs )   ;
            }
            }
         }
      }
   d3go ( temprecno ) ;
   video.saycolor = tempcolor ;

}

int browse_vtotals (row, col, nrecs )
int row, col, nrecs ;
{
   unsigned char tempcolor = video.saycolor ;

   char saybuf [25] ;
   int rec, fld ;
   int n = s_brno ;
   long recno       = d3recno() ;
```

```
long temprecno   = recno ;
long reccount    = d3reccount() ;

for ( rec = 0; rec < nrecs ; rec++ )
   {
   for ( fld = 0 ; fld <= s_br[n].maxfld ; fld++ )
      {
      if ( fld == 0 )
         s_br[n].recs[rec].sum == 0.00 ;
      if ( ( fld % 2 ) ) video.saycolor = color ( BLACK,GREEN,NORMAL) ;
      else video.saycolor = video.oddcolor ;

      if ( s_br[n].flds[fld].type == 'N'
           && s_br[n].flds[fld].total == TRUE )
         {
         s_br[n].recs[rec].sum +=
         ( s_br[n].flds[fld].value = atof (
         s_br[n].recs[fld].buf+ rec* (s_br[n].flds[fld].width+1) ) ) ;

         if ( rec == 0 )   /* calculate sums */
            {
            d3top () ;
          grand_total+=
          ( s_br[n].flds[fld].sum = x3sum ( s_br[n].flds[fld].ref ) ) ;
            sprintf ( s_br[n].recs [fld].buf+ nrecs*(s_br[n].flds[fld].width+1),
            "%*.*lf",
            s_br[n].flds[fld].width+2,
            s_br[n].flds[fld].dec,
            s_br[n].flds[fld].sum ) ;
            }

         /* display sums - do this after sum calculations */
         if ( rec == 1 )
            {
         if ( s_br[n].flds[fld].sum     == 0.00 )
            {
            at_say ( row+fld,
                     col+ nrecs*( s_br[n].flds[s_br[n].maxfld].width+1 ),
                     replicate ( " " , s_br[n].flds[fld].width+1 ) ) ;
            }
         else
            {
                at_say ( row+fld,
                         col+ nrecs*( s_br[n].flds[s_br[n].maxfld].width+1 ),
                         s_br[n].recs[fld].buf+ nrecs*
                        (s_br[n].flds[fld].width+1) ) ;
               }
         }
         if ( fld == s_br[n].maxfld )
            {
         sprintf ( saybuf,
               "%*.*lf",
                s_br[n].flds[fld].width+2,
                s_br[n].flds[fld].dec,
```

```
                    grand_total ) ;

            sprintf ( s_br[n].recs[fld+2].buf+
                         rec*(s_br[n].flds[fld].width+1),
                      "%*.*lf",
                      s_br[n].flds[fld].width,
                      s_br[n].flds[fld].dec,
                      s_br[n].recs[rec].sum ) ;

            if ( s_br[n].recs[rec].sum    == 0.00 )
               {
               at_say ( row+fld+2,
                        col+nrecs*( s_br[n].flds[s_br[n].maxfld].width+1 ),
                        replicate ( " " , s_br[n].flds[fld].width+1 ) ) ;
               }
            else
               {
                   at_say  ( row+fld+2,
                             col+rec*(s_br[n].flds[fld].width+1),
                             s_br[n].recs[fld+2].buf+
                             rec*(s_br[n].flds[fld].width+1) ) ;
                 }
               at_say  ( row+fld+2,
                         col+ nrecs*( s_br[n].flds[s_br[n].maxfld].width+1 ),
                         saybuf ) ;
               }
            }
         }
      }
   d3go ( temprecno ) ;
   video.saycolor = tempcolor ;

}

int br_vtotal_say ( row, col, fld, rec, nrecs )
int row, col, fld, rec, nrecs ;
   {
   int n = s_brno ;
   char saybuf [25] ;
   unsigned char tempcolor = video.saycolor ;

   /* display record total */

   video.saycolor = color ( BLACK,GREEN,NORMAL) ;

   if ( s_br[n].recs[rec].sum    == 0.00 )
      {
      at_say ( row+s_br[n].maxfld+2,
               col+rec*( s_br[n].width+1 ),
               replicate ( " " , s_br[n].width ) ) ;
      }
   else
      {
```

```
     sprintf ( saybuf,
               "%*.*lf",
               s_br[n].width,
               s_br[n].dec,
               s_br[n].recs[rec].sum ) ;
     at_say  ( row+s_br[n].maxfld+2,
               col+rec*( s_br[n].width+1 ),
               saybuf ) ;
   }

if ( fld == -1 )
   {
   video.saycolor = tempcolor ;
   return (0) ;
   }

/* display grand total */

video.saycolor = color ( BLACK, CYAN, NORMAL ) ;

sprintf ( saybuf,
          "%*.*lf",
          s_br[n].flds[fld].width+2,
          s_br[n].flds[fld].dec,
          grand_total ) ;
at_say  ( row+s_br[n].maxfld+2,
          col+ nrecs*( s_br[n].flds[s_br[n].maxfld].width+1 ),
          saybuf ) ;

/* display field total */

if ( ( fld % 2 ) ) video.saycolor = color ( BLACK,GREEN,NORMAL) ;
else video.saycolor = video.oddcolor ;
if ( s_br[n].flds[fld].sum    == 0.00 )
   {
   at_say ( row+fld,
            col+ nrecs*( s_br[n].flds[s_br[n].maxfld].width+1 ),
            replicate ( " " , s_br[n].flds[s_br[n].maxfld].width+2 ) ) ;
   }
else
   {
    sprintf ( saybuf,
    "%*.*lf",
    s_br[n].flds[fld].width+2,
    s_br[n].flds[fld].dec,
    s_br[n].flds[fld].sum ) ;
    at_say ( row+fld,
             col+ nrecs*( s_br[n].flds[s_br[n].maxfld].width+1 ),
             saybuf ) ;
    }

video.saycolor = tempcolor ;
}
```

```
int br_htotal_say ( row, col, fld, rec, nrecs )
int row, col, fld, rec, nrecs ;
   {
   int n = s_brno ;
   char saybuf [25] ;
   unsigned char tempcolor = video.saycolor ;

   /* display field total */

   video.saycolor = color ( BLACK,CYAN,NORMAL) ;
   if ( s_br[n].flds[fld].sum    == 0.00 )
      {
      at_say ( row+nrecs+1,
                 col+s_br[n].flds[fld].col,
            replicate ( " " , s_br[n].flds[fld].width ) ) ;
      }
   else
      {
       sprintf ( saybuf,
       "%*.*lf",
       s_br[n].flds[fld].width,
       s_br[n].flds[fld].dec,
       s_br[n].flds[fld].sum ) ;
       at_say ( row+nrecs+1,
                 col+s_br[n].flds[fld].col,
                 saybuf ) ;
       }

   /* display record total

   if ( s_br[n].recs[rec].sum    == 0.00 )
      {
      at_say ( row+s_br[n].maxfld+2,
               col+rec*( s_br[n].flds[fld].width+1 ),
               replicate ( " " , s_br[n].flds[fld].width ) ) ;
      }
   else
      {
       sprintf ( saybuf,
                 "%*.*lf",
                 s_br[n].flds[fld].width,
                 s_br[n].flds[fld].dec,
                 s_br[n].recs[rec].sum ) ;
       at_say  ( row+s_br[n].maxfld+2,
                 col+rec*( s_br[n].flds[fld].width+1 ),
                 saybuf ) ;
      }
   */
   /* display grand total

   video.saycolor = color ( BLACK, CYAN, NORMAL ) ;

   sprintf ( saybuf,
            "%*.*lf",
```

```
            s_br[n].flds[fld].width+2,
            s_br[n].flds[fld].dec,
            grand_total ) ;
   at_say  ( row+s_br[n].maxfld+2,
            col+ nrecs*( s_br[n].flds[s_br[n].maxfld].width+1 ),
            saybuf ) ;
   */
   video.saycolor = tempcolor ;
   }
```

The scrolling functions are in the source s_scroll.c:

```
/*------------------------------------
Starbase browse functions.
Copyright (c) 1987, 1988, 1989 Steve Straley & Associates

Description:

These functions allow for flexible, two-dimensional views of a database,
just like dBASE's browse, or Clipper's DBEDIT.  Here, however, the
programmer has complete control over the view of the database and the
way information is received from the user.

-------------------------------------*/

#include <stdio.h>      /* standard 'C' */
#include <stdlib.h>     /* standard 'C' */
#include <string.h>     /* standard 'C' */
#include <math.h>       /* standard 'C' */
#include <d3base.h>     /* Code base header file */
#include <s_get.h>      /* Starbase get    system header file */
#include <s_say.h>      /* Starbase video  system header file */
#include <s_browse.h>   /* Starbase browse system header file */

extern double grand_total ;

int browse_hscroll ( row, col, nrecs, direction )
int row, col, nrecs ;
unsigned int direction ;
{
   int fld, rec = 0, end_of_file ;
   int n = s_brno ;
   char *recbuf, searchstr[2] ;
   long recno = d3recno() ;

   switch ( direction )
      {
      recno = d3recno() ;
      case UP:
         /* test for top of file */
         if ( ( end_of_file = d3skip ( -1L ) ) )
            {
            recno = d3recno() ;
            d3top () ;
```

```
      return ( rec = nrecs-1 ) ;
      }
   /* save the last browse record which will scroll off screen */

   d3skip ( (long) nrecs ) ;
   recno = d3recno() ;
   browse_hsave ( nrecs-1, nrecs ) ;

   /* shift the browse records down */

   for ( rec = nrecs-1, end_of_file = FALSE ;
         rec > 0 ;
         rec-- )
      {
      memcpy( s_br[n].recs [rec].buf ,
            s_br[n].recs [rec-1].buf ,
            SIZE_BROWSE_BUF    ) ;
      }
   /* transfer the previous dbf record to the browse record */

   d3skip ( (long) -nrecs ) ;
   recno = d3recno() ;
   recno = d3recno() ;
   recbuf = f3record() ;
   memset ( s_br[n].recs [rec].buf, '\0', SIZE_BROWSE_BUF ) ;

   for ( fld = 0 ; fld <= s_br[n].maxfld ; fld++ )
      {
      memcpy ( s_br[n].recs [rec].buf + s_br[n].flds [fld] .col,
               recbuf + s_br[n].flds [fld] .offset,
               s_br[n].flds [fld] .width )   ;

      if ( s_br[n].flds [fld].type == 'D' )
         {
         memcpy ( s_br[n].recs [rec].buf + s_br[n].flds [fld] .col,
                  c3dt_format (
                  s_br[n].recs [rec].buf + s_br[n].flds [fld] .col,
                  "MM/DD/YY" ),
                  s_br[n].flds [fld] .width )   ;
         }
      }
   /* display the scrolled screen */

   recno = d3recno() ;
   browse_hsay ( row, col, nrecs ) ;
   return ( rec = 0 ) ;
case DOWN:
   /* test for bottom of file */
   if ( ( end_of_file = d3skip ( (long) nrecs ) ) )
      {
      d3bottom() ;
      d3skip ( (long) - (nrecs-1) ) ;
      return ( rec = 0 ) ;
      }
```

```
   /* save the first browse record */
   d3skip ( (long) - nrecs ) ;
   browse_hsave ( 0, 1 ) ;
   for ( rec = 0, end_of_file = FALSE ;
        rec < (nrecs-1) ;
         rec++ )
      {
      memcpy( s_br[n].recs [rec].buf ,
              s_br[n].recs [rec+1].buf ,
              SIZE_BROWSE_BUF    ) ;
      }
   /* transfer the next dbf record to the browse record */
   d3skip ( (long) nrecs ) ;
   recno = d3recno() ;
   recbuf = f3record() ;
   memset ( s_br[n].recs [rec].buf, '\0', SIZE_BROWSE_BUF ) ;

   for ( fld = 0 ; fld <= s_br[n].maxfld ; fld++ )
      {
      memcpy ( s_br[n].recs [rec].buf + s_br[n].flds [fld] .col,
               recbuf + s_br[n].flds [fld] .offset,
               s_br[n].flds [fld] .width )   ;

      if ( s_br[n].flds [fld].type == 'D' )
         {
         memcpy ( s_br[n].recs [rec].buf + s_br[n].flds [fld] .col,
                  c3dt_format (
                  s_br[n].recs [rec].buf + s_br[n].flds [fld] .col,
                  "MM/DD/YY" ),
                  s_br[n].flds [fld] .width )    ;
         }
      }

   d3skip ( (long) - (nrecs-1) ) ;
   recno = d3recno() ;
   browse_hsay ( row, col, nrecs ) ;
   return ( rec = nrecs-1 ) ;

case PGUP:
   browse_hsave ( 0, nrecs ) ;
   /* test for top of file */
   if ( ( end_of_file = d3skip ( (long) - nrecs ) ) )
      {
      d3top() ;
      }
   browse_hform ( 0, nrecs ) ;
   browse_hsay ( row, col, nrecs ) ;
   return ( rec = 0 ) ;

case PGDN:
   browse_hsave ( 0, nrecs ) ;
   /* test for top of file */
   if ( ( end_of_file = d3skip ( (long) ((2*nrecs)-1) ) ) )
```

```
            {
            d3bottom() ;
            d3skip ( (long) -(nrecs-1) ) ;
            }
         d3skip ( (long) -(nrecs-1) ) ;
         browse_hform ( 0, nrecs ) ;
         browse_hsay ( row, col, nrecs ) ;
         return ( rec = 0 ) ;

      case HOME:
         browse_hsave ( 0, nrecs ) ;
         d3top() ;
         browse_hform ( 0, nrecs ) ;
         browse_hsay ( row, col, nrecs ) ;
         return ( rec = 0 ) ;

      case END:
         browse_hsave ( 0, nrecs ) ;
         d3bottom() ;
         d3skip ( (long) -(nrecs-1) ) ;
         browse_hform ( 0, nrecs ) ;
         browse_hsay ( row, col, nrecs ) ;
         return ( rec = 0 ) ;

      default: return ( -1 ) ;
         if ( direction >= SPACEBAR &&
              direction <= STANDARD_END )
            {
            browse_hsave ( 0, nrecs ) ;
            searchstr[0] = s_get.key ;
            searchstr[1] = '\0' ;
            d3seek ( searchstr ) ;
            browse_hform ( 0, nrecs ) ;
            browse_hsay ( row, col, nrecs ) ;
            return ( rec = 0 ) ;
            }
      }
}
int browse_vscroll ( row, col, nrecs, direction )
int row, col, nrecs ;
unsigned int direction ;
{
   int fld, rec = 0, end_of_file ;
   int n = s_brno ;
   char *recbuf ;
   long recno = d3recno() ;

   switch ( direction )
      {
      case LEFT:
      case SHIFTTAB:
         /* test for top of file */
         if ( ( end_of_file = d3skip ( -1L ) ) )
```

```
   {
   d3top () ;
   return ( rec = nrecs-1 ) ;
   }
/* save the last browse record which will scroll off screen */

d3skip ( (long) nrecs ) ;
browse_vsave ( nrecs-1, nrecs ) ;

/* shift the browse records across */
for ( rec = nrecs-1, end_of_file = FALSE ;
     rec > 0 ;
      rec-- )
   {
   for ( fld = 0 ; fld <= s_br[n].maxfld ; fld++ )
      {
      memcpy ( s_br[n].recs [fld].buf+
               rec*(s_br[n].flds[fld].width+1),
               s_br[n].recs [fld].buf+
               (rec-1)*(s_br[n].flds[fld].width+1),
               s_br[n].flds [fld] .width )   ;
      }
   s_br[n].recs[rec].sum = s_br[n].recs[rec-1].sum ;
   br_vtotal_say ( row, col, -1, rec, nrecs ) ;
   }

/* transfer the previous dbf record to the browse record */
 d3skip ( (long) -nrecs ) ;
recno = d3recno() ;
recbuf = f3record() ;
s_br[n].recs[rec].sum = 0.00 ;

for ( fld = 0 ; fld <= s_br[n].maxfld ; fld++ )
   {
   memcpy ( s_br[n].recs [fld].buf+ rec*(s_br[n].flds[fld].width+1),
            recbuf + s_br[n].flds [fld] .offset,
            s_br[n].flds [fld] .width )   ;

   if ( s_br[n].flds [fld].type == 'D' )
      {
      memcpy ( s_br[n].recs [fld].buf + rec*(s_br[n].flds[fld].width+1),
             c3dt_format (
             s_br[n].recs [fld].buf + rec*(s_br[n].flds[fld].width+1),
             "MM/DD/YY" ),
             s_br[n].flds [fld] .width )   ;
      }
   if ( s_br[n].flds [fld].type == 'N' )
      {
         s_br[n].recs[rec].sum +=
         ( s_br[n].flds[fld].value = atof (
         s_br[n].recs[fld].buf+ rec* (s_br[n].flds[fld].width+1) ) ) ;
      }
   }
```

```
        /* display the scrolled screen */
        browse_vsay ( row, col, nrecs ) ;
        br_vtotal_say ( row, col, -1, rec, nrecs ) ;
        return ( rec = 0 ) ;

     case RIGHT:
     case TABKEY:
        /* test for bottom of file */
        if ( ( end_of_file = d3skip ( (long) nrecs ) ) )
           {
           d3bottom() ;
           d3skip ( (long) - (nrecs-1) ) ;
           return ( rec = 0 ) ;
           }
        /* save the first browse record */
        d3skip ( (long) - nrecs ) ;
        browse_vsave ( 0, 1 ) ;
        for ( rec = 0, end_of_file = FALSE ;
              rec < (nrecs-1) ;
               rec++ )
           {
           for ( fld = 0 ; fld <= s_br[n].maxfld ; fld++ )
              {
              memcpy ( s_br[n].recs [fld].buf+
                          rec*(s_br[n].flds[fld].width+1),
                       s_br[n].recs [fld].buf+
                          (rec+1)*(s_br[n].flds[fld].width+1),
                       s_br[n].flds [fld] .width )   ;
              }
           s_br[n].recs[rec].sum = s_br[n].recs[rec+1].sum ;
           br_vtotal_say ( row, col, -1, rec, nrecs ) ;
           }
        /* transfer the next dbf record to the browse record */
         d3skip ( (long) nrecs ) ;
        recno = d3recno() ;
        recbuf = f3record() ;
        s_br[n].recs[rec].sum = 0.00 ;

        for ( fld = 0 ; fld <= s_br[n].maxfld ; fld++ )
           {
           memcpy ( s_br[n].recs [fld].buf+ rec*(s_br[n].flds[fld].width+1),
                      recbuf + s_br[n].flds [fld] .offset,
                 s_br[n].flds [fld] .width )   ;

           if ( s_br[n].flds [fld].type == 'D' )
              {
              memcpy ( s_br[n].recs [fld].buf + rec*(s_br[n].flds[fld].width+1),
                     c3dt_format (
                     s_br[n].recs [fld].buf + rec*(s_br[n].flds[fld].width+1),
                     "MM/DD/YY" ),
                     s_br[n].flds [fld] .width )   ;
              }
```

```
         if ( s_br[n].flds [fld].type == 'N' )
            {
               s_br[n].recs[rec].sum +=
               ( s_br[n].flds[fld].value = atof (
               s_br[n].recs[fld].buf+ rec* (s_br[n].flds[fld].width+1) ) ) ;
            }
         }

      d3skip ( (long) - (nrecs-1) ) ;
      recno = d3recno() ;
      browse_vsay ( row, col, nrecs ) ;
      br_vtotal_say ( row, col, -1, rec, nrecs ) ;
      return ( rec = nrecs-1 ) ;

   case PGUP:
      browse_vsave ( 0, nrecs ) ;
      /* test for top of file */
      if ( ( end_of_file = d3skip ( (long) - nrecs ) ) )
         {
         d3top() ;
         }
      browse_vform ( 0, nrecs ) ;
      browse_vsay ( row, col, nrecs ) ;
      return ( rec = 0 ) ;

   case PGDN:
      browse_vsave ( 0, nrecs ) ;
      /* test for top of file */
      if ( ( end_of_file = d3skip ( (long) ((2*nrecs)-1) ) ) )
         {
         d3bottom() ;
         d3skip ( (long) -(nrecs-1) ) ;
         }
      browse_vform ( 0, nrecs ) ;
      browse_vsay ( row, col, nrecs ) ;
      return ( rec = nrecs-1 ) ;

   case HOME:
      browse_vsave ( 0, nrecs ) ;
      d3top() ;
      browse_vform ( 0, nrecs ) ;
      browse_vsay ( row, col, nrecs ) ;
      return ( rec = 0 ) ;

   case END:
      browse_vsave ( 0, nrecs ) ;
      d3bottom() ;
      d3skip ( (long) -(nrecs-1) ) ;
      browse_vform ( 0, nrecs ) ;
      browse_vsay ( row, col, nrecs ) ;
      return ( rec = 0 ) ;

   default: return ( -1 ) ;
   }
}
```

SUMMARY

In this chapter, we discussed C file handling and introduced some important concepts and introduced the Code Base database engine for those who would like to write database applications purely in C. We also looked at ways to reproduce Clipper's sophisticated screen I/O in C, weighing the merits of various commercial libraries, including the SJSC windowing library. We then discussed date collection from the keyboard in general terms with specific code examples. A great deal of time was spent looking at our own SJSC library for one main reason: to show how easy it is to write a Clipper comparable C language data collection system. Finally, we expanded the SJSC GET system for full screen DBEDIT() screen functionality.

CHAPTER TEN

Interfacing Clipper and C

THE EXTEND SYSTEM

What is the Extend System?

In our introduction to C, we spoke of Clipper's Extend System as a way to interface Clipper and C or Clipper and PC Assembler. Clipper is the only dBASE language product that provides direct access to C. We will now see in detail what the Extend System is and how it works. Programmers often confuse the Extend System with Clipper's Extend.lib. The Extend System and Extend.lib are two separate entities. Extend.lib is a function library containing additional Clipper functions that can be linked to a Clipper application. The Extend System is Clipper's low-level language interface system. We do not need Extend.lib when using the Extend System.

Benefits of the Extend System

To write a C function callable from Clipper, but without the Extend System, we must use the CALL command. The CALL command is the dBASE standard command used for calling any external language functions or subroutines. Setting up a C function to work with the CALL command is not easy, even for experienced C and Assembly language programmers.

With the Extend System, a C function can be called from Clipper once it is correctly compiled and linked to the Clipper application. The only difficulty is that the C function, to be callable from Clipper, must be coded using the Extend System components and procedures. From Clipper's perspective, a C function built via the Extend System is callable in the same way as a Clipper user-defined function.

C Compilers Usable with the Extend System

Since Clipper is coded in Microsoft C 5.1, this compiler is the only one that works fully with the Extend System. Borland's Turbo C works partially. In particular, since Microsoft and Borland use different floating point conventions, floating point operations in Turbo C will not work presently with the Extend System. Sadly, Turbo C's fantastic graphics functions, which rely heavily on floating point operations, will not work presently with the Extend System either.

How to Compile and Link an Extend System Function with Microsoft C

Using Microsoft C, version 5.1, the compiler instruction is:

```
CL -c -AL -l -Oalt - FPa -Gs <filename>.c
```

Using Microsoft Link, version 3.65 or greater, the link instruction is:

```
Link /NOE <clipper object file(s)> <(c object file(s)>,,, clipper ;
```

What the Extend System Does

The Extend System provides a way to send information to and from Clipper without interfering with Clipper's internal memory setup. Normally, C arguments to functions are passed via stack memory. If we changed Clipper's order of variables on the stack with our own C function, we would have to reset the stack to the way it was prior to the function call once we were done. Otherwise, the Clipper application would crash. The Extend System provides the means to pass and retrieve external C function parameters without changing the order of variables in stack memory. A sample Extend System function is:

```
#include <nandef.h>
#include <extend.h>

CLIPPER square_it()
{
double number = _parnd(1) ;     /* call to parameter func. */
_retnd (number*number );        /* call to return value func. */
}
```

In partial pseudocode, here is the above Extend System C UDF:

```
#include <general #defines and typedefs>
#include <extend system #defines, typedefs, macros, function
         prototypes and header data structure>

<typedef to leave stack as is> square_it()
{
double number = < first Clipper parameter passed as a double >
<func to return double parameter to Clipper> (number*number ) ;
}
```

The above Extend C UDF performs the following tasks:

1. Preprocessor directives.

   a. nandef.h is #included. The C UDF thereby gains access to general #define constants and typedefs that an Extend System UDF may require. Among these are logical constants such as TRUE, FALSE, and BOOLEAN and type constants such as NULL and NIL. Note: other header files, such as stdio.h, may declare the same constants. Care should therefore be taken to #include nandef.h and extend.h last in an Extend System C UDF.

b. extend.h is #included. The C UDF thereby gains access to the following preprocessor information specific to the Extend System: (1) The C function return type void pascal #defined as the constant CLIPPER, (2) #define numeric constants for Clipper data types, (3) function prototypes for Extend System parameter functions, (4) function prototypes for Extend System return value functions, (5) function prototypes for Extend System dynamic memory allocation functions, (6) macros to figure parameter count and types, and (7) structure template and declaration for .dbf header information.

2. Header of the Extend System C function. CLIPPER, a #define constant for void pascal, is specified for the return type of the function. When a C function uses the type void pascal, it returns no value and preserves the order of the stack. Note: The keyword pascal is only available in some implementations of the C compiler, such as Microsoft and Turbo C.

   The function is then given a name of up to nine characters. To preserve the order of the stack, the function also has no regular C parameters. Therefore the parameter list to any Extend System function is void. The general header for any extend system function is

```
CLIPPER <name of function> (void)
```

3. Body of the Extend System C function. In the body of the function, automatic variables are declared as they would normally be declared in a C function. Stack memory is also used for these variables. However, because automatic variables are inside the function only they do not interfere with the stack setup outside the function.

   Note: Clipper only has 2K worth of stack memory. Care must therefore be taken not to use more than this amount for automatic variables declared in an Extend System function. If more memory is required, the C standard library or Extend System dynamic space allocation functions must be used. Use of these functions will be detailed later in this section.

   Variables in an Extend System function can also be initialized, just as in a normal C function. In our sample, the double number is declared and initialized with the Extend System parameter function _parnd().

4. Extend System parameter functions.

   a. parnd(1) is invoked to access the first double parameter from Clipper. It is one of a set of _par*() functions that access parameters from Clipper. The following list describes all the _par*() Extend System functions:

Function Header	Description
double _parnd (n [, i]); int n [, i];	Passes from Clipper to C the nth function parameter as a double (6-byte) value. An array index i may be specified.
int _parni (n [, i]); int n [, i];	Passes from Clipper to C the nth function parameter as an int (2-byte) value. An array index i may be specified.
long _parnl (n [, i]); int n [, i];	Passes from Clipper to C the nth function parameter as a long (4-byte) value. An array index i may be specified.
long _pards (n [, i]); int n [, i];	Passes from Clipper to C the nth function parameter as a date. The date is passed to C as a character string pointer where the string is in the form "YYYYMMDD." An array index i may be specified.
long _parl (n [, i]); int n [, i];	Passes from Clipper to C the nth function parameter as a logical value where 0 = FALSE and 1 = TRUE. An array index i may be specified.
char *_parc (n [, i]); int n [, i];	Passes from Clipper to C the nth function parameter as a character string pointer where the string contains a Clipper character expression. An array index i may be specified.

int _parinfo (n);
int n;
	Yields a value representing the Clipper type of the nth parameter or the number of parameters if n = 0. The type values are defined in extend.h as:
	`#define UNDEF 0`
	`#define CHARACTER 1`
	`#define NUMERIC 2`
	`#define LOGICAL 4`
	`#define DATE 8`
	`#define ALIAS 16`
	The above values are bitwise ORed with the values below for the following special Clipper types:
	`#define MPTR 32`
	`#define MEMO 65`
	`#define WORD 128`
	`#define ARRAY 512`

Function Header	Description
int _parinfa(n [, i]); int n [, i];	Same as parinfo(), except an array index i may be specified.
int _parclen(n [, i]); int n [, i];	Yields the length of nth parameter where the nth parameter is a character expression. An array index i may be specified.
int _parcsiz(n [, i]); int n [, i];	Yields the allocated size in bytes of the nth parameter where the nth parameter is a character expression. An array i may be specified.

b. _retnd(number) is called last, to return the C double number to Clipper from C. It is one of a set of _ret*() functions that return values to Clipper. An explicit C return statement cannot be used in an Extend System UDF. The following table describes all the _ret*() Extend System functions:

Function	Description
void _retnd (value); double value ;	Passes a double from C to Clipper as a numeric type.
void _retni (value); int value ;	Passes an int from C to Clipper as a numeric type.
void _retnl (value); long value ;	Passes a long from C to Clipper as a numeric type.
void _retl (value); int value ;	Passes a logical C value or expression to Clipper as a logical type. If the return parameter evaluates to 0 in C, a logical .F. is returned. If the return parameter evaluates to nonzero in C, a logical .T. is returned.
void _retds (date_string); char *date_string ;	Passes a date string from C to Clipper as a date type. The string must be in the form "YYYYMMDD."
void _retc (string); char *string ;	Passes a character string from C to Clipper as a character expression. _retc() ends the expression when it encounters the C terminated Null character (ASCII 0).

Function	Description
void _retclen (str,length); char *str ; int length ;	Passes a character buffer from C to Clipper as a character expression containing n characters. The function treats a Null character in the string like any other character.
void _ret (void) ;	Passes nothing from Clipper to C. This function is required if no other _ret*() function is used.

How an Extend System C UDF is Referenced in Clipper

From Clipper, the C UDF square_it() would be referenced as follows:

```
value = 5 ;
sq_value = square_it (value)
?"The squared value of "+STR(value)+" is "+STR(sq_value)
```

Clipper calls the C UDF just as it calls a Clipper function or Clipper UDF.

MORE EXTEND SYSTEM EXAMPLES USING VARIOUS C AND CLIPPER DATA TYPES

As detailed earlier, C has many numeric data types; in Clipper there is only one. For this reason there is more than one extend system _par*() and _ret*() function for passing numeric type data to and from Clipper and C.

Working with the C Type Int

The Extend System functions for the numeric data type int are most often used. These are _parni(), for passing int parameters from Clipper to C, and _retni(), for returning an int from C to a Clipper type numeric.

What is the reason for the popularity of _parni() and _retni()? Many Extend System functions access DOS internals or the ROM BIOS from C. DOS internal or ROM BIOS data is in the form of single bytes or 2-byte words, where all bits are used. The C type used for a single byte where all bits are used is unsigned char, and the C type used for a word where all bits are used is unsigned int.

In the Summer '87 version of Clipper, no Extend System functions exist for C unsigned types or for type char. However, the Extend System functions for type int can be used in conjunction with casts for the types unsigned int and unsigned char.

In the next section, we have written a function for moving the cursor, called cursor_set_pos(), whose function header is:

```
void cursor_set_pos( row, col )
unsigned char row, col ;
```

The C function cursor_set_pos() can be accessed from Clipper with an Extend System function coded as follows:

```
#include <nandef.h>
#include <extend.h>
#define SCREEN_WIDTH 80

CLIPPER put_curs()
{
int row = _parni(1), col = parni(2) ;
int offset = row * SCREEN_WIDTH + col ;

cursor_set_pos ( (unsigned char) row , (unsigned char) col ) ;
_retni ( offset ) ;
}
```

In Clipper, the function might be referenced as:

```
put_curs (10, 1)
```

This would move the cursor to the tenth screen row, first column.

In put_curs(), _parni() is used to pass the row and column coordinates to the Extend System C function. These coordinates are assigned to two declared integer variables **row** and **col**. In the next statement, the variables row and col are used to figure the offset of the new cursor position from the top of the screen, and this calculation is assigned to the int variable **offset**. The variables row and col are then cast to unsigned char and passed to the function cursor_set_pos to move the cursor. Finally the int variable offset is passed to the function retni(), which returns the offset to Clipper.

Working with the C Type Long

The Extend System functions for the numeric data type long are used less often than those for int. They are very useful, however, when one wishes to use the Extend System for C stream and file I/O. Positions in files are measured as long ints for buffered or unbuffered stream or file I/O functions.

The Extend System functions for the numeric data type long are _parnl(), for passing int parameters from Clipper to C, and _retnl(), for returning an int from C to a Clipper type numeric.

Working with the C Type Double

Since Clipper itself uses a double for its numeric data type, working with doubles is the most natural way to move numeric data using the Extend System. The Extend System functions for the numeric data type long are _parnd(), for passing int parameters from Clipper to C, and _retnd(), for returning an int from C to a Clipper type numeric.

Logical Expressions and the Extend System

As detailed earlier, C has no logical data type. Instead a numeric variable or expression in C is logically false if it evaluates to 0; otherwise it is logically true. The Extend System provides the proper conversion of a Clipper logical to a C logical with the function _parl(), and vice-versa with the function _retl().

Character Expressions and the Extend System

The Extend System provides the proper conversion of a Clipper character expression to a C character string with _parc(). The function _parc() returns a pointer to the string. The function _retc() returns a Null terminated character string to Clipper as a Clipper character expression. The following Extend System C UDF, cl_strrev(), reverses the characters in a character expression. To do this it calls _parc(), _retc(), and the C standard library function strrev(). :

```
#include <string.h>
#include <nandef.h>
#include <extend.h>

CLIPPER cl_strrev()
{
      char *strptr = _parc(1) ;
      _retc ( strrev (strptr) ) ;
}
```

In Clipper, cl_strrev() would be referenced as follows:

```
expression = "DOG"
? cl_strrev ( expression )
```

The Extend System also provides functions to work with character expressions in C without regard to the terminating Null in a C string. This allows for the possibility of embedded Nulls in a Clipper character expression and makes it easier to work with partial strings or substrings.

For example, the Extend System gives us two functions for determining the length of a Clipper character expression passed to C. The first function, _parclen(), is similar to the C standard library strlen() function, which counts characters in a C string up to the first Null byte. The second function, _parcsiz(), gives us the full length of the character expression regardless of embedded Nulls.

We have already seen that _retc() will pass a Null terminated C character string to Clipper as a character expression. In addition the Extend System function _retclen() will return a C character buffer of a specified length to Clipper as a character expression. The specified length may be less than or greater than the position of one or more Nulls in the C character buffer.

PASS BY REFERENCE IN THE EXTEND SYSTEM

Character Expressions

In C we can pass a character string to a function and have the function alter its contents. This occurs because what is passed to the function is the character string's address. The function then changes the contents of what is stored at the address.

In Clipper, an Extend System function will also alter a character expression's contents by reference if the character expression is not a string literal. To prove this, we can reference our C UDF cl_strrev() from Clipper as follows:

```
expression = "DOG"
cl_strrev ( expression )
? expression
```

Clipper Types Other Than Character Expressions

In C a variable of any data type can be passed to a function by reference. This is done by passing the address of the variable. Since in C a string name is itself an address, a C function can always manipulate a string passed to it and alter its contents by reference. For this reason, a character expression passed to an Extend System function can be altered by reference.

In the Summer '87 version of Clipper no mechanism exists for passing the addresses of variables other than character expressions to an Extend System C UDF. Therefore passing by reference will not work with Clipper types other than character expressions. If it is necessary to pass Clipper types other than character expressions by reference, the Clipper type must first be converted to a character expression and then passed to the function.

Parameter Evaluation

The Extend System provides functions and macros for parameter evaluation. The functions for parameter evaluation are parinfo() and parinfa(). The routine parinfa() works the same way as parinfo(), except an array index may be supplied. Several parameter macros are also defined in extend.h. The following table describes them:

Name	Return
PCOUNT	Number of parameters
ISCHAR(n)	True, if nth parameter is a character expression
ISNUM(n)	True, if nth parameter is a numeric expression
ISLOG(n)	True, if nth parameter is a logical expression
ISDATE(n)	True, if nth parameter is a date expression
ISMEMO(n)	True, if nth parameter is a memo field
ISBYREF(n)	True, if nth parameter is an address
ISARRAY(n)	True, if nth parameter is an array
ALENGTH(n)	The length of an array

Dynamic Memory Allocation in the Extend System

An Extend System function has only 2K of stack memory to work with in declaring variables. It is safest not even to rely on this 2K amount of memory for an array or data structure of any significant size. How then do we work with large data variables in the extend system? The answer is through dynamic memory allocation functions. Earlier, we introduced the C standard library dynamic space allocation functions. The two major functions are malloc(), which allocates space to a pointer, and free(), which frees, or deallocates, space from the pointer.

The Extend System provides two embellished forms of the C standard library's malloc() and free(). The Extend System version of malloc() is _exmgrab(), and its version of free() is _exmback(). The function headers are:

```
unsigned char *_exmgrab ( n_bytes )
unsigned int n_bytes ;

void _exmback ( exmgrab_ptr, n_bytes )
```

```
char *exmgrab_ptr ;
unsigned int n_bytes ;
```

The function _exmgrab() works like malloc(). The number of bytes of memory requested is specified and a pointer to the allocated memory is returned by the function.

The difference between _exmgrab() and malloc() is that _exmgrab() always performs memory checking within Clipper. The return value of malloc() can be tested for success or failure within the C UDF. The programmer cannot test, within the UDF, the success or failure of _exmgrab(). If _exmgrab() fails to allocate memory when not enough is available, an Out of Memory message is generated by the Clipper program at run-time. If malloc() is used, an out of memory problem can be checked at compile-time, when the programmer has the option of generating a run-time error message for the program's user or correcting the problem internally.

The difference between _exmback() and free() is that _exmback() requires an additional parameter, which is the amount of memory to give back, free, or deallocate. The C standard library function free() simply deallocates all memory allocated to the memory pointer passed to it.

In practice, using the C standard library dynamic allocation functions in an Extend System UDF offers more flexibility than using _exmgrab() and _exmfree.

We also showed some of the limitations of the Summer '87 Extend System. With Clipper 5.0, Nantucket promises us an improved and enhanced Extend System. To address the Extend System limitations for Summer '87 Clipper, Nantucket has produced an interim set of additional functions known as "C Goodies."

DOS INTERNALS AND THE ROM BIOS

Clipper developers very often build C or Assembler functions with the Extend System to access DOS internals and the ROM BIOS. In this way, programmers have complete control over applications running in the PC and compatible environment. Many third-party function libraries written for Clipper access DOS internals and the BIOS services for lowest-level operating system functions.

On PCs and compatibles, this lowest-level information is controlled by both hardware and software. The absolute, lowest-level hardware control is ROM, or Read Only Memory. ROM information is accessed by PC software through the BIOS or Basic Input Output System. The ROM BIOS controls the following aspects of the computer:

Monitor
Keyboard
Printer

Auxiliary devices
Date and time, via clock
Boot disk device

The next highest level of hardware control is via the operating system kernel, the innermost layer of software on the computer. When MS-DOS is loaded onto a PC or compatible, this operating system kernel is the DOS kernel; it controls the following aspects of the computer:

File management
Memory management
Input/output using a character set such as ASCII
Execution of programs
Access to the clock

Interrupts

Numbered interrupts provide access to either the ROM BIOS or DOS kernel to programs running in MS-DOS. An interrupt is so named because when it is invoked, an activity is performed that interrupts the PC's or compatible's low-level state of hardware operations.

Some interrupts are generated by the hardware itself. These are triggered when a fatal system error occurs, such as that caused by attempting to divide by 0. The other interrupts are generated by software, either by the DOS kernel or the ROM BIOS. These software interrupts are the ones that we can invoke from an application program.

Certain interrupts provide access to the DOS kernel, while others provide access to the ROM BIOS. DOS interrupts are numbered 20H (20 in hex notation) through 2FH. The most commonly used DOS interrupt is 21H.

All other interrupts are for the ROM BIOS. While most of the BIOS interrupts may be accessed from any type of PC or compatible, several are new and work with the AT and/or IBM PS/2. Microsoft reserves BIOS interrupt 33H for Mouse activities.

The DOS Kernel versus the BIOS

Many DOS kernel functions can also be performed by BIOS services and functions. For example, a keystroke can be accessed by either a DOS function or a BIOS service. Why is there this duplication? The answer is that DOS functions are set up to be independent of the hardware, while the BIOS is hardware dependent. DOS is loaded from software into the hardware, while the BIOS function is always in the hardware.

Because the DOS kernel is software based, it is upgradable without regard to the hardware. This allows DOS to be upgraded without altering the hardware. It also allows changes to be made to the hardware, and to the BIOS as a result, without affecting the DOS kernel functions used by application software.

The PC and compatible programming community is told by IBM and PC clone manufacturers that BIOS information may be altered, while DOS functions will remain unchanged, except through additions. Historically, however, the BIOS component of the PC has not changed, except for additions. Most real-world applications accessing the DOS kernel or the BIOS use all the functions and services necessary, whether DOS or ROM BIOS. There are two reasons for this: (1) DOS functions do not perform many of the tasks performed through the lower-level BIOS services and functions and (2) DOS functions for certain tasks call the corresponding BIOS service to perform the task. This may make the DOS service slower, since we are one step removed from the machine.

Calling DOS Internals or the BIOS from C

Microsoft and Turbo C, along with most PC C compilers, provide functions added to the C standard library to work with DOS internals and the BIOS. These DOS internal and BIOS functions are called with the same parameters. The most commonly used functions are the following:

Function	Usage
int86()	Invokes any BIOS interrupt
int21() or intdos()	Call universal DOS functions only

Microsoft and Turbo C also provide additional higher-level C functions specific to commonly used BIOS services. The Microsoft C functions all begin with the prefix _bios. The Turbo C functions all begin with the prefix bios. Microsoft C also provides additional higher-level C functions for commonly used DOS kernel functions. The C functions all begin with the prefix _dos.

The specific action taken by invoking a ROM BIOS interrupt is controlled by a subset of logical services. Within these services, a further subset of logical functions may be invoked for each interrupt. For almost all access to the DOS kernel, a specific interrupt, INT 21H (21 in hex notation), is invoked. INT 21H has a large subset of logical functions, each dedicated to a specific activity.

Functions and Hardware Registers

The parameters to BIOS and DOS kernel services and functions are hardware requests. Information is stored in hardware registers as a byte (an unsigned char) or a word (an unsigned int, containing 2 bytes).

Access to the Registers from C

DOS.H

In Microsoft and Turbo C, assignments to data structures provide access to the byte and word hardware registers. Structure templates are in the header file dos.h and are included in our program with the preprocessor line:

```
#include include<dos.h>
```

The data structures to access the registers are templated, in dos.h, as follows:

1. A template for 2-byte or word registers:

```
struct WORDREGS {
    unsigned int ax;
    unsigned int bx;
    unsigned int cx;
    unsigned int dx;
    unsigned int si;
    unsigned int di;
    unsigned int cflag;
    };
```

2. A template for 1-byte registers:

```
struct BYTEREGS {
    unsigned char al, ah;
    unsigned char bl, bh;
    unsigned char cl, ch;
    unsigned char dl, dh;
    };
```

3. A union to overlays that correspond to word and byte registers:.

```
union REGS {
    struct WORDREGS x;
    struct BYTEREGS h;
    };
```

The use of these data structures will be clearer as we continue with explanations and code samples.

DOS C Language Functions

To access the BIOS services and functions or DOS functions, the function int86() is most often used. Its function header is:

```
#include <dos.h>

int int86(intno,inregs,outregs);
int intno;              /*the number of the interrupt, or BIOS service/*
union REGS *inregs ;    /*contains register values to access from BIOS*/
union REGS *outregs ;   /*contains register values to update BIOS with*/
```

To access the DOS universal functions only, the function intdos() is most often used. Its function header is:

```
#include <dos.h>

int int86(inregs,outregs);
union REGS *inregs ;    /*contains register values to access from BIOS*/
union REGS *outregs ;   /*contains register values to update BIOS with*/
```

The functions int86() and intdos() work the same way, except that intdos() does not require an interrupt number parameter. Instead, intdos() always calls interrupt 21H.

General Form of a C Function Calling int86() or intdos()

A C function calling int86() or intdos() takes the following general form:

```
#include <dos.h>
[<other preprocessor statements>]

<function header>

     union REGS inregs,outregs;
     [other declarations]

     [statements to setup the union inregs]
     [other statements]

     int86 (<interrupt>, &inregs, &outregs ) ;
     /* or */
     int86 ( &inregs, &outregs ) ;
```

```
     [statements to access the union inregs]
     [other statements]

     [return <C UDF return value>]
}
```

EXAMPLES

Getting a Key with a Microsoft C Standard Library Call

To access any key, including special keys, from the keyboard, the function getkey() is used; it is coded as follows:

```
#include <conio.h>

int getkey(void)
{
     int key ;

     if ((key = getch()) )
          return ( key ) ;
     else return ( getch() + 300 ) ;
}
```

Getting a Key via the Dos Kernel Using intdos()

A function that performs identically using intdos() may be coded this way:

```
#include <dos.h>

int key_from_DOS(void)
{
     union REGS inregs,outregs;
     int key ;

     inregs.h.ah = 8;          /* call function 8 */
     intdos( &inregs, &outregs ) ;
     if ( ( key = (int) outregs.h.al ) )  /* return key if ASCII */
          return ( key ) ;
     inregs.h.ah = 8;          /* If it's not ASCII, it's a
                                  scan code for a special
                                  key.  So call function 8
                                  again to get the scan
                                  code. */
```

```
    intdos( &inregs, &outregs ) ;
    return ( outregs.h.al + 300 ) ;   /* Return scan code as
                                         a unique value. */
}
```

The above key_from_dos() C UDF is identical to the getkey() function, except that the key is gotten with a call to universal DOS function 8.

Internally, DOS functions are accessed by first invoking interrupt 21H and setting the .ah register to the number of the function. In a C function, however, this calling sequence is reversed. First the inregs.h.ah member of a data structure, REGS inregs, is assigned the number of the DOS function:

```
inregs.h.ah = 8;      /* Call function 8 */
```

Then the function intdos() is invoked. The intdos() function calls interrupt 21H for us and sets the register(s) with whatever value(s) we placed in REGS inregs. In this case the member inregs.h.ah will pass the value 8 to the high byte of the .ah hardware register. The call to intdos() takes the following form:

```
intdos( &inregs, &outregs ) ; /* call interrupt 21H with
                                 the current inregs
                                 settings.  Return the
                                 new outregs settings.
```

The key is accessed from the outregs.h.al member of the data structure REGS outregs. This contains the low byte of the hardware register .al. In key_from_dos(), the value of outregs.h.al is then assigned to the integer variable **key**.

```
key = (int) outregs.h.al
```

An (int) cast is used because outregs.h.al contains an unsigned char value.

The variable key is tested to see if its assigned value equates to a normal ASCII typewriter key. This will be the case if the assigned value of key is nonzero, or a C logical TRUE value. If the value of key is nonzero, the ASCII value of a typewriter key pressed is then returned by the function. For example, pressing the letter "A" would return the decimal value 65.

If the value of key fails the logical test, the value of key is 0, which indicates that a special key was pressed. When this is the case, as in getkey(), the next byte in the keyboard buffer will contain the scan code of a special key. DOS function 8 is therefore called again in order to access the scan code.

The value of the scan code is then returned, with a magic constant added to it to distinguish it from keys in the ASCII character set. For example, pressing the special key F7 will access a key scan code of decimal 65. Since this code is the same as the ASCII value of the letter "A," we add 300 to the scan code, to make it 365, to distinguish the function key value from the ASCII key value.

Getting a Key via the Bios Using int86()

The following function will also get a key from the keyboard, but it invokes a ROM BIOS service for the key rather than a universal DOS function. The BIOS Interrupt invoked is INT 16H, which is the interrupt for the BIOS keyboard services.

```
int key_from_BIOS()
{
        union REGS inregs, outregs ;

        int key = 0 ;

        inregs.h.ah = 0;
        int86(0x16, &inregs, &outregs ) ;
        if ( ( key = (int) outregs.h.al ) )
             return ( key ) ;
        else return ( (int) outregs.h.ah + 300 ) ;
}
```

First, the inregs and outregs are declared, along with the variable key, as they were in key_from_DOS().

Second, the ROM service request is placed in inregs.h.ah. It will be passed to the .ah register when the int86() function is called. The particular service requested for obtaining a key in a wait state, under INT 16H, is service 0. The C ROM service request statement is therefore:

```
inregs.h.ah = 0;
```

Third, the int86() function is called, specifying INT 16H as the interrupt to invoke:

```
int86(0x16, &inregs, &outregs ) ;
```

Fourth, the key is deciphered from the REGS outregs union. In the BIOS function, this is accomplished differently than in the previous getkey() or key_from_dos() functions. The ROM BIOS services 0 returns the key as a word rather than a byte. This means that both the value of the low and high bytes, containing the possible ASCII value and scan code, are returned as a single value, stored in the ax register. After a call to int86(), the register contents are placed in outregs.x.ax.

The low byte of outregs.x.ax therefore contains an ASCII key value if a typewriter key was pressed. The high byte of outregs.x.ax contains the scan code if a special key was pressed. The low-byte component of outregs.x.ax is referenced as outregs.x.al. The high-byte component of outregs.x.ax is referenced as outregs.x.ah.

Fifth, the value of outregs.x.al is tested to see if it contains an ASCII key value of a typewriter key. If it does, the ASCII value of the key is returned. Otherwise, the scan code value, from outregs.x.ah, is incremented with a magic constant and returned.

With the BIOS key service 0, the function int86() need only be called once since it returns both the possible ASCII and scan code value of the key pressed.

Getting Key States from the BIOS

The previous samples work well for getting a transient key from the keyboard. But certain keys, such as Caps Lock and Num Lock, activate and deactivate key states. How do we access these? The answer is through the same BIOS interrupt but using service 2. Here is a sample program to display active key states, including the code for a function to determine the key states by requesting BIOS service 2 under interrupt 16H:

```
#include <stdio.h>
#include <dos.h>

#define R_SHIFT          1
#define L_SHIFT          2
#define CTRL             4
#define ALT              8
#define SCROLL_LOCK     16
#define NUM_LOCK        32
#define CAPS_LOCK       64
#define INSERT_ON      128

unsigned char get_key_flags()
{
     union REGS inregs, outregs ;
     int key = 0 ;

     inregs.h.ah = 0;
     int86(0x16, &inregs, &outregs ) ;

     inregs.h.ah = 2;
     int86(0x16, &inregs, &outregs ) ;
     return (outregs.h.al) ;
}

main()
{
     unsigned char status, get_key_flags (void) ;
```

```
        int get_bios_key (void ) ;

        get_bios_key() ;

        status = get_key_flags() ;

        if (status & R_SHIFT     ) printf ( "Right Shift\n" ) ;
        if (status & L_SHIFT     ) printf ( "Left Shift\n"  ) ;
        if (status & CTRL        ) printf ( "Ctrl Key\n"    ) ;
        if (status & ALT         ) printf ( "Alt Key\n" ) ;
        if (status & SCROLL_LOCK ) printf ( "Scroll Lock\n" ) ;
        if (status & NUM_LOCK    ) printf ( "Num Lock\n" ) ;
        if (status & CAPS_LOCK   ) printf ( "Caps Lock\n" ) ;
        if (status & INSERT_ON   ) printf ( "Insert Key\n" ) ;
}
```

As is often the case with data stored in registers, each bit of the register byte or word acts as a flag. After int86() is called, a single byte is returned whose bits are flags for the various key states. This byte is in the .al register and is therefore accessed in our C function through outregs.h.al.

In this case, we just return the raw outregs.h.al unsigned character value, as is, from get_carry_flags(). In main(), this value is assigned to the variable status, which is then analyzed via the & (logical and) operator. The logical and is used to determine whether a particular bit in the byte is on or off. If it is on, the if statement will be logically true.

Using the Higher-Level Microsoft C _BIOS Functions

All the BIOS keyboard services we have used so far in this section may be obtained through one higher-level Microsoft C _bios function. This function is one of several such functions and is called _bios_keybrd() The header of _bios_keybrd is:

```
#include <bios.h>

unsigned _bios_keybrd (service_number )
unsigned service_number ;
```

The header file bios.h contains function prototypes for this and other _bios functions. It also contains #define constants for the service numbers used for this function.

Turbo C also has its own, similar set of higher-level BIOS functions. See Turbo C documentation for details.

Placing the Cursor

Another aspect of getting a key is how to echo the key to the screen and move the cursor. In Chapter 9, we mentioned many ways to display information. Now we present a BIOS function to move the cursor. It accesses the ROM BIOS display interrupt 10H, which provides several services for manipulating the screen. Among these is a service to position the cursor, ROM display service 2. The C function to move the cursor is coded as follows:

```
#include <dos.h>

void cursor_set_pos ( row, col )
unsigned char row, col ;
{
   union REGS inregs,outregs ;

   inregs.h.ah = 2 ;        /* will set ah to 2 to call service 2 */
   inregs.h.dl = col ;      /* the dl reg.will contain the column */
   inregs.h.dh = row ;      /* the dh register will contain the row
   inregs.h.bh = 0 ;
   int86 (0x10, &inregs, &outregs) ;
}
```

In this case the BIOS screen interrupt service for moving the cursor is 2, so we set inregs.h.ah = 2. Inregs.h.dl is set to the column position for the cursor, and inregs.h.dh is set to the row position to be set. If we provide an invalid row or column coordinate, the cursor will disappear.

For the cursor movement function, we did not need to make use of the outregs data.

Extend System BIOS Functions

To build an Extend System BIOS function, the BIOS C code is placed in an Extend System C function. This may be done most gracefully by calling the BIOS code as a separate function. We can build an Extend System function out of cursor_set_pos, for example, as follows:

```
#include <nandef.h>
#include <extend.h>
#include <bios.h>
{
CLIPPER cursor_set_pos (void)
     {
     void c_cursor_set_pos (unsigned char row, unsigned char col) ;
     c_cursor_set_pos ((unsigned char)parni(1),(unsigned char)parni(2));
     }

void c_cursor_set_pos (row,col)
unsigned char row, unsigned char col ;
{
     union REGS inregs,outregs ;

     inregs.h.ah = 2 ;
     inregs.h.dl = col ;
     inregs.h.dh = row ;
```

```
    inregs.h.bh = 0 ;
    int86 (0x10, &inregs, &outregs) ;
}
```

The trickiest aspect of Extend System C BIOS calls is performing the correct casting. Almost all BIOS parameters are unsigned values, either unsigned chars when dealing with a byte register or unsigned ints when dealing with a word register. Clipper Summer '87 does not provide a way of passing numeric parameters through the Extend System other than signed ints and doubles. Therefore numeric parameters must be properly cast when used to pass or receive BIOS data.

Thus, building one's own BIOS or DOS kernel functions in C is quite straightforward if one has an understanding of the BIOS and DOS kernel. Making BIOS and DOS kernel C functions callable from Clipper Summer '87 with the Extend System is also not too difficult, except that pains must be taken to perform the proper type conversions of values with C casts. Clipper 5.0 intends to make the Extend System more flexible by allowing us to pass other numeric types to C from Clipper and to return other numeric types from Clipper to C.

The High-Level Versus Low-Level API Crossroads

The higher level a routine is, the more portable it can be. If the high-level routine or set of routines is well thought out, it is also easier for the programmer to use, making it faster to develop an application. On the other hand, a low-level routine, such as one that accesses the BIOS or manipulates the PC via addresses in memory, gives the tightest control and fastest performance for a program in a specific hardware environment.

Teaching and Reference Texts on the DOS Kernel and ROM BIOS

We want to mention three excellent sources for ROM BIOS and DOS kernel knowledge and information. All three are published by Microsoft Press. The first is *Advanced MS-DOS* by Ray Duncan. It covers everything one might want to know about DOS and the BIOS and has many code examples in Assembler and C. The second is *Peter Norton's Guide to the IBM PC/PS 2* by Peter Norton. This book is a thorough teaching and reference text, written in the master's clear English. The third book, purely a reference, is *The PC Programmer's SourceBook*, by Thom Hogan. It lists in one book everything from BIOS information to Hewlett Packard LaserJet II escape sequences.

SUMMARY

This chapter covered the basic interface, practice and principles, between C and Clipper. The beauty of the Clipper language is in its open architecture. It was designed to work with the C language, to expand the impact of your applications and environment. Knowing how to work within that architecture can mean the difference between success and failure.

CHAPTER ELEVEN

A Cross-Reference Between Clipper and C

The following section is devoted to providing as many C equivalent routines for the Clipper dialect as possible.

COMMANDS

@

Clipper:

Syntax:

```
@ <row,column> = [SAY <exp> [PICTURE <clause> ]]
                 [GET <exp> [PICTURE <clause> ]
                 [RANGE <exp>,<exp>]
                 [VALID <exp>]
                 [CLEAR]
```

Description: The @ command is used to display and accept formatted information.

C:

Source: Code Base Windowing and GET functions

```
#include <w4.h>

w4 ( row, column, string )
int row, column ;
char *string ;

g4 ( row, column, string )
int row, column ;
char *string ;

void g4picture ( picture_string )
char *picture_string ;

void g4valid ( user_defined_function )
int (*user_defined_function)() ;

int g4read (void) ;
```

Description: The functions w4() and g4() are the basic routines for data collection of C strings in the Code Base windowing and GET systems, respectively. There are additional Code Base windowing and GET system functions for the display and data collection of other data types.

The function g4() is an initializer in Code Base. The GET is not actually performed until d4read() is called.

The functions g4picture() and g4valid() are called after g4() and prior to g4read() to establish the picture format of the GET and to set up GET validation.

The function g4valid() is passed the address of a user_defined_function to validate the GET. If this C UDF returns 0, the GET is validated; otherwise, it is not validated.

The above scenario works differently from a Clipper @SAY..GET followed by a READ. In Code Base, g4read() causes a GET, set up by previously called GET functions, to be both performed and read. In Clipper, the @ SAY..GET command causes a previously performed GET only to be read, while a READ is used to read information.

When a GET is read, the data gotten from the user is assigned to C variables or written to database fields.

Portability: PCs and compatibles and UNIX systems. Separate versions of Code Base exist for them.

Source: SJSC Library™, Copyright © 1989, Stephen J. Straley & Associates. All rights reserved.

Syntax: SJSC library SAY functions:

```
#include <s_say.h>

at_say      (int row,int col,unsigned char *string);
at_say_to   (int row,int col,unsigned char *buffer,
             int buffer_size);
at_center   (int row, unsigned char *string);
```

SJSC library GET function:

```
#include <s_get.h>

    char *getstr   ( int row, int col, char *string );
```

```
void set_<activity> ( int flag )
int do_<activity> ( void )
```

Description: Several SJSC functions provide @ functionality in C:

at_say() displays a character string at a particular location.

getstr() accepts formatted character string information and returns a pointer to the string. Sister functions are also provided for other data types.

The set_<activity>() functions are called prior to each GET to determine how a GET should perform a particular GET activity.

The do_<activity>() are user-redefinable functions for each GET activity.

@...TO

Clipper:

Syntax:

```
@ <row1, column1> [CLEAR] to <row2,column2>[DOUBLE]
```

Description: The @...TO command is used to format an area of the screen, either as a cleared space or edged with a single- or double-line border.

C:

Source: Code Base window() functions

Syntax:

```
#include <w4.h>

w4border ( box_char_string, attribute )
char *string, attribute ;

w4box (  box_char_string, startrow, starcol,
            end_row, end_col )
char *string ;
int startrow,startcol,endrow,endcol ;
```

Description: These function are used to draw borders around a currently selected Code Base window.

The function w4define() must be called first to define the window.

The box_char_string characters are in the following order:

Top side
Bottom side
Left side
Right side
Upper-left corner
Upper-right corner
Lower-left corner
Lower-right corner

Source: SJSC Library window() functions

Syntax:

```
#include <s_say.h>

   int window (int minrow, /* upper row coordinate  */
   int mincol,     /* upper col coordinate  */
   int maxrow,    /* lower row coordinate  */
   int maxcol,     /* lower col coordinate  */
   unsigned char fill,       /* IBM ASCII char */
   unsigned char type        /* from s_say.h    */
   );

void set_border (box_char_string)
char *box_char_string ;

void at_color     (int row, int col,
                   unsigned char attribute,
                   int times_to_repeat );
```

Source: SJSC Library macro

Syntax:

```
#include <s_say.h>

unsigned char color  (unsigned char foreground,
                      unsigned char background,
                      unsigned char blink_state ) ;
```

Description: The SJSC window() function creates a window anywhere on the screen and draws an optional border and shadow around it based on the value of the **type** parameter. The possible values of type are #defined in the header file s_say.h as follows:

NO_BDR 0
SINGLE 1

DOUBLE 2
CUSTOM 3
NO_BDR_SHADOW 4
SINGLE_SHADOW 5
DOUBLE_SHADOW 6
CUSTOM_SHADOW 7

If CUSTOM is used, the function set_border() determines the window.

Note: All subsequent calls to at_say() and get() functions, once a window function is called, will use window coordinates.

The SJSC Library function at_say_at (row, col) can be used to override window coordinates. at_say_at(0,0) will cause at_say() functions to revert to absolute screen coordinates.

![<exp]

Clipper:

Syntax: ![<exp>]

Description: This logical NOT operator performs the same way as .NOT. It was added in the Clipper Winter '85 release principally because of its popularity among programmers who had used it in C.

C:

Source: C language logical operator

Syntax: ![<exp>]

Description: Logical NOT operator

In C, .NOT. is not implemented. However, a #define preprocessor macro may be used as follows:

#define .NOT. !

?, ??

Clipper:

Syntax: ?, ?? <expression list>

Description: This operator displays and evaluates the value of an expression.

C:

Source: C standard library

Syntax: #include <stdio.h>
printf()

Description: printf() displays and evaluates the value of a single or multiple expressions, and it will work with any data type. printf() can also display these expressions with or without new lines, tabs, and other display formats.

? (single question mark in Clipper) forces a new line. With printf(), a new line may also be forced using the character literal "\n" (backslash n) in the control printf() control string.

Examples:

```
printf ("hello"\n ) ; /* like Clipper's ? */
printf ("hello ) ;    /* like Clipper's ?? */
```

See Chapter 8 for a more complete description of printf() or refer to the C compiler documentation.

==

Clipper:

Syntax: <exp> == <exp>

Description: Logical equality operator

The equality is TRUE if both expressions evaluate to the same value. This has the same result as using the single equal (=) Clipper equality operator and setting SET EXACT ON.

C:

Source: C language equality operator

Syntax: <exp> == <exp>

Description: The equality is TRUE if both expressions evaluate to the same value.

Caution 1: In C the single equal (=) assignment operator is always used to assign values and never to equate them.

Caution 2: In C, character strings cannot be compared with the logical equality operator (==). Character strings must be compared with string comparison functions, such as the C standard library function strcmp(). See the C discussion for SET EXACT ON for a description of the string comparison functions.

ACCEPT

Clipper:

Syntax: ACCEPT [<prompt message>] TO <character memvar>

Description: Prompts the user for specific input. All data input by the user is treated as character type.

C:

Source: C standard library

Syntax:

```
#include <stdio.h>

gets ( string )
char *string ;
```

Description: Waits for the user to input a string. The string must be alphanumeric and is completed (confirmed) with an ASCII 13 (Return) character.

There is no prompt in gets(). If a prompt is desired, write a prompt to the screen and position the cursor first, and then gets(). The standard C library function printf() will write to the screen and position the cursor.

Also see @ for a description of GET functionality using the Code Base and SJSC libraries.

APPEND BLANK

Clipper:

Syntax: APPEND BLANK

Description: This command places a blank record at the end of the file and positions the record pointer or counter at the new blank record.

C:

Source: Code Base library

Syntax:

```
#include <d4base.h>

d4write ( recno )
long recno ;
```

Usage: d4write (–1L) ;

Description: The function d4write(), when passed a –1, places a new record at the end of the currently selected database. The record pointer is not repositioned.

The following C function will act as a Clipper APPEND BLANK command:

Source:

```
int append_blank ( void )
{
memset ( f4record(), ' ', f4record_width() ) ;
d4write ( –1L ) ;
return ( d4bottom () ) ;
}
```

APPEND FROM

Clipper:

Syntax:

```
APPEND FROM [<scope>] [FIELDS <field list>]
FROM <fieldname> [FOR <condition>] [WHILE <condition>]
[SDF/Delimited[WITH BLANK/<delimiter>]]
```

Description: Allows records to be added to the currently selected and opened database from another database or from another file in particular formats.

Command: Standard

Library: Clipper.lib

C:

Source: Code Base library

Syntax:

```
#include <d4base.h>

d4write ( recno )
long recno ;
```

Usage:

```
d4write (–1L) ;
```

Description: The function d4write(), when passed a –1, places a new record at the end of the currently selected database.

The record buffer is first set by (a) Getting a pointer to the record buffer with a call to the Code Base function f4record() and (b) Altering the contents of the record either by manipulating the record buffer directly or with Code Base field writing functions such as f4replace().

After a call to d4write(), the record pointer is not repositioned.

Source: SJSC Library™, Copyright © 1989 by Stephen J. Straley & Associates. All rights reserved.

The functions below call the Code Base functions d4write() and f4record() internally.

Syntax:

```
#include <d4base.h>

void append_dbf ( (char *) dbf_name ) ;
void append_sdf ( (char *) ascii_file_name ) ;
void append_dlm ( (char *) ascii_file_name ) ;
```

Description: append_dbf() appends the contents of a .DBF file to the end of the current file.

append_sdf() appends the contents of an ASCII file in SDF format to the end of the file.

append_dlm() appends the contents of an ASCII file in comma delimited format to the end of the file.

AVERAGE

Clipper:

Syntax: AVERAGE [<scope>] <field list> TO <memvar list> [FOR <condition>] [WHILE <condition>]

Description: Enables an average of specified fields to be calculated based on a specific condition in the currently selected and open database.

Command: Standard

Library: Clipper.lib

C:

Source: None. There is no single function to perform an average of a database field. However, an algorithm may be constructed to perform an average using Code Base functions.

BEGIN SEQUENCE

Clipper:

Syntax: BEGIN SEQUENCE <statements> [BREAK] <statements>..

Description: The BEGIN SEQUENCE command allows you to define program control for error trapping and conditional breaking within the flow of a program. The BREAK statement will turn over program execution to the statement immediately following the matching END statement.

Command: Clipper enhanced — Summer '87

Library: Clipper.lib

C:

Source: C language control statement

Syntax:

```
goto <label> ;
...

<label>:
C statements
```

When goto is encountered, processing jumps from the goto to the label and resumes from there.

BOX

Clipper:

Syntax: @ <top,left,bottom,right BOX <string>

Description: The BOX command is used to draw a box using ASCII characters, including drawing characters expressly for this purpose that are part of the extended IBM ASCII character set. See Programming in Clipper for more detailed information.

Command: Clipper enhanced — Summer '87

Library: Clipper.lib

C:

Source: Code Base and SJSC provide box drawing functions as part of their windowing libraries. See the @...TO.

CALL

Clipper:

Syntax: CALL <process> [WITH <parameter list>]

Description: This command provides access from Clipper to separately compiled and/or assembled routines linked to the Clipper application. These separate routines must be set up as .bin files and return far pointers.

The Clipper Extend System, discussed in Chapter 10, alleviates the need for this command when calling C or PC Assembly functions from Clipper. With the Extend System, separate routines may be linked as .obj files.

C:

Source: C language function call

Syntax: < [return_value =] function name ([<argument list...>]) > ;

Description: In C separately compiled functions may be called using the above syntax. There is no need for a special call command.

Functions may also be in other languages, as long as the separate functions cooperate in their handling of the stack in memory. Certain languages, such as Pascal, place data on the stack in reverse, so it is necessary to instruct the compiler to access the stack properly with the keyword PASCAL. See your compiler documentation for further details.

CANCEL

Clipper:

Syntax: CANCEL

Description: Just as effective as the QUIT command, this command stops the execution of a procedure or command file and the program returns to the operating system.

Command: Standard

C:

Source: C library function

Syntax: exit ((int) exitcode) ;

Description: The exit() function stops the execution of the current process and returns control to the operating system.

CLEAR

Clipper:

Syntax: CLEAR

Description: This command clears the screen and positions the cursor at ROW = 0, COL = 0 or at the upper leftmost corner of the screen. It will also clear all GET/READS from the calling program.

Command: Standard

Library: Clipper.lib

C:

Source: Code Base library

```
#include <w4.h>

void w4clear ( row )
int row ;
```

Description: This function can either be used to clear the entire screen, like the Clipper CLEAR command, or clear the currently selected Code Base window if one has been set up.

If the row parameter is –1, the entire screen is cleared. Otherwise, the screen is cleared starting from the specified window row.

Source: SJSC Library™, Copyright © 1989 by Stephen J. Straley & Associates. All rights reserved.
Screen functions

Syntax:

```
#include <s_say.h>

void clear ( unsigned char attribute ) ;
void cls( void ) ;
void at_say_at ( int new_row, int new_col ) ;
```

Description: These functions clear the video screen and return the cursor to the upper left-hand corner of the screen. clear() can be used to clear the screen to a particular color. cls() will clear the screen to the current color. at_say_at (0,0) will clear row and column coordinates set by previous window commands.

CLEAR ALL

Clipper:

Syntax: CLEAR ALL

Description: This command clears all memory variables, closes all open databases and associated indexes and memo fields (if applicable), and releases any SET RELATION TO and filter conditions. It then SELECTS work area 1.

Command: Standard

Library: Clipper.lib

C:

Source: SJSC Library™, Copyright © 1989 by Stephen J. Straley & Associates. All rights reserved.

Screen functions; Database functions. Code Base functions are called internally.

Syntax:

```
#include <s_say.h>

int clear_all () ;
```

Description: The C function below will work the same way as its Clipper counterpart. Note: Code Base automatically selects work area 0 the next time a file is opened with d4use).

```
#include <d4base.h>
#include <s_say.h>

clear_all()
{
cls() ;
at_say_at (0,0) ;
d4close_all() ;
}
```

CLEAR GETS

Clipper:

Syntax: CLEAR GETS

Description: Used in conjunction with associated @ SAY..GET commands, a CLEAR GETS command releases all GET statements prior to this command.

Command: Standard

Library: Clipper.lib

C:

Source: SJSC Library™, Copyright © 1989 by Stephen J. Straley & Associates. All rights reserved.
Get function data structure flag

Syntax: s_get.quit = TRUE ;

Description: To exit a get() or browse() function, set the member **quit** of the S_GET data structure. This works as a toggle:

```
#include <s_get.h>

s_get.quit = TRUE  ; /* to clear   */
s_get.quit = FALSE ; /* to stay in */
```

CLEAR MEMORY

Clipper:

Syntax: CLEAR MEMORY

Description: This command releases and clears all memory variables from the system.

Command: Standard

Library: Clipper.lib

C:

Source: C standard library

Syntax:

```
#include <malloc.h> or
#include <stdlib.h>

free ( ptr )
void (*ptr) ;
```

Source: C standard library

Syntax:

```
#include <d4base.h>

h4free ( char ** ptr_ref_ptr, int mem_ref )
```

Description: The free() function will free any dynamically allocated memory pointed to by ptr. SJSC functions make little use of dynamically allocated memory, while Clipper and Code Base use it extensively.

Code Base has its own set of functions for memory management that create, allocate, and free memory. h4free() is used to free memory. See Code Base documentation for complete details on using the Code Base memory management system.

CLEAR TYPEAHEAD

Clipper:

Syntax: CLEAR TYPEAHEAD

Description: The CLEAR TYPEAHEAD command clears the keyboard buffer.

Command: Clipper enhanced — Summer '87 release

C:

Source: This functionality does not exist in Code Base or in SJSC or in any other commercial C library, to our knowledge. It is, however, possible to write a function in C that performs direct access to the keyboard buffer. This is done by accessing the address of the keyboard buffer or by calling universal DOS function 0CH.

CLOSE

Clipper:

Syntax: CLOSE <file type>

Description: The CLOSE DATABASES command closes all open databases and all associated indexes.

The CLOSE ALL command is a Summer '87 enhancement; it closes all types of files including alternate files, databases, and index files. It will also release all active files, formats, and relations.

The CLOSE INDEX command closes all open index files that are currently in use.

The CLOSE FORMAT/PROCEDURE command closes all open FORMAT/PROCEDURE files.

C:

Source: Code Base functions

Syntax: #include <d4base.h>

```
int d4close (void) ;
int i4close (void) ;
int d4close_all (void) ;
```

Description: These Code Base functions close Clipper databases and indexes.

d4close() closes the currently used and selected database (.dbf) file and all related opened index files.

i4close() closes the currently used and selected index (.ntx or .ndx) file.

d4close_all closes all the currently used and selected database (.dbf) files and index (.ntx or .ndx) files.

See also FCLOSE() in the "Functions" section later in this chapter.

COMMIT

Clipper:

Syntax: COMMIT

Description: The COMMIT command performs a solid-disk write for all work areas. Before the disk write is performed, all buffers are flushed to DOS.

Command: Clipper enhanced — Summer '87 release

Library: Clipper.lib

Note: This command will only work with DOS versions 3.3 or higher.

C:

Source: None

Explanation: There is no specific COMMIT function in the Code Base or SJSC libraries.

CONTINUE

Clipper:

Syntax: CONTINUE

Description: This command resumes a search initiated by a LOCATE FOR command, continuing to search for records that meet the search criteria.

Command: Standard

Library: Clipper.lib

C:

Source: None. This functionality does not presently exist in any of the libraries mentioned in this book. The C continue statement serves a different purpose from the Clipper CONTINUE command.

COPY FILE

Clipper:

Syntax: COPY FILE <source file> TO <destination file>

Description: The COPY FILE command makes an exact copy of <source file> with the name <destination file>.

C:

Source: C standard library

Syntax:

```
#include <process.h>
system ( "COPY <source path> <destination path>
        [<option flags>]" )
```

Description: Use the system() function to call the DOS copy command to copy the file. Alternatively, the source and destination files may be opened for reading and writing, respectively, and data may be copied from the source to the destination file using C standard library functions.

COPY STRUCTURE

Clipper:

Syntax: COPY STRUCTURE TO <filename> [FIELDS <field list>]

Description: The COPY STRUCTURE command only copies the structure of the currently active database to <filename>.

C:

Source: User-defined function composed of Code Base library functions

Example:

```
#include <stdio.h>
#include <d4base.h>
#define FIELD_MAX 3

int main ( argc, argv )
int argc ;
char *argv[] ;
{
FIELD flds[FIELD_MAX] ;

int test = 0, n = 1 ;
long fref = 0L ;
video_init() ;
test = d4use ( "test.dbf" ) ;

for ( ; n <= f4num_fields() ; n++ )
     {
     strcpy ( flds [n-1].name,
          f4name (fref = f4j_ref (n)) ) ;
     flds [n-1].type     =  f4type    (fref) ;
     flds [n-1].width    = f4width    (fref) ;
     flds [n-1].decimals = f4decimals (fref) ;
     flds [n-1].offset   = f4offset   (fref) ;
     }
d4create ( "name.dbf", n-1, flds, 1 ) ;
d4close_all ( ) ;
}
```

COPY TO

Clipper:

Syntax: COPY TO <filename> [<scope>][FIELDS <field list>][FOR <condition>] [WHILE <condition>] [SDF/DELIMITED WITH BLANK/<delimiter>]

Description: The COPY TO <filename> command copies the currently selected database to another database or to an alternate text file.

Command: Standard

Library: Clipper.lib

C:

Reference: See COPY FILE.

COPY TO STRUCTURE EXTENDED

Clipper:

Syntax: COPY TO <filename> STRUCTURE EXTENDED

Description: The COPY TO STRUCTURE EXTENDED command creates a new database consisting of four fields: field_name, field_type, field_len, and field_dec. Fields of the open database become records in the structure extended database.

C:

Source: SJSC Library™, Copyright © 1989, Stephen J. Straley & Associates. All rights reserved.
Database function
Calls Code Base library functions

Syntax: int struc_extend (filename)
char *filename ;

Code:

```
#include <d4base.h>
#include <string.h>
```

```
extern int v4error ;


int struc_extend ( filename )
char *filename ;
{
static FIELD flds[] = {
     {"FIELD_NAME", 'C', 10, 0, 0 },
     {"FIELD_TYPE", 'C',  1, 0, 0 },
     {"FIELD_LEN",  'N',  5, 0, 0 },
     {"FIELD_DEC",  'N',  2, 0, 0 } } ;

int source, target, n = 1 ;
long fref = 0L ;

char name [11] ;
char type ;
double  width ;
double  decimals ;

source = d4select ( -1 ) ;
if ((target=d4create( filename,4, flds, 0 )) == -1)
     return ( v4error ) ;
d4select ( source ) ;
for ( n = 1; n <=  f4num_fields() ; n++ )
     {
     strcpy (name, f4name (fref=f4j_ref(n))) ;
     type     = f4type               ( fref ) ;
     width    = (double) f4width     ( fref ) ;
     decimals = (double) f4decimals  ( fref ) ;
     d4select ( target ) ;
     f4record() ;
     f4replace (f4ref ("FIELD_NAME"), name      );
     f4replace (f4ref ("FIELD_TYPE"), &type     );
     f4replace (f4ref ("FIELD_LEN"),  &width    );
     f4replace (f4ref ("FIELD_DEC"),  &decimals );
     d4write (-1L ) ;
     d4select ( source ) ;
     }
}
```

Sample:

```
int main ( argc, argv )
int argc ;
char *argv[] ;
```

```
{
      d4use ( "test" ) ;
      struc_extend ( "fields.dbf" ) ;
      d4close_all() ;
}
```

COUNT

Clipper:

Syntax: COUNT [<scope>][FOR/WHILE <conditon>] TO <memvar>

Description: This command counts how many records in the currently active and open database file meet a specific condition and stores that figure to a memory variable.

C:

Source: None

Description: There is no specific COUNT function in the Code Base or SJSC libraries. The following source, however, illustrates how to build a database COUNT algorithm in C using Code Base:

```
#includye <string.h>
#include <d4base.h>
#define TRUE  1
#define FALSE 0

long count ( fieldname, expression )
char *fieldname, *expression ;
{

/* initialization */
int end_of_file = FALSE ;
static long counter = 0L ;

/* database loop */
d4top() ;

for ( ; !end_of_file ; end_of_file = d4skip(1L) )
   {
   /* condition */
   if ( !strncmp ( f4str ( f4ref (fieldname) ),
            expression,
```

```
            strlen (expression) ) )
        counter++ ;
    }
return ( counter ) ;
}

#include <stdio.h>
#include <d4base.h>

int main ()
   {
   long how_many ;
   long count ( char *fieldname, char *expression);

   d4use ( "PHONEBOOK.DBF" ) ;
   how_many = count ( "STORES", "SHOES" ) ;
   printf ( "%ld\n", hom_many ) ;
   d4close () ;
   }
```

CREATE

Clipper:

Syntax: CREATE <database file name>

Description: This command creates a STRUCTURE EXTENDED database consisting of four fields: field_name, field_type, field_dec, and field_len. In this case, the database is blank. The application initializes the fields.

C:

Source: SJSC Library™, Copyright © 1989, Stephen J. Straley & Associates. All rights reserved.
Database function
Calls Code Base library functions

Syntax:

```
int create ( filename )
char *filename ;
```

Code:

```
#include <d4base.h>

int create ( filename )
```

```
char *filename ;
{

static FIELD flds[] = {
     {"FIELD_NAME", 'C', 10, 0, 0 },
     {"FIELD_TYPE", 'C',  1, 0, 0 },
     {"FIELD_LEN",  'N',  5, 0, 0 },
     {"FIELD_DEC",  'N',  2, 0, 0 } } ;
return ( d4create( filename, 4, flds, 0 )) )
}
```

Sample:

```
int main ( argc, argv )
int argc ;
char *argv[] ;
{
     char name [11] ;
     char type ;
     double  width ;
     double  decimals ;
     create ( "fields.dbf" ) ;
     strcpy (name, "WANTED" ) ;
     type = "C"
     width = (double)   25 ;
     decimals = (double) 0 ;     f4record() ;
     f4replace (f4ref ("FIELD_NAME"), name      );
     f4replace (f4ref ("FIELD_TYPE"), &type     );
     f4replace (f4ref ("FIELD_LEN"),  &width    );
     f4replace (f4ref ("FIELD_DEC"),  &decimals );
     d4write (-1L ) ;
     d4close() ;
}
```

CREATE FROM

Clipper:

Syntax: CREATE <newfile> FROM <structure extended file>

Description: The CREATE FROM command forms a new database file based on the contents of a structure extended file.

Command: Standard

C:

Source: Code Base library

Syntax: #include <d4base.h>

int d4create(char *, int, FIELD *, int) ;

Description: The Code Base d4create() function creates a database from a C data structure, rather than a structure extended file. The data structure may be stored in a header file.

DECLARE

Clipper:

Syntax: DECLARE <memvar>[<expn>] [,<array list>]

Description: This command established a Clipper array named <memvar> of <expN> items. The items may be of any type and may be mixed. See *Programming in Clipper, 2nd Ed.,* (Addison-Wesley) which documents the DECLARE command extensively, or see the Clipper manual.

Command: Clipper enhanced

Library: Summer '87 — Clipper.lib
Autumn '86 — Dbu.lib

C:

Source: Declarations of C types: Structures and unions

Syntax:

```
struct/union TEMPLATE_NAME <tag>
{
member declaration1 ;
[ member declaration2 ] ;
.....
[ member declarationN ] ;
} [ <structure declaration [array dimension]> [= <initialization> ]] ;
```

Description: A Clipper array is really an array of C data structures. The facility to address data of any type at any position in the array is provided by a special type of C data structure called a union.

Data structures in C are declared just like any other C data type. They may be global, static, or automatic. Structures and unions that are initialized must be either global or static.

DELETE

Clipper:

Syntax: DELETE [<scope>] [FOR <condition>] [WHILE <condition>]

Description: The DELETE command marks a record(s) in the currently opened database for future deletion.

Command: Standard

Library: Clipper.lib

C:

Source: Code Base library

Syntax:

```
#include <d4base.h>

int d4delete (recno) ;
long recno ;
```

Description: The d4delete() function marks a record in the currently opened database for future deletion. The record number must be explicitly passed to the function as a long integer. To delete the current record use the following syntax:

```
d4delete ( d4recno() ) ;
```

A while or for loop, with conditional if statements, would need to be constructed to delete groups of records matching particular criteria.

DIR

Clipper:

Syntax: DIR [<path>] [<skeleton>]

Description: The Clipper DIR command works like the DOS DIR command, except that if no <skeleton> is passed, only .dbf files are listed.

Command: Standard

Library: Clipper.lib

C:

Source: C standard library

Syntax: #include <process.h>

int system [string] ;
const char string ;

Usage: System ("DIR [<path>] [<skeleton>] [<options>]") ;

Description: Use a DOS system call to execute the DOS directory command from C. The following syntax would be used to produce a wide listing of .dbf files:

System ("DIR *.dbf /w") ;

DISPLAY

Clipper:

Syntax: DISPLAY [OFF][scope] FIELDS <field list> [FOR <condition>] [WHILE <condition> [TO PRINT][TO FILE <file>]

Description: This command allows the contents of fields to be displayed.

C:

Source: SJSC Library™, Copyright © 1989 SJS and Associates. All rights reserved.

Calls Code Base functions internally

Syntax: Browse functions:

int browse_which (browse_no) ;
int browse_no ;

int browse_set (row, col, order, fieldname)
int row,
    int col,

```
    int order ;
char *fieldname ;

int browse_setopts ( valid, confirm, listbox, end,
                     help, edit, picture, insert,
                     total )
int valid          /* global field validation flag       */
int confirm        /* global key exit flag               */
int listbox        /* global listbox flag                */
int end            /* global field exit activity flag    */
int help           /* global field help activity flag    */
int edit           /* global field edit activity flag    */
int picture        /* global field picture flag          */
int insert         /* initial insert key state           */
int total          /* how totals, if any, should show    */ )
int browse ( row, col, reccount, start_rec, mode )
int row ;          /* starting row of the browse         */
int col ;          /* starting column of the browse      */
int reccount ;     /* total records to browse            */
int start_rec ;    /* record to start from               */
int mode ;         /* browse mode - from s_browse.h      */
```

See Chapter 9 of this book.

Reference: The LIST command discussion in this chapter shows how DISPLAY functionality may be achieved by other means.

DO

Clipper:

Syntax: DO <file name> [WITH <parameter(s)>]

Description: The DO command begins execution of a program file or procedure.

Command: Standard

Library: Clipper.lib

C:

Source: C language function call

Syntax: < [return_value =] function name ([<argument list...>]) >;

Description: In C new processes are invoked with function calls. Functions can be in the same or different source files. Source files in C are compiled separately. Each source file produces an object file. The object files are merged into one executable file by the linker.

DO CASE

Clipper:

Syntax:

```
DO CASE
CASE <logical expression is true>
        <commands>
CASE <logical expression is true>
        <commands>
CASE <logical expression is true>
        <commands>
OTHERWISE
        <commands>
ENDCASE
```

Description: In Clipper, when we need to branch execution of a program based on more than two conditions, we can, as an alternative to the IF ELSE command, use the DO CASE and CASE commands.

Command: Standard

Library: Clipper.lib

C:

Source: C language control statement

Syntax:

```
switch ( < numeric expression > )
{
case    < matching numeric expression >:
        statements
case    < matching numeric expression >:
        statements
case    < matching numeric expression >:
        statements
default:
    statements
}
```

Description: The C language provides a case statement, but it works in a different way than in Clipper. In C the case control structure is called a switch case statement, and it allows us to branch program execution based on multiple evaluation of one numeric expression. For complete details and examples see Chapter 9.

DO WHILE

Clipper:

Syntax:

```
DO WHILE    <condition>
            <commands>
ENDO
```

Description: The DO WHILE command allows statements within the DO WHILE and associated ENDDO statement to be repeated so long as the condition specified by the DO WHILE command remains true.

Command: Standard

Library: Clipper.lib

C:

Source: C language control statement

Syntax:

```
   while ( logical expression is true )
   {
   execute statements
   }
do
   {
   execute statements
   }
while ( logical expression is true ) ;
```

Description: The C language provides two types of while loops. The first while loop evaluates an expression in the loop; the second loop, the do..while, allows for a statement to be presented first and then evaluated in a loop.

Clipper's DO WHILE command works like a C while loop (without the do), where expressions are evaluated within the loop until a logical condition is satisfied. For complete details and examples see Chapter 9.

Source: C language control structure

EJECT

Clipper:

Syntax: EJECT

Description: The EJECT command issues a form feed command to the printer.

Command: Standard

Library: Clipper.lib

C:

Source: C statement

Syntax:

```
#include <stdio.h>

#define FORMFEED 12

fprintf ( stdprn, "%c", FORMFEED ) ;
```

Description: This is one way in C to send a form feed to the printer. An ASCII decimal 12 form feed is one of the few universal printer codes.

ERASE

Clipper:

Syntax: ERASE < filename >

Description: The ERASE command removes a file from the disk directory. The use of wild card characters (*,?) are permitted with this command.

Command: Standard

Library: Clipper.lib

C:

Source: C standard library

Syntax:

```
#include < io.h >
#include < stdio.h> /*  Use either header file */

int unlink ( path )
char *path ;
```

Syntax:

```
#include <process.h>

int system [string] ;
const char string ;
```

Usage: System ("ERASE [<path>]") ;

Description: The unlink() function erases a single file from the disk directory. Use system() to erase multiple files. Use of a DOS system() call to erase files is better because, in the case of accidental erasure, the files can be unerased with popular third-party DOS file management tools.

EXIT

Clipper:

Syntax: EXIT

Description: The EXIT command stops the execution of commands within a DO WHILE..ENDDO loop and FOR..NEXT loop and transfers processing to the command statement immediately following the appropriate ENDDO or NEXT command.

Command: Clipper enhanced

Library: Clipper.lib

C:

Source: C control flow statement

Syntax: break ;

Description: The C break statement stops the execution of processing within a while, do while, or for loop and transfers processing to the statements immediately following the loop. A break statement is also used in a switch case statement, where it is placed in a case, to stop processing any more cases. For complete details and examples see Chapter 9.

EXTERNAL

Clipper:

Syntax: EXTERNAL <procedure list>

Description: This command is used to declare a symbol during compiling for later use by the linker. This allows procedures to be placed in overlays.

Command: Clipper enhanced

Library: Clipper.lib

C:

Source: C language function call

Syntax: < [return_value =] function name ([<argument list...>]) >;

Description: In C, separately compiled functions may be called using the above syntax. See your C compiler and linker documentation to see if overlays are supported and how to implement them.

Microsoft Link supports internal, but not external, overlays.

Reference: See FUNCTION.

FIND

Clipper:

Syntax: FIND <expC>/<expN>

Description: The FIND command searches the active, indexed database for the first record with a matching key. The FIND command can only find literal expressions. Use SEEK for variable expressions.

Command: Clipper enhanced

Library: Clipper.lib

C:

Source: Code Base library function

Syntax:

```
#include <d4base.h>

int d4seek ( key_expression )
char *key_expression ;
```

Description: The d4seek() Code Base function searches the active, indexed database for the first record with a matching key expression. d4seek returns the following values:

0 An exact find was made.

1 An inexact find was made, such as when the expression passed to d4seek() matches only the first part of the database key.

2 Returned if the value is not greater than any value in the index file, but a find cannot be made. This works like Clipper's FIND and SEEK commands when SET SOFTSEEK is on.

3 End of File. Returned if the value of the key expression is greater than any value in the index file.

-1 Error.

When searching index files with date keys, key_expression should be in the form "YYYYMMDD."

When searching index files with numeric keys, use the following syntax:

```
double value = <double expression> ;
d4seek ( ( char *) &value ) ;
```

Source: Code Base functions

FOR..NEXT

Clipper:

Syntax: FOR <memvar> = <expN> TO <expN> [STEP <expN>] <commands> [EXIT]...<commands>
NEXT:

Description: The CLIPPER FOR..NEXT command allows looping for a range of values, where the value of <memvar> may increment or decrement by the amount of the STEP expression at each loop.

Command: Clipper enhanced

Library: Clipper.lib

C:

Source: C language control statement

Syntax:

```
for  ( [ initial statements ] ;
       [ logical expression ] ;
       [ modifying statements ] )
{
[ statement(s) ] ;
}
```

Description: C's **for** loop, similarly, allows for initial values to be processed in the loop and values to be modified with each iteration of the loop. This loop is particularly useful for tightly controlled increment and decrement values to be made in a loop.

Each component of the for loop is optional. An endless loop would appear as follows:

for (;;) ;

For complete details and examples see Chapter 9.

FUNCTION

Clipper:

Syntax:

FUNCTION <name>
<commands>
RETURN (<value>)

Description: This command initializes user-defined functions. As with procedures, functions may or may not have parameters passed to them.

Command: Clipper enhanced

Library: Clipper.lib

C:

Source: C language function call

Syntax:

<[return_val=] function name([<argument list...>])
argument list types >;

Description: In C, functions are created using the above syntax. C functions that return and/or pass no arguments should use the void type to specify that nothing is to be returned and/or passed. For example:

```
void Nothing (void)
{
/*  this function does nothing.  It is not alone
    in the world. */
}
```

Functions may also be created in other languages as long as the separate functions cooperate in their handling of the stack in memory. Certain languages, such as Pascal, place data on the stack in reverse so it is necessary to instruct the compiler to access the stack properly with the keyword PASCAL. See your compiler documentation for further details.

GO/GOTO

Clipper:

Syntax: GO/GOTO <exp> TOP/BOTTOM

Description: The GO/GOTO command places the record pointer in the currently selected work area at the specified record or location in the database.

Command: Standard

Library: Clipper.lib

C:

Source: Code Base library

Syntax:

```
#include <d4base.h>

int d4go ( recno ) ;
long recno ;
```

Description: The Code Base d4go() function performs like the GOTO command. Remember to pass the record number as a long integer. When using a literal value, use the following syntax:

```
d4go ( (long) <literal value> )
```

d4go() returns the following values:

0 Successfully went to the record.

1 Record does not exist.

-1 Error.

Locking: The record is locked.

IF

Clipper:

Syntax:

```
IF <logical expression is true>
   execute statements...
[ELSEIF <logical expression is true>
   execute statements...]
[ELSE
   execute statements...]
ENDIF
```

Description: The IF command allows a conditional processing, also referred to as branching.

Command: Standard

Library: Clipper.lib

C:

Source: C language control statement

Syntax:

```
if ( <logical expression is true> )
    {
    [ execute statement(s) ; ]
    }
[ else if ( <logical expression is true> )
    {
    [ execute statement(s) ; ]
    } ]
[ else
    {
    [ execute statement(s) ; ]
    } ]
```

Description: The functionality of the C if statement is close to that of the CLIPPER IF statement. Because of the use of curly brackets to control processing, there is no need for an ENDIF statement.

Note: In C a logical expression can be any expression. The expression evaluates to zero if it is false or nonzero if it is true.

INDEX ON

Clipper:

Syntax: INDEX ON <key expression> TO <file name>

Description: The INDEX command creates an index file for the current, active database. The INDEX file presents a logical view of the database as if it were sorted on <key expression>.

Command: Standard

Library: Clipper.lib

C:

Source: Code Base library

Syntax:

```
i4index ( name, key_expression, unique, safety )
char *name ;
char *key_expression ;
int unique ;
int safety ;
```

Description: The i4index() Code Base function creates, opens, and selects a database. If safety is off (0) and a previous index file with the same name is open, the previous index file will be closed, deleted, and then created once more according to the new specifications.

Note: The unique flag is not compatible with Clipper. It specifies whether each key in the index file must be unique. When using Clipper index files, always set this key to 0.

INPUT

Clipper:

Syntax: INPUT [<expC>] TO <memvar>

Description: The INPUT command accepts user entered data from the keyboard. The INPUT can be of any data type and is completed by striking the Enter key.

Command: Standard

Library: Clipper.lib

C:

Source: C standard library

Syntax:

```
int scanf (format [ , argument... ] ) ;
const char *format ;
```

Description: The standard C library function scanf() accepts user entered data from the keyboard. The data can be of any data type.

Example:

```
#include <stdio.h>
int main()
{
int i = 0. result ;
double f = 0.00 ;
char c, str[81] ;
printf ( "Enter an integer, a double, a character \n
         and a string\n -> " ) ;

total = scanf ( "%d, %lf, %c, %s",&i, &f, &c, str );
printf ( "\nThe number of fields input is %d\n",
           total ) ;
printf ( "The contents are %d, %lf, %c, %s" ,
         i, f, c, str ) ;
```

JOIN

Clipper:

Syntax: JOIN WITH <alias> TO <new filename> FOR <condition> [FIELDS <field list>]

Description: The JOIN command creates a new database based on two open databases by merging specified records and fields to that new file.

Command: Standard

Library: Clipper.lib

C:

Source: None

Description: This functionality does not exist in standard C or in Code Base. See SET RELATION TO.

KEYBOARD

Clipper:

Syntax: KEYBOARD <expC>

Description: This command stuffs the Clipper input buffer with <expC>.

C:

Source: None

Explanation: This functionality does not exist in Code Base or in SJSC or in any other commercial C library, to our knowledge. It is, however, possible to write a function in C that performs direct access to the keyboard buffer. This is done by accessing the address of the keyboard buffer or by using either universal DOS function 0CH or BIOS INT 16H, service 05H. This BIOS service only works on ATs, AT compatibles, and PS/2s.

In the SJSC library GET system, key substitution may be performed within a GET. This may be accomplished in the following ways:

1. The value returned by the SJSC function getkey() may be substituted for another.

2. The values in the s_get structure used by SJS GET functions may be substituted for others, including those of s_get.array, s_get.key, and s_get.lastkey.

Reference: See the SJSC functions discussed under @ in this section and INKEY() in the next section.

LABEL FORM

Clipper:

Syntax: LABEL FORM <file name> [<scope>] [FOR <condition>] [WHILE <condition>] [SAMPLE] [TO PRINT] [TO FILE <file name>]

Description: The LABEL command allows labels to be printed based on the format outlined in a .LBL file on disk.

Command: Standard

Library: Clipper.lib

C:

Source: None

Description: There is no single C function to produce labels from a database. However, database generated labels can be produced using Code Base library functions.

A third-party report writer, such as Concentric Data Systems' R&R Relational Report Writer, provides much better flexibility than the LABEL command for this purpose.

LIST

Clipper:

Syntax: LIST [OFF] [scope]<field list> [FOR <condition>] [WHILE <condition>][TO PRINT][TO FILE <filename>]

Description: The LIST command displays the contents of the database.

Command: Standard

Library: Clipper.lib

C:

Source: None

Description: There is no single C function to produce lists from a database. However, Clipper database generated lists of records can be produced using Code Base library functions.

Here is an example of how this might be done:

```
int main(argc, argv)
int argc ;
char *argv[]
{
/* this function will display the database record specified by the
command line argument */
if ( argc < 2 )
    {
    printf ( "usage: list <.dbf filename>\n" ) ;
    exit (1) ;
    }
if ( d4use ( argv[1] ) != SUCCESS )
    {
    printf ( "error opening .dbf file\n" ) ;
```

```
}

d4top() ;
for ( end_of_file = TRUE ;
    !end_of_file ;
    end_of_file = d4skip (1L )
    {
    printf ( "%s\n", f4record() ) ;
    }
d4close() ;
```

Note: A common technique used by C programmers reading in a record buffer is to create a data structure mask for it so that the fields can be printed out in a formatted way or otherwise manipulated. Say the database structure's fields were as follows:

```
NAME        'C'   4   1
PHONE       'C'   12  5
BIRTHDAY    'D'   8   17
```

The data structure could be declared as follows. Since .dbf files are stored in character format, the structure that reads the raw database buffer would contain only character data:

```
struct FRIENDS
    {
    char name    [30]
    char phone   [12]
    } friends ;
```

The structure serves to divide the buffer into its field components. We can access each field as a non-NULL terminated character buffer with the general syntax:

<declared struct name>.member.

For example, the database reading loop in the above source would be written as follows. Note the string precision ("%.<number>s" is required for the printf control string because the character buffers in the structure, from the raw database buffer, are not NULL terminated:

```
d4top() ;
printf ( "NAME                    ") ;
printf ( "PHONE\n\n") ;
```

```
for ( end_of_file = TRUE ;
   !end_of_file ;
   end_of_file = d4skip (1L )
   {
   memcpy ( (char*) friends, f4record() ;
   printf (  "%.30s  %.12s\n",
             friends.name, friends.phone ) ;
   }
d4close() ;
```

Also note: A third-party report writer, such as Concentric Data Systems' R&R Relational Report Writer, provides enormous flexibility for this purpose.

LOCATE

Clipper:

Syntax: LOCATE [<scope>] [FOR <condition>] [WHILE <condition>]

Description: The LOCATE command searches the open and selected database for the first record that meets the condition specified. LOCATE does not require an INDEX file to be in USE. The LOCATE command performs a sequential search from the top of the database.

C:

Source: User-defined C function using the Code Base library

Syntax:

```
long locate ( fieldname, expression )
char *fieldname, *expression ;
```

Description: This function will scan a database sequentially for a field or partial field that matches an expression. The source below may be altered to fit the need.

Source: SJSC Library™, Copyright © 1989, Stephen J. Straely & Associates. All rights reserved.

This database function calls Code Base functions internally.

```
#include <string.h>
#include <d4base.h>
```

```
#define TRUE  1
#define FALSE 0

long locate ( fieldname, expression )
char *fieldname, *expression ;
{
int end_of_file = FALSE ;

d4top() ;
while ( !end_of_file &&
        strncmp ( f4str ( f4ref (fieldname) ),
            expression,
            strlen (expression) ) )
        end_of_file = d4skip (1L ) ;
return ( d4recno() ) ;
}

#include <stdio.h>
#include <d4base.h>
int main ()
   {
   long locate ( char *fieldname, char *expression);
   d4use ( "TRIP.DBF" ) ;
   locate ( "CITY", "MOSCOW" ) ;
   printf ( "%s\n", f4record() ) ;
   d4close () ;
   }
```

LOOP

Clipper:

Syntax: LOOP

Description: The LOOP command immediately jumps to the beginning of the current DO WHILE..ENDDO loop. Any command or series of commands following the LOOP command are ignored.

Command: Standard

Library: Clipper.lib

C:

Source: C Language control statement

Syntax: continue ;

Description: In C, a continue statement will also have the effect of skipping the processing of the remaining statements in a loop and continuing at the next iteration of the loop. The continue statement will work in while(), do while(), and for() loops.

Note: Whether in Clipper or in C, it is best to avoid much use of LOOP or continue, respectively.

NOTE /*/&&

Clipper:

Syntax: NOTE/* <text>
<command line> && <text>

Description: The NOTE /*/&& command allows text to be entered into the program or procedure code that can be used to describe the action taken by the procedure or command.

C:

Source: C language comments

Syntax:

```
/* text
   text
   text */
```

Description: /* begins comment text. Everything following will be ignored by the compiler until:

*/ ends comment text.

Comments in C work differently than in Clipper. Because C is not source code line oriented, there is no way to comment a line of code in C with one comment marker. Instead, code is commented in blocks.

Warning: Most compilers do a terrible job of telling you if you are missing a comment marker. Instead, erratic problems occur in compiling. Therefore care must be taken to use opening and closing comments.

PACK

Clipper:

Syntax: PACK

Description: The PACK command removes from the currently open and selected database those records that were previously marked for deletion.

Command: Standard

Library: Clipper.lib

C:

Source: Code Base library

Syntax: #include <d4base.h>
d4pack()

Description: The d4pack() command in the Code Base library works the same way as the Clipper PACK command. It, too, reindexes opened databases.

Security: While the current version of d4pack() seems to work well, it is safest to close the packed file and reopen it after using d4pack(). In previous versions of Code Base, this has proven necessary.

PARAMETERS

Clipper:

Syntax: PARAMETERS <parameter list>

Description: The PARAMETERS command assigns local variables with the names given. The values in these variables will be either referenced or valued as determined by the calling program.

Command: Standard

Library: Clipper.lib

C:

Source: C language function call

Syntax: <[return_val=] function name([<argument list...>])
argument list types >;

Description: In C, parameters are passed to functions using the above syntax. In C, every procedure is a function.

Command line arguments are arguments to a program passed from the operating system when the program is invoked. In Clipper the PARAMETERS command allows these arguments to be received into a program. In C, the function main(), the first function called in a C program, receives command line arguments. These arguments are passed to main() using the following syntax:

```
int main ( argc, argv[]
int argc ;        /* the number of arguments */
char *argv[]      /* the argument strings stored in an
                     array of character pointers */
```

PROMPT MESSAGE

Clipper:

Syntax: @ <row>,<col> PROMPT <expC> [MESSAGE <expC>]

Description: The PROMPT..MESSAGE command places menu selections on the screen, highlights menu choices, and allows the cursor to be moved via the cursor pad or direct input.

Command: Clipper enhanced

Library: Clipper.lib

C:

Source: Code Base library menuing routines

Description: Code Base provides a comprehensive set of menuing functions. These allow for the creation of the following menu styles: pull down, pop up, vertical, horizontal, and Lotus-style.

See Code Base documentation for the syntax and use of these functions.

PROCEDURE

Clipper:

Syntax: PROCEDURE <procedure name>

Description: A PROCEDURE is a group of commands that perform a specific task.

Command: Standard

Library: Clipper.lib

C:

Source: C language function call

Syntax: < [return_value =] function name ([<argument list...>]) >;

C language function syntax

```
< [return_value = ] function name ([<argument list...>]) >;
{
statements.... ;
}
```

Description: In C, statements are grouped together in functions rather than procedures. Functions can be in the same or different source files. The functions become known to each other by the linker.

PUBLIC

Clipper:

Syntax: PUBLIC <memvar list>[,Clipper]

Description: The PUBLIC command declares memory variables to be PUBLIC in nature; available to all procedure and functions within an application.

Command: Clipper enhanced

Library: Clipper.lib

C:

Source: C language storage class

Syntax: extern <memory variable list>

Description: The extern storage class in C is equivalent to the PUBLIC storage class in Clipper. The scope of an extern variable in C is the entire application.

Note: When an extern variable is declared in a different source file from the one in which it was previously declared, it must be redeclared and preceded by the keyword extern. See Chapter 9.

Example: contents of main.c:

```
int count ;

main ()
      count = 5 ;
}
```

contents of print.c:

```
#include <stdio.h>

extern int count
{
      printf ( "%d\n", count ) ;
}
```

It is best to make a list of all externs and declare them in a C header file. The header file is then #included in each source file that references the external variables. For example:

contents of globs.h:

```
int count = 5 ;
int flag1 = TRUE ;
int flag2 = FALSE;
```

contents of main.c:

```
#include "globs.h" ;

main ()
{
     if (flag1) count-- ;
}
```

contents of print.c:

```
#include <stdio.h>
#include "globs.h" ;

extern int count
{
     printf ( "%d\n", count ) ;
}
```

QUIT

Clipper:

Syntax: QUIT

Description: The QUIT command closes all open files, clears all memory variables, and returns control to the operating system.

Command: Standard

Library: Clipper.lib

C:

Source: C standard library

Syntax: #include <stdio.h>

int exit (exit_code)
int exit_code ;

Description: The C exit() function closes all open files, clears all variables, and returns control to the operating system.

READ

Clipper:

Syntax: READ [SAVE]

Description: The READ command activates all current @..GETs invoked since the last CLEAR, CLEAR ALL, CLEAR GETS, or READ.

Command: Standard

Library: Clipper.lib

C:

Source: Code Base GET routines

Syntax:

```
#include <w4.h>
int g4read (void) ;
```

A Code Base g4read() call functions differently from a Clipper @SAY..GET followed by a READ. In Code Base, g4read() causes a GET, set up by previously called GET functions, to be both performed and read. In Clipper, the @ SAY..GET command causes a previously performed GET only to be read, while a READ is used to read information.

When a GET is read, the data gotten from the user is assigned to C variables or written to database fields.

Source: SJSC Library™, Copyright © 1989, Stephen J. Straley & Associates. All rights reserved.
GET functions

Description: In SJSC GET functions, what Clipper does with a READ statement is accomplished with other functionality. See the @SAY..GET command discussion at the beginning of this chapter for SJSC GET function syntax. Also see Chapter 8 for additional information.

RECALL

Clipper:

Syntax: RECALL <scope>[[FOR <condition>][WHILE <condition>]]

Description: The RECALL command unmarks those records marked for deletion and reactivates them in the current and open database.

Command: Standard

Library: Clipper.lib

C:

Source: Code Base library

Syntax:

```
#include <d4base.h>

void d4recall(record_number)
long record_number ;

char *f4record()
```

Description: The Code Base d4recall() function recalls a specified record marked for deletion.

When a .dbf file record is marked for deletion, a 1 is placed in the first character position of the record. When the record is unmarked using d4recall(), a space (ASCII decimal value 32) is placed in the first character position.

The Code Base f4record() function, which accesses the entire record buffer at once, can also be used to mark or unmark records for deletion. This is done by changing the initial value of the record buffer returned by f4record():

```
#define SUCCESS 0
#define ERROR_CODE -1

int delete_func(recno)
long recno ;
{
char *record ;

if ( d4go (recno) != SUCCESS )
        return (ERROR_CODE)

record = f4record() ;
*record = '1' ;
```

```
if ( d4write (recno) != SUCCESS )
        return (ERROR_CODE)
else return (SUCCESS )
}

int recall_func(recno)
long recno ;
{
char *record ;

if ( d4go (recno) != SUCCESS )
        return (ERROR_CODE)

record = f4record() ;
*record = ' ' ;

if ( d4write (recno) != SUCCESS )
        return (ERROR_CODE)
else return (SUCCESS )
}
```

REINDEX

Clipper:

Syntax: REINDEX

Description: The REINDEX command rebuilds all of the active index files in the currently open and active work area.

Command: Standard

Library: Clipper.lib

C:

Source: Code Base library

Syntax:

```
#include <d4base.h>
int i4reindex ( index_ref )
int index_ref ;
```

Description: i4reindex() reindexes the specified index file. If index ref is negative, all the index files for the current database will be reindexed.

Returns: If the file or files are successfully reindexed, the function returns 0. Otherwise, i4reindex() returns a -1.

Library: Code Base library

Example:

```
#include <d4base.h>

main()
{
int index_ref, error_code ;

d4use ( "CANDIDATES" ) ;
index_ref = i4open ( "MAYORAL.NTX" ) ;

error_code = i4reindex ( index_ref ) ;
d4close_all() ;

return (error_code ) ;
}
```

RELEASE

Clipper:

Syntax:

RELEASE <memory variable>
RELEASE <memory variable list>
RELEASE [ALL [LIKE/EXCEPT <skeleton>]]

Description: The RELEASE command deletes from memory a memory variable (or variables) and reallocates memory space for future use.

Command: Standard

Library: Clipper.lib

C:

Source: C standard library

Syntax:

```
#include <malloc.h> or
#include <stdlib.h>

void free ( ptr )
void *ptr ;
```

Description: The standard library function free() is analogous to Clipper's RELEASE command. free() deallocates memory allocated to the pointer **ptr**. See STORE.

RENAME

Clipper:

Syntax: RENAME <filename> TO <filename2>

Description: The RENAME command changes the name of the first <filename> to that of the second <filename>.

Command: Standard

Library: Clipper.lib

C:

Source: C standard library

Syntax:

```
#include <process.h>

int system ( dos_command ) ;
char *dos_command ;
```

Usage:

```
system ( "RENAME <filename> <filename2>" ) ;
```

Description: In C it is simplest to invoke a system call, which is analogous to a RUN command in Clipper. Then we can call the internal DOS command RENAME.

REPLACE

Clipper:

Syntax: REPLACE [<scope>]<field> WITH <exp> [, <field> WITH <exp>...][FOR <condition>] [WHILE <condition>]

Description: The REPLACE command changes the contents of specified fields in the active database.

Command: Standard

Library: Clipper.lib

C:

Source: Code Base library

Syntax:

```
#include <d4base.h>

int f4replace ( field_ref, value )
long field_ref ;
void *value ;

char *f4record(void) ;
```

Description: The Code Base f4replace() function replaces the contents of a field in the current record of the active database. A Code Base field reference number identifies the field, or the field can be references by name and passed with a character pointer to a string or as a literal as follows:

```
d4replace ( f4ref (field_name), value ) ;
```

The value parameter to the function can be a character pointer to a string or literal expression or the address of a double numeric value. Dates are passed as character expressions in the form "YYYYMMDD."

REPORT FORM

Clipper:

Syntax:

```
REPORT FORM <file name> [<scope>] [FOR <condition>]
WHILE <condition>] [TO PRINT] [TO FILE <file name>]
[PLAIN][HEADING]<expC>][NOEJECT]
```

Description: The REPORT FROM command allows forms to be printed based on the format outlined in a .FRM file on the disk.

Command: Standard

Library: Clipper.lib

C:

Source: None

Description: There is no single C function to produce labels from a database. However, database-generated labels can be produced using Code Base database library functions.

A third-party report writer, such as Concentric Data Systems' R&R Relational Report Writer, is very useful for this purpose.

RESTORE FROM

Clipper:

Syntax: RESTORE FROM <filename> [ADDITIVE]

Description: The RESTORE FROM command retrieves from disk a memory variable and activates all memory variables stored in that file.

Command: Standard

Library: Clipper.lib

C:

Source: None. This functionality does not exist in standard C, Code Base, or SJSC libraries. It may, however, exist elsewhere in a commercial C library with which we are not familiar.

RESTORE SCREEN

Clipper:

Syntax: RESTORE SCREEN

Description: The RESTORE SCREEN command draws a screen that was previously saved in memory.

Command: Clipper enhanced

Library: Clipper.lib

C:

Source: Code Base library

Syntax: w4write_window (window_ref, screen_buffer)
int window_ref, char *screen_buffer ;

Description: The Code Base function w4write_window() will write the window specified by window_ref to a user-defined character buffer. The character buffer must be large enough for the character spaces of the window multiplied by 2, since each character is paired with an attribute byte.

Portability: Code Base screen I/O functions will work on PCs and compatibles and Unix machines.

Source: SJSC Library™, Copyright © 1989, Stephen J. Straley & Associates. All rights reserved.

restore_screen (screen_number)
int screen_number ;

Description: The SJSC screen function will restore a screen from memory that has been previously saved with the SJSC screen function save_screen (screen_number).

SJSC allocates space for and declares the number of screens available in the header file s_say.h. This can be modified by the user for the need at hand. Each screen requires 4K of RAM.

Portability: SJSC screen functions are optimized for PCs and compatibles.

RETURN

Clipper:

Syntax: The RETURN command restores control to the program or procedure that originally called the current program or procedure. If there is no program file or procedures to return control to, control is returned to DOS.

Description: Basically, this returns control to the calling procedure, function, or routine.

Command: Standard

Library: Clipper.lib

C:

Source: C language function return statement

Syntax: return (<function type> variable) ;

Description: The return statement in C restores control to the function that calls it. If a return statement is made in main(), control returns to the operating system.

The variable returned must be of the same data type as the data type of the function it is returning from. When returning from a function of type void, the return statement can be omitted, or return is referenced as return() with no variable in parentheses.

RUN/ !

Clipper:

Syntax: RUN <MS/IBM DOS command>/
! <MS/IBM DOS command>

Description: Runs a DOS command by first loading a copy of command.com.

Command: Standard

Library: Clipper.lib

C:

Source: C standard library

Syntax:

```
#include <process.h>

int system ( dos_command ) ;
char *dos_command ;
```

Description: In C a system call is analogous to a RUN command in Clipper. A copy of command.com is loaded when a system call is invoked.

Note: In C there are alternative commands for running programs as child processes from the current program or parent process. These functions are the C standard library functions **spawn**() and **exec**(). They do not load a copy of command.com but fork the child process directly into memory.

Refer to compiler documentation for complete syntax and discussion of spawn() and exec() functions.

SAVE SCREEN

Clipper:

Syntax: SAVE SCREEN [TO <memvar>]

Description: This command SAVEs the display to a memory variable.

Command: Clipper enhanced

Library: Clipper.lib

Syntax:

```
save_screen ( screen_number )
int screen_number ;
```

C:

Source: SJSC Library™, Copyright © 1989, Stephen J. Straely & Associates. All rights reserved.

Description: The SJSC save_screen() function will save a screen in memory, which can then be restored with the SJSC screen function restore_screen (screen_number).

SJSC allocates space for and declares the number of screens available in the header file s_say.h. This can be modified by the user for the need at hand. Each screen requires 4K of RAM.

Portability: SJSC screen functions are optimized for PCs and compatibles. They can be modified to run on other machines.

Source: Code Base library windowing functions

Syntax:

```
#include <w4.h>

w4read_window ( window_ref, screen_buffer )
int window_ref, char *screen_buffer ;
```

Description: The Code Base function w4read_window() will read the window specified by window_ref to a character_buffer. The character buffer must be large enough for the character spaces of the window multiplied by 2 since each character is paired with an attribute byte.

Note: This function will not restore window borders.

Portability: Code Base screen I/O functions will work on PCs and compatibles and UNIX machines.

SAVE TO

Clipper:

Syntax: SAVE TO <filename> [ALL LIKE/EXCEPT <skeleton>]

Description: The SAVE TO command stores all or part of the current set of memory variables to a designated file.

Command: Standard

Library: Clipper.lib

C:

Source: None. This functionality does not exist in standard C, Code Base, or SJSC libraries. It may, however, exist elsewhere in a commercial C library with which we are not familiar.

SEEK

Clipper:

Syntax: SEEK <expression>

Description: The SEEK command searches for the first record in a database file with a key of an open index file that matches <expression>.

Command: Standard

Library: Clipper.lib

C:

Source: Code Base library

Syntax:

```
#include <d4base.h>

int d4seek ( key_expression )
char *key_expression ;
```

Description:

The d4seek() Code Base function searches the active, indexed database for the first record with a matching key expression. d4seek() returns the following values:

0 An exact find was made.

1 An inexact find was made, such as when the expression passed to d4seek() matches only the first part of the database key.

2 Returned if the value is not greater than any value in the index file, but a find cannot be made. This works like Clipper's FIND and SEEK commands when SET SOFTSEEK is on.

3 End of File. Returned if the value of the key expression is greater than any value in the index file.

-1 Error.

When searching index files with date keys, key_expression should be in the form "YYYYMMDD."

When searching index files with numeric keys, use the following syntax:

```
double value = <double expression> ;

d4seek ( ( char *) &value ) ;
```

SELECT

Clipper:

Syntax: SELECT <expN>/<expC>

Description: The SELECT command moves Clipper's internal primary focus and allows changes in the selected work area.

Command: Standard

Library: Clipper.lib

C:

Source: Code Base library

Syntax:

```
#include <d4base.h>

int d4select(database_ref_no)
int database_ref_no ;
```

Description: Code Base's d4select() function similarly changes the selected work area. Work area values are termed database reference numbers. Unlike Clipper, these numbers are not assigned by the programmer but by Code Base when it opens each database with the function d4use().

Code Base's d4select() function, when passed a -1, will return the current work area, or database reference, number for the database in use.

SET ALTERNATE TO

Clipper:

Syntax: SET ALTERNATE TO [<filename>]

Description: The SET ALTERNATE TO command creates a text file for the SET ALTERNATE ON command to port to.

Command: Standard

Library: Clipper.lib

C:

Source: C standard library

Syntax:

```
#include <stdio.h>

FILE *freopen (new_stream_name,access_mode,stream )
char *new_stream_name, *access_mode ;
FILE *stream ;
```

Description: The freopen() function will cause a file_descriptor to be associated with a different input or output stream.

Library: Standard C

SET ALTERNATE

Clipper:

Syntax: SET ALTERNATE ON/OFF

Description: The SET ALTERNATE ON/OFF command tells the computer that program output information to follow is to be redirected to the file specified by the SET ALTERNATE TO command.

Information displayed with @..SAY/GET commands is not redirected to the file.

Command: Standard

Library: Clipper.lib

C:

Syntax: See SET ALTERNATE TO.

SET BELL

Clipper:

Syntax: SET BELL ON/OFF

Description: The SET BELL command toggles the bell to sound whenever the last character position in a GET is entered or if an invalid data type is entered into a GET.

Default: ON

Command: Standard

Library: Clipper.lib

C:

Source: Code Base library

Syntax:

```
g4bell_set (toggle)
int toggle ;

g4bell() ;
```

Description: These functions cause the bell to sound in the Code Base GET system:

g4bell_set(0) is equivalent to SET BELL OFF.

g4bell_set(1) is equivalent to SET BELL ON.

g4bell() will sound the computer's bell if a previous call to g4bell_set() was made and the toggle parameter is TRUE (any nonzero value).

A call to g4read() in conjunction with a Code Base GET will cause the bell to sound after entry into the GET field.

Default: The Code Base GET system bell is turned off.

Source: SJSC Library™, Copyright © 1989 Stephen J. Straley & Associates. All rights reserved.

Syntax:

```
#include <s_get.h>

void set_end(flag)
int flag ;

int do_end (void) ;
```

Description: The SJSC GET functions can be used to turn the bell on globally for GETs in an application.

Usage: Calling function code fragment:

```
#define RING_BELL 10
int set_up_get(void)
{
   int user_defined_flag = RING_BELL ;
   set_end (user_defined_flag) ;
```

```
    get (row,col,string) ;
}
```

The C UDF do_end() code_fragment:

```
if ( s_get.end == RING_BELL )
  putc (7) ; /* causes bell to sound */
```

The C UDF do_end() is called internally by get(). The GET structure member s_get.end contains the flag passed to set_end() outside the GET.

Default: No bell sounds at the conclusion of a GET.

SET CENTURY

Clipper:

Syntax: SET CENTURY ON/OFF

Description: The SET CENTURY ON/OFF command allows the input and the display of dates within the century prefix. It will be in standard "MM/DD/YYYY" format.

Command: Clipper enhanced

Library: Clipper.lib

C:

Source: Code Base library

Syntax:

```
#include <d4base.h>

char *c4dt_format( dbf_date, picture ) ;
char *dbf_date, *picture ;
```

Description: This is not a global set function. The function is used in local situations to convert a date from its raw .dbf file form "YYCCMMDD" to a form specified in the picture string. The picture form is composed of any arrangement of the substrings "CC," "MM," "YY," and "DD." The use of "CC" is optional. For example:

```
printf ( c4dt_format "19890630", "MM/DD/CCYY" ) ;
```

will display 06/30/1989

printf (c4dt_format "19890630", "MM/DD/YY") ;

will display 06/30/89

SET COLOR TO

Clipper:

Syntax: SET COLOR TO [<standard> [, <enhanced> [, <border> [, <background [,unselected]]]]]

Description: This command changes the colors displayed on the screen.

Command: Clipper enhanced

Library: Clipper.lib

C:

Source: Code Base library

Syntax:

```
#include <w4.h>

int w4attribute ( attribute )
int attribute ;

#include <g4.h>

int g4attribute ( attribute )
int attribute ;
```

Description: These functions set the attribute byte of the display. The window function w4attribute() sets the color for the current window. The GET function g4attribute() sets the color for subsequent GETs.

The Code Base manual shows examples of how the attribute may be set using Code Base #defines. For more flexibility, however, use the SJSC color() macro with color constants to code the attribute byte. Source code for these is given below.

Source: SJSC Library™, Copyright © 1989 Stephen J. Straley & Associates. All rights reserved.

```
#include <s_say.h>

void set_color ( attribute )
unsigned char attribute ;

void set_getcolor ( attribute )
unsigned char attribute ;

attribute = color ( fore,back,blink)
unsigned char back, fore,blink ;
```

General Usage:

```
set_color     (color(fore,back,blink) ) ;
set_getcolor  (color(fore,back,blink) ) ;
```

These functions also set the attribute byte of the display. The function set_color() sets the color of at_say() strings with or without windows. The function set_getcolor() sets the color for subsequent GETs.

The macro color() provides a user-friendly means to set the attribute byte. It is #defined as follows:

```
#define color(fore,back,blink) (fore|(back<<4)|blink)
```

The values for fore (foreground) and back (background) are #defined as:

```
#define BLACK     0
#define BLUE      1
#define GREEN     2
#define CYAN      3
#define RED       4
#define MAGENTA   5
#define BROWN     6
#define WHITE     7
```

Other values for fore are #defined as:

```
#define LT_WHITE     8   /*foreground only */
#define LT_BLUE      9   /*foreground only */
#define LT_GREEN     10  /*foreground only */
#define LT_CYAN      11  /*foreground only */
#define ORANGE       12  /*foreground only */
#define LT_MAGENTA   13  /*foreground only */
```

#define YELLOW 14 /*foreground only */
#define LT_WHITE 15 /*foreground only */

Values for blink are #defined as:

#define BLINK 128
#define NORMAL 0

The above #defines are in the SJSC header file s_say.h

Sample:

```
#include <s_say.h>
#include <s_get.h>

main()
{
     static char name[] = "              " ;

     video_init() /* function to determine monitor

     type and initialize video data
               structure  */

     set_color (color (WHITE,BLUE,NORMAL)
     at_say ( 10, 2, "Name: " ) ;
     set_getcolor (color (BLACK,WHITE,NORMAL)
     get ( 10, 8, name ) ;
}
```

SET CONFIRM

Clipper:

Syntax: SET CONFIRM ON/OFF

Description: With the SET CONFIRM ON command, the Enter key is required for each and every GET.

Default: OFF

Command: Standard

Library: Clipper.lib

C:

Source: SJSC Library™, Copyright © 1989, Stephen J. Straley & Associates. All rights reserved.

Syntax:

```
#include <s_get.c>

void set_confirm(flag)
int flag

int do_confirm(void)
```

Description: These functions can set any single or set of characters, or no character, to be used to confirm a GET.

Usage: Calling function code fragment:

```
#define RETURN    1
#define SPECIAL   2
#define NONE      0

function(<parameter list>)
<parameter type list> ;
{
   int user_defined_flag = RETURN ;

   set_confirm (user_defined_flag) ;
   get (row,col,string) ;
}
```

User-defined function do_confirm() code fragment:

```
#include <s_get.h>

#define RET       1
#define SPECIAL   2
#define NONE      0

unsigned int key = s_get.key ;

user_defined_flag = s_get.confirm ;

switch ( user_defined_flag )
   {
      case NONE:
```

```
        return (TRUE) ;
    case RET:
        if ( key == RETURN ) return (TRUE) ;
        else return (FALSE) ;
    case SPECIAL:
        switch (key)
        {
    case RETURN:
    case TABKEY:
    case F10:
        return (TRUE)
    default:
        return(FALSE) ;
        }
    default:
        return(FALSE) ;
}
```

The C UDF do_confirm() is called internally by get(). The structure member s_get.confirm contains the flag passed to set_confirm() outside the get.

Key names are in a header file named s_keys.h #included within s_get.h.

Default: Field confirmation is on. Return, Tab, and Escape keys will confirm a GET.

SET CONSOLE

Clipper:

Syntax: SET CONSOLE ON/OFF

Description: The SET CONSOLE command turns the screen either off or on for screen display other than @..SAY commands.

Default: ON

Command: Standard

Library: Clipper.lib

C:

Syntax: #include <stdio.h>

```
freopen ( filename, mode, stream ) ;
char *filename, *mode, *stream ;
```

Usage:

```
freopen ( "nul", "w", stdout ) ;
```

Description: freopen () causes a stream to be redirected to or from the stream named by filename. In MS-DOS, the reserved filename "nul" is used to redirect output of a program to nowhere. In C, the macro stdout refers to standard output, which is the display.

This only works with functions other than SJSC at_say() and GET functions and Code Base window functions. It also only works with C functions that by default write to stdout, such as printf().

SET CURSOR

Clipper:

Syntax: SET CURSOR ON/OFF

Description: The SET CURSOR command toggles the cursor on and off.

Default: ON

Command: Clipper enhanced

Library: Clipper.lib

C:

Source: Code Base library

Syntax: #include <w4.h>

```
void w4cursor ( row, col )
int row,col ;
```

SJSC: void set_cursor_pos (row, col)
char row,col ;

Description: Negative row and/or column values, or values greater than the maximum screen rows and/or columns, will cause the cursor to disappear.

SET DATE

Clipper:

Syntax: SET DATE AMERICAN/ANSI/BRITISH/FRENCH/GERMAN/ITALIAN

Description: The SET DATE command sets the date type format for function arguments and returned values and for display purposes.

Command: Clipper enhanced

Library: Clipper.lib

C:

Source: Code Base library

Syntax: char * c4dt_format(dbf_date, picture) ;
char *dbf_date, *picture ;

Description: This is not a global set function. The function is used in local situations to convert a date from its raw .dbf file form "YYCCMMDD" to a form specified in the picture string. The picture form is composed of any arrangement of the substrings "CC," "MM," "YY", and "DD." The use of "CC" is optional. For example:

```
printf ( c4dt_format "19890630", "MM/DD/CCYY" ) ;
```

will display 06/30/1989

```
printf ( c4dt_format "19890630", "MM/DD/YY" ) ;
```

will display 06/30/89

SET DECIMALS TO
SET DECIMALS TO <expN>

Clipper:

Syntax: SET DECIMALS TO

Description: The SET DECIMALS TO command establishes the number of decimal places that Clipper will use for display in mathematical calculations, functions, memory variables, and fields.

Command: Standard

Library: Clipper.lib

C:

Source: None. Numeric precision in C is controlled by providing a variety of data types. Floating point value decimal precision is locally defined. Generally, one of the printf() family of C standard library functions is used to display a floating point value with decimal precision.

```
double value = 1.12845 ;
printf ( "%.2lf, value ) ;
```

The above sample will be output to the display as:

1.13

When a C variable is known always to be an integer with no fraction, it is generally declared as nonfloating point type, such as an int or a long.

SET DEFAULT TO

Clipper:

Syntax: SET DEFAULT TO <disk drive>/<path>

Description: The SET DEFAULT TO command changes the drive and directory used for reading and writing of database, index, memory, and alternate files.

Default: Current drive when the process, e.g., the Clipper program, was started up.

Command: Standard

Library: Clipper.lib

C:

Source: None. This functionality does not exist in Code Base or in other libraries, to our knowledge.

SET DELETED

Clipper:

Syntax: SET DELETED ON/OFF

Description: The SET DELETED command is, in essence, a filter placed on the database to mask out those records marked for deletion. A SET DELETED ON command is just as effective as a SET FILTER TO .NOT. DELETED

Default: OFF

Command: Standard

Library: Clipper.lib

C:

Source: Code Base library

Syntax:

```
#include <d4base.h>

void x4filter ( filter_routine )
int (*filter_routine)() ;
```

Usage:

```
x4filter ( d4deleted ) ;
```

Description: The above usage is equivalent to a Clipper SET FILTER TO .NOT. DELETED

SET DELIMITERS

Clipper:

Syntax: SET DELIMITERS ON/OFF

Description: The SET DELIMITERS ON command allows specific characters to delimit field area input. See SET DELIMITERS TO.

Default: OFF

Command: Standard

Library: Clipper.lib

C:

Discussion: See SET DELIMITERS TO.

SET DELIMITERS TO

Clipper:

Syntax: SET DELIMITERS TO [<expC>][DEFAULT]

Description: The SET DELIMITERS TO command changes the characters that delimit the area before and after field or variable input.

Default: OFF

Command: Standard

Library: Clipper.lib

C:

Source: Code Base library

Syntax: #include <w4.h>

```
char *g4delimiter ( delimiter )
char *delimiter ;
```

Description: Subsequent calls to GETs in the Code Base GET system will use the specified delimiter characters.

A non-NULL terminated character buffer containing the pair of delimiters is returned.

Source: SJSC Library™, Copyright © 1989 Stephen J. Straley & Associates. All rights reserved.

Syntax:

```
#include <w4.h>

void set_display(flag)
int flag ;

void do_display(void)
```

Description: The do_display() function can format field display any way a user wishes, including placing delimiters, or window borders, around a field. The function do_display() can display different fields in different ways, according to the flag set by the function set_display.

Usage: Calling function code fragment:

```
#define QUOTES    1
#define WINDOW  2
#define NONE        0

function(<parameter list>)
<parameter type list> ;
{
   set_display (QUOTES) ;
   get (row,col,string) ;
}
```

Called user defined function do_display() code fragment:

```
#include <s_get.h>

int row   = s_get.row ;
int col   = s_get.col ;
```

```
int width = s_get.width ;
    unsigned char saycolor = s_win.saycolor ;

    save_window () ;    /* save's previous window
                           parameters */

    switch ( s_get.display )
        {
        case QUOTES:
            at_say (row,col-1, "\"") ;
            at_say (row,col+width,"\"") ;
            break ;
        case WINDOW:
            window   ( row-1,col-1,
                       row+1,col+width,
                       ' ', SINGLE_BORDER) ;
        case NONE:
        default:
            break ;
        }
    at_say_at(0,0); /* use absolute screen coords */
    at_say ( row,col, s_get.array ) ;
    restore_window() ; /* restores previous window's
                          parameters and colors */
    }
```

The C UDF do_display() is called internally by get(). The structure member s_get.display contains the flag passed to set_display() outside the GET.

SET DEVICE TO

Clipper:

Syntax: SET DEVICE TO <PRINT/SCREEN>

Description: The SET DEVICE TO command determines where @..SAY commands will be displayed (either the screen or the printer).

Default: Screen

Command: Standard

Library: Clipper.lib

C:

Source: None. Code Base does not support redirection of its window functions, and SJSC does not support redirection of the at_say() function.

SET ESCAPE

Clipper:

Syntax: SET ESCAPE ON/OFF

Description: The SET ESCAPE ON commands allows an Alt-C to terminate execution of a program and ignores VALID. If the SET ESCAPE OFF command is issued, Alt-C will not terminate an operation and no escape from a READ (VALID) is possible.

Default: ON

Command: Clipper enhanced

Library: Clipper.lib

C:

Source: C standard library

Syntax:

```
#include <signal.h>

void signal  (int sig,void(*func)
             (int sig[,int subcode])))(int) ;
```

Description: The function signal() is used to perform an overriding activity when a key is pressed. The most common activity is to terminate the program when Ctrl-Break or Ctrl-C is pressed. See the example for SETCANCEL() in the following section.

SET EXACT

Clipper:

Syntax: SET EXACT ON/OFF

Description: The SET EXACT command determines how much of a comparison will be performed between two character expressions.

Default: OFF

Command: Standard

Library: Clipper.lib

C:

Source: C standard library

Syntax:

```
#include <string.h>

int strcmp (string1,string2)
char *string1,string2 ;

int strncmp (string1,string2, length)
char *string1,string2 ;
int length ;

int stricmp (string1,string2)
char *string1,string2 ;

int memcmp (string1,string2,length)
char *string1,string2 ;
int length ;

int memicmp (string1,string2,length)
char *string1,string2 ;
int length ;
```

Description: In C, separate strings are not compared using equality or logical equality operators. Instead C standard library string comparison functions are used.

The functions strcmp() and memcmp() perform an exact comparison. Use strcmp() to compare two NULL terminated character strings. Use memcmp() to compare non-Null-terminated character buffers up to a specified length.

The functions stricmp() and memicmp() ignore the case of characters when the comparison is made; therefore "And" and "ANd" will compare.

The function strncmp() will compare only the specified number of characters from string2 to string1.

Return Values: If the comparison is successful, a 0 is returned. Otherwise, the lexigraphical difference between the strings is returned as either a positive or negative value.

SET EXCLUSIVE

Clipper:

Syntax: SET EXCLUSIVE ON/OFF

Description: The SET EXCLUSIVE ON/OFF command determines the way in which the database and related memo and index files are opened. OFF means files are shared between users in a local area network environment; more than one user can access the same file at the same time. ON means files cannot be shared on the network; each file can only be accessed by one user at a time.

Default: ON

Command: Clipper enhanced

Library: Clipper.lib

C:

Source: None

Description: In Code Base, a database is unlocked when opened. Each database in use, or portion thereof, must be explicitly locked with a call to the function d4lock() to exclude others from using it on a network.

SET FILTER TO

Clipper:

Syntax: SET FILTER TO [<expression>]

Description: The SET FILTER TO command masks a database so that only those records that meet the condition prescribed by the <expression> will be shown.

Default: No filter set

Command: Standard

Library: Clipper.lib

C:

Source: Code Base library

Syntax:

```
#include <d4base.h>

void x4filter ( filter_routine )
int (*filter_routine)() ;

int x4filter_pop(void) ;

void x4filter_reset() ;

int x4filter_do() ;
```

Description: The Code Base x4filter() function allows filter conditions to be set on a database. The conditions are determined by a function passed by reference to x4filter(). This function may be a Code Base function or a C UDF. The C UDF must return one of the following flags:

1 Filter the record

0 Use the record

-1 Error

The x4filter() function may be called multiple times to set up a number of filters.

x4filter_pop() will remove the previous filter condition.

x4filter_reset() will remove all filters.

Use of filtering in Code Base requires using a special set of Code Base functions for queries of the database. This set of functions is prefixed by "x4" instead of "d4." For example the Code Base function x4skip() is used with filtering instead of d4skip().

The "x4" prefix Code Base functions are slower than "d4" prefix functions because "x4" prefix functions must perform filtering and check for relations.

SET FIXED

Clipper:

Syntax: SET FIXED ON/OFF

Description: The SET FIXED command activates a systemwide fixed placement on the number of decimal places shown for all numeric output.

Default: OFF

Command: Standard

Library: Clipper.lib

C:

Source: None. Numeric precision in C is controlled by providing a variety of data types. Floating point value decimal precision is locally defined. Generally, one of the printf() family of C standard library functions is used to display a floating point value with decimal precision.

```
double value = 1.12845 ;
printf ( "%.2lf, value ) ;
```

The above sample will be output to the display as 1.13.

SET FORMAT TO

Clipper:

Syntax: SET FORMAT TO <filename>

Description: The SET FORMAT TO command selects a custom format that has been previously stored in a format (.FMT) file.

Default: No file

Command: Standard

Library: Clipper.lib

C:

Source: None. This functionality does not exist in Code Base, SJSC, or any other commercial C function library, to our knowledge.

SET FUNCTION

Clipper:

Syntax: SET FUNCTION <expN> TO <expC>

Description: The SET FUNCTION TO command allows each function key to be reprogrammed to represent a character expression.

Default: No keys set

Command: Standard

Library: Clipper.lib

C:

Explanation: This functionality does not exist in Code Base, SJSC, or in any other C library, to our knowledge.

SET INDEX

Clipper:

Syntax: SET INDEX TO [<file list>]

Description: This command opens an index file in the current, active database. If more than one file is listed in <file list>, the order of the database will be determined by the first index file in the <file list>. All file operations will be based on the first index file; however, all index files in the <file list> will be updated if the database is updated.

Default: None

Command: Standard

Library: Clipper.lib

C:

Source: Code Base library

Syntax:
```
int i4select(index_ref)
int index_ref ;
```

Description: i4select() will select a specified index file that has previously been opened. The specified index file becomes current and is used by d4seek(), d4top(), and d4bottom() to search the record.

SET INTENSITY

Clipper:

Syntax: SET INTENSITY ON/OFF

Description: The SET INTENSITY command sets the filed input color to either highlighted (inverse video) or normal color.

Default: ON

Command: Standard

Library: Clipper.lib

C:

Source: None

Source: SJSC macro

Syntax: #define set_intensity_on color (color|8)

SET KEY TO

Clipper:

Syntax: SET KEY TO

Description: SET KEY <expN> TO [<proc>]

This command is used where <expN> is equal to the value given by INKEY() for any keyboard key, and <proc> is a procedure.

Note: This command was introduced with the Autumn '86 release.

Default: No key SET except F1 TO HELP.PRG, if HELP.PRG is present.

Command: Clipper enhanced

Library: Clipper.lib

C:

Source: SJSC Library™, Copyright © 1989, Stephen J. Straely & Associates. All rights reserved.

Syntax:

void set_<action>(flag)
int flag ;

get() ;

int do_<action>(void)

Description: set_<action>(flag) and do_<action>(flag) functions are part of the SJSC GET system. This system is detailed in Chapter 10. The set_<action>(flag) functions cause a specific GET activity to occur when a key is pressed.

SET MARGIN TO

Clipper:

Syntax: SET MARGIN TO <expN>

Description: The SET MARGIN TO command adjusts the left-hand print margin for all printed output according to the value expressed as <expN>.

Default: 0

Command: Standard

Library: Clipper.lib

C:

Source: None

Description: There is no single function in the C standard library, in Code Base, or in SJSC that performs this. However, this functionality can easily be coded in C using fprintf() as follows:

```
int main()
{
int margin = 10 ;

fprintf ( stdprn, "%*s\r\n",
(int)strlen(string)+margin, /* minimum print len */
string ) ;
}
```

SET MESSAGE TO

Clipper:

Syntax: SET MESSAGE TO <expN> [CENTER]

Description: This command is designed to work with the MENU TO and PROMPT commands. With the SET MESSAGE TO command, chose a line number between 1 and 24 inclusive where a special prompt will appear.

Default: 24

Command: Clipper enhanced

Library: Clipper.lib

C:

Source: Code Base library menuing routines

Description: Code Base provides a comprehensive set of menuing functions. These allow for the creation of the following menu styles: pull down, pop up, vertical, horizontal, and Lotus-style.

See Code Base documentation for the syntax and use of these functions.

SET ORDER TO

Clipper:

Syntax: SET ORDER TO [<expN>]

Description: The SET ORDER TO command selects a new active index from the index list. If <expN> is 0, the current index list order will be maintained.

Default: 1

Command: Clipper enhanced

Library: Clipper.lib

C:

Source: Code Base library

Syntax:

```
int i4select(index_ref)
int index_ref ;
```

Description: i4select() will select a specified index file that has previously been opened. The specified index file becomes current and is used by d4seek(), d4top(), and d4bottom() to search the record.

SET PATH TO

Clipper:

Syntax: SET PATH TO <expC>

Description: This command will change the system path.

Default: None

Command: Standard

Library: Clipper.lib

C:

Source: C standard Library

Syntax: setenv()

Description: setenv() can be used to set any environment variable, including the path command.

Note: When the DOS environment is reset in a process, such as a Clipper or C program, the new settings will be ignored when the process terminates.

SET PRINT

Clipper:

Syntax: SET PRINT ON/OFF

Description: The SET PRINT command directs all output that is not controlled by the @..SAY command to the printer and the console.

Default: OFF

Command: Standard

Library: Clipper.lib

C:

Source: Standard C library

Syntax:

```
#include <stdio.h>

FILE *freopen (new_stream_name,access_mode,stream )
char *new_stream_name, *access_mode ;
FILE *stream ;
```

Description: The freopen() function will cause a file_descriptor to be associated with a different input or output stream.

SET PRINTER TO

Clipper:

Syntax: SET PRINTER TO [<device>/<filename>]

Description: If you are redirecting the full screen output to a file or special output device, the SET PRINTER TO command is used in conjunction with SET DEVICE TO.

Default: The standard printer port, which in MS-DOS is LPT1.

Command: Clipper enhanced — Autumn '86

Library: Clipper.lib

C:

Source: Standard C library

Syntax:

```
#include <stdio.h>

FILE *freopen (new_stream_name,access_mode,stream )
char *new_stream_name, *access_mode ;
FILE *stream ;
```

Description: The freopen() function will cause a file_descriptor to be associated with a different input or output stream.

SET PROCEDURE TO

Clipper:

Syntax: SET PROCEDURE TO <filename>

Description: The SET PROCEDURE TO command allows a series of procedures that are contained in a .PRG file to be pulled into the application and used accordingly.

Default: None

Command: Standard

Library: Clipper.lib

C:

Source: None. In C, functions are used to accomplish what a procedure does in Clipper. C function and Clipper procedures are an encapsulated set of programming instructions.

In C, functions may be in one or several source files. When functions are in several source files, source files are separately compiled into .obj files. The .obj files are then linked together with the linker, creating an executable (.exe) file.

The scope of C functions by default is applicationwide. Therefore functions in separate files that have been linked together are known throughout the application.

In C an extern (global) variable declared in one source file needs to be pseudoredeclared in another source file (or files) referencing the variable. Otherwise a compiler error will result when an attempt is made to reference the variable.

Example: Contents of hello.c:

```
char hello[] = "Hello world." ;

int main()
{
     void say_hi(void) ;

     say_hi() ;
   }
```

Contents of say_hi.c:

```
#include <stdio.h>

extern char hello[] ;

void say_hi()
{
```

```
     printf ( hello ) ;
}
```

Compile with:

```
cl -c [<other options>] hello.c ;
cl -c [<other options>] say_hi.c ;
```

Link with:

```
link hello, say_hi, hello, [<link list>], ;
```

SET RELATION TO

Clipper:

Syntax: SET RELATION [ADDITIVE] TO <keyexp> /RECNO/<expN> INTO <alias> [,TO <key exp> / RECNO()/ <expN> INTO <alias>...]

Description: The SET RELATION TO command links two or more database files according to a key expression that is common to all files.

Command: Standard

Library: Clipper.lib

C:

Source: Code Base library

Syntax:

```
#include <d4base.h>

x4relate ( key, base_ref, index_ref, miss_code ) ;
char *key ;
int base_ref, index_ref ;
long miss_code ;
```

Description: x4relate() sets up a database relation according to a key expression. Use of this function requires using a special set of Code Base functions for queries of the database. This set of functions is prefixed by “x4” instead of “d4.” For example the Code Base function x4skip() instead of d4skip().

The "x4" prefix Code Base functions are slower than "d4" prefix functions because "x4" prefix functions must perform filtering and check for relations.

SET SCOREBOARD

Clipper:

Syntax: SET SCOREBOARD ON/OFF

Description: The SET SCOREBOARD command will toggle the display area in the upper-right corner of the screen for the READ command and the MEMOEDIT() function.

Default: ON

Command: Clipper enhanced

Library: Clipper.lib

C:

Source: None. This functionality does not exists in Code Base or SJSC or other commercial C libraries, to our knowledge.

SET SOFTSEEK

Clipper:

Syntax: SET SOFTSEEK ON/OFF

Description: The SET SOFTSEEK command toggles for a "relative" seeking condition to exist. If the SET SOFTSEEK command is ON, if a SEEK or FIND command is issued, and if no match is found, the record pointer will be set to the next record in the index with a higher key value than the expression in the SEEK or FIND command.

Default: OFF

Command: Clipper enhanced — Summer '87

Library: Clipper.lib

C:

Source: Code Base library

Syntax: #include <d4base.h>

```
int d4seek ( key_expression )
char *key_expression ;
```

Usage: In Clipper: SET SOFTSEEK ON
In C, when the following expression is TRUE:
d4seek (key_expression) >= 0

In Clipper: SET SOFTSEEK OFF
In C, when the following expression is TRUE:
d4seek (key_expression) == 0

Description: The d4seek() Code Base function searches the active, indexed database for the first record with a matching key expression; it returns the following values:

0 An exact find was made.

1 An inexact find was made, such as when the expression passed to d4seek() matches only the first part of the database key.

2 Returned if the value is not greater than any value in the index file, but a find cannot be made, and the inexact find test also fails. This works like Clipper's FIND and SEEK commands when SET SOFTSEEK is on.

3 End of File. Returned if the value of the key expression is greater than any value in the index file.

-1 Error.

When searching index files with date keys, key_expression should be in the form "YYYYMMDD."

When searching index files with numeric keys, use the following syntax:

```
double value_pointer = (double *) <&value> ;

d4seek ( (char *) value_pointer ) ;
```

SET TYPEAHEAD

Clipper:

Syntax: SET TYPEAHEAD

Description: The SET TYPEAHEAD command sets the size of the keyboard buffer.

Command: Clipper enhanced — Summer '87

Library: Clipper.lib

C:

Explanation: This functionality does not exist in Code Base or in SJSC or in any other commercial C library, to our knowledge. It is, however, possible to write a function in C that performs direct access to the keyboard buffer. This is done by accessing the address of the keyboard buffer.

SET UNIQUE

Clipper:

Syntax: SET UNIQUE

Description: The SET UNIQUE command determines whether all records with the same value on a key expression will be included in the index file.

Default: OFF

Command: Standard

Library: Clipper.lib

C:

Source: Code Base library

Syntax:

```
#include <d4base.h>

i4index (name, expr, unique, safety )
char *name, expr ;
int unique, safety ;
```

Description: When i4index() is used to create an index, and the index is a .ndx (dBASE compatible index) file, passing the **unique** parameter as a 1 has the same effect as SET UNIQUE ON.

If .ntx (Clipper compatible index) files are used, however, unique indexing is not supported by Code Base. With .ntx files, the unique parameter of i4index() must be 0.

SET WRAP

Clipper:

Syntax: SET WRAP ON/OFF

Description: The SET WRAP command toggles MENU wrapping.

Default: OFF

Command: Clipper enhanced — Summer '87

Library: Clipper.lib

C:

Source: None. It in not in the standard, Code Base, or SJSC libraries. This functionality may, however, presently exist in other commercial C libraries. General pop-up window word wrapping is, for example, supported by Vermont Creative Software's Vermont Views (formerly Windows for C and Windows for Data).

SKIP

Clipper:

Syntax: SKIP [<expN>] [ALIAS <expN>/<expC>]

Description: The SKIP command moves the record pointer in either the active database or any other database. SKIP works with either indexed or nonindexed databases.

Command: Clipper enhanced

Library: Clipper.lib

C:

Source: Code Base library

Syntax: #include <d4base.h>

```
int d4skip ( recs_to_skip )
long recs_to_skip ;
```

Description: The d4skip() command moves the record pointer in either the active or inactive database. d4skip() works with either indexed or non-indexed databases. To change aliases, use this function in conjunction with d4select() (see the SELECT command).

SORT

Clipper:

Syntax: SORT <scope> TO [<newfile>] ON <field> [/A][/C][/D] [,<field2>] [/A][/C][/D] [FOR <condition>] [WHILE <condition>]

Description: The SORT command copies the currently selected database of <newfile> with the records in alphabetical, chronological, or numerical order as specified by the ON <field> clause.

Command: Standard

Library: Clipper.lib

C:

Source: Code Base library

Syntax:

```
void u4sort ( (void* base,
(size_t) num,
(size_t) width,
(int) (*compare) (void *) e1,
(void *) e2) )
```

Description: This function is Code Base's version of the qsort function in the Microsoft C library.

STORE

Clipper:

Syntax: STORE <expression> TO <memory variable> / <memory variable list>

Description: The STORE command initializes a memory variable(s) to be a specific value. An acceptable alternate syntax would be:

<memory variable> = <expression>

Command: Standard

Library: Clipper.lib

C:

Source: C variable declaration syntax

Syntax: [<storage class>] <variable type> <variable name> [<subscripts>] [= {initializer(s)}]

Source: C dynamic allocation of space setup

Syntax: [#include <malloc.h>
<variable pointer> = malloc (size) ;]

Description: C variables must all be explicitly declared, and necessary storage must allocated to arrays using subscripts and/or initializers.

A C pointer, however, may be declared and storage can be allocated to it later. This technique is known as dynamic allocation of space. The C standard library has a set of functions for dynamic space allocation. The major function in this set is malloc().

Clipper uses dynamic allocation of space when a memory variable is assigned a context using the STORE command.

Great care should be taken when using C dynamic space allocation functions. In particular, dynamically allocated space remains in a program until it is freed with the following function:

```
free ( ptr )
void *ptr ;
```

The argument to free is the same pointer that was returned by malloc().

In practice, it is safest to avoid using dynamic space allocation functions when explicit declarations of arrays and other data types will work just as well.

SUM

Clipper:

Syntax: SUM <scope> <filed list> TO <MEMVAR LIST> [FOR <condition>] [WHILE <condition>]

Description: The SUM command sums to a <memvar> the values of fields in a database, depending upon the condition set.

Command: Standard

Library: Clipper.lib

C:

Syntax:

```
#include < d4base.h >

double x4sum     ( field_ref )
(long) field_ref ;
```

Description: The Code Base x4sum() function sums a particular field in a database. It uses filtering and works with database relations. If filtering or relations are not used, it is best to construct a SUM UDF that loops through the database records and sums the desired field or fields.

TEXT

Clipper:

Syntax:

```
TEXT [TO PRINT/TO FILE <filename>]
        <commands>
ENDTEXT
```

Description: The TEXT command prints large quantities of information without using the @..SAY command.

Command: Standard

Library: Clipper.lib

C:

Syntax:

```
#include <stdio.h>

int printf ( format [argument list]...)
const char *format ;

int fprintf (stream_ptr,format [argument list]...)
FILE *stream_ptr;
const char *format ;

#include <stdio.h>

main ()
{
static char text[] = {
"This can be a large amount of text to print.\r\n\
This can be one long string with embedded new lines\
.\r\n.     Remember to use \\r\\n combinations for \new lines
on PCs/compatibles. \
\r\nStrings bigger than 64K bytes in size \
must be compiled with the huge memory model. \r\n.  A single
\\ character is required to continue\r\n \
literal text to the next line in a C source file" } ;

printf ( text ) ;
fprintf ( stdprn, text ) ;
}
```

TYPE

Clipper:

Syntax: TYPE <file name> [TO PRINT]/[TO FILE <filename>]

Description: The TYPE command types to screen, printer, or file the contents of an ASCII file.

Command: Standard

Library: Clipper.lib

C:

Syntax:

```
#include <process.h>

int system ( dos_command ) ;
char *dos_command ;
```

Usage: system ("TYPE <filename> [> prn/<filename>]

Description: In C it is simplest to invoke a system call, which is analogous to a RUN command in Clipper. Using the DOS TYPE command, we can redirect output to the printer using the reserved DOS name prn or to a file whose name we specify.

UNLOCK

Clipper:

Syntax: UNLOCK [ALL]

Description: The UNLOCK command releases the file or record lock in the selected work area. If the [ALL] clause is used, all current locks in all work areas will be removed.

Command: Clipper enhanced — Summer '87

Library: Clipper.lib

C:

Source: Code Base library

Syntax:

```
#include <d4base.h>

int d4lock ( lock_code, do_wait )
long lock_code ;
int do_wait ;

int d4unlock ( lock_code )
long lock_code ;
```

Description: d4lock() locks the currently opened and selected database or a part thereof. The lock_code, when passed as a positive long integer, is used to lock a specific record. If lock_code is passed as a -1, the entire database is locked, as with FLOCK(). The second parameter do_wait, when passed as a 1, will suspend processing until the file is locked. If do_wait is 0, no waiting will occur.

d4unlock() removes locks on the currently selected database as specified by lock_code. If lock_code is passed as a 1 and a specific record is locked, it will be unlocked. If lock_code is -1, all locks on the currently selected database and associated index files will be removed. See Code Base documentation for additional information.

Portability: Database and index functions: ANSI C
Screen functions: Optimized for PCs and compatibles
Library source provided with the product.

UPDATE ON

Clipper:

Syntax: UPDATE ON <key field> FROM <Alias> REPLACE <field> WITH <exp> [,<field2> WITH <exp>...] [RANDOM]

Description: The UPDATE command uses data from an existing file and changes data records accordingly in the currently selected database. The alterations are made by matching records in the two database files on a single key field.

Command: Standard

Library: Clipper.lib

C:

Source: None. There is no UPDATE ON command available in Code Base or in the SJSC library. Using Code Base, however, this functionality can be created in C.

USE

Clipper:

Syntax: USE [<file name>] [INDEX <index file list>] [ALIAS <expC>]

Description: The USE command opens an existing database in the selected work area.

Command: Standard

Library: Clipper.lib

C:

Source: Code Base library

Syntax: int reference_number = d4use (char *name) ;

Description: The Code Base function opens and selects the specified database. If no file extension is specified, .DBF is assumed.

The Code Base system returns a handle, or reference number, for the database, which is analogous to a Clipper work area value. The major difference is that the Code Base reference number for a database is initially determined by Code Base and not by the user. Reference number values begin with 0 for the first file in a program opened with d4use() and increment by 1 with each new database opened with d4use(). The reference number for a current database previously opened with d4use() can be ascertained as follows:

current reference_number = d4select (-1) ;

WAIT

Clipper:

Syntax: WAIT [<expC>][TO <memvar>]

Description: The WAIT command pauses all processing and execution until any key is pressed.

Command: Standard

Library: Clipper.lib

C:

Source: Standard C

Portability: ANSI C

Syntax: #include <stdio.h>

getc() ;
getchar() ;

Source: Standard C

Portability: MS-DOS only

Syntax: #include <stdio.h>

getch()

Source: SJSC Library™, Copyright © 1989, Stephen J. Straley & Associates. All rights reserved.

Portability: MS-DOS only

Syntax: #include <s_get.h> /* or */
#include <s_keys.h>

Description: The standard C library function getc(), the macro getchar(), and the MS-DOS C library function getch() will suspend processing until a key is pressed. The getc() function and getchar() macro, which calls getc(), only return the values of alphanumeric and punctuation keys once a key is pressed. These functions will not tell whether a function key is pressed or what value a function key has.

The SJSC function getkey() will similarly suspend program execution and wait for a key to be pressed. It has the advantage of returning a value for any key pressed on an IBM PC keyboard. See Chapter 8 for a complete description of the function and its use in the context of GET operations in C.

ZAP

Clipper:

Syntax: ZAP

Description: The ZAP command removes all records from the active database.

Command: Standard

Library: Clipper.lib

C:

Source: Code Base library

Syntax: #include <d4base.h>

int d4zap (start_record, end_record)
long start_record, end_record ;

Description: The Code Base d4zap() command removes some or all records from the active database. To remove all records use the following syntax:

d4zap (1L, d4reccount()) ;

FUNCTIONS

$ — SUBSTRING COMPARISON

Clipper syntax: <<expC1>> $ <<expC2>>

C function name: strstr()

C library source: Standard library

C portability: ANSI C

C function header: #include <string.h>
char *strstr (str1, str2)
char *str1, *str2 ;

C function return: Character pointer to the first occurrence of str2 in str1.

Description:

Clipper: $ returns a logical true (.T.) if the character or string in <<expC1>> is found in <<expC2>>.

C: strstr() returns a character pointer to the first occurrence of str2 in str1 if it is found. Otherwise it returns NULL.

Samples:

Clipper:

```
?? "A" $ "ABCDEF" .AND. "NY $ "CANYNJCT"
```

C:

```
#include <stdio.h>
#include <string.h>

int main ( argc, argv )
int argc ;
char *argv[] ;
{
char *substr ;

if ( ( substr = strstr ( "ABCDEF", "B" ) ) != NULL )
     printf ( "B is the 1st character in %s", substr )

if ( argc < 3 )
     {
     printf ( "usage: <string>, <string in string>\n" ) ;
     return (1) ;
     }

if ( ( substr = strstr ( argv[1], argv[2] ) ) != NULL )
     printf ( "Found %s in %s\n", argv[2], argv[1]" ) ;
else
     printf ( "Couldn't find %s in %s\n" ) ;

return (0) ;
}
```

ABS()

Clipper syntax: ABS (<expN>)

Clipper parameter: <numeric expression>

Clipper return: <numeric expression>

C function name: abs()

C library source: Standard library

C portability: ANSI C

C function header:

```
#include <string.h>
int abs(n)
int n ;
```

Description:

Clipper: Returns the absolute value of a numeric expression.

C: Returns the absolute value of a variable of type int.

Samples:

Clipper:

```
? ABS (-5) && This will yield a 5
```

C:

```
#include <stdio.h>
#include <stdlib.h>

int main()
{
printf ("%d\n" abs ( -5 )) ; /* this will also
                                yield a 5 */
return(0) ;
}
```

ACHOICE()

Clipper syntax: ACHOICE (<expN1>, <expN2>, <expN3>, <expN4>, <array1> [,<array2, [, <expC1> [, <expN4>>
[<expN6>]]]])

Clipper parameters: <top>,<left> <bottom>, <right coordinates>, <array name> [,<array name>[,<function name>[,<numeric value>[,<numeric value]]]]

Clipper return: <numeric expression>

C function name: browse() ;

C function library: SJSC Library™, Copyright © 1989, Stephen J. Straley & Associates. All rights reserved.

C portability: Optimized for PCs and compatibles

Description:

Clipper: This function displays a list-box from an array, with an optional array and user defined function passed for additional controls. See *Programming In Clipper, 2nd Edition*, for a more complete description.

C: See Chapter 8.

ACOPY()

Clipper syntax: ACOPY (<expC1>, <expC2> [, <expN1> [, <expN2> [,<expN3>]]])

Clipper parameters: <array name>, <array name> [,<numeric expression> [,<numeric expression>[,<numeric expression>]]]

Clipper return: Nothing

C function name: memcpy()

C library source: Standard library

C function header:

```
#include <memory.h> /* or */
#include <string.h>

void *memcpy ( buffer_to, buffer_from, count )
void *buffer_to
const void *buffer_from
unsigned int count ; /* how much to copy */
```

C function return: A pointer to the destination buffer

C function name: memccpy()

C library source: Standard library

C function header:

```
#include <memory.h> /* or */
#include <string.h>
void *memccpy ( buffer_to, buffer_from, c, count )
void *buffer_to ;
const void *buffer_from ;
int c ;                 /* last character to copy */
unsigned int count ;    /* or how much to copy,
                           whichever comes first */
```

C return: A pointer to the destination buffer

C portability: ANSI C

Description:

Clipper: ACOPY() copies Clipper array elements from <expC1> to <expC2>.

C: In C, the function memcpy() provides this functionality at a lower level. C's memcpy() copies any sequence of bytes to any other sequence of bytes. Therefore we can use memcpy() to copy C data structures, such as those used to contain Clipper arrays.

The arguments to memcpy() copies are the addresses of the buffers to be copied. Since the name of a character buffer in C is an address, character buffers are copied by supplying the names of the buffers as arguments to memcpy().

When data types other than character buffers or pointers to character buffers are passed to memcpy(), the following rules apply:

1. The address of operator "&" must be used.

2. The parameters must be cast as pointers to character buffers using (char *).

To copy data structures using memcpy(), the general syntax is:

```
memcpy ((char *) &struc_to,    (char *) &struc_from,
sizeof (struc_to)) ;
```

Related functions: memccpy() performs just like memcpy(), except that copying stops after the first occurrence of a specified character is copied from the source buffer to the destination buffer.

ADEL()

Clipper syntax: ADEL (<expC>, <expN>)

Clipper parameters: <array name>, <array position>

Clipper return: Nothing

C function name: None. There is no counterpart for this function in C.

Description:

Clipper: The function deletes an element in the named array at the array position specified.

C: In C, it would be necessary to build an algorithm to delete an element in an array of structures or linked list. Using an array of structures, here's an example of how this would work:

C sample:

```
#include <stdio.h>
#include <string.h>
/* here we create a template for, declare, and
initialize a global array of structures */
struct SUPER_CARS {
     char model[80] ;
} super_cars [] = { "JAGUAR","MERCEDES",
"ROLLS ROYCE","YUGO","STEVE'S CAR", NULL }
#define YUGO 3

int main ()
{
int i = 0 /* in C start counting arrays, including
               arrays of structures, from element 0 */
printf ( "Alleged super cars are:\n" ) ;
for ( i = 0 ; *super_cars[i].model != NULL ; i++ )
     printf ( "\t%s\n", super_cars[i].model ) ;
/* delete Yugo with the following while loop, since it
   cannot fit Steve or Dave in it */
i = YUGO ;
while ( *super_cars[i].model != NULL )
     {
     strcpy (super_cars[i].model,
super_cars[i+1].model)
     i++ ;
     }
printf ( "Truly super cars are:\n" ) ;
for ( i = 0 ; *super_cars[i].model != NULL ; i++ )
     printf ( "\t%s\n", super_cars[i].model ) ;
return(0) ;
}
```

ADIR()

Clipper syntax: ADIR (<expC>, <expC>)

Clipper parameters: <array name>, <array position>

Clipper return: Nothing

C function names: u4file_first(), u4file_next()

C library source: Code Base library

C syntax:

```
#include <d4base.h>

int u4file_first ( pattern, buffer ) ;
char *pattern, buffer ;
int u4file_next ( pattern, buffer ) ;
char *pattern, buffer ;
```

Description:

Clipper: ADIR returns the number of files that match a pattern specified by the first <expC> on the currently logged disk and directory. The pattern may use DOS wild card characters, such as "*.*," or "?.ext."

C: The pair of Code Base functions u4file_first() and u4file_next() may be used to read DOS directories using wild cards.

u4file_first() is called to write the first item in the list.

u4file_next() is called in a loop to fill in the rest of the list.

AFIELDS()

Clipper syntax: AFIELDS (<expC1> [, <expC2> [, <expC3> [, <expC4>]]])

Clipper Return: <array expression> [,<array expression>
[, <array expression> [,<array expression>]]]

C function name: d4ptr() ;

C library source: Code Base library

C portability: Database and index functions: ANSI C

Screen functions: Optimized for PCs and compatibles

Library source provided with the product.

C function headers:

```
#include <d4base.h>
BASE *d4ptr()
unsigned int header(void)
```

Description:

Clipper: AFIELDS reads each field in the database structure into arrays.

C: d4ptr() points to Code Base's internal database data structure describing the currently active and selected database, including the database's structure. A member variable of this data structure, struct fields, contains field information. To access this variable, the following C statement is used:

```
d4ptr()->fields->name ;
```

ALIAS()

Clipper syntax: ALIAS (<expN>)

Clipper parameters: <numeric expression>

Clipper return: <character expression>

C function name: <none>

C operation: #define <expn> ALIAS_NAME

Description:

Clipper: This function yields the alias name of the work area specified by <expN> or the alias name of the current work area if <expN> is not passed to the function.

C: In C, aliases are not needed because of the C preprocessor; the #define preprocessor statement can be used to give any value a macro name.

Clipper Sample:

```
USE History
?

USE History
? ALIAS()  && Displays the word 'history'
? ALIAS(2) && Displays a null string
```

C Sample:

```
/* this example uses Code Base functions introduced
in Chapter 8 */

#include <stdio.h>
#include <d4base.h>

#define HISTORY 0
#define HISTORY 1

main()
{
/* Code Base begins numbering its work areas from 0,
   not 1 */

d4use ( "History" ) ;
d4use ( "Philosophy" ) ;
d4select ( HISTORY ) ;

printf ( d4ptr()->name ) ;
d4close_all() ;
}
```

ALLTRIM()

Clipper syntax: ALLTRIM (<expC>)

Clipper parameters: <character expression>

Clipper return: Nothing

C function name: alltrim()

C function library: SJSC Library™, Copyright © 1989, Stephen J. Straley & Associates. All rights reserved.

C function header:

```
#include <string.h>
char *alltrim ( char *string) ;     /* required
                                       declaration */
char *alltrim ( string )
char *string ;
```

C portability: ANSI C

Description:

Clipper: ALLTRIM() returns a character expression stripped of leading and trailing blanks.

C: alltrim() returns a pointer to string stripped of leading and trailing blanks. It also strips the string provided as an argument via call by reference.

C source:

```
#include <string.h>

char *alltrim (string)
char *string ;
{
unsigned int n ;

for ( n = strlen(string) ; string[n-1] == ' ' ; n-- ) ;
string [n] = '\0' ;
for ( n = 0 ; string[n] == ' ' ; n++ ) ;
return ( strcpy (string, string+n ) ) ;
}
```

C usage:

```
#include <stdio.h>
main()
{
char *alltrim (char *string) ; /*function declaration*/
static char hello[] = "  HELLO   " ;
printf ( "%s\n", hello ) ; /* original string */
printf ( "%s\n", alltrim (hello) ) ; /*return string*/
printf ( "%s\n", hello ) ;     /*  string changed by
                                   reference*/
}
```

AMPM()

Clipper syntax: AMPM (<expC>)

Clipper parameter: <character expression as time string>

Clipper return: <character expression as time string>

C function names: time() to get system time
localtime() to convert to local time zone
asctime() to display the time

C library source: Standard library

C portability: ANSI C

C function headers:

```
#include <time.h>

char *_strdate (date)
char *date ;

long time(timeptr)
long *timeptr ;

struct tm*localtime (timeptr)
long *timeptr ;

char *asctime(timeptr);
struct tm *timeptr ;
```

Description:

Clipper: AMPM expects <expC> to be in the form of a time string.

AMPM() then returns an 11-byte character string based on the time string in the 12-hour a.m. and p.m. format.

C: Below is an example of how to use ANSI standard C time functions to get the date and format and display it as a.m. or p.m.:

```
#include <stdio.h>
#include <time.h>
#define TRUE  1
#define FALSE 0
```

```
main()
{
struct tm *ourtime ;
int afternoon = TRUE ;
long ticktock ;

time ( &ticktock ) ;
ourtime = localtime (&ticktock) ;
if (ourtime->tm_hour < 12 ) afternoon = FALSE ;
if (ourtime->tm_hour > 12 ) ourtime->tm_hour -=12 ;
if (afternoon )
   printf ( "%.19s %s\n", asctime(ourtime), "PM" ) ;
else
   printf ( "%.19s %s\n", asctime(ourtime), "AM" ) ;
}
```

ASC()

Clipper syntax: ASC (<expC>)

Clipper parameters: <character expression>

Clipper return: Nothing

C function: None

C operation: Use the C indirection operator (*) on the name of a string.

Description:

Clipper: ASC() returns the ASCII value for the leftmost character of any character expression.

C: The indirection operator yields the first byte of the name of the string that follows it. This byte can be manipulated as a value or displayed by printf(). Printf() can either show the ASCII character, with "%c," or the ASCII value, with the "%d" control string.

```
#include <stdio.h>

int main()
{
static char hello[] = "HELLO" ;

printf (
```

```
"The ASCII value of %c, the first letter in %s, is %d\n",
*hello, hello, *hello );

return(0) ;
}
```

ASCAN()

Clipper syntax: ASCAN (<expC>, <exp> [,<expN> [<expN>]])

Clipper parameters: <array name>, <search expression> [,<numeric expression> [, <numeric expression>]]

Clipper return: Nothing

C function name: None. There is no counterpart for this function in C.

Description:

Clipper: The function scans the contents of an array named <expC> for <exp>. The returned value is the position in the array in which it was found. If <exp> is not found, 0 is returned.

C: In C, it would be necessary to build an algorithm to scan an array of structures or linked list.

AT()

Clipper syntax: AT (<expC>,<expC>)

Clipper parameters: <character expression>,<character expression>

Clipper return: <numeric expression>

C function name: strstr()

C library source: Standard library

C portability: ANSI C

C function header:

```
#include <string.h>
char *strstr ( str1, str2 )
char *str1, *str2 ;
```

C function return: Character pointer to the first occurrence of str2 in str1

Description:

Clipper: The AT() function searches the second string expression for the starting position of the characters in the first string expression. A zero is returned if no match is found.

C: The strstr() function works the same way as AT(), except that the search parameters are reversed and strstr() returns a pointer to the first occurrence of str2 in str1. Pointer arithmetic can be used to find the numeric index of the string by taking the difference between str1 and the return pointer from strstr(). This is illustrated in the sample below.

Clipper: STORE "Bert" TO search

Sample:

```
STORE "Bill Jim  SteveRogerRay  Bert David" to string
STORE AT (search,string) TO which_one
? "B in 'BERT' is the " && This will display a 26
?? which_one
?? "the character in the string."
```

C sample:

```
#include <stdio.h>
#include <string.h>

int main()
{
static char search[] = "Bert" ;
static char string[] = "Bill Jim  SteveRogerRay  Bert David" ;

printf
     ( "B in 'BERT' is the %dth character in the string",
     ( strstr ( string,search ) - str1 ) + 1 ) ;
}
```

BIN2I()

Clipper syntax: BIN2I (<expC>)

Clipper parameter: <character expression>

Clipper return: <numeric expression>

BIN2L()

Clipper syntax: BIN2I (<expC>)

Clipper parameter: <character expression>

Clipper return: <numeric expression>

BIN2W()

Clipper syntax: BIN2W (<expC>)

Clipper parameter: <character expression>

Clipper return: <numeric expression>

C function name: fread()

C function header:

```
#include <stdio.h>
size_t fread (buffer, size, count, stream)
void *buffer ;        /* where data will be stored */
int size ;            /* the data type size */
int count ;           /* how many bytes to read */
FILE *stream ;        /* which file or I/O stream */
```

Description:

Clipper: These functions exist in Clipper to convert binary file data previously read into character expressions with Clipper's low-level file functions.

C: In C, the function fread() allows binary file data to be converted into the appropriate data type as the file is being read.

C Example: The following program reads the database record count from a .dbf file header into a long integer.

```
#include <stdio.h>

main()
{

long file_item ;
int num_read ;
FILE *stream = fopen ( "test.dbf", "rb") ;
```

```
if ( stream == NULL )
     printf ( "Error opening file test.dbf\n" ) ;

/* skip 4 bytes from the beginning of the file to
where the record count binary value is stored */

fseek ( stream, 4L, SEEK_SET ) ;

/* now read the next 4 bytes into 1 long integer with
fread() */

num_read = fread ( (char *) &file_item, sizeof(long),
1, stream ) ;

/* display the number of items read and the number of
records found in the .dbf file header */

printf ( "Number Read = %d\n", num_read ) ;
printf ( "The number of records in the .dbf are
%ld\n", file_item ) ;

fclose (stream) ;
}
```

BOF()

Clipper syntax: BOF()

Clipper parameters: Nothing

Clipper return: <logical expression>

C function name: tell() or ftell()

C function headers: #include <io.h>
long tell (file_handle)
int file_handle ;
long ftell (stream)
FILE *stream ;
C function return:
0L, (long) 0, if beginning of file, a positive long integer if not.

CDOW ()

Clipper syntax: CDOW (<expD>)

Clipper parameters: <date expression>

Clipper return: <character expression>

C function name: cdow()

C library: SJSC Library™, Copyright © 1989, Stephen J. Straley & Associates. All rights reserved.

C portability: ANSI C

C function header:

```
char *cdow (date)
long date ;
```

Description:

Clipper and C: CDOW returns the day of the week from a date expression.

CHR()

Clipper syntax: CHR (<expN>)

Clipper parameters: <expression number>

Clipper return: <character expression>

C function: fputc() and fputchar(), the printf() family of functions: printf(), cprintf(), sprintf()

C library source: Standard library

C portability: ANSI C

C operation: An ASCII value can be directly assigned to a character in a string, whether the value is displayable or not.

Description:

Clipper: ASC() returns the ASCII character code for <expN>. The number must be an integer within the range of 0 to 255, inclusive. This is the range of the ASCII character set on IBM PCs and compatibles.

The CHR() function is often used for generating nonprintable ASCII codes for printer escape sequences and the like.

C: An ASCII value in the range of 0 to 255 can be directly assigned to a character in a string, whether the value is displayable or not. For generating escape sequences and the like, one of the printf() functions can be used with the %c control string, as in the following C example.

Clipper sample:

```
* ring the bell
? CHR (7)
```

C sample:

```
/* ring the bell */
#include <stdio.h>

int main()
{
     char long_bell[5] ;
     int i = 0 ;

     /* ring the bell once
     printf ( "%c", 7 ) ;
     /* or this example of direct assignment
        will ring the bell 4 times */

     i = 4 ;
     long_bell[i] = 0 ; /* assign an ASCII 0 to signal
                           an end to the string */
     while ( --i >= 0 )
          long_bell[i] = 7 ;

     printf ( long_bell ) ;
}
```

CMONTH ()

Clipper syntax: CMONTH (<expD>)

Clipper parameters: <date expression>

Clipper return: <character expression>

C function name: cmonth()

C library: SJSC Library™, Copyright © 1989, Stephen J. Straley & Associates. All rights reserved.

Source provided below

C portability: Uses ANSI C functions

C function header:

```
char *cmonth (date)
long date ;
```

Description:

Clipper and C: This function returns the name of the month from a date expression.

COL()

Clipper syntax: COL()

Clipper parameters: Nothing

Clipper return: <numeric expression>

C functions: col()
get_curs()

C library: SJSC Library™, Copyright © 1989, Stephen J. Straley & Associates. All rights reserved.

Source provided below.

C portability: col() is IBM PC- and compatible-specific. It calls a subfunction get_curs(), which in turn makes a PC ROM BIOS call to figure the screen location.

C headers:

```
int col(void) ;
void get_curs ( rowptr, colptr )
unsigned char *rowptr ;
unsigned char *colptr ;
```

Description:

Clipper: COL() returns the current column position of the cursor on the screen().

C: A separate col() and row() function can be used to get the current column and row position of the cursor, respectively. But better yet, one function called get_curs() can return both row and column coordinates using call by reference. Below we provide source for these functions.

C source col():

```
int col ( void )

{
unsigned char col = 0, row = 0 ;
void get_cursor    (  unsigned char *rowptr,
                      unsigned char *colptr ) ;
get_cursor ( &row, &col ) ;
return ( (int) col ) ;
}
```

C source getcurs():

```
#include <stdio.h>
#include <dos.h>

void get_cursor ( rowptr, colptr )    /*  use BIOS to get
                                          cursor position */
unsigned char *rowptr, *colptr ;
{
union REGS inregs,outregs ;
inregs.h.ah = 3 ;
inregs.h.bh = 0 ;
int86 (0x10, &inregs, &outregs) ;
*colptr = outregs.h.dl;
*rowptr = outregs.h.dh;
}
```

CTOD()

Clipper syntax: CTOD (<expC>)

Clipper parameter: <character expression>

Clipper return: <date expression>

C function name: ctod()

C library: SJSC Library™, Copyright © 1989, Stephen J. Straley & Associates. All rights reserved.

Source provided below.

C portability: Uses ANSI C functions

C function header:

```
long ctod (string)
char *string ;
```

Description:

Clipper: CTOD converts a character expression of a date in the form "MM/DD/YY" into a date expression in the form "YYYYMMDD."

C: Using sprintf(), we write a crude CTOD() function, as follows:

```
#include <stdlib.h>

long ctod( string)
char *string ; /* must be in the form MM/YY/DD */
{
   sprintf ( string, "%.2s%.2s%.2s",
             string, string+3, string+6 ) ;
   return ( atol ( string ) ;
}
```

With Code Base, we can also write another version of CTOD. It uses the Code Base function c4dt_unformat(), which returns a character string stripped of its Clipper or dBASE picture format:

```
#include <stdlib.h>

long ctod( string)
char *string ; /* must be in the form MM/YY/DD */
{
   return (atol (c4dt_unformat (string, "MM/DD/YY" )));
}
```

CURDIR()

Clipper syntax: CURDIR (<expC>)

Clipper parameter: <character expression>

Clipper return: <character expression>

C function name: getcwd()

C function library: Exists in most PC C compiler standard libraries, including Microsoft and Turbo C. See your compiler documentation.

C portability: MS-DOS specific

C function header:

```
#include <direct.h>

char *getcwd ( path, max_length )
char *path ;
int max_length ;
```

Description:

Clipper: CURDIR() returns the current DOS directory path of a specified drive. If <expC> is not specified, the current logged drive is assumed.

C: getcwd() returns the current DOS directory path of the current drive.

DATE()

Clipper syntax: DATE()

Clipper parameter: Nothing

Clipper return: <date expression>

C function names: Microsoft C: strdate()

ANSI C: time() to get system time
localtime() to convert to local time zone
asctime() to display the time

C function headers:

```
#include <time.h>

char *_strdate (date)
char *date ;

long time(timeptr)
long *timeptr ;

struct tm*localtime (timeptr)
long *timeptr ;
```

```
char *asctime(timeptr);
struct tm *timeptr ;
```

Description:

Clipper: DATE returns the current system date, set by MS-DOS, as a date expression.

C: _sysdate() returns the current system date, set by MS-DOS, as a string in the form "MM/DD/YY." Use the C function ctod() to convert the string to a long date variable in the form "YYYYMMDD." Below is an example of how to use ANSI standard C time functions to get the date and format and display it:

```
#include <stdio.h>
#include <time.h>

#define TRUE  1
#define FALSE 0

main()
{
struct tm *ourtime ;
int afternoon = TRUE ;
long ticktock ;

time ( &ticktock ) ;
ourtime = localtime (&ticktock) ;

if ( ourtime->tm_hour < 12 )  afternoon = FALSE ;
if ( ourtime->tm_hour > 12 )   ourtime->tm_hour -=12 ;

if ( afternoon )

   printf ( "%.19s %s\n", asctime(ourtime), "PM" ) ;
else
   printf ( "%.19s %s\n", asctime(ourtime), "AM" ) ;
}
```

DAY()

Clipper syntax: DAY (<expD>)

Clipper parameter: <date expression>

Clipper return: <numeric expression>

C function: day()

C library: SJSC library

C header:

```
int day ( date )
long date ;
```

Description:

Clipper: The DAY function returns a number that represents the day of a given date expression.

C: The function below does the same in C:

C source:

```
/* SJSC day() function, Copyright © 1989, Stephen J.Sraley &
Associates. All rights reserved. */

#include <stdlib.h>

int day ( date )
long date ;
{
char datestr [9] ;
ltoa ( datestr, date, 10 )
return ( atoi ( datestr+6 ) ) ;
}
```

DAYS()

Clipper syntax: DAYS()

Clipper parameter: <numeric expression>

Clipper return: <numeric expression>

C source: None

Description:

Clipper: This function converts <expN> seconds to the equivalent number of days.

C: This functionality is not provided in a C function. It would be necessary to create a C algorithm to provide it.

DBEDIT() See Chapter 9.

DBF()

Clipper syntax: DBF()

Clipper parameter: Nothing

Clipper return: <character expression>

C function: int d4select(int refno)

C source: Code Base library

C usage: dbf_ref = d4select(-1)

Description:

Clipper: The Clipper function() returns the ALIAS name of the current work area as a character expression.

C: The Code Base d4select() function will select a different work area if passed a positive value. If passed a negative value, it will return the identity of the current work area.

While in Clipper the identity of the current work area may be a character expression, in Code Base it is always a value, a database reference number.

A unique database reference number is first assigned when a database is opened with a call to d4open(). The first database to be opened is always assigned a database reference number of 0. Each subsequent database to be opened is assigned the reference number of the previous database plus 1.

In C, an alias can be given to any value with a #define preprocessor statement.

DBFILTER()

Clipper syntax: DBFILTER()

Clipper parameter: Nothing

Clipper return: <character expression>

Description:

Clipper: Returns as a character expression the filter condition for the current database, if any.

C: This functionality does not exist in Code Base, in SJSC, or in any other library, to our knowledge.

DBRELATION()

Clipper syntax: DBRELATION (<expN>)

Clipper parameter: <numeric expression>

Clipper return: <character expression>

Description:

Clipper: Returns as a character expression the linking expression between two related databases: the current database and the one whose work area is specified by <expN>.

C: This functionality does not exist in Code Base, in SJSC, or in any other library, to our knowledge.

DBRSELECT()

Clipper syntax: DBRSELECT (<expN>)

Clipper parameter: <numeric expression>

Clipper return: <numeric expression>

Description:

Clipper: The DBRSELECT() function returns the work area number that is tied, via the SET RELATION TO command, to the work area expressed as <expN>.

C: d4select() is used to select between related and unrelated database files. The selection is made with the database's unique database reference number. See the discussion for the SELECT command for further information.

DELETED()

Clipper syntax: DELETED()

Clipper parameter: <nothing>

Clipper return: <logical expression>

C function name: deleted()

C function library: Code Base library

C header: #include <d4base.h>
int deleted (void)

C return: 0 — Not marked for deletion

1 — Marked for deletion

Description: In Clipper or Code Base, this function indicates whether a record in the current database has been marked for deletion.

DESCEND()

Clipper syntax: DESCEND (<exp>)

Clipper parameter: <expression>

Clipper return: <expression>

C function name: None

Description:

Clipper: The DESCEND() function is used to create and seek On indexes in descending order.

C: Code Base plans to support descending indexes in its next release. Currently, the only way to create descending indexes with Code Base is to modify the indexing source that comes with Code Base. This is only recommended for experienced C programmers.

DISKSPACE()

Clipper syntax: DISKSPACE (<expN>)

Clipper parameter: <numeric expression>

Clipper return: <numeric expression>

C function name: <<MS C BIOS function>>

C function library: Microsoft's version of the C standard library; PC-specific function

Description:

Clipper: Determines the number of bytes left on a specified disk drive. The drive is passed by number, where 1 = A, 2 = B, 3 = C, etc.

C: There is no specific C function for this purpose. The universal DOS function 1CH may be called in a C source file to obtain drive information.

DOSERROR()

Clipper syntax: DOSERROR()

Clipper parameter: Nothing

Clipper return: <numeric expression>

C function name: None

C function library: C standard global system error variable

Description:

Clipper: DOSERROR() returns any error from a previous call to a DOS command.

C: In C, a global variable (or variables) records system errors, such as those returned by MS-DOS. See your compiler documentation for the naming convention of the variable(s). In Microsoft C, this variable is **_doserrno**.

DOW()

Clipper syntax: DOW (<expD>)

Clipper parameter: <date expression>

Clipper return: <numeric expression>

C function name: dow()

C function library: SJSC Library™, Copyright © 1989, Stephen J. Straley & Associates. All rights reserved.

C function header:

```
int dow (date)
long date ;
```

Description:

Clipper and C: The DOW() and dow() functions return a number representing the day of the week. Sunday returns a 1 while the remaining days of the week return consecutive values.

In the C dow() function the date must be a long integer in the form "CCYYMMDD."

DTOC()

Clipper syntax: DTOC (<expD>)

Clipper parameter: <date expression>

Clipper return: <character expression>

C function name: dtoc()

C function library: SJSC Library™, Copyright © 1989, Stephen J. Straley & Associates. All rights reserved.

C function header:

```
int dtoc (date)
char *date ;
```

Description:

Clipper: The DTOC() function returns a Clipper date as a character expression.

C: The dtoc() function returns a long date parameter in the form "CCYYMMDD" as a pointer to a character string in the form "MM/DD/YY."

Note: To parse the date into other date formats, use the SJSC function dtos() and the Code Base function c4dt_format().

DTOS()

Clipper syntax: DTOS (<expD>)

Clipper parameter: <date expression>

Clipper return: <character expression>

C function name: dtos()

C function library: SJSC Library™, Copyright © 1989, Stephen J. Straley & Associates. All rights reserved.

C function header:

```
int dtos (date)
char *date ;
```

Description:

Clipper: The DTOS() function returns a Clipper date as a character expression.

C: The dtos() function returns a long date parameter in the form "CCYYMMDD" as a pointer to a character string in the same form.

Note: To parse the date into other date formats, use the Code Base function c4dt_format().

ELAPTIME()

Clipper syntax: ELAPTIME (<expC>, <expC>)

Clipper parameter: <character expression>, <character expression>

Clipper return: <character expression>

C function name: None. A single function that performs as ELAPTIME() does not exist in any commercial C library, to our knowledge.

EMPTY()

Clipper syntax: EMPTY (<exp>)

Clipper parameter: <expression>

Clipper return: <logical expression>

C function name: None. A single function that performs this action does not exist in any commercial C library, to our knowledge.

Description:

Clipper: This function is used to test variables and database fields for an EMPTY condition.

EOF()

Clipper syntax: EOF()

Clipper parameter: Nothing

Clipper return: <logical expression>

C function name: eof() or feof()

C function library: Code Base library

C function headers: #include <io.h>

```
long eof (file_handle)
int file_handle ;
```

C eof() return: 1 if end of file, 0 if not end of file, or -1 if a bad file handle was passed.

```
#include <stdio.h>

long feof (stream)
FILE *stream ;
```

C feof() return: 1 if end of file, 0 if not end of file.

ERRORLEVEL()

Clipper syntax: ERRORLEVEL ([<expN>])

Clipper parameters: [<numeric expression>]

Clipper return: <numeric expression>

C environment variable name: _doserrno

C function name: getenv()

C function library: Microsoft C

C portability: MS-DOS only

C function headers: #include <stdlib.h>

```
char *getenv (variable_name)
const char *variable_name ;
```

Description:

Clipper: ERRORLEVEL() returns the current DOS error level. If <expN> contains a value, that value will be used to set the DOS error level;

C: The Microsoft C environment variable _doserrno is always set to the value of ERRORLEVEL and is the easiest means of access to the current DOS error level.

The C standard library function getenv() returns the contents of any environment variable sent to it, including ERRORLEVEL. The contents are returned as a string.

EXP()

Clipper syntax: EXP (<expN>)

Clipper argument: <numeric expression>

Clipper return: <numeric expression>

C function name: exp()

C function library: Microsoft C

C portability: ANSI C

C function header: #include <math.h>

```
double exp ( value )
double value ;
```

Description:

Clipper: Returns the exponential of any given real number.

C: Returns the exponential, as a double, of any given real number passed as a double. Remember to link with em.lib or the floating point math library when compiling on a PC or compatible.

FCLOSE()

Clipper syntax: FCLOSE (<expN>)

Clipper argument: <numeric expression>

Clipper return: <logical expression>

C function names: close()
fclose()

C function library: Microsoft C

C function headers: #include <io.h>

```
int close ( handle )
int handle ;

int fclose ( stream )
FILE *stream ;
```

C function returns: Both functions return 0 if the file or stream is successfully closed.

C portability: ANSI C

Description:

Clipper: Closes a file opened with the low-level functions FOPEN() or FCREATE().

C: close() closes a file opened with open(); fclose() closes a stream opened with fopen().

FCOUNT()

Clipper syntax: FCOUNT()

Clipper argument: Nothing

Clipper return: <logical expression>

C function name: f4num_fields()

C function library: Code Base library

C portability: Database and index functions: ANSI C
Screen functions: Optimized for PCs and compatibles
Library source provided with the product.

C function header: #include <d4base.h>

int f4num_fields (void)

Description:

Clipper: FCOUNT() returns the number of fields in the current and active database.

C: f4num_fields returns the number of fields in the current and active database.

Clipper sample:

```
USE ( "travel" ) ;
? "The number of fields in the database is"
?? FCOUNT()
CLOSE ALL
```

C sample:

```
#include <stdio.h>
#include <dBASE.h>
```

```
d4use ( "travel" ) ;
printf ("The number of fields in the database is
%d\n", f4num_fields() ) ;
d4close_all()
```

FCREATE()

Clipper syntax: FCREATE (<expC> [,<expN>])

Clipper argument: <character expression> [,<numeric expression>]

Clipper return: <numeric expression>

C function names: open()
fopen()

C function library: Standard library

C portability: ANSI C

C function headers: #include <io.h>

int open ( )
int handle ;

#include <stdio.h>

int fopen (stream)
FILE *stream ;

C portability: ANSI C

Description:

Clipper: Creates a new file with the name expressed as <expC>; <expN> is defaulted to 0 and contains the DOS attribute of the new file <expC>.

C: open() and fopen() can create a new file or open an existing one. See the description of these functions under FOPEN().

FERROR()

Clipper syntax: FERROR()

Clipper argument: Nothing

Clipper return: <numeric expression>

C function names: error()
ferror()

C function library: Standard library

C portability: ANSI C

C function headers:

```
#include <io.h>

int error(handle)
int handle ;

#include <stdio.h>

int ferror ( stream )
FILE *stream ;
```

C portability: ANSI C

Description:

Clipper: Returns the DOS error from the last file operation. A 0 is returned if there is no error condition present.

C: error() returns any file error on the file opened with open() and designated by the file handle passed to it as an argument; ferror() returns any stream error on the stream opened with fopen() and designated by the stream pointer passed to it as an argument.

FKLABEL()

Clipper syntax: FKLABEL (<expN>)

Clipper argument: <numeric expression>

Clipper return: <character expression>

C function name: none

C operation: # define <key> <name>

Description:

Clipper: This function returns the name assigned to the function key specified by <expN>.

FIELDNAME()

Clipper syntax: FIELDNAME (<expN>)

Clipper argument: <numeric expression>

Clipper return: <character expression>

C function names: f4name()
f4jref()

C function library: Code Base library

C portability: Database and index functions: ANSI C
Screen functions: Optimized for PCs and compatibles
Library source provided with the product.

C function headers:

```
#include <d4base.h>

char *f4name ( field_ref )
long field_ref ;

long f4jref ( nth_field )
int nth_field ;
```

Description:

Clipper: FIELDNAME() returns the name of the <expN>th field in the current and active database.

C: f4name() returns the name of the field referred to by the field reference variable **field_ref** in any opened database.

f4jref() returns the field reference variable for the nth_field in the current and active database.

To match the functionality of the Clipper fieldname() function, call f4jref() as an argument to f4name() as follows:

```
char *fieldname = f4name ( f4jref ( nth_field ) ) ;
```

Clipper sample:

```
USE ( "INVOICE" )
? fieldname ( 2 )
```

C sample:

```
#include <stdio.h>
#include <d4base.h>

int main()
{
     d4use ( "invoice" ) ;
     printf ( "%s\n" , f4name ( f4jref ( 2 ) ) ;
     return (0) ;
}
```

FILE()

Clipper syntax: FILE (<expC>)

Clipper argument: <character expression>

Clipper return: <logical expression>

C function names: access(), stat(), fstat(), open(), fopen()

C function library: Standard library

C portability: ANSI C

C function headers:

```
#include <sys\types.h>
#include <sys\stat.h>

int access (path, mode)
char *path ;
int mode ;

int stat ( path, info_buffer )
char *path ;
struct stat *info_buffer ;

int fstat ( file_handle, buffer )
int file_handle ;
struct stat *info_buffer ;
```

See FOPEN() discussion for file headers for C open() and fopen() functions. See USED() discussion for file headers for d4use() and d4index().

Description:

Clipper: Returns a logical true (.T.) if the file exists. Otherwise a logical false (.F.) is returned.

C: Use any one of five C functions depending on how much information is needed about the file.

access(), open(), stat(), and fstat() return -1 if the file named in path cannot be found.

fopen() returns a NULL if the file named in the path cannot be found.

access() is the simplest function to use just to check for file existence. It can also be used to see if the file is read only. To check for file existence, pass the file's name as the first parameter and 0 as the second parameter to access(). See the sample below.

open() or fopen() open a file and check for file existence at the same time. Code Base d4use() and d4index() functions can also check for file existence when opening dBASE and Clipper database and index files in C.

stat() and fstat() will provide a full laundry list of information pertaining to a file. This list is placed into struct stat *info_buffer, which points to a data structure. The form, or template, for this data structure is in the include file \sys\stat.h. See your compiler documentation for more specifics.

Clipper sample:

```
IF FILE ( "contras" )
     ? "The file exists.  Bring it to Congress."
ELSE
     ? "The file doesn't exist.  The shredders were
here."
```

C sample:

```
#include <io.h>
#include <stdio.h>

int main()

if ( ( access ( "contras", 0 ) ) == -1 )
     {
     printf ( "The file exists.  Bring it to Congress.\n") ;
```

```
          return (1) ;
          }
     else
          {
          printf ( "The file doesn't exist" ) ;
          printf ( "The shredders were here.\n ) ;
          return (0) ;
          }
     }
```

FLOCK()

Clipper syntax: FLOCK()

Clipper argument: Nothing

Clipper return: <logical expression>

C function name: d4lock()

C function library: Code Base library

C portability: Database and index functions: ANSI C
Screen functions: Optimized for PCs and compatibles
Library source provided with the product.

C function header:

```
#include <d4base.h>

int d4lock ( lock_code, do_wait )
long lock_code ;
int do_wait ;

int d4unlock ( lock_code )
long lock_code ;
```

Description:

Clipper: If the currently opened and selected database is unlocked, FLOCK() attempts to lock the currently opened database and returns a logical true (.T.) if successful. If the database is already locked, FLOCK() unlocks the database.

C: d4lock() locks the currently opened and selected database or a part thereof. The lock_code, when passed as a positive long integer, is used to lock a specific record. If lock_code is passed as a –1, the entire database is locked, as with FLOCK(). The second parameter do_wait, when passed as a 1, will suspend processing until the file is locked. If do_wait is zero(0), no waiting will occur.

FOPEN()

Clipper syntax: FOPEN (<expC>,<expN>)

Clipper argument: Nothing

Clipper return: <logical expression>

C function names: fopen()
open()

C function library: Standard library

C portability: ANSI C

C function headers:

```
#include <stdio.h>

FILE *fopen ( path_name, access_type )
const char *path_name ;
const char *access_type ;

#include <io.h>
#include <fcntl.h>
#include <sys\types.h>
#include <sys\stat.h>

int open ( path_name, access_type [,permission] )
char *path_name ;
int access_type ;
int permission ;
```

Description:

Clipper: FOPEN() function opens the file expressed as <expC>. The value of <expN> determines how the file will be opened, with the default value being 0. The possible values are: 0 = read only; 1 = write only; 2 = both read and write.

If FOPEN() opens a file successful, it returns a unique integer value to identify the file, called a file_handle.

C:

fopen() and open() similarly open a file passed as path_name. The second argument to these C functions, like Clipper's FOPEN(), is a variable that specifies how the file is to be opened. Both functions also return a unique variable to identify the file.

fopen() is a higher-level function that performs buffered file I/O, affording some protection against a file being corrupted while it is opened. C's open() function is a lower-level function that performs no buffered file I/O but allows more options on opening and handling the file.

fopen()'s second parameter is a character string containing file access codes. open()'s second parameter is an integer defining file access composed of ORed bit values. See your compiler's documentation for specific access codes for fopen() and ORed bit values for open().

open() allows an optional third parameter that controls shared access to a file on a multitasking or networked environment.

If successful, fopen() returns a file pointer that uniquely identifies the open file. Otherwise it returns a NULL. This file pointer is of type *FILE. FILE is a typedef in stdio.h, whose macro reference is an internal data structure.

If successful, open() returns a file handle, an integer value, which uniquely identifies the open file. Otherwise it returns a -1.

Both fopen() and open() may be used to create a file that does not exist. Whether a new file is to be created or an existing file opened is determined by the second argument to either fopen() or open().

Clipper sample:

```
fhandle = FCREATE ("the_file.txt",0 )
FWRITE (fhandle, "hello" )
FCLOSE (fhandle)
```

C sample:

```
#include <stdio.h>

main()
{
/* create a new file for writing */
FILE *fptr = fopen( "the_file.txt","w" ) ;
fprintf ( fptr, "hello" ) ;
fclose (fhandle)
```

```
}

#include <io.h>
#include <fcntl.h>
#include <sys\types.h>
#include <sys\stat.h>

main()
{
static char hello[] = "hello" ;
int fhandle = open( "the_file.txt",
                    O_WRONLY | O_CREAT,
                    S_IREAD | S_IWRITE ) ;
write ( fhandle, hello, strlen ( hello ) ) ;
close ( fhandle ) ;
}
```

FOUND()

Clipper syntax: FOUND()

Clipper argument: Nothing

Clipper return: <logical expression>

C function name: None

C operation: Test return value of C functions used in file seeking operations.

Description:

Clipper: FOUND() returns a logical true (.T.) if the previous SEEK, LOCATE, CONTINUE, or FIND was successful.

Since in Clipper commands do not return values, as do functions, this separate FOUND() function is required to test the success of a SEEK, LOCATE, CONTINUE, or FIND.

C: In C, functions are used in file I/O operations. These functions return unique values indicating whether the file I/O operation was successful or not. See FSEEK() following and SEEK in the command section.

FREAD()

Clipper syntax: FREAD (<expN1>), @<expC>, <expN2>)

Clipper argument: <numeric expression, @<character expression>, <numeric expression>

Clipper return: <numeric expression >

C function names: read()
fread()

C function library: Standard C

C portability: ANSI C

C function headers: read():

```
#include <io.h>

read ( file_handle, buffer, count )
int file_handle ;
char *buffer ;
unsigned int count ;
```

fread():

```
#include <stdio.h>

long fread ( buffer, size, count, stream_ptr )
void *buffer ;
long size ;
long count ;
FILE *stream_ptr ;
```

Description:

Clipper: The FREAD() function reads <expN2> characters from a file whose file handle is <expN1> into a predefined memory variable, passed by reference as <expC>.

C: fread() reads **count** characters from the stream pointed to by **stream_ptr** in blocks of **size** bytes at a time. The characters are stored in the storage variable specified by **buffer**, which may be either a character array or other buffer cast to the correct size to receive data from the file. **buffer** must have been declared, prior to calling the function, to be big enough for the data placed in it by the read() function.

read() works similarly to fread(), except that a file handle is used to identify the file, data is always read 1 byte at a time, and the type of the receiving buffer must always be a character buffer.

FREADSTR()

Clipper syntax: FREADSTR (<expN1>, <expN2>)

Clipper argument: <numeric expression, <numeric expression>

Clipper return: <character expression>

C functions: read(), fread()
fgets()

C function library: Standard C

C portability: ANSI C

C function header: #include <stdio.h>

```
char *fgets ( buffer, count, stream_ptr )
char *buffer ;
int count ;
FILE *stream_ptr ;
```

see FREAD() function headers for read() and fread()

Description:

Clipper: FREADSTR() returns <expN2> characters of a character expression from a file specified by <expN1>

C: fgets() fills buffer with characters from a file or stream specified by stream_ptr. The buffer will contain count characters but with the following condition: If a new line character (ASCII 10) is encountered in the file or stream before count is reached, buffer will contain only characters up to and including the new line character from the file.

fgets() will also return a pointer to the character buffer upon success or NULL upon failure.

C note: The file or stream must be opened in text mode (the compiler default) for fgets() to read new lines correctly.

C sample:

```
/* this will work like the MS-DOS-type command */
#include <stdio.h>
#define LINESIZE 512

int main(argc,argv)
int argc ;
char *argv[] ;
{
FILE *fileptr = NULL ;
char buffer [LINESIZE+1] ;
char *bufptr = NULL ;

if ( argc < 2 )
     {
     printf ( "usage: requires the name of a file\n"
) ;
     return (1) ;
     }
if ( ( fileptr = fopen(argv[1], "r") ) == NULL )
     {
          printf ( "error: file does not exist\n" ) ;
          return (1) ;
          }
     while ((bufptr = fgets (buffer,LINES-
IZE,fileptr))!= NULL )
          printf ( bufptr ) ;

     fclose ( fileptr ) ;
     }
```

FSEEK()

Clipper syntax: FSEEK (<expN1>, <expN2> [, <expN3>])

Clipper argument: <numeric expression, <numeric expression>
[, <numeric expression>]

Clipper return: <numeric expression>

C function names: fseek(), lseek()

C function library: Standard C

C portability: ANSI C

C function headers:

```
#include <stdio.h>

long fseek ( stream_ptr, offset, origin )
FILE *stream_ptr ;
long offset ;
int origin ;

#include <io.h>

long lseek ( file_handle, offset, origin )
int file_handle ;
long offset ;
int origin ;
```

Description:

Clipper: The FSEEK() function moves the file pointer in the file represented by file handle <expN1> and moves the file pointer by <expN2> bytes from the file position <expN3>. The returned value is the relative position of the file pointer from the beginning of the file.

C: The lseek and fseek() functions move the file pointer in the file represented by file_handle, in the case of lseek(), and stream_ptr, in the case of fseek(). The file pointer is moved offset bytes from origin. origin can be one of three #defined constant values in <stdio.h> or <io.h>:

#defined name	Value	Definition
SEEK_SET	0	Beginning of file
SEEK_CUR	1	Current position in file
SEEK_END	2	End of file

lseek() and fseek() return the new offset, in bytes, from the beginning of the file. The return offset is a long integer.

FWRITE()

Clipper syntax: FWRITE (<expN1>, <expC1> [, <expN2>])

Clipper argument: <numeric expression>, <character expression>
[, <numeric expression>]

Clipper return: <numeric expression>

C function names: write(), fprintf(), fputs(), fputc()

C function library: Standard C

C portability: ANSI C

C function headers:

```
#include <io.h>

int write (handle, buffer, count);
int handle;
char *buffer;
unsigned int count;

#include <stdio.h>

int fputs ( string, stream_ptr )
char *string ;
FILE *stream_ptr ;

int fputc ( char, stream_ptr )
int char ;
FILE *stream_ptr ;

int fprintf (stream_ptr,format [argument list]...)
FILE *stream_ptr;
const char *format ;
```

Description:

Clipper: The FWRITE() function writes the contents of <expC> to the file represented by handle <expN1>. If used, <expN2> is the maximum number of bytes to write.

C: A variety of functions can be used to write to a file in C. With unbuffered files opened with open(), use the function write(), which works like FWRITE(); write() writes the contents of buffer to the file represented by file_handle. With C's write() function, a length argument is also required. If writing a character string, write() can be called as follows:

```
write ( file_ptr, buffer, strlen ( buffer ) ;
```

For buffered files or streams opened with fopen(), writing to a file in C is more flexible. Here the function fprintf() can write printf()-style formatted data to a file or stream. fprintf() takes the same arguments as printf(), except that another, first argument has been added: the stream pointer steam_ptr.

Using fputs() or fputc(), a string or single character can be written to the file or stream using less memory overhead than fprintf().

See your compiler documentation for additional details.

GETE()

Clipper syntax: GETE (<expC>)

Clipper argument: <character expression>

Clipper return: <character expression>

C function name: getenv()

C function library: Standard C

C portability: MS-DOS only

C function header: #include <stdlib.h>

```
char *getenv (variable_name)
const char *variable_name ;
```

Description:

Clipper: The GETE function returns a string that contains what was assigned to the environment variable <expC>, stored at the DOS level with the SET command or putenv() function.

C: The getenv() function returns a pointer to a character string that contains what was assigned to the environment variable variable_name, stored at the DOS level with the SET command or putenv() function.

Note: Any DOS environment setting made during the execution of a process, e.g., from a program while it is running, will be lost when the process is terminated, e.g., when the program stops running and control is returned to DOS. This is true when using putenv() or making a RUN or system call to change the environment.

HARDCR()

Clipper syntax: HARDCR (<expC>)

Clipper argument: <character expression>

Clipper return: <character expression>

C function name: hardcr()

C function library: SJSC Library™, Copyright © 1989, Stephen J. Straley & Associates. All rights reserved.

C portability: ANSI C

C header:

```
char *hardcr ( buffer )
char *buffer ;
```

Description:

Clipper: This function replaces all soft carriage returns [CHR(141)] with hard ones.

C: The following C function accomplishes the same function:

```
char *hardcr ( str )
char *str ;
{
/* use an unsigned char pointer to force the compiler
   to recognize char values > 127 */
unsigned char *retstr = (unsigned char *) str ;

while ( *retstr != NULL )
    {
    if (*retstr==141 && *(retstr+1) ==10 )*retstr=13 ;
```

```
    retstr++ ;
    }
return ( str ) ;
}
```

HEADER()

Clipper syntax: HEADER()

Clipper argument: Nothing

Clipper return: <numeric expression>

C function name: header()

C function library: SJSC Library™, Copyright © 1989, Stephen J. Straley & Associates. All rights reserved.

C function name: d4ptr()

C function library: Code Base library

C portability: Database and index functions: ANSI C
Screen functions: Optimized for PCs and compatibles
Library source provided with the product.

C function headers:

```
#include <d4base.h>

BASE *d4ptr()
unsigned int header(void)
```

Description:

Clipper: Returns the number of bytes in the header of the currently active and selected database.

C: d4ptr() points to Code Base's internal database data structure describing the currently active and selected database. A member variable of this data structure, unsigned header_len, contains the length of the database header. To access this variable, the following C statement is used:

```
d4ptr()->header_len ;
```

To create our own C function named header(), which functions like the Clipper function HEADER(), the statement appears as follows:

```
#include <d4base.h>

unsigned int header(void)
{
   return ( d4ptr()->header_len ) ;
}
```

C function name: i2bin()

C function library: SJSC Library™, Copyright © 1989, Stephen J. Straley & Associates. All rights reserved.

I2BIN()

Clipper syntax: I2BIN (<expN>)

Clipper argument: <numeric expression>

Clipper return: <numeric expression>

C function name: i2bin()

C function library: SJSC Library™, Copyright © 1989, Stephen J. Straley & Associates. All rights reserved.

C portability: Works only on Intel 808X machines and computers recognizing an integer as a 16-bit (2-byte) data type. The function would have to be modified for machines such as the Digital VAX where an integer is a 32-bit (4-byte) data type.

Description:

Clipper: This function translates a 16-bit unsigned int value into a character expression. The purpose of this is to write a file with binary data.

C: The function we wrote below does this in C and also illustrates the technique for making this conversion with any data type: by using a specialized form of data structure called a union. In a union, each of the members of the structure is used to look at the same piece of data in different ways, using different data types.

Note: The return character buffer is not NULL terminated.

```
#include <string.h>

union I2CHARS
    {
    unsigned int value ;
    unsigned char buf[2] ;
    } convert ;

unsigned char *i2bin( value )
unsigned int value ;
{
    convert.value = value ;
    return ( convert.buf ) ;
}
main()
{
    unsigned char *i2bin (value) ;

    unsigned int value = 16 ;
    printf ( "%s\n", i2bin(value) ) ;
}
```

IF()

Clipper syntax: IF (<exp1>, <exp2>, <exp3>)

Clipper argument: <condition> <expression>,<expression>

Clipper return: <expression>

C operator: ?:

C usage: <exp1> ? <exp2> : <exp3>

C portability: ANSI C

Description:

Clipper: Returns the result of <exp2> if <exp1> evaluates to a logical true. Otherwise, if <exp1> is evaluated to a logical false, the result of <exp3> is returned.

C: An operator called the ternary operator is provided, which accomplishes the same task.

INDEXEXT()

Clipper syntax: INDEXEXT()

Clipper argument: Nothing

Clipper return: <character expression>

C function name: u4full_name()

C function library: Code Base library

C portability: Database and index functions: ANSI C
Screen functions: Optimized for PCs and compatibles
Library source provided with the product.

C function header: #include <d4base.h>

void u4fullname (result, name, extension)
char *result, char *name, char *extension ;

Description:

Clipper: Returns either .ndx or .ntx, depending on the type of index file in use.

C: u4fullname will place in **result**, the extension name of any filename passed as **name**.

INDEXKEY()

Clipper syntax: INDEXKEY (<expN>)

Clipper argument: <numeric expression>

Clipper return: <character expression>

C function name: i4eval()

C function library: Code Base library

C portability: Database and index functions: ANSI C
Screen functions: Optimized for PCs and compatibles
Library source provided with the product.

C function header: #include <d4base.h>

```
char *i4eval (index_ref )
int index_ref ;
```

Description:

Clipper: INDEXKEY() returns the key expression of an active index file where <expN> is the place of the file in a list of open index files.

C: i4eval() returns the key expression of an active index file where index_ref is the place of the file in a list of open index files. index_ref would be 0 for the first file opened, 1 for the second, and so on.

INDEXORD()

Clipper syntax: INDEXORD()

Clipper argument: Nothing

Clipper return: <numeric expression>

C function name: i4ref()

C function library: Code Base library

C portability: Database and index functions: ANSI C
Screen functions: Optimized for PCs and compatibles
Library source provided with the product.

C function header: #include <d4base.h>

```
intchar *i4eval ((int) index_ref )
```

Description:

Clipper: INDEXORD() returns the position in a list of opened indexes of the index file currently in use.

C: The function i4index(), given the correct arguments, and i4select(), when passed a –1, will return the position in a list of opened indexes of the index file currently in use. The function i4ref(name) will return the position in a list of opened indexes of any index file passed by name. In the Code Base system, this return value acts as a file handle for the index file. See INDEX ON in the command section.

INKEY()

Clipper syntax: INKEY ([expN])

Clipper argument: <numeric expression>

Clipper return: <numeric expression>

C function names: getc()
getchar()

C function library: Standard C

C portability: ANSI C

C function name: getch()

C function library: Standard C

C portability: MS-DOS only

C function name: getkey()

C function library: SJSC Library™, Copyright © 1989, Stephen J. Straley & Associates. All rights reserved.

C portability: MS-DOS only

C headers: See Chapter 8.

Description:

Clipper: Returns a value for any key pressed on an IBM PC keyboard. <expN1> is a wait state.

C: The Standard C library function getc(), the macro getchar(), and the MS-DOS C library function getch() only return the values of alpha numeric and punctuation keys once a key is pressed. These functions will not tell whether (a) a function key is pressed or (b) what value a function key has.

getkey() will wait for a key to be pressed and then return a value for any key pressed on an IBM PC keyboard. See Chapter 3 for a complete description of the function and its use in the context of GET operations in C.

INT()

Clipper syntax: INT (<expN>)

Clipper argument: <numeric expression>

Clipper return: <numeric expression>

C operation: cast

C function library: Microsoft C

C use: (int) <expN>
(unsigned int) <expN>

Description:

Clipper: Returns a Clipper numeric type as an integer.

C: A cast is used to force a numeric variable to be read as an integer or unsigned integer.

ISALPHA()

Clipper syntax: ISALPHA (<expC>)

Clipper argument: <character expression>

Clipper return: <logical expression>

C macro (function): isalpha()

C function library: Standard C

C portability: ANSI C

C header: ctype.h

C usage: isalpha (character)

Description:

Clipper: This function returns a logical true (.T.) if the first character of <expC> is a letter in the range [A-Z][a-z].

C: This macro returns nonzero if the value of character is the ASCII value of a letter in the range [A-Z][a-z].

C also provides the following related macros:

Macro	Logical Return
isupper(c)	True if value is in range [A-Z]
islower(c)	True if value is in range [a-z]
isdigit(c)	True if value is in range [0-9]
isspace(c)	True if value is [' '], decimal 32
ispunct(c)	True if value is a punctuation character
isalnum(c)	True if value is in range [a-z][A-Z][0-9]
isprint(c)	True if value is in range [a-z][A-Z][0-9] or value is a punctuation or space character
isgraph(c)	True if value is in range [a-z][A-Z][0-9] or value is a punctuation character; false if value is a space character or any other character
iscntrl(c)	True if ASCII value is < decimal 32

ISCOLOR()

Clipper syntax: ISCOLOR (<expC>)

Clipper argument: Nothing

Clipper return: <logical expression>

C function name: See Chapter 8.

Description:

Clipper: This function returns a logical true (.T.) if a color graphics card has been installed in the computer.

C: This functionality is achieved in C, as in Clipper, by reading ROM BIOS information, which usually correctly stores the type of graphics card installed on the computer. Automatic detection, however, is by no means fail safe. See Chapter 8 for more information about the ROM BIOS and Screen I/O in C.

ISLOWER()

Clipper syntax: ISLOWER (<expC>)

Clipper argument: <character expression>

Clipper return: <logical expression>

C macro (function): islower()

C function library: Standard C

C portability: ANSI C

C header: ctype.h

C usage: islower (character)

Description:

Clipper: This function returns a logical true (.T.) if the first character of <expC> is a letter in the range [a-z].

C: This macro returns nonzero if the value of character is the ASCII value of a letter in the range [a-z].

C also provides the following related macros:

Macro	Logical Return
isupper(c)	True if value is in range [A-Z]
isalpha(c)	True if value is in range [a-z][A-Z]
isdigit(c)	True if value is in range [0-9]
isspace(c)	True if value is [' '], decimal 32
ispunct(c)	True if value is a punctuation character
isalnum(c)	True if value is in range [a-z][A-Z][0-9]
isprint(c)	True if value is in range [a-z][A-Z][0-9] or value is a punctuation or space character
isgraph(c)	True if value is in range [a-z][A-Z][0-9] or value is a punctuation character; false if value is a space character or any other character.
iscntrl(c)	True if ASCII value is < decimal 32

ISUPPER()

Clipper syntax: ISUPPER (<expC>)

Clipper argument: <character expression>

Clipper return: <logical expression>

C macro (function): isupper()

C function library: Standard C

C portability: ANSI C

C header: ctype.h

C usage: isupper (character)

Description:

Clipper: This function returns a logical true (.T.) if the first character of <expC. is a letter in the range [A-Z].

C: This macro returns nonzero if the value of character is the ASCII value of a letter in the range [A-Z].

C also provides the following related macros:

Macro	Logical Return
islower(c)	True if value is in range [a-z]
isalpha(c)	True if value is in range [a-z][A-Z]
isdigit(c)	True if value is in range [0-9]
isspace(c)	True if value is [' '], decimal 32
ispunct(c)	True if value is a punctuation character
isalnum(c)	True if value is in range [a-z][A-Z][0-9]
isprint(c)	True if value is in range [a-z][A-Z][0-9] or value is a punctuation or space character
isgraph(c)	True if value is in range [a-z][A-Z][0-9] or value is a punctuation character; false if value is a space character or any other character
iscntrl(c)	True if ASCII value is < decimal 32

L2BIN()

Clipper syntax: L2BIN (<expN>)

Clipper argument: <numeric expression>

Clipper return: <numeric expression>

C function name: l2bin()

C function library: SJSC Library™, Copyright © 1989, Stephen J. Straley & Associates. All rights reserved.

C portability: Works on computers recognizing a long integer as a 32-bit (4-byte) data type.

Description:

Clipper: This function translates a 32-bit unsigned long integer value into a character expression. The purpose of this is to write a file with binary data.

C: The function source below does the same job. See also the description of I2BIN().

Note: The return character buffer is not NULL terminated.

```
#include <string.h>

union L4CHARS
   {
   unsigned int value ;
   unsigned char buf[4] ;
   } convert ;

unsigned char *l2bin( value )
unsigned int value ;
{
   convert.value = value ;
   return ( convert.buf ) ;
}

main()
{
unsigned char *l2bin (value) ;
```

```
unsigned long value = 100000 ;
printf ( "%s\n", l2bin(value) ) ;
}
```

LASTKEY()

Clipper syntax: LASTKEY()

Clipper argument: Nothing

Clipper return: <numeric expression>

C function name: lastkey()

Depends on: get<var>()

C function library: SJSC Library™, Copyright © 1989, Stephen J. Straley & Associates. All rights reserved.

See Chapter 8.

C function header: #include <s_get.h>

unsigned int lastkey(void)

Description:

Clipper: This function returns a number representing the ASCII value of the last key pressed or an INKEY() special key value if a function key or other special key is pressed.

C: We provide the source code for this function below. It assumes that the last key hit was during a call to SJSC library GET functions, described in Chapter 8.

SJSC GET functions place global information pertaining to a GET in the global data structure, s_get. One of the members of this data structure is s_get.key, which contains the value of the last key hit in the GET. Special key values are the same as for the function getkey() and can be referenced in the header file s_keys.h

```
#include <s_get.h>

unsigned int lastkey( void)
{
```

```
    return (s_get.key) ;
}
```

LASTREC()

Clipper syntax: LASTREC()

Clipper argument: Nothing

Clipper return: <numeric expression>

C function name: d4reccount()

C function library: Code Base library

C portability: Database and index functions: ANSI C
Screen functions: Optimized for PCs and compatibles
Library source provided with the product.

C function header: #include <d4base.h>

long d4reccount()

Description:

Clipper: LASTREC() returns the number of records present in the active database.

C: The Code Base function d4reccount() also returns the number of records present in the active database. In C, where numeric data types are varied, the returned number of records is a long integer.

LEFT()

Clipper syntax: LEFT (<expC>, <expN>)

Clipper argument: <character expression>, <numeric expression>

Clipper return: <character expression>

C function name: sprintf()

C function library: Standard C

C portability: ANSI C

C function header: #include <stdio.h>

int sprintf (buffer, format [,argument]...) ;

Description:

Clipper: This function returns the leftmost <expN> characters of <expC>.

C: sprintf() is used to copy formatted data to a string, including data from another character string. See your compiler documentation for the printf() family of functions for specific format rules.

Clipper? LEFT ("This is a test", 4) && This would yield 'This' sample:

C sample:

```
#include <stdio.h>

main()
{
char buffer[80] ;

sprintf ( buffer, "%.4s\n", "This is a test" ) ;
printf ( buffer ) ;

/* or */

printf ( "%.4s\n", "This is a test" ) ;
}
```

LEN()

Clipper syntax: LEN (<expC>)

Clipper argument: <character expression>

Clipper return: <numeric expression>

C function name: strlen()

C function library: Standard C

C portability: ANSI C

C function header:

```
#include <stdio.h>

        unsigned int strlen ( string ) ;
        char *string ;
```

Description:

Clipper: This function returns the length of <expC>.

C: This function returns the length of **string** as an unsigned integer.

Clipper ? LFT ("This is a test", 4) && This would yield 'This' sample:

C sample:

```
#include <stdio.h>

main()
{
char buffer[80] ;

sprintf ( buffer, "%.4s\n", "This is a test" ) ;
printf ( buffer ) ;

/* or */

printf ( "%.4s\n", "This is a test" ) ;
}
```

LENNUM()

Clipper syntax: LENNUM (<expN>)

Clipper argument: <numeric expression>

Clipper return: <numeric expression>

C function name: None

Description:

Clipper: This function will yield the length in bytes of <expN> if it is a character expression. Similar functionality can be achieved with the following:

```
#include <string.h>

int main()
{
char buffer [80] ;

sprintf ( buffer, "%ld", number ) ;
length = strlen ( buffer ) ;

return (0) ;
}
```

LUPDATE()

Clipper syntax: LUPDATE()

Clipper argument: Nothing

Clipper return: <date expression>

C function name: lupdate()

C function library: SJSC Library™, Copyright © 1989, Stephen J. Straley & Associates. All rights reserved.

C function name: d4ptr()

C function library: Code Base library

C portability: Database and index functions: ANSI C
Screen functions: Optimized for PCs and compatibles
Library source provided with the product.

C function headers:

```
#include <d4base.h>

BASE *d4ptr()
long lupdate(void)
```

Description:

Clipper: Returns the date DOS entered when the selected and active database was last written to disk.

C: d4ptr() points to Code Base's internal database data structure describing the currently active and selected database. Three member variables of this data structure, char YY, char MM, and char DD contain the last update date of the database.

To create our own C function named lupdate(), which functions like the Clipper function LUPDATE(), we code the function as follows:

```
#include <stdio.h>
#include <d4base.h>

unsigned int header(void)
{
   sprintf ( datestr, "19%s,%s%s",
             d4ptr()->yy,
             d4ptr()->mm,
             d4ptr()->dd ) ;
return ( atol ( datestr ) ) ;
}
```

LOG()

Clipper syntax: LOG (<expN>)

Clipper argument: <numeric expression>

Clipper return: <numeric expression>

C functions: log()
log10()

C function library: Standard C.

C portability: ANSI C

C function headers:

```
double log(x)
double x ;

double log10(x)
double x;
```

Description:

Clipper and C: The log() function returns the natural logarithm of the number passed to it.

LOWER()

Clipper syntax: LOWER (<expC>)

Clipper argument: <character expression>

Clipper return: <character expression>

C function name: strlower() /* converts entire string */

C function library: Standard C

C portability: ANSI C

C header: #include <string.h>

```
char *strlower ( string )
char *string
```

C macro (function): tolower() /* converts one character */

C header: ctype.h

C function library: Standard C

C portability: ANSI C

C usage: tolower(character)

Description:

Clipper: Converts the first character of <expC> to its lowercase representation.

C: Use strupper() to convert all uppercase characters in an entire character string to lowercase.

Use tolower() to convert an uppercase ASCII value to a lowercase one.

LTRIM()

Clipper syntax: LTRIM (<expC>)

Clipper parameters: <character expression>

Clipper return: Nothing

C function name: ltrim()

C function library: SJSC Library™, Copyright © 1989, Stephen J. Straley & Associates. All rights reserved.

C function header:

```
#include <string.h>

char *alltrim ( char *string ) ;    /* required
                                       declaration */
char *alltrim ( string )
char *string ;
```

C portability: ANSI C

Description:

Clipper: LTRIM() returns a character expression stripped of leading blanks.

C: ltrim() returns a pointer to a string stripped of leading blanks. It also strips the string provided as an argument via call by reference.

C source:

```
#include <string.h>

char *ltrim (string)
char *string ;
{
unsigned int n ;

for ( n = 0 ; string[n] == ' ' ; n++ ) ;
return ( strcpy (string, string+n ) ) ;
}
```

C usage:

```
#include <stdio.h>
main()
{
char *ltrim (char *string) ; /*function declaration*/
static char hello[] = "  HELLO" ;
printf ( "%s\n", hello ) ; /* original string */
printf ( "%s\n", ltrim (hello) ) ; /*return string*/
printf ( "%s\n", hello ) ;    /*  string changed by
                                  reference*/
}
```

MAX()

Clipper syntax: MAX (<expN>)

Clipper parameter: <numeric expression>

Clipper return: <numeric expression>

C macro (function): max()

C library source: Standard library

C portability: ANSI C

C function header: #include <stdlib.h>

```
type max(a,b)
type a,b ;
```

Description:

Clipper: The MAX() function returns the larger of the two passed expressions. The macro will work with dates or numbers.

C: This function will work with any numeric type, including dates formatted as long integers, whether using C or dBASE-Clipper date formats.

MEMOEDIT()

Clipper syntax: MEMOEDIT (<expC1>,<expN1>,<expN2>,<expN3>,
<expN4>,[,<expL>[,expC2>[,<expN5>[,<expN6>,
[,<expN7>[,<expN8>[,<expN9>[,<expN10>]]]]]]]])

Clipper arguments: MEMOEDIT (<memo field>/<character expression>,
<numeric expression>,<numeric expression>,
<numeric expression>,<numeric expression>,
[,<logical expression>[,<character expression>
[,<numeric expression>[,<numeric expression>,
[,<numeric expression>[,<numeric expression>
[,<numeric expression>[,<numeric expression>
]]]]]]]]))

Clipper return: <character expression>

C function name: m4edit()

C library source: Code Base library

C portability: Database and index functions: ANSI C
Screen functions: Optimized for PCs and compatibles
Library source provided with the product.

C function header:

```
#include <d4base.h>

int m4edit ( field_ref, recno, editor, size )
long field_ref ;  /* Code Base field number    */
long recno ;      /* the record number         */
char *editor ;    /* which editor to use       */
int size ;        /* maximum size              */
```

Description:

Clipper: MEMOEDIT() is an extremely high-level function for editing memo fields. It has its own built-in word processor.

C: m4edit() is a much simpler function that requires invoking a separate text editor, via a DOS system call, in order to work.

See *Programming in Clipper, 2nd Edition* or Code Base documentation for more information and examples.

MEMOREAD()

Clipper syntax: MEMOREAD (<filename>)

Clipper argument: <character expression>

Clipper return: <character expression>

C function name: m4read()

C library: Code Base library

C portability: Database and index functions: ANSI C
Screen functions: Optimized for PCs and compatibles
Library source provided with the product.

C function headers:

```
#include <d4base.h>
```

```
m4read (field_ref, recno, string, str_len)
long field_ref, recno
char *string ;
int str_len ;
```

Description:

Clipper: This function returns the contents of <filename> as a character expression.

C: The Code Base function m4read() reads str_len characters from a memo field into string. string must be declared as a character array or buffer with enough storage for the memo field data. On completion, string will be null terminated.

MEMOTRAN()

Clipper syntax: MEMOTRAN (<expC>)[,hard_fix][,soft_fix])

Clipper argument: <character expression>[,<character expression>]

Clipper return: [,<character expression>]

C function name: memotran()

C function library: SJSC Library™, Copyright 1989, Stephen J. Straley & Associates. All rights reserved.

C function header: #include <string.h>

```
char *memotran ( string, hard_fix, softfix ) ;
char *string ;
unsigned char hard_fix, softfix ;
```

Description:

Clipper: This function returns <expC> with the hard carriage returns and/or soft carriage returns replaced with a special value.

C: The C function will do the same, except that both arguments are required. If you wish to keep a hard carriage return, pass an ASCII 13 as the first value. If you wish to keep a soft carriage return, pass an IBM ASCII 141 as the second argument.

The C function will also return the converted string by reference, as well as return a pointer to the converted string.

```
#define HARDCR 13
#define SOFTCR 141

char *memotran ( str, hfix, sfix )
char *str ;
unsigned char hfix, sfix ;
{
/*  use an unsigned char pointer to force the compiler
    to recognize char values > 127 */
unsigned char *retstr = (unsigned char *) str ;

while ( *retstr != NULL )
    {
    if (*retstr == HARDCR ) *retstr = hfix ;
    if (*retstr == SOFTCR ) *retstr = sfix ;
    retstr++ ;
    }
return ( str ) ;
}
```

MEMOWRIT()

Clipper syntax: MEMOWRIT (<filename>)

Clipper argument: <character expression>

Clipper return: <character expression>

C function name: m4write()

C library: Code Base library

C portability: Database and index functions: ANSI C
Screen functions: Optimized for PCs and compatibles
Library source provided with the product.

C function headers:

```
#include <d4base.h>

m4write (field_ref, recno, string, str_len)
long field_ref, recno
char *string ;
int str_len ;
```

Description:

Clipper: This function writes the <expC> to <filename>.

C: The Code Base function m4write() writes str_len characters from string into a memo field.

MIN()

Clipper syntax: MIN (<expN1>,<expN2>)

Clipper parameter: <numeric expression>

Clipper return: <numeric expression>

C macro (function): min

C library source: Standard library

C portability: ANSI C

C function header: #include <stdlib.h>

type min (a,b)
type a,b ;

Description:

Clipper: The MIN() function returns the smaller of the two passed expressions. The function will work with dates or numbers.

C: This C macro will work with any numeric type, including dates formatted as long integers, whether using C or dBASE-Clipper date formats.

MLCOUNT()

Clipper syntax: MLCOUNT (<expC>, <expN>)

Clipper argument: <character expression>[,<numeric expression>]

Clipper return: <numeric expression>

C function name: mlcount()

C function library: SJSC Library™, Copyright © 1989, Stephen J. Straley & Associates. All rights reserved.

C portability: Works only with IBM extended ASCII character set

C function header:

```
#include <string.h>

int mlcount ( string, line_size ) ;
char *string ;
int line_size ;
```

Description:

Clipper: This function returns the number of soft carriage returns within <expC> based on the line size specified by <expN>.

C: The C function returns the number of soft carriage returns within <expC> based on the line size specified by <expN>.

```
#define SOFTCR 141

int mlcount ( str, line_size )
unsigned char *str ;
int line_size ;
{
int index = 0, count = 0 ;

while ( index < line_size  )
   {
   if (*(str+index) == SOFTCR ) count++ ;
   index++ ;
   }
return ( str ) ;
}
```

MLPOS()

Clipper syntax: MLPOS (<expC>, <expN1>, <expN2>)

Clipper argument: <character expression>[,<numeric expression>]

Clipper return: <numeric expression>

C function name: mlpos()

C function library: SJSC Library™, Copyright © 1989, Stephen J. Straley & Associates. All rights reserved.

C portability: Works only with IBM extended ASCII character set

C function header:

```
#include <string.h>

int mlpos ( string, line_size ) ;
char *string ;
int line_size ;
```

Description:

Clipper: This function determines the offset of a specified line number <expN2> in a string or memo field expressed as <expC> with <expN1> characters per line.

C: This function determines the offset of line_number in string with line_size characters per line.

```
#define SOFTCR 141

unsigned int mlpos ( str, line_size, line_number )
unsigned char *str ;
int line_size, line_number ;
{
}
```

MOD()

Clipper syntax: MOD (<expN1>,<expN2>)

Clipper parameter: <numeric expression>, <numeric expression>

Clipper return: <numeric expression>

C operator: <expN> % <expN>

C portability: ANSI C

Description:

Clipper: The function returns the remainder of <expN1> divided by <expN2>. The Clipper function returns 0 upon division by 0; dBASE's MOD() function returns <expN1>.

The Summer '87 version of Clipper supports the % operator, described below.

C: The modulus operator (%) is used to determine the remainder of two numeric expressions.

MONTH()

Clipper syntax: MONTH (<expC>)

Clipper parameters: <character expression>

Clipper return: Nothing

C function name: month()

C function library: SJSC Library™, Copyright © 1989, Stephen J. Straley & Associates. All rights reserved.

C function header:

```
#include <string.h>

char *month (date) ; /* required declaration */
long date ;
```

C portability: ANSI C

Description:

Clipper: The MONTH() function returns a number that represents the month of a given date expression.

C: The C function provided below does the same:

```
#include <stdlib.h>

int month ( date )
long date ;
{
char datestr [9] ;
ltoa ( datestr, date, 10 )
*(datestr+6) = '\0' ;
return ( atoi ( datestr+4 ) ) ;
}
```

NDX()

Clipper syntax: NDX()

Clipper argument: Nothing

Clipper return: <character expression>

C function name: u4fullname

C function header: #include <d4base.h>

```
void u4fullname ( result, name, extension )
char *result, char *name, char *extension ;
```

Description:

Clipper: Returns the root file name for the <expN>th selected index.

C: Returns the name of the index file in use.

NETERR()

Clipper syntax: NETERR()

Clipper argument: Nothing

Clipper return: <logical expression>

C function: None

C operation: Test return value of C functions used in file opening operations.

Description:

Clipper: NETERR() returns a logical true (.T.) if the previous USE, APPEND BLANK, or USE..EXCLUSIVE failed in a network environment.

Since Clipper commands do not return values, as do functions, this separate NETERR() function is required in Clipper.

C: C functions, whether from the Standard library or a third-party library such as Code Base, are used in file I/O operations. All these functions return unique values indicating whether the file I/O operation was successful or not. Therefore, in C, a separate error function is not needed.

NETNAME()

Clipper syntax: NETNAME()

Clipper argument: Nothing

Clipper return: <character expression>

C function: None

Description:

Clipper: NETNAME() returns the name of the network station.

OS()

Clipper syntax: OS()

Clipper argument: Nothing

Clipper return: <character expression>

C function: None

Description:

Clipper: OS() always returns MS- or PC-DOS.

PCOL()

Clipper syntax: PCOL()

Clipper argument: Nothing

Clipper return: <numeric expression>

C function: ftell() ;

C library source: Standard library

C portability: ANSI C

C function headers:

```
#include <stdio.h>

long ftell( stream_ptr )
FILE *stream_ptr ;
```

Description:

Clipper: PCOL() returns the column position of the printer.

C: ftell() returns the current offset in the stream pointed to by stream_ptr. The standard stream_ptr in the case of a print stream is named **stdprn**. On MS-DOS machines it refers to the stream of data sent to port LPT1.

```
main()
{
   fprintf ( stdprn, "Hello" ) ;
   printf ("The printer column position is %ld",
            ftell ( stdprn ) % LINE_WIDTH ;
}
```

PCOUNT()

Clipper syntax: PCOUNT()

Clipper argument: Nothing

Clipper return: <numeric expression>

C function: None

Description:

Clipper: This function returns the number of successful parameter matches issued. It can be used to test to see if the parameter name is “U” (undefined).

PROCLINE()

Clipper syntax: PROCLINE()

Clipper argument: Nothing

Clipper return: <numeric expression>

C function: None

Description:

Clipper: This function returns the source code line number of the currently running program or procedure.

PROCNAME()

Clipper syntax: PROCNAME()

Clipper argument: Nothing

Clipper return: <numeric expression>

C function: None

Description:

Clipper: This function returns the name of the program or procedure currently running.

PROW()

Clipper syntax: PROW()

Clipper argument: Nothing

Clipper return: <numeric expression>

C function name: ftell()

C library source: Standard library

C portability: ANSI C

C function headers: #include <stdio.h>

```
long ftell( stream_ptr )
FILE *stream_ptr ;
```

Description:

Clipper: PROW() returns the row position of the printer.

C: ftell() returns the current offset in the stream pointed to by stream_ptr. The standard stream_ptr in the case of a print stream is named **stdprn**. On MS-DOS machines it refers to the stream of data sent to port LPT1.

```
main()
{
   fprintf ( stdprn, "Hello" ) ;
   printf ("The printer row position is %ld",
            ftell ( stdprn ) / LINE_WIDTH ;
}
```

RAT()

Clipper syntax: RAT (<expC1>, <expC2>)

Clipper argument: <character expression>, <character expression>

Clipper return: <numeric expression>

C function name: strrchr()

C library source: Standard library

C portability: ANSI C

C function headers: #include <string.h>

```
char *strrchr( string, ascii_char )
char *string ;
int ascii_char ;
```

Description:

Clipper: The R(ight)AT function searches through <expC2> for the last occurrence of <expC1> and returns the offset in <expC2> where it is found.

C: The Standard library function strrchr() searches through string for the last occurrence of ascii_char. strrchr() returns a character pointer to the string that begins at the offset where the last occurrence is found.

Clipper sample:

```
? "The current directory is "+ ;
SUBSTR ( CURDIR(), RAT("\",CURDIR()) -1 )
```

C sample:

```
#include <stdio.h>
#include <string.h>
#include <direct.h>
#define PATH_SIZE 128

main()
{
char path [PATH_SIZE] ;

printf ("The current directory is %s\n",
        strrchr ( getcwd ( path, PATH_SIZE ), '\\' ) ;
}
```

READEXIT()

Clipper syntax: READEXIT (<expCL>)

Clipper argument: <logical expression>, <character expression>

Clipper return: <numeric expression>

C function names: get*(), browse()

C function library: SJSC Library™, Copyright © 1989, Stephen J. Straley & Associates. All rights reserved.

C portability: MS-DOS only

C function headers: See Chapter 8.

Description:

Clipper: The READEXIT() function checks and toggles the Up and Down array keys as exit keys to a READ command.

C: In the SJSC current GET and browse functions, what Clipper does with a READ statement is accomplished with other functionality. See Chapter 8 for details.

READINSERT()

Clipper syntax: READINSERT (<expC1>)

Clipper argument: <logical expression>, <character expression>

Clipper return: <numeric expression>

C function names: get*(), browse() ;

C function library: SJSC Library™, Copyright © 1989, Stephen J. Straley & Associates. All rights reserved.

C portability: MS-DOS only

C function headers: See Chapter 8.

Description:

Clipper: The READEXIT() function checks and toggles the Insert key for all READS and the MEMOEDIT() command.

C: In the current SJSC GET and browse functions, what Clipper does with a READ statement is accomplished with other functionality. See Chapter 8 for details.

READKEY()

Clipper syntax: READKEY()

Clipper argument: <numeric expression>

Clipper return: <numeric expression>

C function names: get*(), browse()

C function library: SJSC Library™, Copyright © 1989, Stephen J. Straley & Associates. All rights reserved.

C portability: MS-DOS only

C headers: See Chapter 8.

Description:

Clipper: Returns a value for any key pressed that exits a Clipper full edit mode.

C: This value is placed in s_get.key when SJSC browse or GET functions are used. See INKEY() for a table of the return values; also see LASTKEY().

READVAR()

Clipper syntax: READVAR()

Clipper argument: Nothing

Clipper return: <character expression>

C function names: get*(), browse()

C function library: SJSC Library™, Copyright © 1989, Stephen J. Straley & Associates. All rights reserved.

C portability: MS-DOS only

C headers: See Chapter 8.

Description:

Clipper: Returns the name of a variable in the current GET/MENU.

C: This value is placed in the s_get.array when SJSC browse or GET functions are completed. When browse() is used as a menu, the menu selection chosen is also placed in s_get.array. When browse() is used as a list-box, the item chosen from the list-box is also placed in s_get.array.

RECCOUNT()

Clipper syntax: RECCOUNT()

Clipper argument: Nothing

Clipper return: <numeric expression>

C function name: d4reccount()

C function library: Code Base library

C portability: Database and index functions: ANSI C
Screen functions: Optimized for PCs and compatibles
Library source provided with the product.

C function header: #include <d4base.h>

long d4reccount()

Description:

Clipper: RECCOUNT() returns the number of records present in the active database. RECCOUNT() does not exist in the Autumn 86 version of Clipper; use LASTREC() instead.

C: The Code Base function d4reccount() also returns the number of records present in the active database. In C, where numeric data types are varied, the returned number of records is a long integer.

RECNO()

Clipper syntax: RECNO()

Clipper argument: Nothing

Clipper return: <numeric expression>

C function name: d4recno()

C function library: Code Base library

C portability: Database and index functions: ANSI C
Screen functions: Optimized for PCs and compatibles
Library source provided with the product.

C function headers: #include <d4base.h>

long d4recno(void)

Description:

Clipper: Returns the current record number, e.g., the position of the record pointer, in the current and active database.

C: The Code Base d4recno() number performs the same function as RECNO(). The data type of a record number in C is a long integer.

RECSIZE()

Clipper syntax: RECSIZE()

Clipper argument: Nothing

Clipper return: <numeric expression>

C function name: f4record_width

C function library: Code Base library

C portability: Database and index functions: ANSI C
Screen functions: Optimized for PCs and compatibles
Library source provided with the product.

C function headers: #include <d4base.h>

int f4record_width(void)

Description:

Clipper: Returns the number of bytes used by a single record in the currently selected and active database file.

C: The Code Base f4record_width() performs the same function as RECSIZE(). However, the data type of the returned size is an integer (16-bit) value.

REPLICATE()

Clipper syntax: REPLICATE (<expC>, <expN>)

Clipper parameters: <character expression>, <numeric expression>

Clipper return: Nothing

C function name: replicate()

C function library: SJSC Library™, Copyright © 1989, Stephen J. Straley & Associates. All rights reserved.

C function header:

```
#include <string.h>

unsigned char *replicate ( string, repeat )
unsigned char *string ;
int repeat ;
```

C portability: ANSI C

Description:

Clipper: The REPLICATE function returns a string composed of <expN> repetitions of <expC>.

C: The C function whose source code is below performs the same function:

```
unsigned char *replicate ( string, repeat )
unsigned char *string ;
int repeat ;
{
   static char buffer [256] ;
   int i, strsize = strlen (string) ;

   if ( strsize > 256 ) return (NULL) ;

   strcpy (buffer, string ) ;

   for ( i = 1 ; i < repeat ; i++ )
         {
         if ( strsize*i > 256 ) return ( NULL ) ;
         strcat ( buffer,string ) ;  }
   return ( buffer ) ;
}
```

RESTSCREEN()

Clipper syntax: RESTSCREEN (<expN1>, <expN2>, <expN3>, <expN4>, <expC1>)

Clipper parameters: <numeric expression>, <numeric expression>, <numeric expression>, <numeric expression>, <character expression>

Clipper return: Nothing

C function name: restore_window()

C function library: SJSC Library™, Copyright © 1989, Stephen J. Straley & Associates. All rights reserved.

C function header: #include <s_say.c>

void restore_window() ;

C portability: IBM PCs and compatibles only

Description:

Clipper: The RESTSCREEN() function restores the screen contents of <expC1> at window coordinates <expN1> through <expN4>

C: The restore_window() function restores the contents of a window area of the screen defined with the SJSC function window() and saved with the function save_window(). See Chapter 8 for more details.

C: The C function whose source is below performs the same function:

```
unsigned char *replicate ( string, repeat )
nsigned char *string ;
int repeat ;
{
   static char buffer [256] ;
   int i, strsize = strlen (string) ;

   if ( strsize > 256 ) return (NULL) ;

   strcpy (buffer, string ) ;

   for ( i = 1 ; i < repeat ; i++ )
         {
         if ( strsize*i > 256 ) return ( NULL ) ;
         strcat ( buffer,string ) ;      }
   return ( buffer ) ;
}
```

RIGHT()

Clipper syntax: RIGHT (<expC>,<expN>)

Clipper parameter: <character expression>, <numeric expression>

Clipper return: <character expression>

C function name: ltrim()

C function library: SJSC Library™, Copyright © 1989, Stephen J. Straley & Associates. All rights reserved.

C function header:

```
#include <string.h>

char *right ( string, len ) ;
char *string ;
unsigned int len ;
```

C portability: ANSI C

Description:

Clipper: The RIGHT() function returns the right-most <expN> characters of <expC>.

C: The right() function below will do the same:

C source:

```
#include <string.h>

char *right (string, len )
char *string ;
unsigned int len ;
{
return ( strcpy (string,string+strlen(string)-len) ) ;
}
```

C usage:

```
#include <stdio.h>
main()
{
char *right (char *string, int len ) ;    /* function declaration*/
static char hello[] = "  HELLO" ;
printf ( "%s\n", hello ) ;                 /* original string */
printf ( "%s\n", right (hello, 5 ) ) ;     /* return string*/
printf ( "%s\n", hello ) ;                 /* string changed by
                                              reference*/
}
```

ROUND()

Clipper syntax: ROUND (<expN>,<expN>)

Clipper argument: <numeric expression>,<numeric expression>

Clipper return: <numeric expression>

C function name: round()

C library source: SJSC Library™, Copyright © 1989, Stephen J. Straley & Associates. All rights reserved.

C portability: ANSI C

C function header:

```
double round ( number, precision )
double number ;
int precision ;
```

Description:

Clipper: The ROUND() function rounds off the first <expN> to the number of decimal places specified by the second <expN>

C: Rounding in C is accomplished via a two-step process:

1. Create a numeric formatted string using sprintf().

2. Use the function atof() to convert the string back to a double or float rounded value.

Here is the source for our round() function in C, which uses this process:

```
#include <stdio.h>
#include <math.h>

double round ( number, precision )
double number ;
int precision ;
{
char string[80] ;
sprintf (string, "%.*lf ", precision, number ) ;
return ( atof (string) ) ;
}
```

ROW()

Clipper syntax: ROW()

Clipper parameters: Nothing

Clipper return: <numeric expression>

C functions: row() ;
get_curs() ;

C function library: SJSC Library™, Copyright © 1989, Stephen J. Straley & Associates. All rights reserved.

Source provided below.

C portability: row() is IBM PC and compatible specific. It calls a subfunction get_curs() that in turn makes a PC ROM BIOS call to figure the screen location.

C headers:

```
int row(void) ;
void get_curs ( rowptr, colptr )
unsigned char *rowptr ;
unsigned char *colptr ;
```

Description:

Clipper: ROW() returns the current row position of the cursor on the screen().

C: Separate col() and row() functions can be used to get the current column and row position of the cursor, respectively. But better yet, one function called get_curs() can return **both** row and column coordinates using call by reference. Below is the source for these functions.

C source col():

```
int row ( void ) {
unsigned char col = 0, row = 0 ;
void get_cursor   (   unsigned char *rowptr,
                      unsigned char *colptr ) ;
get_cursor ( &row, &col ) ;
return ( (int) row ) ;
}
```

C source getcurs():

```
#include <stdio.h>
#include <dos.h>

void get_cursor ( rowptr, colptr )    /* use BIOS to get
                                         cursor position */
unsigned char *rowptr, *colptr ;
{
union REGS inregs,outregs ;

inregs.h.ah = 3 ;
inregs.h.bh = 0 ;
int86 (0x10, &inregs, &outregs) ;
*colptr = outregs.h.dl;
*rowptr = outregs.h.dh;
}
```

SAVESCREEN()

Clipper syntax: SAVESCREEN (<expN1>,<expN2>,<expN3>,<expN4>)

Clipper parameters: <numeric expression>,<numeric expression>, <numeric expression>,<numeric expression>

Clipper return: <character expression>

C function names: save_screen(), save_window()

C function library: SJSC Library™, Copyright © 1989, Stephen J. Straley & Associates. All rights reserved.

C portability: Screen I/O functions are optimizes for PCs and compatibles.

C function headers:

```
#include <s_say.h>

void save_screen(void) ;
void save_window(void) ;
```

Description:

Clipper: SAVE_SCREEN() returns the current row position of the cursor on the screen().

C: save_screen() saves an entire screen;

save_window() saves a window area of the screen defined in a last called to window().

SECONDS()

Clipper syntax: SECONDS()

Clipper argument: Nothing

Clipper return: <numeric expression>

C function name: seconds()

C function library: SJSC Library™, Copyright © 1989, Stephen J. Straley & Associates. All rights reserved.

C function header: long seconds(void)

Description:

Clipper: The SECONDS() function returns a numeric value representing the number of seconds that have elapsed since 12:00 a.m. according to the system clock.

C: The SJSC function seconds() returns the same value, expressed as a long integer.

C sample:

```
#include <time.h>

long seconds(void)
{
struct tm *ourtime ;
long ticktock ;
static char timestr[9] ;

time ( &ticktock ) ;
ourtime = localtime (&ticktock) ;

return (
(long) (ourtime->tm_min) * 60L +
(long) (ourtime->tm_hour) * 3600L +
(long) ourtime->tm_sec ) ;
}

#include <stdio.h>

int main()
```

```
{
long seconds(void) ;
printf ( "%ld\n", seconds() ) ;
return (0) ;
}
```

SELECT()

Clipper syntax: SELECT ([<expC>])

Clipper parameters: Nothing

Clipper return: <numeric expression>

C function name: d4select()

C function use: d4select(-1) ;

C function library: Code Base library

C portability: Database and index functions: ANSI C
Screen functions: Optimized for PCs and compatibles
Library source provided with the product.

C function headers: #include <d4base.h>

int d4select(database_ref_no)
int database_ref_no ;

Description:

Clipper: Returns the currently selected work area or work area of an alias if provided as an argument to the function.

C: Code Base's d4select() function, when passed a -1 will return the current work area, which Code Base also calls a database reference number.

SETCANCEL()

Clipper syntax: SETCANCEL ([<expL>])

Clipper parameters: Nothing

Clipper return: [<logical expression>]

C function name: signal()

C library source: Standard library

C portability: ANSI C

C function header: #include <signal.h>

void signal (int sig,void(*func)
(int sig[,int subcode])))(int) ;

Description:

Clipper: The function checks and toggles the Alt-C (termination) key.

C: Signal() is used to perform an overriding activity when a key is hit. The most common activity is to terminate the program when Ctrl-Break or Ctrl-C is pressed.

C example:

```
#include <stdio.h>
#include <signal.h>

void trap (int sig)
{
printf ( "Program terminated with user signal.\n" ) ;
exit(1) ;
}

main()
{
     signal ( SIGINT, trap );
     for ( ; ; )
     printf ( "Stop me...\n" ) ;
}
```

SETCOLOR()

Clipper syntax: SETCOLOR ([<expC>])

Clipper parameters: [<character expression>]

Clipper return: <character expression>

C function name: set_color()

C function library: SJSC Library™, Copyright © 1989, Stephen J. Straley & Associates. All rights reserved.

C portability: Screen I/O functions are optimized for PCs and compatibles.

C function headers: #include <s_say.h>

void setcolor (attrib) ;
unsigned char attrib ;

unsigned char color (fore, back, blink_state) ;
unsigned char fore, back, blink_state ;

Description:

Clipper: SETCOLOR(), when passed no parameters, returns the current color setting; with a parameter it sets the color and returns the previous color setting.

C: set_color() sets the current color setting. It is passed an attribute value that is the actual screen attribute value for the display in text mode.

To create this attribute value from logical color names, use the macro color() and color values from the color table color.h

SETPRC()

Clipper syntax: SETPRC (<expN1>,<expN2>)

Clipper parameters: <numeric expression>, <numeric expression>

Clipper return: Nothing

C function name: fseek() ;

C function library: Standard C

C portability: ANSI C

C function headers: #include <stdio.h>

long fseek (stream_ptr, offset, origin)

```
FILE *stream_ptr ;
long offset ;
int origin ;
```

Description:

Clipper: SETPRC() sets internal PROW() and PCOL() pointers to new printer row and column values. This counteracts the incrementing of these internal pointers when nonprinting characters are sent to the printer.

C: In C these internal values are not kept. However, the standard library function fseek() can be used to reposition a stream I/O file pointer, including stdprn.

SPACE()

Clipper syntax: SPACE (<expN>)

Clipper parameters: <numeric expression>

Clipper return: <character expression>

C function name: space (<expN>)

C function library: SJSC Library™, Copyright © 1989, Stephen J. Straley & Associates. All rights reserved.

C portability: ANSI C

C function header:

```
char *space ( size ) ;
unsigned int size ;
```

Description:

Clipper: This function generates a string consisting of <expN> blank spaces.

C: The C function below, which calls our function replicate(), has the same functionality:

```
char *space ( size ) ;
unsigned int size ;
{
```

```
return ( replicate ( " ", size ) ) ;
}
```

SQRT()

Clipper syntax: SQRT (<expN>)

Clipper parameters: <numeric expression>

Clipper return: <numeric expression>

C function name: sqrt (<expN>)

C function library: Standard C

C portability: ANSI C

C function header:

```
double sqrt ( x ) ;
double x ;
```

Description:

Clipper: The SQRT() function returns the square root of <expN>.

C: The C function returns the square root of **x**.

The passed and returned values are doubles.

STR()

Clipper syntax: STR (<expN>,[<length>[,[decimals>]])

Clipper parameters: <numeric expression>[,<numeric expression>
[,<numeric expression>]]

Clipper return: <character expression>

C function names:
sprintf()
itoa()
ltoa()
fcvt()
gcvt()
ecvt()

C function library: Standard library

C headers:

```
/* converts any type to a string */
#include <stdio.h>
int sprintf ( buffer, format [,argument]...) ;

/* converts int to string */
#include <stdlib.h>
char *itoa (int value, char *string, int radix)

/* converts long to string */
#include <stdlib.h>
char *ltoa (long value, char *string, int radix)

/* converts double to string */
#include <stdlib.h>
char *fcvt ( double value, int num_digits,
            int *dec, int *sign )
```

Description:

Clipper: The STR() function transforms a numeric expression into a string. The second parameter sets the length of the string and the third parameter sets the number of decimal places to be included.

C: The function sprintf() can transform an expression of any data type into a string, using printf() control codes. We can also specify a length and number of decimal places.

The functions itoa(), ltoa(), and fcvt() use less memory than sprintf(). While itoa() and ltoa() are simple to use instead of sprintf(), fcvt() is more complex.

Here is an example of how sprintf() is used to convert a double;

```
#include <stdio.h>
main()
{
   char string [80] ;
   double value = 2314.124567
   int width = 3
   int dec_places = 2 ;

   /* string will contain 314.12 */
   sprintf ( string, "%3.2f", value ) ;
   printf ( "%s\n", string ) ;
```

```
/* string will also contain 314.12 */
sprintf ( string, "%*.*f", width, dec_places, value ) ;
printf ( "%s\n", string ) ;

/* we can also display the same value this way */
printf ( "%*.*f\n", width, dec_places, value ) ;
```

STRZERO()

Clipper syntax: STRZERO (<expN1>,[<expN2> [,<expN3>]])

Clipper parameters: <numeric expression>, [,<numeric expression> [,<numeric expression>]]]

Clipper return: <character expression>

C function name: sprintf()

C function library: Standard library

C header:

```
/* converts any type to a string */
#include <stdio.h>
int sprintf ( buffer, format [,argument]...) ;
```

Description:

Clipper: The STRZERO() function returns a numeric string with leading 0s instead of blanks.

C: The sprintf() function can format a numeric string with leading 0s instead of blanks as follows:

```
#include <stdio.h>
main()
{
    char string [80] ;
    int value = 2314 ;

    sprintf ( string, "%06d", value ) ;
    printf ( "%s\n", string ) ;
}
```

STUFF()

Clipper syntax: STUFF (<expC1>, <expN1>, <expN2>, <expC2>)

Clipper parameters: <character expression>, <numeric expression> <numeric expression>, <character expression>

Clipper return: <character expression>

C function name: stuff() ;

C function library: SJSC Library™, Copyright © 1989, Stephen J. Straley & Associates. All rights reserved.

C header:

```
char *stuff  (char *str1,char* str2,
              unsigned offset, unsigned length );
```

C function name: sprintf() ;

C function library: Standard library

C header:

```
#include <stdio.h>

int sprintf ( buffer, format [,argument]...) ;
```

Description:

Clipper: STUFF() returns a character expression of <expC1> overlayed by <expC2>.

C: The SJSC stuff() function works the same way as the Clipper function. In C there is a lot more flexibility for creating formatted strings using sprintf(). sprintf() can create a string representation of any data type or combination of data types, including a reformatting of the string itself.

Note: In C, it is important to declare any converted string that is larger than the original string with enough storage to contain its new contents. See the samples below, where the string hello has been declared with 80 characters. In general practice and if memory requirements permit, it is always best to allow some extra room for strings that are created with sprintf() or with other string formatting and copying functions.

```
#include <stdio.h>
#include <string.h>
```

Example 1 using stuff():

```
int main()
{
static char from[] = "from " ;
static char hello[80] = "Hello Steve." ;

char *stuff (char *str1,char* str2,
             unsigned offset, unsigned length ) ;

stuff ( hello, from, 6, 5 ) ;
printf ( "%s\n",hello ) ;
return (0) ;
}

char *stuff ( str1, str2, offset, length )
char *str1, *str2 ;
unsigned int offset, length ;
{
/* the stuff function requires only two calls to
   the same function, memcpy().  The string is
   changed by reference and a pointer to itself is
   returned */

memcpy ( str1+offset+length, str1+offset,length ) ;
memcpy ( str1+offset,str2,length ) ;
return ( str1 ) ;
}
```

Example 2 using sprintf():

```
#include <stdio.h>

int main()
{
static char from[] = "from " ;
static char hello[80] = "Hello Steve." ;
static char newhello[80]  ;

sprintf ( newhello, "%.6s%s%s, hello, from, hello+6 )
;
printf ( newhello\n" ) ;
return (0) ;
}
```

SUBSTR()

Clipper syntax: SUBSTR (<expC1>, <expN1>[,<expN2>])

Clipper parameters: <character expression>, <numeric expression> <numeric expression>

Clipper return: <character expression>

C function name: substr() ;

C function library: SJSC Library™, Copyright © 1989, Stephen J. Straley & Associates. All rights reserved.

C header: char *substr (char *str1, unsigned offset, unsigned length) ;

C function name: sprintf() ;

C function library: Standard library

C header: #include <stdio.h>

int sprintf (buffer, format [,argument]...) ;

Description:

Clipper: The SUBSTR() function returns a character string composed of <expC>, starting at the position <expN1> and continuing for a length of <expN2> characters.

C: The substr() function below works the same way, except that the length argument is required. Note, however, that the initial array position in a C string is element 0, not 1.

```
#include <string.h>

char *substr ( str1, offset, length )
char *str1 ;
unsigned offset, length ;
{
if (offset > ( maxlen = strlen (str1) )
    offset = maxlen ;
if (length > ( maxlen = strlen (str1) )
    length = maxlen ;

str1+length = '\0' ;
return ( str1 = str1+offset ) ;
```

TIME()

Clipper syntax: TIME()

Clipper parameters: Nothing

Clipper return: <character expression>

C function name: hhmmss()

C function library: SJSC Library™, Copyright © 1989, Stephen J. Straley & Associates. All rights reserved.

C function header: char *hhmmss(void)

Description:

Clipper: The TIME() function returns the system time as a character string in the form HH:MM:SS.

C: The hhmmss() function below calls standard C time functions to obtain the current time and time format and returns a character string in the form HH:MM:SS.

Note: In standard C, there is already a function named time(), which the hhmmss() function calls.

```
#include <time.h>

char *hhmmss(void)
{
struct tm *ourtime ;
long ticktock ;
static char timestr[9] ;

time ( &ticktock ) ;
ourtime = localtime (&ticktock) ;
sprintf ( timestr, "%02d:%02d:%02d",
        ourtime->tm_hour ,
        ourtime->tm_min ,
        ourtime->tm_sec ) ;
return ( timestr ) ;
}
```

example:

```
#include <stdio.h>

int main()
{
char *hhmmss(void) ;
printf ( "%s\n", hhmmss() ) ;
return (0) ;
}
```

TRANSFORM()

Clipper syntax: TRANSFORM (<exp>,<expC)

Clipper parameters: <character expression>/<numeric expression>, <picture expression>

Clipper return: <character expression>

C function name: str_picture (string, expression)

C function library: SJSC Library™, Copyright 1989, Stephen J. Straely & Associates. All rights reserved.

Description:

Clipper and C: Returns <exp> in the format of the picture expression passed to the function as <expC>.

TRIM()

Clipper syntax: TRIM (<expC>)

Clipper parameters: <character expression>

Clipper return: Nothing

C function name: trim()

C function library: SJSC Library™, Copyright © 1989, Stephen J. Straley & Associates. All rights reserved.

C function header: #include <string.h>

char *trim (char *string) ; /* required declaration */

```
char *trim ( string )
char *string ;
```

C portability: ANSI C

Description:

Clipper: TRIM() returns a character expression stripped of trailing blanks.

C: Trim() returns a pointer to a string stripped of trailing blanks. It also strips the string that is provided as an argument via call by reference.

C source:

```
#include <string.h>

char *trim (string)
char *string ;
{
unsigned int n ;

for ( n = strlen(string) ; string[n-1] == ' ' ; n-- ) ;
string [n] = '\0' ;
return ( string ) ) ;
}
```

C usage:

```
#include <stdio.h>
main()
{
char *trim (char *string) ;          /*function declaration */
static char hello[] = "HELLO   " ;
printf ( "%s\n", hello ) ;           /*original string */
printf ( "%s\n", trim (hello) ) ;    /*return string */
printf ( "%s\n", hello ) ;           /*string changed by reference */
}
```

TSTRING()

Clipper syntax: TSTRING (<expN>)

Clipper parameters: <numeric expression>

Clipper return: <character expression>

C function name: tstring () ;

C function library: SJSC Library™, Copyright © 1989, Stephen J. Straley & Associates. All rights reserved.

C function header: char *string (int secs) ;

Description:

Clipper: The TSTRING() function yields a time string of <expN> seconds.

C: The tstring() function yields a time string from seconds. If the number of seconds exceeds DAY, only the remaining seconds are calculated.

Note: Seconds must be passed as an integer.

```
#include <stdio.h>

#define DAY ( 24*60*60 )
#define HOUR ( 60*60 )
#define MINUTE ( 60 )

char *tstring (seconds )
int seconds ;
{
int days = 0, hours = 0, minutes = 0 ;
static char timestr[9] ;
if ( seconds > DAY )  seconds = seconds % DAY ;

hours       = seconds/HOUR ;
minutes     = (seconds % HOUR) / MINUTE ;
seconds     = (seconds % HOUR) % MINUTE ;

sprintf    ( timestr, "%02d:%02d:%02d",
             hours, minutes, seconds ) ;
return ( timestr ) ;
}
```

TYPE()

Clipper syntax: TYPE (<exp>)

Clipper parameters: <expression>

Clipper return: <character expression>

C operator: sizeof () ;

C function library: Standard library

C portability: ANSI C

Description:

Clipper: This function returns a code for the data type of <exp>.

C: The sizeof operator returns the data type size of the variable passed to it.

UPDATED()

Clipper syntax: UPDATED()

Clipper argument: Nothing

Clipper return: <logical expression>

C function names: get*(), browse() ;

C function library: SJSC Library™, Copyright © 1989, Stephen J. Straley & Associates. All rights reserved.

C portability: MS-DOS only

C function headers: See Chapter 8.

Description:

Clipper: The UPDATED() function checks to see if the last READ() statement updated any data when GETs were used.

C: In SJSC GET and browse functions, what Clipper does with a READ statement is accomplished with other functionality. The updated status of a GET can be found by comparing the original string going into the GET, stored in the global array s_get.clear, with the current GET string in the global array s_get.array.

UPPER()

Clipper syntax: UPPER (<expC>)

Clipper argument: <character expression>

Clipper return: <character expression>

C function name: strupper() /* converts entire string */

C function library: Standard library

C portability: ANSI C

C header: #include <string.h>

```
char *strupper ( string )
char *string
```

C macro (function): toupper() /* converts one character */

C header: ctype.h

C function library: Standard library

C portability: ANSI C

C usage: toupper(character)

Description:

Clipper: Converts the first character of <expC> to its uppercase representation.

C: Use strupper() to convert all lowercase characters in an entire character string to uppercase.

Use toupper() to convert a lowercase ASCII value to a uppercase one.

USED()

Clipper syntax: USED()

Clipper argument: Nothing

Clipper return: <logical expression>

C function name: d4select()

C function use: d4select(work_area) ;

C function library: Code Base library

C portability: Database and index functions: ANSI C
Screen functions: Optimized for PCs and compatibles
Library source provided with the product.

C function headers: #include <d4base.h>

```
int d4select(database_ref_no)
int database_ref_no ;
```

Description:

Clipper: USED() returns a logical true if a database is in use in the selected work area.

C: d4select() returns a -1 if no database is in use in the selected work area.

VAL()

Clipper syntax: VAL()

Clipper argument: <character expression>

Clipper return: <numeric expression>

C function name: None

Description:

Clipper: VAL() converts a character into a numeric expression.

VERSION()

Clipper syntax: VERSION()

Clipper argument: Nothing

Clipper return: <character expression>

C function name: None

Description:

Clipper: VERSION() returns the current release of Clipper as a character expression.

WORD()

Clipper syntax: CALL <procedure> WITH WORD (<expN>)

Clipper argument: <numeric expression>

Clipper return: <character expression>

Description:

Clipper: WORD() converts a numeric expression to an integer (16-bit unsigned value) when it is passed to a CALLed procedure.

C: A cast can be used to convert a C numeric expression to an integer. The general form of the cast is:

```
integer_value = (int) other_value ;
```

APPENDIX

Data Generation Program

Below is the main file that generates the databases, indexes, memo file, text file, and subsequent data for the Clipper programs and examples contained in this book. Please read the notation in the header of the file for complete compiling, linking, and ancillary information.

```
********************
* Name      Data.prg
* Author    Stephen J. Straley
* Notice    Copyright (c) 1989 Stephen J. Straley & Associates
*           All Rights Reserved.
* Date      July 1, 1989
* Compile   Clipper Data -m
* Release   Summer '87
* Link      PLINK86 FI Data FI ToolkiTA LIB Clipper LIB Extend
* Note      This file is to produce the data
*           for the Addison-Wesley Book "Advanced
*           Programming in Clipper with C"
*           All rights reserved.
*
*           Additional power provided by a
*           special version of Steve Straley's
*           ToolkiT - Release 2 published by
*           Four Seasons Publishing Co., Inc.
*           All Rights Reserved.
*
*           Many external references are made to
*           the following functions:
*
*           Ismono()     Publics()     Setup()     Savesys()
*           Palate()     Windowpush()  Windowpop() Wsayget()
*           Op()         Dbfmake()     Dbfindex()  Selecting()
*           Wdepth()     Prompt()      Pan()       Nosubdr()
*           Drnames()    Stats()       Sjs_read()
*
*           These functions can be obtained by contacting
*           Four Seasons Publishing at (212) 599-2141. Only some
*           of the code for these functions is available in
*           the above-mentioned book.
*
********************

CLEAR SCREEN
scrmono = Ismono(24,00)
Publics()
Setup(.F.)
Savesys()
Palate(2)
Windowpush(5,20,18,60)
Wsayget(1,2, "First, generate the file structures")
Filestru()
Wsayget(2,2, "Now, create the first database")
Op(A->(Dbfmake("Ontap", file1)))
Op(A->(Dbfindex("Ontap", "files")))
```

```
Op(A->(Selecting("Ontap", "Ontap")))

Wsayget(3,2, "Now, create the second database")
Op(B->(Dbfmake("Clients", file2)))
Op(B->(Selecting("Clients")))

Wsayget(4,2, "Now, create the third database")
Op(C->(Dbfmake("Trans", file3)))
Op(C->(Selecting("Trans")))

Wsayget(5,2, "Now, create the fourth database")
Op(D->(Dbfmake("Statcode", file4)))
Op(D->(Selecting("Statcode")))

Wsayget(6,2, "Now, create the fifth database")
Op(E->(Dbfmake("Disknos", file5)))
Op(E->(Dbfindex("Disknos", "disk_no")))
Op(E->(Selecting("Disknos", "Disknos")))

Wsayget(7,2, "Now, create the sixth database")
Op(F->(Dbfmake("Filenos", file6)))
Op(F->(Dbfindex("Filenos", "sub_no + file_name", "Filenos")))
Op(F->(Dbfindex("Filenos", "sub_no + sub_name",  "Filesub")))
Op(F->(Dbfindex("Filenos", "sub_no + file_type", "Filetype")))
Op(F->(Selecting("Filenos", "Filenos/Filesub/Filetype")))

Wsayget(8,2, "Now, create the seventh database")
Op(G->(Dbfmake("Statbase", file7)))
Op(G->(Selecting("Statbase")))

Wsayget(9,2, "Now, create the eighth database")
Op(H->(Dbfmake("Notap", file8)))
Op(H->(Dbfindex("Notap", "files")))
Op(H->(Selecting("Notap", "Notap")))

Wsayget(Wdepth(), 2, "Ready for next phase? ")
Prompt()
Pan(8)

Wsayget(1, 2, "Adding Information to first file")
Op(A->(Withone()))

Wsayget(2, 2, "Working with second file")
Op(B->(Withtwo()))

Wsayget(3, 2, "Adding Transactions to file")
Op(C->(Withthree()))

Wsayget(4, 2, "Storing Code information...")
Op(D->(Withfour()))

Wsayget(5, 2, "Making the Help Files....")
Mhelp()
```

```
Wsayget(6, 2, "Searching through the drive")
DECLARE array[NOSUBDR("C:")]
DRNAMES(array, "C:")

Wsayget(7, 2, "Obtaining File Information!")
Wsayget(8, 2, "         Secondary File ...")
Op(E->(Obtain()))

Wsayget(9, 2, "Adding State Information.")
Op(G->(Statbase()))

Wsayget(10,2, "Now adding the final piece.")
Op(H->(Final()))

Wsayget(Wdepth(), 2, "Any key for final screen ")
INKEY(0)
Pan(4)
Windowpop()
Stats()
IF LASTKEY() = 27 .OR. LASTKEY() = 13
   Sjs_hello()
ENDIF
CLEAR SCREEN

******************

PROCEDURE Filestru

   PUBLIC file1[ 5]
      file1[ 1] = "files/C/12"
      file1[ 2] = "sizes/N/12"
      file1[ 3] = "datestamp/D/ 8"
      file1[ 4] = "times/C/ 8"
      file1[ 5] = "notes/M/10"
   PUBLIC file2[15]
      file2[ 1] = "status/C/1"
      file2[ 2] = "account/C/6"
      file2[ 3] = "name/C/25"
      file2[ 4] = "address1/C/20"
      file2[ 5] = "address2/C/20"
      file2[ 6] = "city/C/15"
      file2[ 7] = "state/C/2"
      file2[ 8] = "zip/C/9"
      file2[ 9] = "current/N/16/2"
      file2[10] = "due/N/16/2"
      file2[11] = "phone/C/14"
      file2[12] = "contact/C/5"
      file2[13] = "indate/D/8"
      file2[14] = "active/C/1"
      file2[15] = "paired/L/1"
   PUBLIC file3[ 4]
      file3[ 1] = "account/C/6"
      file3[ 2] = "adate/D/8"
      file3[ 3] = "now_due/N/10/2"
```

```
      file3[ 4] = "paid/L/1"
   PUBLIC file4[ 2]
      file4[ 1] = "status/C/1"
      file4[ 2] = "descript/C/20"
   PUBLIC file5[10]
      file5[ 1] = "disk_no/C/10"    && The Disk Number
      file5[ 2] = "sub_no/C/3"      && The Number of Subs
      file5[ 3] = "disk_name/C/50"  && The Disk Name
      file5[ 4] = "disk_comm/C/40"  && The Disk Comment
      file5[ 5] = "date_add/D/8"    && The Date Add to File
      file5[ 6] = "date_up/D/8"     && The Date Last Updated
      file5[ 7] = "disk_label/M/10" && The Disk's Label
      file5[ 8] = "bytes_left/N/10" && Bytes availables
      file5[ 9] = "hardflop/L/1"    && Hard/Floppy Toggle
      file5[10] = "drivelet/C/2"    && The Drive Letter
   PUBLIC file6[11]
      file6[ 1] = "disk_no/C/10"    && The Disk Number
      file6[ 2] = "sub_no/C/3"      && The Number of Subs
      file6[ 3] = "sub_name/C/40"   && The Sub-Directory Name
      file6[ 4] = "file_no/C/5"     && The File Number
      file6[ 5] = "file_name/C/12"  && The File Name
      file6[ 6] = "file_type/C/3"   && The Type of File/Code
      file6[ 7] = "file_size/N/10"  && The File Size
      file6[ 8] = "file_date/D/8"   && The File Date Stamp
      file6[ 9] = "file_time/C/10"  && The File Time Stamp
      file6[10] = "file_comm/C/50"  && The File's Comments
      file6[11] = "is_arc/L/1"      && Is this an ARC file
   PUBLIC file7[ 3]
      file7[ 1] = "state/C/2"
      file7[ 2] = "zpre/C/1"
      file7[ 3] = "ppre/C/3"
   PUBLIC file8[ 8]
      file8[ 1] = "files/C/12"
      file8[ 2] = "sizes/N/12"
      file8[ 3] = "datestamp/D/8"
      file8[ 4] = "times/C/8"
      file8[ 5] = "comment/M/10"
      file8[ 6] = "file_use/C/40"
      file8[ 7] = "subdrive/C/50"
      file8[ 8] = "per_used/N/8/4"

*******************

PROCEDURE Withone

   how_many = ADIR("*.*")
   DECLARE afiles[how_many], asizes[how_many], ;
           adate[how_many], atimes[how_many]
   ADIR("*.*", afiles, asizes, adate, atimes)
   FOR x = 1 TO how_many
      APPEND BLANK
      REPLACE files WITH afiles[x], sizes with asizes[x], ;
              datestamp WITH adate[x], times WITH atimes[x]
   NEXT
```

```
********************

PROCEDURE Withtwo

   Adding("3", "100000", "Nantucket Corporation", ;
         "1255 Jefferson Blvd", "", "Los Angeles", ;
         "CA", "90066", 1000.00, 23.00, ;
         "1-800-231-1521", "Ray",   DATE(), "", .F.)
   Adding("1", "200000", "Stephen Straley & Assoc.", ;
         "319 Barrow Street", "Suite 7A", "Jersey City",;
         "NJ", "07302", 230000.00, 12.00, "1-201-432-8189",;
         "Steve", DATE(), "", .F.)
   Adding("6", "200001", "Falcon Software, Ltd.",;
         "319 Barrow - Ste 7A", "", "Jersey City", "NJ",;
         "07302", 200.00, 2.00, "1-201-432-8189", "Steve",;
         DATE(), "", .T.)
   Adding("1", "200010", "Number One Software", "", "", "",;
         "", "", 2.00, 1221.00, "", "", DATE(), "", .F.)
   Adding("3", "300000", "Ashton-Tate", "", "", "", "", "",;
         23.00, 13.00, "", "", DATE(), "", .F.)
   Adding("1", "323333", "Lotus Development", "", "", "",;
         "", "", 14525.00, 2313.00, "", "", DATE(), "", .T.)
   Adding("1", "352231", "MicroSoft, Corp.", "", "", "", "",;
         "", 7472374.00, 8482348.00, "", "", DATE(), "", .F.)
   Adding("1", "400000", "IBM", "", "", "", "", "", 8237.00,;
         76674.00, "", "", DATE(), "", .F.)
   Adding("2", "511001", "Panasonic", "", "", "", "", "", ;
         1625.00, 95945.00, "", "", DATE(), "", .T.)
   Adding("1", "610000", "Sony", "", "", "", "", "", 0.00, ;
         0.00, "", "", DATE(), "", .T.)
   Adding("2", "714442", "Tandy International", "", "", "", ;
         "", "", 0.00, 0.00, "", "", DATE(), "", .T.)
   Adding("1", "740000", "Texaco Limited", "", "", "", "", ;
         "", 0.00, 0.00, "", "", DATE(), "", .F.)
   Adding("4", "830000", "Magnus Production", "", "", "", ;
         "", "", 0.00, 0.00, "", "", DATE(), "", .F.)
   Adding("1", "831000", "MacIntosh Corp.", "", "", "", "",;
         "", 0.00, 0.00, "", "", DATE(), "", .F.)
   Adding("1", "845500", "Hayes MicroComputer", "", "", "",;
         "", "", 0.00, 0.00, "", "", DATE(), "", .F.)
   Adding("8", "860000", "Sharp Images", "", "", "", "",;
         "", 0.00, 0.00, "", "", DATE(), "", .F.)
   Adding("2", "900000", "Ford Motorcars", "", "", "", "",;
         "", 0.00, 0.00, "", "", DATE(), "", .F.)
   Adding("9", "910000", "Chrysler Corporation", "", "", "",;
         "", "", 0.00, 0.00, "", "", DATE(), "", .F.)
   Adding("9", "920000", "General Motors", "", "", "", "",;
         "", 0.00, 0.00, "", "", DATE(), "", .F.)
   Adding("9", "930000", "Nisan Motors", "", "", "", "", "",;
         0.00, 0.00, "", "", DATE(), "", .F.)
   Adding("9", "931000", "Totyota", "", "", "", "", "", ;
         0.00, 0.00, "", "", DATE(), "", .F.)
   Adding("9", "933100", "Isuzu", "", "", "", "", "", 0.00, ;
         0.00, "", "", DATE(), "", .F.)
```

```
   Adding("9", "935000", "Honda Motocars", "", "", "", "",;
          "", 0.00, 0.00, "", "", DATE(), "", .F.)
   Adding("9", "939300", "Subaru", "", "", "", "", "", ;
          0.00, 0.00, "", "", DATE(), "", .F.)
   Adding("9", "940000", "ABC", "", "", "", "", "", 0.00, ;
          0.00, "", "", DATE(), "", .F.)
   Adding("9", "945000", "Fox Television", "", "", "", "", ;
          "", 0.00, 0.00, "", "", DATE(), "", .F.)
   Adding("9", "950000", "NBC", "", "", "", "", "", 0.00, ;
          0.00, "", "", DATE(), "", .F.)
   Adding("9", "955000", "CBS", "", "", "", "", "", 0.00, ;
          0.00, "", "", DATE(), "", .F.)

********************

PROCEDURE Adding

   PARAMETERS a1, b1, c1, d1, e1, f1, g1, h1, ;
              i1, j1, k1, l1, m1, n1, o1

   APPEND BLANK
   REPLACE  status WITH a1,  account WITH b1,;
              name WITH c1, address1 WITH d1, ;
          address2 WITH e1,     city WITH f1, ;
             state WITH g1,      zip WITH h1, ;
           current WITH i1,      due WITH j1, ;
             phone WITH k1,  contact WITH l1, ;
            indate WITH m1,   active WITH n1, ;
            paired WITH o1
   Wsayget(2, 35, RECNO(), "", "999")

*******************

PROCEDURE Withthree

   Anotadd("100000", CTOD("02/18/88"),  25452.23,  .F.)
   Anotadd("200000", CTOD("02/18/88"),  54512.23,  .F.)
   Anotadd("200001", CTOD("02/18/88"),  545213.23,  .F.)
   Anotadd("200010", CTOD("02/18/88"),  5412.23,  .F.)
   Anotadd("300000", CTOD("02/18/88"),  512.23,  .F.)
   Anotadd("323333", CTOD("02/18/88"),  5412.23,  .F.)
   Anotadd("352231", CTOD("02/18/88"),  5122.32,  .F.)
   Anotadd("400000", CTOD("02/18/88"),  2.33,  .F.)
   Anotadd("511001", CTOD("02/18/88"),  52.36,  .F.)
   Anotadd("610000", CTOD("02/18/88"),  3.54,  .F.)
   Anotadd("714442", CTOD("02/18/88"),  1.25,  .F.)
   Anotadd("740000", CTOD("02/18/88"),  0.01,  .F.)
   Anotadd("830000", CTOD("02/18/88"),  221.22,  .F.)
   Anotadd("831000", CTOD("02/18/88"),  84.50,  .F.)
   Anotadd("845500", CTOD("02/18/88"),  7014.00,  .F.)
   Anotadd("860000", CTOD("02/18/88"),  21.00,  .F.)
   Anotadd("900000", CTOD("02/18/88"),  7.01,  .F.)
   Anotadd("910000", CTOD("02/18/88"),  10.25,  .F.)
   Anotadd("920000", CTOD("02/18/88"),  2.50,  .F.)
```

```
Anotadd("930000", CTOD("02/18/88"),  6.00,  .F.)
Anotadd("931000", CTOD("02/18/88"),  10.00,  .F.)
Anotadd("933100", CTOD("02/18/88"),  0.01,  .F.)
Anotadd("935000", CTOD("02/18/88"),  24.12,  .F.)
Anotadd("939300", CTOD("02/18/88"),  15.24,  .F.)
Anotadd("940000", CTOD("02/18/88"),  0.12,  .F.)
Anotadd("945000", CTOD("02/18/88"),  5.21,  .F.)
Anotadd("950000", CTOD("02/18/88"),  48.21,  .F.)
Anotadd("955000", CTOD("02/18/88"),  4.21,  .F.)
Anotadd("100000", CTOD("02/18/88"),  47.21,  .F.)
Anotadd("200000", CTOD("02/18/88"),  4.21,  .F.)
Anotadd("200001", CTOD("02/18/88"),  42.65,  .F.)
Anotadd("200010", CTOD("02/18/88"),  2.21,  .F.)
Anotadd("300000", CTOD("02/18/88"),  4.84,  .F.)
Anotadd("323333", CTOD("02/18/88"),  5.21,  .F.)
Anotadd("352231", CTOD("02/18/88"),  2.14,  .F.)
Anotadd("400000", CTOD("02/18/88"),  78.21,  .F.)
Anotadd("511001", CTOD("02/18/88"),  43.26,  .F.)
Anotadd("610000", CTOD("02/18/88"),  32.12,  .F.)
Anotadd("714442", CTOD("02/18/88"),  34.21,  .F.)
Anotadd("740000", CTOD("02/18/88"),  3721.12,  .F.)
Anotadd("830000", CTOD("02/18/88"),  34.71,  .F.)
Anotadd("831000", CTOD("02/18/88"),  29482.72,  .F.)
Anotadd("845500", CTOD("02/18/88"),  31.43,  .F.)
Anotadd("860000", CTOD("02/18/88"),  273.13,  .F.)
Anotadd("900000", CTOD("02/18/88"),  243.13,  .F.)
Anotadd("910000", CTOD("02/18/88"),  234.73,  .F.)
Anotadd("920000", CTOD("02/18/88"),  2156.83,  .F.)
Anotadd("930000", CTOD("02/18/88"),  22.09,  .F.)
Anotadd("931000", CTOD("02/18/88"),  542.56,  .F.)
Anotadd("933100", CTOD("02/18/88"),  4273.26,  .F.)
Anotadd("935000", CTOD("02/18/88"),  4.32,  .F.)
Anotadd("939300", CTOD("02/18/88"),  36.14,  .F.)
Anotadd("940000", CTOD("02/18/88"),  5.78,  .F.)
Anotadd("945000", CTOD("02/18/88"),  4.95,  .F.)
Anotadd("950000", CTOD("02/18/88"),  1.23,  .F.)
Anotadd("955000", CTOD("02/18/88"),  64.51,  .F.)
Anotadd("100000", CTOD("02/18/88"),  24.20,  .F.)
Anotadd("200000", CTOD("02/18/88"),  2314.21,  .F.)
Anotadd("200001", CTOD("02/18/88"),  0.15,  .F.)
Anotadd("200010", CTOD("02/18/88"),  4.26,  .F.)
Anotadd("300000", CTOD("02/18/88"),  1.23,  .F.)
Anotadd("323333", CTOD("02/18/88"),  1.24,  .F.)
Anotadd("352231", CTOD("02/18/88"),  7.25,  .F.)
Anotadd("400000", CTOD("02/18/88"),  8.14,  .F.)
Anotadd("511001", CTOD("02/18/88"),  0.26,  .F.)
Anotadd("610000", CTOD("02/18/88"),  7.19,  .F.)
Anotadd("714442", CTOD("02/18/88"),  8.23,  .F.)
Anotadd("740000", CTOD("02/18/88"),  47.20,  .F.)
Anotadd("830000", CTOD("02/18/88"),  47.21,  .F.)
Anotadd("831000", CTOD("02/18/88"),  7.23,  .F.)
Anotadd("845500", CTOD("02/18/88"),  47.51,  .F.)
Anotadd("860000", CTOD("02/18/88"),  8.32,  .F.)
Anotadd("900000", CTOD("02/18/88"),  47.22,  .F.)
```

```
Anotadd("910000", CTOD("02/18/88"), 1.00, .F.)
Anotadd("920000", CTOD("02/18/88"), 23.32, .F.)
Anotadd("930000", CTOD("02/18/88"), 8.00, .F.)
Anotadd("931000", CTOD("02/18/88"), 0.23, .F.)
Anotadd("933100", CTOD("02/18/88"), 0.32, .F.)
Anotadd("935000", CTOD("02/18/88"), 0.32, .F.)
Anotadd("939300", CTOD("02/18/88"), 5.32, .F.)
Anotadd("940000", CTOD("02/18/88"), 0.32, .F.)
Anotadd("945000", CTOD("02/18/88"), 3.32, .F.)
Anotadd("950000", CTOD("02/18/88"), 3.32, .F.)
Anotadd("955000", CTOD("02/18/88"), 334273.13, .F.)
Anotadd("100000", CTOD("02/18/88"), 2.73, .F.)
Anotadd("200000", CTOD("02/18/88"), 2342.37, .F.)
Anotadd("200001", CTOD("02/18/88"), 32134.13, .F.)
Anotadd("200010", CTOD("02/18/88"), 27.43, .F.)
Anotadd("300000", CTOD("02/18/88"), 2831314.32, .F.)
Anotadd("323333", CTOD("02/18/88"), 3382.34, .F.)
Anotadd("352231", CTOD("02/18/88"), 231.38, .F.)
Anotadd("400000", CTOD("02/18/88"), 32.32, .F.)
Anotadd("511001", CTOD("02/18/88"), 1.00, .F.)
Anotadd("610000", CTOD("02/18/88"), 2.00, .F.)
Anotadd("714442", CTOD("02/18/88"), 3.00, .F.)
Anotadd("740000", CTOD("02/18/88"), 6.00, .F.)
Anotadd("830000", CTOD("02/18/88"), 4.00, .F.)
Anotadd("831000", CTOD("02/18/88"), 5.00, .F.)
Anotadd("845500", CTOD("02/18/88"), 7.00, .F.)
Anotadd("860000", CTOD("02/18/88"), 85.00, .F.)
Anotadd("900000", CTOD("02/18/88"), 212.00, .F.)
Anotadd("910000", CTOD("02/18/88"), 236.00, .F.)
Anotadd("920000", CTOD("02/18/88"), 0.31, .F.)
Anotadd("930000", CTOD("02/18/88"), 2323.00, .F.)
Anotadd("931000", CTOD("02/18/88"), 25.12, .F.)
Anotadd("933100", CTOD("02/18/88"), 241.74, .F.)
Anotadd("935000", CTOD("02/18/88"), 32.96, .F.)
Anotadd("939300", CTOD("02/18/88"), 5.28, .F.)
Anotadd("940000", CTOD("02/18/88"), 7.23, .F.)
Anotadd("945000", CTOD("02/18/88"), 425412.36, .F.)
Anotadd("950000", CTOD("02/18/88"), 2475.92, .F.)
Anotadd("955000", CTOD("02/18/88"), 3.65, .F.)
Anotadd("100000", CTOD("02/18/88"), 0.13, .F.)
Anotadd("200000", CTOD("02/18/88"), 542.13, .F.)
Anotadd("200001", CTOD("02/18/88"), 23.00, .F.)
Anotadd("200010", CTOD("02/18/88"), 64.13, .F.)
Anotadd("300000", CTOD("02/18/88"), 267.13, .F.)
Anotadd("323333", CTOD("02/18/88"), 264.13, .F.)
Anotadd("352231", CTOD("02/18/88"), 721.29, .F.)
Anotadd("400000", CTOD("02/18/88"), 1542.73, .F.)
Anotadd("511001", CTOD("02/18/88"), 126437.13, .F.)
Anotadd("610000", CTOD("02/18/88"), 267.13, .F.)
Anotadd("714442", CTOD("02/18/88"), 2642373.16, .F.)
Anotadd("740000", CTOD("02/18/88"), 2.31, .F.)
Anotadd("830000", CTOD("02/18/88"), 3165.23, .F.)
Anotadd("831000", CTOD("02/18/88"), 16432.31, .F.)
Anotadd("845500", CTOD("02/18/88"), 9.03, .F.)
```

```
Anotadd("860000", CTOD("02/18/88"),  121.24,  .F.)
Anotadd("900000", CTOD("02/18/88"),  37.12,  .F.)
Anotadd("910000", CTOD("02/18/88"),  31.13,  .F.)
Anotadd("920000", CTOD("02/18/88"),  27912.42,  .F.)
Anotadd("930000", CTOD("02/18/88"),  7325.12,  .F.)
Anotadd("931000", CTOD("02/18/88"),  14.72,  .F.)
Anotadd("933100", CTOD("02/18/88"),  331324.72,  .F.)
Anotadd("935000", CTOD("02/18/88"),  38.53,  .F.)
Anotadd("939300", CTOD("02/18/88"),  4237.13,  .F.)
Anotadd("940000", CTOD("02/18/88"),  24.72,  .F.)
Anotadd("945000", CTOD("02/18/88"),  312337.52,  .F.)
Anotadd("950000", CTOD("02/18/88"),  3.15,  .F.)
Anotadd("955000", CTOD("02/18/88"),  67.22,  .F.)
Anotadd("100000", CTOD("02/18/88"),  3328.53,  .F.)
Anotadd("200000", CTOD("02/18/88"),  21234.53,  .F.)
Anotadd("200001", CTOD("02/18/88"),  28231.23,  .F.)
Anotadd("200010", CTOD("02/18/88"),  825.12,  .F.)
Anotadd("300000", CTOD("02/18/88"),  35268.03,  .F.)
Anotadd("323333", CTOD("02/18/88"),  1234.72,  .F.)
Anotadd("352231", CTOD("02/18/88"),  31235.22,  .F.)
Anotadd("400000", CTOD("02/18/88"),  38321.28,  .F.)
Anotadd("511001", CTOD("02/18/88"),  32.12,  .F.)
Anotadd("610000", CTOD("02/18/88"),  37235.23,  .F.)
Anotadd("714442", CTOD("02/18/88"),  423832.13,  .F.)
Anotadd("740000", CTOD("02/18/88"),  21328.22,  .F.)
Anotadd("830000", CTOD("02/18/88"),  31325.23,  .F.)
Anotadd("831000", CTOD("02/18/88"),  1235.12,  .F.)
Anotadd("845500", CTOD("02/18/88"),  3279513.22,  .F.)
Anotadd("860000", CTOD("02/18/88"),  321.23,  .F.)
Anotadd("900000", CTOD("02/18/88"),  423.12,  .F.)
Anotadd("910000", CTOD("02/18/88"),  31564.23,  .F.)
Anotadd("920000", CTOD("02/18/88"),  167232.13,  .F.)
Anotadd("930000", CTOD("02/18/88"),  6.12,  .F.)
Anotadd("931000", CTOD("02/18/88"),  313.23,  .F.)
Anotadd("933100", CTOD("02/18/88"),  24.28,  .F.)
Anotadd("935000", CTOD("02/18/88"),  742.25,  .F.)
Anotadd("939300", CTOD("02/18/88"),  12.32,  .F.)
Anotadd("940000", CTOD("02/18/88"),  56412.23,  .F.)
Anotadd("945000", CTOD("02/18/88"),  52141.23,  .F.)
Anotadd("950000", CTOD("02/18/88"),  25.23,  .F.)
Anotadd("955000", CTOD("02/18/88"),  1.25,  .F.)
Anotadd("100000", CTOD("02/18/88"),  2.23,  .F.)
Anotadd("200000", CTOD("02/18/88"),  62.36,  .F.)
Anotadd("200001", CTOD("02/18/88"),  5.21,  .F.)
Anotadd("200010", CTOD("02/18/88"),  42.23,  .F.)
Anotadd("300000", CTOD("02/18/88"),  102.12,  .F.)
Anotadd("323333", CTOD("02/18/88"),  32.20,  .F.)
Anotadd("352231", CTOD("02/18/88"),  315.08,  .F.)
Anotadd("400000", CTOD("02/18/88"),  1.70,  .F.)
Anotadd("511001", CTOD("02/18/88"),  9.10,  .F.)
Anotadd("610000", CTOD("02/18/88"),  9.72,  .F.)
Anotadd("714442", CTOD("02/18/88"),  3084.02,  .F.)
Anotadd("740000", CTOD("02/18/88"),  5137.13,  .F.)
Anotadd("830000", CTOD("02/18/88"),  568.23,  .F.)
```

```
   Anotadd("831000", CTOD("02/18/88"),  2.23,  .F.)
   Anotadd("845500", CTOD("02/18/88"),  24.02,  .F.)
   Anotadd("860000", CTOD("02/18/88"),  645.73,  .F.)
   Anotadd("900000", CTOD("02/18/88"),  3426723.12,  .F.)
   Anotadd("910000", CTOD("02/18/88"),  3309725.31,  .F.)
   Anotadd("920000", CTOD("02/18/88"),  328321.02,  .F.)
   Anotadd("930000", CTOD("02/18/88"),  38235.13,  .F.)
   Anotadd("931000", CTOD("02/18/88"),  28322.13,  .F.)
   Anotadd("933100", CTOD("02/18/88"),  283.13,  .F.)
   Anotadd("935000", CTOD("02/18/88"),  2832.13,  .F.)
   Anotadd("939300", CTOD("02/18/88"),  2831.03,  .F.)
   Anotadd("940000", CTOD("02/18/88"),  283.13,  .F.)
   Anotadd("945000", CTOD("02/18/88"),  235.73,  .F.)
   Anotadd("950000", CTOD("02/18/88"),  123.03,  .F.)
   Anotadd("955000", CTOD("02/18/88"),  2137.30,  .F.)
   Anotadd("100000", CTOD("02/18/88"),  231.23,  .F.)
   Anotadd("200000", CTOD("02/18/88"),  23023.00,  .F.)
   Anotadd("200001", CTOD("02/18/88"),  1543.23,  .F.)
   Anotadd("200010", CTOD("02/18/88"),  23.03,  .F.)
   Anotadd("300000", CTOD("02/18/88"),  22354.03,  .F.)
   Anotadd("323333", CTOD("02/18/88"),  273123.00,  .F.)
   Anotadd("352231", CTOD("02/18/88"),  3231.30,  .F.)
   Anotadd("400000", CTOD("02/18/88"),  212.21,  .F.)
   Anotadd("511001", CTOD("02/18/88"),  4.12,  .F.)
   Anotadd("610000", CTOD("02/18/88"),  1.12,  .F.)
   Anotadd("714442", CTOD("02/18/88"),  3.20,  .F.)
   Anotadd("740000", CTOD("02/18/88"),  3.12,  .F.)
   Anotadd("830000", CTOD("02/18/88"),  34.02,  .F.)
   Anotadd("831000", CTOD("02/18/88"),  3.23,  .F.)
   Anotadd("845500", CTOD("02/18/88"),  0.23,  .F.)
   Anotadd("860000", CTOD("02/18/88"),  1.03,  .F.)
   Anotadd("900000", CTOD("02/18/88"),  0.23,  .F.)
   Anotadd("910000", CTOD("02/18/88"),  157.53,  .F.)
   Anotadd("920000", CTOD("02/18/88"),  0.90,  .F.)
   Anotadd("930000", CTOD("02/18/88"),  0.12,  .F.)
   Anotadd("931000", CTOD("02/18/88"),  0.40,  .F.)
   Anotadd("933100", CTOD("02/18/88"),  0.27,  .F.)
   Anotadd("935000", CTOD("02/18/88"),  0.12,  .F.)
   Anotadd("939300", CTOD("02/18/88"),  23.00,  .F.)
   Anotadd("940000", CTOD("02/18/88"),  24.13,  .F.)
   Anotadd("945000", CTOD("02/18/88"),  3212.42,  .F.)
   Anotadd("950000", CTOD("02/18/88"),  37231.42,  .F.)
   Anotadd("955000", CTOD("02/18/88"),  337.43,  .F.)

*******************

PROCEDURE Anotadd

   PARAMETERS a, b, c, d

   APPEND BLANK

   IF SELECT() = 3
      REPLACE account WITH a, adate WITH b, ;
```

```
            now_due WITH c, paid WITH d
      Wsayget(SELECT(), 35, RECNO(), "", "999")
   ELSEIF SELECT() = 4
      REPLACE status WITH a, descript WITH b
      Wsayget(SELECT(), 35, RECNO(), "", "999")
   ELSEIF SELECT() = 7
      REPLACE state WITH a, zpre WITH b, ppre WITH c
      Wsayget(SELECT()+2, 35, RECNO(), "", "999")
   ENDIF

*********************

PROCEDURE Withfour

   Anotadd("1", "Normal Account")
   Anotadd("2", "Inventory Account")
   Anotadd("3", "Special")
   Anotadd("4", "Fortune 500")
   Anotadd("5", "Premier Account")
   Anotadd("6", "Gold Card Member")
   Anotadd("7", "Inventory Control")
   Anotadd("8", "Unassigned")
   Anotadd("9", "Development")
   Anotadd("A", "Additional Account")
   Anotadd("T", "Tax Account")

********************

PROCEDURE Mhelp

   carriage = "CHR(141) + CHR(10)"
   a1 = "Pressing the ESC Key will abort " + &carriage.
   a2 = "the window of PROMPTS and return " + &carriage.
   a3 = "you to the main DBEDIT() window  "
   MEMOWRIT("HELPTXT1.TXT", a1+a2+a3)
   a1 = "Pressing the F1 in most systems will " + &carriage.
   a2 = "generate some type of help.  In this " + &carriage.
   a3 = "example, TOPIC ORIENTED HELP is "  + &carriage.
   a4 = "the main focus.  With this, the user " + &carriage.
   a5 = "can identify what area of help is " + &carriage.
   a6 = "required BEFORE actually viewing text " + &carriage.
   a7 = "on it."
   MEMOWRIT("HELPTXT2.TXT", a1+a2+a3+a4+a5+a6+a7)
   a1 = "Pressing the F10 key on the first field " + ;
        &carriage.
   a2 = "will mean that another DBEDIT() will be " + ;
        &carriage.
   a3 = "called showing all of the legitimate " + &carriage.
   a4 = "account names for the coded values enter." + ;
        &carriage. + &carriage.
   a5 = "Pressing the F10 key on any other field " + ;
        &carriage.
   a6 = "will show the account balance DUE from " + ;
        &carriage.
```

```
   a7 = "that customer."  + &carriage.  + &carriage.
   a8 = "This means that keystrokes may not only be" + ;
       &carriage.
   a9 = "manipulated, but they may be by field location" + ;
       &carriage.
   a0 = "as well."
   MEMOWRIT("HELPTXT3.TXT", a1+a2+a3+a4+a5+a6+a7+a8+a9+a0)

******************

PROCEDURE Obtain

   FOR x = 1 TO LEN(array)
      APPEND BLANK
      Wsayget(7,34,RECNO(),"", "9999")
      REPLACE Disknos->disk_no    WITH "        1", ;
              Disknos->sub_no     WITH TRANSFORM(x, "999"),;
              Disknos->disk_name  WITH "Master Disk", ;
              Disknos->date_add   WITH DATE(), ;
              Disknos->date_up    WITH DATE(), ;
              Disknos->bytes_left WITH DISKSPACE(), ;
              Disknos->hardflop   WITH .T., ;
              Disknos->drivelet   WITH "C:"
      Op(F->(Restofit()))
   NEXT

********************

PROCEDURE Restofit

   DECLARE sarray[1]
   submany = ADIR("C:"+array[x]+"\*.*", "","", ;
                  "","", sarray)
   DECLARE snames[submany], stypes[submany], ;
           ssizes[submany], sdates[submany], ;
           stimes[submany]
   ADIR("C:"+array[x]+"\*.*", snames, ssizes, ;
       sdates, stimes, stypes)
   FOR y = 1 TO submany
      APPEND BLANK
      Wsayget(8,34,RECNO(), "", "9999")
      REPLACE Filenos->disk_no   WITH Disknos->disk_no, ;
              Filenos->sub_no    WITH Disknos->sub_no, ;
              Filenos->sub_name  WITH array[x], ;
              Filenos->file_no   WITH TRANSFORM(y, "99999"),;
              Filenos->file_name WITH snames[y],;
              Filenos->file_type WITH stypes[y], ;
              Filenos->file_size WITH ssizes[y], ;
              Filenos->file_date WITH sdates[y], ;
              Filenos->file_time WITH stimes[y], ;
              Filenos->is_arc    WITH (".ARC"$snames[y])
   NEXT
```

```
********************

PROCEDURE Statbase

   Anotadd("AR", "4", "501")
   Anotadd("AZ", "9", "602")
   Anotadd("AK", "9", "907")
   Anotadd("AL", "3", "205")
   Anotadd("CO", "8", "303")
   Anotadd("CT", "0", "203")
   Anotadd("DE", "1", "302")
   Anotadd("HA", "9", "808")
   Anotadd("NM", "7", "505")
   Anotadd("MD", "1", "301")
   Anotadd("ME", "0", "207")
   Anotadd("OE", "9", "503")
   Anotadd("UT", "8", "801")
   Anotadd("WV", "2", "304")
   Anotadd("WY", "6", "307")
   Anotadd("ND", "6", "701")

**********************

PROCEDURE Final

   how_many = ADIR("*.*")
   DECLARE afiles[how_many], asizes[how_many],;
           adate[how_many], atimes[how_many]
   ADIR("*.*", afiles, asizes, adate, atimes)
   FOR x = 1 TO how_many
      APPEND BLANK
      Wsayget(10,35,RECNO(), "", "999")
      REPLACE files WITH afiles[x],    ;
              sizes WITH asizes[x],    ;
              datestamp WITH adate[x], ;
              times WITH atimes[x],    ;
              per_used WITH (asizes[x] / DISKSPACE()) * 100,;
              subdrive WITH CURDIR()
   NEXT

* End of File
```

INDEX